THE DIARY
OF VIRGINIA
WOOLF

Volume Four:
1931-1935

THE DIARY of VIRGINIA WOOLF

Edited by
Anne Olivier Bell
Assisted by Andrew McNeillie

VOLUME FOUR
1931-1935

Harcourt Brace Jovanovich, Publishers

New York and London

HBJ

Library of Congress Cataloging in Publication Data

Woolf, Virginia Stephen, 1882–1941.
The diary of Virginia Woolf.

Includes index.
CONTENTS: V. 1. 1915–1919.—V. 2. 1920–1924.—
V. 3. 1925–1930.—V. 4. 1931–1935.
1. Woolf, Virginia Stephen, 1882–1941—Diaries.
2. Authors, English—20th century—Biography.
PR6045.072Z494   1977   823'.9'12   [B]   77-73111
ISBN 0–15–125602–0

B C D E

CONTENTS

The Diary

EDITOR'S PREFACE

The last entry in the previous volume of Virginia Woolf's diary left her sitting over the fire at Monks House, writing of *The Waves*: 'it is I think rather good'; five years later to the day, 30 December 1935, the present volume concludes rather sadly with her contemplating the coming struggle of revising and condensing what had, after many baptisms and re-baptisms, become *The Years*. Looking back at her career as a novelist from a distance of half a century, we may perceive that the publication of *The Waves* in 1931 marked the triumphant culmination of a progress, begin-ning with *Jacob's Room*, in which Virginia Woolf explores ever more interesting provinces of what had become her chosen territory; and whether we think of *To the Lighthouse* or *The Waves* as the zenith of that happy exploration, there can be little doubt that the 1920s was a time of ever increasing mastery and ever increasing fulfilment, whereas the 'thirties, during which she completed *The Years* and wrote *Flush*, *Three Guineas*, and *Roger Fry: A Biography*, cannot be regarded as a period of equally prosperous creativity.

Nonetheless, at the outset Virginia was very far from considering *The Years* an unpromising venture: she was excited and absorbed by her con-ception. *Flush* she never took very seriously; and throughout most of the decade she is gathering material, sometimes in a spirit of jubilant ridicule, sometimes with deep anger, for that polemic which, after an array of tentative forms and titles (including *On Being Despised* and *The Next War*), finally became *Three Guineas*. The feminist note, scarcely audible in the previous volume, now sounds clear and often. *Three Guineas* is how-ever not simply a woman's protest against the arrogance, stupidity, and cruelty of men in their relations with the opposite sex; it is also a savage complaint. Men have ruled the world since the beginning of history, and what have been the results? During these years it was becoming in-creasingly evident that the hideous slaughter of 1914-18 had produced nothing save the conditions for a still larger and more horrible convulsion; these are the years when fascism and extreme nationalism began their irresistible march towards another war, years during which, in England, the bright hopes of the 1920s were extinguished by a reactionary govern-ment which, while countenancing domestic misery, showed itself incap-able of opposing foreign tyrants. The worst is yet to come, but already by the end of 1935 the picture is becoming clear: unemployment at home, appeasement abroad.

To this ominous development of public life were added private sorrows of a grievous kind. Lytton Strachey died in 1932 and with him faded a whole chapter of Virginia's youth. His death was shortly followed by the suicide of Dora Carrington, a tragedy made more poignant by the fact that Virginia herself stood so close to it. In 1934 came the death of Roger Fry, a loss which affected Virginia more immediately, partly because of its devastating effect upon her sister, and partly because she herself had grown increasingly appreciative of his qualities and personality. Lytton had for some years been living in a circle of his own, whereas Roger remained much closer to what one might call the heart of Bloomsbury—if, that is, we think of Virginia Woolf and Vanessa Bell as the core of that elusive entity. Roger Fry had enriched his friends' lives with his genial warmth, his eternal youthfulness of spirit, his adventurous and well-stocked mind, and his death impoverished their world, leaving it barren and bereft of the old joyous mixture of fun, argument, and intellectual probity which his presence invariably engendered. Finally, in 1935 Francis Birrell—a comparatively young man—was struck down and killed by a cancer of the brain. Frankie had never been important to Virginia as Lytton and Roger were important, but no-one who knew him could fail to love him or to be appalled by the cruelty of a fate which removed so wholly delightful a person. His death moved her also in another way, for he met it with a clearsighted and cheerful philosophy which resulted not from religious belief but from a stout-hearted rationalism.

Intensely interested in her own reputation, Virginia nevertheless was unwilling to accept the public rewards which now resulted from the growing recognition of her achievement. The Clark Lectureship at Cambridge, an Honorary Degree at Manchester, the Companionship of Honour: all were offered and each politely refused. And yet, while she seemed to regard these tributes almost as trivialities, she could not so easily dismiss the hostile jibings of Swinnerton, of Mirsky, of Wyndham Lewis. While the tributes afforded little pleasure, her detractors could inflict real pain.

Such were the miseries of her life: Virginia's frequent echoing of the phrase in Wesley's anecdote usually alludes (as he does) to the magnification of trivial vexations; and indeed, while feeling keenly enough the larger tragedies, she notes the lesser distresses of her life without seeking to minimise their consequence to herself, and, in particular, reverts over and again to her familiar predicament—the conflict between her desire for the stimulus of society and her need for solitude and tranquillity.

From the forgoing it might be anticipated that these pages will prove a record of unmitigated woe, but this is very far from the case. Virginia Woolf was—as she often remarks—essentially a happy woman, and she had a genius for enjoying and for expressing joy in life—the world 'life' here being taken to mean everything from landscape to friendship. The creative perceptiveness of her observation of people and places and, it must be stressed, the accuracy, is evident all through these diaries, whether she turns her attention to a little maid-servant in a French hotel or records the discourse of Yeats or Shaw or Eliot; whether she is describing the weather in the Ouse valley or the plains of Marathon. Perhaps the most spirited and pleasurable pages in this volume are those devoted to the foreign journeys which she and Leonard Woolf undertook during these years, to France, to Italy, to Greece, to Holland and Germany, and above all, that to Ireland in 1934. Although Virginia could speak French and some Italian (and read both languages), her ability to communicate in them was limited; whereas in Ireland she found a people who spoke her own tongue with a verve and an abundance which delighted her and made her respond to the Irish as fellow craftsmen in her own medium.

Her own medium is naturally the underlying concern of Virginia's existence, and the triumphs and tribulations of this concern are expressed throughout this diary, whether in relation to her own work or that of others. She wrote much less criticism than formerly (though she revised and published the second series of *The Common Reader*), largely because the success of her own books removed the necessity to make money in this way; but as always she read voraciously, including, it should be remembered, innumerable manuscripts submitted for publication to the Hogarth Press—that by now substantial enterprise which increasingly she felt to be a millstone round her and Leonard's necks. In 1931 they found a promising manager in John Lehmann, but after eighteen months he left (to return three years later), and her efforts to weaken Leonard's attachment to his creation and to leave both of them freer were unsuccessful. But lest this dissension should be seized upon as a grain of support for the reckless mythology recently propounded, wherein Leonard and Virginia are depicted as mutually inimical—a theory which would be laughable were it not taken apparently seriously—these diaries should serve to convince the unprejudiced reader that, despite minor differences and disagreements which it would be surprising not to find between two such exceptional characters, her marriage was the bedrock of Virginia's life: a truly fortunate, prosperous, and happy alliance.

Editorial Note

(What follows is virtually a condensed repetition of the information on editorial measures given in previous volumes.)

The original manuscript diaries from which these volumes are transcibed have since 1970 been preserved in the Henry W. and Albert A. Berg Collection of English and American Literature in the New York Public Library (Astor, Lenox, and Tilden Foundations) under an arrangement entered into by Leonard Woolf in 1958. The diaries are listed (and the arrangement described) in Volume I of the present 5-volume publication. The text for the five years 1931-35 in this fourth volume is taken from part of Diary XX through to Diary XXIV, plus three pages from the beginning of Diary XXV.

The transcription follows Virginia Woolf's manuscript as closely and completely as possible: any omissions—practically none—are indicated. My uncertainties or failures in making out single words in her inconsiderately scribbled pages—usually written on her knee in the depths of an easy chair, sometimes perched on a bed in a strange hotel—are indicated by square brackets (reserved for editorial use) and question marks. I have followed her corrections where she has made them, occasionally retaining the cancelled word or words within angled brackets: ⟨ ⟩. Her mis-spellings—though these are rare—are preserved unless I judge them to be purely inadvertent, when they are silently corrected; after her sometimes phonetic spelling of proper names, the correct form is supplied in square brackets or a footnote. Her almost invariable use of the ampersand is retained to suggest the pace of her writing, although unfortunately the symbol in its printed form rather negates this intention.

The dating of the entries has been standardised for general convenience; some dates have been corrected, supplied, or suggested on internal or external evidence—particularly that of Leonard Woolf's laconic pocket diaries, now in the Library of the University of Sussex.

I have distinguished paragraphs in Virginia's normally unindented pages where they suggest themselves; and I have very sparingly—for the unpremeditated nature of this writing should remain apparent—tidied up the punctuation, adding or eliminating a full point, a bracket, or an inverted comma to clarify the sense. And where appropriate, I have bodied out her abbreviations in the text rather than resort to a footnote.

Such annotations as I judge to be necessary are given at the foot of the page to which they relate, and are numbered in sequence within each month. The footnotes are intended for a very wide range of putative readers, and those who do not need them should resist the temptation to read them. Some are inevitably very dull; but many do seem to me to furnish information essential to an understanding of Virginia Woolf's thought. I have attempted to identify every person to whom she refers; the regulars of her world I have again relegated to an Appendix on p. 364; the less frequent, and the new arrivals, are normally introduced in footnotes on their first appearance: the index should discover them all. As more and more people crowd into her pages, with often less and less said about them, I have likewise reduced my summaries to a minimum.

Virginia's own published writings are identified according to B. J. Kirkpatrick's indispensable *Bibliography of Virginia Woolf* (the splendid third edition of which was published in 1980), her numbering here prefixed by *Kp*. Books published by the Hogarth Press are also identified, from J. Howard Woolmer's *Checklist of the Hogarth Press, 1917-38*; *M&M* denotes the volume on Virginia Woolf, edited by Robin Majumdar and Allen McLaurin, in the *Critical Heritage* series, which usefully reprints critical reactions to her published works. A list of abbreviations here regularly employed for books and names is to be found on p. 362; other books are cited by their author, full title, and date of publication in England, except for Virginia Woolf's own works, when reference is made, unless otherwise stated, to the Uniform Edition, published in London by the Hogarth Press and in New York by Harcourt Brace Jovanovich.

Acknowledgments

I am fortunate in having at hand in my home a pretty extensive library, formed to some degree by natural accumulation and natural acquisitiveness, but greatly augmented by inheritance from my father, A. E. Popham, from my father-in-law Clive Bell, and finally, seeing that we already had a house chock-full of books, Duncan Grant mischievously left us all of his. Blessed be their memory, all three. Though deficient in the sciences, the range is broad, from old maps and guide books to the *Dictionary of National Biography*, from the classics of French literature to English poetry, from the history of art to the history and memoirs of men and women. This favourable circumstance (despite the difficulty of *finding* anything in a family home) has enabled me and my assistant Andrew McNeillie to do the greater part of our work on these volumes in this house, thereby reducing the time and money spent on travelling and pursuing information in less convenient places. Nonetheless, pursuit in other places has been imperative, and has not been shirked. Again the London Library, and the Library and Documents Centre of the University of Sussex, have provided the most effective help in the most congenial conditions, and I would like to thank the librarians and staff of both these noble institutions for their assistance; as too the Librarian and the Modern Archivist of King's College Library, Cambridge, who have answered my many letters with a fulness and a care for detail which is most welcome to me. I have had access also, by proxy, to a great repository of knowledge in the University of Cambridge since Harry (Sir Henry) Lintott—who helped me so much with the last volume—and his wife Margaret moved to that city; his resourcefulness in supplementing and his benevolent severity in criticising my notes have been of immense benefit, not only to me, but without doubt to readers of this volume. My gratitude is none the less warm for his assurance that he enjoys the self-imposed task.

Nigel Nicolson and Joanne Trautmann have now completed their monumental six-volume edition of *The Letters of Virginia Woolf*, and the value to me of having these beside me cannot be exaggerated; in addition, Nigel Nicolson, with his particular knowledge and experience of the period and the problems, has responded to every question I have put to him with fraternal clarity and precision. Dr Brenda Silver of Dartmouth College was good enough to send us in typescript her impressively researched *Bibliographic Guide to Virginia Woolf's Reading Notebooks* which—even at that stage minus an index—has been extremely useful; I hope it may soon be published. I have been particularly lucky in having as Foreign Correspondents Dr Tadhg Foley in Galway City and my brother Philip Sherrard in Greece; to them and to the following friends and correspondents I would like to express my sincere gratitude for information and for help of various kinds:

Dr Igor Anrep; Lord and Lady David Cecil; Mrs T. S. Eliot; Mr & Mrs R. Gosden; Dr A. D. Harris; Mrs Grace Higgens; Professor A. N. Jeffares; Dr Milo Keynes; Mr Philip Keyte; Professor Mitchell A. Leaska; Dr Paul Levy; Professor Norman Mackenzie; Mr Robert Medley; Professor D. E. Moggridge; Mr Richard Morphet; Mrs Karmen Newman; Mr David Nye; Sir Edward Playfair; Mrs Ian Parsons; Mrs Ralph Partridge; the Marchesa Iris Origo; Mrs Angela Richards; Dr G. H. W. Rylands; Miss Daphne Sanger; Mr Richard Shone; Dr Frances Spalding; Mr George Spater; Mrs Peggy Stangroom; Mrs Ann Synge; Mr J. Howard Woolmer.

I also wish to acknowledge the courtesy and assistance I have received from officials or staff of the following:

The Museum and Historical Research Section, The Bank of England; The Bodley Head Ltd; Buckinghamshire County Library, and Buckinghamshire County Record Office; Peter Davies Ltd; *The New Statesman & Nation*; The Scottish Record Office, Edinburgh; H.M. Registry, Somerset House; The Tate Gallery; The Theatre Museum.

Once again, credit for much essential preparatory work, indexing, and typing, must go to Victoria Walton, Virginia Bell, and Sandra Williams; without their willing and reliable activity we should never have got done.

Last Spring I was again able to visit the actual repository of Virginia Woolf's diaries, the Berg Collection in New York (the perfect refuge from the transport strike and torrential rain), to whose Curator Dr Lola L. Szladits I offer both my gratitude and respect: it is, above all, her high standards and expectations of probity in scholarship which I have sought to emulate and hope to satisfy.

To Mrs Norah Smallwood of the Hogarth Press, her admirable colleagues, and her excellent printers, I am sincerely grateful for their patience, understanding, and professional skills; Mr John Ferrone of Harcourt Brace Jovanovich, New York, has provided both moral and practical support.

The copyright holders in Virginia Woolf's work, her niece and nephew Angelica Garnett and Quentin Bell, are unique witnesses of many of the circumstances and characters touched on in these diaries and, living as I happily do in close proximity (especially to the latter, my husband), I have greatly benefited from their experience and help.

In conclusion, I think it proper to acknowledge the fact that the publication of Virginia Woolf's diaries in this extended form is only possible because royalties from her copyrights inherited by my husband have been used to defray the costs of preparation and research. Whether she would have been more appalled or amused that her earnings from beyond the grave should be put to such use is a question I often ask myself; but for better or for worse, the freedom and independence of judgement this allows me is something I think she would approve.

ANNE OLIVIER BELL

Sussex, May 1981

1931

1931

The Woolfs had driven to Monks House on 24 December; on arrival, VW had gone to bed with a temperature, and was virtually laid up until the end of the year. She continued to write her diary in the book she had been using since September—DIARY XX.

[*Friday 2 January*]

This is the turn of the tide. The days are lengthening. Today was fine from start to finish—the first we have had, I think, since we came. And for the first time I walked my Northease walk & saw the moon ride at 3, pale, very thin, in a pure blue sky above wide misty flattened fields, as if it were early on a June morning.

Here are my resolutions for the next 3 months; the next lap of the year.

First, to have none. Not to be tied

Second, to be free & kindly with myself, not goading it to parties: to sit rather privately reading in the studio.

To make a good job of The Waves.

To care nothing for making money.

As for Nelly, to stop irritation by the assurance that nothing is worth irritation: if it comes back, she must go. Then not to slip this time into the easiness of letting her stay.[1]

Then—well the chief resolution is the most important—not to make resolutions. Sometimes to read, sometimes not to read. To go out yes—but stay at home in spite of being asked. As for clothes, I think to buy good ones.

This morning Sandles brought Miranda, & she is now stood in her alcove. We went over to Charleston yesterday, & I fought, rather successfully with the usual depression. Is it their levity?—a sneer? But nothing so bad as usual. Duncan there. We came in, & the scene had the usual red cave effect—red cave in the profound winter hollow.[2]

---

1. Nelly Boxall, who had been the Woolfs' living-in cook-housekeeper since 1916, had a serious operation in May 1930; VW took the occasion of her long convalescence to employ non-resident domestics, which she found a preferable system. She resolved not to have Nelly back, but after a long talk (see *III VW Diary*, 12 November 1930), had agreed to her returning for a three-month trial from 1 January 1931.
2. Sandles was a Lewes carrier, delivering to Rodmell on Tuesdays and Fridays. 'Miranda'—a life-size figure of a half-draped woman which LW acquired (like most of his garden statuary) from Ballard's general store at Barcombe, near Lewes—was first placed against the front of Monks House, but later moved into the orchard. For Duncan Grant, see Appendix.

The Woolfs returned from Rodmell to 52 Tavistock Square by car on the afternoon of Wednesday 7 January.

Wednesday 7 January

Well, we have just got back, had our tea, Francis Birrell has called & been dismissed, & there are two hours to dinner. What am I to do with two hours? I dont want to spend them fuming over my new established & respectable household—Nelly in the kitchen & Lottie attempting concealment in the bed room. And I cant settle to read The Enormous Room, nor Madame du Deffand either. L. is busy coping with Miss Belsher & correspondence.[3]

My head is not in the first spring of energy: this fortnight has brought me no views of the lapping downs—no fields & hedges—too many firelit houses & lit up pages, & pen & ink—curse my influenza. It is very quiet here—not a sound but the hiss of the gaz. Oh but the cold was too great at Rodmell. I was frozen like a small sparrow. And I did write a few staggering sentences. Few books have interested me more to write than The Waves. Why even now, at the end, I'm turning up a stone or two: no glibness, no assurance; you see, I could perhaps do B[ernard]'s soliloquy in such a way as to break up, dig deep, make prose move—yes I swear—as prose has never moved before: from the chuckle & the babble to the rhapsody. Something new goes into my pot every morning—something thats never been got at before. The high wind can't blow, because I'm chopping & tacking all the time. And I've stored a few ideas for articles: one on Gosse—the critic as talker; the armchair critic; one on Letters—one on Queens—[4]

Now this is true: The Waves is written at such high pressure that I cant take it up & read it through between tea & dinner; I can only write it for about one hour, from 10 to 11.30. And the typing is almost the hardest part of the work. Heaven help me if all my little 80,000 word books are going in future to cost me two years! But I shall fling off, like a cutter

---

3. For Francis Birrell, see Appendix. When the Woolfs moved from Richmond to Bloomsbury in 1924, Nelly's friend and fellow-servant Lottie Hope went to the Adrian Stephens in nearby Gordon Square; she was dismissed in 1930, and suffered a period of insecurity until becoming cook to Clive Bell early in 1932. Peggy Belsher had been secretary-clerk at the Hogarth Press since March 1928. *The Enormous Room* (1922) by e e cummings; *Lettres de la Marquise du Deffand à Horace Walpole*, publiées par Mrs Paget Toynbee, 3 vols., 1912.

4. 'Edmund Gosse', an article stimulated by the publication in 1931 of *The Life and Letters of Sir Edmund Gosse* by Evan Charteris, appeared in *The Fortnightly Review*, 1 June 1931 (Kp C331); 'the armchair critic' was probably that published as 'All About Books' in the *NS&N*, 28 February 1931 (Kp C329). Apparently the other ideas were not realised.

leaning on its side, on some swifter, slighter adventure—another Orlando perhaps.

I looked out at dawn once or twice—a redness, like wood fire cinders, in a frosty sky; frost thick on the fields; the candles alight in some of the cottages, & so back to bed, wrapping my clothes round me. And every morning I took the bellows & chafed up my logs, & made a game of it, & almost always won my blazing fire by the time L. came up.

How I dislike servants voices & giggles. Enough—enough.

We shall play the Grosse Fugue [Beethoven] tonight—Ethel, I daresay, will ring up. I shall go down & get the post. Tom, Lyn & Ethel have written: I am asked to contribute to a symposium on Love—& thats about all. But already we are committed to 'see' 6 people before Monday—the only one of importance is John Lehmann. And shall I now write to Arthur Symons about his novel? O dear. What machine is there for making 1 hour & 35 minutes blaze?[5]

[Saturday 10 January]

Rather stirred by reading my own essay on Poetry in Fiction I write here instead of breaking my back over Dante.[6] (Its true, I get more thrill from Dante, read after an hours Waves, than from almost any reading—hence the effort). And Clive is looking in for 5 minutes to say good bye. "And to see how you are" he says. "And how are you?" I say. "Blind" he says, rather dolefully. Such is the state of our relationship at 10 to 6 on Saturday Jan. 10th 1931. Lord lord, what a queer thing life is![7]

We walked through the little dingy streets of Seven Dials Leonard & I

5. For T. S. (Tom) Eliot, Ethel Smyth, and John Lehmann, see Appendix. Lyn Lloyd Irvine (1901-73), daughter of a Scottish minister of religion, was educated at Aberdeen and Cambridge Universities (Girton 1924-27). She had contributed to the N&A when LW was that paper's literary editor, and was to edit Ten Letter-Writers for the Hogarth Press (HP Checklist 293). In December 1934 she married Maxwell Newman, lecturer in Mathematics at Cambridge 1927-45. An American intellectual quarterly called The Symposium (which published two substantial articles on VW in 1932) had been started in 1930; this may be relevant to the otherwise unexplained invitation. Arthur William Symons (1865-1945), poet, translator and critic. It is unlikely that he wrote any novel after his severe breakdown in 1908, but he may have sent the Hogarth Press his translation of a French novel.

6. VW's essay 'Poetry, Fiction and the Future' had been published in the New York Herald Tribune in August 1927 (Kp C284); some of the ideas it embodies were amplified in the book on fiction which she embarked on in 1925 for the Hogarth Press but never completed, although chapters, including one on 'The Poets', were published as 'Phases of Fiction' in the N.Y. Bookman in 1929 (Kp C312).

7. For Clive Bell, see Appendix. He was about to spend six weeks in a Zurich clinic undergoing treatment for a deteriorating condition of the eye which had hampered him since the previous autumn.

this afternoon, to Charing Cross Road. What a mood of tears I was in—of pathos, for Leonard, for myself; & said to him Would you like half a crown to buy a squirrel? Suddenly one is overcome with sorrow for people.

But to be connected—Lehmann may do: a tight aquiline boy, pink, with the adorable curls of youth; yes, but persistent, sharp. Shall I be paid if I come as apprentice? Can I have the Hogarth Press books? Not much atmosphere; save perhaps that his eyes are imaginative: Lord knows. And we ask 4 or 5 thousand as his share.

Now those figures have driven away my stir & the spirit of delight, whose wings were brushing me. in spite of our solid middleclass household (servants again) & over cooked meat.

I think a little Dante is indicated—Canto XXVI.

Tuesday 20 January

I have this moment, while having my bath, conceived an entire new book—a sequel to a Room of Ones Own—about the sexual life of women: to be called Professions for Women perhaps—Lord how exciting! This sprang out of my paper to be read on Wednesday to Pippa's society. Now for The Waves. Thank God—but I'm very much excited.[8]

(This is Here & Now I think. May. 34.)

Friday 23 January

Too much excited, alas, to get on with The Waves. One goes on making up The Open Door, or whatever it is to be called. The didactive demonstrative style conflicts with the dramatic: I find it hard to get back inside Bernard again.

8. To this moment may be traced the conception of two books which, after a convoluted and entangled history, were eventually to be published (in 1937 and 1938) as *The Years* and *Three Guineas*. *Here and Now* was the second of ten titles considered by VW for the former (i.e.: *The Pargiters; Here and Now; Music; Dawn; Sons and Daughters; Daughters and Sons; Ordinary People; The Caravan; Other People's Houses; The Years*). Before she finally (in November 1936) decided on *Three Guineas* as the title for the 'sequel to *A Room of One's Own*', VW successively attached the following to it: *Professions for Women; The Open Door; Opening the Door; A Tap at the Door; 'Men are like that'; On Being Despised; P. & P.; The Next War; What Are We to Do?; Answers to Correspondents; Letter to an Englishman; Two Guineas*.
   Philippa (Pippa) Strachey (1872-1968), the third of Lytton Strachey's five sisters, was Secretary to the National Society for Women's Service; she had invited VW to speak to the London branch on 21 January 1931. For VW's speech, and further discussion of the evolution of *The Years*, see *The Pargiters*, edited by Mitchell A. Leaska, 1977.

The speech took place; L. I think slightly exacerbated: an interesting observation if a true one. Two hundred people; well dressed, keen, & often beautiful young women. Ethel in her blue kimono & wig. I by her side. Her speech rollicking & direct: mine too compressed & allusive. Never mind. Four people wish the speeches printed.[9] Naturally I am rather used up—cant make the effort this morning of going on with The Waves. And am 99: & get headaches very easily—Lord, how often this drains my last chapters of their strength! And now Open Door is sucking at my brain too. Such accidents cant be avoided.

Vita last night: "If I, who am the most fortunate of women, can ask What is life for?, how can other people live at all?" in a vague mood of depression. She says she gets more pain than pleasure from praise of her books, which I believe to be true. Never was there a more modest writer. And yet she makes £74 in a morning—I mean a cheque drops in for a story.[10]

Monday 26 January

Heaven be praised, I can truthfully say on this first day of being 49 that I have shaken off the obsession of Opening the Door, & have returned to Waves: & have this instant seen the entire book whole, & how I can finish it—say in under 3 weeks. That takes me to Feb. 16th; then I propose, after doing Gosse, or an article perhaps, to dash off the rough sketch of Open Door, to be finished by April 1st. (Easter [Friday] is April 3rd). We shall then, I hope, have an Italian journey: return say May 1st & finish Waves, so that the MS can go to be printed in June, & appear in September. These are possible dates anyhow.

Yesterday at Rodmell we saw a magpie & heard the first spring birds: sharp egotistical, like [illegible]. A hot sun; walked over Caburn; home by Horley & saw 3 men dash from a blue car & race, without hats across a field. We saw a silver & blue aeroplane in the middle of a field, apparently unhurt, among trees & cows. This morning the paper says three men were killed—the aeroplane dashing to the earth: But we went on, reminding me of that epitaph in the Greek anthology: when I sank, the other ships sailed on.[11]

9. A report of this 'hilariously serious' occasion appeared in Vera Brittain's column 'A Woman's Notebook' in the NS&N of 31 January 1931 (reprinted in The Pargiters, p. xxxv).
10. For Vita Sackville-West, see Appendix.
11. Mount Caburn is the bare down dominating the Ouse Valley on the far side of the river from Rodmell. The crashed aircraft was an Avro 40K from Gatwick aerodrome, where the three dead men were employed. 'I am the tomb of a shipwrecked man; but set sail, stranger: for when we were lost, the other ships voyaged on.' Theodoridas, no. 282 in book VII of The Greek Anthology, Loeb edition.

FEBRUARY 1931

My memory of todays headlines is this: *Gandhi set free. Pavlova to be buried at Golders Green. Ripper murder on Blackheath. Death of Lady St Helier*—who was so d—d condescending to me, 30 years ago.[12]

Monday 2 February

I think I am about to finish The Waves. I think I might finish it on Saturday.

This is merely an author's note: never have I screwed my brain so tight over a book. The proof is that I am almost incapable of other reading or writing. I can only flop wide once the morning is over. Oh Lord the relief when this week is over, & I have anyrate the feeling that I have wound up & done with that long labour: ended that vision. I think I have just done what I meant: of course I have altered the scheme considerably; but my feeling is that I have insisted upon saying, by hook or by crook certain things I meant to say. I imagine that the hookedness may be so great that it will be a failure from a reader's point of view. Well, never mind: it is a brave attempt, I think, ⟨& marks⟩ something struggled for. Oh & then the delight of skirmishing free again—the delight of being idle, & not much minding what happens; & then I shall be able to read again, with all my mind—a thing I haven't done these 4 months I daresay. This will have taken me 18 months to write: & we cant publish it till the autumn I suppose.

William P. talked more of his new novel, the Autobiography or Experiences? of an Emigrant the other night than L. has talked of his books all his life.[1]

Wednesday 4 February

A day ruined, for us both. L. has to go every morning at 10.15 to the

12. Gandhi, held in prison in India for civil disobedience since May 1930, was released on 25 January. The Russian ballerina Anna Pavlova (1881-1931) died at The Hague on 22 January; she was cremated at Golders Green, North London, on 29 January. The murder of Louise Maud Steel, whose body was found on Blackheath on 23 January, gave rise to a crop of sensational rumours about missing girls in the district. Lady St Helier, 'indefatigable in the service of the poor, and in Society famed for her brilliant art of entertaining' (*Who's Who*), published her *Memories of Fifty Years* in 1909. Her husband, a judge, was raised to the peerage shortly before his death in 1905, and it would have been under her previous appellation of Lady Jeune that she condescended to VW, a reluctant debutante.

1. William Plomer (1903-1973), poet and novelist. He sent his first novel *Turbott Wolfe* to the Hogarth Press from South Africa, where he grew up, and the Woolfs published it in 1925. After two years spent in Japan, he first met them on returning to England in 1929. His new novel *Sado*, which they published in September 1931 (*HP Checklist* 266), was set in Japan.

Courts, where his jury is still called, but respited always till 10.15 the next day; & this morning, wh. should have dealt a formidable blow at The Waves—B[ernard]. is within 2 days I think of saying O Death—was ruined by Elly, who was to have come at 9.30 sharp but did not come till 11. And it is now 12.30, & we sat talking about the period & professional women, after the usual rites with the stethoscope, seeking vainly the cause of my temperature. If we like to spend 7 guineas we might catch a bug—but we dont like. And so I am to eat Bemax [*a tonic*] &—the usual routine.[2]

How strange & wilful these last exacerbations of The Waves are! I was to have finished it at Christmas.

Today Ethel comes. On Monday I went to hear her rehearse at Lady Lewis's. A vast Portland Place house with the cold wedding cake Adams' plaster: shabby red carpets; flat surfaces washed with dull greens. The rehearsal was in a long room with a bow window looking on, in fact in, to other houses—iron staircases, chimneys, roofs—a barren brick outlook. There was a roaring fire in the Adams grate. Lady L. a now shapeless sausage, & Mrs Hunter, a swathed satin sausage, sat side by side on a sofa. Ethel stood at the piano in the window, in her battered felt, in her jersey & short skirt conducting with a pencil. There was a drop at the end of her nose. Miss Suddaby was singing the Soul, & I observed that she went through precisely the same attitudes of ecstasy & inspiration in the room, as in a hall.[3] There were two young or youngish men. Ethel's pince nez rode nearer & nearer the tip of her nose. She sang now & then; & once, taking the bass, made a cat squalling sound—but everything she does with such forthrightness directness that there is nothing ridiculous. She loses self-consciousness completely. She seems all vitalised; all energised: she knocks her hat from side to side. Strides rhythmically down the room

2. Dr Frances Elinor Rendel (1885-1942), a niece of Lytton Strachey, had been VW's doctor since the Woolfs moved to Tavistock Square in 1924.

3. Lady Lewis (1845-1931) was the German-born widow of the eminent Victorian solicitor Sir George Lewis; their house at 88 Portland Place had been a meeting place for society and the leading artists, writers, and musicians of their day. She died in September 1931. Mary Hunter (1857-1933), Ethel Smyth's elder sister, was the widow (since 1916) of an immensely wealthy coal-owner, whose fortune she used to dispense patronage and hospitality on a scale that eventually ruined her (see below, 13 May 1931). Ethel Smyth was rehearsing her setting for voice and orchestra of her friend Henry Brewster's metaphysical poem *The Prison*, which shortly afterwards had its first performance in Edinburgh under her baton, prior to its London performance at the Queen's Hall on 24 February under Adrian Boult. Elsie Suddaby (b. 1893) was in the front rank of concert sopranos between the wars; she and the bass-baritone Stuart Robertson took the two solo parts in *The Prison*.

to signify to Elizabeth that this is the Greek melody;[4] strides back; Now the furniture moving begins, she said, referring to some supernatural gambols connected with the prisoner's escape, or defiance or death. I suspect the music is too literary—too stressed—too didactic for my taste. But I am always impressed by the fact that it is music—I mean that she has spun these coherent chords harmonies melodies out of her so practical vigorous, strident mind. What if she should be a great composer? This fantastic idea is to her the merest commonplace: it is the fabric of her being. As she conducts, she hears music like Beethoven's. As she strides & turns & wheels about to us perched mute on chairs she thinks this is about the most important event now taking place in London. And perhaps it is. Well—I watched the curiously sensitive, perceptive Jewish face of old Lady L. trembling like a butterflies antennae to the sound. How sensitised to music old Jewesses are—how pliable, how supple. Mrs Hunter sat like a wax figure composed, upholstered [?], transfixed, with her gold chain purse.

Saturday 7 February

Here in the few minutes that remain, I must record, heaven be praised, the end of The Waves. I wrote the words O Death fifteen minutes ago, having reeled across the last ten pages with some moments of such intensity & intoxication that I seemed only to stumble after my own voice, or almost, after some sort of speaker (as when I was mad). I was almost afraid, remembering the voices that used to fly ahead. Anyhow it is done; & I have been sitting these 15 minutes in a state of glory, & calm, & some tears, thinking of Thoby & if I could write Julian Thoby Stephen 1881-1906 on the first page. I suppose not. How physical the sense of triumph & relief is! Whether good or bad, its done; & as I certainly felt at the end, not merely finished, but rounded off, completed, the thing stated—how hastily, how fragmentarily I know; but I mean that I have netted that fin in the waste of waters which appeared to me over the marshes out of my window at Rodmell when I was coming to an end of To the Lighthouse.[5]

What interests me in the last stage was the freedom & boldness with which my imagination picked up used & tossed aside all the images & symbols which I had prepared. I am sure that this is the right way of using them—not in set pieces, as I had tried at first, coherently, but simply as

4. Elizabeth Williamson (1901-80), grand-daughter of Mrs Hunter, a favourite great-niece and frequent companion of Ethel Smyth, taught mathematics and astronomy at University College, London.
5. See *III VW Diary*, 30 September 1926: 'One sees a fin passing far out. What image can I reach to convey what I mean? . . . All I mean to make is a note of a curious state of mind. I hazard the guess that it may be the impulse behind another book.'

images; never making them work out; only suggest. Thus I hope to have kept the sound of the sea & the birds, dawn, & garden subconsciously present, doing their work under ground.

Friday 14 February

And I had my hair curled two days ago. With some difficulty I controlled my bottomless despair when Nessa disapproved. I will front the world curled, I said to myself at 6 o'clock a m: very valiantly; I like my experimental temper.

Janet Case yesterday, shrivelled, narrowed, dimmed, aged, & very poverty struck. I noted her cheap shoes & dirty old velvet hat. I suppose over 70 now; & yet I always think of her as 45. She clings to youth. "But we never see any young people" & so reads Tom Eliot &c: has her wits about her: but oh dear, the pathos when our teachers become our learners. She has had I suppose a far harder life than I knew—illness, poverty, & all the narrowness of living; alone with Emphie; without any luxury, & the thought—I dont know about this—of leaving E. or being left. She was staying with an old man of 91. A curious clutching anxious sense such old age gives one: her face has become pointed, whitened; shrunk; her eyes remain. How I used to wait for her lesson: & then the arguments, the excitements. I was 17 she said when she came. She felt unsuccessful.[6]

Tuesday 17 February

And I feel us, compared with Aldous & Maria, unsuccessful. They're off today to do mines, factories . . black country; did the docks when they were here; must see England. They are going to the Sex Congress at Moscow, have been in India, will go to America, speak French, visit celebrities,—while here I live like a weevil in a biscuit. The fog thickens. My electric lamp is broken; (because we are having fires put [in]). Lord, how little I've seen, done, lived, felt, thought compared with the Huxleys —compared with anyone.[7] Here we toil, reading & writing, year in year out. No adventure, no travel; darker grows the fog. Here, by some

6. Janet Elizabeth Case (1862-1937), Classical scholar, had taught VW Greek at the beginning of the century. She and her sister Euphemia ('Emphie') now lived in retirement at Minstead in the New Forest.

7. Aldous Huxley (1894-1963) and his Belgian wife Maria (1898-1955) had their home in France, but were avid travellers; they were at this time spending some weeks in England, partly to gather material for articles on industrial Britain. They intended to accompany his brother Julian and others to the USSR in late spring on a visit organised by Intourist with the object of bringing British and Russian scientists in contact with each other; but in the event they did not go. The Huxleys dined with the Woolfs on 16 February.

invisible rope, we are bound. Add to this my gnats perception of fila-
mentary relations. With Nessa for example. I think she plumes & prides
herself: I think she exists self sufficient: I think her beauty is praised; I
think she does not want me; I think a million things a minute. My boasts
do me harm. My reality is unknown. So I go on—this is the truck [?] of
The Waves.[8] My ship has sailed on. I toss among empty bottles & bits of
toilet paper. O & the servants: Lottie. Mrs M. [*charwoman*] Nelly comfortably installed for life.

And I am to write 6 articles straight off about what? And a story.[9]
About what? All I like is my own capacity for feeling. If I werent so
miserable I could not be happy. And the Huxleys are now approaching
Chesterfield, where they will interview managers. Aldous takes life in
hand. Whether that damages his writing I dont know. He is 'modern'.
He is endlessly athletic & adventurous. He will be able to say he did not
waste his youth. Some bitterness is the goad which drives him on. Death
comes; nothing matters; at least let me see all that there is to be seen, read
all there is to be read. I fancy no one thing gives him the immense satisfaction things give me. Thats all the comfort I find.

Monday 9 March

And then I went, more than a week ago to Lady Rosebery's—blank
sealit room, buffet, elderly butlers or peers. Lady R. young & shorn.
Lord Revelstoke exemplary. Caviare. Lady Oxford. A curious fierce, dart
in her eye: strung; pinioned. I knew your father: your mother.. &c. Is to
come to tea. Wants me to write about her book. Sense of drum & blare:
of Ethel's remorseless fangs: her irresistible vanity, & some pang too for
her child's craving for a party—how tawdry how paltry: her facing out
the failure of The Prison; her desperate good cheer; her one bouquet; her
old battered wigged head. How mixed my feelings were—& how exhausted & windswept & disillusioned I was—with my ears ringing, & no
warmth depth comfort slippers & ease anywhere: but all effort & strain:
& the sense of the futility of it all.[1]

8. 'truck': the apposite word might be *trough*; and it is worth remarking that VW
would have pronounced this *truff*, which may account for a slip.
9. VW had undertaken to write six articles for *Good Housekeeping*, which were to be
published at intervals in the twelve months from December 1931 (see Kp C332.1;
C332.2; C333.1; C333.2; C334.1; C335.1). Five of the essays were reprinted in book
form by Frank Hallmann, New York, in 1975 under the title *The London Scene*
(Kp A43). The story has not been identified.
1. On 24 February the Woolfs had been to hear the first London performance of Ethel
Smyth's *The Prison* at the Queen's Hall, and afterwards VW went on to a party
given for Ethel at 38 Berkeley Square by the Countess of Rosebery (b. 1892),
second wife of the 6th Earl. Cecil Baring, 3rd Baron Revelstoke (1864-1945), was

Monday 16 March

These few & rather exacerbated entries show, I think, the back wash of The Waves. I am writing little articles of a morning, & should have been sketching the Houses of the Great this moring, but that I have not the material. This afternoon I shall try to see Carlyle's house & Keats' house. Tomorrow I lunch with George & Margaret to meet the Rothensteins. Miss Holtby is writing a book on me.[2] So we go on, until, with the sun out & the birds singing as I hope, we end this lap of the year with 3 weeks holiday. I'm ready this year for holiday. I think indeed that I have seldom worked harder, one way & another. Emotionally there has been the slight perpetual restraint with Nelly; & one fine blaze, about Lady Rosebery's party with Ethel—that valiant truculent old moss-trooper of a woman. She is so gritty to be brother with. And I respect her capacity for ignoring me. She took to reading Dean Inge, she says, when she assumed from my voice—exhausted, cold & gruff—that 'all was over.' Her strength of feeling is her power over one. This drives her head-long. Her Press has been catcalling—whistling. Never mind. She has other schemes on foot at once. A curious problem—what she minds, what she thinks, about her music. She descends to explanations in Time & Tide which seem deplorably low down. No, I cannot write this morning.[3]

---

an elder brother of Ethel's friend Maurice Baring. The Countess of Oxford (1864-1945), widow of the Liberal Prime Minister H. H. Asquith and better known as Margot Asquith, was a prominent and influential figure in politico-intellectual society; she published several books, and VW had already written unsigned reviews of two of them (Kp C262.4, Kp C283.1); her next book was *More Memories* (1933).

2. 'Great Men's Houses' was published as the third in VW's series for *Good House-keeping* (see above, 17 February 1931, n. 9). It describes her impressions of Thomas and Jane Carlyle's house at no. 5 (now 24) Cheyne Row, Chelsea; and of Keats's house in Keats Grove, Hampstead, to which LW drove her this afternoon. Sir George Duckworth (1868-1934), the elder of VW's half-brothers, and his wife Margaret (*née* Lady Margaret Herbert), had a London house in Mayfair. Sir William Rothenstein (1872-1945), the painter, since 1920 Principal of the Royal College of Art (and recently knighted), had known George since the 1890s; he had just published the first volume of his *Men and Memories*, in which he describes visiting Hyde Park Gate, and meeting George's 'step-sisters' Vanessa and Virginia Stephen, all in black. Winifred Holtby (1898-1935), the writer; her book on VW was published in October 1932.

3. See *IV VW Letters*, no. 2335 for VW's blaze about the party. The Very Rev. W. R. Inge (1860-1954), Dean of St Paul's 1911-34, known as 'the gloomy Dean', was a prolific writer on theological, philosophical, and political matters, and from 1921-46 wrote a regular column in the *Evening Standard*. Ethel Smyth's response to un-favourable press criticism of *The Prison* was to appear in the form of articles published in *Time and Tide* on 21 March and 4 April, and in the *NS&N*, 9 May: 'Composers and Critics'.

Barbara, Julian & Betty Jenkins the other night—Julian in a stew about his poems. And so my quiet weekend at Rodmell next week will be spent discussing Pope &c. How I grudge it—& yet cant deny the young. Ann Toby Henderson & I go to Tantivy Towers. But enough of this moping & groping.[4]

There is no doubt that a low mood, betokening dispiritment is more enlivening to our friends than one blown with triumph & success:—[5]

Thursday 19 March

Ethel yesterday, very uneasy about her character; & possible mis-representations. I think deluding herself about her own motives in countering reviewers: (purely for the sake of other musicians, women in particular: I've nothing to lose: have suffered neglect &c all my life). I think uneasy about her own greatness, requiring assurance, & snatching it rather hastily from such vague remarks as I could make "Thats just what I wanted you to say"—she plays a losing game very gallantly. "But I detest Bohemianism. I want fresh air, above everything. Therefore I took care to afficher myself. I was the friend of the Empress. The Ambassador was an old friend of mine. I couldn't afford to be declassée. Couldn't have borne it (about her standing in Roman society).[6]

It seems possible to me that nature gave her everything except the power of expression in music: hence the race & violence & restlessness of

4. Barbara (b. 1911) was the only daughter of Mary and St John Hutchinson (see Appendix). Julian Heward Bell (1908-37), the elder of Clive and Vanessa Bell's two sons, went up to King's College, Cambridge, in 1927 and read History and English; in 1930 King's granted him a research studentship in order to write a dissertation on Pope. His first book of poems, *Winter Movement*, had been published by Chatto & Windus in the autumn of 1930. These two had dined with the Woolfs at the Ivy Restaurant on 13 March, and were joined afterwards at 52 Tavistock Square by Elizabeth Jenkins (b. 1905), scholar and graduate of Newnham, who was now teaching English at King Alfred's School, Hampstead; her first novel, *Virginia Water*, had been published in 1929.

    The Woolfs took VW's niece Ann Stephen (b. 1916), the elder of VW's brother Adrian's two daughters, and Joan Cedar ('Toby', b. 1916), daughter of the former editor of the *N&A* Hubert Henderson, to the Lyric Theatre, Hammersmith, on 27 March to see the successful light opera by A. P. Herbert and Thomas F. Dunhill.

5. This appears to be a note of another writer's (Keats?) thought rather than VW's own. On the *verso* of the page she has copied a passage from a letter from Keats to Benjamin Robert Haydon, dated 22 December 1818 (p. 212 in Sydney Colvin's edition): "'I should say I value more the privilege of seeing great things in loneliness than the fame of a Prophet" Keats. Letters, 212.'

6. The Smyth family had been Surrey neighbours of the Empress Eugénie (1826-1920) when she lived at Farnborough Hill, and she subsequently became one of the pivots of Ethel Smyth's life (see her *Streaks of Life*, 1921).

her nature: the one outlet is stopped up. And she for ever batters at the door; it remains locked; she flows away over me, Lady Cunard—whoever it may be with the vehemence of a tortured & baffled spirit. But she would die rather than allow this. Hence her terrific egotism: her insatiable desire for praise, since she is denied the only true satisfaction. An exhausting companion, therefore.

Christabel last night.

I put Leonard higher than anybody here—above you, who are above the rest.

My fourth child is not by my husband.

Why these candours & confessions?

She did not like me, or trust me, last night

Desmond, ⟨Velinda⟩ Benita?, Vanessa, Raymond, Vita, Lord David Duncan Julian[7]

[*Wednesday 25 March*]

And here I sit, waiting to go to the Richmonds, having lunched with Clive, about to dine with the Wolves. Wine at lunch flushes me & floats me. So with Tom. A bad thing. My hair came down. Yesterday at the docks with Harold. Tomorrow, Ethel's party at Nessa's. Friday Tantivy Towers—wh. reminds me to write more letters before I change. Lord Lord.[8]

Saturday 28 March

Arnold Bennett died last night; which leaves me sadder than I should

7. Lady ('Emerald') Cunard (1872-1945), the American-born widow of the wealthy Sir Bache Cunard, was a prominent London hostess and patroness of the arts. On 18 March, VW dined with Clive Bell. Christabel, the Hon. Mrs Henry MacLaren (1890-1974), became Lady Aberconway on the death of her father-in-law in 1934. Benita Jaeger was at this period Clive's most frequent companion. Lord David Cecil (b. 1902), younger son of the 4th Marquess of Salisbury, critic and biographer and a Fellow of Wadham College, Oxford; his life of Cowper, *The Stricken Deer*, had been published in 1929. For Desmond MacCarthy and Raymond Mortimer see Appendix.

8. This entry is undated, but it was on 25 March that VW lunched with Clive Bell and T. S. Eliot. She went to tea in Kensington with Bruce Lyttelton Richmond (1871-1964), editor of the *TLS*, and his wife Elena (1878-1964), and LW fetched her from Kensington for a family dinner with his mother, a sister and brother, and their spouses. On 20 March VW had visited the docks in a Port of London Authority launch with a party which included LW, V. Sackville-West, and the Persian Ambassador; she returned with Harold Nicolson (see below, 7 August 1931, n. 7); and used her impressions in one of her articles on 'The London Scene' for *Good Housekeeping* (see above 17 February 1931, n. 9).

have supposed.[9] A lovable genuine man; impeded, somehow a little awkward in life; well meaning; ponderous; kindly; coarse; knowing he was coarse; dimly floundering & feeling for something else. Glutted with success: wounded in his feelings: avid; thick lipped: prosaic intolerably; rather dignified; set upon writing; yet always taken in; deluded by splendour & success; but naïve; an old bore; an egotist; much at the mercy of life for all his competence; a shop keepers view of literature; yet with the rudiments, covered over with fat & prosperity & the desire for hideous Empire furniture, of sensibility. Some real understanding power, as well as a gigantic absorbing power.—These are the sort of things that I think by fits & starts this morning, as I sit journalising; I remember his determinat[ion] to write, 1000 words daily; & how he trotted off to do it that night: & feel some sorrow that now he will never sit down & begin methodically covering his regulation number of pages in his workmanlike beautiful but dull hand. Queer how one regrets the dispersal of any body who seemed—as I say—genuine; who had direct contact with life—for he abused me; & I yet rather wished him to go on abusing me; & me abusing him. An element in life—even in mine that was so remote—taken away. This is what one minds.[10]

On Saturday 28 March the Woolfs drove to Liphook to stay the night at Passfield Corner as guests of Sidney and Beatrice Webb; on Monday they went to the House of Commons (Cf. "This is the House of Commons", Good Housekeeping, *Kp C334.1); on 31 March they attended the memorial service for Arnold Bennett at St Clement Danes in the Strand. On Thursday 2 April they drove to Monks House for Easter, returning to London on 9 April.*

Saturday 11 April

Oh I am so tired of correcting my own writing—these 8 articles—I have however learnt I think to dash: & not to finick. I mean the writing is free enough: its the repulsiveness of correcting that nauseates me. And the cramming in & the cutting out. And articles & more articles are asked for. For ever I could write articles.[1]

9. Arnold Bennett died at his Baker Street flat on 27 March of typhoid fever contracted through drinking tap water in Paris at the New Year. VW's last meeting with him was at a dinner party of Ethel Sands' on 1 December (see *III VW Diary*, 2 December 1930).

10. Cf. VW's essay on Edmund Gosse published in the *Fortnightly Review* in June 1931 (Kp C331), in which she adverts to Bennett's unaffected bluntness and sincerity towards other writers and contrasts this favourably with the decorous self-importance of Gosse.

1. Besides the London articles for *Good Housekeeping* and that on Gosse for the *Fortnightly Review*, VW at this time also wrote two articles for the *TLS*, on 'Lockhart's Criticism' and '"Aurora Leigh"' (Kp C330, C332, the latter also published in the *Yale Review*).

But I have no pen—well, it will just make a mark. And not much to say. or rather too much & not the mood.

We came back on Thursday. The sun at once rose[;] all the leaves pushed; the grass in the Square was literally liquid emerald. And so on. Imagine my regrets for Monks House: & how I start in the night—my early mornings are terrible battles—Fight fight—yet later I cant remember what the fights about—saying Curse, oh God, curse: as I remember that hideous new house on the top of my down; the rampart so often looked at on my evening walk. They are building the garage now; so we dig ourselves in.[2]

And I saw Pernel & of course, on top of Pernel Peter [Lucas]; so she was cross & he was pertinacious, & I had to skim the two of them with talk about Mrs Hunt's life of E. Siddal: not what I wanted to say. But these lovers have the pertinacity of gnats round flames: must talk, even if not about Sheilah.[3]

On Thursday we have our fortnight in France. I intend to keep a diary so as to make each day last longer. I think I shall like La Rochelle best: I shall want to live there. I shall take a house there: I shall dream of walking there when I am old & full of sleep.

The Woolfs left Rodmell for their French tour on 16 April, crossing at night from Newhaven to Dieppe, to return there on 30 April. LW's diary (LWP, Sussex) records in detail their itinerary and the hotels at which they stayed.

Here I will paste in—though it is hardly worth the trouble, the fitful flying notes I made, generally very cold, rather wet, with a rug round my knees, for the weather—everybody is talking about the weather. The worst April for 50 years.

That we retrieved so much from it that was lovely, ravishing, amusing & had so many good hours, spinning along the wet roads, under a

2. Bleak House, or as VW calls it elsewhere 'Hancock's Horror', was built at the top of Mill Hill above Rodmell for F. R. Hancock, the (unsuccessful) Labour candidate for Lewes constituency in the general elections of 1931 and 1935.
3. (Joan) Pernel Strachey (1876-1951), Principal of Newnham College, Cambridge, 1923-41, fourth of Lytton's five sisters. Frank Laurence ('Peter') Lucas (1894-1967), Fellow of King's College, Cambridge, and since 1926 University Lecturer in English Literature; he and his wife had separated two years previously, and he was now in love with Sheelah (1903-36), a graduate of Newnham and wife of the painter and art-critic, Alan Clutton-Brock. Violet Hunt's sensational and unreliable book, *The Wife of Rossetti, Her Life and Death*, was considered for publication by the Hogarth Press, but declined; it was published in 1932 by John Lane.

complete grey cloud, speaks well for the state of our souls. After being married since August 1912

$$\begin{array}{r} 1931 \\ 1912 \\ \hline 19 \end{array}$$

nineteen years, how moving to find this warmth, curiousity, attachment in being alone with L. If I dared I would investigate my own sensations with regard to him, but out of laziness, humility, pride, I dont know what reticence—refrain. I who am not reticent.

Diary of Tour
to La Rochelle,
Brantome
&c.
April 16th 1931

Thursday 16 April

Newhaven: dinner. hotel lately done up in modern style.[4] Guests surprising. 2 young men in trousers are women. One is Mrs Pilkington [*unidentified*]. Conversation on phone. "Oh darling Judy . . longing to see you—Ethel too marvellous. In bed at 2.30 this morning. Now at New-haven". Yet her stride & gestures male: check shirt. The other had feminine face: was the woman of the two: but trousers. Nobody stared. Ordered cocktails. Other guests, man like Tartarin: bushy black beard sprouting from chin: bare ankles: yatchting cap: but English. Others a newly married pair; bride in full evening dress. Rung up. Maybe the family—her's presumably. Elderly married couples, crossing, like ourselves, looked too respectable in this comedy film star atmosphere—at Newhaven of all places. And a fairly good dinner.

Friday 17 April

Very wet: very cold: horrid seaside marine atmosphere: all drenched & shrubs blown as usual at Dieppe. Breakfast in the usual hotel [du Rhinet de Newhaven]. Started. Wind & rain: almost black air. Rain came through. At the ferry at Quilleboeuf L. saw blue sky. Great rejoicing. Lunch at Inn by ferry—cheap, coarse; burnt fish. Old man & woman country people lunching. He had a thimble of brandy in his coffee. On again. Cold but fine in bouts. Along country roads. No houses. Came to Alençon. A

4. The Woolfs dined at the Bridge Hotel—'by Appointment to the King of France'—in Newhaven, where in 1848 Louis Philippe spent his first night of exile in England.

white elegant old town, with a great magnolia tree all stuck thick with flowers. Heard a loudspeaker in an old house, where a girl sat under rows of jars writing. Odd little scene. Vast bare Place for soldiers. Dined badly—save for wine; a whole bottle. Guests: 4 French businessmen & one Chinese business man: a girl like Fredegond [Shove, *VW's cousin*] & very old man. Talk about trains to Paris. Cold water in our bath; for which we paid heavily. Bitter cold: but suffocated with hot air early in the morning. Started for Saumur. Drove more slowly. April weather. bitter cold. Not enough clothes on. Lunch at Sablé-sur-Sarthe: not good food yet. Little old town on river. Saw old castle at Durtal: turned into alms-houses or hotel; dusty with waterproof peaked towers.

Saturday 18 April

Saumur, cold & wet, with gleams, though. The Loire—vast, without a single boat. France very empty. Hotel improved. hotter water. Women said they had been wearing cotton dresses—weather unknown. Saw the big round church by the river. A market. Started; having forgotten change of time. Bad morning. Went to Fontevrault. Saw beautiful bare old convent church. Dont take off your hat, said man. Its not sacred. The tombs of Plantagenets: like Edith Sitwell: straight, narrow side by side: re-painted, blue & red. Now all this great convent where filles de France educated a prison. Prison bells ringing for their dinner. Fountain where the girls washed before dinner. The cold must have been worse then. The Abbesses had themselves painted in frescoes—fat, sensual, highnosed faces.[5]

Went on in rain across country: narrow yellow roads: old women sitting in fields under umbrellas near sheep. Biblical. Behind time. Lunch at Thouars: the food still no better than food in English Inns L. says.

Monday 20 April

Gradual southerly feeling—men playing boules. Old men getting out of cars to pick flowers in the woods. Roads as straight as rods; some of them entirely lined with trees; their tops touching. But the worst weather so far. Car shut all day. Reached Niort at 6: determined to push on 40

5. The Abbey of Fontevrault, founded in the 11th century and converted into a prison by Napoleon in 1804, had housed religious communities, both presided over by an abbess, of monks and nuns, the latter drawn largely from aristocratic families. The Romanesque church contains eight Plantagenet royal tombs, including those of Henry II and Richard I. The frescoes are in the chapter-house opening off the cloisters. The poet Edith Sitwell (1887-1964) prided herself on her Angevin blood.

miles to La Rochelle. Arrived at 7.30—so quick one drives: I forgot our 2 punctures. One at Thouart [Thouars]; kept us, as the man did not mend it while we lunched. I read Sons & Lovers [*by D. H. Lawrence*], every word: a merry go round. Wished for fur coat. Another puncture 10 miles later. Had to stand in rain & change wheel. Scraped a hole in the road. On & off again. Went into hotel on the place. Found them dancing: so came here (de France et Angleterre) Exactly right—very ciré floors: quiet: a garden: ruins; lilac; flower pot roofs; but still gray this morning. Window open though; & not actually raining.

Tuesday 21 April

To Marennes. Cold & dark at first; gradually cleared. Our finest day. People at once begin lounging: put shutters up. Went to Marennes, across an emerald green marsh: deserted, a cow or two: a tall spare woman dressed in black like a clergyman. At Bourgeant ? [Brouage]—a town in an old wall; tufted with grass. Lovely country. a ferry. aeroplanes looping loop. Church in Marennes; old ship slung from ceiling. The hotel of the oysters 2 Ki. on. Sat at green table in the sun & drank coffee: L. had 12 oysters: alive: twisted in his mouth he said; green: with distorted shells. A pine wood; all silent; no bungalows. low sea. boats out at oyster banks. Very lovely drive back across the marsh. Tall marsh grasses fine yellow like babies' hair: broad brown river. Friendly men on ferry. Home. Now colder. Car jammed. First wholly fine day. Lunch off paté & croissants in the marsh. Hotel food soon bores.

Saturday 25 April

Angouleme. Fair, concours agricole braying: a loudspeaker too under a vast blue & yellow cardboard tower, higher than this hotel, on wh. is written Huiles et Tourbeaux: they sell ices at a little opening. We have been to the concours: saw dogs: Belgian hares; mechanical saws; bees in hives. Then walked, in high wind & black clouds, round battlements. Slightly reminded me of Clifton—high airy terraces, overlooking breadths of cloud darkened country. Girls drinking port & eating cakes in Thé Salon.

Before this, we went to Castillon: an adventure, driving on narrow country roads, further south than Brantome. Arrived late. Asked for dinner at Boule d'Or. Walked by the Dordogne—of majestic brea[d]th, empty like all France, save for one racing boat. We slept here very well in soft warm beds, though there was no hot water & the cold was so great we had to go to bed. Next day was fine & warm. I went into the Church; after the school children had left. I always wonder at the immense fund of ancient piety, dragging these blocks into mere villages. Lovely spring day. Drove 7 or 8 miles to Montaigne. Rang at Castle door.

No one came.[6] Women tending cows in ancient stables. A tower at one end. A garden with flowering trees. The usual renovated peaked & black tiled Chateau: over the door Que S'cais-je— A woman came. Took us up narrow stone steps, worn; opened thick nail studded door. This is his bedroom; this is his dressing room. Here he died. Here he went down— he was very small—to Chapel. Upstairs again is his library. The books & furniture are at Bordeaux. Here is his chair & table. He wrote those inscriptions on the beams. Sure enough it was his room; a piece of an old wooden chair might be his. A circular tower, very thick; 3 small windows looking along the wall to another tower. All that remains of the fire wh. burnt the old Chateau in 1880—or thereabouts. We wandered on the terrace. Saw the vineyards below; the shaped reddish hills & terraces: one or two brooding brown farms—much his view—the curious musing man must have halted to look at what we saw. So lovely now; as then. Americans &c. Every day of the year the woman said. A dog went with us fetching a chestnut & putting it on the parapet to be thrown. So on, through lovely shaped fields, like the south, but subtler, to Bergerac, where we had our best—our only good meal L. says. Indeed when the novelty is gone, the food is ranker & commoner & less interesting than I remembered; save for this lunch; off Monbazillac wine; pâte; eggs & so on.

To Perigueux: old furniture shops: expensive chairs: a church with green domes; scraped; renewed. All worshippers are old women; all in black; all woollen; decrepit. A random priest ambling along with different gestures. Tom's religion. (I must read his Lambeth tonight, having read myself almost out of books[7]). So to Brantôme—in the evening sun. Man felling poplar in a flat meadow: boy fishing; a ring & loop of waters under old bridges; smoky cave dwellings lived in since Charlemagne. Cheap, clean, elementary Inn—no. Letters. Kauffer. Ethel. Vita—about my bibliography: papers: Nessa at Okehampton in floods; determined that England is intolerable—Children so excited she cant give up the tour.[8]

6. It was on Thursday 23 April that the Woolfs visited the Château at St Michel-de-Montaigne to the west of Castillon, birthplace and home of the sceptical moralist Michel Eyquem de Montaigne (1533-1592), for whom LW had a particular veneration as the first civilised modern man. The château was largely destroyed by fire in 1885 and replaced by a modern edifice, but the round tower on the walls used by Montaigne as his retreat survives.
7. T. S. Eliot's *Thoughts After Lambeth* had been published in March 1931 as 'Criterion Miscellany, No. 30'; VW's copy was sold at Sotheby's, 27 April 1970, lot 50.
8. Edward McKnight Kauffer (1890-1954), American artist-designer, who had settled in London in 1914; he designed the alternative wolf's-head colophon used on some Hogarth Press publications from 1930 onwards. VW's bibliography, unexplained. Vanessa, for a school holiday treat, was driving her daughter and a friend to Cornwall and back.

Walk yesterday. Forgot the size of maps. Found Champagnac beyond us. Went wrong at Les Roches. Arrived at an old house on a green sward, with trees & walled garden. O to live here, we said. So much subtler, gentler, lovelier than Cassis. The land is flat & green as a lawn; with elongated quivering poplars just fledged; then the spade pressed hills I love; & the river, by which we walked—the river so deep, so romantic, taking the blue thunder clouds, the willows, twisting them nonchalantly, flowing on. Clumps of purple gentian in the reeds. An Elizabethan meadow—cowslips, bluebells. But the thunder roared out. We ran. We sheltered under a ruined cave of some sort. Then dashed home 2 miles of road or more; thighs aching; thunder & lightning at Cemetery. All the tin shelters & metal wreaths gleamed. Girls, mourners, took arms & ran. Home before the main shower, very heavy.

Fair. All the women in black with kids & sheep. Pens of pigs. Man said his sister in law said fish cheaper in Paris. Clerks from the Societe Generale for lunch. One black literary man. The other very southern; mobile[;] talked about cars.

Sunday 26 April

On to Poitiers. Went to Movies last night after a good dinner at the hotel we shd. have stayed at. Laughed violently at animals in hotel. A light risible method—the French—of telling the story of a cycle race— done by quick drawings on a sheet. Out into cold town—all spread for sun, which does not come. Cold windy drive this morning. Country might be Hampshire, save for emptiness. No cars. Poitiers for lunch. A Restaurant. Officers lunching & their young ladies—rather provincial. Enormous meal made by a thick slab of a man—painful to see soufflé disappear. Visited churches, heard women baa-ing responses like sheep. Rain & cold by fits; so came back to read & write till dinner. A quiet homely hotel; room looking onto courtyard. but still cold. [*Written on 27 April:*] No central heating that night; so had to go to bed for warmth, as before.

Monday 27 April

Cloud of Sunday lifted; but heavy in the skies. Drove over high ground to Chinon; showery: a discreet charming grey & white town. Got our letters. Pleasant to be asked to wire about making a speech; & know one cant answer. A first rate lunch—one of our great successes. No comparison with White Hart at Lewes possible. Climbed the steep path to Castle. Tapped at door. Went away relieved. No woman summoned us back. Explored castle alone as usual. Not a single tourist, & only 3 English the whole tour. Saw the high unroofed room in wh. Jeanne stood before the King. The very chimney piece perhaps.[9] Walls cut through by thin windows. Suddenly one looks down, down on roofs. How did the middle ages get through the evenings? A stone crypt in wh. J. lived: people carve their names everywhere. River silken serpentine beneath. Liked the stone roofless rooms; & the angular cut windows. Sat on the steps to hear 2 struck by the clock wh. has rung since the 13th Century: wh. J. heard. Rusty toned. What did she think? Was she mad? a visionary coinciding with the right moment. Drove on; showers; cold; bad roads; never mind —cheerful enough, till we landed at Chateau le-noir [Château-du-Loir] hoping for a small country Inn. Women holding the ends of sheets in the hall. Perpetual washing & ironing at hotels. Small child in Bureau playing with paper. Good dinner of its kind. Then the Movies began in the court-yard—talk & laughing till 12.30 or so. This damp place did its best to rejoice—valiantly, unfortunately for us. And bad breakfast in the public room, smelling of wine. So off: the day cold, but rather brighter. They call this La lune Rousse. They say it happens every year. Whether red or Russian I dont know.[10]

So to Le Mans. Another grey & white curved, dignified, flat windowed ancient town. Letters. The Cathedral. Bought umbrellas; pen tray; lunched. The tournedos underdone & expensive. Very little good meat in town restaurants I should say; at Chinon, though, whatever it was—duck I think—excellent. Here not much to pit against the White Hart Lewes— our staple comparison. In this great argument I am always for France; L. for England. Expense seems higher than 3 years ago. I voted for Dreux; so we went there—to Hotel de Paradis; & coming in heard the violins, & saw thinly dressed girls; cheap; rigged out in ready mades from the local shop. A wedding. Dancing already at 5.30. This is the Inn that has old cupboards.[11] Had to dine across the yard, as the dining room was danced in. Strawberries for dinner. An ice; but remembering A. Bennett, refused it. All very slow & cold. People driving up in cars all the time. Little boys scampering about in black velvet. Small girl perfectly dressed & very prim. Whole families invited: small business people I imagine. The dancing went on till 11. Then we saw the wretched waiters carrying tables across—how cynical all waiters must be & chambermaids—how terribly aware of the transitoriness of life—& the music stopped. They ate. Then at 12 or 1 (I was woken) cars began tuning up: people shouting, laughing saying goodbye. I had seen the bride dancing—a pale girl in

9. It was in the *grande salle* of the Château du Milieu at Chinon on 9 March 1429 that Jeanne d'Arc recognised Charles VII concealed among his courtiers.
10. *Lune rousse*: lunar month occurring after Easter; often accompanied by frosts and cold winds, which rust (*font roussir*) the young shoots.
11. The Woolfs had stayed there in April 1928 on their return journey from Cassis.

spectacles—& thought of her borne off to fulfil her duties in some small suburban house outside Dreux, for she was marrying a clerk I should think: & they now begin to replenish the race.

This morning was our finest. I put on my shady hat & left off my jersey. So did L. And I was cajoled into considering seriously a desk; £10: then stopped in Nonancourt: found a gigantic old furniture shop—cultivated man in knee breeches well cut—sporting—a connoisseur—too aware—perhaps shall buy a bed. Then lunched at our Clara's Bois Joli—my word![12] A chateau furnished each room in its own period; a chicken turned over the fire on a spit; old custom; pretty maids in pretty dresses; the usual fake; amusing; American; she said of the cowslips "Look at these baby primroses—arent they cute?" How I hate foreigners bad French. Our lunch admirable: but cost £1.10. This is Clara's idea of heaven. Not mine. A glorified Drusilla's teashop. Sickened me of old French furniture. Lovely as they are, things lose infinitely from being preserved not used. The sham, & the effort to tickle our vanity & feed on our money disagreeable. Lots of ancient summer houses & Skittles. An old caleche the most pleasant thing—rolled off with some rubbish in a doorway—18th Century. So here: Caudebec: & the weather is now (our last day) set fine. So be it.

[End of inserted pages]

Sunday 3 May

52 Tavistock Square.

Yes, thats all very well; but how to begin, & why begin? I mean what do these diaries amount to? O merely matter for a book, I think: & to read when I have a headache. After all, Percy could burn the lot in one bonfire. He could burn them at the edge of the field where, so we think, we shall lie buried. That was our conclusion after attending Arnold Bennett's funeral.[1]

But now, say I have a 3 months lap ahead of me: the 3 summer months. What shall I do? We are going to regulate 'seeing' people. There is to be a weekly black hole; a seething mass of people all eating tea together. We shall thus have more evenings free. In those evenings I intend to walk; to read, Elizabethans; to be mistress of my soul. Yes. And I intend to investigate Edinburgh & Stratford on Avon. Also to finish off The

12. A restaurant at Tillières-sur-Avre presumably recommended by LW's younger sister Clara. Drusilla's was (and is) a country tea shop between Berwick and Alfriston in Sussex.

1. Percy Bartholomew of Park Cottages, Rodmell, since 1928 the Woolfs' gardener at Monks House; both Virginia's and Leonard's ashes are buried within the garden there. The service for Arnold Bennett was at St Clement Danes, Strand, on 31 March.

Waves in a dashing masterly manner. D H Lawrence has given me much to think about—about writing for writings sake. Two days are to be set aside for reading MSS: & they are not to leak into other compartments. These two decisions—the Black Hole, & Hogarth Press MSS, will I think make for an orderly & satisfactory summer. Then of course, being now so well off, with 2 frigidaires & everything handsome, I need not fritter & fribble about clothes; & having little sense of the duty of society left, shall hope to take my way about unhasting unresting. I want to see the fields & flowers, one or two new places; to write some good articles. At the moment, I seem able to write criticism fearlessly. Because of a R. of ones Own I said suddenly to myself last night.

Wednesday 13 May

Unless I write a few sentences here from time to time I shall, as they say, forget the use of my pen. I am now engaged in typing out from start to finish the 332 pages of that very condensed book The Waves. I do 7 or 8 daily; by which means I hope to have the whole complete by June 16th or thereabouts. This requires some resolution; but I can see no other way to make all the corrections, & keep the lilt, & join up, & expand & do all the other final processes. It is like sweeping over an entire canvas with a wet brush.

[Friday 15 May]

But it is a happy life. Those rules I made have so far kept my week orderly. Yesterday I went to Mrs Hunter's sale, & before I had been in the room 5 minutes had bought through Mr Marchment of Shepherds Bush a large old rosewood & satinwood secretaire for £6.16. Heavens! The wood alone was worth that.[2] It was a sordid, emulative, exciting, depressing scene. The trade was there in force. Jews, smoking pipes. Many winks & nods interchanged. Poor old Mrs Hunter's little odds & ends were peered at & snatched; everybody seemed to be finding out flaws, & offering the least money. Marchment kept saying to me "Buy it—buy it— it'll grow into money". Thus solicited I did buy a shawl for 35/- & a little cabinet for £3.15. This I regretted; & I let slip—oh never mind. One must take these bargains & slips philosophically, in order to attain the perfectly buoyant & energised life which is now my aim. O yes, I dont waste a moment: I am always on the hop, with so much licence too

2. Ethel Smyth's sister Mrs Charles Hunter, having ruined herself by her extravagant and open-handed hospitality and patronage of artists and musicians, was compelled to sell her pictures and furnishings. The Woolfs went to view the contents of her house at 2 Gloucester Square on 8 May, and to the sale on the premises on 14 May.

allowed for sheer frivolity. Most plans of life are far too strict. I allow a liberal margin for pleasure.

The faces of Mrs H.'s rich friends disgusted me. Nothing is quite so coarse, cruel, meaningless, & sensual as a fashionable woman's face, who is about 50: has done nothing but scavenge about London in cars; eating & drinking; marrying; coveting, tittle tattling. The Smyth-Hunter circle centres I think round the shires; the golf courses; the purlieus of the Bath Club & Whites. They are horsey, dressy; but not aristocratic, not distinguished. They are very well off; but lose money largely—or so at least I diagnose them. But their philosophy requires them to take tumbles bravely. When we went in on Friday to look at the things, Mrs H. was sitting at the desk which I want to buy, as cool & self-possessed as if she were giving a house warming, instead of seeing all her possessions, beds & blankets, paper knives & pen trays, all go for two or three shillings. "I see you so seldom. Do sit down for a moment & talk!" And what was I to say, to a woman old enough to be my mother, in that predicament?

Tuesday 19 May

A quarter of an hour:—yes, & what to say in a quarter of an hour.

Lytton's book: very good.[3] Thats his line. The compressed yet glowing account which requires logic, reason, learning, taste, wit order & infinite skill—this suits him far better, I think than the larger scale, needing boldness, originality, sweep. I'm delighted too, to have an argument in favour of writing v. non-writing. Compare with Lawrence. These things wont tarnish & drop & let fall their petals. They hint at force; at reserve; at the strength to leave things unsaid; the strength required not to preach; not to extemporise. Like Max, though, a small talent sedulously cultivated. And I respect that. But I dont respect Logan. I loathe the vulgarity, the fribbery & frivolity of Logan (afterthoughts).[4]

Lytton & Raymond to dinner tonight. Desmond t'other night. He needs £300. Cant handle his book—makes excuses for leaving it with us. Much obliterated in the struggle for life.[5]

Mrs Hunt Hueffer: "I dont remember names after my illness. But I heard my mother talking to old Mr Black as I went upstairs. I did not

3. *Portraits in Miniature and Other Essays* by Lytton Strachey was published in May 1931.

4. See letter from Max Beerbohm quoted by David Cecil in *Max: A Biography* (1964), p. 393: 'My gifts are small. I've used them very well and very discreetly, never straining them; and . . . made a charming little reputation.' *Afterthoughts* by Logan Pearsall Smith (1865-1946) was published in May 1931 as a sequel to *Trivia* (1918) and *More Trivia* (1922).

5. Desmond MacCarthy's book was *Portraits*, the first in the uniform series of his collected essays and journalism; it was published by Putnam in November 1931.

know what it meant—intimate relations—at the time. afterwards I found out" as she has, Hugh says, with diverse people: perhaps Hugh; who winced at her name. William also (our first black hole) about his book: rather a disappointment—an Episode.[6]

Thursday 28 May

Soon after this, I started a headache—flashes of light raying round my eyes, & sharp pain; the pain cut into me by Ethel's voice, as she sat telling me—"You've got to listen"—about Adrian Boult, & how he ordered her to leave the room.[7] And then to Rodmell, where the same thing happened—the light round my eyes, but as I could lie still in bed in my big airy room, the pain was much less. If it were not for the divine goodness of L. how many times I should be thinking of death; always knocked over as I am; but now the recoveries are full of infinite relief. Moreover, on Whit Monday the sun blazed, making the grass semi-transparent. And space & leisure seemed to lie all about; & I said, not once in an exstasy, but frequently & soberly, This is happiness. Why should I feel now calmer, quieter than ever before? Partly my disposition of life; partly Nessa Roger & Clive being away so that I am not hauled about & ruffled. Partly The Waves coming to an end—partly—I really dont know.[8]

We went to Firle last night & brushed the buttercups on to our shoes, walking through the Park. A lovely country, even counting the villas. At Monks House we had electric light, & the Frigidaire is—today of course —working. When the electric light fused, we could hardly tolerate

6. (Isobel) Violet Hunt (1862-1942), who for some years from 1911 lived as his wife with Ford Madox Hueffer, adopting his name (the cause of legal proceedings and public scandal), was a prolific writer; her parents had moved in the social circle of the pre-Raphaelites, and her life of Elizabeth Siddal (see above, 11 April 1931, n. 3) was inspired by hearsay. Hugh Seymour Walpole (1884-1941), highly successful novelist; in 1928 he had presented the Femina-Vie-Heureuse prize to VW for *To the Lighthouse*; her subsequent friendship with him was somewhat equivocal, comprehending personal affection and a sardonically critical view of his work. Plomer's book was *Sado* (see above, 2 February 1931, n. 1).
7. An extended account of Ethel Smyth's conduct when she came to tea on 20 May is contained in *IV VW Letters*, no. 2375, to Vanessa Bell. Adrian Boult (b. 1889), Director of Music at the BBC since 1930, had conducted the first London performance of Smyth's *The Prison* at the Queen's Hall in February; she had chosen a particularly inopportune moment to demand that he repeat the performance for broadcasting, and her resentment at his refusal was poured out on VW. The Woolfs drove next morning to Monks House for Whitsun and returned to London on 28 May.
8. Clive Bell was in France, Vanessa in Rome, where she and Duncan Grant were joined by Roger Fry and Helen Anrep (see Appendix).

Aladdin lamps, so soon is the soul corrupted by comfort. Yesterday men were in the house all day boring holes for electric fires. What more comfort can we acquire? And, though the moralists say, when one has a thing one at once finds it hollow, I dont at all agree. I enjoy my luxuries at every turn, & think them wholly good for what I am pleased to call the soul.

Four young people smashed into Beddingham level crossing gates on Saturday & were cut in pieces by the 9.40 train. One man was found stripped naked, save for the hem of one trouser. Disappointed, reading lightly though, by The man who died, D. H. L.'s last. Reading Sons & Lovers first, then the last I seem to span the measure of his powers & trace his decline. A kind of Guy Fawkes dressing up grew on him it seems, in spite of the lovely silver-bright writing here & there: something sham. Making himself into a God, I suppose.[9]

I am much interrupted again by my wish to write A Knock on the door. For some weeks I have not thought of it. It suddenly forces itself on me, & I go on making up sentences, arguments, jokes &c. Then several people have written to me lately about A Room.

Saturday 30 May

No, I have just said, it being 12.45—I cannot write any more, &
p. 162 therefore indeed I cannot: I am copying the death chapter: have
halfway. in 26 re-written it twice. I shall go at it again & finish it, I
days. shall finish hope, this afternoon. But how it rolls into a tight ball the
by 1st July muscles in my brain! This is the most concentrated
with luck. work I have ever done—& oh the relief when it is
finished. But also the most interesting. ⟨p. 137⟩

A letter from Desmond this morning to say that he is sending his book to Putnam because, alas, it represents his life work; & though once he thought he could have done more, he now sees this is all, & therefore must seek a more durable publisher than the Hogarth Press.

To annoy me, Mary H[utchinson]. rings up & says they are thinking of taking Southease this summer. Surrounded by fashion & bungalows, I feel like a fish in a frying pan. But no doubt shall skip out. I dont like the idea of meeting Mary & Barbara appropriately dressed on the downs. Happily, some menial of the Pritchards is now hammering, & I have an excuse to go up to luncheon.[10]

9. D. H. Lawrence's story 'The Escaped Cock', published by the Black Sun Press in Paris six months before his death, was reissued in London by Martin Secker in March 1931 under the title *The Man Who Died*.
10. William Burchell Pritchard (d. 1940) was senior, his son George junior, partner, and his sister chief clerk, in the firm Dollman and Pritchard, Solicitors, the Woolfs' tenants on the ground and first floors of 52 Tavistock Square.

Thursday 2 June

Yes, it is very important to write a few sentences, or I shall forget how. All this correcting—all this hammer hammer hammer on the hard high road.[1]

Ethel again—All my ills, such as they are, spring from liver: I am a very strong woman, who needs calomel. After swallowing this terrific insult to the celebrated sensibility of my nervous system, I try to find out what motive lies behind Ethel & her calomel. I think; (but then I am not a psychologist) that she wants me to be everlasting: that she wants me to be unhurt by any amount of talk about the Prison: that she wants to have things—to her own will: that she dislikes other peoples illnesses which interfere with her vitality; that she likes to rationalise everything: that she suspects, on principle, all shrinking, subtlety & sensibility. Also she is remorseful for having sent me the picture of a sick monkey, but feels that if she can prove that the monkey was not sick but shamming, she is absolved. I dont know. It is very characteristic, & akin to the methods she pursues about her music. There too, to explain her lack of success, she fabricates a theory (about her kinship with the common man, & her consequent failure to attract the sophisticated, who control the Ring, so that Bax Vaughan Williams &c—are done. but she not).[2]

Monday 8 June

Dreams.

I had three lately: one of Katherine Mansfield: how we met, beyond death, & shook hands; saying something by way of explanation, & friendship: yet I knew she was dead. A curious summing up, it seemed, of what has passed since she died.

Then the dream of Daphne Sanger, & how she was proved to be the heir to the throne of England. And Charlie was there. And another dream which L. coming in to say that Jean Stewart wants to come to tea, has caused me to forget.[3] I diagnose, by the way, a coldness on the part of Ethel. No communications since last Tuesday save one rather formal card. I shall lie low & do nothing.

1. 'It ain't the 'unting as 'urts 'un, it's the 'ammer, 'ammer, 'ammer along the 'ard 'igh road.' *Punch*, vol. xxx, p. 141 (1856).
2. Arnold Bax (1883-1953) and Ralph Vaughan Williams (1872-1958), English composers.
3. Katherine Mansfield died in 1923. Daphne Sanger (b. 1905), a social worker since graduating from Newnham in 1928, was the only child of C. P. (Charlie) Sanger (1871-1930), to whom VW had been very attached, and his wife Dora. Jean Stewart (b. 1903), Faculty Lecturer in the University of Cambridge, was the author of *Poetry in France and England*, which the Hogarth Press published in May 1931 (*HP Checklist* 272).

Oh dear me no—no quarrel at all.

Two notes: the woman in white stamping on bread in Kensington Gardens: the Indian looking woman ferreting in the litter box—both wild, outlandish, in shabby finery, within a hands pace. This was last week.

Wednesday 17 June

L. finished the first volume of his book on Sunday: begun over 10 years ago. We shall bring it out in the autumn & a reprint of The Village. He has been asked to give 6 Broadcast talks in the autumn on politics.[4]

[Tuesday 23 June]

And yesterday, 22nd June—when, I think, the days begin to draw in, I finished my re-typing of The Waves. Not that it is finished—oh dear no. For then I must correct the re-re-typing. This work I began on May 5th, & no one can say that I have been hasty or careless this time; though I doubt not the lapses & slovenlinesses are innumerable.

A dark kind of summer. The cloud that hung over La Rochelle in April still hangs over London. In spite of this, owing to good resolutions, my little life has been adventurous & more stable than usual. There was Duncan's show; & considerable content, indeed a kind of bubbling rapture I think, in Fitzroy Street.[5] I must ask Nessa why we are so happy. Clive is in Cassis. Julian has grown a bristling beard like a chimpanzee & is off with volumes of Pope in MS to France. Tonight we go to the Gala Opera with Christabel. Stalls costing 25/- each.

I mean to record some literal conversations one of these days. Goldie wrote a qualified letter of praise about L.'s book: new & important ideas: the style repetitive & tedious. I distrust this, since Goldie's own mechanical style, the mould made in Greece, since considerably smoothed out, never takes my fancy: in fact I should not exaggerate if I said that I detest it: & its currency, plausibility & general first class aspect.[6]

4. The first volume of LW's ambitious projected study of the psychology of man as a social animal, *After the Deluge*, was published in October 1931 (*HP Checklist* 278). He had recovered the rights in his novel, *A Village in the Jungle*, published by Edward Arnold in 1913, and the first Hogarth Press edition appeared in September 1931 (*HP Checklist* 277). His six broadcasts, under the general title 'The Modern State', were to be given each Thursday from 1 October to 5 November on the National Service of the BBC (and were printed in *The Listener*).

5. The exhibition of 'Recent Paintings by Duncan Grant' at the Cooling Galleries, 92 New Bond Street, was opened by Lady Ottoline Morrell on 10 June; VW had lunched beforehand in Vanessa's studio with a family party.

6. Goldsworthy ('Goldie') Lowes Dickinson (1862-1932), Fellow of King's College, Cambridge, and an Apostle, was an influential teacher and writer on ethical and political matters whom LW had known and respected since his undergraduate days.

On Wednesday-tomorrow-Ethel comes, & we have a party. Such is life—so gliding on. It is 12.30.

[*Wednesday 24 June*]

Last night we went to the gala opera; sat in the stalls, 2 rows from the stage, with Christabel & a woman, who came in late, called Lady Abingdon.[7] Her fortune has been spent on her face. Perfectly agile, direct, slim. She has only a thin rigid trickle of a mind, & no play, range, or more than an inch of depth. But she is perfectly energised: knew what she was after. Christabel, to weld these incompatibles (L[eonard]. &c) told stories of Princess Mary at Mrs Marshall's party: how she stopped, jerked; was short clumsy, dressed like the upper housemaid in peacock blue. In the interval, old bibulous Maurice Baring red as a turkey cock, a survival from the Regency as I feel, came following, to clear Gosse's character; which he did—but Evan Charteris had already done it—amiably enough. He has pink eye starting, & long equine teeth. Then Mrs Grenfell, whose chin, as C. said (C. is witty in her skimming way, & exactly fits this kind of thing) should have an inch or two hammered off.[8] People passing. Old women like Roman matrons, ample, tightly girt; girls wand like: many large clear stoned necklaces & long dresses. I got the feeling of this traditional English life; its garden like quality; flowers all in beds & rows; & the ceremony that has been in being so many years. Between the acts we all stood in the street; a dry brilliant night, with women all opening their cloaks: then came dribbling through us a draggled procession of poor women wheeling perambulators & carrying small, white haired dazed children; going across Waterloo bridge. I watched Lady A's expression to see if she had children; but could only gather a momentary schoolboyish compunction. The women, involved in this garish feathered crowd, pushed on stolidly. There was Tom Bridges; a gallant, irresistible General, with one leg, his head on one side; off the stage as it seemed, so typical of the distinguished elderly Beau. He has broken many hearts said

7. The Gala Performance on 23 June during Sir Thomas Beecham's 'Season of Russian Opera and Ballet' at the Lyceum Theatre, consisted of performances of acts from three operas, *Don Quixote*, *Prince Igor*, and *La Fiancée du Czar*, and the ballet *Petrouchka*. Lady Abingdon (1896-1978) was Elizabeth, *née* Stuart-Wortley, wife of the 8th Earl of Abingdon; they had no children.
8. Maurice Baring (1874-1945), diplomat, man of letters, and a particular friend of Ethel Smyth. VW, in her own words (*IV VW Letters*, no. 2345), had been 'candid and caustic' about Edmund Gosse in her *Fortnightly Review* article (Kp C331); his biographer, Evan Charteris, had written to her about it (see *IV VW Letters*, no. 2403), but his letter does not survive. Florence Grenfell (d. 1971), wife of the banker and Conservative MP E. C. Grenfell, later Lord St Just, was a friend of Lydia Keynes (see Appendix).

C. but I don't like him.[9] C. said she might be summoned away before the end of Prince Igor. And so she went, liking this little amorous mystery. Lady A. stalked off without a good night or glance in our direction. Each of her nails was red, & cut out like a small rose petal. L. who had been reading The Lady said this was considered in bad taste; & that men, according to The Lady, dont like it. So home, by cab. Oh & my hair stood the strain very well. I believe I can now with care master my hair.

The woman who has been standing in the square for some 6 hours daily came yesterday with a sword, upon which she leant as she pretended to read the paper. This finally got upon the household nerves, & Miss Talbot summoned her in. She then spoke (said Nelly) very nicely; regretted having annoyed anybody, & said she was waiting for Dr Rowe, of the Clinic, from which we infer that she is an ex-patient with a grievance.[10]

I was also made to waste half an hour looking at silk stockings by Mr Lowe, & lost my temper, on being asked to deposit 3/—a thing I greatly enjoy, because it makes me seem so vigorous. Now to continue Rhoda's speech. Oh this book!——

Monday 29 June

I had an idea for a book last night—a voyage round the world, imaginary, hunting, climbing, adventurous people, shooting tigers, submarines, flying & so on. Fantastic. Some character: partly the result of L.'s saying if we go to America we shd. not make one bite of the cherry but go round the world. Then W.A. Forster said And write an Orlando of your tour.[11]

Tuesday 30 June

Yesterday Nessa gave me the picture of Angelica.

9. Lt. Gen. Sir (George) Tom (Molesworth) Bridges (1871-1939) retired from the army in 1922 after a particularly dashing career, including losing a leg at Passchendaele in 1917. He was a nephew of the poet Robert Bridges; in 1938 he published a book of reminiscences, *Alarms and Excursions*. See MHP, Sussex, B 2a for VW's notes on this book.

10. The Tavistock Square Clinic (for functional nervous disorders) was at 51 Tavistock Square, next door to the Woolfs and their solicitor-tenants, where Miss Talbot was clerk. Dr Constance Rowe was assistant-physician at the Clinic.

11. William Arnold-Forster (1885-1951), husband of VW's old friend 'Ka' Cox, had trained as a painter at the Slade, but now devoted much of his energy towards furthering the ideals of the League of Nations. He was, like LW, a member of the Labour Party Advisory Committee on International Affairs. On 27 June he both breakfasted and lunched with the Woolfs at Tavistock Square and attended a committee meeting of the Fabian Society there.

Yesterday Ethel's indignity reached its sordid & ridiculous climax.[12]

Wednesday 1 July

Today Mary [Hutchinson] & Tommy dine with us & Ottoline comes in afterwards.

We go to Easdale's concert at 3. & so on.[1]

Jack, as a wedding gift to Miss Mary Ashton, has stopped, not only my allowance but Nessa's & Adrian's.[2]

Our takings, what with the Press & my work, have given me a bonus of £860.

And now I must go up & find Ethel's sentimental & hysterical sheets & underline the most sentimental & hysterical passages for her benefit. Pah—as people say in Shakespeare. And John Bailey is dead, aged 67.[3] (which makes me think—no this refers to Jack—that I will read Stendhal de l'Amour).

12. Angelica Bell (b. 1918) was Vanessa's daughter by Duncan Grant; she was at boarding school in Essex. This oil painting of her sewing hung in LW's London house at his death; present whereabouts unknown. On 27 June VW had answered Ethel Smyth's request for criticism of her article on 'Composers and Critics' (published in the *NS&N* on 9 May) which she was revising for inclusion in a collection later published as *Female Pipings in Eden* (1933), with a letter 'written in a hurry ... with all its faults on its face'; Ethel's hysterical response, which VW returned to her with passages underlined (see below, 1 July 1931) is preserved in the Berg with VW's own frosty reply. (See *IV VW Letters*, nos. 2393, 2396.)

1. For Lady Ottoline Morrell, see Appendix. The Hon. Stephen ('Tommy') Tomlin (1901-1937), sculptor, son of Lord Justice Tomlin, had married Julia Strachey (see below, 12 March 1932, n. 4) in 1927; since first meeting VW he had wished to model her head (see *II VW Diary*, 21 December 1924), and during this month she grudgingly gave him (and Vanessa) six sittings in his studio at 8 Percy Street, WC1. The original plaster model of the resulting portrait head is at Charleston; lead casts are at Monks House and the National Portrait Gallery. The Woolfs had come into contact with the Easdale family, mother, son, and daughter Joan, through the latter sending her poems to the Hogarth Press, which published them in February 1931 (*HP Checklist* 253). The son was a composer, and he and his sister gave a performance of his settings of her poems in Bumpus's bookshop in Oxford Street.

2. Rt. Hon. John ('Jack') Waller Hills (1867-1938), MP, widower of VW's half-sister Stella Duckworth (1869-97), in 1931 married Mary Grace Ashton. Stella died intestate, and income from her substantial marriage settlement had been transferred by Hills to her step-father Leslie Stephen (see his *Mausoleum Book*, edited by Alan Bell, 1977, p. 104); and on his death this had devolved upon his children.

3. John Cann Bailey (1864-1931), man of letters, clubman, and constant contributor to the *TLS* since its inception; as a figure in the literary and Kensington world he had been known to VW since early in the century.

JULY 1931

Tuesday 7 July

O to seek relief from this incessant correction (I am doing the interludes) & write a few words carelessly. Still better, to write nothing; to tramp over the downs, blown like thistle. as irresponsible. And to get away from this hard knot in which my brain has been so tight spun—I mean The Waves.

Such are my sentiments at half past twelve on Tuesday July 7th—a fine day I think & everything, so the tag runs in my head, handsome about us. L. is now floating on the tide of celebrity: odd how the strings all begin to tug at once: asked to Broadcast, asked to go to America, asked to write the Weekly Wayfarer in the Statesman. And I am not jealous.[4]

But I am fearful of what I call (though this much puzzles Fraulein Gulde) Life. (Fr. G. is studying my works in the Brit. Mus. & cannot be sure what life is, so writes to ask me.)[5] Clive is back, & as I observe instantly on opening the door, favourably disposed towards me. For example he says What lovely flowers! Ethel has been penitent after her fashion for her letter. That is she came yesterday, after an intermission of almost a fortnight, & defended & explained herself in a speech which lasted 20 minutes by my watch. She raised her cup of tea 6 times to her lips but always thought of some new parenthesis or qualification & put it down untouched. Her zeal, sincerity & vitality of course convince; though I'm glad to drive my stake in firmly & so avoid complete over-whelming. I shout obloquies at her like gun shots. She takes them on her solid old body with a thud like that on an elephant's hide. Staggers, recovers herself, & stands pendant & prominent—for she has a paunch—over me. I dominate by silence—a phenomenon to her very formidable. And off she goes at 6.45 subdued—like Pinka [*the Woolfs' cocker spaniel*], L. says, when she has been grouting in the rubbish heap. We kiss—she passionately in the hall, while Miss Pritchard shelters behind her door, slightly alarmed I think. But what care I might be Ethel's song: & for that I like her.

I am reading Don Juan; & dispatch a biography every two days.
So no more.

Long discussion the other night between Ott., Tommie, Mary & ourselves upon being in the cage: Mary rampant; like a horse when a train passes a field. Must escape. Must find a brazen man & go to Spain. Why dont we do anything? Change our lives? She live with L. I with Jack? Why this hedge of telephone calls daily? Why not expose a different self?

---

4. *Much Ado About Nothing* IV. ii. 83. Dogberry: '. . . [a fellow] that hath two gowns, and everything handsome about him . . .' LW did not contribute a weekly column to the *NS&N*.

5. This was possibly Fraülein Ruth Grüber, who was to publish a study of VW in 1935 (see below, 31 May 1935).

Tuesday 14 July

It is now twelve o'clock on the morning of July 14th—& (Bob has come in to ask me to sign a paper to get Palmer a pension. Bob says . . . mostly about his new house, washing basins, can he use a candle still to go to bed with, Bessy is moving in today, he is off to Italy for a month, will I send a copy of my new book to Count Morra, all Italians are Counts, once he showed four Counts round Cambridge, Palmer . . . & so on: shuffling from foot to foot, taking his hat off & putting it on again, moving to the door & returning. O & about Desmond's book. Desmond stole some of the articles—Putnam wrote him a very severe letter—)[6]

& I had meant to say that I am now (here Nelly comes in with a bill for 4/6 to pay for my shoes)

I had meant to say that I have just finished correcting the Hampton Court scene (This is the final correction, please God.)

But my Waves account runs, I think, as follows:—

I began it, seriously about September 10th 1929:
I finished the first version on April 10th 1930

Sept 10th to Apr 7 months

I began 2nd version May 1st 1930.
I finished 2nd version Feb. 7th 1931

9
3
———
19 months

I began to correct the 2nd version May 1st 1931
finished 22nd. June. 1931
I began to correct the typescript 25th June 1931
Shall finish (I hope.) ⟨28 June⟩ 18th July. —

Then remain only the proofs.

The Woolfs drove to Monks House on the afternoon of Friday 17 July, and returned to Tavistock Square on Sunday.

Friday 17 July

Yes. This morning I think I may say I have finished. That is to say I have once more, for the 18th time, copied out the opening

which I then lost.

sentences. L. will read it tomorrow; & I shall open this book to record his verdict. My own opinion,—oh dear—, its a difficult book. I don't know that I've ever felt so strained. And I'm nervous, I

6. Herbert Edward Palmer (1880-1961), poet and critic; in 1921 he had given up teaching for a full-time literary career. The Hogarth Press had published three books of his poetry (*HP Checklist* 72, 140, 230). Robert ('Bob') Calverly Trevelyan (1872-1951), poet and classical scholar and an old friend, and his Dutch wife Bessy, moved a few miles from Leith Hill to their new home, The Shiffolds, Holmbury St Mary in Surrey. Conte Umberto Morra di Lauriano (who after the second World War became Cultural Attaché to the Italian Embassy in London) published a number of articles on VW in Italian literary journals between 1927 and 1946.

confess, about L. For one thing he will be honest, more than usually. And it may be a failure. And I can't do any more. And I'm inclined to think it good but incoherent, inspissate: one jerk succeeding another. Anyhow it is laboured, compact. Anyhow I had a shot at my vision & if its not a catch, its a cast in the right direction. But I'm nervous. It may be small & finicky in general effect. Lord knows. As I say, repeating it to enforce the rather unpleasant little lift in my heart, I shall be nervous to hear what L. says when he comes out, say tomorrow night or Sunday morning to my garden room, carrying the MS & sits himself down & begins "Well!

Sunday 19 July

"It is a masterpiece" said L. coming out to my lodge this morning. "And the best of your books". This note I make; adding that he also thinks the first 100 pages extremely difficult, & is doubtful how far any common reader will follow. But Lord! what a relief! I stumped off in the rain to make a little round to Rat Farm in jubilation, & am almost resigned to the fact that a Goat farm, with a house to be built, is now in process on the slope near Northease.

The Woolfs returned to Rodmell for their two month's summer respite on Thursday 30 July.

Friday 7 August

Monks House Rodmell

I have just written those august words, Rodmell. August 1931. And its as good, no better than I thought. Who else in the whole of Sussex can say that? Weather all sorts; river running; boat swimming; loud speaker, camera, Electric Light, frigidaire—thus I run through those material blessings which one ought to say make no difference.[1] Yet they do—Heal beds too: my wide empty room to wake in; to go to bed in crossing the garden by the pale flowers—the garden lit by our bright lights. We were at Oare, & I like this country better for comparing it. And I made no note of Sydney, save that he has been given the tip by God—a queer feeling; spreads round him an oily surface of superficial calm.[2] Then I sat to Tommie. Oh dear, what a terrific hemp strong heather root obstinate

---

1. The boat was an inflatable rubber dinghy for use on the nearby tidal reaches of the River Ouse. LW had bought a Zeiss Ikon camera on 23 July.
2. Sydney Waterlow (1878-1944), diplomat, from 1929-33 British Minister in Sofia, thereafter in Athens. He was an old, if by the nature of his career, intermittent friend. He married Margery Eckhard in 1913, had three children, and in England his home was Parsonage House, Oare, in Wiltshire. The Woolfs drove there for a rainy twenty-four-hour visit on Saturday 25 July.

fountain of furious individuality shoots in me—they tampered with it, Nessa & Tommy—pinning me there, from 2 to 4 on 6 afternoons, to be looked at; & I felt like a piece of whalebone bent. This amused & interested me, at the same time I foamed with rage. T. was late. T. couldn't change his plans & so on. And I had to plod along the dusty streets there.

And Rosamond Lehmann dined with Lord David; & I liked her;[3] & at last, at last, at last, on Thursday 30th we got into the car, slammed the door, & made off. And how satisfactory it has been, is being. I writing Flush of a morning, half seriously to ease my brain, knotted by all that last screw of The Waves:[4] L. doing his broadcast & correcting proofs, no one coming, except Bells: no one ringing up; no one to say dinner's ready, or to be stumping about in the kitchen. Annie, composed, neat, nimble, has everything disposed of by 3—which reminds me I must go & put the pie in the oven, I think.[5] And lights & shadows & walks—today over to Northease & back by the marsh; almost forgiving the pink slate abortion on the Telscombe horizon. Goat Farm isn't so much of an eyesore as might have been. True, one day I was frittered into fury by Worthing & Mrs W. & her sudden curious revival of arch airs that had charmed diamond merchants in the 70s.[6] How odd that sudden spurt of sex in a woman of 80! How repulsive to me that flutter of rather cheap attractiveness—that value for Mr Legge's good opinion—he had taken her to the Pavilion & hired a special car. "Nice eh?" she laughed, as if she were on some beach with other Jewesses 50 years ago. So it seemed. And then one saw her old & pink & wattled & overdressed, demanding amusement, pleasure, cakes, drives—but enough (as they say): I wrote these very words last summer, & this summer all will be over, with one smashing family tea, by the 25th.

Lovely are the curves of the grey clouds sweeping; & the long barns

3. Rosamond Nina, the second of John Lehmann's three elder sisters, had been a scholar of Girton, and in 1928 had married the painter the Hon. Wogan Philipps. Her successful first novel *Dusty Answer* had been published in 1927; VW had read her second, *A Note in Music*, 'with some interest and admiration' (see *III VW Diary*, 28 August 1930).

4. This is the first reference in the Diary to *Flush: A Biography* (of Elizabeth Barrett Browning's spaniel), published in October 1933 (Kp A19), which VW had embarked upon as a relief from *The Waves*.

5. Annie Thomsett was a Rodmell village girl who did the necessary domestic work at Monks House when the Woolfs were there; two years previously they had bought a cottage for her to live in.

6. LW's mother Marie Woolf, *née* de Jongh (1850-1939) was Dutch born; she had been a matriarchal widow since 1892, and, after her nine children left home, lived in hotels in Earls Court, with a summer migration to Worthing. The Woolfs went to tea with her on 4 August.

37

lying; Vita writes this morning about K M's letters & says how she longs for all poets in a garden; no more; whereas Harold is becoming, they say, editor of a new morning paper & has resigned from the Standard. And are you fond of me? she asks.[7]

Monday 10 August

No I will not let this day be a bad one, though it has every sign of so being. First an argument with L. at breakfast about seeing his family: the usual rather embittered argument: which deprives me of my box[?]; & then a headache is incipient; which is caused, partly, by Charleston; where we were very gay; & I gave away prizes; & then involved myself in one of my miserable edge sitting tenebrous exquisitely uneasy dialogues with Raymond: shd. I ask him to stay—should I not? Nessa did: Nessa who has Roger, & will have Jean.[8] And now we were to ask R. to come; & now I sit in the lodge this grey pale morning & will not go on with Flush, because of my head; & we have a day in London tomorrow; & should begin to correct my first proofs; & perhaps shall when I've done this. No, I say, I will not let this day be a bad one: but by what means? Quiet & control. Eating apples—sleeping this afternoon. Thats all. And now for Waves.

I have now 10.45, read the first chapter of The Waves, & made no changes, save 2 words & 3 commas. Yes, anyhow this is exact & to the point. I like it. And see that for once my proofs will be dispatched with a few pencil strokes. Now my brood mounts: I think "I am taking my fences . . We have asked Raymond. I am forging through the sea, in spite of headache in spite of bitterness—I may also get a box[?]." I will now write a little at Flush.

Saturday 15 August

I am in rather a flutter - proof reading. I can only read a few pages at a time. So it was when I wrote it, & Heaven knows what virtue it all has,

7. 'Lovely are the curves of the white owl sweeping'—cf. George Meredith, *Love in the Valley*. Katherine Mansfield's letters, selected and edited by her husband J. Middleton Murry, had been published in two volumes in 1928; VW describes at length her relationship to her in her reply to Vita of 8 August (see *IV VW Letters*, no. 2418). Vita's husband, Harold Nicolson (1886-1968) gave up his career in the Diplomatic Service and joined the *Evening Standard* in 1930; in March this year he had joined Sir Oswald Mosley's New Party, and was now leaving the *Standard* to become editor of the party's journal *Action*, the first issue of which was to appear on 8 October 1931.

8. The Woolfs went to tea at Charleston on Sunday 9 August. Jean Campbell lived with Colonel Teed, Vanessa's landlord at Cassis, in the Château de Fontcreuse, and the Woolfs stayed with them during their visits to Cassis in 1928 and 1929.

this pressed [?] ecstatic book. All I note here though is that I feel vibrational; get violent impressions from Roger Raymond, Sibyl, Vita. Sibyl came by her own request yesterday; & I wondered after 2 hours jerking barren gossip, what satisfaction she got from it.[9] Once she looked at the downs. The worst of being Sibyl is that one suspects every action of some motive. "I am proving myself a woman who loves the country". One never feels, This is what she likes, as I do when Vita stumbles over the marsh & hardly has a word to say. S. looks at chairs & tables; sums one up: has a magpies eye, a larder of facts which she will hand on at her next meeting. Nobody scarcely will let themselves be themselves: & I am a sinner sometimes. Then, as we stood at the door, she tried to make us invite her to stay. And I resisted; why should she want us to ask her to stay? I asked. She had been at the Gages', again, I suppose, self invited.[10] As you see, S.'s company does not lead to lofty reflections; does not put one on one's mettle, except to show off. Old Vita shaggy & stiff, writing another novel; but as careless about it all as ever. Eddy had written to abuse A.P.S. She was annoyed; then tore up his letter.[11] Harold is starting a new paper Action on Oct. 1st: costing 2d. Cold, wet, lights at luncheon; the cat kittened in the coalhole; the valuable spaniel bitch died in childbed next door. A wet wild August, the coldest for 14 years; & the farmers here burning their hay. Meanwhile the country is in the throes of a crisis. Great events are brewing. Maynard visits Downing Street & spreads sensational rumours. Are we living then through a crisis; & am I fiddling? & will future ages, as they say, behold our predicament (financial) with horror?[12] Sometimes I feel the world desperate; then walk among the downs. Last night, after Sibyl, after thunder & rain, specially [?] various, tender, fleeting, evanescent, I stood by the gate & watched Asheham hill cloud & kindle like the emerald it is. And all round the hills lay, low in cloud.

9. Sybil (d. 1950), wife of Sir Arthur Colefax, KC, was an indefatigable hostess, entertaining fashion and culture at her Chelsea home, Argyll House.
10. Henry Rainald, 6th Viscount Gage (b. 1895), of Firle Place, one of the great Sussex landowners (both Charleston and Tilton are on his estates), this year married the Hon. Imogen Grenfell (1905-69) younger daughter of Lord Desborough.
11. The Hon. Edward Sackville-West (1901-65), Vita's cousin and heir to the Sackville title and estates, was himself a novelist; the book by Vita which he abused was *All Passion Spent* (*HP Checklist* 270) published in May 1931; she was now writing *Family History* (*HP Checklist* 307).
12. For John Maynard Keynes see Appendix. In England the repercussions of the international financial crisis were leading to the resignation of the Labour Party Prime Minister Ramsay MacDonald on 24 August, his formation of a 'National' Government, and Britain's abandonment of the gold standard on 21 September 1931.

Sunday 16 August

I should really apologise to this book for using it as I am doing to write off my aimlessness; that is I am doing my proofs—the last chapter this morning—& find that I must stop after half an hour, & let my mind spread, after these moments of concentration. I cannot write my life of Flush, because the rhythm is wrong. I think The Waves is anyhow tense & packed; since it screws my brain up like this. And what will the reviewers say? And my friends? They cant, of course, find anything very new to say.

L. is in the house making his Index & printing the photographs we developed last night.

The reason why Colefax is so dull is that she never feels or thinks for herself. That is why I should suffocate of dust if she spent a night here. Also she is forever collecting facts about one, not from interest, but from curiosity. It is a warning not to go to places like Argyll House again, because one is expected to make some return.*

* The poor woman today Wednesday writes a pathetic letter about other summers & regrets, & how all the same they drank (A. & she) their delights to the full; & the sight of us tho' it stirred these sorrows comforted her.

It is a good idea I think to write biographies; to make them use my powers of representation reality accuracy; & to use my novels simply to express the general, the poetic. Flush is serving this purpose.

We had a perfectly happy day yesterday. I set up some of Dadie's poems in the new room;[13] walked on the marshes. L. cut the apple trees; it was a lovely day—indeed this broken weather has the merit of an extraordinary capricious beauty. I doubt that I have ever seen the downs lovelier. I am in a fix though about Ethel, who with considerable brutality to back her, asks if she may come here. When people—G.L.D[ickinson] for instance—put us off, we are almost shocked; & then feel an amazed relief. Is it possible that there is someone who does not want to see us? Such royalty we have become—in our set, as Ethel says. She annoys me by telling Lady Craik that I live in a set, & am a recluse.[14] Now, alas, I must back to Bernard (on P[ercival]'s death)

One of Sibyl's sayings, or insinuations: "Ah, if only Arthur & I could

---

13. George ('Dadie') Rylands (b. 1902), had worked at the Hogarth Press during the latter half of 1924; since 1927 he had been a resident Fellow of King's College, Cambridge. His *Poems* was published in an edition of 350 numbered and signed copies in December 1931 (*HP Checklist* 269).

14. Mary, Lady Craik (b. 1895), widow of Sir George, 2nd Bt, was the only daughter of the Rt Hon. Alfred Lyttelton, KC, MP. Ethel Smyth had described VW in a letter to her which she sent to VW to read and forward (see *IV VW Letters*, no. 2420).

afford a country cottage"—with her Rolls Royce & her chauffeur at the door.

Monday 17 August

Well now, it being just after 12.30 I have put the last corrections in The Waves; done my proofs; & they shall go tomorrow—never, never to be looked at again by me, I imagine.

Wednesday 19 August

My proofs did go: went yesterday; & I shall not see them again.

Tuesday 1 September

And so a few days of bed & headache & overpowering sleep, sleep descending inexorable as I tried to read Judith Paris, then Ivanhoe.[1] A note on Judith Paris: its a London museum book. Hugh bouncing with spurious enthusiasm—a collection of keepsakes bright beads—unrelated. Why? No central feeling anywhere—only "I'm so vital—so big—so creative". True, its competent enough, spare in the wording—but words without roots. Yes thats it. All a trivial litter of bright objects to be swept up.

Scott: a note. A pageant. And I know the man (I forget his name) will hit the mark. So I'm not excited. Almost incredible that my father shd. have taken this scene seriously.[2] But I think some roots. A perfectly sincere desire surely to amuse, now & then ruffled (but oh how seldom!) by some raid from the sub-conscious—only in the humour tho. Rowena, Rebecca, hairdressers ornaments—Madame Tussaud sham jewels. Its the design thats interesting—all flat, daubed. But I think I trust him & like him, better than Hugh. Question of morality. That we are all moralists; with a temporary standard. My anger that S[cott]. wont be more intense partly the result of England's crisis this summer. (if summer it can be called).

Man came this morning when I was in my night gown to put up Nessa's tiles in the top room. L. in London. Joyce's birthday.[3] Hot still September morning. Rooks gathering, cawing

1. *Judith Paris* by Hugh Walpole had been published in August 1931. *Ivanhoe* (1819) by Sir Walter Scott.
2. The character is Locksley [Robin Hood]; see *Ivanhoe*, chapter 13. See also Leslie Stephen: 'Sir Walter Scott', *Hours in a Library* (1892), vol. 1, p. 158.
3. Joyce Wethered (b. 1901), four times British Ladies Open Golf champion, was a particular favourite of Ethel Smyth's, at whose Surrey home VW had met her in July 1930. In 1937 she married Sir John Heathcote Amory.

Thursday 3 September

I am taking, this is the last day—my weeks holiday, with very good results. My brain is soft & warm & fertile again, I feel fresh & free with energy for talk. Yes, I can even envisage 'seeing' people without a clutch & a shudder. Odd how I drink up rest—how I become dry & parched like a withered grass—how then I become green & succulent. By the way, Elizabethan prose is magnificent: & all that I love most at the moment. I bathed myself in Dekker last night as in my natural element. Surely this is a nobler instrument than Scott or the 18th Century. We listened to a Bach concert with the clouds thickening purple over Caburn, the lights springing, & the pale cadaverous glow in the chalk pit.[4] At one moment the brown horses stampeded—flinging out their great legs wildly. The worst of it is that my brain fills too fast—overflows. Waiting for breakfast I read Montaigne this morning & found a passage about the passions of women—their voracity—which I at once opposed to Squire's remarks & so made up a whole chapter of my Tap at the Door or whatever it is, just when I was hoping to let my mind slide off on to a second Common Reader, & the Elizabethans.[5] No letter from Vita, to whom I wrote from my bed; & none from Nessa, to whom I sent £50. A few letters from American lunatics which I must answer, must I?—& stop writing. Will I write a statement What I believe for the American Nation. No. But what do I believe? Other people do this sort of thing. Why not I?[6]

And what was I saying? Oh I was annoyed with Desmond's usual sneer at Mrs Dalloway—woolgathering.[7] I was inspired to make up several phrases about Desmond's own processes—none of which, I suppose, will ever be fired off in print. His worldliness, urbanity, decorum as a writer; his soft supple ways. His audience of teaparty ladies & gentle-

---

4. Thomas Dekker (1570?-1632), playwright. The Promenade Concert, conducted by Sir Henry Wood, was relayed from the Queen's Hall; the works performed were: Brandenburg Concerto No. 2 in F; Fantasy and Fugue in C Minor; and Suite No. 5 for Oboe and Strings.

5. The passage from Montaigne is probably from his essay 'Sur des vers de Vergile', book III, chap. V. J. C. Squire (1884-1958), editor of the *London Mercury* 1919-34, was a prominent and prolific figure in London's literary world; his 'Idle Thoughts', broadcast on 13 August, may have provoked VW.

6. *The Nation* (New York) ran a series of several articles under this title, the contributors to which included Rose Macaulay and Beatrice Webb.

7. Desmond MacCarthy's 'sneer' occurs in an essay 'The Bubble Reputation' in *Life & Letters*, September 1931; in discussing the development of the novel, he wrote: 'In the latest kind of novel—Virginia Woolf's, for example—events have become merely interruptions in a long wool-gathering process, a process that is used chiefly to provide occasions for little prose poems. . . .; as when the tiny gathers in some green silk Mrs Dalloway is sewing on to her belt remind her of summer waves . . ., waves described in a passage of delicate and rhythmical prose.'

men. His timidity. How he wraps everything in flannel. (Browning said this of a cold morning in Paris). And there's truth in what I say of Desmond, not only spite. Then his ridiculous hesitations & nervousness as a writer, about publishing. His perpetual condescension. His now permanent stoop in the back. His aloofness—in the bad sense. I mean he never takes a nettle by the leaves: always wears gloves. His garrulity. Well, let me hope that all his 8 volumes will fail, that he wont be able to pay his income tax & that Michael will be eaten by leopards. Then I shall meet him & my eyes will fill with tears.[8] But its true—a snub—even praise—from Desmond, depresses me more than the downright anger of Arnold Bennett—it saps my vitality.

I open this book again to record the fact that this is the 3rd of September. The battle of Dunbar: the battle of Worcester, & the death of Cromwell. A heavy flagging windy cloudy day with breadths of sun: not actually raining. Its odd how I always remember father saying that at St Ives on this day, & how I am always writing something in a diary on this day & generally it is crisp & clear.[9]

Tuesday 15 September

I have come up here, trembling under the sense of complete failure—I mean The Waves—I mean Hugh Walpole doesn't like it—I mean John L. is about to write to say he thinks it bad—I mean L. accuses me of sensibility verging on insanity—I mean I am acutely depressed & already feeling rising the hard & horny back of my old friend Fight fight. Never mind. Here I need not disguise my tumult of feelings. Lord how I hate that Hugh shd. be running about London saying the new V W. is a disappointment—all about nothing—exquisitely written of course. Ought I not then to say that Brace thinks— Oh well, do let me try to give up weighing opposite impressions.[10] Anyhow my mind is crammed with books, & Lord, I tried to speak the truth, bombastic as the remark sounds, wrung it drop by

This was true: Hugh wrote to say he thinks it "unreal". It beats him.

8. Cf. *IV VW Letters*, no. 2373 of 14 May 1931 in which VW retails to Vanessa Desmond's account of his elder son Michael's (1907-73) farming activities, pursued first in Southern Africa and then in South America.
9. See *III VW Diary*, 3 September 1928: 'The battle of Dunbar, the Battle of Worcester, & the death of Cromwell—how often it seems to me I said that to my father . . . at St Ives; standing bolt upright in the dining room at Talland House.'
10. Donald Clifford Brace (1881-1955), VW's American publisher; his thoughts on *The Waves* are not preserved, but Harcourt Brace & Co. published the book on 22 October, a fortnight later than the Hogarth Press edition. For Hugh Walpole's reactions to *The Waves* see below 16 November 1931 n. 5.

drop from my brain. So essentially I am not horrified. But The Waves, I predict, marks my decline in reputation.

[*Wednesday 16 September*]

Oh but this morning I'm like a bee in the ivy bloom—cant write for pleasure.[11] John says "But I loved it, truly loved it, & was deeply impressed & amazed by its achievement in an entirely new method. . . . There seems to me only the thinnest wall between such a novel & poetry. You somehow maintain the speed of prose & the intensity of poetry . . ." And its very difficult he adds; & so on. But my brain is flushed & flooded & I'm at once inspired to write a Letter to a Young Poet.[12]

Lord what a weathercock—no a wave of emotion is in me.

Saturday 19 September

And the last few days have been heavenly— At last some heat; & then, with this book done—for I don't feel much anxiety now—think that John has hit off the cultivated view—I'm calm; oh & walk; oh & have to record the horror of 2 bungalows on the top of the hill. Yes. This iniquity is being inflicted on the downs for ever by our 'prospective labour candidate' [Hancock]. He shan't have my vote. I swept off into dreams of a house far away in Dorsetshire. But O—again—how happy I am: how calm, for the moment how sweet life is with L. here, in its regularity & order, & the garden & the room at night & music & my walks & writing easily & interestedly at Donne of a morning, & poems all about me. I've come to read poetry with intensity—bought Skelton at Tunbridge Wells. For we went to the Easedales one fine hot day & saw the stuffed wolf; & I must now change for Angelica's birthday party. George & Margaret [Duckworth, to tea] yesterday.[13]

11.   'He will watch from dawn to gloom
              The lake-reflected sun illume
              The yellow bees in the ivy-bloom,
              Nor heed nor see, what things they be;'
                        Shelley, *Prometheus Unbound*

12. Cf. *IV VW Letters*, no. 2437 of 17 September to John Lehmann; also his autobiography *The Whispering Gallery* (1955), p. 170. VW's *A Letter to a Young Poet* was to be published as no. 8 in the 'Hogarth Letters' series in July 1932 (Kp A17).

13. VW's essay 'Donne After Three Centuries' was published in *The Common Reader, Second Series*, 1932 (Kp A18). The Woolfs had driven on 15 September to Tunbridge Wells to travel Hogarth Press books; after lunch they called on Dorothy Wellesley (see below, 27 September 1931, n. 26) at her house Penns-in-the-Rocks; and went on to Crouch to tea with the Easdale family (see above, 1 July 1931, n. 1) —a visit described in *IV VW Letters*, no. 2436 to Vita Sackville-West. Angelica, who was born on Christmas Day 1918, was customarily assigned *his* birthday, 19 September, by Clive Bell.

Monday 21 September

Here am I writing about Donne, & we have 'gone off the Gold Standard' this morning. Maynard & Kahan like people in the war. We sat talking economics & politics. Guards out: Tower defended (this a joke on M.'s part). Telephones: late edition of the paper. We're off, & I write about Donne. Yes; & what could I do better, if we are ruined, & if everybody had spent their time writing about Donne we should not have gone off the Gold Standard—thats my version of the greatest crisis &c &c &c—gabble gabble go the geese, who cant lay golden eggs.[14]

Tuesday 22 September

And Miss Holtby says "It is a poem, more completely than any of your other books, of course. It is most rarely subtle. It has seen more deeply into the human heart, perhaps, than even To the Lighthouse. . . ." & though I copy the sentence, because it is in the chart of my temperature, Lord, as I say, that temperature which was deathly low this time last week, & then fever high, doesn't rise: is normal. I suppose I'm safe; I think people can only repeat. And I've forgotten so much. What I want is to be told that this is solid & means something. What it means I myself shant know till I write another book. And I'm the hare, a long way ahead of the hounds my critics.

Sunday 27 September

Lyn & the Kingsley Martins are in the house, & I have crept out here, as I say, to write letters. But talking jangles the nerves at the back of my head. And we had the Easedales too. "Mr E. was one of those jealous gentlemen, & so he left me". Silence on my part. "I was very young, & should have taken a stronger line." "How terrible that a friendship like that should have been broken off!" said Joan. And we went round the garden.[15]

14. Britain suspended the Gold Standard, to which it had returned a little more than six years previously, as from 21 September 1931. Maynard Keynes had written against the earlier return to the Gold Standard in his pamphlet *The Economic Consequences of Mr Churchill* (1925, *HP Checklist* 66). Richard Ferdinand Kahn (b. 1905), economist, Fellow of King's College, Cambridge, from 1930, and a close collaborator of Keynes.

15. Basil Kingsley Martin (1897-1969), editor of the *New Statesman & Nation* from the date of the merger of these two periodicals earlier this year until his retirement in 1960. His marriage in 1926 to Olga Walters (1901-64) had been unhappy, and they separated in 1934. They and Lyn Irvine stayed at Monks House from Saturday to Monday; the Easedales came to tea on the Saturday—an occasion described by Mrs Easedale in her book, *Middle Age, 1885-1932*, published anonymously by Constable in 1935. This Sunday Julian and Quentin Bell and Roger Fry came to tea at Monks House.

Ethel must be in fine feather. General, & I think sincere praise of The Wreckers. I telegraphed—dont want to write. Dotty's mother dead. Vita going off abroad with her. And we shall publish on 8th in spite of the G[eneral].E[lection]: dont expect sales anyhow.[16]

Wednesday 30 September

I have come up here on this the last evening to clear up papers. All is softly grey: L.'s yellow dahlias are burning on the edge of the terrace. I have been over to Asheham, in the clear pale autumn afternoon, along Mandrill walk, which we walked the night of our marriage. How proud I was of my new despatch box, I remember! So its over, this summer too; & I regret it, & want to stay on, & soothe my mind with (here a wretched little post comes in) with Elizabethan poets. Instead we go up tomorrow, & doesn't the lift of my heart tell me that strain, about The Waves, friends, reviewers, sales, &c. will then begin to make a fiddle string in my side, stretched tight, on which lots of people will carelessly twang this winter. No help for it—So it always is with a book out.

And it will be out in one week tomorrow. But I am slightly less naked than usual, as I've had 3 outside opinions & shan't I suppose get any very great variety of praise or blame. I must make up my mind about the autumn lap, & my bearing. And do some quiet work: & 'see' people not so wearily.

But here I am saying the summer is over—the wet, driven, rather headachy summer—so August was. September improved. How happy I was writing about Donne, up here, how happy a dozen times on solitary walks, in what a rage the day I found Hancock's horror building on the hill, & then we had many & many a game of bowls, & there was the great financial crisis, & then going to Dotty & the Easedales, & the tremendous talk carnival—which I went through with shut lips—I mean looking for no pleasure—last week end. And now apple baskets are filling in the drawing room, & I must seriously set to & destroy & mass together two months of papers.

16. Ethel Smyth's opera *The Wreckers*, first performed in London in 1909 (when VW had heard it) was revived for the current 'Season of Opera in English' at Covent Garden. Dorothy ('Dotty'), Lady Gerald Wellesley (1891-1956), an intimate friend of Vita Sackville-West, was a poet, who sponsored and edited the 'Hogarth Living Poets' series; her mother, the Countess of Scarborough, died on 24 September. The all-party 'National' government formed by the Labour Party Prime Minister Ramsay MacDonald in August as a temporary expedient for overcoming the financial crisis, sought (and obtained) a mandate in the general election called for 27 October. Publication date for *The Waves* had been planned for 8 October.

Monday 5 October

52 Tavistock Sqre.

A note, to say I am all trembling with pleasure—cant go on with my Letter [to a Young Poet]—because Harold Nicolson has rung up to say The Waves is a masterpiece. Ah hah—so it wasn't all wasted then. I mean this vision I had here has some force upon other minds. Now for a cigarette, & then a return to sober composition.

[Thursday 8 October]

Well, to continue this egotistic diary: I am not terribly excited: no: at arm's length more than usual all this talk, because if The W. is anything it is an adventure which I go on alone: & the dear old Lit Sup. who twinkles & beams & patronises—a long, & for The Times, kind & outspoken review—dont stir me very much. Nor Harold in Action either.[1] Yes; to some extent; I shd. have been unhappy had they blamed, but Lord, how far away I become from all this; & we're jaded too, with people, with doing up parcels.

I wonder if it is good to feel this remoteness—that is, that The W. is not what they say. Odd, that they (The Times) shd. praise my characters when I meant to have none. But I'm jaded; I want my marsh, my down, & quiet waking in my airy bedroom. [LW] Broadcasting tonight; to Rodmell tomorrow. Next week I shall have to stand the racket.

Friday 9 October

Really, this unintelligible book is being better 'received' than any of them. A note in The Times proper—the first time this has been allowed me.[2] And it sells—how unexpected, how odd that people can read that difficult grinding stuff!

Wednesday 14 October

A note. For since The Waves my brain wont stand hard writing—writing that must fetch a compass. I'm muscularly strained. So I stop my Letter to John & note that The W. has beaten all my books: sold close on

1. *The Waves* was reviewed in the *TLS*, 8 October 1931 (*M&M*, p. 263). Harold Nicolson's review appeared in *Action*, 8 October 1931 (*M&M*, p. 266).
2. From *The Times*, 9 October 1931: 'Like some old Venetian craftsman in glass, Mrs Woolf spins the coloured threads, and with exquisite, intuitive sensibility fashions ethereal frailties of enduring quality.'

5,000; we are reprinting: so far, save for Hayward & Ethel, no letters.[3] None of my presentees have written. This silence always lasts a week or two. The reviews I think the warmest yet. And so on. But Vita found it desperately dull—anyhow for 100 pages. What shall I say to Virginia? I cant get through it. Up rings Dotty. Cant get through it. Two hours later "I'm getting along better" Still, V. finds it absolutely intellectual: all one person speaking: profound loneliness of the soul; will never like it as much as the others . . Dear me, I spent 20 minutes dashing off a cooks talk—so much I need random rollicking humour.[4] Oh what a grind that was! It comes over me now. Literally I have a pain in my head—but my head has many pains—when I try to stretch another book— And yet of course I envisage The Tree. But help help, stop stop I cry to my brain. Dont torture me again. Wreckers tonight & supper with Vita, L. & Ethel at the Eiffel Tower afterwards.

[*Thursday 15 October*]

Conversation last night. Stulik at the Eiffel Tower.[5] I am talking about Schnitzler: I tell you he had six potatoes here & a bag of flour. He said "Give them to my people. I do not want them." He had six potatoes & a bag of flour. He said "My people are starving. I do not want your alms.". . . .

E[thel] S[myth]: But they have not heard of Schnitzler. We are not musical . . . the English are not artists. You belong to the only race where every man one meets in the street is an artist . . .

Of course these people have heard of Schnitzler . . . And he said Take them—I do not want them. Give them to the people who are starving. He had six potatoes & a bag of flour . . .

Stulik has had a fit & was mildly drunk.

My heart beat when I saw you—(bowing to me with his hand on his heart) come in . . It is long years since you used to come here—you lived

3. The first printing of *The Waves* was about 7,000 copies; a second impression of almost 5,000 was issued later this month. John Davy Hayward (1905-65), bibliophile and editor; VW had met him at Cambridge in 1925.
4. See MHP, Sussex, A13d & e: two typescript drafts of 'The Cook'—a portrait based on Sophia Farrell (c. 1861-1942), the loyal family cook at Hyde Park Gate who followed the orphaned Stephens to Bloomsbury, and worked for VW until her marriage; she then went to the George Duckworths, and had only recently retired to live in Brixton.
5. VW and Vita, after dining and going to *The Wreckers* together, took Ethel Smyth to supper at the Eiffel Tower restaurant in Percy Street, the resort of higher Bohemia, whose proprietor from 1908-37 was the Viennese Rudolf Stulik. (LW, who did not go to the opera, probably joined the party here.) Arthur Schnitzler (1862-1931), the Austrian playwright and novelist, died a week later.

48

in Bedford Square—you had a studio—& there was Lady Utto—she used to come— And my heart leapt, Sir, when I saw you again after all these years. When you came into the room, I felt. . . .

Going through contortions like one swimming with his arms crossing themselves on his breast There sat Rex Whistler & Malcolm Bullock in a corner.[6] E. held forth about Parsifal; & our quarrel—dressed in pale blue with white shoes pinned with safety pins. And some of the W[reckers]. was vigorous & even beautiful; & active & absurd & extreme; & youthful: as if some song in her had tried to issue & been choked [?].

Saturday 17 October

More notes on The Waves. The sales, these past 3 days have fallen to 50 or so: after the great flare up when we sold 500 in one day, the brushwood has died down, as I foretold. (Not that I thought we should sell more than 3,000). What has happened is that the library readers cant get through it & are sending their copies back. So, I prophesy, it will now dribble along till we have sold 6000 & then almost die, yet not quite. For it has been received, as I may say, quoting the stock phrases without vanity, with applause. All the provinces read enthusiastically. I am rather, in a sense, as the M's would say, touched. The unknown provincial reviewers say with almost one accord, here is Mrs Woolf doing her best work; it cant be popular; but we respect her for so doing; & find The Waves positively exciting. I am in danger, indeed, of becoming our leading novelist, & not with the highbrows only. To show how slow a book it is, not only do Vita & Dotty find the first 100 pages boring in the extreme, but I have as yet (10 days after publication) had only 3 letters about it. Nessa's enthusiasm is the brightest spot.[7] And, to annotate further, the lack of sales has had the providential effect of steadying & quieting me, so that I can get back to work, & have already lost the flush & flutter of what seemed like complete success. So now, what shall I work at? So many works hover over me.

Tuesday 20 October

I trotted out yesterday & laid in a stock of Elizabethans. I should like

6. Rex Whistler (1905-44), artist-decorator and illustrator in a vogueish eighteenth-century manner. Captain Malcolm Bullock (1890-1966), Scots Guards 1914-21; Conservative MP 1923-53; and chairman 1930-46 of the Sadler's Wells Society.
7. Vanessa wrote from Charleston (n.d., Berg): 'I have been for the last 3 days completely submerged in The Waves—& am left rather gasping, out of breath, choking, half drowned, as you might expect. I must read it again when I may hope to float more quietly—but meanwhile I'm so overcome by the beauty . . .'

to write a chapter called Some Ethans as prelude to the 2nd Common Reader.[8]

I had a visit from Peter Lucas t'other night. No, he had not read The W. But he has written an Epic. He is working as usual like a miner—bright red all over—egotistic—nice, charming, boyish, hard, imperceptive, not a writer I mean, though set on writing, & indeed has a play being acted.[9] Both our books move slowly; but L.'s I suspect with a giants foot, like an elephant through the undergrowth. Laski says, as reviewers say these things, it is a masterpiece.[10] We makers of masterpieces remain very calm, very well content. We went to the Motor Show, for instance, last Saturday (autumn deepening) & approved The Star, which indeed we could buy if we wished. It's a queer reversal. Here's Lottie out of a place & Mrs Hunt wont accept fees as places aren't to be had. How things have spun these 2 or 3 years then![11]

Oh its blue again over my skylight—please God it stays blue over our week end, the blessed Rodmell week end. Vaguely looking for houses again, & turning over plans for removing. All houses pale though before this one. I'm asked to be Godmother to Noel Richards' daughter. Yet she wont dine here. Election rampant. Plomer & DoBree dined the other night. He a nimble secondrate man: his grandfather the pawnbroker in Vanity Fair.[12]

8. 'The Strange Elizabethans' is the first essay in *The Common Reader: Second Series*, 1932 (Kp A18).

9. F. L. Lucas's poem *Ariadne* was published by the Cambridge University Press in 1932; he probably told VW that his first play, *The Bear Dances*, was going to be acted; it was performed at the Garrick Theatre in November 1932.

10. Harold J. Laski (1893-1950), professor of Political Science at the London School of Economics since 1926; his review of LW's *After the Deluge* vol. I appeared in the *NS&N*, 17 October 1931.

11. The Star Motor Co. of Wolverhampton showed four models at the 1931 Motor Exhibition held at Olympia from 15-24 October; the Little Comet Fourteen at £345 was the novelty and may have attracted the Woolfs, but they did not buy it. Mrs Hunt ran an agency for domestic servants.

12. Dr Noel Richards, *née* Olivier (1892-1969), with whom Rupert Brooke, James Strachey, and Adrian Stephen had all been in love, had married a fellow doctor in 1920; VW agreed to act as *soi-disant* godmother to their third child, who was named Virginia after her. William Plomer and Bonamy Dobrée (1891-1974), author and editor, and lately Professor of English Literature in Cairo, dined with the Woolfs on 15 October. According to his obituary in *The Times*, Dobrée was 'proud that both his Bonamy and Dobrée ancestors, bankers, were mentioned in Thackeray.' There is a pawnbroker called Dobrée in *Pendennis* (ch. 36), not *Vanity Fair*; a Bonamy is mentioned in *Vanity Fair* (ch. 3)—but he is an East India Company civil servant.

[Friday 23 October?]

Oh but I have been made miserable—damped & disheartened—this is no exaggeration—because the Lit Sup. only gave half a column of belittlement to After the Deluge.[13] Not that I should have cared more than a moments damn at them for the usual insignificant spiteful methods —wreaking their politics upon books they dont agree with. But L. says— & honestly believes—that this puts an end to the book— Yes he says no less than that. He says his ten years work are wasted, & that he sees no use in going on. His argument is that he wrote this book for the wider public; that this public is at the mercy of Librarians; that librarians take their orders from the Lit Sup; that they judge by the length of the review; that no librarian will advise spending 15/- after this review; so that, however Laski & the experts may applaud, as they do, in the serious weeklies, his book is dead; his work wasted. He remains with a public of experts who are poor; his sales wont reach 500 in 6 months & so on. For my own part I think this a very curious illustration of his psychology. On Sunday he told me that this was bound to happen; yet we have seldom been happier—True he said he expected one col. or one & $\frac{1}{2}$ of abuse instead of $\frac{1}{2}$;—Oh but the arguments which we have beaten out I daresay for 6 hours, walking in the Sqre, sitting over the fire—utterly cloud my mind. Its his curious pessimistic temper: something deeper than reason, strangling, many coiled, that one cant deal with. Influenza has exactly the same effect, liberating the irrational despondency which I see in all Woolves, & connect with centuries of oppression. The world against us &c. How can one laugh off the $\frac{1}{2}$ column therefore? And when I say this morning incautiously, "I'm reviewed in the M[ancheste]r Guardian" L. says "Is it a long review?" And I say, feeling like a mother to a hurt & miserable little boy, Yes. Lord what human beings are![14]

Now it pours; & are we to go to Rodmell?

Friday 30 October

Happily that morbidity of L.'s is over. Other things have intervened, & praise & some sale. And the General Election which has returned I think 26 Labour members to Parliament. But as I went to James's to hear the results, was in the midst of a chattering crowd (Nina Hamnet drunk)

13. 'The Social Animal', *TLS*, 22 October 1931, a half-column review of *After the Deluge*. While complimenting LW's skill in collating and analysing his material the reviewer also accused him of 'cheapness' in dealing with the General Strike and cautioned him against being 'too rigidly logical'.
14. See 'Books of the Day', *Manchester Guardian*, 23 October 1931, an entirely favourable review of *The Waves* signed C.M., entitled 'The Rhythm of Life' and extending over two-thirds of a column.

my head aches. I rubbed the ache in dining at the Woolf family party last night. Cant write, cant read.[15] Oh—yesterday we made an offer for 47 Gordon Sqre—a house where we may die; for its a 24 years lease. Strange to anchor there again. In order that these notes may remain solid I make them; but cannot comment.

Monday 16 November

But we are not to live & die in 47. The Bedford Estate wont house a publisher; would create a precedent; vans would stop at the door. Unexpectedly complaisant, though, Mr Upton told us that we may stay on here past our term: the side of the Sqre is to be pulled down; but times are bad for building; & they will treat us with consideration. So we stay on, anyhow this next year.[1] With John doubtful (I murmur this in secret) it is wisest so: & Lord, how I love the chance of any escape—from what? to what?

I'm disoriented; have been to the City & seen St Bartholomew's. Came back to wait Vita. Vita has to take Dotty to a nursing home, so cant come; my evening spoilt—mind cant settle. Whats to become of Lottie, still out of a place? Nessa rings up. Will Clive have her? I am reading Clive's book.[2]

Here I will give myself the pleasure—shall I?—of copying a sentence or two from Morgan's unsolicited letter on The Waves:—

"I expect I shall write to you again when I have re read The Waves. I have been looking in it & talking about it at Cambridge. Its difficult to express oneself about a work which one feels to be so very important but I've the sort of excitement over it which comes from believing that one's encountered a classic"[3]

I daresay that gives me more substantial pleasure than any letter I've had about any book. Yes, I think it does, coming from Morgan. For one thing it gives me reason to think that I shall be right to go on along this very

15. The composition of the House of Commons after the General Election on 27 October 1931 was as follows: National Government supporters, 551 seats; Labour, 52; Independent Liberal, 4; Independent, 1. James Strachey, see Appendix; his party was on 27 October. Nina Hamnet (1890-1956), painter and bohemian. Mrs Woolf's birthday dinner was on 29 October; she was 81.

1. Messrs Upton, Britton & Lumb, solicitors, of Bedford Square, acted for the Woolfs' landlord, the Duke of Bedford's London Estates, which planned to demolish and redevelop 52 Tavistock Square and adjacent properties; in the event these plans were postponed, and the Woolfs stayed on until July 1939.

2. Clive Bell's *An Account of French Painting* was published in November 1931. Lottie Hope was to become his cook-housekeeper at 50 Gordon Square in the new year.

3. Forster's letter of 12 November 1931, now in the Berg, continues: 'We shall see— or rather the next fifty years will, when you and I won't see any longer.'

lonely path. I mean in the city today I was thinking of another book—about shopkeepers, & publicans, with low life scenes; & I ratified this sketch by Morgan's judgment. Dadie agrees too.[4] Oh yes, between 50 & 60 I think I shall write out some very singular books, if I live. I mean I think I am about to embody, at last, the exact shapes my brain holds. What a long toil to reach this beginning—if The Waves is my first work in my own style!

To be noted, as curiosities of my literary history: I sedulously avoid meeting Roger & Lytton whom I suspect do not like The Waves. I suspect that it is dubbed a failure also by Ottoline, Colefax, Mary, & Christabel. Lord David does not care for it, nor Hugh Walpole. I sit tight here in my fastness, only sedulously avoiding any meeting with Roger & Lytton. Why do I imagine that they are both hostile towards me, because of The Waves? It is unlikely—No; I disliked Lytton for writing Q. Eth. I remember.[5]

But oh the happiness of this life—

I was thinking to myself today, few people in Cheapside can be saying "It is too good to be true—that L. & I are going to dine alone tonight."

Then of course, for no reason, L. is rather silent & sad at tea; Vita does not come; I cant get on with Philip Sidney; & so my perfect crystal globe has a shadow crossing it. L. is now printing; & perhaps dinner will be all I planned. And if its not, my happiness is too substantial to be tarnished. [*Added later*:] But dinner was very good.

I am working very hard—in my way, to furbish up 2 long Elizabethan articles to front a new Common Reader:[6] then I must go through the whole long list of those articles. I feel too, at the back of my brain, that I can devise a new critical method; something far less stiff & formal than these Times articles. But I must keep to the old style in this volume. And how, I wonder, could I do it? There must be some simpler, subtler,

4. Rylands' letter is in MHP, Sussex.
5. See *III VW Diary*, 28 November 1928, for VW's reaction to Lytton Strachey's 'lively superficial meretricious book' *Elizabeth and Essex* and its author. He, now suffering from the gastric disorder that was to prove fatal, did not in fact read *The Waves*; see *Holroyd*, p. 1051: '"It's perfectly fearful," he admitted to Topsy Lucas (4 November 1931). "I shudder and shiver—and cannot take the plunge. *Any* book lying about I seize up as an excuse for putting it off."' Hugh Walpole had written on 4 November (copy MHP, Sussex) to congratulate VW on the issue of a second impression of *The Waves*, but admitted he found it 'unreal'—a point she takes up in her reply (*IV VW Letters*, no. 2467). No record has been found of the reactions of the other people listed by VW—though Lord David Cecil had tea with VW on 4 November.
6. These were published as 'The Strange Elizabethans' and 'The Countess of Pembroke's Arcadia', for which VW was reading Gabriel Harvey and Philip Sidney, in *The Common Reader, Second Series*.

closer means of writing about books, as about people, could I hit upon it.

[*Added later:*] (The Waves has sold more than 7,000. The Deluge is selling very well)

Theres always somebody playing a concertina if one has the window open at the back—a kind of bagpipe concertina. That reminds me, I scribble a page of what is called, I think, Diary or Calendar every morning, before setting to upon Harvey, in which I catch such reflections—& shall one day publish them in a square grey-papered covered volume, very thin: a kind of copy book, with a calendar of the month stamped upon it.

Tuesday 17 November

Yes I forget, why do I want to write here, what do I want to say? with half an hour to lunch. A foggy morning; & Vita rings up; & I say (chiefly owing to my dream that she had gone off with someone, very markedly, at a party, in a small house whose room I was about to make into my study by knocking down a wall—I still see it: I hear Nessa saying She's tired of you: then my teeth broke; then as I say Vita went off triumphantly with somebody, being sick of me; & so I woke, about 4.30, & decided that I would be firm if she rang me up & asked me to lunch with her & Gerald Heard.[7] In truth she did do this: & I was firm; & she was charming & warm & trusty & friendly, & said she would come in this evening then, as she so much wanted to see me. Really my firmness was due to my dream).

Isnt it odd that I'm really, I believe, ostracised by some of my friends, because of The Waves, & lifted to the highest pinnacle by others, because of it? Dadie, for instance, & Goldie: but Morgan is the only one, either side, that matters.[8]

On the evening of 17 November the Woolfs went to a concert, and two days later to the cinema; they went to Rodmell from Friday until Sunday. On Monday they gave a dinner party, and on Tuesday 24 November dined in company and went to The Master Builder *at the Duchess Theatre; on that day LW noted: 'VW headache', and for the next month she followed a semi-invalid routine—'a hermit's life, without pleasure or excitement' (IV VW Letters, no. 2478). In mid-December the Woolfs learnt that Lytton Strachey*

7. Gerald Heard (1889-1971), scientific and philosophical writer, who was described by E. M. Forster (BBC, 13 August 1931) as 'one of the most penetrating minds in England.' He was a friend of Harold Nicolson.
8. G. L. Dickinson wrote to VW in praise of *The Waves* on 23 October, and again, after re-reading, on 13 November 1931. Transcriptions of his almost undecipherable typewritten letters in MHP, Sussex, are published on pp. 192-4 of the Abinger Edition, 1973, of E. M. Forster's *Goldsworthy Lowes Dickinson*, 1934.

was seriously ill, and from Rodmell, where they drove on 22 December, they telephoned each day for news of him. They remained at Monks House until 10 January 1932.

Friday Xmas morning

Lytton is still alive this morning. We thought that he could not live through the night. It was a moonlit night. Nessa rang up at 10 to say that he has taken milk & tea after an injection. When she went to Hungerford yesterday they were in great despair sitting round. He had taken nothing for 24 hours & was only half conscious. This may be the turn, or may mean nothing.[1] We are lunching with the Keynes'. Now again all one's sense of him flies out & expands & I begin to think of things I shall say to him, so strong is the desire for life—the triumph of life.

A soft misty morning.

After writing the last page, Nov. 16th, I could not go on writing without perpetual headache; & so took a month lying down; have not written a line; have read Faust, Coningsby &c. & seen Clive, Christabel, Nessa, Miss Bowen, Alice Ritchie: until the last 14 days, when I heard about Lytton.[2] He has been ill a month. I have lived through again all grades of feeling: then the telephone; then Angelica coming; then going to see James; then coming here last Tuesday, a dark drive, a tree reminding me of Lytton. Brighton yesterday. All very quiet, misty; a blue sky & white clouds last night. Talk to L. last night about death: its stupidity; what he would feel if I died. He might give up the Press; but how one must be natural. And the feeling of age coming over us: & the hardship of losing friends; & my dislike of the younger generation; & then I reason, how one must understand. And we are happier now.

Sunday 27 December

Last night—I go to Miss Dixey's to telephone—"the improvement continues".[3] I say this must mean that the stout Strachey constitution has triumphed. For 48 hours L. has been better, & now, Nessa says, realises that he is better, & eats; whatever he is allowed. I am therefore freely

1. Clive and Vanessa, who with their children were spending Christmas with his widowed mother at Seend in Wiltshire, drove over to Ham Spray on Christmas Eve to enquire after Lytton.
2. Elizabeth Bowen (Mrs Alan Cameron, 1899-1973), the Irish-born novelist, whom VW had met at Lady Ottoline Morrell's; she had tea with the Woolfs on 3 December. Alice Ritchie (1897-1941), graduate of Newnham and novelist; from 1928 she acted as traveller for Hogarth Press books.
3. Miss Dicksee and Miss Emery lived at Charnes Cottage, next to Monks House; they bred Fox Terriers.

DECEMBER 1931

imagining a future with my old serpent to talk to, to laugh at, to abuse:
I shall read his book on Sh[akespea]re; I shall stay at Ham Spray; I shall
tell him how L. & I sobbed on Christmas Eve.

But this page is one of my trials to test my brain. If successful I shall go
out to the Lodge tomorrow, light my electric fire, & potter about. I am
cross with Desmond, for talking about dreaming subjectivity & The
Waves; I have been making phrases about his damnable tepidity—he
who neither loves nor hates—in short I'm in a healthy condition.[4] And it
is, remarkably, April the First. L. cant come in. I've been pacing the
terrace. The sun is flooding the downs. The leaves of the plant in the
window are transparent with light. My brain will be filling. We shall go to
Lewes tomorrow. All is again released, though I shall have some trepidation about the telephone. Lunching with the Keynes, they took Lytton
philosophically. "Is he alive?" Lydia asked. She had 3 helps of turkey.
Maynard said that Lytton's last relations had been very thin. He was not
sure when he saw him last. He was not really changed; nothing of importance had happened. They did not go to Ham Spray because Lydia
disapproves of the immorality of Carrington. She is a dog in the manger.
The relationships are hypocritical.[5]

And what d'you feel about immortality, Maynard? I asked. "I am an
idealist," said Maynard, "& therefore on the whole I suppose I think that
something may continue. Clearly the brain is the only exciting thing—
matter does not exist. It follows therefore. . . . but one is very vague."
So, more or less, he said. And L. said death was stupid like a motor
accident. And M. said that Mrs Courtauld was dying, might be dead that
moment.[6] And he wished one cd. die at once: there should be death
arranged for couples simultaneously, like himself & Lydia, me & Leonard.
But he always supposed he would die before Lydia, & I, I said, before
Leonard. Then Lydia & Leonard will marry. They will combine all these
dogs— (dogs were wandering about.) And so home. And I kissed
Maynard. And they are coming to tea.

I can write so far, if it is to be called [writing,] not an effusion of this

4. Desmond MacCarthy's column 'The World of Books', *Sunday Times*, 27 December
1931, was devoted to a survey of the year's publishing. 'In the hands of poetic and
imaginative novelists,' MacCarthy wrote, 'the inner-monologue and the "fantasia"
have proved fruitful . . . in *The Waves* Virginia Woolf pushed her method of
dreaming subjectivity to its extreme limit.'
5. For Lydia Keynes, see Appendix. Dora de Houghton Carrington (1893-1932),
painter, had married Ralph Partridge (1894-1960) in 1921, while he was working
for the Hogarth Press. She was deeply devoted to Lytton Strachey, and he to
Ralph, and their triangular ménage at Ham Spray, though not based on sexual
fidelity, was closely interdependent.
6. Elizabeth, wife of Samuel Courtauld (1876-1947), the industrialist, art-collector,
and Trustee of the Tate and National Galleries, died on 28 December 1931.

old pen, without racing or pain. But when it comes to the screw—the screw that I give, & Desmond doesn't—

Tuesday 29 December

Lytton is, if anything, better. I need not ring up Nessa today, which is a matter of exquisite relief. It seems as if he were now to be seriously ill with ups & downs for some time. They say it is positively not typhoid but ulcerated colon. Well, we have lived through every grade of feeling—how strong, how deep—more than I guessed, though that cavern of horror is well known to me. Soon the whole being can suffer no more: I cant feel anything, I say as I lift the receiver, sitting on Miss Dixey's bed & eying with intensity her shining table & the two pale blue wine glasses; the tea caddy; & the gilt framed picture of a Victorian lady. There was also a little pile of books, a few letters, & The Dog World. In these acute states emotions are much simplified—there is none of the complexity that I feel this morning about Lytton, when I expect him to recover. I feel annoyance, humour, the desire to laugh with him.

It is a bitter windy morning, & Caburn, when I came in was white with snow. Now it is black. Shall I ever 'write' again? And what is writing? The perpetual converse I keep up. I've stopped it these 5 or 6 weeks. That excitement, which becomes a habit, is over. Why take to it again? I am dispassionate. Books come gently surging round me, like icebergs. I could write a book of caricatures. Christabel's story of the Hall Caines suggested a caricature of Country house life, with the red-brown pheasants,[7] Then there's Flush: theres the Knock on the door; there's the appalling novel; theres Common Reader . . . there's my little letter to a Poet. But I'm deficient in excitement; dont feel, as I did after many such illnesses, if I dont write I shall whizz into extinction like an electric globe fused.

That makes me think that our 3 black swans came last night. I will finish this book, & begin another for 1932. And now I have a vast choice of reading matter, & feel no sort of inclination to reply to the flattering invitation of Chatto that they should reprint my books. So Faber wishes too. And L. has sold his 450; & I 9400—what figures!

7. Sir (Thomas Henry) Hall Caine (1853-1931), the popular novelist; he died at his home, Greeba Castle, on the Isle of Man in August of this year.

1932

1932

The following entry is the last in DIARY XX. *On 2 January the Woolfs went up to London for the day.*

[*Friday 1 January*]

This is to be quite frank the 1st Jan. 1932, but I will pretend that it is still 1931: so that I may spend the 25 minutes to lunch writing here. I will bring a new book down tomorrow. The truth is I cannot write—but must scribble. My attempt to polish up John's letter in the lodge yesterday was a failure. Am I more severe, deeper, less of a flibbertigibbet now than of old, so that writing exacts a closer screw?—& my head is twisted with the effort? I think that possible. Anyhow, I must sail over the 7 days left here as smoothly, vacantly, serenely as may be. And use this page to sail on.

Waves have sold 9,650—Deluge 440 (?)

Yesterday we had Keynes's & Bells to tea. Mrs Courtauld is dead. Lytton, as I must believe, very slowly mending. And I must repay a vow made in my sorrow—to send £10 yearly to old Sophie. Only when my brains dry up I feel nervous. Action is dead[1]—O these dogs—thats my present curse. And one must learn to overcome it somehow. This irregular sharp bark is the devil. Ear stoppers? Clive as bright as a bullfinch. We talked of going to bed in front of Angelica. And of Desmond's maniacal lies—"I have posted the article" when he hasn't written it. And of the Stracheys—Nessa's description of the lounge at the Bear filled with Stracheys reading detective novels in despair. In comes Ralph. Silence. "Would you like to come, Pernel?" Pernel elongates herself & goes to get ready. "Gently fading away?" says Oliver. Ralph nods. Dorelia is summoned to be with Carrington, who will commit suicide they think. She leaves. Wires for a little bag with some money that she took out of John's dressing gown—he might be annoyed. A man appears with the bag. Is this yours? They look & find £300 in notes inside. (I am now stopped against the dogs; but it is difficult to write stoppered; & foolish; & an extravagant demand on me by Miss Dixey; & if a knock were to come I should not hear—& the dog after all may stop barking.) Carrington moving about scarcely knowing people: Pippa violently self-controlled;

1. Sophia Farrell, see above, 14 October 1931, n. 4. The last issue of *Action*, the weekly journal of Oswald Mosley's New Party edited by Harold Nicolson, appeared on 31 December 1931.

Saxon helping by—I forget what; Tommie helping, too, but summoned to comfort his parents for the death of Garrow in an air spill; & the Stracheys, all grey, all woollen, all red nosed, swollen eyed, logical, quiet, exact, doing cross word puzzles; thinking of Lytton. And that afternoon (Christmas Eve) Lytton said "If its only keeping me alive a little longer, dont". And so they did nothing; but then he drank tea & milk with brandy & enjoyed them, & the Dr happily had some serum, injected it, & so the turn—if turn they call it—began. This is a scene I can see; & see Lytton too, always reasonable, clear, giving his orders; & dying as he thought; & then, as reasonably, finding some strength returning, deciding to live. And L. & I sobbing here. And I expect Nessa & Clive sitting over the fire late, with some tears, at Seend.[2]

During the last days here, they have been putting up a great erection of girders on the bank opposite Asheham. Is this an overhead railway or an engine house?[3] So another view of the downs is lost forever. And Anny repeats vague gossip that there is to be a series of factories between Newhaven & Lewes: are we doomed to go—or to stay on & be worried out of all walks, all views, & become crusted over with villas?

The Woolfs returned to 52 Tavistock Square on 10 January. The following entry marks the beginning of DIARY XXI.

Wednesday 13 January

Oh but this is, as I always say, making an apology myself to myself, not the first day of the year. It is the thirteenth, & I am in one of those lassitudes & ebbs of life when I cannot heave another word on to the wall. My word, what a heaving The Waves was, that I still feel the strain! We came back from Rodmell last Sunday afternoon—a wet evening, & comfortable to be back, here high up in the air, beyond barking dogs.

2. During Lytton's illness, the Bear Inn at Hungerford had become virtually an annexe of Ham Spray where his anxious friends and relatives congregated; those referred to in VW's record of Vanessa's account of her visit there on Christmas Eve include Carrington's husband Ralph Partridge, Lytton's sisters Pernel and Pippa, his elder brother Oliver (1874-1960), who worked for the Foreign Office as a cryptographer, as well as his youngest brother James. Dorelia (1881-1969), wife of the painter Augustus John, was a friend of long standing particularly congenial to Carrington at this period. Saxon Sydney Turner (1880-1962), Treasury official, had been a contemporary of Lytton, Clive, and LW at Trinity College, Cambridge. 'Tommy' Tomlin's elder brother, the Hon. George Garrow Tomlin, had been killed in an aeroplane crash at Nazeing in Essex on 13 November.
3. This was a vast hangar-like construction built at Asheham for the Alpha Cement Company, which subsequently engulfed Asheham House and excavated chalk and clay from the surrounding downlands (it was demolished in 1981).

"I shall go bankrupt if those dogs bark any more" I said to Anny with some vehemence, & this, implying her ruin, made her speak to Elsie, & the dogs fell silent. Miss Belsher is reported 'very ill'. L. is to see father Belsher this afternoon, & I am to see Mrs Thring 'on a private & confidential matter' which I guess to be the printing of a little book of poems by herself. Time—3.30 to be exact—will prove. Then Miss Cashin is ill too; the press is supported on 2 legs, one the stout leg of good-natured Walton.[4] John labours too, more nervously, & feels jaded, & wants a week off, & wants also, to be our manager, not partner, but to stay in that capacity. So, perhaps, & perchance—for I make no rash boasts—the dear old Press to which I owe so much labour—witness the pile of MSS before me—& fun—oh yes, a great deal of variety & oddity, life on tap down here whenever it flags upstairs—may now settle down for life. For our lives. How long will they be? Can we count on another 20 years? I shall be fifty on 25th, Monday week that is; & sometimes feel that I have lived 250 years already, & sometimes that I am still the youngest person in the omnibus. (Nessa said that she still always thinks this, as she sits down.) And I want to write another 4 novels: Waves, I mean; & the Tap on the Door; & to go through English literature, like a string through cheese, or rather like some industrious insect, eating its way from book to book, from Chaucer to Lawrence. This is a programme, considering my slowness, & how I get slower, thicker, more intolerant of the fling & the rash, to last out my 20 years, if I have them. Lytton goes on, now better, now not so well. And one has taken him back after those sepulchral days when he seemed vanished as part of life. Leonard said "We must make up our minds that we shall never see Lytton again";—or something like that, which made us feel bereft; the end of a section; & now I say it is not the end.

And Vita supports the weight of the Nicolsons on her shoulders, working, working working so that she cant sleep o'nights, Ethel says Hilda says.[5] But why? People should ride life like a horse. This money accumulating, keeping sons at Eton & Long Barn & Siss[inghurs]t in full swing seems to me a little servile: save that she loves generosity & is industrious, & has that queer vein in her of thinking the slogging money

Marginal note: No: it was to get money— she was a notorious swindler who did Hugh out of £70.

---

4. Katherine Thring was the wife of the Secretary to the Society of Authors, G. H. Thring; the marginal note was probably added after Hugh Walpole had been to tea with VW on 26 February. Peggy Belsher, Molly Cashin, and Peggy Walton were all clerks in the Hogarth Press office.

5. Hilda Matheson (1888-1940), an intimate friend of Vita's, was first Director of Talks at the BBC, which she left in 1932. Harold Nicolson had at this time no regular work or income.

making ant like worker, the independent, the professional, romantic. And so she scribbles reviews, broadcasts—pray heaven I may never fall into the money-trap!

Monday 18 January

And then we heard that Lytton was very ill again—they had thought him dying on Sunday. "Give him morphia—it makes no difference" the Dr said. So down we went to Ham Spray on Thursday.[6] So hot, so fresh. The larks singing over the petrol pumps I remember on the Great West Road as we stopped to fill up. They were strained, silent, held in a lock [?]. Then tears—Pippa sobbing on my shoulder at the Bear after lunch— hopeless almost—he is so ill—how can he get better? Then back to Ham Spray—how lovely, with its flat lawn, & the trees grouped & the down rising & the path climbing the down: this I noted, with envy thinking of my dogs barking, my downs ruined, as we sat at tea. I long sometimes for this sealed up, silent, remote country: long for its little villages; its muddy roads, its distance from Brighton & Peacehaven—the roads that go on to Bath, to Oxford, driving through solid England. And so home again, leaving them in the frail lovely house, with hospital nurses popping in & out, all orderly arranged as after long weeks of illness: a light in Lytton's room, the shadow of a screen. He said he liked our coming. Odd to come thus, after all these years. Again today Carrington writes he is slightly better.

Thursday 21 January

And last night Lytton was dying "much worse" Oliver telephoned; & this morning "much better again". So we go to Angelica's party in fancy dress. It is like having the globe of the future perpetually smashed— without Lytton—& then, behold, it fills again.[7]

Friday 22 January

Much better was much weaker. Lytton died yesterday morning.
I see him coming along the street, muffled up with his beard resting on his tie: how we should stop: his eyes glow. Now I am too numb with all the emotion yesterday to do more than think thoughts like this. Well, as I know, the pain will soon begin. One toys about with this & that. How queer it was last night at the party, the tightness round everyone's lips— ours I mean. Duncan Nessa & I sobbing together in the studio—the man looking out of the mews window—a sense of something spent, gone: that

6. The Woolfs' only previous visit to Ham Spray had been in October 1924.
7. The party was in Vanessa Bell's studio, 8 Fitzroy Street.

is to me so intolerable: the impoverishment: then the sudden vividness. Duncan said "One misses people more & more. It comes over one suddenly that one will tell them something. Then the pang comes over one, after years". Nessa said, What would one like if one died oneself? that the party should go on. He is the first of the people one has known since one was grown up to die she said. It was very hopeless. One knows now how irremediable—but no: I cant think of any words for what I mean, & yet go on writing, numb, torpid as I am. We are going down to Rodmell this afternoon I think. Pippa & James come up today. Carrington & Ralph tomorrow. What is to happen now to Carrington? Yes, 20 years of Lytton lost to us, stupidly: the thing we shall never have again.

Saturday 30 January

Oliver to dinner last night. His cheeks are softer, fatter: he looks a codger, a card; an old buffer. I am alert now to take these signs, as if I saw us all becoming figures: rigid, inert. Well: we talked. "Never never have I known so odd a character as Karin. Women *want* children. Ray wants *babies*. I wont have them. Theres no money for anybody. Of course I'm odd—so cold, unemotional. I haven't any feelings as a parent. I saw Ruby in November—after 10 years. Oh yes we shall meet. Why shouldn't we? She was a liar—thats all—couldn't tell the truth. But very attractive. The boy is Hunter's son. But they call him Strachey on his birth certificate. Do you know both the boys are Stracheys—said Ruby. She's had 5 children, never by the same man.[8] Lytton was a great man. Oh the excitement. I came back from India starved, & found—all that." Lytton has left all books printed before 1841 to Senhouse. Why before 1841? "Some private joke I imagine. Senhouse might have preferred £1000.[9] The unfortunate thing was that Lytton fell in love with Ralph. . . . You know what Jeans says? Civilisation is the thickness of a postage stamp on the top of Cleopatra's needle; & time to come is the thickness of postage stamps as high as Mont Blanc. Possessiveness is the devil. Inez is a little too possessive. The ideal is to cease being in love simultaneously & then it passes into another state. Nobody can be in love for more than 5

8. Oliver Strachey's second wife, whom he married in May 1911 and by whom he had two children, was Rachel (Ray) Costelloe (1887-1940), elder sister of Adrian Stephen's wife Karin—who had two daughters. In 1900 Oliver had married Ruby Meyer in India, where he was an official of the East India Railway Company, and their only child Julia was born in 1901. See Richard Strachey, *A Strachey Child*, 1979: 'Eventually Ruby bolted to the hills . . . but for some years, and with the regularity of the monsoon, Ruby continued to add to our family stock.'

9. Roger Senhouse (1900-70) had for the last five years of Lytton's life been his great love; a bibliophile, he became a partner in the publishers Secker & Warburg in 1936. His books, including those left him by Lytton, were sold at Sotheby's, 18-20 October 1971.

years.[10] They cant leave Carrington alone. She says she will kill herself—quite reasonable—but better to wait until the first shock is over & see. Suicide seems to me quite sensible. We've been born too early. Soon they'll have found a way of curing these growths. Yes—there was an autopsy. Pippa came down—we had kept it from her—& said Oughtn't we to have one? It had just been done. It was cancer, an early stage. Nobody guessed it—nobody could have guessed it—" This led to a long argument about doctors. Oliver is a tough old buffer: with one flame inside of him. What the Americans call 'culture'. "*Thats* the only thing: to realise the legacy thats been left us. To read. To do nothing from 18 to 22 but read. Thats what we did. Thats why we shant grow old—we shant come to an end. But you cant do it if you dont do it then. A great man, Roger. He made things transcendent—showed them lifted up. He was at Yattendon—oh that was the greatest time of my life: & then there was the Aholibah; & then the Easter at Corfe: Lytton, Henry & I at one Inn; Ray Elly &—at another. Lytton had the mumps. Ottoline came down & stood beneath his window, & he leant out & they blew each other kisses. She used to take the stiles in one stride. "Such long legs" said Lytton "She cant be a woman". Henry was his most serious love affair.[11] Senhouse is a very nice young man—nice looking, nice manners—but no character, nothing. No Mary [Hutchinson] was rude to Inez; cut her in the street, so I cant see her. Its all a question of little Mary, nothing abstract. But I like her—only not that way of life—so absurd—that fun: but I like old Jack's stories. Well I must go. Thank you, Virginia."

Sunday 31 January

Having just finished, as I say, the final version as I call it, of my Letter to a young poet, I can take a moments liberty. From the cynical tone of this sentence I see that my finality is not secure. Writing becomes harder & harder. Things I dashed off I now compress & re-state. And for pur-

10. Sir James Jeans, FRS, became popular as an expositor of physical science and astronomy through publication of *The Mysterious Universe* (1930) and other books; for this particular exemplification see *The Universe Around Us* (1929), p. 342. Oliver's love affair with Inez Jenkins, *née* Fergusson, flourishing at the end of the war, had passed into another state after her marriage in 1923.

11. Oliver Strachey, divorced from Ruby, returned on leave from India early in 1911. The Manor House, Yattendon, was the home of the poet Robert Bridges, who had married a cousin of Roger Fry. The *Aholibah* was a launch on the river Cam hired by Walter Lamb (1882-1968), a contemporary of Lytton's at Cambridge and then a lecturer in Classics at the University, for a party he gave on 7 June 1911. The 'Easter at Corfe' is described in *Holroyd*, pp. 458-9, and in Barbara Strachey, *Remarkable Relations* (1980), pp. 254-5. Henry Lamb (1883-1960), the painter, was Walter's brother, and Elly, Elinor Rendel (1885-1942), Lytton's niece; she became VW's doctor in 1924.

poses which I need not go into here, I want to use these pages for dialogue for a time. Let me race down the subdued & dulled interview with my mother in law.[12] Oh the heat in that rose pink bed sitting room, with 3 fierce lights on, the tables crowded with flowers; & with cakes, a fire blazing. Mrs W. sitting upright with her feet on a stool on a high straight backed chair: more pink silk cushions behind her: pearl necklaces swinging. I came in late; she was talking about—I forget: had been talking about the girl whom Cecil might have loved: the daughter of a solicitor at Colchester: Oh yes: she had had influenza & gone to a house kept up by funds left by Mr Andrews. And she was reluctant at first—a home you know. But when she got there what was her amazement? All gentlewomen: flowers everywhere; a cupboard with tonics & sweets to take after them; & Georgian silver on the dinner table; & a garden; & a saloon car to take them out; & grounds; & hot milk at eleven, or chocolate; & the wireless, & a page boy coming for orders; & gardeners. Everything you could wish & not a penny to pay for it! Thats so rare—charity that is really thoughtful; charity for educated women with nice feelings who have fallen on bad times. Well Virginia—& whats your news? Oh & there's Captain Steel: every Christmas he has a card from the Duke of Gloucester: & he now sells Hoovers for £2.10 a week. But what can one do, in these days? One must do what one can. And what is your news, Virginia? Exodus? Dont you know Exodus? I sometimes scold myself that I haven't read the Bible lately. Deuteronomy? Oh yes—thats about the building of the Temple. I dont say its all true; but what stories to tell children! I shall never forget telling Bella. Of course a first child is always a wonder child. She used to have her dinner with me when she was 2. And she said what a pity it was summer when Eve stole the apple. If it had been winter, there wouldn't have been an apple. And she said too: I know where gold comes from—that's in the ground: but where do picture frames come from? We had large gilt picture frames with family portraits in the dining room. (V.) Well why dont you write about your children? Oh no: I couldn't say all I think about them. And you're going so soon? But you haven't hardly come. And you'll dine with me next week? She came down to the hall, & was I think going into the lounge to talk to some flushed women playing cards.

Monday 1 February

Last night at Roger's: present; ourselves, Gerald Heard, Igor. Roger rather sunk & aged after influenza. G.H. in full discourse: about the

12. The Woolfs went to tea with LW's mother on 30 January; her next-youngest son Cecil (1887-1917), who was killed at the Battle of Cambrai, had been stationed at Colchester early in the war. Bella (1877-1960), now Mrs Thomas Southorn, was the eldest of her eight surviving children.

67

experiment made by the Yorkshireman who married 4 millions, in Devonshire.[1]

H[eard]. Its intensely interesting (all he says becomes dust). I went round the works with him. The Germans send a man all charges paid for a week. But the vats aren't ready. All the machinery comes from Belgium. They say it'll be delivered on a certain day: & it is. The English make excuses: always some reason why they cant deliver. He says he can keep his community supplied all except oranges & (perhaps) dates. Give him 3 months & he could supply Plymouth. Wood planting neglected in England. He buys woods ahead—9 acres, 4 acres, here & there: then the fields with stumps—whats to be done? No aboriculture in England. . . .

Helen here captured me with questions, flattering, sub-acid, about my writing. And about Roger: & not seeing us; & Baba. She lies in bed & talks about Leonard: he was with the esquimaux & gnawed the shoes of the wives, & so sent for a puppy—her delirium. All youth is mad, I said . . .

Heard said something highly well informed about a Satanic picture. He is a lean starting eyed lobster man: a man of the future, without senses. In with Wells, Plunket &c: but essentially a nobody.[2] Duncan feels this strongly. Science running thin as magnesia or quinine in his veins. Story telling about Things &c began & feeling his irrelevancy, for he knows all facts & no feelings, has no humour, no richness, only advanced ideas, he left. So the air became riper. Roger talked about games; children; his design for a curtain;[3] & N[essa] & D[uncan] were almost too severely malicious.

[*Tuesday 2 February*]

Conversation piece: Monday Feb. 1st 1932. 5.30 pm.
   I am reading Wells' science of life, & have reached the hen that became

1. The Woolfs had joined Roger Fry and Helen Anrep (see Appendix) at their Bernard Street home after dinner on Sunday evening. Igor and Anastasia ('Baba'), now in their late 'teens, were her children by the Russian mosaicist Boris Anrep, whom she had left in 1926 to live with Roger Fry. Gerald Heard's discourse was on the subject of the experiment in rural industry and education conducted by Leonard Elmhirst (1893-1974) and his wife the wealthy American widow Dorothy Whitney Straight, at Dartington Hall, which they had bought on their marriage in 1925.
2. Sir Horace Plunkett (1854-1932), the influential pioneer of agricultural co-operation, who coined the slogan 'better farming, better business, better living.' Heard acted as his personal secretary and assistant for some years.
3. Fry was designing curtains for Jane and Kenneth Clark (see below, 1 November 1934, n. 1); see *II Fry Letters*, nos. 673, 678.

a cock or vice versa.[4] Nelly talks at the door. I hear a characteristic slow & heavy stamp. Then a bold tap at the drawing room door. In comes Ethel Smyth in her spotted fur, like an unclipped & rather overgrown woodland wild beast, species indeterminate. She wears, as usual, her 3 cornered Frederick the Great hat, & one of her innumerable relay of tweed coats & skirts. She carries a leather satchel. Before she has sat down she is talking. "Really I think that building of the kind you describe at Rodmell is worse than death. After all one may say of death its natural: but this is a wanton desecration. Why your downs? Oh I know L. wouldn't agree; but theres my Rupert Gwynne. He said, he pounced like a wolf on the fold the other day when they were talking against landlords—We, & I hope all my family for ever, he said, refuse to sell our land. We think beauty is something to keep. We sacrifice money[5]— Well—Yes I'm exhausted—Two hours injection . . Not tea, no: but vermouth. It wont make me tipsy? Oh I'm worn out (but she looks like a ruddy sea captain or old apple woman.) Now—questions. But I had such a good visit from Eddy. He's writing a novel to show that the virtues of the aristocracy, in which I firmly believe though L. doesnt—must survive.[6] Why not in his own person then I asked? Be noble magnanimous serene, instead of petty spiteful & egotistical. Oh thats his digestion: I assure you he's a pheno-menon. Musical. How I pity him! forced to live in England with that gift—you dont know the loneliness. Compare the people at [*illegible*]. They talk of cricket golf: in Berlin, they have their ham & beer & talk of the way the violin plays the G sharp. Eddy has the duties of his position—a very great one: very real duties. He's a man of the world—L. despises that. I love it. What was I going to say—He played Der Wald. He said nobody knows Ethel Smyth till theyve heard all this. Who made the theme? I did. Well its the pure flower of the romantic movement. And we sat reading our books & he played & played. He has a character of his own—an original point of view. Oh yes I agree. And he has a deep feeling for you. But how could I make anything of Mary Dodge under four years he said? She'd look wild, & hook the salt cellar to her with her silver claw.[7] V. would make something very amusing of it. Does not

---

4. See the case of a 'a three-year-old Buff Orpington' in Section 7, 'Reversal of Sex', vol. II, p. 374 of H. G. Wells' *The Science of Life*, 1930.

5. Lt.-Col. Roland Vaughan Gwynne (1882-1971), of Folkington Manor, near Polegate, was a considerable local landowner, as was his brother at Piddinghoe, near, Rodmell.

6. Edward Sackville-West's novel *The Sun in Capricorn* was to be published in 1934; for VW's reactions to it, see below, 14 October 1934.

7. *Der Wald* was Ethel Smyth's second opera, first produced in Dresden in 1901. Mary Dodge, a rich American who settled in England before the war, was a great supporter of Ethel's, subsidising the production of her opera *The Wreckers* in 1909, and the purchase of land near Woking on which she built her house, Coign.

everybody take a back place once you've known V. I asked. Poor Eddy pumped up the necessary affirmation. Oh my dear dont I know it all— (reference to Lytton) those poor Stracheys: & you who care for so few people. But I must catch my train this time. I'm taking care of myself. I'm worn out. Here are the tickets for the lecture tomorrow in case you can come. My dear V. dont freeze me off—I beg of you. No I cant write to you—I'm completely taken up—three treatments a week. Beecham rang up at eleven. He's going to do the Prison this year. And I wrote to Mrs Snowden—I'm old enough to be your mother.[8] You say. . . . (these final words were rattled off on the doorstep).

Wednesday 3 February

These conversation pieces are artfully contrived to assuage me, about 11.30, after toiling at correcting Donne, who is to introduce the second volume of the Common Reader. I cant go on squeezing my sentences dry of water; & so write here for 20 minutes; then I think read Donne; then finish with a [unidentified ms] novel upon Hamlet, clever, oh yes—novels about Hamlet always are. Then lunch: then—Oh Ottoline this evening. Yet I am so much interested in Donne, or in my views that I cannot begin.

Last night then, at Clive's. Roger, Nessa, Duncan. Clive in his brown tea cosy with the strap hanging down indecently like a tail between his legs. Roger rather shrunk up. Sherry. Lottie says dinner. Down we go to the lovely gay room with blue & white chairs. The character of Gerald Heard. D. makes a subtle distinction. "No its not that he prevents me from doing my little owl. Its not that I dislike his facts—I can absorb facts from some people. It is that he sets up no relation between himself & me so that I cannot relate his facts to anything." R.: But he has passion of mind. V.: He is an ascetic. He refused my cigar. R.: Yet he doesn't disapprove of the senses. D. He sees nothing. Clive: He loves me, but I find him dryer, more juiceless than a banana. He walks down Bond Street with Raymond & says What a wonderful companion Raymond is because he notices the flags. (Van:) "he notices nothing sensual. We live in our senses. He pours forth all those intelligent remarks about the Satanist picture." Here I saw Clive look at Lytton's picture. "Dont have it moved. Have it cleaned, by all means, but it looks very nice there. Its the best thing of Lytton. R. And that horrid vulgar picture by Henry is the one people will know him by. Thats rather summary of course (to D.) Vir: But its far the most like. R. I did a portrait of Lytton, writing E.

8. VW did not go to Ethel's lecture given at King's College, London, on 2 February; she dined with Clive Bell. Sir Thomas Beecham eventually 'did' *The Prison* in January 1934 in a Jubilee concert at the Queen's Hall devoted to Ethel's works. Ethel Snowden was the wife of the Chancellor of the Exchequer, Philip Snowden.

Victorians at Durbins.[9] Vir: I'm a little annoyed that he left all his old books to Senhouse. Clive. And his will? I've heard nothing. No, Roger, I dont think you understand. Nothing, humanly speaking, is more unlikely, in fact impossible, than that R[alph]. should go back to Carrington. He opened his heart to me once . . . D.: Well, I'm fonder of Frances than of any of them; but I think as a human being, she might have behaved differently. I think so. C. But you dont understand, Duncan. She was passionately in love—is still—with R. So when it came to the point—I mustn't come this week end—one shade of pressure from him—how could she resist it?[10] Lytton's letters couldn't be published—they would hurt everybody too much. We protested. Well what about the Nortons? "I've just met a youth who has been a bugger since the age of puberty?" Vir: Oh buggery's exploded—nobody could mind that now.[11]

Wells on life: facts: Roger & I love to have facts poured over us. Clive only likes facts if they are related to something human. A great many small vegetables, handed by Lottie. The ice too hard.

So we went upstairs & then we said—that France was combining against Japan. L. gave his views on the subject of war with China & Japan. We said that war is the dullest of all things. Not naval war, said Duncan. He had a cousin Admiral Arbuthnot, who lost all his ships. That was exciting. Only for ten minutes, I said.[12] Roger said could we not get up a society of artists to protest against the protection of works of art. Meninsky is ill & has sent the hat round. There is no public fund for

9. Clive owned the full-length portrait of Strachey by Duncan Grant (Collection Mrs Barbara Bagenal) painted at Asheham in 1913, when both Vanessa Bell and Roger Fry painted him too. Fry's earlier portrait, signed and dated 1917, is now in the Humanities Research Centre, University of Texas. The Henry Lamb portrait of 1914 is in the Tate Gallery (T 118).

10. Carrington's husband Ralph Partridge, while maintaining close and affectionate links with her and Lytton, had been living since 1926 with Frances Marshall in London, returning at weekends (sometimes with Frances) to Ham Spray, where his qualities of geniality and practicality were essential components of the joint household there. They were married later this year, after Carrington's death.

11. H. T. J. Norton (1886-1937), mathematician and one-time Fellow of Trinity College, Cambridge, to whom Lytton had dedicated *Eminent Victorians* in gratitude for friendship and financial support, was a member of a rich and conventional family which could be shocked and upset by indiscreet references in Lytton's letters.

12. The Sino-Japanese conflict over Manchuria was seriously threatening foreign interests in Shanghai; the French had now agreed to join Britain and the USA in urging the Japanese government to respect the neutrality of the Shanghai trade concessions. Rear-Admiral Sir Robert Arbuthnot (1864-1916) was in command of the 1st Cruiser Squadron when his flagship *Defence* was sunk with all hands at the Battle of Jutland; he was a distant kinsman of Duncan Grant.

helping painters—only writers.[13] What about William Jowitt said Clive, rubbing his hands. Thats a good joke—Poor William's off to the West Indies. I'm glad morality is vindicated, I said. No, I dont think politics ought to be a matter of Oxford & Cambridge, said Roger. Thats what I wrote & told him when the row was on, said Clive. Lesley liked it—she liked dressing up & being at Court. It was she who forced him to it—telephoning from the basement among the black beetles, I said.[14] Good Earth is a wonderful book, Roger said. It has a quality of objectivity & calm; a new kind of beauty, though the woman's name is Pearl Buck & she's an American. Baron Corvo is a good writer said Clive. Once when I was editing the Athenaeum he wrote & said he cdn't get absolution & though not destitute required more money in order to write. He had my entire sympathy.[15]

Roger went early; stopping his car by the pillarbox, venturously; twice he left the room to see if it were stolen. So to stories of Julian, the war game, Quentin's love affair, & so all talking we parted, Clive to be away in Rome for two months.

[Thursday 4 February]

One of the curious things I am now proving—now that I am going through the stages of Lytton's death—is that for us fame has no existence. We say we cant publish Lytton's letters for 50 years, if at all. We can't write about him. He has no funeral. I dont know where his ashes are buried.[16] There is no commemoration any more, except when we meet & talk; or in the usual ways, alone at night, walking along the streets (but

13. The painter Bernard Meninsky (1891-1950), a member of the London Group, taught life drawing at the Westminster School of Art, upon which he depended for his livelihood.
14. The Rt. Hon. Sir William Jowitt (1885-1957), KC, left the Liberal Party in 1929 to become Attorney-General in Ramsay MacDonald's administration. In the October 1931 general election he failed to win one of the two Combined Universities seats (a result, perhaps, of his earlier support for a proposal to abolish university representation); in spite of efforts by MacDonald to secure him a safe seat and amid considerable publicity, he was forced to resign his office on 24 January 1932. Lesley was his wife, very interested in the arts, and rather a friend of Clive.
15. The best-selling novel The Good Earth by Pearl S. Buck (1892-1973) was published in 1931. Frederick William Rolfe (1860-1913), self-styled 'Baron Corvo', author of Hadrian the Seventh (1904), and a convert to Roman Catholicism. Clive was acting editor of the Athenaeum for a short period during 1910.
16. Lytton Strachey was cremated at Golders Green; there was no ceremony, and James Strachey and Saxon Sydney-Turner were the only witnesses. Later on a commemorative tablet was placed in the Strachey family chapel in the church at Chew Magna in Somerset.

these states in my case have yet to be verified: all sensation now: I mean what Lytton's death means I dont yet know). Hence to think of fame is superfluous: what people will say when I'm dead. The solid statue that father left—that exists no longer.

Talk yesterday with Ottoline. Philip discovered in the dining room, with its yellow cloth, reddish shades, reading letters & eating scones. Ott out—selling Lawrence first editions (how I'd like to tell that to Lytton!) We discussed Dryden: P. said he can do nothing but read poetry, gets into an exalted state. I had been buying Dryden for Julian.[17] Talk of celebrated passages. In came Ott: she had toast & tea. Talk of Bertie's autobiography, private: he devotes a chapter to abuse of her. Katherine Mansfield had disillusioned him. "I heard them discussing me all night through the floor." She uses too much scent & powder. She had meant nothing to him. "This he sends me—I could only write back Et tu Brute?"—I've had Lawrence, Aldous, Cannan, Osbert—now Bertie.[18] He replied he was astonished I should mind, but that he always hurts those he loves . . . So to the yellow drawing room. So to Lytton: his charm, long thin fingers, "time I knew him about 1908, with Henry [Lamb] . . . But no letters could be published. He was so considerate. I wrote to him last summer—he answered with great affection, about the past. One could always count on that, though one never saw him much. I've asked James to send back my letters. Sprott told me he had read them—I dont want them to be handed round.[19] And do you think he was happy? with Carrington? with Senhouse?"

So to Tom & Vivienne [Eliot] & the dog that makes messes: to Molly [MacCarthy] & her deafness; to The Waves—Jinny made me think of Mary—& Rhoda made me cry with a vision of you. But how could you write that book? the strain, the intensity—at which I kindle, as always, & say I will give her Johnson's Lives of the Poets. And she says she is

17. See *V VW Letters*, no. 2520; Julian Bell was twenty-four on 4 February. For Philip Morrell, see Appendix.
18. Bertrand Russell eventually published his autobiography in three volumes in 1967, 1968, and 1969; see vol. II, p. 27: 'She [KM] hated Ottoline because Murry did not. It had become clear to me that I must get over the feeling that I had for Ottoline, as she no longer returned it sufficiently to give me any happiness. I listened to all that Katherine Mansfield had to say against her . . .' Lady Ottoline was caricatured by D. H. Lawrence in *Women in Love* (1920), and by Aldous Huxley in *Crome Yellow* (1921); Osbert Sitwell portrayed her as Lady Septuagesima Goodley in *Triple Fugue* (1921); Gilbert Cannan habitually used his friends as models for characters in his numerous novels: but it was perhaps his title *Pugs and Peacocks* (1921) which hurt Ottoline.
19. W. J. H. ('Sebastian') Sprott (1897-1971), since 1928 Reader in Philosophy at University College, Nottingham; an Apostle; he had acted as amanuensis to Lytton and had filed all his correspondence.

reading Eth Bowen who tries to write like me, & will L. come & meet Hodgson who breeds bull dogs; & I say I am an aristocrat in writing; & she confirms this & abuses Vita for writing about Knole, being ignobly conscious of noble blood, & I praise Vita—denounce her novels; & Philip 'works' next door; & there is Ott's pug like a small Chinese lion on the chair in the hall; & Philip pops out with a copy of Dryden's poems in double columns, & I think how I would describe this to Lytton, & so home, embraced, loved perhaps—anyhow here's a letter this morning to ask me to think well of her when she's dead. & to send her The Waves.[20]

Monday 8 February

Why did I ever say I would produce another volume of Common Reader? It will take me week after week, month after month. However a year spent—save for diversions in Greece & Russia—in reading through English literature will no doubt do good to my fictitious brain. Rest it anyhow. One day, all of a rush, fiction will burst in. These remarks are jotted down at the end of a long mornings work on Donne, which will have to be done again, & is it worth the doing? I wake in the night with the sense of being in an empty hall: Lytton dead, & those factories building. What is the point of it—life, when I am not working, suddenly becomes thin, indifferent. Lytton is dead, & nothing definite to mark it. Also they write flimsy articles about him. Jack Squire for instance—as if he had not mattered very much.[21]

And we go on—at Rodmell for the week end; & went over to Caburn, & walked among those primeval downs, like a Heal bed, L. said, so comfortable: bowl shaped shadows; half circles; curves; a deep valley. Quentin last night: how mature, in some way; speaking with deliberation. Calmly explaining his situation with John. All Nessa's sense, & Clive's shrewdness. Suddenly he asks in his drawling childish voice for books upon Italian history, for some account of some armament deal; for he is notably objective, interested in politics, in behaviourism, in psycho-analysis. This was what our talk was of. And Benita, he says, is too much afraid of me to send me her memoirs. Some reproach implied—unless

20. VW replied this day (see *V VW Letters*, no. 2521): 'You bamboozled me into dreadful boasting I'm afraid—I never meant that my own writing is aristocratic, only my attitude to writing in general.' V. Sackville-West drew upon Knole in several of her books, notably *All Passion Spent* (1930) and *The Edwardians* (1931), both published by the Hogarth Press (*HP Checklist* 235 and 270). The poet Ralph Hodgson (1871-1962) was noted as a breeder of bulldogs.

21. J. C. Squire, in his editorial notes in the February issue of the *London Mercury*, devoted seven paragraphs to Lytton Strachey: 'His books, being carefully carven works of art, will continue to be read. But his influence has not been good. Strachey was learned, witty, fastidious . . .' &c.

this is merely the result of "Mrs Woolf's palpitating sensibility unmatched since Sterne"—a phrase from an article on music in the M. Guardian, rather tickling my vanity.[22]

Thursday 11 February

My mind is set running upon A Knock on the Door (whats its name?) owing largely to reading 'Wells on Woman'—how she must be ancillary & decorative in the world of the future, because she has been tried, in 10 years, & has not proved anything.[23] So in this mood I record Mary's telling me last night how she loved cigars; but Jack refuses to let her smoke them—against his idea of what his wife should do—silly affectation—or to let her dress in a dress cut low at the back. Cant go out with you in that frock. Go & put on another. Its indecent—yet will praise Diana [Cooper] for wearing the same. "I threw everything out of the window once" she said. "He treats us—Barbara & me—as if we were tame leopards—pets belonging to him". As indeed they do, since neither has a penny except of Jack's earning & giving. She burst into tears, about Lytton: her best, her most intimate friend—"And now I live merely with barbarians. I have nobody to talk to. Lytton came every week. He told me about all his boys. He sat sobbing bitterly, when Roger [Senhouse] was cruel to him. Oh he loved him—just loved him— Thats what I couldn't understand, & you could, I said. And he was so brilliant, so alive, last winter. I went to him about a fortnight before he was ill. I was in an ecstasy. I said You're wonderful, wonderful— He was so vigorous, giving a party to five young men. We stood in the hall. There was a letter from one of them refusing to come. And he kissed me. He was so sweet. He would come in. There was the coat he wore. He would talk of everything; tell me everything. And all the time there was this growth in him; & here Virginia & Mary sit talking of him & he's dead. I cant believe it"

22. Writing of a Hallé concert in the *Manchester Guardian* of 5 February, Neville Cardus observed: 'nobody has so far commented upon the obvious fact that English music is at the present time following very closely a certain line of development of English fiction. . . . A man might as well hang himself as look for a story, a plot, in "To the Lighthouse" of Mrs Woolf, or in the Third Symphony of Arnold Bax. . . . But there is more than headwork in the art of it all; there is muscle and nervous fibre, despite the lack of insinuating heart-throbbing tunes—just as Mrs Woolf has acute sensibility, perhaps the most palpitating since Sterne despite her indifference to the appeal of an Old Wive's [*sic*] tale.'

23. See H. G. Wells's *The Work, Wealth and Happiness of Mankind* (1932), which LW was reviewing for the *NS&N*, chapter 11, 'The Rôle of Women in the World's Work'; this ends: 'Hitherto the rôle of women has been decorative and ancillary. And today it seems to be still decorative and ancillary. . . . Her recent gains in freedom have widened her choice of what she shall adorn or serve, but they have released no new initiative in human affairs. . . .'

Saturday 13 February

I break off from my plain duty which is to read the Anatomy of the World, to record Roger's lecture: last night.[24] Roger rather cadaverous in white waistcoat. A vast sheet. Pictures passing. He takes his stick. Gets into trouble with the lanternist. Is completely at his ease. Elucidates unravels with fascinating ease & subtlety this quality & that: investigates (with his stick) opposing diagonals: emphasises the immediate & instantaneous in French art. Here a Queen about to fling out her fingers: here a mother "turning to look at something & losing herself in pensive & tender reverie, while her child struggles to look the other way, & she restrains it, unconsciously, with perfect ease & control." In the interval we talked to Mary, about the affair of Potocki which is filling our house, & making ring our telephone. (This man is sentenced to 6 months prison because he submitted for private publication the MS of a poem dedicated to John Penis in the Mount of Venus, to pay for which effusion Leonard has committed himself to find £20).[25] Up drifted Nessa & Duncan & Raymond in a tiger sweater; & so back to more lecture; & so home, through icy streets—winter is on us—I write with both sides of my fire on, & my winter jersey—so to Nessa's, where the stove was kindled, & there was hot soup & cold meat, & coffee & biscuits—all with the usual skill & organising capacity. There we laughed & exaggerated: about the lecture; about Bob & his outburst—'I cant stay in your house—I must leave, if you impute such motives to my friend—he's dying—a better socialist than you are—I am appalled at the meanness of human nature. Heres Allen, the wisest political thinker of our time—& you've nothing but abuse of him for taking a peerage. It dont matter of course—he'll kill himself—he'll be dead by next year. No I oughtn't to say this—I'm sorry I lost my temper. I apologise' (eating muffins; seizing the teapot, like some shaggy, surly, unkempt old animal—And then we had to give him a lift to Chelsea . .)[26]

24. *An Anatomie of the World* (1611) by John Donne. Roger Fry gave two illustrated lectures on French Art at the Queen's Hall in connection with the great winter exhibition at Burlington House.

25. 'Count' Geoffrey Potocki de Montalk, a New Zealander of Polish descent, had been found guilty on 8 February of uttering an obscene libel—which consisted of seeking to commission a printer to print his indecent poems for private circulation —and was sentenced to six months imprisonment. Potocki's friend Douglas Glass sought LW's help in organising an appeal, which, with St John Hutchinson KC appearing for the defence, was heard on 7 March and rejected. See *IV LW*, pp. 134-8.

26. R. C. Trevelyan had tea with the Woolfs on 11 February; his friend Clifford Allen (1889-1939), who was prominent as a Fabian socialist, a pacifist, and a member of the League of Nations Union, supported Ramsay MacDonald's

And we talked about a new life of Jesus, which offers two proofs of his existence—witness Roger's intellectual vitality after speaking to the Queen's Hall for 2 hours—really excited about the reality of Jesus. Quentin quoted French with a nice accent. Duncan had bought a pine apple with the extra 25/ I paid on his money for the screen—that now lights up the drawing room. I brought it home on Thursday. Bob never noticed.[27]

Tuesday 16 February

And I have just 'finished' I use inverted commas ironically, my Donne, a great but I think well intentioned grind. And I'm fuming, slightly, over Nelly's typical servant meanness. After you said you didn't want Lottie hanging about here, —but I didnt say that Nelly—Oh we thought thats what you meant—not very nice to hang about—you said you wouldn't have her doing that—of course I told her she must take a place at once: she's gone to the lady at Victoria—this to revenge themselves on me: to make me feel uncomfortable. But I promptly lost my temper, a great relief, & told Nelly that this is the last time I help Lottie or interest myself in their affairs—whereupon she cringes & withdraws, & says she meant nothing. Then Miss McAfee has rejected my article on Skinner, & asks for one on Q. Elizabeth instead, which she shant get; then I have to dine with Ethel Sands tonight, & must go to Bradleys to try on; & must have my hair curled.[28] And I'm quivering & itching to write my—whats it to be called?—"Men are like that?"—no thats too patently feminist: the sequel then, for which I have collected enough powder to blow up St Pauls. It is to have 4 pictures. And I must go on with the C. Reader—for one thing, by way of proving my credentials. To sit to Nessa; gay & debonair; to tie up parcels; to the Busch Quartet

---

National Government in 1931, and in the New Year Honours 1932 was raised to the peerage as 1st Baron Allen of Hurtwood 'for political and public services'.

27. This was a panel in cross-stitch, designed by Duncan Grant and worked by his mother, framed and mounted as a firescreen; it is now at Monks House.

28. Helen McAfee (1884-1956) was the managing editor of the *Yale Review*; VW had sent her an article (later to be included in *The Common Reader: Second Series*) animated by reading *The Journal of a Somerset Rector* a year earlier (see *III VW Diary*, 29 December 1930); for VW's reply to Miss McAfee, see *V VW Letters*, no. 2529. Ethel Sands (1873-1962), American-born painter who divided her year between the Château d'Auppegard, near Dieppe, which she shared with her life-long friend Nan Hudson (1869-1957), and her house at 15 The Vale, Chelsea. Wealthy and gregarious, she was an active and benign hostess and patron of the arts. Bradleys was a large and superior emporium in Chepstow Place, Bayswater.

where I met Elena R. & reflected upon the transiency of human beauty, passion, & illusion; & so up to lunch.[29]

Friday 26 February

Now I have 'finished' the Arcadia, & have 25 minutes in which I ought to correct my Letter to a Young Poet & give it to John. John is fractious & irritable, said to be the effect of love. And what a mint of people I've seen; dining with Ethel, having Desmond & Lord David & Ottoline & the Keynes', & going to Monks House—so march-white & lovely, the fields, & the river where the man caught a large sea trout, trout die if you draw blood, he said, speaking very slowly, wind bitten, that bitter cold day: & then I saw—oh the Keynes—yes—they say Julian's dissertation is no good, quite uneducated—& talked of Lytton, & how Maynard thought we really carried unconvention too far—no service, no farewell. When Ramsey died his friends went to Golders Green & the coffin was carried through them. But with Lytton there was no mark to say This is over.[30] And he met Senhouse a fortnight later & was the first to tell him that Lytton had left him his books.

Then I've not seen Ethel this 2 weeks, because of the rush; & today Sibyl & Hugh & Eth Williamson all come, knocking on each others heels to tea; & we go to the Camargo on Sunday; & must go in to the Woolf 50 birthday—this will happen yearly now[—]after dinner tonight. And to the French pictures.[31]

And Ka shut me in the middle class bedroom effectively last night—so condescending, so self approving, with her docile stories of respectable lunches with the Cornish aristocracy & Mrs Leverton Harris. Who is Mrs L.H.? "Oh dont you know—she signs letters on George Moore's 80th birthday. And I do hope you will do more Common readers. I prefer them to — —" This little bit of patronage annoyed me more than

29. The Busch Quartet, with Rudolf Serkin, piano, played Brahms, Dvořák, and Beethoven at the Wigmore Hall on 15 February. Mrs Bruce Richmond, as Elena Rathbone before her marriage in 1913, was part of the young Stephens' social circle, and was particularly admired by VW's brother Thoby.

30. The Keyneses dined with the Woolfs on 24 February. Frank P. Ramsey (1903-30), Fellow of King's and an Apostle, whose brilliant promise as a philosopher and mathematician was cut short by his untimely death.

31. The Camargo Ballet Society was founded in 1930 to promote the development of British ballet; the Woolfs went to the Society's matinée at the Savoy Theatre on 28 February; the programme included a performance of Walton's *Façade* with Lydia Lopokova and Frederick Ashton. The fiftieth birthday was LW's younger brother Harold's, and old Mrs Woolf was giving a party for the occasion.

it should. The day Ka came too we sold the ten thousandth copy of The Waves: which thus beats all my novels, unexpectedly.[32]

Monday 29 February

And this morning I opened a letter; & it was from 'yours very sincerely J. J. Thompson"—the Master of Trinity; & it was to say that the council have decided to ask me to deliver the ⟨Ford⟩ Clark Lectures next year. Six of them.[33] This, I suppose, is the first time a woman has been asked; & so it is a great honour—think of me, the uneducated child reading books in my room at 22 H.P.G.—now advanced to this glory. But I shall refuse: because how could I write 6 lectures, to be delivered in full term, without giving up a year to criticism; without becoming a functionary; without sealing my lips when it comes to tilting at Universities; without putting off my Knock at the Door; without perhaps shelving another novel. But I am rather inclined to smile, as I lunch with Miss Dodge today, & she gives me a book with Donne's autograph; as I buy a pair of shoes at Babers;[34] as I sit down dutifully to correct an article for the Common Reader. Yes; all that reading, I say, has borne this odd fruit. And I am pleased; & still more pleased that I wont do it; & like to think that father would have blushed with pleasure could I have told him 30 years ago, that his daughter—my poor little Ginny—was to be asked to succeed him: the sort of compliment he would have liked.

[Thursday 3 March]

And now, Thursday 3rd March, I am rather upset because the devil whispered, all of a sudden, that I have six lectures written in Phases of Fiction; & could furbish them up & deliver the Clark lectures, & win the esteem of my sex, with a few weeks work. True, L. says since the middle 4 were published in America I could not do this without complete re-

32. 'Ka' Cox (1887-1937) had been a close and dependable friend to VW before her marriage in 1918 to Will Arnold-Forster; in 1920 they had moved to Cornwall, where the Woolfs visited them. Mrs Leverton Harris was the widow of the politician and collector Frederick Leverton Harris PC; they had been friends of George Moore and she was one of the numerous signatories of a message of congratulation on his 80th birthday published in *The Times* on 25 February 1932.
33. Sir J. J. Thomson (1856-1940), OM, FRS, had been Master of Trinity College, Cambridge, since 1918. VW's father Leslie Stephen gave the first Clark lectures in 1883, taking 18th century literature as his subject.
34. Mary Dodge's present to VW was John Donne's copy, with his signature and notes, of the first edition (1605) of *Regales Disputationes Tres* by Alberico Gentilis; see lot 143 of Sotheby's sale of books, 27 July 1970. Charles H. Baber of Upper Regent Street were specialists in foot fitting.

writing; & I ought therefore to dismiss the whole thing.[1] Yet, such is the perversity of my mind, I can now think of nothing else; my mind is swarming with ideas for lectures; things I can only say in lectures; & my refusal seems lazy & cowardly. Yet two days ago I was repugnant to the thought: longed only for freedom in which to write a tap at the door; & was convinced that I should be a time serving pot hunter if I accepted. I've no doubt the fizz will subside—still what should I do if some friendly fellow of Trinity asked me to think it over? Soberly, I know that if I sat down to rewrite Phases of Fiction it would mean complete immersal for some weeks: I should have to re-cast, re-read: I should be impregnated with the lecturing manner: its jocosity, its emphasis; then I should be jaded by the time I approached a tap; & when I had done A tap, I should be 2 or 3 years distant from The Waves. Anyhow, I'm thankful that I wrote decidedly in the mood I was then in, before the devil whispered, & I went to my drawer & found that old MS; so well written, so full of thought—all the work done for me. The sensible thing to do would be to talk it over quietly next week end with Dadie. Moreover, L. is definitely against it. But then Nessa & Alice Ritchie were instinctively in favour.

[*Tuesday 8 March*]

Oh but I am too tired to write this morning—cant finish my Dorothy Osborne, all because of the Polish Count & Court yesterday.[2]

[*Thursday 10 March*]

And the peaches were bad last night.

And we had Roger Jack & Mary to dine. And they said the saddle was raw, but it wasn't.

And oh dear I had lunched with Raymond to meet Mrs Keppel;[3] a swarthy thick set raddled direct (My dear, she calls one) old grasper: whose fists have been in the money bags these 50 years: but with boldness:

1. VW never completed her projected book for the Hogarth Press on Fiction (see *III VW Diary*, 7 December 1927, n. 7), but an introduction and six sections were published in three successive issues of the New York *Bookman* in 1929 under the title 'Phases of Fiction' (Kp C312); LW's reference to 'the middle 4' appears to be misleading.
2. VW was revising her 1928 article on Dorothy Osborne's letters (Kp C304) for inclusion in *The Common Reader: Second Series*. For the Polish Count, see above, 13 February 1932, n. 25.
3. Alice Keppel (1869-1947), wife of Lt-Col. the Hon. George Keppel, had been the mistress of King Edward VII and one of the great Edwardian hostesses. According to her daughter Violet Trefusis, Raymond Mortimer 'had offered to sponsor an encounter.' (See *Don't Look Round*, 1952, pp. 107-8.)

told us how her friends used to steal, in country houses in the time of Ed. 7th. One woman purloined any jewelled bag left lying. And she has a flat in the Ritz; old furniture; &c. I liked her, on the surface. I mean the extensive, jolly, brazen surface of the old courtezan; who has lost all bloom; & acquired a kind of cordiality, humour, directness instead. No sensibilities as far as I could see; nor snobberies: immense superficial knowledge, & going off to Berlin to hear Hitler speak. Shabby under dress: magnificent furs: great pearls: a Rolls Royce waiting—going off to visit my old friend the tailor; & so on— But I'm fuddled with talk, & we're starting for Ham Spray to talk to Carrington—dear, dear—a lovely day though.

Oh & Eddy says The Waves is a failure: a miss. Eddy pushed his way in; & I liked him for pushing, once I had done hating him. How formidable I must be.

Saturday 12 March

So we went to Ham Spray—a lovely bright day, & got there at 1.30. "I thought you weren't coming" said C. She came to the door, in her little jacket & socks with a twisted necklace. Her eyes were very pale. "I sent a telegram; but I do everything wrong. I thought you didn't get it". She was pale, small, suffering silently. very calm. She had hot soup for us. I looked at the trees. We sat in the cold dining room. I didnt light the fire, she said. She had cooked us a nice hot lunch, succulent, with her own hands. We talked of Mary & Lytton. She had discovered whom Mary loves, owing to an indiscretion. But Lytton made her swear not to tell. So she didn't. We talked with effort; did she want us? Did she resent our coming to spy on her? She was bitter, laughing at Barbara [Bagenal]. "She asked how she could help. I told her to cut sandwiches. But she took an hour, talking to Tommy." Then we sat on the verandah. We asked her to make us woodcuts for notepaper. And to do designs for Julia's book.[4] We tried to gossip—about Mrs Keppel: about Saxon; she laughed once or twice: & her eyes seemed to get bluer. Then it got cold & we went & sat in Lytton's study—all beautifully neat, his notepaper laid out—a great fire; all his books exactly fitting the shelves, with the letters over them. We sat on the floor round the fire. Then L. suggested a walk. She took us to her grove. She said the trees had a flower wh. smelt very sweet in

4. Barbara Bagenal, née Hiles (b. 1891) was one of Carrington's oldest friends; they had been fellow students at the Slade before the war. Julia (1901-79), Oliver Strachey's daughter by his first marriage, married 'Tommy' Tomlin in 1927, and they both became very close friends of Carrington; the dust-jacket of her first novel, Cheerful Weather for the Wedding, which the Hogarth Press published in September 1932 (HP Checklist 309), was designed by Duncan Grant.

summer. She said she had some notes to write & would we go by ourselves. We only walked to the bottom of the long low down. Then L.
went to do the car, & I wandered in the garden & then back into the
sitting room. I was taking out a book when C. came in & asked if we
would have tea before we went. She had made it. She & I went upstairs,
arm in arm; & I said Let me see the view from the window. We stood
looking out— She said Dont you think one ought to keep a room
exactly as it was? We went to Dorothy Wordsworth's house. Her room
has been kept exactly as she left it. There are even the same prints & little
things on the table.[5] I want to keep Lytton's rooms as he had them. But
the Stracheys say this is morbid. Am I romantic about it d'you think? Oh
no, I'm romantic too, I said. And we went back to L.'s sitting room. She
burst into tears, & I took her in my arms. She sobbed, & said she had
always been a failure. "There is nothing left for me to do. I did everything for Lytton. But I've failed in everything else. People say he was
very selfish to me. But he gave me everything. I was devoted to my
father. I hated my mother. Lytton was like a father to me. He taught me
everything I know. He read poetry & French to me." I did not want to
lie to her—I could not pretend that there was not truth in what she said.
I said life seemed to me sometimes hopeless, useless, when I woke in the
night & thought of Lytton's death. I held her hands. Her wrists seemed
very small. She seemed helpless, deserted, like some small animal left.
She was very gentle; sometimes laughing; kissing me; saying Lytton had
loved his old friends best. She said he had been silly with young men.
But that was only on the top. She had been angry that they had not
understood how great he was. I said I had always known that. And she
said I made too much of his young friends. She said Roger was "as
Lytton said, very dim in the intellect." He could never have a real
intimacy—it wasn't sharing everything—only Roger was very high
spirited & liked going to Rome, & rather liked Lytton reading aloud to
him—but they couldn't talk. And this last year Lytton made up his mind
to be middle aged. He was a realist. He faced the fact that Roger could not
be his love. And we were going to Malaga & then he was going to write
about Shakespeare. And he was going to write his memoirs, which would
take him ten years. It was ironical, his dying, wasnt it. He thought he was
getting better. He said things like Lear when he was ill. I wanted to take
you to see him the day you came, but I was afraid to—James & Pippa
said one must not run any risk, & it might have upset him. "No, of
course not" I said. "Roger will take the books of course—he will have
to." And what else did we say? There was not much time. We had tea &
broken biscuits. She stood by the fireplace. Then we said we must go.
She was very quiet & showed no desire for us to stay.

5. Dove Cottage, Grasmere, where Wordsworth and his sister lived from 1799-1808.

Then, as we were leaving the room to go she suddenly picked up a little French box with a picture of the Arc de Triomphe upon it & said "I gave this to Lytton. Take it. James says I mustnt give away Lytton's things. But this is all right. I gave it him." So I took it. There is a coin in it. How frightened she seemed of doing wrong—like a child who has been scolded.[6]

She came down into the front of the house. She kissed me several times. I said "Then you will come & see us next week—or not—just as you like?" "Yes, I will come, or not" she said. And kissed me again, & said Goodbye. Then she went in; & turned & I waved & she waved back & she went into the house. Next morning at 8.30 the gardener heard a noise in her bedroom. He went in & found she had shot herself through the thigh. She died in 3 hours. She was conscious when Ralph & Alix & Bunny came.

(She also took me into Lytton's bedroom. I saw his great bed; & the Anrep mosaic; his cupboard & things.)[7]

Thursday 17 March

So Carrington killed herself; & again what L. calls "these mausoleum talks" begin again. We were the last to talk to her, & thus might have been summoned to the inquest; but they brought it in an accident. She maintained this, even to Ralph. Her foot slipped as she was shooting a rabbit.

And we discuss suicide; & I feel, as always, ghosts ⟨dwindling⟩ changing. Lytton's affected by this act. I sometimes dislike him for it. He absorbed her[,] made her kill herself. Then the romantic completeness which affects Mary. 'a beautiful gesture—her life & her death'. Nonsense says Leonard: it was histrionic: the real thing is that we shall never see Lytton again. This is unreal. So we discuss suicide. and the ghosts as I say, change so oddly in my mind; like people who live, & are changed by what one hears of them. Now we have to see Pippa, & James & Alix. Then to Rodmell: then—perhaps—to Greece with Roger & Ha.[8] A venture that would be: & I think we're both in the mood for ventures

6. This paragraph, written later on the facing page, is inserted as indicated by VW.
7. The mosaic decoration by Lytton's friend Boris Anrep (1883-1969), was on the chimney-breast, and incorporated a reclining hermaphrodite figure. For David ('Bunny') Garnett and Alix (Mrs James Strachey), see Appendix.
8. 'Ha' was (Sara) Margery Fry (1874-1958), the fifth of Roger's six unmarried sisters, with whom he shared a home in London from 1919 until 1926, when she went to Oxford for five years as Principal of Somerville College. A woman of great intelligence, energy, and wide interests, the principal focus of her life's work was penal reform.

after this morbid time; so much talk of death; & there death is of course.

We went from Cambridge on Saturday to Kings Lynn; through the lovely lonely coast that lies between that & Cromer, where I intend to go again: green meadows against the sea; & trees, & complete solitude, & now & then a line of little old houses: & Stiffkey with its hall; & some village spread out, as in a mediaeval picture, upon the rise of a dune; & lovely stubborn unknown place names; & wild roads; & Blickling, Holt, & Coke of Norfolk & Houghton; & the Pastons—all this jumble somehow shadowed by Carrington's death: the name Partridge of course appearing on tombs & grocers' shops.[9]

Friday 18 March

Last night at William Plomer's: talk, talk talk. Let me try to remember: on cooking: breadmaking; peaches rotten; Glaspells: going over the house; Tony's studio; Tony bald, innocent, blue eyed & slow stumbling; William compact & robust. An eye for furniture. Tony's tables, beds & sofas, in the Empire style. Gas fire. Talk of The Fountain. Oh & Tony's fathers first wife died of apoplexy in C[onstantino]ple, through running to catch the boat on a hot day, a very fat woman. Mary Butts. "I cannot say anything of my sister—She is a bad woman—pretentious—I can see no merit in her books—pretentious. She corrupts young men. They are always committing suicide. She now has married Gabriel Atkins—without any character. They were given 25 decanters for their wedding." Tony is ashamed of Mary, who thus defiles the Butts blood.[10] In came Louise Morgan, the interviewer, nerve drawn, lined, crimson, agile; & Mrs Paul Robeson, negroid, vivacious, supple, talking like a woman on the stage:

9. On Saturday 12 March the Woolfs drove to Cambridge to see the Marlowe Society's *Hamlet*, produced by George Rylands; the following day they spent in North Norfolk, an area where the Paston family (on whom VW had written in *The Common Reader*), Sir Robert Walpole (builder of Houghton Hall, 1722-31), and Thomas, Earl of Leicester (Coke of Norfolk, the agricultural reformer and owner of Holkham Hall), had all been great landowners; on 14 March they spent the night with Roger Fry at his Suffolk home, Rodwell House, Baylham, returning next day to Tavistock Square.

10. William Plomer and his rich and lively Etonian friend Anthony Butts (1900-41), a painter, shared a house in Canning Place, off Palace Gate. Butts and his sister Mary (1893-1937) were the children of a father born in 1830 and his young second wife. Mary led an extravagantly bohemian life, published several books, and had now married an artist, Gabriel Atkin (born Aitken). 'Glaspells' possibly refers to the American story and play writer Susan Glaspell (1876-1948), who had been in London for the production of her one-act play *Trifles* at the Duchess Theatre. *The Fountain* was a recently published novel by Charles Morgan (see below, 6 March 1935, n. 4).

chiefly to L. about negroes. And Janin, who admires my books, & has a friend who wants to translate; a thin skinned Frog all gesture & wrinkle; a coffee merchant ex diplomat; despises society; stories of Colefax, French Embassy. The Duke of Vendome—"Que c'est mêlée, mon monde!"[11] Talk, talk, talk. And cold; & a glass of green water; & so home to bed. William rather pompous, ceremonious, & considerate.

Tea with Nessa, Julian & Mrs Ramsey: the dissertation: Nessa wishes him to give it up. Robustly [?] satisfied with him whatever he does.[12] How dull this is to me—who like faults. Talk of Carrington: how long shall we talk of Carrington? Dispute as to how she got her gun. Mary's story of the 3 rabbits on the lawn.

[Thursday 24 March]

I am not sure of the precise day, save that it is Thursday & tomorrow is Good Friday & therefore we are at Rodmell on the loveliest spring day: soft: a blue veil in the air torn by birds voices. I am glad to be alive & sorry for the dead: cant think why Carrington killed herself & put an end to all this. True, they are building the vast elephant grey sheds at Asheham, but I intend to see them as Greek temples; & Percy says they are building 60 cottages—but we wait to see if this is so.[13] And the country is lovelier & lovelier; more friendly, charming, brilliant, still with great empty spaces, where I want to walk, alone, & come to terms with my own head. Another book? What? Merciful to be free, entirely to think this out; needn't write a line I dont want to, or squander a moment on repetition. Two books on Virginia Woolf have just appeared—in France & Germany. This is a danger signal. I must not settle into a figure.[14]

Perhaps we are becoming more sociable. Mrs Hawkesford wants to

11. Louise Morgan (d. 1964), journalist, was currently editing the monthly magazine *Everyman*; Eslanda Goode (d. 1965) married the negro singer and actor Paul Robeson in 1921; at this time they were living in London, where she attended the London School of Economics. René Janin, son of a French general, according to Plomer 'moved with ease and amusement in social, intellectual, diplomatic and commercial spheres in any country where English, French, German or Spanish are spoken.'
12. Lettice Ramsey, Julian's current *inamorata*, was the widow of Frank Ramsey (see above, 26 February 1932, n. 30). Julian's Fellowship dissertation on Pope, which he had submitted at the end of 1931, had just been rejected by the Electors of King's College; but he embarked on another, with the working title 'The Good and All That'.
13. A group of council houses was built in Mill Lane, Rodmell, in the 1930s.
14. These were: *Le roman psychologique de Virginia Woolf* by Floris Delattre, Paris 1932; and *Die Sprache Virginia Woolfs* by Ingeborg Badenhausen, Marburg 1932 —a doctoral dissertation limited almost solely to the accidence of grammar.

bring her daughter to tea.[15] I think we shall go to Greece with Roger & Margery. And—well, we go to tea with M. Baring on Monday.

I'm drowsing in this heat & quiet. Cant correct any more C.R. articles; nor write letters; yet it isn't lunch time yet. And there's the paper to read. Odd that Lytton didn't write more. Which life should one lead— the life one likes. I like writing. I like change. I like to toss my mind up & watch to see where it'll fall. Nessa off to Cassis. Clive coming back. Then the London Season: then here again. A happy life. But encompassed by solitude—human life I mean. Miss Bowen, stammering, shy, conventional, to tea [*on 18 March*].

Friday 25 March

Such is the atmosphere of days, that I thought this was Sunday, because it is Good Friday. The weather is Sunday weather—divinely good, warm, unclouded— Oh how lovely my view would be if it weren't for the grey galvanised sheds—how am I to absorb them into the view? And I want to write a little story, before I go into Good Friday goose. I'm tired of my own criticism— But isn't it futile to get away into that life—where all the proportions are different—when I still have Lord knows how many brilliant articles—all cut out rounded, coloured, like magic lantern slides, to correct? An odd gulf between the one world & the other. I think I'll go into the house & fetch my de Quincey who comes next. I am sober & desultory, cant string all my ideas on one thread. Leonard is in a pickle with Wells, & cant get hold of the facts with which to confute him.[16] On the other hand, the dogs are thinking more & barking less, the result of my letter. One poor beast is they say 'taped'— has his mouth—sealed: not altogether: barking again. A good walk might be wholesome. Percy steals the anthracite, & says didn't we hear Pinka barking all one night—a rustic attempt at mystification which fails to convince. Why is there always this relationship between master & servant?—Maynard says its the same in offices. Always deceit & distrust. Our Transition Age, perhaps. Perhaps we go to Sissinghurst tomorrow: there are 2 people with their house for life.

15. The widow of the Rev. James Hawkesford, Rector of Rodmell 1896-1928.
16. LW's review of H. G. Wells's *The Work, Wealth and Happiness of Mankind* had appeared in the *NS&N* on 27 February; in praising his achievement ('no living man but Mr Wells . . . could have written [850 pages on industry and economics] and made it readable and valuable'), LW referred to 'one of the younger generation' having dismissed Wells 'as a thinker who could not think'—at which Mr Wells took umbrage. It was the source of this opinion which now eluded LW. See *III LW*, pp. 194-7.

[Tuesday 29 March]

We went to Sissinghurst—I'm so tired with correcting Dr Burney that I must run my pen here—& it was a fine goose grey morning.[17] Odd the merging of Sussex into Kent. The sloping hop oasts do it, I think: then the little sunk away villages: what led people to pitch on the 18th century where they did? A tudor house, alone; on the road: why build there? L. notices the way; I these little facts. Harold came out in a torn jacket: Vita in breeches & pink shirt. We went over the grounds. H. said I'm getting nobler & nobler as we get poorer. I've refused an offer to write for the American papers. Oh but there are myriads of things to do here. "Yes we want to turn those stables into guest bedrooms: & build a library across the courtyard", said Vita. All is planned. H. has drawn it in his note book. Walls have been built & turf laid. Lunch in the boys cottage. Talk of Beaverbrook's party to wh. H. went with Enid Jones— Oh so lovely—the clothes; then to Heinemann: people seemed to have dust scattered on them. Enid became quite upset. How she wants to write, but has to give parties for her husband. And I was sleepy & afraid the Rolls Royce wd. get to the Temple too quick & she'd not have finished her story. But she had finished it. And next day I got a letter to say that she had almost—killed herself? I suggested—no, broken down. She wants to be a writer. Envies the genius of Mrs Belloc Lowndes.[18]

So we ate cold salmon & raspberries & cream & little variegated chocolates given by Lady Sackville,[19] now at their feet, & drank oh lots of drinks; & then climbed Vita's tower; lovely pink brick; but like Knole, not much view, save of stables that are to be guest rooms. So home. And then a very wet Sunday & a prodigious reading & drowsing—I've now carried to perfection the art of sleeping & reading & make up half my book in the wildest way asleep, improvising, & then surprised to wake up & find none of it true.

Yesterday we went to Rottingdean to tea with Maurice (as I'm now to call him.) He & Elizabeth [Williamson] in a long sunny room full of books, tables, plants; rather bad taste; rich; nothing very nice to look at; two sweating dusty footmen brought in innumerable plates.[20] In came Ethel: in grey tweed; & a chinless Cavalry Captain called Grant, who is Peter Davies' partner: the very spit & image of a soldier in Punch: many

17. VW was revising 'Dr Burney's Evening Party' (Kp C313) for inclusion in *The Common Reader: Second Series*; the Woolfs' visit to Sissinghurst was on Saturday 26 March.
18. The writer Enid Bagnold (1889-1981) married Sir Roderick Jones, the Chairman of Reuters, in 1920; Mrs Belloc Lowndes (d. 1947) was the sister of Hilaire Belloc and a prolific and popular novelist.
19. Lady Sackville (1862-1936) was Vita's autocratic and wilful widowed mother.
20. In 1930 Maurice Baring bought a villa called Half Way House at Rottingdean.

peoples ideal, I daresay; so suave, masculine, foolish; exactly a round peg in his hole. All the slang right & the snobbery & the culture & the self-possession. Had killed animals in every part of the East. Talk, of course, wildly detailed & emphatic & useless about Greece. You must see Meleora—where's the map? You get out of the train—you get a car—no we couldnt—go to Giolman in Athens—oh & dont forget Aegina: you must hire a boat—oh that evening. . &c &c.[21] And then talk about publishing: & I slipped my anchovy sandwich into my bag, & took it out, thinking it was my lighter. Ethel balanced by the fire: told us stories about Empresses: Maurice prompted: laughed at her. "I've known him 40 years & he's always shocked—feels what people feel at the other end of the room. Nice feelings. I haven't any. I'm going to write a book called The Mole, the Cesspool & Mrs Woolf. You've kept my letters you say—Yes she's a strange woman—loves getting letters—so I write, sheet after sheet. Nothing I like better. I used to keep a diary. Since I knew her, two years ago in February, I've written only letters . . ."

And Mrs Woolf we want you to write a biography for us in 30,000 words. You'd pay a devil £15 to get up the facts for you. Then you'd have nothing to do but dash it down. You'd do it in two months. By way of bargain I'll offer you the MS of a gardening book. Oh we've lost heavily over our expensive books. Dizzy's edition fills our cellar.[22] I've come in to make us less high brow. I want novels. Ideas. Thats whats the fun. Making suggestions to authors— That chinless man to suggest to me. Pah! So home; after seeing M[aurice]'s bedrooms &c. A shy, lobster coloured skinless man; tripping about the room to fetch things. Keeps his house, I think, for his friends. Drinks. Sentimentalises. Would like to be taken seriously.

Monday 11 April

The eddy of travel—wisps & straws—is already whirling round. I have a list of things to buy on my table. We start at 10 on Friday; shall be sailing down the Dalmatian coast this time next week. Embedded as I am in Tavistock Sqre I cant make much play with this. Also it is fiendishly cold, wet, blowing, like last year in France. I like this adventure of Greece all the same; & the fact that we are sociably going with Roger & Margery; & that—intimacy—will be part of our journey. The result of Lytton's death—this desire to be with friends. I am muddled headed. This per-

21. Captain Alistair Edward Grant was a partner in Peter Davies Ltd, who published Ethel Smyth's collection of articles, *Female Pipings in Eden*, in 1933. Ghiolman Bros., of Constitution Square, Athens, old-established travel agents.

22. In 1926-7 Peter Davies published the *Bradenham Edition of the Novels and Tales of Benjamin Disraeli* in 5 volumes at 10/6d each.

petual criticism tires my brain. I've almost done de Quincey though, & am well on with the book.

As for external facts—it seems likely that our John will not stay. That is he wishes to work half time in order to write. Elizabeth Williamson is a possibility—rain rain—it drums on my skylight. L. is doing Press accounts & it looks as if we should net £2000.

Hail now; & camel coloured sky. I am waiting for lunch. Dear me, I ought to read some hideously obscure poems. Tomorrow we go to Monks House to take Pinka. This is a little girls writing—like a childs letter. I've seen the Nicolsons, & Ethel, & Kingsley Martin. Harold up to be looked at for that job.[1] And James & Alix. Lytton left masses of poems & unfinished plays—not much good, James says. And box upon box of letters. Ours still lost. What to do? said James. He said nasty things about everyone. How can they be published? Could one extract a philosophy? He had meant to write one more book for money on Washington & then burn his boats: declare himself & live abroad. Declare what? Everything. His hatred [?] &c. Sex: love: But I doubt it. There was Ham Spray.

At 10 am on Friday 15 April the Woolfs, *with Roger Fry and his sister Margery, set off from Victoria Station; travelling* via *Dover-Calais, they dined in Paris and continued their journey overnight, reaching Venice the next afternoon, where they stayed at the* Casa Petrarca *on the Grand Canal. At 12.30 pm on Sunday they sailed for Athens via Brindisi on the s.s. Tevere. The following account of their travels, written on 28 white pages pasted in to* DIARY XXI, *is at places very difficult to decipher.*

Monday 18 April

On board the Tevere, off the coast of Italy. Yes, but I've forgotten to get out my ink pot, & thus the splendour of these first words is committed to the gold pen.

My mind—but is this to be a record of 'my mind'—truth is I've not thought of a form for this book—shall it have one—or none? I was so knife-splitting, flower expanding that morning at Victoria: I felicitated myself upon being a writer. Whatever I saw was so complex. There was a bride, dressed in the colours of the Union Jack, brand new handbag. And Helen [Anrep], the full blown rose petals dewed with moisture, come to say Good bye: & the Yak that is M[argery Fry]: for she is thick as an oak, & wears a rough white pelt, constrained by a girdle—the Yak said

---

1. There was a possibility (unrealised) that Harold Nicolson might succeed R. Ellis Roberts as Literary Editor of the *NS&N*.

"If you'd brought a dog I should have said Good bye." I divined antagonism. This has developed only into a pervasive inferiority complex. I'm one of those superior beings, she thinks, who exist by virtue of their white petals; this little nervousness I vanquish by visiting her in her carriage alone, while L. & R. play chess & teach each other Greek. R. is sweet, rich, accommodating, infinitely serious, & rolls out rich Italian commands to the gondoliers, all waiting for foreigners who dont come, for no one travels this year, by the canal, at the end of St Mark's. We take a gondola for one hour, & so cross to San Giorgio; & see the miraculous apse, & peer; & climb; & smooth our soles on the red yellow rosy pavement, raying out like the sea, with inlaid flowers: & Venetian light is pale & bright: the palaces, says R. pretty frauds, examples of inlay & carpentry. That old fraud Ruskin—we were now in St Mark's Square, looking at Adam & Eve. There are chapters about that.[2] He was too virtuous. thats a great pity. everything had to be squared—even these finicking palaces must be morally Good—which theyre not—oh no—merely slices of coloured stone. Dinner at the Cavallo—the old one gone bankrupt. Out after the play, in the theatre slung with green glass beads, onto the black tossing water, so silent, so swaying: & the poor people asked us not to overpay the traghetto; & there were cactuses; & a man singing in the morning;[3] & R. & I went to the Tiepolo church;[3] & the thick yellow service with the priests weaving a web in incantation, & the little boys & the reverence & secularity & ancientness made us say This is the magic we want: & magic there must be; so long as magic keeps its place. So on board our spacious orderly well found ship, now passing the coast of Italy.

Thursday 21 April

Athens [*Hotel Majestic*]

Yes, but what can I say about the Parthenon—that my own ghost met me, the girl of 23, with all her life to come: that; & then, this is more compact & splendid & robust than I remembered.[4] The yellow pillars— how shall I say? gathered, grouped, radiating there on the rock, against the most violent sky, with staring ice blue, & then cinder black; crowds flying as if suppliants (really Greek schoolchildren). The Temple like a

---

2. Adam and Eve—The Fall of Man—are carved on the column at the Piazzetta-Molo corner of the *Palazzo Ducale*—which Ruskin (*Stones of Venice*, volume II, chapter VIII) calls the 'fig tree angle'.

3. LW notes: 'Accademia morn.'; so the church visited by VW and Roger was probably the nearby *Gesuati* on the Zattere.

4. VW's previous visit to Greece had been in the autumn of 1906, with Vanessa, her brothers Thoby and Adrian, and their friend Violet Dickinson.

ship, so vibrant, taut, sailing, though still all these ages. It is larger than I remembered, & better held together. Perhaps I've washed off something of the sentimentality of youth, which tends to makes things melancholy. Now I'm 50 (I signed this boldly in the hotel book—the good Yak refrained—another proof of inferiority complex), now I'm grey haired & well through with life I suppose I like the vital, the flourish in the face of death. Then there's Athens like crumbled egg shells beneath, & the black grey bush tufted hills. "The Germans come out like things hidden in a pocket" I said. Sure enough, when the storm passed over, out they came, honest [?], perspiring unattractive people, claiming, we thought, more of the Acropolis than any other nation. We wandered; Roger said Awfully swell, awfully swell. At the Museum in the morning he said They dont compose. Thats a star fish shape. Look at the thinness of the lines: & no background. There were—& still are—myriads of Greek black & red or red & black pots, each capable of inspiring a volume, & before them trail tired children, tired mothers, the oddest shabbiest raggiest house-maids & clerks, whose whole fortune has been spent on the ticket, & they'll go home, & dominate some little suburban street on the strength of "I was in Athens in April 1932": witness the pure white marble bust after Pheidias on the mantlepiece. This is depressing in museums.

I like Athens about 7, when the streets are hurrying clamouring, flitted across by all those black whitefaced women, & shawled women, & dapper little men who come with the bats & the evening primroses in Southern towns, ari lalagos. Margery, listening to the talk at Averrov tonight said the pitch is the same as the English.[5] She is full of reasonable & well instructed remarks—as that Christ is never painted being washed; that the priests are allowed hairpins gratis, since they wear their hair long & might be tempted into effeminate ornament. This was said by the garden where all the flowers were this morning—ranunculus like pink & violet shells many folded; the flapping black white specked irises. The other remark was made in the Byzantine Church at Daphnis. "Oh awfully swell—better than I'd any notion of" said Roger depositing his hat stick pochard & two or three guides & dictionaries on a pillar. Then we all stared up at the white vindictive Christ, larger than a nightmare, in blue & white mosaic on the ceiling. We liked that Church very much. It is high & rugged, & arched, & the mosaic is mostly peeled. And one looks out of the door on those tufted green trees which seem each tufted with a sun lit & clouded wave—so bright so dark are the green waves in the wood in which we walked. A Greek family keeps the church—middle-aged men & women, sitting in town clothes (the men) with overcoats & gold rings reading a paper at 3.30. Such idleness, such aimlessness I've

---

5. *ari lalagos*: chattering, babbling, garrulous. Averov, in the odos Stadiou, was one
of the best restaurants in Athens.

never seen in England. At last the youngest, a woman, in shawl slippers & cotton dress, strolls off, climbs a ruined wall & begins to pick yellow flowers—nothing else to do. So we drove on down to the sea—& how lovely the pure lip of the sea is touching a wild shore; with hills behind, & green plains, & Eleusis in the distance & green, & red rocks, & one steamer starting.

Friday 22 April (as I think)

It was bitter cold. That one always forgets. The wind whistled through the uncovered sides of Giolmann's Hupmobile. L. sneezed: I shivered. All the floor was covered with painting boxes. We lunched on a table in the sun at Suniun—the chalk white pillars set high like a lighthouse. The flowers all in miniature made a bright turf—M. uprooted little irises. What did we say? Nothing much. After a week one talks only at dinner. And then drove home; that is through the plumed trees, by the red shaped fields, with the sudden carpets of deep red poppies, past the gipsies huts, made like wigwams out of pressed ferns; there a girl wandered spinning from a lump of sheeps wool; & women sat at the door—I thought of Piccadilly at this hour. How strange the patiently amenable flat land is, set with biblical trees, grazed by long woolled sheep, & not a house to be seen. This is England in the time of Chaucer. So at Sunium, the sea breaks upon green stone & red stone, & the slate-coloured slanting sailed ships go by—all as in the time of Chaucer or Homer, not a pier, not a parade; no one looking. At Salamis the Greek Army were carrying little sacks of earth to the top of the Tomb of the dead soldiers to make it [*word illegible*]. A tuft of flowers was on the top. Oh the cold, the cold.[6]

Sunday 24 April

Oh the rain, the rain! That was next day at Aegina. That lovely shelving island with the baked narrow path, the sea & the beach, the little pink & yellow houses, the thyme, the steep hillside, the Temple, skeletal, dominant, the bays flowing filled with sea—all this was nothing but chill, mist, rain, Americans clustering round a thin professor; & we cowering under a pine tree which let the rain on us. Even so— Roger said awfully swell; this is superb—a sandstone temple better than Sunium. Marvellous what genius can do in a little space—heres the perfectly moving proportions—& the rain drove us down to our boat as soon as we could. They

---

6. The day's expedition was to the Temple of Poseidon at Sunium, and, after lunch there, by way of Marathon (not, as VW has mistakenly written, Salamis) back to Athens. The Sorós in the middle of the plain of Marathon is a mound some 12 m high raised over the bodies of the Athenians who fell in the battle of 490 BC.

had caught red fish & octopus. How? Well they put onions, bread & so on down, & the fish settle on them, then they drop a charge & pouf!—it goes up like that, & the fish come to the top dead, & they spear them. Its not allowed. But nobody can see you, round there. Such was the account given by the stoker with the lovely Greek smile—the smile the muleteers have & the taximen. For R. & M. were mounted, & very queer they looked, jolting up the hill—the polie makria [*far distant*] hill, as the bright faced girl called it. For the people are desperately poor, & come, offering flowers, & are given the remains of lunch.

Today—how happy today was—at the little round Byzantine Church on the slopes of Hymettus. Why cant we live for ever like this, I said to myself, not that it was hot enough; but the rain blew over; & life seemed very free, & full of the good things—wildness, thyme smelling, cypresses, the little courtyard where R. & M. sat absorbed painting; with the great marble white dog asleep in a corner, & the usual frail slippered women padding about in their swallow rooms built upstairs, with old bits of carved marble for the doorposts. I got a handful of wild anemomes & orchids. One drives the dull part & scrambles when the ruts throw us too violently backward & forward.

Talk today about Max Eastman's book: Roger's theories of art; & stories. M. tells stories of falling off a horse in Canada; of Julian's life; of Mrs Masefield—unintimate stories, for she has no foothold among us; & will slip off this rock into her obscure waters when we go back—not that she needs us. She is punctilious about trains, & has a passion for cheese—We start tomorrow early for Nauplia, in a car.[7]

Monday 2 May

Well it is five minutes to ten: but where am I, writing with pen & ink? Not in my studio. In the gorge, or valley, at Delphi, under an olive tree, sitting on dry earth covered with white daisies. L. is reading his Greek grammar beside me; there goes, I think, a swallow tail. Shelves of grey rock rise opposite me, each set with olive trees, & little bushes, & if I follow up, there comes the huge bald gray & black mountain, & then the perfectly smooth sky. And so back to the hot earth, & the flies sitting in yellow hearts of the daisies. There is a tinkling of goat bells; an old man has ridden off on his mule—we're right at the bottom of the hill on top of

7. Max Eastman's book: *The Literary Mind: Its Place in an Age of Science*, 1931. Before she took up her appointment as Principal of Somerville in 1926, Margery Fry travelled across Canada to visit her nephew Julian Fry (b. 1901), Roger's son, who after leaving Cambridge in 1923 became a cattle-rancher in British Columbia; she had been thrown from a horse and badly hurt in remote country, and the circumstances had called for considerable fortitude. Constance, *née* Crommelin (d. 1960), who was her school teacher in 1891-2, married the poet John Masefield in 1903.

which is Delphi, & Roger & Margery sketching. And a locust has just perched on the olive tree.

Thus I try to make visible this scene which will soon be gone forever. & perhaps too try to avoid that demon which says, perhaps so unnecessarily, that one ought to write down how we went to Corinth, Nauplia, Mycenae, to Mistra to Tripolitza, & so back to Athens, when the sun blazed, & I wore a silk dress, & we went to the gardens, & then started at 7 on Saturday morning for Delphi. I ought to write about all these places, & try perhaps to solidify some of these floating sequences that go through my mind as we drive. For the drives were very long; Oh & the wind & the sun, & how ones lips swelled & blackened & cracked & one's nose peeled, & one's cheeks were hot & dry as if sitting unshaded by a hot fire. All vanity has long died out. One is becoming a peasant. This reminds me of the start of joy with which I saw a tolerably well-dressed woman in the Salon at the Hotel Majestic drinking with a voluble old Greek gentleman the afternoon we came back, dry dusty red, gold, black, brown, creased, (M.'s wrinkles are marked like the stripes on the coat of a wild beast). After four or five days of the peasants & their solid draped beauty, the sharpness & subtlety of civilisation excite one's upper scale of nerves—the violin notes.

Greece then, so to return to Greece, is a land so ancient that it is like wandering in the fields of the moon. Life is receding (in spite of that donkey). The living, these worn down, for ever travelling the roads Greeks, cannot master Greece any longer. It is too bare too stony, precipitous for them. We met them always on the high mountain passes padding along beside their donkeys, so small, existing so painfully, always marching in search of some herb, some root, mastered by the vast distances, unable to do more than dig their heels in in the rock. Such solitude as they must know, under the sun, under the snow, such dependence on themselves to clothe & feed themselves through the splendid summer days is unthinkable in England. The centuries have left no trace. There is no 18th 16th, 15th century all in layers as in England—nothing between them & 300 B.C. 300 B.C. somehow ⟨dominated⟩ conquered Greece & still holds it. So it is the country of the moon; I mean, lit by a dead sun. If one finds a bay it is deserted; so too with the hills & the valleys; not a villa, not a tea shop not a kennel anywhere; no wires, no churches, almost no graveyards.

But to be accurate, Nauplia & Mycenae lie in a rich soft prosperous plain, there are even occasional villages, where we stop & R. & M. get out their paint boxes, because the accent is there right for painting—where there is a house; for there there are aspens & cypresses & roofs to stand against the plains & the mountains.

What then happens (we've been a walk still further into the valley which still winds itself deeper & deeper, left leaves to mark the path, coming back lost it, peeled a stick for me & here we are, having shifted, owing to the sun, higher, under the olive tree; & I've taken off my shoes for coolness) what then happens is that the villagers come up & begin, like friends, to talk about things in general. Last night on the hill above Delphi in the evening light with Itea beginning to flash & sparkle by the sea, one ship in the bay & the snow mountains standing out in the background, & the foreground still running rich green & red brown, where the goats & sheep were grazing, & the cars passing slowly on the winding road beneath, last night as we sat there, the goat girl came bounding up as if to rick her sheep, but it was only to talk to us. No slinking past, no tittering, no shyness. She stopped before us, as a matter of course. M. made her look through her glasses, first the right way, then the wrong. Then she told us words for things. Skotos her rough thick coat, ouranos the sky, a flower lullulin (?) [luludi] my watch orologe [orologiou], the car—I've forgotten. She shouted with laughter. She was small brown, will make a shrewd broad old woman; unconstrained, friendly. Her brother came, 18, quick, shrewd, small eyed. I took his stick & water bottle. Then there was the difficulty about the coins. First she wouldn't take them or M.'s handkerchief: then followed us, putting her hand on her chest, asking complaining, but about what? L. repeated his gift. She took it. But not with joy. And the boy brought us a great saucepan of yaot [yoghurt]. & so home, with the electric lights coming out; & they danced after dinner in the public house, young men, punctiliously, bowing & twisting & keeping their feet on the right spot, dressed in trousers & shirts.

halfway up. It occurs to me that the ridge seen from the top is like a badly peeled pear, when lines of peel are left on the edges.

Also that Lawrence writes his books as I write this diary in gulps & jerks: & has not the strength to come down in one blow: no welding, no shaping—the result of a false anti-literariness perhaps.

Also that the male virtues are never for themselves, but to be paid for. This introduces another element into their psychology—to be paid for: what will pay. This can be sublimated but the alloy remains. (I'm thinking of the book again)

Sunday 8 May

Here it is, the last evening; very hot, very dusty. The loudspeaker is braying; L. reading, not with sympathy, Ethel Smyth;[1] it is 2 minutes to 7 & therefore I have about 30 minutes in which to fill this book. I've only used 10 of my 100 nibs: my ink is still deep; how many white pages remain. This is the result of the best holiday these many years. It was so

1. See *V VW Letters*, no. 2572: 'We're taking—L. is going to study—your book'. i.e. *A Three-Legged Tour in Greece* by Ethel Smyth, 1927.

nice going off to the Post Office after our plain roll & honey; & it was so hot, & then there was always something doing. (I dont like Sundays, not even here: the little yellow cardboard looking boys are now drumming, & the dogs barking).

We went to Aegina [*on 6 May*]: sun & blue gradually rolling up the mist; & L. & I found a desert bay lapped by water pale & pure—no—not pale—but pure as some liquid jelly, laid quivering over stones, & shells, & anemones. L. went staggering out across the stones & flung himself in; I paddled. My bare feet burnt on the sand. I dried them by letting them burn a minute. And this was virgin sea. The island looked from the Temple like a south sea island with naked natives gathering to see the boats come in. M.—whose humanity grows & waxes, or perhaps is allowed fuller expression, became sad by the number of donkeys provided, & we only took two. Here the girls [?] pulled my hands—Ride ride they kept saying, very hot, very steep. So we pretended to shiver—said riding was too cold. And the children came pressing irises & yellow poppies.

Even so, I shant fill my book—even by writing so quickly. I've scarcely read either—only Roger's Eastman, & Wells, & Murry.[2] Oh but I've thought too much, about my little book. The truth is this sight seeing, this sitting, as we've just sat, in the [Zappeion] garden & watching the whiskered maniac against the wall laughing, as if his insanity were merely too much ripeness, & the woman with gold teeth, & the love struck boy who ate a chocolate cake, while M. painfully commiserates the poverty of the Greeks, who look anxious, she says, & the hotel keeper she says has consumption— Couldnt she give the bootblack our toast— oh yes, she cant resist the little boy with a roll of peppermints—this is her suppressed, half Quaker, half virgin attitude to the world—as I was saying while I watch all this, & wonder what the hectic lady with rouged cheeks is laughing at—is it my straw hat trimmed of half its brim last night, or can it be Roger's paintboxes with which he's painfully slung—as I meditate such important events, as they slip & slide & catch on the surface of my mind, I'm subterraneously sunk in scenes for my little book: make up arguments, see pictures, keep dropping something new into the cauldron, which must bubble as richly as possible before its poured & stilled & hardened—as I do this, & accept whatever suggestion the shaking cypresses & aspens, the orange flower smell, the man selling penny toys of monkeys on sticks offer me, time passes: I'm not sure if I'm in Greece or London: but think it more likely I'm in Greece, happy, easy, friendly with everything swimming easily forward. L. discussing prison reform with Marjorie, informing Roger about the break up of the atom.

2. Probably *Son of Woman. The Story of D. H. Lawrence* by J. Middleton Murry, 1931.

And then behold we come to a stop before an aviary. L. picks a tassel of grass; & the budgerigars find it & peck it to bits. On we loaf again. Its odd why khaki is used I say: & R. says thats how they see the country; then we watch a mediæval soldier in white leggings, & tufted shoes, & kilt. R. has been painting in the Parthenon, hadn't liked to ask him to sit. We spent 3 hours a day eating says M. M. wants to give away our food says L. & Roger runs across the road for it. These are our jokes: kindly sensitive jokes. M. is still conscious of inferiority, likes to talk of her parents & to palliate R.'s severity. Would like to begin life again, I think. What is lack of charm? I ask myself. Why dont these good qualities cut more ice? And whats just [?] untied the bunch in her so that shes in-effective? Yet has every art at command; can compell yaot to breed in her house; travels; sketches; has sympathy far more widely than I have for beggars, children, state of the people. But not charm.

Then I had the vision, in Aegina, of an uncivilised, hot new season to be brought into our lives—how yearly we shall come here, with a tent, escaping England, & sloughing the respectable skin; & all the tightness & formality of London; & fame, & wealth; & go back & become irres-ponsible, livers, existing on bread yaot, butter, eggs, say in Crete. This is to some extent a genuine impulse, I thought, coming down the hill with easy strides; London is not enough, nor Sussex either. One wants to be sunbaked, & taken back to these loquacious friendly people, simply to live, to talk, not to read & write. And then I looked up & saw the mountains across the bay, knife shaped, coloured, & the sea, brimming smooth; & felt as if a knife had scraped some incrusted organ in me, for I could not find anything lacking in that agile, athletic beauty, steeped in colour, so that it was not cold, perfectly free from vulgarity, yet old in human life, so that every inch has its wild flower that might grow in an English garden, & the peasants are gentle people; & their clothes, worn & burnt, are subtly coloured, though coarse. Now there are sympathies between people & places, as between human beings. And I could love Greece, as an old woman, so I think, as I once loved Cornwall, as a child.

For this reason then, that we shall come back, & because L. wants to go to dinner, & I think there is a hair in my pen, I doubt that I shall make any more ceremony about coming to an end—'Now get ready & dont talk so much—' I must end.

Still the last night, & L. playing chess still with Roger, & I've lain in one of those interesting torpors on my bed, with Lawrence to read, & have now woken & cant but try to fix these last minutes for L. will be in then—if I can. The Greeks, who dont dine till 9, are now at it—that is are chattering, hooting, driving in the street. I hear them though our window opens on the back.

It is a fine still night. Now & then a few single words become audible. The top half of a building is cadaverous. Now the loudspeaker begins, &

will so reel hoarsely through a few bars, & then suddenly stop. Everything rattles & jerks as if it were a jingling ill jointed but rapid cart.

So the days in Athens will get hotter & hotter—tonight they were dining on the pavement at Costis—& the nights will get noisier & gayer. I forgot to write about the Parthenon yesterday—all a glare—an oblong of blue sky made oblong by white pillars—the compact rush of the Parthenon—a slip of shade along the Erechtheum, in which we sat. And a loose lipped good tempered blue eyed man lounged up & said might he look at L.'s stick (the ringed one, bought at Sparta). So he picked at it & we said it was Greek, & he said no. It was a banana cane from Canada—had never been made in Greece. From that he went on to talk about Greek peasants. To see how they live would make you cry he said. Always working & nothing to eat but black bread so hard you cant cut it, (this with excruciated gestures) & perhaps they make a little cheese & come & sell it but there is plenty of wine always. So to the war. Everything has been wrong since then. Before the pound was stable & so was the drachma. Now one day theyre up: another down. What does sugar cost by the kilo in England? A kilo is 3 lbs: well, its cheaper in Greece. The Government protect it. But anything that comes from abroad is dear—shoes, clothes. And we make hardly any flour. All this in tortured French, with the young French officer sitting beside us & his wife & sister reading a guide book. A French battle ship was in the bay, & an Italian, & soon the English would come & the sailors would walk about the town & say they had seen Greece. Indeed here came a guide leading the French sailors. Only French sailors would know the names of pediments & columns, said Roger, always in love with the French. The French would cook this better or do that better. Now the French President has been killed by a White Russian. M. pricks up her ears commiserates & reflects intelligently what effect this will have on politics.[3] So we went to the hill which the driver called Phillipappos [Philopappos], all in one gulp, but it was wired off, & we therefore turned back & went on to the theatre [of Dionysos], with its curved marble seats each cut with the name of a priest seat holder as they stick cards on the boxes at Covent Garden. One, the pawed one, the lion one, was for the priest of Dionysos, & had a carving of goats prancing & vines pendant. Here L. sat & we said that Sophocles Euripides & Aristophanes must have sat here & seen—Anyhow the hills were before them, as before us. And if the 2000 years have laid a few light rubbishy stucco houses on the earth, in the way, very little has been done to damage the view—nothing solid & immense & lasting has been built. Poverty & war & misery have prevented any

3. Paul Doumer (1857-1932), President of the Third Republic since June 1931, was assassinated in Paris on 6 May by Pavel Gorgulov, who was reported as having described himself as 'chief of the Russian Fascists'.

obliteration—here or elsewhere. Indeed one might ask for more care, & more custody, not less. This afternoon the Greek raggamuffin boys were shying stones at a marble ruined arch, & pitting it, so that in some years it will be irrecoverably damaged. And the graves are nettled, tin-canned, dirty, dissolute, though the Greeks made the tombs with their own hands—no the land is too exhausted even to guard its own interests any longer—no doubt Lord Elgin's excuse for stealing the statues from the Parthenon & the pillars from the tomb of Agamemnon at Mycenae.[4]

Still L. plays chess & it is nearly twelve. But Athens shows no sign of sleep, so I can't complain. A howling whistling sound is made by the trams. This time tomorrow we shall be nearing Salonika: I shall be turning on my shelf, L. on his, & so for 3 nights till we reach Rodmell & sleep in our soft beds, in the cool English May:

Tuesday 10 May

Only the most hardened scribbler could attempt to write in the Orient Express—for the letters are swept out of my hand—heads & tails. Here we are, 10.30, in Jugo Slavia, a tamer more subjugated country far than Greece, the last of which we saw last night—crossing a terrific stone gorge on a crazy bridge & looking down till I quivered from our window, sitting down to dinner with Venus colliding with the moon, & a shepherds hut, & two men in long coats lit up by the electric lights of our restaurant car. Curious contrasts! Our sufficiency & civilisation drawing all compact through want, poverty, desolation, shepherds, sheep, torrents, lonely rivers winding through rocks. We dined, on the usual smoke grey china. Another bride & groom on board. Gathered in the salon at the station were all their friends come with boxes of chocolate. She said in English "Looking through my things I found this belt" & gave it to the young man with the choc. box. A few sentences—specially intimate—arch—coquettish?—in English; then a babble of Greek again. A language one doesn't understand is always unaccented, sibyllant, soft, wavy, unidentifiable with words. Last night was bad. Very hot. Then interruptions. At Salonika (1.30) they came in to ask about money. We had been advised to hide all except 600 drachmas—where? In the electric light bell he said. An impossible idea—so we disposed them all over—in the pockets of Baedeker, in an envelope. In Yugo Slavia the same question. So on, stopping & starting all night. We woke, & washed, looking at

4. Thomas Bruce, 7th Earl of Elgin (1766-1841), British envoy to the Ottoman Porte from 1799-1803, secured permission to record and then to remove Greek antiquities within the Turkish dominion; his great collection of sculptures, taken chiefly from the Parthenon but including the two green marble columns from the Treasury of Atreus at Mycenae, were shipped to England and in 1816 bought for the nation for £35,000; they are now in the British Museum.

mountains. But the time had changed back & we had to wait 2 hours for coffee. Now for Rousseau.

Wednesday 11 May

again this heroism in the attempt at pen & ink; but I am tired of reading Rousseau: it is 6 o'clock; & we have just said that by this time tomorrow we shall be in Monk's House. L. will be talking to Pinka. As it is, we are shaking & rattling through Lombardy towards the Alps: & shall wake near Paris. It is a flat country set with small red houses. All is tame & rich & civilised after Greece. We went out in the rain & walked up the broad stucco streets of Belgrade yesterday: we saw nothing but very tall men in tight fitting clothes: two women in looping breeches & Turkish handkerchiefs; & so back to the train again. We saw Trieste in the same way this morning, but hot sunny [?], with its sea spread silky & boats & there attached ourselves to England by buying The Times. The paper reads empty & provincial—these good Englishmen making such a bother about the Academy & motor cars when all the time there is Athens & the Greek islands. In kindness to my eyes now & to come I stop.

[*Sunday 15 May*]

And now, Whit Sunday, here we are at Monks House, & Greece is perceptibly melting: just for a moment England & Greece stood side by side, each much enlivened by the other. When we landed, the English coast seemed long low sweeping empty. I exclaimed at the extraordinary English green—with its silver mixture; & L. said the earth had an unbaked look—no red in it; & the lines of the hills so sloping. Now our road seems a garden path. This was Greece still active in our eyes. But its force is waning. Already my mind is hard at work (in my absence) arranging, editing, bringing forward, eliminating, until it will present me, unasked, with visions, as I walk, of Aegina, of Athens—the Acropolis with the incandescent pillars; the view from the goatherds hill at Delphi—no, the process is not yet complete enough for me to have detached pictures. Last nights gossip at Charleston has further strewn sand over Greece. And my head has settled down; & my body is rapidly using itself to arm chairs & soft beds & English meat & Jam.

[*End of inserted pages*]

The Woolfs returned by car from Monks House to Tavistock Square on the afternoon of Whit Sunday, 15 May.

Tuesday 17 May

What ⟨should be⟩ is the right attitude towards criticism? What ought

I to feel & say & do when Miss B. devotes an article in Scrutiny to attacking me?[5] She is young, Cambridge, ardent. And she says I'm a very bad writer. Now I think the thing to do is to note the pith of what is said—that I dont think—then to use the little kick of energy which opposition supplies to be more vigorously oneself. It is perhaps true that my reputation will now decline. I shall be laughed at & pointed at. What should be my attitude—clearly Arnold Bennett & Wells took the criticism of their youngsters in the wrong way. The right way is not to resent; not to . . be long suffering & Christian & submissive either. Of course, with my odd mixture of extreme rashness & modesty (to analyse roughly) I very soon recover from praise & blame. But I want to find out an attitude. The most important thing is not to think very much about oneself. To investigate candidly the charge; but not fussily, not very anxiously. On no account to retaliate by going to the other extreme— thinking too much. And now that thorn is out—perhaps too easily but then of course John interrupted.

[Thursday 19 May]

John has interrupted to some purpose. All last night Nessa put his case for him & against the irascible Leonard & the hard work & the underpay. And today we have to discuss with him his 'feelings'—I'm not specially sympathetic, thinking of all the time we've spent. And Hilda M[atheson]. lunches tomorrow with a view to—Oh dear, the Press, the Press—how much time it has cost us.[6]

[Monday 23 May]

Here is a little scene that I will write, bored as I am with refurbishing Dickens.[7]

Yesterday we were driving home [from Richmond]. As we came to Mortlake Bridge I saw some heads bobbing in the river. I thought they were boys bathing; I thought it odd; why bathe on Sunday under a bridge! And then I saw a boat flopping on its side; & then a crowd; &

5. M. C. Bradbrook in 'Notes on the Style of Mrs Woolf', Scrutiny, May 1932 (see M&M, p. 308) concludes thus: 'To demand "thinking" from Mrs Woolf is clearly illegitimate: but such deliberate repudiation of it and such a smoke screen of feminine charm is surely to be deprecated'. Muriel Bradbrook (b. 1909), later (1965) Professor of English at Cambridge, and (1968) Mistress of Girton, had recently been elected to a fellowship at that college.
6. For John Lehmann's relations with the Hogarth Press at this period, see his Thrown to the Woolfs (1978), p. 32ff, and below.
7. VW did not in the end include her refurbished 'David Copperfield', published originally in 1925 in the N&A (Kp C266), in her second Common Reader.

then putting two & two together realised that this silent bobbing scene meant that here was an accident. We stopped & got out & watched three or four people swimming very slowly in full dress the few yards to shore. Then a sound of snoring sobbing was heard. Nobody moved. Nobody was excited active or amused. One red faced dishevelled woman was lying on her back. A man was pulling & pushing her. At last they touched shore; & a bright eyed elderly man scrambled up the steep bank, ran quickly, dripping in black trousers plastered to his legs, to the parapet, where he had left a hat & an overcoat. It was a sordid, silent spectacle— this heroic rescue. Middle class people in full Sunday dress immersed in cold water. I thought of a picture of a miracle; people fully dressed floating: there was a touch of the grotesque; none of terror or sublimity. The boat lay like a log boat, on its side.

So home: & Hilda is willing; & therefore, late last night John comes & renews his application. The mixture of emotionalism & grasping is so odd: as hard as nails, & then quivering.

Wednesday 25 May

Now I have "finished" David Copperfield, & I say to myself cant I escape to some pleasanter atmosphere? Cant I expand & embalm & become a sentient living creature! Lord how I suffer! What a terrific capacity I possess for feeling with intensity—now, since we came back, I'm screwed up into a ball; cant get into step; cant make things dance; feel awfully detached; see youth; feel old; no, thats not quite it; wonder how a year or 20 perhaps is to be endured. Think, yet people do live; cant imagine what goes on behind faces. All is surface hard; myself only an organ that takes blows, one after another; the horror of the hard raddled faces in the [Chelsea] flower show yesterday; the inane pointlessness of all this existence; hatred of my own brainlessness & indecision: the old treadmill feeling, of going on & on & on; for no reason: Lytton's death; Carrington's; a longing to speak to him; all that cut away, gone. Eddy's idiotic letter; the peevishness & egotism of Eddy; of John; the hardness & competitiveness of life; no space which one can expand in & say Time stand still here;[8] L.'s goodness, & firmness; & the immense responsibility that rests on him. What to do about the press, about Hilda, about John; women; my book on professions; shall I write another novel; contempt for my lack of intellectual power; reading Wells without understanding; Nessa's children; society; buying clothes; Rodmell spoilt; all England spoilt; terror at night of things generally wrong in the

8. VW had encountered E. Sackville-West at a party given by Adrian Stephen on 19 May; for her reply to his 'idiotic' letter, and a later conciliatory one, see *V VW Letters*, nos. 2591, 2598. Cf. Mrs Ramsay: 'Life stand still here.' *To the Lighthouse*, pp. 249, 250.

universe; buying clothes; how I hate Bond Street & spending money on clothes; worst of all is this disjected barrenness. And my eyes hurt; & my hand trembles.

A saying of Leonard's comes into my head in this season of complete inanity & boredom "Things have gone wrong somehow". It was the night Carrington killed herself. We were walking along that silent blue street with the scaffolding. I saw all the violence & unreason crossing in the air: ourselves small; a tumult outside: something terrifying: unreason. Shall I make a book out of this? It would be a way of bringing order & speed again into my world.

Thursday 26 May

And now today suddenly the weight on my head is lifted. I can think, reason, keep to one thing, & concentrate. Perhaps this is the beginning of another spurt. Perhaps I owe it to my conversation with L. last night. I tried to analyse my depression: how my brain is jaded with the conflict within of two types of thought, the critical, the creative; how I am harassed by the strife & jar & uncertainty without. This morning the inside of my head feels cool & smooth instead of strained & turbulent.

[Friday 27 May]

Last night at Adrian's evening. Zuckerman on apes. Doris Chapman sitting on the floor.[9] I afraid of Eddy coming in—I wrote him a sharp, but well earned, letter. Adrian so curiously reminiscent—will talk of his school of Greece of the past as if nothing had happened in between: a queer psychological fact in him—this dwelling on the past, when there's his present & his future all round him: D.C. to wit, & Karin coming in late, predacious, struggling, never amenable or comforting as poor woman no doubt she knows: deaf, twisted, gnarled, short, stockish—baffled, still she comes. Dick Strachey. All these cold elements of a party not mingling. L. & I talk with some effort. Duncan wanders off. Nessa gone to Tarzan.[10] We meet James & Alix in the door. Come & dine says James with the desire strong in him I think to keep hold of Lytton. Monkeys can discriminate between light & dark: dogs cant. Tarzan is made largely of human apes. People have libraries of wild beast 'shots' let out on hire.

9. Solly Zuckerman (b. 1904 in S. Africa), zoologist and from 1928-32 Demonstrator in Anatomy at University College, London, had just published *The Social Life of Monkeys and Apes*. Doris Chapman, with whom Adrian had fallen in love, was a painter currently showing her work at the Wertheim Gallery.
10. Richard (Dick) Strachey (1902-76), writer, elder son of Lytton's brother Ralph. The 'screen sensation' *Tarzan the Ape Man*, with Johnny Weissmuller and Maureen O'Sullivan, was showing at the Empire Leicester Square.

Question how the lion fight was done. Real. Probably the lion was doped or had its claws cut. Talk of Greece. Talk of Spain. Dick was taken for a ghost.[11] A feeling of distance & remoteness. Adrian sepulchral, polite, emaciated, elongated, scientific, called Adrian by Solly; then in come rapid small women, Hughes, & I think his wife.[12] We evaporate at 11.20: courteously thanked for coming by Adrian. Question what pleasure these parties give. Some, presumably, or these singular figures wouldn't coagulate. A pouring wet day, & we're off to Rodmell for the week end. As for the Press, we're to see Harold's woman on Tuesday & contemplate a re-arrangement: no John, no Hilda, but competent underlings; Belsher coming back after her holiday. Now for more articles. But I think one fortnight will see me through.

Wednesday 1 June

(Derby day.) Oh dear, oh dear, I dont like dining with Clive—not altogether. It is true I conquered, at 8, my profound trepidation about my clothes. "I wont wear my new dress I said, in case I should be laughed at". This philosophy shivered on the doorstep, when I saw two 20 horse power cars drawn up, apparently, at his door. Again I fluctuated & shivered, like a blown candle flame, when I came in & found only steamy, grubby inarticulate Rex Whistler. Why have I dressed at all I asked. Then Lord David, then Bea Howe, then Mrs Quennell. Thats all. So to dinner. And the boasting! Clive rattling out noble names. Memories of Cecils, & Godolphins: how Jack Caermarthen was engaged to Mary Baker: how the deaf duchess gondoled with the deaf Mrs Baker: but I played my tricks: jumped over the candlestick; & co operated with Clive in the great business of impressing, I think it was, Mrs Quennell. *She* could only remember diplomatic society in Tokio. Clive luxuriated in the Embassy at Rome. "Lady—I've forgotten her name oh of course, Cynthia Graham".[1] Then, drawing round after dinner, he put me through my paces about Eddy. And he became teasing, malicious; & he said "But

11. Spanish gipsies mistook him for a mythological beast, the *Mantiquera*; see D. Garnett, *The Familiar Faces* (1962), p. 30.
12. Richard Hughes (1900-76), author of *A High Wind in Jamaica* (1929); in November 1931 he had written to VW about *The Waves* (letter, MHP, Sussex). He was recently married.
1. Clive's dinner party was on 31 May. Beatrice Howe, a writer, had married Mark Lubbock in 1930. The first Mrs Peter Quennell (they were soon to part) spent 18 months in Japan when he was a Professor of English in Tokyo. Mary Baker and her mother were wealthy Americans living and entertaining in Italy; Clive had seen a good deal of her during the preceding autumn and spring, much of which he had spent in Venice where she rented a palazzo, or in Rome. John Godolphin Osborne

you've never known anything—once you were out of your mind—that's all." & he said "Now tell the truth. You were extremely disagreeable to Eddy . . ." Well, well; these little hooks only scratch the surface; & there were moments of brilliant fluency which I enjoyed; when I said its far better to be here, rubbing my wits with these charming people than reading Rousseau in my drawing room; then I revoked that opinion; then I floated again; then I landed in the scrannels. No, I dont think I like Clive's partys anymore—though theyre stirring enough. I pick up too many thorns, one way & another. His oblique method of getting his own back always exacerbates. His own—what did I steal 20 years ago that he should never feel the debt paid? Anyhow, why not refuse the next party, & rummage on my own? My own pie is full enough: Mary, Christabel, Ld David tonight, Peter Lucas, Ethel tomorrow: &c.

[*Thursday 2 June*]

Lord David's party last night. Half across London. Derby night. Great motors full of men with buttonholes. A rose pink girl tripping across Sh[aftesbur]y Avenue hand in hand with a young man: all fluff & roses. Edwardes Sqre very large leafy silent Georgian refined: so too no. 41 with its white & green; its one print—but nothing definite eno' for my taste: Ly Salisbury by Sargent over the mantelpiece; a butler; an orange cat; Ld D. & Eth Bowen talking by the fire; then Puffin, then John Sparrow.[2] Not a good dinner: meagre; exiguous; & I took too many asparagus. All adroit kind nice talk—the note of the Asquiths & Cecils. 'How very true'—'Yes, I agree entirely'—so different from B[loomsbur]y. Theres more body to us. Still I dont complain. A little confabulation about Eddy: then about crying at crowds, at theatres, at films; what is tragic; about football. Sp[arrow]. is a baller, a solid young man, just called to Chancery Bar who writes a life of Donne after dinner. Talk about Auden & Naomi Mitchison: her review of Auden read aloud: Aeschylus "& all that lot". How she went to a party with corn in her hair: how her group knocks people down; how they pig in the Ellis's [?] hotel; how she

(1901-63), Marquess of Carmarthen, succeeded his father as 11th Duke of Leeds in 1927; the deaf Duchess was his mother; he married three times, but never Mary Baker. Lady Sybil Graham was the wife of the British Ambassador in Rome, 1921-33, Sir Ronald Graham.

2. The Sargent portrait of Lord David Cecil's mother Lady Salisbury is a charcoal drawing. The Hon. Anthony ('Puffin') Asquith (1902-68), only son of Herbert and Margot Asquith—since 1925 the Earl and Countess of Oxford and Asquith—was a film director. John Sparrow (b. 1906), scholar and barrister, elected fellow of All Souls in 1929, practised at the Chancery Bar from 1931-9.

loves, poses, writes but its not really good, says David.[3] Then they talked about the German youth movement: about bad people: about—Lindsey who likes lice in the head; about Murry; & I wore my new dress, too white & young perhaps; & so came home across London, & must now wash for Maynard's lunch & the Bernard Shaws—oh damn, oh damn—not an idea in my head or a wish to be brilliant

[*Friday 3 June*]

I dont like old ladies who guzzle. My comment upon Ethel Smyth last night—no doubt a harsh one. But she champed & chopped; & squabbled over her duck; & then was over eaten & had to go home.

My comment upon the Shaws:
he said "I am not sufficiently fond of myself to wish for immortality. I should like to be different. I should like to be a performer in music, & a mathematician. So I dont keep a diary. I destroy all my letters. So did [*blank in ms.*] He had had letters from every great man. He took them out in the garden & burnt them. But I couldnt burn Ellen Terry's. They were works of art. It would have been like burning a page of the Luttrell psalter. The handwriting was a work of art. She scribb[l]ed them—never thought of a phrase. But I admit that when our correspondence was published I thought—I admit—I shall be the hero: not a bit of it: I have to admit that Ellen was the superior. She comes out far the better of the two. Frank Harris—his life of me was a life of himself. Theres no truth in it about me. No life of me has a word of truth in it. They say my father was persecuted, & that I was persecuted, as a boy—sent to a Wesleyan School. Desmond MacCarthy says he's going to write my life—well, he may say so.[4] He comes & talks—I cant tell the truth yet, about myself. The Webbs looked lonely somehow going off to Russia. He's not growing old—no, I dont find that. I've always quarrelled with the Webbs. You see Webb has a gigantic faculty for absorbing information. He could have gone to Oxford—found some flaw in the statutes—proved it to the examiners. But didn't go: only wanted to be in the right. And so, when I first knew him, I had to overcome an immense amount of useless knowledge. He had to forget things he had learnt. I always tell a story to illustrate this. When I was a boy I asked my father "What is a Unitarian" And he thought for a time & then he said, "Unitarians believe that after

3. Naomi Mitchison, *née* Haldane (b. 1897), spirited and forceful writer and socialist; she had promoted W. H. Auden's reputation by publishing and reviewing his early poems; her review of his recently published *The Orators* appeared in the *Weekend Review* of 28 May 1932.
4. See *Ellen Terry and Bernard Shaw. A Correspondence*, edited by C. St John, 1931; Frank Harris, *Bernard Shaw*, 1931. Desmond MacCarthy did not write a life of Shaw.

Christ was crucified he got down off the Cross & ran away on the other side of the hill." Years later, when I was 30 or so, I was staying with the Trevelyans at Wellcomb; & the talk got upon Unitarians, & it flashed upon me, this cannot be the true story—but I'd always seen Christ running down the hill all those years. Webb would be much more effective if he'd one drop of the artist. But he has, not one. Beatrice is in despair about it. Cant make a good speech therefore.[5] People think my style as speaker is spontaneous, colloquial. Its the most artificial ever known. I've taken long railway journeys & spent them saying the letters of the alphabet aloud so as to make my vowels strike out. Then they forget I'm an Irishman—I think quicker than the English. No I dont mug things up—when I write history I dont read it. I imagine the sort of things people would have done & then I say they did them & then I find out facts—one always can—that prove it. The great pleasure of the Broadcasting to me is that I can sit at home & conduct The Meistersinger myself. I sit with the book of the score & conduct & I'm furious when they dont follow me. That way one finds how often the singers make howlers—come in a bar early or late. Beecham—(here he sang a piece of the Magic Flute) turned *that*—which is solemn, slow, processionly [?]—into a hornpipe. I leapt in my seat (he leapt up his knees & clasped them in agony—[6] he is never still a moment—he clenches his fists—he flings himself this way & that; he sprang up to go, as if he were 22, not 74 as L. remarked. What life, what vitality! What immense nervous spring! That perhaps is his genius. Immense vivacity—& why I dont read him for pleasure. His face is bright red; his nose lumpy: his eyes sea green like a sailors or a cockatoos. He doesnt much notice who's there. Told stories about the fortunes of plays to Maynard who was rung up 3 or 4 times at lunch by his colleagues at the Savoy. The ballet starts on Monday & he has no notion if it will crash or flourish. People no longer book ahead. Shaw said they used to book 6 weeks ahead.[7]

(I skipped this page, so will insert here how I heard Maynard say to Mrs Shaw "Well, we're about as bad as we can be. Never been so bad. We may go over the edge—but as its never been like this, nobody knows.

5. Sidney and Beatrice Webb, friends of Shaw and fellow Fabians since the 1880s, left England in May for a three-month visit to Russia (after which they declared they had 'fallen in love with Soviet Communism'). Welcombe House, near Stratford-on-Avon, was one of the homes of Sir George Otto Trevelyan, the statesman and historian.

6. At this point VW inadvertently turned over two pages to go on with her account of Shaw; the paragraph below and the entry for 4 June were written later on the intervening page.

7. The Camargo Society, in which Keynes was very active, was promoting a four-week season of ballet at the Savoy Theatre, 6 June-2 July, in which Lydia Lopokova danced. The Woolfs went to the first night.

One would say we must"—which was uttered in the low tone of a doctor saying a man was dying in the next room; but didnt want to disturb the company. This referred to the state of Europe, while we lunched—very well too.

Saturday 4 June

And last night we stopped the car in Hyde Park & I watched a people on the verge of ruin. How many Rolls Royces, & other low, pink, yellow, very powerful cars werent booming through the park like giant dorbeetles, with luxurious owners, men & women, lying back, on their way to some party. A Rolls Royce means £5000 a year. Then the children in perambulators with nurses. Then the strollers & saunterers. Then the mauve grey green trees, flushed with livid pinks & yellows; the may & the laburnum scarcely burning, like colour under water that cloudy, rainy, thunder yellow evening. So back through the West End—more cars blocked; & we on the verge of a precipice.

This is written, not so much for the sake of its historical interest, as to get the taste of Madame Bolotine's memoirs out of my mouth. The influence is perceptible. Queer, the pervasiveness of bad writing. And still queerer, the fact that this emotional, unreal badly written, flimsy book is dearer to the writer than a child, has to be delivered by hand, & is the record of a tempestuous violent Russian life yet feebler than Mrs Bartholomew's memoirs.[8]

[Monday 6 June]

Last night, Sunday, dining at Clive's. Just back from Wiltshire. Brown. Good tempered. Nessa heating dinner. C. cross with Lottie—too many dishes—too much fuss—does the napkins into shapes—chatter, gossip; ballet; attack on Bolitho's Price Consort;[9] Quentin thinks Emperor Napoleon attractive; Clive swears he's wrong; story of Merimée in love with the Empress Mother; so to Tommy & Raymond. Some acrimony. Duncan says "Raymond needs an arboreous bush". Nessa says T. wd. appreciate that; Raymond wouldn't; I say T.'s a screeching gull, & ought to be happy in a lovely young wife; Nessa laughs; they say thats the

8. Mme Bolotine's memoirs: presumably a ms. submitted to the Hogarth Press. Mrs Bartholomew, *née* Lydia Green, was the daughter of a well-to-do miller in the Eastern counties who lost his money through drinking; she became a nurse in Brighton, where she met and married Percy Bartholomew, then working as a hospital porter, and they came to live in Rodmell near his brother William and sister Rose; he became the gardener at Monks House, and both women on occasion worked in the house.

9. Hector Bolitho: *Albert the Good: a Life of the Prince Consort*, 1932.

agony—he isn't happy. What worse torture? says Clive. One would agree to try living with her in Lambs Conduit St. & then the memory of happier days (always thus lyrical about lovers). And he's falling flat says Nessa: Angus no longer loves him, nor Barbara.[10] Raymond can make a story out of life, T. cant, I say, for all his sitting in public houses. Oh but he can, says Nessa. Raymond only sits in drawing rooms, says D. testy. (He has been testy about Cassis gossip). So to bed: a man says I lunched with Mrs —— & she has a heavenly bull pup 7 weeks old

[*Monday 13 June*]

Back from a good week end at Rodmell—a week end of no talking, sinking at once into deep safe book reading; & then sleep: clear transparent; with the may tree like a breaking wave outside; & all the garden green tunnels, mounds of green: & then to wake into the hot still day, & never a person to be seen, never an interruption: the place to ourselves: the long hours. To celebrate the occasion I bought a little desk & L. a beehive, & we drove to the Lay; & I did my best not to see the cement sheds. The bees swarmed. Sitting after lunch we heard them outside; & on Sunday there they were again hanging in a quivering shiny brown black purse to Mrs Thompsett's tombstone. We leapt about in the long grass of the graves, Percy all dressed up in mackintosh, & netted hat. Bees shoot whizz, like arrows of desire: fierce, sexual; weave cats cradles in the air; each whizzing from a string; the whole air full of vibration: of beauty, of this burning arrowy desire; & speed: I still think the quivering shifting bee bag the most sexual & sensual symbol. So home, through vapours, tunnels, caverns of green: with pink & yellow glass mounds in gardens—rhododendrons. To Nessa's. Adrian has told Karin that he must separate She demurs. They are to start separate houses, he says, in the autumn.

Last week was such a scrimmage: oh so many people: among them Doris [Chapman] & Adrian: she like a dogfish: that circular slit of a mouth in a pale flesh: & an ugly rayed dress: but said by Nessa to be nice. Why the bees should swarm round her, I cant say. Now Vita rings up: may she & Harold dine tonight: then Ethel: I look ahead to my fortnights week end.

Saturday 18 June

Adrian rings up & says "Can you suggest a tenant for two rooms? We're in the throes of dividing things up." Whether he goes & Karin stays, I dont know. John stays, on a revised basis, as adviser; Miss Scott

10. Angus Davidson (1898-1980), charming and ineffective Cambridge graduate, worked for three years as potential manager in the Hogarth Press before resigning in December 1927.

Johnson as permanent manager; & I am to consult & help John more, & not to sit here "with a red cross on your door, so that I daren't come in." My advice is that he shall be more malleable, & less pernickety. He craves influence & authority, to publish the books of his friends: wishes to start a magazine; is poor; ⟨cant do without pay;⟩ must economise; live with Peggy in Pimlico.[11] Am I too aloof—partly so as not to chatter, partly to get to my own work? Ought one to be more sympathetic; but oh so many people to see & things to fit in already: nevertheless I'll try, if the new method is to be tried. He says Leonard is "so deep: & plans things; & never comes out at once with what he means; so that I dont know how to behave." I daresay we've spent 10 hours talking about all this. Ethel more than usually controlled. Headaches skirmishing. Oh & I'm finishing the C.R.: I trust to God; have done the last article, & hope to send off to be typed tomorrow. Desmond's criticism rather sends my value up in my eyes: can't make a dint in a pat of butter. Man of the word. Respectable, acute, astute, to the point.[12]

Nessa & Duncan's private view. Tatlock smelling of drink. Horsey [?] arty people. Agnews. Mrs Grant. Mrs Rendel. All this moving round the pictures, & I meeting Ethel [Smyth] in electric blue & Quentin: & she telling us at Stewarts how Miss Liddell rolled down the steps at Marl-borough House dead drunk.[13]

Friday 24 June

On the verge of my fortnightly dip at Monk's House. Dinner at the Hutchinsons last night: sat between Desmond & Lord Balniel. Lord & Lady Derwent also there; & Lord David [Cecil] only absent because of a

11. The proposed changes within the Hogarth Press are clarified in John Lehmann's *Thrown to the Woolfs* (1978), pp. 33-6. Miss Scott Johnson acted as manager for little over six months. Peggy was Beatrix Lehmann (1903-79), the actress, the youngest of Lehmann's three sisters.

12. *Criticism*, the second volume of Desmond MacCarthy's collected essays, was published in June 1932; in his long essay 'Notes on the Novel' he refers to VW's attempt in *Jacob's Room* to find a form without employing the novelist's usual methods: 'Mrs Woolf gave us, as it were, not the train itself, but the draught a train makes as it flies by —'.

13. The private view of 'Recent Paintings by Duncan Grant, Vanessa Bell and Keith Baynes' was at Thomas Agnew & Sons, 43 Old Bond Street, on Tuesday 14 June; all three painters resigned from the London Artists' Association in July 1931 and their work was now handled by Agnews. Robert Rattray Tatlock (1889-1954), editor of the *Burlington Magazine*, 1920-33, and art critic of the *Daily Telegraph*, 1924-34. Mrs Rendel, *née* Elinor Strachey (1860-1945), was Lytton's eldest sister and mother of VW's doctor. Stewart's tea shop, on the corner of Old Bond Street and Piccadilly, near Agnews.

sprained ankle; & Lord Chichester ringing up. "So good for Leonard" Jack said, "all these Lords."[14] A certain thin spread tightness in the talk. Champagne necessary. Two footmen. Lady Balniel simple hard direct plain confident young with children. aristocratic. Desmond back from Cambridge & Abbott [*a friend*]. Very cheerful: & I think his book so bad. How then can he be cheerful? The thin stretched whipped up champagne talk was about—oh, I said to Lord B. some nonsense about pictures: & he said my writing (I'm so well known now) was more real than his politics. "I go about in my wife's country, & up in Lancashire: I meet the oddest people; very nice: we talk: I've got to make a speech at a bazaar about the Christian attitude to the unemployment question. What does it mean? And so dont get much time for pictures. David Cecil & I always loved pictures, even at Eton." Ly D. Roumanian, passionate, dumb. Jack small talk with Lady B. Mary expanding about Sadlers Wells to B. about Courthauld. B. smoking a cheroot. D. saying what it felt like to be sick. So to the Zoo: a mist rising; white bears elongated like El Grecos: stinking meat held near my nose: bear bit a boy's arm off; bears dived; white explosion; red & yellow fairy lamps; distant music; the sea lions, rushing like torpedoes, flouncing up the rocks; in silk coats; the blind bear; one swollen white eye; birds flying under the livid green; baby sea lions, like puppies; Mary tipping the man: her sexual response: home with Desmond till 1.

Tuesday 28 June

Just "finished De Quincey". Thus am I trying to keep pace with the days & deliver the 2nd C.R. done on the last of June—which I see with dismay is Thursday. I spent last summer thus toiling over The Waves. This is less severe by a long chalk (whats the origin of that? cricket pitch? billiards?)[15] Anyhow it blazes; swoons; the heat. Royal, imperial, are the words I fumble with in the Square. So hot yesterday—so hot, when

14. LW didn't benefit: he was chairing a lecture. David Lindsay, Lord Balneil (1900-75), Conservative MP for Lonsdale in Lancashire, 1924-40 (when he succeeded his father as 28th Earl of Crawford and Balcarres), had become a Trustee of the Tate Gallery and was beginning his distinguished career of service to the arts; his wife Mary, *née* Cavendish, was a niece of the Duke of Devonshire. George Harcourt Johnstone, 3rd Baron Derwent (1899-1949), author and diplomat; his *Fifty Poems* had been published in 1931 (*HP Checklist* 252); his wife Sabine, *née* Iliesco, was the daughter of the former Chief of Staff of the Roumanian Army. John Buxton Pelham, 8th Earl of Chichester (1912-44), diplomat. The Hutchinsons lived at 3 Albert Road, opposite Regent's Park and the Zoo.
15. 'A reference to the custom of making merit marks with chalk, before lead pencils were so common.' Brewer's *Dictionary of Phrase and Fable*.

Prince Mirsky came with his dubious fluent Russian lady:[16] I mean she was full of temperament; had the free gestures of the Slav; but Mirsky was trap mouthed; opened & bit his remark to pieces: has yellow misplaced teeth; wrinkles his forehead; dispair, suffering, very marked on his face. Has been in England, in boarding houses for 12 years; now returns to Russia 'for ever'. I thought as I watched his eye brighten & fade—soon there'll be a bullet through your head. Thats one of the results of war: this trapped cabin'd man: but that didnt lubricate our tea.

Vita came in; then Alix; both relieved of their books (Vita's is said to be bad) & so rather elated. Vita is driving west, alone, for 4 days today. An American has offered her £250 for 2,000 words; & will offer the same to me. I doubt it.[17] Alix like a red Indian; so large boned, & with wrinkles, & sunburn like an Indians. And tonight, to my considerable alarm, at opening an entirely new door, into an entirely new room, I dine with Katharine Furse.[18] And here's Morgan come to lunch. So enough.

Wednesday 29 June

The room was a very sumptuous room; a wide staircase led to it; a broad hall. I was early. "What a magnificent cabinet!" I said to hide my nervousness, with this old charwoman in the tight dress & black stockings. All her hair has shrunk. She has the hardened, lined, drawn face of a very unhappy woman. Why, in that light she looked terrible to me. Where had the handsome Katharine gone: she who strode; had firm red cheeks; & was decisive, masterly, controlled even in the great trench [?] of her unhappiness? Heavens, what an injury life inflicts! To have replaced that

16. Prince Dmitri Syvatopolk Mirsky (1890-c.1940), Russian literary historian and critic, lecturer in Russian literature, King's College, University of London. He did return to Russia, and apparently perished in a labour camp. See *IV LW*, pp. 23-7. Perhaps his companion on this visit was the Mme Bolotine whose memoirs VW had been reading (see above, 4 June 1932)?

17. The books—or mss.—which had been delivered to the Hogarth Press, which published both later in the year, were *Family History* by V. Sackville-West (*HP Checklist* 307), and Alix Strachey's edition and translation of Melanie Klein's *The Psycho-Analysis of Children* (*HP Checklist* 295). For the American offer, see below, 8 July 1932 and *V VW Letters*, no. 2603; the medium for these lavish proposals appears to have been the literary agent Nancy R. Pearn ('Pearnie'), then of Curtis Brown Ltd.

18. Dame Katharine Furse (1875-1952), youngest daughter of John Addington Symonds and sister of Madge Vaughan whom VW had once idolized; she was the widow of the painter Charles Furse (1868-1904). She became the first Director of the Women's Royal Naval Service, 1917-19, and was now Director of the World Association of Girl Guides and Girl Scouts. She lived at 5 Cheyne Walk, Chelsea, with the American philosopher and philanthropist Mary Parker Follett (1868-1933).

dashing youth with this almost intolerable look of suffering: a grudging look; a scraped bare look; the ugly poor woman look. By dint of arrangement, by looking through half closed eyes I could, as the evening wore on & the light faded piece together something fine: her eyes; small but penetrating; her gestures—they are still free & bold, though so much hampered by bare arms & tight ugly black & blue dress. What is fine is that she conceals nothing; has no shrinking left; has been wrung & mangled out of the softnesses & sensibilities. How white her face is, too; yet she commanded her table—her & Follett's table—with the old mastery; but as if nothing gave her any pleasure. She never relaxed. Never lost her look of suffering the whole evening. To harden to blunt to coarsen that is the worst damage age—& I daresay she's only 8 years older than I am—can inflict. Is this all Charles' death? Or what? The talk spattered & sprinkled. A dry precise old pepperbox called Cabot, professor of Harvard, his vague wife,[19] Mary Follett, verbose, diffuse—that was the party & we sat & let the light turn grey & cold & all the cabinets grow dim—all very elderly & ugly. Was that contained in my dismay with Katharine—the sense I look like that too. Perhaps. Then Leonard came in, in his grey suit & blue tie, sunburnt; & I felt that we are still vigorous & young. And so kissed Katharine the old woman on the doorstep. Yes, last time we met she was driving a dogcart: & it was a cold winters day, & she was going to the docks to look at treasure.

[Sunday 3 July]

Whenever I suck my pen, my lip is covered with ink. And I have no ink with which to fill my pot; & it is 10 minutes past 12; & I have just finished Hardy; & I promise myself that the C.R. will be finally done by Wednesday next. And today is Sunday. Last night at 10. the Zeppelin came past with a string of light hanging from its navel. This consoled me for not having gone to the last night of the [Camargo] ballet.[1]

Now I have cleaned my table; which John inherits while I'm away. And I should now attack Ch. Rossetti. But Lord, how tired one gets of one's own writing.

[Wednesday 6 July]

Today is Wednesday & the CR I confess is not yet quite done. But then—well I had to re-write the last article, which I had thought so good,

19. Richard Clarke Cabot (1868-1939), professor of Medicine and of Social Ethics at Harvard; his wife, Ella Lyman Cabot, was a teacher and writer on ethics.

1. The German airship *Graf Zeppelin* passed over London on Saturday and Sunday on her flights between her base at Friedrichshafen and Hanwell airpark, where she took on passengers for a circuit tour of Great Britain.

entirely. Not for many years shall I collect another bunch of articles. Many many people, too, & parties still to be transacted. On Sunday the Bussies; he detached ironic Gallic; she intense, worried, ineffective rather; money troubles; war loan investments vanished; they're left with £80 income. But we shall go to Spain in September said Simon. Then to Angelica, passing the funeral in Epping forest; Nessa made her dress for the ballet party sitting in a field after lunch, while Quentin & Angelica wandered & L. made up an article & spoke to an old man in a hedge.[2] Then Adrian came on Sunday night, garrulous & cheerful; talking science: then [on 4 July] we dined with the James's: Alix Red Indian: James trying to extend a feeler from his hard nut. I'm an old friend, Lytton's friend. Will we choose books. How Carrington lied to him the night before Lytton died: said she wd not kill herself; was found unconscious in the car later. How regular your books are I said: a mere weed, he said of Eddy in Lytton's way

These days have been very hot & very busy: books out tomorrow, Plomer, my letter & Hugh's.[3]

[Friday 8 July]

And so I fainted, at the Ivy: & had to be led out by Clive. A curious sensation. Feeling it come on; sitting still & fading out: then Clive by my side & a woman with salts. And the odd liberation of emotion in the cab with Clive; & the absolute delight of dark & bed: after that stony rattling & heat & Frankie shouting; & things being churned up, removed.

I write this on a blazing morning, because L. is instructing Miss C[ashin]. how to arrange the books: so that I cant correct articles. "Everywhere I look everything is hopeless. . . . Either the Northern Saga ought not to be here at all—or it ought to be in the other room. . . . (John is ill: publishing day yesterday; Harold drivelling snapping, when I hoped for 'serious criticism'—why go on hoping?) the whole of thats going over—Here are 3 things of Nature has no tune of wh. we dont sell a copy a year. . . ."[4]

2. The French painter Simon Bussy (1870-1954) married Lytton Strachey's sister Dorothy (1866-1960) in 1903; they lived at Roquebrune on the Mediterranean, but normally spent some weeks in England each summer. On Saturday 2 July the Woolfs drove Vanessa and Quentin Bell to Essex to give Angelica an outing from her school, Langford Grove.
3. *The Case is Altered* by William Plomer; *A Letter to a Young Poet* by VW; and *A Letter to a Modern Novelist* by Hugh Walpole (*HP Checklist* nos. 302, 314, 312).
4. The books referred to are *The Northern Saga* (1929) by E. E. Kellett and *Nature Has No Tune* (1929) by Sylva Norman (*HP Checklist* nos. 198, 203). Harold Nicolson's review of VW's and Hugh Walpole's *Letters* . . . appeared in the *NS&N* on 9 July 1932.

Oh dear, I've twenty minutes to use; & cant 'correct' any more. What a fling I shall have into fiction & freedom when this is off! At once, an American comes to ask me to consider writing articles for some huge figure. And (hushed be this said) I sent Nessa a cheque for £100 last night: & Leonard gave his mother £50, & Philip [*his youngest brother*] £50. These are among the solid good things, I think: Nessa's £100 will buy her some release from worry, I hope: Clive saying they must spend £600 a year less. Roger to have his operation, said to be slight, tomorrow. Adrian fretted to death—almost to fainting in the street—must anyhow stumble in to Nessa's & ask for water & spend the evening—by the vagaries of his Doris. This is what Francis foretold: a girl of dubious morality, & to me like a codfish in her person. And there are fleas at M[onks].H[ouse].: to which we go; & black beetles here, & said to be mice also.

Monday 11 July

I will take a new pen & a new page to record the fact which is now a fact that I have slipped a green rubber band round the Common Reader, second series, & there it lies, at 10 minutes to one, ready to take upstairs. There is no sense of glory; only of drudgery done. And yet I daresay its a nice enough book to read—I doubt that I shall write another like it all the same. I must find a quicker cut into books than this. But heaven be praised, not now. Now I'm taking a holiday. That is to say, what shall I write tomorrow? I can sit down & think.

Wednesday 13 July

I have been sleeping over a promising novel. Thats the way to write. Its a livid hot day; & Clive has been summoned to take Mary Baker to Claridges—Oh dont think me too frivolous—& may I know who was coming—what young lady—& we've got Morgan instead—a change all to L.'s liking. Almost our last party.[5]

I'm ruminating, as usual, how to improve my lot; & shall begin by walking, alone, in Regents Park this afternoon. What I mean is why do a single thing one doesn't want to do—for instance buy a hat or read a book? Old Joseph Wright & Lizzie Wright are people I respect. Indeed I do hope the 2nd vol. will come this morning. He was a maker of dialect dixeries: he was a workhouse boy—his mother went charing. And he married Miss Lea a clergyman's daughter. And I've just read their love

5. The 'young lady' was Rosamond Lehmann; she and Forster were the Woolf's dinner guests and William Plomer came in afterwards.

letters with respect.[6] And he said "Always please yourself—then one person's happy at any rate". And she said "make details part of a whole—get proportions right"—contemplating marriage with Joe. Odd how rare it is to meet people who say things that we ourselves could have said. Their attitude to life much our own. Joe a very thick sturdy man—'I am unique in certain respects' he said. 'We must leave some record of Joe & Lizzie to posterity'. Had his old working mother to Oxford. She thought All Souls would make a good Co-op. Had a fist & struck boys. His notion of learning. I sometimes would like to be learned myself. About sounds & dialects. Still what use is it? I mean, if you have that mind why not make something *beautiful*? Yes, but then the triumph of learning is that it leaves something done solidly for ever. Everybody knows now about dialect, owing to his dixery. He is a coarse, sturdy variety of Sidney Webb & Walter Leaf—stockish, hairy; more humorous & forcible than either.[7] Could work all night, wash, & work all next day. Miss Weisse, Tovey's lady, brought them together—made Lizzy give up arranging the flowers in the Rectory & go to Oxford.[8] She a woman of character. Wouldnt accept Jo's offer of a job because he made her feel like a bear at the end of a chain. But she married him. They were lost in the woods by Virginia Water in 1896: & sat on a seat & had an hour of great suffering, after which she accepted him—they got on a bakers cart & were taken back to Miss Weisse. An absorbing story. Joe knew all about servants. Joe taught himself to read at 14; taught mill boys in a bedroom for 2d a week; a surly but very sensitive man, apparently. Now this is a testimony to Joe & Lizzy that I've been thinking how I should have liked to see them—would now like to write to her. A fine face with bright big eyes—yes—but what happens in volume two?

Thursday 14 July

'Immunity' I said to myself half an hour ago, lying back in my chair.

6. VW was reading *The Life of Joseph Wright* by his wife, published in 2 volumes in 1932. Joseph Wright (1855-1930), compiler of *The English Dialect Dictionary* (6 volumes, 1896-1905), was from 1901-25 Professor of Comparative Philology in the University of Oxford; in 1896 he had married a former student of his from Lady Margaret Hall, Elizabeth Mary Lea, daughter of the rector of Tedstone Delamere, Herefordshire.

7. Walter Leaf (1852-1927), Homeric scholar and from 1919 Chairman of the Westminster Bank, was the husband of Charlotte (Lotta) Symonds, sister of Madge Vaughan and Katharine Furse.

8. Donald Francis Tovey (1875-1940), one of the greatest musical personalities of his day, and from 1914-40 Reid Professor of Music in the University of Edinburgh, gained a music scholarship at Balliol College, Oxford, in 1894; he owed his upbringing and education to the teacher Miss Sophie Weisse (1852-1945), who virtually adopted him and fostered his precocious and remarkable gifts.

Thats the state I am (or was) in. And its a holy, calm, satisfactory flawless feeling— To be immune, means to exist apart from rubs, shocks, suffering; to be beyond the range of darts; to have enough to live on without courting flattery, success; not to need to accept invitations; not to mind other people being praised; to feel This—to sit & breathe behind my screen, alone, is enough; to be strong; content; to let Nessa & D. go to Paris without envy; to feel no one's thinking of me; to feel I have done certain things & can be quiet now; to be mistress of my hours; to feel detached from all sayings about me; & claims on me; to be glad of lunching alone with Leonard; to have a spare time this afternoon; to read Coleridge's letters.[9] Immunity is an exalted calm desirable state, & one I could reach much oftener than I do.

[Saturday 16 July]

Stella Benson last night:[10] as quiet, as controlled, white, drawn as usual, also deaf: with steady honest eyes; said she had been to a great many parties. "I just say nothing. I feel none of these people matters. They say how much they liked my book . . I was given a medal. The old gentleman couldnt remember what for. He pinned it on. Both my dogs are dead. I liked one for bounding. But that was only a sign of Stannard's disease. I go back in August—to Linlon (or some such name) a mud island. I hate Hong Kong. They play games. At Government House they give you a slip of paper with names of games on it: you have to put a cross next the one you play. Sitting out is one. James & I choose that. So we sit out together." That was her style in a very weak but persistent voice; she coughs; & then goes on with a mild persistent patience. She is bleached; even her blue eyes are bleached. But at the same time she's practical; realistic: talked, of course, of "Pearnie"—doesnt like her—& making money by stories; & Harpers & so on; in a sensible matter of fact way, like a working class woman. Then smiles with her charming steady eyes. The light faded grey in the drawing room, & she sat there lying back telling us in a very low voice, which went on steadily about the slave trade in H.K.; about James & his little Chinese destroyer, manned by ex-officers from England; how they steam out after sailing ships: the ships

9. *S. T. Coleridge's Unpublished Letters*, edited by E. L. Griggs, had just been published in 2 volumes.
10. Stella Benson (1892-1933), writer, was in 1932 awarded both the *Femina Vie Heureuse* prize and the Royal Society of Literature's Benson silver medal for her novel *Tobit Transplanted* (1931). Since her marriage in 1921 to James Carew O'Gorman Anderson of the Chinese Customs Service she had lived mainly in China. During this prize-gathering visit to England she wrote the *Time and Tide* feature 'Notes on the Way' for a month.

117

cant escape; they throw out bales of cotton & flannel: which float: James goes aboard & discovers the deck laden with opium, heroin; man cries out "That little parcel's for my father. Let me have that". Then all the other men say that the cement &c is a present for an aunt. There's always fighting. Chinese planes come over very low down. Shoot with revolvers. She sits in her kitchen. All the inhabitants crowd round, thinking the English safe—pretend they're selling eggs. Chinese generals come to dine & stand rifles on each side of their chairs: send soldiers into the kitchen to see that the food isn't poisoned. She goes back for another two years. Writes & writes. Must buzz home in her little Morris Cowley to write 8 pages of her monthly notes for Time & Tide. I ask why? Oh its good pay. Has bought a house in Kensington. Will come back for 2 years with James, who will be The O'Gorman. All this serious, weary, intent. I like her & was glad to sign her Waves.

[Monday 18 July]

Clive & Mary [Baker] last night, small, pink, underbred; not a woman of the world; without distinction; nice; rich; has lived above her means, spiritually & socially; has a little edge to her mind; tells her little story. Clive's bad manners—how she almost married Ld C[armar]then; might stand in a Tobacconists — — waspish; enamoured; C. bending over her cigarette case; fetching her coat (black: expensive): all this strained; incredible to spend weeks with her: no prestige attached; no glow; a little pickety, nervous, enthusiastic, hysterical dog—for all the world like the little yapping dog that ran mad round the Round Pond. Nessa (next day, going to the carpet shop) says Ah yes, but think of the speed boat!

Thursday 21 July

Oh but I'm so tired—I sometimes think people cant know what they do to me when they ask me to 'see' them: how they hold me in the scorching light: how I dry & shrivel: how I lie awake at night longing for rest—this is true. But know that I'm to be pitchforked up into the light & the glare again next day. Mary [Hutchinson] yesterday; Ethel today; Adrian tomorrow: & Ju[lia Strachey]. Since Monday, Nessa, Angelica: Tom & Eth Bowen; Katharine & Follett; then Adrian's suicidal face at night gave me the nightmare. And my head aches; & my back; & I'm sapped; wilted. Never mind. I shall lie in the cool at Monks House.

Alice Ritchie ringing me up about dinner, said "One thing I want to say. Please dont go so far away in your next book". She had just re-read The Waves: magnificent: but loneliness almost unbearable. Mrs Hardy writes that she has often wished, after my wonderful article on Hardy, that she had asked me to write his life. Had I consented she would have given me all the materials. And how proud I was to be asked to do the T.L.S. article![11]

On the other hand, my poet letter passes unnoticed.

[*Friday 22 July*]

I do not like Ethel when she is doing the powerful stunt—or whatever stunt it is: proclaiming that all is over; denouncing me; protesting her love; whipping up a scene; being august; despairing; melodramatic, & wobbly & weak all at the same time. No I do not like it: & also I am bored. This is the old fashioned version of an emotional scene—the tactics are to leave the other person in a hole—where indeed I would willingly have been left, if I had not remembered then all the letters I should have to write & the telephones: so I shouted after her, as she stumped down stairs, "Do you want your letters?" & as she tied them up—the HB letters[12]—I teased & railed, & felt the hollowness of it all, & her unattractive old age—not much else, so dusty & jaded I am—& she went—in what mood I do not know. Its the superficiality of these things that disenchants one: her lust for emotion. Or so I felt. Seeing herself, dramatising herself instead of being anything.

But I am distraught & lazy: I am frittering away these last mornings experimenting with little stories; but, as L. says, the change makes all work impossible: the sorting[;] packing; like a dog one senses the move; then there's Adrian tonight, & Julia & so on: then there's Welwyn I think tomorrow.[13] Nessa is gone; oh & my proofs will soon be coming; oh & I want to think out certain problems: & to be more vagarious: not yet to eat myself into a book. I want to go to Ireland, could that be managed. Are we too aloof, & absorbed—this work—whats the use of so much money— familiar thoughts: also another novel: Desmond gets between, why[?]: his tepid praise; & the difficulty: peoples minds & bodies to be separated; & clothes; & demeanour; & the autumn; & our relations with people. Dine & sleep parties. &c.

11. VW's commissioned article 'Thomas Hardy's Novels' (Kp C294) appeared as the anonymous leading article in the *TLS* on 19 January 1928, a week after his death. Florence Hardy published the life of her husband in two volumes (1928 and 1930) virtually prepared by Hardy himself. The occasion for the present exchange of letters was VW's broken engagement to lunch with Mrs Hardy on 7 July, the day after she fainted at the Ivy; see *V VW Letters*, no. 2607.

12. In 1930 Ethel Smyth had asked VW to read the letters written to her by her beloved friend Henry Brewster (1859-1908), the Anglo-American philosopher and poet, whose words she set to music in *The Wreckers* and *The Prison*.

13. On 23 July LW drove to Welwyn for a conference of the Society for Sexual Information and Progress, the brainchild of Dr C. W. Saleeby; it is not clear whether VW went too.

AUGUST 1932

The Woolfs drove to Monks House for their summer vacation on Tuesday afternoon, 26 July.

Friday 5 August

Rodmell

Yesterday L. came in to my room at Breakfast & said Goldie is dead. One of those muddles apparently; he refused to tell his sister; took advice only of Morgan & Gerald Heard; was anxious to be economical; went to Guys; had an operation, secretly, a week ago; Roger saw him on Tuesday (I think) thought the little cubicle dirty; talked; supposed him to be recovering; he died suddenly that night, of an internal haemorrhage. There was no time to send for anybody. These are the dismal details of the end of that fine charming spirit—so much a spirit that my thought was, anyhow he wont mind. And then, how much of a piece with our friends, like him, we are; it is thus we die, when they die. Regrets for not having had him here. He made his farewell intentionally at the [Apostles'] dinner in June: spoke of death & not minding it. I never knew him well but had the common feeling that I have with those trusty Cambridge fellows; & was pleased, of course, by what he wrote of The Waves; & so came nearer. I get the strangest feeling now of our all being in the midst of some vast operation: of the splendour of this undertaking—life: of being capable of dying: an immensity surrounds us. No—I cant get it—shall let it brood itself into 'a novel', no doubt. (Its thus I get the conception from which the book condenses). At night L. & I talked of death again the second time this year: we may be like worms crushed by a motor car: what does the worm know of the car—how it is made? There may be a reason; if so not one we, as human beings, can grasp. Goldie had some mystic belief.

And now we have been to Lewes races & seen the fat lady in black with parts of her person spilling over the shooting seat on which her bulk is so insecurely poised: seen the riff raff of sporting society all lined up in their cars with the dickies bulging with picnic baskets: heard the bark of bookies; & seen for a second the pounding straining horses with red faced jockeys lashing them pound by. What a noise they made—what a sense of muscle hard & stretched—& beyond the downs this windy sunny day looked wild & remote; & I could rethink them into uncultivated land again.

So people will go on dying until we die, Leonard said. Lytton, Carrington, Goldie—all last August to be spoken to—or let go, alas, because of the many times one would see them. That is one of my results: not to let friends lapse. But what can one do? One has to follow ones bent—mine often to be moody, irritable, longing for solitude. I will try to write to Helen: to ask Saxon down. These are the little efforts I make against death

—& am at the same time, annoyed that my clean dress hasn't come, & that I've re-arranged the drawing room to L.'s liking to my disliking.

Wednesday 17 August

Now I think I have corrected the CR till I can correct no longer. And I have a few minutes holiday, before I need take the proofs in to L. Shall I then describe how I fainted again?—That is the galloping horses got wild in my head last Thursday night as I sat on the terrace with L. How cool it is after the heat! I said. We were watching the downs draw back into fine darkness after they had burnt like solid emerald all day. Now that was being softly finely veiled. And the white owl was crossing to fetch mice from the marsh. Then my heart leapt; & stopped; & leapt again; & I tasted that queer bitterness at the back of my throat; & the pulse leapt into my head & beat & beat, more savagely, more quickly. I am going to faint I said & slipped off my chair & lay on the grass. Oh no I was not unconscious. I was alive; but possessed with this struggling team in my head: galloping, pounding. I thought something will burst in my brain if this goes on. Slowly it muffled itself. I pulled myself up, & staggered, with what infinite difficulty & alarm, now truly fainting & seeing the garden painfully lengthened & distorted, back back back—how long it seemed—could I drag myself?—to the house; & gained my room & fell on my bed. Then pain, as of childbirth; & then that too slowly faded; & I lay presiding, like a flickering light, like a most solicitous mother, over the shattered splintered fragments of my body. A very acute & unpleasant experience.

Saturday 20 August

A curious day in London yesterday. I said to myself standing at L.'s window, 'Look at the present moment because its not been so hot for 21 years.' There was a hot wind, as if one passed over a kitchen, going from the studio to the Press. Outside girls & young men lying in white on the Square grass. So hot we couldn't sit in the dining room. L. fetched & carried & hardly let me walk upstairs carrying my own body. Coming back we had the car shut & the windscreen open—thus sat in a hot rough gale, which, as we came to the lanes & woods became deliciously cold & green. The coolest place is the front seat of a car going at 40 or 50 miles with the windscreen open. Today, at 12.30 a wind rose: clouds descended; now at 3.45 its almost a normal warm summer day. For 10 days this heat has lasted. After my faint my head soon throbs: or so I think. I think, a little, of dying suddenly. & reflect well then go about eating & drinking & laughing & feeding the fish. Odd—the silliness one attributes to death—the desire one has to belittle it, & be found as Montaigne said, laughing with girls & good fellows. And L. is staking out the dewpond; & I am going in to be photographed.

Three more books appearing on Mrs Woolf; which reminds me to make a note, some time, on my work.[1]

Between 20 August and 2 September the Woolfs paid a number of visits by car—to Charleston, to Tilton, to Lewes Races, to the Adrian Stephens at Thorpe-le-Soken, calling in at 52 Tavistock Square on the return journey. The following lists are written on the verso of p. 92, facing p. 93 of the ms. diary on which the entry for 20 August and the beginning of that for 2 September is written:

Reading this August:[2]	People this August
Souvenirs de Tocqueville	Nessa. Julian
Any number of biographies—	Clive. F. Marshall
Coleridge—one or two poems.	Maynard Lydia
Lord Kilbracken memoirs.	Sheppard. Roger.
Shaw Pen portraits.	Alice Ritchie (to stay)
Ainslie memoirs.	Tom & Vivienne.
Vita's novel	Adrian & Karin
MSS.(Livingstones)	Judith
Nothing much good—	Nicolsons.
except de T:	

Coleridges letters; but failed to finish the 2nd vol.

Friday 2 September

After this the wind blew & released all the prisoners—so I thought, walking on the down above Lewes in the sudden slaty chill. But thats long past; & it is a sea fret today, as we had meant to go to Canterbury. As we had meant—but whats the good of meaning when at any moment

1. Two of these books never appeared: see *V VW Letters*, no. 2622 of 16 August 1932 to Harmon H. Goldstone, an American, concerning his proposed book, and in which VW mentions that the novelist Dorothy Richardson 'is engaged upon a study of my works'; the third book, Winifred Holtby's, was published in October 1932.
2. The *Souvenirs* of the French political historian Alexis de Tocqueville (1805-59) were first published in 1893; Lord Kilbracken (1847-1932), who as Sir Arthur Godley was Permanent under-Secretary of State for India from 1883-1909, published his *Reminiscences* in 1931; Bernard Shaw, *Pen Portraits and Reviews*, 1931; Ainslie Memoirs: *Adventures Social and Literary* (1922) by Douglas Ainslie (1865-1945), diplomat and man of letters; *Livingstones. A Novel of Contemporary Life* by Derrick Leon was published by the Hogarth Press in February 1933 (*HP Checklist* 323).

there's a tap—behold Tom & Vivienne [Eliot]: we cant buy our fish for dinner. But it was a friendly thought,—she wild as Ophelia—alas no Hamlet would love her, with her powdered spots—in white satin, L. said; Tom, poor man, all battened down as usual, prim, grey, making his kind jokes with her. "Oh but why didn't they tell me Adrian Stephen was your brother. Why? Why! Nobody mentioned it. They kept it from me." Then her chops & changes. Where is my bag? Where—where—then a sudden amorous embrace for me—& so on: trailing about the garden—never settling—seizing the wheel of their car—suddenly telling Tom to drive—all of which he bears with great patience: feeling perhaps that his 7 months of freedom draw near.[1] In the middle of their tea the post came with an astonishing letter from John to say that he does not intend to carry out our agreement. He has left the press. L. says he will send no answer. What could one say indeed? What a blessing! That egotistical young man with all his jealousies & vanities & ambitions, his weakness & changeableness is no loss. But we—or L. has lost an infinity of time. I suppose the severity with wh. L. was speaking to him on Friday when I came in to say Teas ready upset his trembling apple cart: his vanity could no longer endure: so he threw up the sponge, but I must say with the least possible good manners or consideration. On the whole though what a mercy. Now I can roam about the basement unperturbed. And, coming from him, with this crashing folly, one can take the line of least resistance—needn't attempt the amicable go between—needn't ask him to dinner.[2]

A happy lively summer this—& I enjoy my freak of writing Flush—& think it a good idea—this easy indolent writing once in a way—to let my brain cool; & here I am, asked to write about 'my father' in the Times. No.[3] So to give old Mrs Grey her basket of plums. The Common Reader went off on Monday last.

Friday 16 September

I'm in such a tremor that I've botched the last—penultimate chapter of Flush—is it worth writing that book—& can scarcely sit still, & must therefore scribble here, making myself form my letters, because—oh

1. Eliot had been invited to give the Charles Eliot Norton lectures on Poetry at Harvard; he sailed for America in October and did not return to England until the end of June 1933.
2. The 'revised basis' of John Lehmann's position in the Hogarth Press agreed in June (see above, 18 June 1932), was to have come into force on 31 August on the termination of his original agreement. 'In the end, & at the last moment, I made up my mind to go . . .' (*Thrown to the Woolfs*, p. 37).
3. VW changed her mind: 'Leslie Stephen, the Philosopher at Home: a Daughter's Memories' (Kp C335) was published in *The Times* on 28 November 1932, the centenary of his birth.

ridiculous crumpled petal—Wishart is publishing L.'s snap shot of me instead of the Lenare photograph & I feel that my privacy is invaded; my legs show; & I am revealed to the world (1,000 at most) as a plain dowdy old woman.[4] How odd! I never gave the matter a thought till this morning. I sent the photographs off with some compunction at being too late. Now I'm all of a quiver—cant read or write; & can, rightly, expect little sympathy from L. What an ill joined web of nerves—to be kind— my being is! A touch makes the whole thing quiver. What can it matter? The complex is: privacy invaded, ugliness revealed—oh & that I was trapped into it by Wishart. Lord! One of the contributory causes is the auctioneers catalogue of the Rodmell sale. My ivy blooming walk is to be sold for building (the bees on the ivy bloom—quoted one afternoon by Tom). A road is to be made from Deans to the down path.[5] All is to be houses inside. Shall we try to buy? Is it worth saving one crumb when all is threatened? Yet on my walk—too long—I was tired—& leapt in my bed dreaming that Angelica was dead—what a dream—how vivid—on my walk I almost felt my mind glow like hot iron—so complete & holy was the old habitual beauty of England: the silver sheep clustering; & the downs soaring, like birds wings sweeping up & up—I said [to] myself that beauty had become almost entirely satisfactory (oh my legs in the snapshot). I mean, I can fasten on a beautiful day, as a bee fixes itself on a sunflower. It feeds me, rests me, satisfies me, as nothing else does—(well thats not quite true: when Nessa, Duncan & the children come I brim equally; but with a thinner, more exciting ardour—I think a better heat[?] & rapture—but not this.) This has a holiness. This will go on after I'm dead.

A very good summer, this, for all my shying & jibbing, my tremors this morning. Beautifully quiet, airy, powerful. I believe I want this more humane existence for my next—to spread carelessly among one's friends —to feel the width & amusement of *human* life: not to strain to make a pattern just yet: to be made supple, & to let the juice of usual things, talk, character, seep through me, quietly, involuntarily before I say—Stop, & take out my pen. Yes, my thighs now begin to run smooth: no longer is every nerve upright.

Yesterday we took plums to old Mrs Grey. She is shrunk, & sits on a hard chair in the corner, the door open. She twitches & trembles. Has the wild expressionless stare of the old. L. liked her despair: I crawls up to

---

4. LW's snapshot, which was reproduced (*sans* legs) as the frontispiece of Winifred Holtby's study of VW published by Wishart, also forms the frontispiece of volume II of Quentin Bell's biography (1972); the preferred Lenare photograph is reproduced opposite p. 106 of *IV VW Letters*.
5. 'The yellow bees in the ivy-bloom': Shelley, *Prometheus Unbound*, I, 737. Deans— the blacksmith's at the Rodmell cross-roads.

bed hoping for the day; & I crawls down hoping for the night. "I'm an ignorant old woman—cant write or read. But I prays to God every night to take me—oh to go to my rest. Nobody can say what pains I suffer. Feel my shoulder" & she began shuffling with a safety pin. I felt it. "Hard as iron—full of water—& my legs too"—She pulled down her stocking. The dropsy. "I'm ninety two; & all my brothers & sisters are dead; my daughters dead; my husband is dead . . ." She repeated her misery, her list of ills, over & over; could see nothing else; could only begin all over again; & kissed my hand, thanking us for our pound. This is what we make of our lives—no reading or writing—keep her alive with parish doctors when she wishes to die—Human ingenuity in torture is very great.[6]

Between the last entry and their return to Tavistock Square on 1 October, the Woolfs had William Plomer and Charles Siepmann, who had succeeded Hilda Matheson as Director of Talks, BBC, to stay, and drove with them to Sissinghurst to see a performance of The Land; *they entertained Angus Davidson, Ethel Smyth, and the Keyneses; and hobnobbed with the Charlestonians.*

Sunday 2 October

London

Yes. I will allow myself a new nib. Odd how coming back here upsets my writing mood. Odder still how possessed I am with the feeling that now, aged 50, I'm just poised to shoot forth quite free straight & undeflected my bolts whatever they are. Therefore all this flitter flutter of weekly newspapers interests me not at all. These are the soul's changes. I dont believe in ageing. I believe in forever altering one's aspect to the sun. Hence my optimism. And to alter now, cleanly & sanely, I want to shuffle off this loose living randomness: people; reviews; fame; all the glittering scales; & be withdrawn; & concentrated. So I shant run about, just yet, buying clothes, seeing people. We are off to Leicester tomorrow, to the Labour party conference.[1] Then back to the fever of publishing. My C.R. doesnt cause me a single tremor. Nor Holtby's book. I'm interested in watching what goes on for the moment without wishing to take part—a good frame of mind, when one's conscious of power. Then I am backed now by the downs: the country: how happy L. & I are at Rodmell: what a free life that is—sweeping 30 or 40 miles; coming in

6. Cf. 'Old Mrs Grey' in *The Death of the Moth* (Kp A27).
1. The Woolfs travelled to Leicester by train on the afternoon of 3 October to attend the Annual Conference of the Labour Party, held at the de Montfort Hall, 3-7 October; they returned to London on 5 October.

when & how we like; sleeping in the empty house; dealing triumphantly with interruptions; & diving daily into that divine loveliness—always some walk: & the gulls on the purple plough; or going over to Tarring Neville—these are the flights I most love now—in the wide, the indifferent air. No being jerked, teased, tugged. And people come easily, flowering into intimacy in my room. But this is the past, or future.

I am also reading DHL. with the usual sense of frustration.[2] Not that he & I have too much in common—the same pressure to be ourselves: so that I dont escape when I read him; am surfeited; what I want is to be made free of another world. This Proust does. To me Lawrence is airless, confined: I dont want this, I go on saying. And the repetition of one idea. I dont want that either. I dont want 'a philosophy' in the least; I dont believe in other people's reading of riddles. What I enjoy (in the Letters) is the sudden visualisation: the great ghost springing over the wave (of the spray in Cornwall) but I get no satisfaction from his explanations of what he sees. And then its harrowing: this panting effort after something; & 'I have £6.10 left' & then Government hoofing him out, like a toad; & banning his book; the brutality of civilised society to this panting agonised man: & how futile it was. All this makes a sort of gasping in his letters. And none of it seems essential. So he pants & jerks. Then too I dont like strumming with two fingers—& the arrogance. After all English has one million words: why confine yourself to 6? & praise yourself for so doing. But its the preaching that rasps me. Like a person delivering judgment when only half the facts are there; & clinging to the rails & beating the cushion. Come out & see whats up here—I want to say. I mean its so barren; so easy; giving advice on a system. The moral is, if you want to help, never systematise—not till you're 70: & have been supple & sympathetic & creative & tried out all your nerves & scopes. He died though at 45. And why does Aldous say he was an 'artist'? Art is being rid of all preaching: things in themselves: the sentence in itself beautiful: multitudinous seas; daffodils that come before the swallow dares:[3] whereas L[awrence]. would only say what proved something. I havent read him of course. But in the Letters he cant listen beyond a point; must give advice; get you in to the system too. Hence his attraction for those who want to be fitted; which I dont: indeed I think it a blasphemy this fitting of Carswells into a Lawrence system. So much more reverent to leave them alone: nothing else to reverence except the Carswellism of

2. *The Letters of D. H. Lawrence*, edited and with a long introduction by Aldous Huxley, was published in September 1932.
3. '. . . This my hand will rather/The multitudinous seas incarnadine,/Making the green one red.' *Macbeth* II ii 61;
  '. . . daffodils,/That come before the swallow dares, and take/The winds of March with beauty.' *The Winter's Tale* IV iii 116.

Carswell.[4] Hence his minds schoolboy tweaking & smacking of anyone offered to him: Lytton, Bertie,—Squire—all are suburban, unclean. His ruler coming down & measuring them. Why all this criticism of other people? Why not some system that includes the good? What a discovery that would be—a system that did not shut out.

Thursday 13 October

It was an odd sight—Desmond with Rachel on his arm.[5] Everybody stood up. The white & red procession with the cross in front went ahead. Then very small, smooth, pale & sleek appeared Rachel & Desmond arm in arm. I have never seen him as a father. Now he was that—gentle, kind—leading his daughter. She was a wax work—with her diamond cross; very pale; very small; carrying a white book. Oh but the inadequacy of the service—the sense of its being the entirely obsolete & primitive voice of a defunct tribal magnate, laying down laws for the government of the tribe: & then these civilised sceptical people letting themselves pretend that they obey. That clogged & diluted all the real feeling. And David's high collar & tails: & their sober, decorous backs kneeling there: & the respectability & the wavering watery music: the perpetual compromise. I sat with Hope. Opposite were the sort of women one sees in Oxford St. at midday. (11.30). The bridegrooms side was notably better tailored & more distinguished than ours—where, as I imagine, all the Ritchies & so on had come, saying well, I'm a first cousin so I needn't buy new gloves. Molly was much as a pouter pigeon in some maroon dress with a yellow bunch.[6] The ceremony went decorously forward in that grey brown church. Now & then one heard a shout from the market. No I dont like the ceremony. They hauled a dilapidated bishop up by the armpits to give the blessing which he did in a trembling overemphatic

4. Catherine Roxburgh Carswell, *née* Macfarlane *quo* Jackson (1879-1946), writer, was an ardent friend and disciple of Lawrence whom she first met in 1914; her book *The Savage Pilgrimage: A Narrative of D. H. Lawrence*, published in the Spring, had been withdrawn because of threats from Murry, and a slightly revised version was issued by a different publisher later in 1932.

5. The marriage of Rachel MacCarthy, only daughter of Desmond and Mary (Molly) MacCarthy, and Lord David Cecil, younger son of the Marquess and Marchioness of Salisbury, was solemnized on the morning of 13 October at the church of St Bartholomew the Great, Smithfield; the Archdeacon of St Albans, assisted by Bishop Talbot and Canon Savage, officiated.

6. For Molly (Mrs Desmond MacCarthy) see Appendix. Both Rachel, through her mother, and VW were related to the ubiquitous Ritchie family. LW did not go to the wedding; VW sat with Hope Mirrlees (1887-1978), writer, whom she had known since the end of the war, and whose poem *Paris* was among the first productions of the fledgling Hogarth Press (*HP Checklist* 5).

voice, as if he were scrubbing the heads of David & Rachel as he called them. Then a sort of inner play went forward behind glass doors. One saw Salisburys & MacCs signing books. Then a dribble back of relatives. Then the Wagner wedding march. Then David & Rachel arm in arm sleep walking down the aisle preceded by a cross which ushered them into a car & so into a happy long life, I make no doubt—but thats not the ceremony I like—oh no not at all. And following in the wake of the sleep walkers came the Salisburys & the MacCarthys arm in arm: dwindling into Dermod & a wizened old lady—presumably old Mrs M. [*Rachel's brother and grandmother.*] "Theyre hideously plain" Hope kept saying—indeed green grey light at midday off old stone is not genial—oh & I wanted some rapture—some precious stone to hold. None. None. Only endless small observations—Hubert C[ornish, *Rachel's uncle*]. carrying two umbrellas—Ralph & Frances in grey tweeds—late—taking prominent places. Lady Oxford, Lady Hartington, Ly Colefax, Maurice Baring & so on. A queer little dolls face, Rachel's, to harbour a passion, to bear children. And I got washed up against the Bishop going out, & heard him apologise to the cleric. But it is an honour to support a Bishop, said that man. And then they began talking about so & so, Colonel of the Scotts guards, & so to the episcopal motor car, which was holding up the meat salesmen—with its gold cross. And now Desmond is stretched out by the fire in slippers, preparing his BBC talk I daresay: & Rachel & David are—shall we say—in a first class reserved carriage going to Sherborne: & he is putting the rug straight over her knees; & she is looking at the fields, thinking Why has the whole world been given me: then they have tea: I should think he will be shy tonight.

Today the CR is out & I havent give it a thought, being entirely absorbed in my Essay, which I began yesterday.[7] The last 3 or four days I've done parcels in a daze: Belsher ill; 6,000 Family History [by V. Sackville-West] to be despatched: a great bundle of orders found last night hidden in a drawer.

But I still see the two doll figures kneeling—for all the world like a picture—what do I mean? I'm too sleepy to say. And now for Spender.[8]

---

7. See Mitchell A. Leaska's introduction to *The Pargiters by Virginia Woolf. The Novel-Essay Portion of The Years* (1978). 'On 11 October Virginia Woolf, with an almost fresh manuscript volume before her, dipped her pen and wrote: "THE PARGITERS: An Essay based upon a paper read to the London/National Society for Women's Service".'

8. Stephen Spender (b. 1909), poet, had been included in the anthology *New Signatures/Poems by Several Hands* published by the Hogarth Press in February, and in 1931 submitted a novel which VW advised him to scrap. He was invited to dine on 11 October (*V VW Letters*, no. 1642) but presumably came to tea (on 13 October) instead.

Wednesday 2 November

He [Stephen Spender] is a rattle headed bolt eyed young man, raw
boned, loose jointed who thinks himself the greatest poet of all time. I
daresay he is—it's not a subject that interests me enormously at the
moment. What does? My own writing of course. I've just polished up the
L[eslie].S[tephen]. for the Times—a good one, I think, considering the
currents that sway round that subject in the Times of all papers. And I
have entirely remodelled my 'Essay'. Its to be an Essay-Novel, called the
Pargiters—& its to take in everything, sex, education, life &c; & come,
with the most powerful & agile leaps, like a chamois across precipices
from 1880 to here & now—Thats the notion anyhow, & I have been in
such a haze & dream & intoxication, declaiming phrases, seeing scenes,
as I walk up Southampton Row that I can hardly say I have been alive at
all, since the 10th Oct. Everything is running of its own accord into the
stream, as with Orlando. What has happened of course is that after
abstaining from the novel of fact all these years—since 1919—& N[ight].
& D[ay]. indeed, I find myself infinitely delighting in facts for a change, &
in possession of quantitities beyond counting: though I feel now & then
the tug to vision, but resist it. This is the true line, I am sure, after The
Waves—The Pargiters—this is what leads naturally on to the next stage
—the essay-novel. Then of course being so excited, so incandescent, I
must needs fire up about Priestley & his priestliness, & write an essay,
wh. L. very rightly advised against sending to the N. Statesman. So I
have cellared it, against a rainy day, when I shall re-write it as an essay—
Middlebrow.[1] And then all this incandescence led to the galloping horses
in my heart the night before last. I lay in bed reasoning that I could not
come smash. Death I defy you, &c. But it was a terrific effort, holding on
to the reins. So at 2.30 I woke L. & asked, very reasonably, for ice, which
he got me. And my horses calmed down—he was so sensible. And I slept
after a time, but Elly [Rendel] came yesterday & says I am putting a
strain on my heart, which of course gives out, at the Ivy, or in the garden,
though there's nothing wrong; so I take this as permission not to go to
parties, like Mary's at Sadlers Wells, not to do anything I dislike. And
thats a great discovery. I think I shall have thus a very reasonable happy
winter, writing The Pargiters, but for Gods sake, I must be careful, & go

1. The first of a series of BBC talks called 'To an unnamed Listener' was given on
10 October by J. B. Priestley and addressed 'To a Highbrow'; the second, a fortnight later: 'To a Lowbrow', was by Harold Nicolson. In the *NS&N* of 29 October
'Critic' praised the latter 'who took up the cudgels against Mr Priestley and gave
the low-brow a tremendous doing-down.' VW's essay, in the form of a letter
addressed to the Editor of the *NS&N* acknowledging the favourable review of her
second *Common Reader* on 15 October, was not sent, but was published as 'Middlebrow' in the posthumous collection *The Death of the Moth* in 1942 (Kp A27).

quietly, & order my litter of excitements—people like Logan & Eddy who torment me with their vanity; I must brood & chew & dream, & be entirely natural, feeling as I do for the first time that this book is important. Why do I feel this, & I never felt it in the least about the others? I have joined Pippa's Society; we dined with Pippa [on 27 October] & she told us stories about cows & chimney pots.

Thursday 10 November

I am taking a morning off, having done the child scene—the man exposing himself—in the Pargiters: to polish my LS. (done) & then to write letters. Theres Ott's memoir—a queer thing that Ott shd. come, after all these years, old shabby tender to my sofa; & I liked her; its her integrity thats sloppy; thats what we all slipped on. Cant tell the truth about love—but then thats so interesting, & not discreditable, considering her upbringing—Welbeck, the young men servants. So she lent me her memoirs, full as they are of love letters, & copulation. I must now write to her—& to Margaret Ll.D. & so on. Janet Case comes to tea today, & then theres Derick Leon & Julia to dinner—[2] A long day for me, who must must must be quiet & spacious this autumn, to finish the P[argiter]s. How important I feel it!—well, this is the merest note . . And we've bought a Lanchester: to be delivered on Dec. 10th. Grey & green. I dont think we've ever been so happy, what with one thing & another. And so intimate, & so completely entire, I mean L. & I. If it could only last like this another 50 years—life like this is wholly satisfactory. to me anyhow. So to my letters.

[Undated]

Yes it was a long day & I had two days of jump jump afterwards; but owing to the caution of the cat on broken glass, I am now steadier. I was

2. Lady Ottoline Morrell's memoirs, which VW encouraged her to write, were published after her death in two volumes (1963, 1974) edited by Robert Gathorne-Hardy; she came to see VW after tea on 4 November. No letter of 10 November 1932 to Lady Ottoline survives; but see *V VW Letters*, no. 2664 for that to Margaret Llewelyn Davies (1861-1944), formerly General Secretary of the Women's Co-operative Guild and, like Janet Case, a very old friend—particularly of LW's. Derrick Leon (d. 1944) was the author of *Livingstones*, the ms of which VW read in August (see above, p. 122); he had a job in the furniture department of Fortnum & Mason's. After dinner William Plomer and Count Potocki de Montalk came in; the latter gave his version of the evening in 'Quack Quack', the first chapter of his *Social Climbers in Bloomsbury*, privately printed for his own *The Right Review* in 1939.

not 'on the sofa' yesterday; which has been my refuge after tea. And I've fought with Eddy; & with Logan; & L. is fighting with John; & we are the victors, I think, in all these fights: I'm rid of Eddy, have Logan to tea on his own terms; & John is in tears consulting his lawyer.[3] But oh, how I've written since Oct 11th! So much that my fingers cant write, of an evening: my brain spins scene after scene. Its only the signs of some fatigue, & depression that leave me ten minutes now before lunch for this starved book.

[? *Sunday 4 December*]

I must finish the first part—which is to be called 1880—in a day or two; & then freshen up: & read, for the next part—1880-1900.

On Wednesday we gave our party: notable for its peeresses, its chatter, its cocktails: Ott, Ly Oxford, the Gages—& so on. Us two hussies entertaining the peerage: & boys in white jackets handing blue green yellow drinks. And my money £100—lent them—did the trick. Rather a fertile way of spending money. though I may be landed with 4 great panels. My carpet, Duncan's, for the drawing room is come & down: & we have risen socially to the rank of the younger sons of baronets—it is like being real gentry, sitting with our feet embedded in pile.[1]

And then, on Friday, we went to Brixton to Sophie. Maud a stout matron. Sophy presiding like a born lady. "This is more of a party to me" she said; indeed it was—more than the cocktail one.[2]

Saturday 17 December

I have precisely 4 minutes before luncheon in which to record Rebecca West at dinner—oh yes a very clever woman, rather rubbed about the thorax: with a great supply of worldly talk: & much go & humour; a

3. VW had been provoked by Logan Pearsall Smith into engaging in a Bloomsbury v. Chelsea sparring match; see *V VW Letters*, nos. 2652, 2658, 2671, 2677, and his letters to her in MHP, Sussex (copies).
1. A 'Music Room' with furnishings, fabrics, and decorations by Duncan Grant and Vanessa Bell was installed at the Lefevre Gallery, Bruton Street, and on 30 November Vanessa and VW gave a Private View party there; this was financed by an advance from VW who thereby acquired a carpet and an embroidery-framed mirror designed by Duncan Grant, and a threefold screen with life-size female figures by Vanessa. See *Shone*, pp. 237-42.
2. Maud was housemaid and Sophie Farrell cook-housekeeper at 38 Brunswick Square—the household that VW shared with her brother Adrian, Maynard Keynes, and LW before her marriage.

silky careening society voice; flowers from her afterwards to apologise for staying till 1.30.[3]

And Logan—lord, what a bore: a dogmatic cultivated American bore; no truth in him; but an uneasy worm squirming for compliments. This I could see through his shallow water; & was 'very severe' L. says (L. is always a judge of my severity: & I of his) but I cant keep my temper when people thrust. Its not playing the game. And then—oh ever so many people; & a wind up with L.'s family & then the Frys to dinner: & we're cheated of the car for Christmas, God damn their souls: all this is very helter skelter: & dinner with Hope last night: her stuffed black dachshund sausage stretched along my knee; & so to Rodmell on Tuesday. I've almost written out my first fury—234 typewritten pages since Oct 10th—& shall put my brain to rest for a few days at Monks House. But the fun of the book is to come, with Magdalena & Elvira.[4]

[Monday 19 December]

Yes, today, Dec. 19th, Monday, I have written myself to the verge of total extinction. Praised be I can stop & wallow in coolness & downs, & let the wheels of my mind—how I beg them to do this—cool & slow & stop altogether. I shall take up Flush again to cool myself. By Heaven, I have written 60,320 words since Oct. 11th. I think this must be far the quickest going of any of my books: comes far ahead of Orlando or The Lighthouse. But then those 60 thousand will have to be sweated & dried into 30 or 40 thousand—a great grind to come. Never mind. I have secured the outline & fixed a shape for the rest. I feel, for the first time, No I mustn't take risks crossing the road, till the book is done. And though to me it is so important, I receive, at Clive's—at George, Ring the Bell & Run Away's—the first of the little pricks which will be so lavishly provided when The Pargiters comes out.[5] Oh but by then I shall have perfected my social technique. I am practising with Eddy, & intend to make further experiments, when opportunity serves, with Logan. Yes,

3. Rebecca West (b. 1892), novelist, political journalist and literary critic, dined with the Woolfs on 13 December. Her husband, Henry Maxwell Andrews (1894-1968), a merchant banker, did not come with her. The phrase 'rubbed about the thorax'— suggesting a somewhat shiny, shabby appearance—is derived from VW's early activities as a 'bug-hunter' or lepidopterist. Logan Pearsall Smith came to tea on 15 December.
4. In the published version of *The Years* (1937), Magdalena (Maggie) Pargiter's sister became Sara (Sally) instead of Elvira.
5. The Woolfs gave dinner to Roger Fry and Helen Anrep on Sunday 18 December, after which they all went round to Clive Bell's, where they found Vanessa, Frankie Birrell and Raymond Mortimer. See VW's definition (*Three Guineas*, p. 311, n. 11): "'A-ring-the-bell-and-run-away-man.'" This word has been coined in order to

I will be free & entire & absolute & mistress of my life by Oct. 1st 1933. Nobody shall come here on their terms; or hale me off to them on theirs. Oh & I shall write a poets book next. This one, however, releases such a torrent of fact as I did not know I had in me. I must have been observing & collecting these 20 years—since Jacob's Room anyhow. Such a wealth of things seen present themselves that I cant choose even—hence 60,000 words all about one paragraph. What I must do is to keep control; & not be too sarcastic; & keep the right degree of freedom & reserve. But oh how easy this writing is compared with The Waves! I wonder what the degree of carat gold is in the 2 books. Of course this is external: but there's a good deal of gold—more than I'd thought—in externality. Anyhow, what care I for my goose feather bed? I'm off to join the raggle taggle gipsies oh! The Gipsies, I say: not Hugh Walpole & Priestley—no.

In truth The Pargiters is first cousin to Orlando, though the cousin in the flesh: Orlando taught me the trick of it. Now—oh but I must stop for 10 days at least—no 14—if not 21 days—now I must compose 1880-1900 chapter which needs skill. But I like applying skill I own. L. is off to the Lanchester's in a rage.[6] I am going to polish off my jobs: & tomorrow we go.

A very fruitful varied & I think successful autumn—thanks partly to my tired heart: so I could impose terms: & I have never lived in such a race, such a dream, such a violent impulsion & compulsion—scarcely seeing anything but the Pargiters.

The Woolfs drove to Rodmell for Christmas on 20 December. The following entry (23 December) has been inserted, and the subsequent one (31 December) written, in a fresh book, DIARY XXII, *prepared for 1933.*

Friday 23 December

This is not the first day of the new year; but the discrepancy may be forgiven. I must write off my dejected rambling misery—having just read over the 30,000 words of Flush & come to the conclusion that they won't do. Oh what a waste—what a bore! Four months of work, & heaven knows how much reading—not of an exalted kind either—& I cant see

---

define those who make use of words with the desire to hurt but at the same time to escape detection.'—derived from the nursery rhyme:

> 'Georgie Porgie, pudding and pie
> Kissed the girls and made them cry;
> When the boys came out to play,
> Georgie Porgie ran away.'

6. LW ordered a new Lanchester car on 3 November; through (nowadays familiar) prevarications and delays he did not finally get it until 14 January 1933.

how to make anything of it. Its not the right subject for that length: its too slight & too serious. Much good in it but would have to be much better. So here I am two days before Christmas, pitched into one of my grey welters. True, its partly over writing The Pargiters. But I cant get back into Flush, ever, I feel: & L. will be disappointed; & the money loss too—thats a bore. I took it up impetuously after The Waves by way of a change: no forethought in me; & so got landed: it would need a months hard work—& even then I doubt it. In that time I might have done Dryden & Pope. And I'm thus led to begin—no to end the year with a doleful plaint. It is blazing hot; like spring, with the bees on the flowers. Never mind; this is not a reverse of the first order—not at all.

Saturday 31 December

This is in fact the last day of 1932, but I am so tired of polishing off Flush—such a pressure on the brain is caused by doing ten pages daily— that I am taking a morning off, & shall use it here, in my lazy way, to sum up the whole of life. By that phrase, one of my colloquialities, I only mean, I wish I could deliver myself of a picture of all my friends, thoughts, doings, projects at this moment. Vita is on the high seas, sailing to America. Our new car came, vicariously, yesterday—we are lent one. And I had a long letter from Ottoline, of sheer affection, & one still longer from Ethel Smyth, of dubious jealousy & supressed temper & love strangled & out bursting. And Anrep wants to put me on the floor of the Bank of England as Clio, &—cards, thanks, catalogues of winter sales.[7] On Monday we go up to Angelica's party. On Tuesday we come back. And we shall be here till the 14th of Jan. And Miss Scott Johnson doesn't do. And we are us usual needing manuscripts; the dew pond is filling; the gold fish are dead; it is a clear pale blue eyed winters day; &—&—&— my thoughts turn with excitement to The Pargiters, for I long to feel my sails blow out, & to be careering with Elvira, Maggie & the rest over the whole of human life.

And indeed I cannot sum this up, being tired in my head. I think of Lytton too. Yes, of course this autumn has been a tremendous revelation. You will understand that all impediments suddenly dropped off. It was a great season of liberation. Everything appeared very distinct, amazingly

7. Vita and Harold Nicolson sailed from Southampton on 30 December for a lecture-tour of America which lasted until April. Ottoline Morrell's letter, dated 28 December, is in MHP, Sussex; Ethel Smyth's, of 30 December, is in the Berg: '. . . Its well I do love [Vita] as otherwise what you . . . write about being bereft of her till April would make me jealous. No—it wouldn't.' Boris Anrep 'put' VW on the floor of the National Gallery (where she is represented as Clio in the 'Awakening of the Muses' on one of the vestibule landings); he was concurrently executing mosaic decorations for the new Bank of England building.

exciting. I had no restrictions whatever, & was thus free to define my attitude with a vigour & certainty I have never known before. I laid about me & cut down the nettles. I said I will no longer be fettered by any artificial tie. I therefore spoke out in my own voice to Eddy & tried to ⟨subdue⟩ circumscribe Logan. Well—it is always doubtful how far one human being can be free. The ties are not purely artificial. One cannot cut a way absolutely straight. However, I secured a season of intoxicating exhilaration. Nor do I intend to let myself pay for it with the usual black despair. I intend to circumvent that supervening ghost—that which always trails its damp wings behind my glories. I shall be very wary, very adept—as now—writing languidly to avoid a headache. To suppress one self & run freely out in joy, or laughter with impersonal joys & laughters —such is the perfectly infallible & simple prescription.

For example, with Julian & Lettice Ramsay last night—why not simply become fluid in their lives, if my own is dim? And to use ones hands & eyes; to talk to people; to be a straw on the river, now & then— passive, not striving to say this is this. If one does not lie back & sum up & say to the moment, this very moment, stay you are so fair, what will be one's gain, dying? No: stay, this moment. No one ever says that enough. Always hurry. I am now going in, to see L. & say stay this moment.[8]

8. 'Verweile doch! du bist so schön!' (Goethe, *Faust*).

135

1933

1933

The Woolfs drove to London on the afternoon of 2 January to go to Angelica's fancy-dress fourteenth birthday party in Vanessa's Fitzroy Street studio, and returned next day to Rodmell. VW having left her new diary in the country made the following entry in her last year's book, DIARY XXI.

Tuesday 3 January

This is a little out of place, but then so am I. We are up for Angelica's party last night, & I have half an hour to spend before shooting in the new Lanchester (not ours—one lent) back to Rodmell. We have been there just short of one fortnight, & I ate myself into the heart of print & solitude—so as to adumbrate a headache. And to wipe off the intensity of concentration—trying to re-write that abominable dog Flush in 13 days, so as to be free—oh heavenly freedom—to write The Pargiters,—I insisted upon a night of chatter. Let me see.

I fell into the arms of Nan [Hudson] & Ethel [Sands]—the two discreet ladies. Nan had a banana brown mask; Ethel the head of a Parisian cocotte. I like masks. I like the disorientation they give my feelings (here I lapsed for 5 minutes into Elvira's thoughts about civilisation—indeed, its a good discipline, this new one, of forcing one's brain the other way for a time— see how vigorously it spurts back—) Then I was settled with Nan; & she poor woman, tried to conciliate the powers which were then in the ascendant & said she "infinitely preferred this to the Beau Monde. Oh how much hungrier I am for this meal than for my own dinner! Yes, Virginia, I'm a bohemian at heart. I have just slipped into the other. There is a certain charm in it. But our Butler is the most Bohemian of all.[1] And then dear Ethel—" Now stop, I said, you're going to celebrate the perfections of Ethel. I cant allow that. For I assure you, Ethel's humanity is mere superficiality—"Oh my dear, I assure you you're wrong. She has a very subtle sense of society—I haven't. She gets things from Ldy Oxford for instance, that I dont. If she has a fault it is that she never sees anyones faults, which tends of course to make them—I mean, its a little lacking in salt, that is to me". While this ambling & pacing went on—I always whip myself up to say something entire I give myself that credit— but its often very silly & something I've said before—Ethel was sitting

1. Ethel and Nan's butler from 1925-34, Henry Lomas, was an exceptional character whose only fault as a servant was his occasional weakness for the bottle. (See Wendy Baron, *Miss Ethel Sands and her Circle* (1977), pp. 194-6.)

by us, on the models throne talking to Raymond. And we were eating ham & chicken & ices & rolls & paté sandwiches—& drinking wine—Nessa's commissariat was lavish & opportune—I daresay there were 60—or 40—people there. Wogan drifted up. We talked. I was very polite, because of John. He was very polite. Rosamund I thought a little chill—no, shy I daresay. Wogan said The Waves shd. be filmed: I in my vague way, said V. Isham wants to do it—but she meant to broadcast, & oddly enough, when I came home I found a letter from her saying so.[2] Then W[ogan]. talked about the autumnal Ottoline calling R[osamond]. to her upstairs & leaving him to hear Dryden read by Pipsey [Philip Morrell]: to walk in the garden & get advice about trees & pagodas. W. lives a little—but lives joyously, & I daresay wantonly—in the shadow of R. who, modest I think, is yet a best seller; an American success—a musical, rapt girl or woman: too easily content though with familiar melodies. Wogan wears well cut trousers—was a sporting man—& a red jersey to symbolise that he is now disowned by his father, a painter. R. later got into talk with L. about John; & was vague, grieved, apologetic, yet sisterly. Couldn't, I think, put up much defense. And dear old Marjorie performed. My word! she is now an elderly fat woman—grey as a badger, but so stout, so pendulous—so much an old fireside matron for all her witch ways—which are in truth obscene with her peculiar touch of genius in being blatantly obscene. She has few, black, crooked (so it seemed to me) teeth. She opens her mouth, grimaces, claws, paws, stumps, projects, hawks, pirouettes—should have been on the stage—a Marie Lloyd. And Cory, up for his Bohemian night & determined to be Bohemian as he signified by saying in a loud voice under the lee of Nan "My family call him the Arch-Bugger"—Cory was much taken by her, & stretching a long arm I pulled one strand of her hair, & introduced them.[3] She gets moth eaten, she says, in the country: seemed to feel it damp, clayey; is driven in on herself; reads too much; cant escape; has no one to rub up with—yet—Wogan said—is the life & soul of Leicester: plays games

2. Wogan Philipps (b. 1902), painter, eldest son of Sir Laurence Philipps, 1st Bt (later, 1939, 1st Baron Milford); in 1928 he had married John Lehmann's sister Rosamond; he joined the Communist Party, fought with the International Brigade in Spain, and succeeded his father as 2nd Baron in 1962. Virginia Isham (b. 1898), actress, was the only daughter of Sir Vere Isham and VW's cousin Millicent, née Vaughan. For VW's reply to her letter, see *V VW Letters*, no. 2690.

3. Marjorie Colville Strachey (1882-1964), nicknamed 'Gumbo', teacher; she was the youngest of Lytton's five sisters. Her party piece was a rendering of English nursery songs in a manner both funny and obscene. Marie Lloyd (1870-1922), music-hall entertainer (see *II VW Diary*, 8 April 1921). Lt.-Col. William Cory Heward Bell (1875-1964), Clive's elder brother, was Unionist MP for Devizes 1918-23, High Sheriff of Wiltshire 1932, and from 1931-46 was a county councillor; he lived at Pewsey in Wiltshire.

with the hunting set—according to him the most barbarous of all people. Children come down with blood on their foreheads for 3 days after a hunt: mustn't wash it off. Then there was Saxon bowing & smiling in silence like a Chinese mandarin—so I bowed & smiled in silence swaying off my throne to him. "We know each other so well, we smile now" I said, reflecting that I should ask him to dinner; but I doubt if he wants it.

(my 30 minutes is stretching.) L. is talking to Miss [Scott] Johnson, who won't do. And last night Belsher rang up to say her fur coat was stolen: might she borrow one from me: so up she came, & accused Miss Johnson's protegé an unemployed man who is allowed in; significant of the relations between Miss J. & B.—strained. The coat was worth £30, Miss B. said: too poor to buy another: & this morning she rings up to say she is ill, & so is all her family. What then about Porter? I wonder—that strapping American?[4] Oh the future of the Press—for the millionth time it is melting again.

I daresay this will be my last appearance in this book, because I think I have destroyed this pen, tired my hand, & nothing but thin water comes from my brain, having written so much, so quickly. It is 12.35 on Tuesday January 3rd 1933.

VW here continues her 1933 diary in the new book (DIARY XXII) *which she had broached at Rodmell on 31 December 1932.*

Thursday 5 January

I am so delighted with my own ingenuity in having after only ten years or so, made myself, in 5 minutes, a perfect writing board, with pen tray attached, so that I cant ever again fly into a fury bereft of ink & pen at the most critical moment of a writers life & see my sudden sentence dissipate itself all for lack of a pen handy—& besides I'm so glad to be quit of page 100 of Flush—this the third time of writing that Whitechapel scene, & I doubt if its worth it, that I cant help disporting myself on this free blue page, which thank God in heaven, needs no re-writing. It is a wet misty day: my windows out here are all fog. And I daresay we shall drive our new car, though it is still only a substitute, twenty miles or so this afternoon, by way of a test. It is like travelling first instead of third.

Bunny's new Pochantos is reviewed in the Lit. Sup. this morning, & I augur a great success, I think without any serious pangs of jealousy.[5] But

4. VW not only lent, but gave Peggy Belsher a moleskin coat of her own to replace the missing one. Louise Porter, an apparently affluent American, was an ardent admirer of VW's books who turned up at the Hogarth Press and eventually prevailed upon Miss Belsher to arrange for her to meet her idol.

5. *Pocahontas or The Nonpareil of Virginia* by David Garnett was praised in the *TLS*, 5 January 1933, as a 'lovely and true book'.

that of course, has yet to be proved. Jealousy may slink out its green paws, being the uncertain fabric I am. But I think not, if only because I'm in sublime reading fettle: seriously I believe that the strain of The Waves weakened my concentration for months—& then all that article compressing for the C.R. I am now at the height of my powers in that line, & have read, with close & powerful attention, some 12 or 15 books since I came here. What a joy—what a sense as of a Rolls Royce engine once more purring its 70 miles an hour in my brain: so that if Bunny's book is a good one, there will be another stretch of road ahead of me for a few days. What I hitherto have disliked in Bunny is the falsetto. Assuming a mask to speak through: out comes his own voice stylised, mincing, though well articulated & controlled. Lytton's saying "Ye old Cocke & Balls" of one of them sums up my meaning. I am also encouraged to read by the feeling that I am on the flood of creativeness in The Pargiters— what a liberation that gives one—as if everything added to that torrent— all books become fluid & swell the stream. But I daresay this is a sign only that I'm doing what is rather superficial & hasty & eager. I dont know. I've another week of Flush here, & then shall come to grips with my 20 years in one chapter problem. I visualise this book now as a curiously uneven time sequence—a series of great balloons, linked by straight narrow passages of narrative. I can take liberties with the representational form which I could not dare when I wrote Night & Day—a book that taught me much, bad though it may be. And now I must write to N. Darwin about her Jemmy Button. Hampson's new novel is so bad we are going to advise against publishing it.[6]

Sunday 15 January

I have come out here, our last morning, to write letters, so, naturally, I write this book. But then I haven't written a line these 3 weeks—only typed Flush, which, Heaven be praised, I 'finished', almost without inverted commas, yesterday. Ah but my writing Flush has been gradually shoved out, as by a cuckoo born in the nest, by The Pargiters. How odd

6. Nora Darwin (b. 1895) had married Alan Barlow in 1911; in 1933 she published an edition of her grandfather Charles Darwin's *Beagle* diary. Lady Barlow does not now (1980) recall why she and VW should have corresponded about 'her Jemmy Button'; Jemmy Button was one of the four native Fuegians brought to England in 1830 by Captain Fitzroy of *HMS Beagle* so that on being returned to Tierra del Fuego they might enlighten their compatriots in Christian morality and the use of tools. The Hogarth Press had published two novels by John Hampson (the pseudonym of John Simpson, 1901-55), *Saturday Night at the Greyhound* (1931) and *O Providence* (1932), *HP Checklist* 256 and 290; the novel VW now condemned was possibly revised and re-submitted later in the year (see below, 20 October 1933, n. 14).

the mind's functions are! About a week ago, I began the making up of scenes—unconsciously: saying phrases to myself; & so, for a week, I've sat here, staring at the typewriter, & speaking aloud phrases of The Pargiters. This becomes more & more maddening. It will however all be run off in a few days, when I let myself write again.

I am reading Parnell.[7] Yes; but this scene making increases the rate of my heart with uncomfortable rapidity. While I was forcing myself to do Flush my old headache came back—for the first time this autumn. Why should The P.s make my heart jump, why should Flush stiffen the back of my neck? What connection has the brain with the body? Nobody in Harley St could explain, yet the symptoms are purely physical & as distinct as one book is from the other.

Meanwhile, L.'s hired stock has given him some form of itch. He picks what he thinks black insects off his neck—I can imagine nothing more terrible than to have insects under ones skin—I should see them parading in squads. Now I will try to call in my mind from The P.s, & attach it to Mr Shaw Desmond, to Tom, to Holtby, to K. Furse; but not I think to E. Smyth.[8]

And I was forgetting to say that The Deluge [*Lanchester car*] came yesterday. It was expected at 1.15. At 3 Julian & Angelica arrived. at 4 as A. &. J. were going to the shop to buy sweets L. pruning, cried out its come. And it had gone. It swept up the village past us, but returned. In colour & shape it is beyond the wildest dreams—I mean it is elegant green silver beautifully compact modelled firm & not too rich—not a money car. We drove it to Lewes, & shall now take it to London; & so, I say, write letters. A cloudy, goose wing day with silver shields.

Thursday 19 January

It must be confessed that The Pargiters are like cuckoos in my nest—which should be Flush. I have only 50 pages to correct & send to Mabel [*typist*]; & these cursed scenes & dialogues will go on springing up in my head; & after correcting one page, I sit mooning for 20 minutes. I daresay this will increase the blood pressure when I come to write. But it is a tiresome bewildering distraction now.

Then we began London briskly with Leonard's lice—his incurable & disgusting skin disease. We went to a Wimpole Street specialist—happily

7. *The Life of Charles Stewart Parnell*, 2 vols (1898) by R. Barry O'Brien.
8. Of the letters VW intended to write this morning, only that to T. S. Eliot in America is known (*V VW Letters*, no. 2696); it threw light upon the source of LW's affliction: 'We went to a fancy dress party at Vanessa's, and [Leonard] had the temerity to dress up as an English gentleman of the old school in hired clothes... the itch was in the stock.' Shaw Desmond (1877-1960) was a prolific Irish writer.

his house was almost opposite Flush's so that I could count the storeys & verify the knockers—its true they have none, but the houses are very well pointed—while L. & Elly [Dr Rendel] were inside the consulting room. Finally the dr. said L. had never been bitten at all. And so, as the day wore on, the incurable disease was cured.[9]

Then came Plomer & Marjorie [Strachey] to dine; & we went to Sadler's Wells & saw Pomona with Nessa's designs[19]—dresses, scenery— all very pale & bright—I mean Fra Angelico against a background of Cassis—but dear (said to be from dieu) knows I cant keep my wits at the ballet; cant throw a ring round so many wild horses—music, dancing, decoration: & so hop on my perch, & merely make parrot noises of appreciation—when, at Fitzroy Street [*Vanessa's studio*], we all had hot sausages. Large dishes of hot, writhing sausages, looking indecent, like black snakes amorously intertwined, were handed round. There was Bunny, flushed with triumph (I sent back Pocahontas unread—cant read with my head stuffed with Pargiters) & I said I had dreamt I was in his arms, so he took me in his arms—pale phantom of old love—the love of men & women—in the pantry. Roger was there,—is he older, less volatile? He makes his signal to Helen sooner than of old & drives off in that blind bull of a car—it charges with its head down—but not before, as I maliciously observed, he had cross-questioned me about his lectures. This insistent egotism has its charm. I never ask him to read my essays.[11]

So home in the new car.

Saturday 21 January

Well, Flush lingers on & I cannot despatch him. Thats the sad truth. I always see something I could press tighter, or enwrap more completely. There's no trifling with words—cant be done: not when they're to stand 'for ever'. So I am battening down my Pargiters say till Wednesday—it shant be later, I swear. And now I grow doubtful of the value of those

9. LW saw the dermatologist Henry MacCormack (d. 1950) at 23 Wimpole Street; the Barretts had lived at no. 50. See *Flush*, pp.19-20: '. . . one has only to go to Wimpole Street . . . to admire the brass knockers and their regularity . . . a prayer rises in the heart and bursts from the lips that not a brick of Wimpole Street may be repointed . . . for as long as Wimpole Street remains, civilisation is secure.'
10. *Pomona*, a ballet to music by Constant Lambert, with choreography by Frederick Ashton and the set and costumes designed by Vanessa Bell, was given its first performance at Sadler's Wells on 17 January 1933.
11. Roger Fry had adapted his two lectures on French Art given the previous winter at the Queen's Hall (one of which VW had attended—see above 13 February 1932) and they were about to be published by Chatto and Windus as *Characteristics of French Art*; he had perhaps sent VW an advance copy of the book.

figures. I'm afraid of the didactic; perhaps it was only that spurious passion that made me rattle away before Christmas. Anyhow I enjoyed it immensely, & shall again—oh to be free, in fiction, making up my scenes again—however discreetly. Such is my cry this very fine cold January morning.

In 10 minutes Angelica comes & we go to Don Giovanni at Sadler's Wells. I have seen this week besides Plomer & Marjorie, Cotter Ludby who has been found in a Police Court, strapped to a bed in St Pancras Infirmary—been raging mad, as I can believe—& Robson & Ethel Smyth.[12] Mrs Hunter is dead. Died standing eating drinking dressing penniless, ruined discredited, having got through 40,000 a year, not all of her own; but they say she was a great hostess & all is forgiven—rightly I think, though in another class she would have been in prison. Such is the price we pay for our great hostesses. Witness Sibyl Colefax working in a shop.[13]

Thursday 26 January

Well, Flush is, I swear, despatched. Nobody can say I dont take trouble with my little stories. And now, having bent my mind for 5 weeks sternly this way, I must unbend them the other—the Pargiter way. No critic ever gives full weight to the desire of the mind for change. Talk of being many sided—naturally one must go the other way. Now if I ever had the wits to go into the Shakespeare business I believe one would find the same law there—tragedy comedy, & so on. Looming behind the P.s I can just see the shape of pure poetry beckoning me. But the P.s is a delightful solid possession to be enjoyed tomorrow. How bad I shall find it.

Not a letter has come my way these 2 days (oh but several parcels) & I therefore lapse into the healing sanctuary of anonymity. I think The Beau Monde has given me up—Ethel Sands is undoubtedly & no doubt reasonably annoyed with what Logan has chosen to purvey of my letters. So I say I will rout further in the bran pie; & go to my Club & meet young working women. I am going to learn Italian. Bianca my unknown

12. William Alexander Robson (1895-1980), lecturer at the London School of Economics (and later Professor of Public Administration there); he was joint editor with LW of the *Political Quarterly*, a journal he and Kingsley Martin had launched in 1930 with the backing of LW and others. Cotter Ludby was Helen Cotter, *née* Morison (d. 1939), wife of the artist Max Ludby, and daughter of Leslie Stephen's friend, the Positivist James Cotter Morison.

13. Ethel Smyth's sister Mary Hunter died at her home, 138 Ashley Gardens, on 18 January. In 1932 Lady Colefax had started a business in Mayfair as an interior decorator.

adorer is to teach me. And I am to have Holtby to tea today. So perhaps I can make do without Chelsea.[14]

I have bought several things freely & cheaply for the first time at the Winter Sales. Yesterday at Mar[shall] & Snelgrove's I said, by way of a joke to the girl, If that coats rubbed, they should sell it me for £3. And took me seriously. I heard an acrid conversation behind a screen. The girl was a greenhorn. You've no right to tell customers the coat is rubbed. Thats what its reduced for & so on. To my surprise my 3.19.6—formerly £5.10 coat was given me—all for my joke—for £3.10. Oh dear—the world of shops!

Thursday 2 February

No we are not deserted by the world—oh dear no: dinner Mary Monday; dinner here Friday; James & Alix dinner Wednesday—to talk about Lytton's things, says James. "I want to see you both alone". Hope [Mirrlees], will you come to dinner again? Ethel, will you lunch at Woking; Margaret West to tea on Sunday—a possible Press manager (S[cott].J[ohnson]. to go)[1] & Bianca to tea today: on top of which we have to decide about 35 Gordon Square on Saturday. By chance, Martins [*estate agent*] sent us an order; we saw it; well, it might do—Its a great big corner house; a warren of a basement; a studio, a bad dining room & kitchen; but great rooms looking on to the square; & quiet, with gardens behind; with a side door, so that publishing is possible—they say: altogether, I expect we shall take it for 9 years, at much the same rent as this, & the Pritchards will share. Not that I much want a move in March, with The Pargiters on my hands. I am going however to work largely, spaciously, fruitfully on that book. Today I finished—rather more completely than usual—revising the first chapter. I'm leaving out the interchapters—compacting them in the text; & project an appendix of dates. A good idea?[2]

And Galsworthy died two days ago, it suddenly struck me, walking just now by the Serpentine after calling on Mrs W[oolf]. (who's been

14. VW's 'Club' must have been the Society for Women's Service at Marsham Street, Westminster, where she and Ethel Smyth had spoken on 21 January 1931. Bianca Weiss gave VW some dozen lessons in Italian between early February and mid-April.

1. Miss Margaret West (recommended by Lady Rhondda) did succeed Miss Scott Johnson as manager of the Hogarth Press soon after this—and remained until her death in January 1937.

2. For a record of the development and changes in VW's conception of *The Pargiters* which lead to its final emergence as *The Years*, see Mitchell A. Leaska's introduction, p. xiv ff, to *The Pargiters*, 1977.

dying—is recovering) with the gulls opening their scimitars—masses of gulls. Galsworthy's dead: & A. Bennett told me he simply couldn't stick Galsworthy. Had to praise Jack's books to Mrs G. But I could say what I liked against Galsworthy. That stark man lies dead.[3]

[*Friday 17 February*]

I steal time from my Italian verbs. Yes I think I know them. I am having 2 lessons weekly from Bianca; she suggests three; but as I have to get in Ethel &c. Oh yesterday it was like being a snail shell & having a thrush tapping till the beak of her incessant voice broke my skull. I always say "Poor old lady". For I rather think she came all the way from Woking for this dry brittle hour. I am half ashamed—yet cant see that I'm to blame. And now she goes to Bath for 5 weeks—yes, to my relief I own. Because I cant bear being a snail shell. And she is so positive, so insistent. Being Ethel is so habitual to her.

I'm launched again in The Pargiters, in this blank season of the year— Nessa at Charleston, Clive in Jamaica, Roger in Tangier—Vita in America—which of my friends is left. But Desmond dined the night before last; Morgan came in last night; Holtby today—so there's no lack of people. Now of course the P.s runs a little slack. This fact recording is too flat.

There are no entries in VW's diary between 17 February and 15 March; LW's little engagement diary notes their outings—to Rodmell, to Hampstead, to Ivinghoe Beacon, to the RHS Flower Show; their entertainments—a René Clair film, ballet at Sadler's Wells, four concerts by the Busch Quartet; and their visits and visitors, who, among the less familiar, included VW's cousin Harry Stephen, Elizabeth Bowen, and Rose Macaulay.

Saturday 25 March

It is an utterly corrupt society I have just remarked, speaking in the person of Elvira Pargiter, & I will take nothing that it can give me &c &c: now, as Virginia Woolf, I have to write—oh dear me what a bore— to the Vice Chancellor of Manchester Un[ivers]ty & say that I refuse to be made a Doctor of Letters. And to Lady Simon, who has been urgent in

3. John Galsworthy (1867-1933), novelist and playwright, died at his Hampstead home on 31 January.

the matter, & asks us to stay.[1] Lord knows how I'm to put Elvira's language into polite journalese. What an odd coincidence! that real life should provide precisely the situation I was writing about! I hardly know which I am, or where: Virginia or Elvira; in the Pargiters or outside. We dined with Susan Lawrence two nights ago. A Mrs Stocks of Man[cheste]r U[niversit]y was there. How delighted my husband will be to give you your degree in July! she began. And had rattled off a great deal about the delight of Manchester in seeing me honoured, before I had to pluck up courage & say, But I wont take it. After that there was a general argument, with the Nevinsons (Evelyn Sharp), Susan Lawrence &c.[2] They all said they would take a degree from a University though not an honour from the state. They made me feel a little silly, priggish & perhaps extreme: but only superficially. Nothing would induce me to connive at all that humbug. Nor would it give me, even illicitly, any pleasure. I really believe that Nessa & I—she went with me, & used my arguments about the silliness of honours for women—are without the publicity sense. Now for the polite letters. Dear Vice Chancellor—

Tuesday 28 March

The polite letters have been sent. So far I have had, nor could have had any answer. No, thank Heaven, I need not emerge from my fiction in July to have a tuft of fur put on my head. It is the finest spring ever known —soft, hot, blue, misty. The trees all out, the other day in the park, when we took Bunny's child to Hayling Island. It was a June day. Poor Ray like a slum woman, so gaunt, so grim. He had a boat. It was cold on the beach—the Island is spotted with houses, like the rest of the world. And then down to Maidenhead in June weather—more bungalows.[3] And

1. For VW's letters of refusal, see *V VW Letters*, nos. 2719, 2720. The Vice-Chancellor of Manchester University from 1928-36 was Walter Moberly (1881-1974). (Dorothy) Shena Simon, *née* Potter (1883-1972), educated at Newnham College, Cambridge, 1904-7, was the wife and working partner of Sir Ernest Simon (created Lord Simon of Wythenshawe in 1947), ex-Lord Mayor and twice Liberal MP for Manchester; she was a Manchester City Councillor and in 1932 chairman of the Education Committee. She first met VW at Tavistock Square on 29 June 1933.
2. Susan Lawrence (1871-1947), Labour politician and MP, 1923-4, 1926-31, chairman of the Labour Party 1929-30. Mary Stocks, JP (b. 1891), created a Life Peer in 1966, lectured at Manchester University where her husband J. L. Stocks (1882-1937) was Professor of Philosophy. Henry Woodd Nevinson (1856-1941), journalist, married the author and suffragist Evelyn Sharp (d. 1955) as his second wife in 1933.
3. On 24 March the Woolfs drove Ray (Rachel Alice, *née* Marshall, 1892-1940), whom David Garnett had married in 1921, and their elder son Richard (b. 1923) to Hayling Island, and the following day visited LW's brother Herbert and his wife at Cookham, near Maidenhead.

dinner with Ly Rhondda. I felt her a disappointed woman. Should have had 10 children perhaps. She was sitting alone, shawled dowdy in an old Hampstead half [?] flat with a garden with great trees. She is what they call, I expect, 'inhibited'—something tentative furtive. Discussed Time & Tide &c. She lives for T. & T. but is a little under the thumb of Mr Ellis Roberts.[4] Then on to Clive; back from Jamaica. "The steward came in; & was surprised to find a young lady stark naked brushing her teeth." True Clive. Julian has failed to get his fellowship, & thinks, or Nessa thinks, of Burma.

Thursday 6 April

Oh I'm so tired! I've written myself out over The Pargiters this last lap. I've brought it down to Elvira in bed—the scene I've had in my mind ever so many months, but I cant write it now. Its the turn of the book. It needs a great shove to swing it round on its hinges. As usual, doubts rush in. Isnt it all too quick, too thin, too surface bright? Well, I'm too jaded to crunch it up, if thats so; & so shall bury it for a month— till we're back from Italy perhaps; & write on Goldsmith &c meanwhile. Then seize on it fresh, & dash it off in June July August September. Four months should finish the first draght—100,000 words I think. 50,000 words written in 5 months—my record

This is a time of ending. I've ever so many people to see. Ott tomorrow. The people of Manchester have written, very politely, with additional respect for me, because I dont take honours. And I'm going to Hugo [*Language Institute*] to hear Sigrun Martyn talk Italian. Mine is hopeless. She dashes on about her car—I limp & fumble. Bianca is in Italy. Nessa & the others at Charleston. Last night Lord Olivier, a jolly old bore, has been a dog in his day, dined here.[1] And Pippa came in later—grown very thick, but looks unhappy. And we went to Bedford [*travelling books*] on

4. Margaret Haig Thomas, Viscountess Rhondda (1883-1958), succeeded to her father's title under special remainder in 1918; married in 1908, she had no children and divorced her husband in 1923. In 1920 she founded, and from 1926 edited, the weekly *Time and Tide*, to which she devoted her energies and her fortune. She lived at 1B Baytree Lodge, Frognal. Richard Ellis Roberts (1870-1953), formerly of the *NS&N*, was literary editor of the paper from 1933-4, before becoming editor of *Life and Letters* (1934-5) and vice-President of the PEN Club.
1. Sydney Haldane Olivier (1859-1943), one of the founding fathers of the Fabian Society and a now retired Colonial administrator, had been raised to the peerage in 1924 so that he might serve as Secretary of State for India in the first Labour Government; his books were published by the Hogarth Press (*The Myth of Governor Eyre* appeared in October of this year, *HP Checklist* 327).

Tuesday in this June weather & to St Neots & saw the carved ceiling. I began the four great vols of Goldsmith this morning.[2]

Thursday 13 April

No I have worked myself too dry this time. There is not one idea left in the orange. But we go [*to Rodmell*] today, & I shall sun, with only a few books. No I will *not* write; I will *not* see people. A little nip from Gissing in the TLS. which I must answer.[3] But indeed I cant find words—use the wrong ones—thats my state: the familiar state after these 3 months writing—what fun that book is to me! And pressing in Italian, & seeing a mint of people—the state I say is quite familiar; & will vanish; yes, & then there's Italy to come. I have my new corduroys; & Mr Ronald Murray is appointed my dress maker.

Sibyl lunched—one hears her dry claws tapping the perch as she hops—then Pernel, ample gentle silver grey, & very—what is the word?—there I go forgetting. The word I like—integrity. Now I must collect my things. Nelly by the way touchingly friendly. Age is like lichen on roofs—knowing people I mean: gives our relationship some yellow red glow, so I think. Ann & Judy dined here. Ann at the stage where she likes action, rather than detective plays. Judy as candid as a boy of 10. And I want to

2. VW inherited the four volumes of James Prior's edition of *The Miscellaneous Works of Oliver Goldsmith* (1837) from her father. (See *Holleyman*, VS I, p. 32.) She was intermittently working on an article on Goldsmith for the rest of this year; her reading notes on the subject are in MHP, Sussex, B3d. It finally appeared in the *TLS* on 1 March 1934 (Kp C342), linked to the publication of a reprint of *The Citizen of the World* and *The Bee*.

3. Early in 1933 Jonathan Cape (with her permission) reprinted an article by VW on George Gissing (see Kp B9, C280) as the introduction to their Travellers' Library edition of his *By the Ionian Sea* (1901). In March VW heard from Cape that Gissing's son had made objections to it (see *V VW Letters*, no. 2717) and, after an exchange of letters in the *TLS* (13, 20 and 27 April), VW finally replied (*TLS*, 4 May 1933) to A. C. Gissing's seven specific complaints: 'I am sorry to find that in my introduction . . . I have left out three dots to indicate that the words "with a cart" are omitted. Otherwise the quotation is accurate. I also regret that I may have led the reader to suppose that Gissing dined off lentils a year after he had given up eating them; still got up at five when he had stopped getting up at five; took six journeys to a bookseller when in fact he took only two; referred to a fog and a landlady when there was not a fog or a landlady; and used the phrase "as he died" instead of "two days before he died". Such mistakes do not seem to me, I admit, of a serious nature. But I apologise for having stated that the Gissings had "to scrape together what education they could get" when it appears that there was no shortage of money for educational purposes.'

write on Goldsmith, Halifax & Turgenev.[4] And Ethel is "cutting the painter" (between us—for the 100th time). And—no, I must really learn a smoother narrative style.

The Woolfs spent Easter at Monks House, returning to London on 23 April; they exchanged visits with the Keyneses and the Bells.

Tuesday 25 April

No, we didn't see nobody at Rodmell. Lydia & Maynard arrived before we had been there half an hour; & we dined with them, & were invited to the royal party at Shelleys—Mr Hambro being the uncle of the proprietor; & the friend of Timmy & of the Gleichens; & they had crab, but the chicken was tough, so we did not go.[5]

Thats all over—our ten days: & I wrote daily, almost, at Goldsmith—dont much see the point of my Goldsmiths & so on—& read Goldsmith, & so on. Yes; I should now be correcting Flush proofs—I doubt that little book to some extent: but I'm in a doubting mood: the scrambled mood of transience, for on Friday 5th we go to Siena; so I cant settle, & make up my story, in which lies permanence. And as usual I want to seethe myself in something new—to break the mould of habit entirely, & get that escape which Italy & the sun & the lounging & the indifference of all that to all this brings about. I rise, like a bubble out of a bottle. And my eyes hurt, & I must go & see Mr Doggett—Sheppard's Johnny—today.[6] And have 7 Italian lessons; & see Vita, Christabel, &c.

But The Pargiters. I think this will be a terrific affair. I must be bold & adventurous. I want to give the whole of the present society—nothing less: facts, as well as the vision. And to combine them both. I mean, The

4. Ann (b. 1916) and Judith (1918-72) were VW's nieces, daughters of her brother Adrian Stephen and his wife Karin (VW later—26 July 1933—describes them as 'Amazons'); the Woolfs took them to see Paul Robeson and Flora Robson in Eugene O'Neill's play *All God's Chillun* at the Piccadilly Theatre on 3 April. VW did write on Goldsmith (see above, 6 April 1933, n. 2) and on Turgenev ('The Novels of Turgenev' was published in the *TLS* of 14 December 1933, Kp C341); but not apparently on the seventeenth-century political pamphleteer Lord Halifax.

5. This 'royal party'—to which the Woolfs did not go—at Shelley's Hotel, Lewes (proprietor M. R. Heriot) was so called by VW as both Lord Edward Gleichen (1863-1937) and 'Timmy' (the Hon. Gerald) Chichester (1886-1939) held appointments at Court; the latter was a friend of Duncan Grant, at whose studio VW had met him (see *V VW Letters*, no. 2717). Ronald Olaf Hambro (1885-1961) became chairman of Hambro's Bank in 1933; both he and Lord Edward Gleichen lived in Sussex, and he had been High Sheriff of the County.

6. James Hamilton Doggart (b. 1900), ophthalmic surgeon, whom J. T. Sheppard brought to dine at Hogarth House in 1920 (see *II VW Diary*, 17 January 1920).

Waves going on simultaneously with Night & Day. Is this possible? At present I have assembled 50,000 words of 'real' life: now in the next 50 I must somehow comment; Lord knows how—while keeping the march of events. The figure of Elvira is the difficulty. She may become too dominant. She is to be seen only in relation to other things. This should give I think a great edge to both of the realities—this contrast. At present, I think the run of events is too fluid & too free. It reads thin; but lively. How am I to get the depth without becoming static? But I like these problems, & anyhow theres a wind & a vigour in this naturalness. It should aim at immense breadth & immense intensity. It should include satire, comedy, poetry, narrative, & what form is to hold them all together? Should I bring in a play, letters, poems? I think I begin to grasp the whole. And its to end with the press of daily normal life continuing. And there are to be millions of ideas but no preaching—history, politics, feminism, art, literature—in short a summing up of all I know, feel, laugh at, despise, like, admire hate & so on.

Friday 28 April

A mere note. We got out of the car last night & began walking down to the Serpentine. A summer evening. Chestnuts in their crinolines, bearing tapers: grey green water & so on. Suddenly L. bore off; & there was Shaw, dwindled shanks, white beard; striding along. We talked, by a railing, for 15 mins.[7] He stood with his arms folded, very upright, leaning back; teeth gold tipped. Just come from the dentist, & 'lured' out for a walk by the weather. Very friendly. That is his art, to make one think he likes one. A great spurt of ideas. "You forget that an aeroplane is like a car—it bumps—We went over the great wall—saw a little dim object in the distance. Of course the tropics are the place. The Ceylon[?] people are the original human beings—we are smudged copies. I caught the Chinese looking at us with horror—that we should be human beings! Of course the tour cost thousands; yet to see us, you'd think we hadnt the price of the fare to Hampton Court. Lots of old spinsters had saved up for years to come. Oh but my publicity! Its terrifying. An hours bombardment at every port. I made the mistake of accepting [blank] invitation. I found myself on a platform with the whole university round me. They began shouting We want Bernard Shaw. So I told them that every man at 21 must be a revolutionary. After that of course the police imprisoned them by dozens. I want to write an article for the Herald pointing out what Dickens said years ago about the folly of

---

7. Bernard Shaw and his wife had only recently returned to England from New York, having embarked in December 1932 on a world cruise in the *Empress of Britain* which had taken them to the Far East.

Parliament. Oh I could only stand the voyage by writing. I've written 3 or 4 books. I like to give the public full weight. Books should be sold by the pound. What a nice little dog. But aren't I keeping you & making you cold (touching my arm)—Two men stopped along the path to look. Off he strode again on his dwindled legs. I said Shaw likes us. L. thinks he likes nobody. What will they think of Shaw in 50 years? He is 76 he said; too old for the tropics.

[*Saturday 29 April*]

Last night—to relieve myself for a moment from correcting that silly book Flush,—oh what a waste of time—I will record Bruno Walter.[8] He is a swarthy, fattish, man; not at all smart. Not at all the "great conductor". He is a little Slav, a little semitic. He is very nearly mad; that is, he cant get 'the poison' as he called it of Hitler out of him. "You must not think of the Jews" he kept on saying "You must think of this awful reign of intolerance. You must think of the whole state of the world. It is terrible—terrible. That this meanness, that this pettiness, should be possible! Our Germany—which I loved—with our tradition—our culture—We are now a disgrace." Then he told us how you cant talk above a whisper. There are spies everywhere. He had to sit in the window of his hotel in Leipzig? a whole day, telephoning. All the time soldiers were marching. They never stop marching. And on the wireless, between the turns, they play military music. Horrible horrible! He hopes for the monarchy as the only hope. He will never go back there. His orchestra had been in existence for 150 years: but it is the spirit of the whole that is awful. We must band together. We must refuse to meet any German. We must say that they are uncivilised. We will not trade with them or play with them—we must make them feel themselves outcasts—not by fighting them; by ignoring them. Then he swept off to music. He has the intensity—genius?—which makes him live every thing he feels. Described conducting: must know every player.

The Woolfs left London in their new car on Friday 5 May and made the Newhaven-Dieppe crossing that evening; they drove through France and via the Grande Corniche to Siena, which they reached on 13 May and where they spent four nights; after a further four days touring they left Italy on 21 May for the return journey through France, and arrived at Monks House

8. Bruno Walter (1876-1962), musician and conductor, was from 1925-33 Director of the *Städtisches Oper* in his native Berlin, and concurrently (1920-33) of the Gewandhaus Concerts in Leipzig; he had been forced to leave Germany following Hitler's rise to power in January 1933. He later worked in Austria and France and from 1939 in America, where he died. His meeting with the Woolfs was arranged by Ethel Smyth.

on 27 May. The details of their itinerary are recorded in LW's diary (LWP, Sussex); VW's record which follows is written on 17 smaller white sheets pasted on to the blue pages of DIARY XXII.

Tuesday 9 May

Juan les Pins

Yes, I thought: I will make a note of that face—the face of the woman stitching a very thin, lustrous green silk at a table in the restaurant where we lunched at Vienne. She was like fate—a consummate mistress of all the arts of self preservation: hair rolled & lustrous; eyes so nonchalant; nothing could startle her; there she sat stitching her green silk with people going & coming all the time; she not looking, yet knowing, fearing nothing, expecting nothing—a perfectly equipped middle class French woman.

At Carpentras last night there was the little servant girl with honest eyes, hair brushed in a flop, & one rather black tooth. I felt that life would crush her out inevitably. Perhaps 18. not more; yet on the wheel, without hope; poor, not weak but mastered—yet not enough mastered but to desire furiously travel, for a moment, a car. Ah but I am not rich she said to me—which her cheap little stockings & shoes showed anyhow. Oh how I envy you—able to travel. You like Carpentras? But the wind blows ever so hard. You'll come again? Thats the bell ringing. Never mind. Come over here & look at this. No, I've never seen anything like it. Ah yes, she always likes the English ('She' was the other maid, with hair like some cactus in erection). Yes I always like the English she said. The odd little honest face, with the black tooth, will stay on at Carpentras I suppose: will marry? will become one of those stout black women who sit in the door knitting? No: I foretell for her some tragedy; because she had enough mind to envy us the Lanchester.

Thursday 11 May

Rapallo

Yesterday there was Miss Cotton. She is one of the army of spinsters, on half or quarter pay. She finds she can live at Diano Marina for 8/- a day. Her friends say But what is there to do? She says, oh there are the beauties of nature. She burst out, directly she came in to dinner, dressed in greenish dressing gown: by her side the dour Miss Thread. How was France? Was it cheap? Oh it was Liberty Hall here. Then she described the wife, the husband, of the inn: & the servants; & how there had once been an Earthquake. Meanwhile came in the 2 guests [?] in evening dress, the deaf lady & the voluble; also the powdered white lady with the red scarf: & after dinner—they often give us asparagus, she said—& they had their own bottles of wine—the two parties settled in at their own tables—

where they are now & played bridge. Now this half pay spinster will dwindle on, beside the sea under the mountain, chatting, till she dies.

No we dont like the French Riviera, or the Italian much; but if it has to be, Rapallo does it best: its bay stretched with gold silk this evening, humming scented villas; all orange blossom. Quiet women reading to children, little boats, high cliffs; a sauntering indolent luxurious evening place, where one might spend ones last penny; grown old.

But we dont like these villas—like the Bussys'—laid like eggs on ledges, so that you cant go up or down but must merely sit, & for ever behold the sea & the roof of the Casino. Dorothy & Janie taking their coffee like ladies in a perfectly neat, spaced, yellow room with a large leaved tree outside;—the tree Dorothy & Simon planted 30 years ago.[1] But we dont wish to live here, shredding out our days, in these scented villas, sauntering round the harbour.

Friday 12 May

Pisa

Yes Shelley chose better than Max Beerbohm. He chose a harbour; a bay; & his home, with a balcony, on which Mary stood, looks out across the sea.[2] Sloping sailed boats were coming in this morning—a windy little town, of high pink & yellow Southern houses, not much changed I suppose; very full of the breaking of waves, very much open to the sea; & the rather desolate house standing with the sea just in front. Shelley, I suppose, bathed, walked sat on the beach there; & Mary & Mrs Williams had their coffee on the balcony. I daresay the clothes & the people were much the same. At any rate, a very good great man's house in its way. What is the word for full of the sea? Cant think tonight, sky high in a bedroom at the Nettuno in Pisa, much occupied by French tourists. The Arno swimming past with the usual coffee coloured foam. Walked in the Cloisters; this is true Italy, with the old dusty smell; people swarming in the streets; under the—what is the word for—I think the word for a street that has pillars is Arcade. Shelley's house waiting by the sea, & Shelley not coming, & Mary & Mrs Williams watching from the balcony & then Trelawney coming from Pisa, & burning the body on the shore—thats in my mind. All the colours here are white bluish marble against a very

1. The Bussys' villa, La Souco, was built on the steep terraced hillside at Roquebrune, overlooking Monte Carlo; the Woolfs had called in there on Wednesday.
2. Max Beerbohm had chosen to make his home at Rapallo in 1910. The Shelleys and the Williamses moved into the Casa Magni, on the shore between San Terenzo and Lerici, in May 1822; on 8 July, returning in their boat from Leghorn to Lerici, Shelley and Williams were drowned. Shelley's body was burnt near Viareggio, where it had been washed ashore, on 16 August in the presence of Byron, Trelawny, and Leigh Hunt.

light saturated sky. The tower leaning prodigiously. Clerical beggar at the door in a mock fantastic leather hat. The clergy walking.

It was in these cloisters—Campo Santo—that L. & I walked 21 years ago & met the Palgraves & I tried to hide behind the pillars. And now we come in our car; & the Palgraves—are they dead, or very old? Now at any rate we have left the black country, the bald necked vulture country with its sprinkling of redroofed villas. This is the Italy one used to visit in a railway train with Violet Dickinson—taking the hotel bus.[3]

Saturday 13 May

Siena

Today we saw the most beautiful of views & the melancholy man. The view was like a line of poetry that makes itself; the shaped hill, all flushed with reds & greens; the elongated lines, cultivated every inch; old, wild, perfectly said, once & for all: & I walked up to a group & said What is that village? It called itself [*blank in ms*]; & the woman with the blue eyes said wont you come to my house & drink? She was famished for talk. Four or five of them buzzed round us, & I made a Ciceronian speech, about the beauty of the country. But I have no money to travel with, she said, wringing her hands. We would not go to her house—or cottage on the side of the hill, & shook hands; hers were dusty; she wanted to keep them from me; but we all shook hands, & I wished we had gone to her house, in the loveliest of all landscapes. Then, lunching by the river among the ants, we met the melancholy man. He had five or six little fish in his hands, which he had caught in his hands. We said it was very beautiful country; & he said no, he preferred the town. He had been to Florence; no, he did not like the country. He wanted to travel, but had no money: worked at some village; no he did not like the country, he repeated, with his gentle cultivated voice; no theatres, no pictures, only perfect beauty. I gave him 2 cigarettes; at first he refused, then offered us his 6 or 7 little fish. But we could not cook them at Siena, we said. No, he agreed; & so we parted.

It is all very well, saying one will write notes but writing is a very difficult art. That is one has always to select; & I am too sleepy, & hence merely run sand through my fingers. Writing is not in the least an easy art. Thinking what to write, it seems easy; but the thought evaporates, runs hither & thither. Here we are in the noise of Siena—the vast

3. Leslie Stephen had known the poet Francis Turner Palgrave (1824-97), and at Easter 1901 his widow had lent the Stephen family her house at Lyme Regis for a fortnight's holiday. It is not known which members of the Palgrave family VW and LW encountered at Pisa in 1912 in the course of their honeymoon journey. Violet Dickinson (1865-1948), who had become a close friend, accompanied VW and Vanessa during part of their excursion to Italy after their father's death in 1904.

tunnelled arched stone town, swarmed over by chattering shrieking children.

Sunday 14 May

Yes I am reading—skipping—the Sacred Fount [*by Henry James*]—about the most inappropriate of all books for this din—sitting by the open window, looking across heads & heads & heads—all Siena parading in gray & pink & the cars hooting. How finely run along those involuted threads? I dont—thats the answer. I let 'em break. I only mark that the sign of a masterly writer is his power to break his mould callously. None of H. J.'s timid imitators have the vigour, once they've spun their sentence, to smash it. He has some native juice—figure; has driven his spoon deep into some stew of his own—some swarming mixture. That—his vitality—his vernacular—his pounce & grip & swing always spring fresh upon me, if at the same time I ask how could anyone, outside an orchis in a greenhouse, fabricate such an orchid's dream! Oh these Edwardian ladies with pale hair, these tailored "my dear men"! Yet compared to that vulgar old brute Creevey—L. is here bitten by a flea—H.J. is muscular, lean. No doubt the society of the Regent—the smell of brandy & bones, the painted velvet Lawrence women—the general laxity & lustiness & vulgarity are here at their superlative. Of course the Shelleys the Wordsworths the Coleridges existed on the other side of the hedge. But when it comes gushing out of Creevey's page, its for all the world like—something between Buckingham Palace, Brighton; & the Queen's own italic style—so uncurbed, so weak: & how can one hope for or care for a single person? There's all the dreary Lords & Ladies ogling & over eating; & plush & gilt; & the Princess & the Prince—I think dissolution & obesity taking hold of the 18th Century & swelling it into a puff ball efflorescence. 1860 is considerably more to the point.[4]

Monday 15 May

This should be all description—I mean of the little pointed green hills; & the white oxen, & the poplars, & the cypresses, & the sculptured shaped infinitely musical, flushed green land from here to Abbazia—that is where we went today;[5] & couldn't find it, & asked one after another of the charming tired peasants, but none had been 4 miles beyond their range, until we came to the stone breaker, & he knew. He could not stop

4. See *The Creevey Papers*, selected from the correspondence and diaries of the Whig MP and gossip Thomas Creevey (1768-1838). The Woolfs had a copy of Herbert Maxwell's 1928 edition.
5. This afternoon the Woolfs had driven to the *Abbazia di S. Antimo*, the 12th century travertine basilica standing in a lonely valley to the south of Montalcino.

work to come with us, because the inspector was coming tomorrow. And he was alone, alone, all day with no one to talk to. So was the aged Maria at the Abbazio. And she mumbled & slipped her words, as she showed us into the huge bare stone building; mumbled & mumbled, about the English—how beautiful they were. Are you a Contessa? she asked me. But she didnt like Italian country either. They seem stinted, dried up; like grasshoppers, & with the manners of impoverished gentle people; sad, wise, tolerant, humorous. There was the man with the mule. He let the mule gallop away down the road. We are welcome, because we might talk; they draw round & discuss us after we're gone. Crowds of gentle kindly boys & girls always come about us, & wave & touch their hats. And nobody looks at the view—except us—at the Euganean, bone white, this evening: then there's a ruddy red farm or two; & light islands swimming here & there in the sea of shadow—for it was very showery— then there are the black stripes of cypresses round the farms; like fur ridges; & the poplars, & the streams & the nightingales singing & sudden gusts of orange blossom; & white alabaster oxen, with swinging chins— great flaps of white leather hanging under their noses—& infinite empti- ness, loneliness, silence: never a new house, or a village; but only the vineyards & the olive trees, where they have always been. The hills go pale blue, washed very sharp & soft on the sky; hill after hill;

On the afternoon of 16 May the Woolfs drove out to see the Abbey of Monte Oliveto Maggiore, and the following day left Siena for Lucca, stopping for lunch at San Gimignano; from Lucca they went to Lerici, and on 19 May on to Piacenza.

Friday 19 May

Piacenza

Its a queer thing that I write a date. Perhaps in this disoriented life one thinks, if I can say what day it is, then . . . Three dots to signify I dont know what I mean. But we have been driving all day from Lerici over the Apennines, & it is now cold, cloistral, highly uncomfortable in a vast galleried Italian inn [*Croce Bianca*], so ill provided with chairs that now at this present moment we are squatted, L. in a hard chair by his bed, I on the bed, in order to take advantage of the single light which burns between us. L. is writing directions to the Press. I am about to read Goldoni.

Lerici is hot & blue & we had a room with a balcony. There were Misses [?] & Mothers—misses [?] who had lost all chance of life long ago, & could with a gentle frown, a frown of mild sadness, confront a whole meal—arranged for the English—in entire silence, dressed as if for cold Sunday supper in Wimbledon. Then there's the retired Anglo-Indian, who takes shall we say Miss Toutchet for a walk, a breezy red faced man, very fond of evensong at the Abbey. She goes to the Temple; where 'my brother' has rooms. Et cetera Et cetera.

Of the Apennines I have nothing to say—save that up on the top theyre like the inside of a green umbrella: spine after spine: & clouds caught on the point of the stick. And so down to Parma; hot, stony, noisy; with shops that dont keep maps; & so on along a racing road to Piacenza, at which we find ourselves now at 6 minutes to 9 P.M. This of course is the rub of travelling—this is the price paid for the sweep & the freedom—the dusting of our shoes & careering off tomorrow—& eating our lunch on a green plot beside a deep cold stream. It will all be over this day week—comfort & discomfort; & the zest & rush that no engagements, hours, habits give. Then we shall take them up again with more than the zest of travelling.

[Sunday 21 May]

To write to keep off sleep—that is the exalted mission of tonight—tonight sitting at the open window of a secondrate inn in Draguignan—with plane trees outside, the usual single noted bird, the usual loudspeaker. Everyone in France motors on Sunday; then sleeps it off at night. The hotel keepers are gorged, & scarcely stop playing cards. But Grasse was too plethoric—we came on here late. We leave here early. I dip into Creevey; L. into Golden Bough.[6] We long for bed. This is the tax for travelling—these sticky uncomfortable hotel nights—sitting on hard chairs under the lamp. But the seduction works as we start—to Aix tomorrow—so home— And 'home' becomes a magnet, for I cant stop making up The P.s: cant live without that intoxicant—though this is the loveliest & most distracting alternative. But I'm full of holiday—& want work—ungrateful that I am!—& yet I want the hills near Fabbria too, & the hills near Siena—but no other hills—not these black & green violent monotonous Southern hills— We saw poor Lawrence's Phoenix picked out in coloured pebbles at Vence today, among all the fretted lace tombs.[7]

Tuesday 23 May

I have just said to myself if it were possible to write, those white sheets would be the very thing, not too large or too small. But I do not

6. LW had an abridged one-volume edition (1929) of J. G. Frazer's *The Golden Bough*, first published in 12 volumes 1890-1915. See *Holleyman* VS VI, p. 15.
7. D. H. Lawrence was buried in the cemetery at Vence on 4 March 1930; in 1935 he was disinterred and cremated, and his ashes taken to New Mexico. His gravestone, with the Phoenix in a mosaic of pebbles designed by Dominique Matteucci, is now in the Council Chamber at Eastwood, Nottingham, his birthplace.

wish to write, except as an irritant. This is the position. I sit on L.'s bed; he in the only armchair. People tap up & down on the pavement. This is Vienne. it is roasting hot—hotter & hotter it gets—& we are driving through France; & its Tuesday & we cross on Friday & this strange interval of travel of sweeping away from habitations & habits will be over. On & on we go—through Aix, through Avignon, on & on, under arches of leaves, over bare sandy roads, under grey black hills with castles, beside vines: & I'm thinking of The Pargiters; & L. is driving; & when we come to poplars, we get out & lunch by the river; & then on; & take a cup of tea by the river, fetch our letters, learn that Lady Cynthia Mosley is dead; picture the scene; wonder at death; & drowse & doze in the heat, & decide to sleep here—hotel de la Poste; & read another letter, & learn that the Book Society will probably take Flush, & speculate what we shall do if we have £1,000 or £2,000 to spend.[8] And what would these little burghers of Vienne, who are drinking coffee do, with that sum, I ask? The girl is a typist; the young men clerks. For some reason they start discussing hotels at Lyons, I think; & they havent a penny piece between them; & all the men go into the urinal, one sees their legs; & the Morocco soldiers go in their great cloaks; & the children play ball, & people stand lounging, & everything becomes highly pictorial, composed, legs, in particular—the odd angles they make, & the people dining in the hotel; & the queer air it all has, since we shall leave early tomorrow, of something designing [?] Vienne on my mind, significantly. Now the draw of home, & freedom, & no packing tells on us—oh to sit in an arm chair, & read & not to have to ask for Eau Minerale with which to brush our teeth!

[End of inserted pages]

Tuesday 30 May

52 Tavistock Square

Yes but of all things coming home from a holiday is undoubtedly the most damned. Never was there such aimlessness, such depression. Cant read, write or think. Theres no climax here. Comfort yes: but the coffee's not so good as I expected. And my brain is extinct—literally hasnt the power to lift a pen. What one must do is to set it—my machine I mean—on the rails & give it a push. Lord—how I pushed yesterday to make it start running along Goldsmith again. Theres that half finished article. Lord Salisbury said something about dished up speeches being like the cold remains of last nights supper. I see white grease on the pages of my

8. Lady Cynthia Mosley, daughter of Lord Curzon, died of acute appendicitis on 16 May 1933; VW had noted her wedding to Oswald Mosley in 1920 (see *II VW Diary*, 11 May 1920). *Flush* was the Book Society's choice for October 1933, the month of its publication.

article. Today its a little warmer—tepid meat: a slab of cold mutton. Its coldish, dullish here. Yes, but I hear the clock tick, & suspect, though I must not look, that the wheels are just beginning to turn on the rails. We go to Monks House for Whitsun, which is Monday—the suburban, the diminished Monks House. No, I cant look at The Pargiters. Its an empty snail shell. And I'm empty with a cold slab of a brain. Never mind. I shall dive head foremost into The Pargiters. And now I shall make my mind run along Italian—whats his name—Goldoni. A few verbs I think.

It occurs to me that this state, my depressed state, is the state in which most people usually are.

Wednesday 31 May

I think I have now got to the point where I can write for 4 months straight ahead at The Pargiters. Oh the relief—the physical relief! I feel as if I cd. hardly any longer keep And I am at once called out to draw lots in our Derby sweepstake. No favourite this year they say. back—that my brain is being tortured by always butting against a blank wall—I mean Flush, Goldsmith, motoring through Italy: now, tomorrow, I mean to run it off. And suppose only nonsense comes? The thing is to be venturous, bold, to take every possible fence. One might introduce plays, poems, letters, dialogues: must get the round, not only the flat. Not the theory only. And conversation; argument. How to do that will be one of the problems. I mean intellectual argument in the form of art: I mean how give ordinary waking Arnold Bennett life the form of art? These are rich hard problems for my 4 months ahead. And I dont know my own gifts at the moment. I'm disoriented completely after 4 weeks holiday—no 3—but tomorrow we go to Rodmell again. And I must fill up the chinks with reading—& dont want to settle down to books—

Well, now I have to go up to Murray about my dress: & theres Ethel round the corner; but no letters; disorganisation from Whitsun again. I thought, driving through Richmond last night, something very profound about the synthesis of my being: how only writing composes it: how nothing makes a whole unless I am writing; now I have forgotten what seemed so profound. The rhododendron like coloured glass mounds at Kew. Oh the agitation, oh the discomfort of this mood.

[?*Thursday 8 June*]

Very well: the old Pargiters are beginning to run off: & I say oh to be done. I mean, writing is effort: writing is despair: & yet of course t'other day in the grilling heat at Rodmell, I admit that the perspective—this I think was something like my profound thought at Richmond—shifts into focus: yes: the proportion is right; though I at the top suffer strain, suffer, as this morning grim despair & shall O Lord when it comes to re-writing, suffer an intensity of anguish ineffable (the word only means one cant express it); holding the thing—all the things—the innumerable things—together.

We burst 'the proportion'—I'm amused to compare the thing done with this inner oddity—& went to Leonards Lee, where I saw Nelly Cecil. She escaped—flying old white attenuated: I couldnt summon force to stop her. And she vanished. Violet was in the offing. So to tea in a stable with Mrs Woolf, Sylvia buying frigidaires because there's nothing else to do; & Edgar glum, gloomy, solemn.[1]

Tuesday 13 June

Apostle dinner last night. Morgan on Goldie. Adrian dined with me: wine; peach fed ham; Karin with inflamed eye from tattoo; Kapp: wine; cigars; in comes Hope [Mirrlees]: lost her neck. grown stubby waxy but affable. Talk of lunch to Ott: Would she like it? Yes, they say. Mention Pipsy [Philip Morrell]. And what is happening to Nan Warmington? Husband found dead in bed. And Ka. And Lottie. And Mrs Millington ⟨has⟩ hopes to inherit a fortune. Chancery opens once in 50 years.[2]

And so on; like birds; very garrulous. The black dachshund on Hope's knee. Has a snappy screech. Mary to call it by. Logan's malice. His version of John & the Press. Resolved to make Logan pay for this. L. comes in. Says he must go again round to James [Strachey]. On with our stories: father, childhood. Was he utterly bad? Had friends, A. says. Cruel, says Hope, making me walk.

I am in full flood with P.s rather think it tends to a play: anyhow am floated. L. depressed, partly because of Shaw lunch, because of Pinka's eczema; people—Bunny & E. Bowen tomorrow, Shaws, Bussys,

1. The woodland gardens at Leonardslee, Sussex, laid out by Sir Edmund Loder, Bt in the 1880s, and inherited by his grandson Sir Giles, were noted for their rhododendrons, azaleas, and other flowering shrubs; they were opened to the public at Whitsun; the Woolfs had arranged to meet LW's mother, his third brother Edgar (1883-1981) and his wife Sylvia there. Lady Eleanor Cecil (1868-1956), who shared with VW a serious interest in writing, had been a friend both of her and Violet Dickinson since early in the century; she and her husband Lord Robert Cecil had a Sussex home at Chelwood Gate. See also *V VW Letters*, no. 2742, about this expedition to Leonardslee.
2. Edmond X. Kapp (1890-1978), draughtsman and painter, known particularly for his character studies of prominent people. Mrs Warmington and Mrs Millington, unidentified. For the outcome of the proposal that her friends should give a luncheon party for Lady Ottoline, see below, 16 June 1933.

Camargo;[3] & now, instantly B[arbara]. Hutchinson, to ask a favour, then
to hat shop & Nelly Cecil.

Friday 16 June

Anrep coming in half an hour—10-10—so I cant even pretend to
settle down to write. (Elvira scene finished). Oh yesterday! Oh yesterday!
Figure to yourself lunch on a hot day at the Shaws. Long narrow
room overlooking river & white sepulchral buildings. The Binyons. He
a plethoric bolt eyed congested little man; she, washy watery.[4] Mrs Shaw
small gimleteyed. In comes Shaw, alert for business, but not in the mood.
No one in the mood. Lunch in another long narrow room. Unreal hotel
lunch. butlers. Service Kitchen. Shaw's paddle actually out of the water.
Cutting no ice. Had to make a speech to friends of the Nat. Libraries that
afternoon; didnt know what their object was; but hoped to say something
unpleasant about the conference.[5] And I talked. And I said This is d—d
dull. I said it at intervals. Nothing flourished. Every saying died as
spoken. All I retrieved was: Shaw does not visualise. I think of the sharp
key as brass [?]—thats all. I never see my characters. I feel them in
another way. Also, he had been sounded about the O. M. Baldwin said,
he'll only guy us. "I said I have already conferred the Order of Merit on
myself". Stories—about China: some he'd told us already. L.'s hand
clattered.[6] Story about his fathers love, which I share, of anti-climax.
Throw them all into the Liffey—of his ancestors bones, when they wanted
to make a new church. And I kept saying no the drug won't work. Never
once did it work; & we were all glad—Shaw glad—when Mrs S. whose
mild babble is continuous—moved; & we never sat down, but had one
look at the river, & Shaw escorted us along the black & white passage—

3. Simon Bussy's exhibition 'Pastels of Morocco and Zoo Studies' was at the Leicester
   Galleries, which the Woolfs went to on 9 June; they also went to a gala performance
   at Covent Garden on 27 June given by the Camargo Society in honour of the
   delegates to the World Economic Conference.
4. The Bernard Shaws lived in a flat on the fourth floor of Whitehall Court, a vast
   block of service flats facing the Thames from the Victoria Embankment. Laurence
   Binyon, CH (1869-1943), was Keeper of Prints and Drawings in the British Museum
   1932-3, and succeeded T. S. Eliot as Charles Eliot Norton Professor of Poetry at
   Harvard this year.
5. Shaw addressed the second annual conference of the Friends of the National
   Libraries in the rooms of the British Academy, Burlington House, on 15 June; he
   had nothing but praise for their work.
6. Stanley Baldwin (1867-1947), leader of the Conservative Party, was Lord President
   of the Council in Ramsay MacDonald's National Government, 1931-5. All his life
   LW suffered from a congenital nervous tremor of the right hand, which increased
   markedly under stress.

very jaunty, upright—sea green eyes red face to the lift. A man of perfect poise—spring—agility—never to me interesting—no poet, but what an efficient, adept, trained arch & darter! His wires, his spring, at 76 entirely astonishing. And the hands flung out in gesture: he has the power to make the world his shape—to me not a beautiful shape—thats all. So home.

Very hot. Very hot. Had to write a letter for M. Fry about opening Squares.[7] At 3.20 Anrep—to Ott's. Ott in blue & red muslin—dangling earrings. What is it? Our affection for you Ott: we wish you to lunch ————Oh dear, no I couldnt, I couldnt. Philip come & protect me!! Enter P. rather moth eaten. I am entirely on Ott's side. Publicity. Too like Jack Squire. Besides, we still see our friends. And Clive has done very well without us. Do you think we are over? And so on—rather suspicious, rather hurt, rather on the high horse. And Ott genuinely disliking the ceremony. And Boris genuinely anxious expostulatory, deliberate rotund —grasping his hat & making a speech—determined. And P. saying, rather with intent, Ott has been at death's door (yes, & we were none of us very kind then) & now, as you dont realise, cant stand any strain. Oh but we arent suggesting that she should give more parties—(And you'll never come to parties she does give. This was sub-acute). Anyhow we walked up to T[avistock].S[quare]. with her—she to have her feet tended—& then B[oris]. so he said, overcame her & kissed her in the street. So back here Then the wallet with the pass to the Pullman Cars picked up in the street. Then Ethel—oh & I was dumb, chill, completely insentient; & she tried to stage a quarrel & failed—failed, poor old woman, in all her effects—with the pinks too—was very unattractive— felt it—suggested going. Did I care? No. I could feel nothing, was dazed, impotent, so led her down the stairs, she, perhaps, suffering, perhaps not—& off she went, & I sank at last—at last—into silence. For had we not had Barbara Hutchinson twice, about her lover: had I not signed books, & gone to tea with Nelly Cecil, & picked up my ears with Lord Bob—& then the dinner with Bunny—taciturn, monolithic—& E[lizabe]th Bowen, conventional—& so on: all this I say has been whizz-ing & buzzing; & now Boris comes with Maynard's letter of invitation to the Ott tea: whereupon out drops Ott's refusal. No, no no, I cant. So thats over.[8] And now to Rodmell this very hot June day.

7. VW's letter, written at the instigation of Margery Fry and the London Council of Social Services, was published in the *NS&N* on 24 June; it suggested that London Squares, normally reserved for residents, might be opened during part of the summer to those without the means to leave town in the holiday season.

8. 'In a moment of weakness, under the charm of Boris—I said yes . . . but my real self says "No" "No" . . . "No". . . . I don't think private friendship can be ever acknowledged en masse.' Ottoline Morrell to VW, 15 June 1933, MHP, Sussex. For VW's reply, see *V VW Letters*, no. 2750.

Tuesday 20 June

Its a very ugly thing, a ceremony. I detest them more & more. This refers to my waste of a morning at the WCG Jubilee today.[9] Margaret & Lilian, in grey blue, & coffee colour—how characteristic!—presented a banner. M.'s white hair, tied with black bow, wears thin. Their shoulders hunch a little. Otherwise I noted little change. The great hall full. The women all in pinks & blues. Fine old housekeepers; of the Sophie type; massive; determined. Now & then a great laugh; & very queer accents. Mrs Jones of Brighton pronounced twenty different ways. But all was ceremony. Margaret Bondfield: Susan Lawrence—& so on: the bigwigs: & they say things that arent true: they say we are on the brink of a new world; they talk of the triumph of co[-operatio]n. Thats why I hate ceremonies—not a word that fits—all wind blown, gaseous, with elementary emotions. Years ago I got something out of the mere conglomeration, the stir, the multitude. But today, I was not annihilated, dispersed; I said to myself The P.s is more real, truer harder, more veined with blood than all this, & longed to be back, working. How odd to spend a morning merely vacant, regardant!—How many I spend concentrated! Then we shook, & smiled with others intervening Margaret's, Lilian's hands: emotions not extreme; & found a back way out. I must now read Wainwrights, a possible East End novel.[10] I am in flood again with The P.s.

Monday 26 June

The present moment. 7 o'clock on June 26th: L. printing: hot: thunderous: I after reading Henry 4 Pt one saying whats the use of writing; reading, imperfectly, a poem by Leopardi; the present moment, in my studio. A bucket banged in the mews; dog barks; woman, 'I didn't know if you were out here.' Leaves door open: far away horns; a bee buzzing. Bobo's first night; King lays stone of London Un[iversity]. Doctors, scarlet, purple in streets; poor little students in gowns: so to dine, & read

9. The Jubilee Congress of the Women's Co-operative Guild was held in the Central Hall, Westminster. Lilian Harris (c. 1866-1949) was, like her friend and companion Margaret Llewelyn Davies, a veteran of the WCG, from which they had retired in 1921 as Assistant-Secretary and General Secretary respectively. The Rt. Hon. Margaret Bondfield (1873-1953), Minister of Labour in the Labour Party administration of 1929-31, represented the Trade Union movement, and Susan Lawrence (see above, 25 March 1933), brought greetings from the Labour Party.
10. *The Wainwrights. A Novel, not a Saga* by Edgar Meredith was published by Grayson & Grayson in 1935.

Archibald Marshall's memoir; & music; thunder, I dare say; & so to open my windows, & go up: the moment done.[11]

Thursday 6 July

Dinner at Roger's yesterday. Company, S. Sitwells, Brennan, Oliver. All sat round about in Helen's bedroom, eating cold things off a table. I next Georgia & Roger.[1] Talk of patent medicines. "And then I found it was an aphrodisiac" G. says. She buys every patent medicine, by way of sedative. Bounds, abounds, halloos dogs on lawn: brown chocolate eyed; vital as they say not intellectual. Made the salad with cheese. Mrs B[renan]. said to be sympathetic & soft & amusing by L. The Quennells: I in my desire not to be crushing perhaps too friendly. Francis Birrell. All chatter. Stayed late. Not much satisfaction—yet amusing enough, as such things are: Helen's pin points; Roger reading French poetry to Mrs Q. & Gloria [Georgia]. "Gloria" says Helen, on the doorstep "has fallen in love with Dutuit. Caught her sighing at breakfast. My maid is going to have a child. Nonsense Gloria. Well, to tell the truth, I'm headlong in love—so's he."[2] Gaily blinking, clumsy, moleish, attractive, always jerking from thing to thing. Knows nothing. Thats what lies behind the aphrodisiac, & the bounce I suppose.

Also to sit with George [Duckworth]—a solid mound in pink pyjamas: Margaret tender & solicitous; given eau de Cologne; also Roger's show: also—now to the London Library meeting.[3] Two days of misery writing Goldsmith, forced respite from Pargiters.

Friday 7 July

Being headachy after Pargiters & Goldsmith & ever so many people

11. Beatrice ('Bobo') Mayor, *née* Meinertzhagen (1885-1971), an old, if not very close, friend; her play, *Little Earthquake*, had its first night at the Q Theatre, Kew Bridge, on 26 June; on this day, King George V, accompanied by Queen Mary, laid the foundation stone of the vast building to the north of the British Museum which was to become the headquarters of the University of London amid 'animated scenes of academic pageantry' (*The Times*). Archibald Marshall (1866-1934), author and novelist, published his *Out and About, Random Reminiscences* in 1933.

1. Sacheverell Sitwell (b. 1897), writer and aristocrat, had married Georgia Doble (d. 1980) in 1925. Gerald Brenan (b. 1894), also a writer, normally lived at Yegen in Southern Spain, where the Woolfs had stayed with him in 1923, as had Roger Fry and Helen Anrep this Spring; his wife was the American poet Gamel Woolsey (1899-1968). Peter Quennell (b. 1905), biographer and literary journalist, whose *Letter to Mrs Virginia Woolf* had been published by the Hogarth Press in October 1932 (*HP Checklist* 305); he and his wife were on the verge of separation.

2. Georges Duthuit (1891-1973), French art critic and son-in-law of Matisse.

3. The exhibition of 'Pictures by Roger Fry' was at Agnew's, 43 Old Bond Street. The Annual General Meeting of the London Library was held on 6 July.

I have spent the whole morning reading old diaries, & am now (10 to 1) much refreshed. This is by way of justifying these many written books. And we have a party tonight—Wests, Hutchinsons, Plomer—so I need rest my head. The diary amuses me.[4]

Monday 10 July

Bella [*LW's sister*] arrived & knocked her head upon the window of the car. She cut her nose & was dazed. And then I was in 'one of my states'—how violent how acute & walked in Regent's Park in black misery & had to summon my cohorts in the old way to see me through, which they have done more or less. A note made to testify to my own ups & downs; many of which go unrecorded though they are less violent I think than they used to be. But how familiar it was—stamping along the road, with gloom & pain constricting my heart; & the desire for death in the old way all for two, I daresay careless words.

It seems possible that Tom has finally deserted Vivienne.[5] Jack Hutch. came to our frosty sticky party, with the meticulous fish blooded cultivated Andrews—Rebecca merely a hard painted woman, that night, living in society—& Hutch. told us how V. has heard by cable that Tom sailed on 26th & he has not arrived. She has by today worked herself into frenzy—in bed, with a nurse; & then Jack telephoned to Faber—L.'s idea—& they say mysteriously that they cannot discuss the matter on the telephone, but if V. will pull herself together she will realise that there is no reason for anxiety. This we interpret to mean that Tom is back; has told Faber that he is parting from her; but it is kept secret. until he gives leave—which he may do today. Anyhow, V. is clearly concealing something. J[ack]. read one of Tom's last letters, & describes it as a very cold & brutal document, saying that he has made no money. I should expect that after his 6 months thought & absence he has decided to make the break here: has warned V. & provided for her. But she shuts the letters in the cupboard with the sealed string. L. is made her executor. So I go up to lunch to hear.

Thursday 20 July

This was quite a correct statement of the Eliot position. He has left her

4. Rebecca West and her husband Henry Andrews dined with the Woolfs on 7 July; St John (Jack) Hutchinson and William Plomer came in afterwards.
5. T. S. Eliot returned to England late in June after six months' absence lecturing in America, and went at once to stay with Frank Morley, a fellow-director of Faber & Faber, and his family in Surrey, where he remained for several months. A formal Deed of Separation had already been drawn up by his lawyers and sent, with an explanatory letter from Eliot, to his wife.

"irrevocably"; & she sits meanwhile in a flat decorated with pictures of him, & altars, & flowers. Sometimes she prevails on a stranger—like E. Bowen to believe her story, at others lapses into sense. We dine with the Hutchinsons tonight, & shall I expect found some sort of Vivienne fund. It is said that there is a Convent next door to M[ary]. in which she might pass her days, praying for Tom.

I am again in full flood with The P.s after a week of very scanty pages. The trouble is to get the meat pressed in: I mean to keep the rhythm & convey the meaning. It tends more & more, I think—at any rate the E[lvira].M[aggie]. scenes—to drama. I think the next lap ought to be objective, realistic, in the manner of Jane Austen: carrying the story on all the time.

Vita dined [on 18 July]; Nigel has appendicitis; Vita that night had slightly painted her lips, but unskilfully. Now why?

Friday 21 July

Dinner at the Hutchinsons last night; in the garden, though there might have been a shower. Very cloudy, sultry & completely still. The white cat came out & played about. Mary in white, like a mummy; with a yellow turban, hanging down: chalk white face, like a pierrot. I said I would put her in The Pargiters. She might come in the last scene, or going half jockey too to a party. Like a little horse. We were much more natural & easy than usual. Lobster & cutlets in aspic. We talked of the Eliots a little; then of B[arbara]. & Victor: how both Desmond & I said he was jealous.[6] Then the lights began to flicker on the faces of the houses & on the trees. Mary became rather restless & said would we like to go to the Zoo. We might meet people there, she said. She wanted to go. Jack not much, nor I not much. But we went. And we met Simon [Bussy] & two frenchmen, Masson the ballet maker, in the reptile house.[7] Mary twined the heavy scaly pythons round her: they have bright electric blue bloom on them. They feel like muscles moving under a shiny plated skin; L. took one & it wound itself round his head like a toque, sticking its head out & flicking its tongue at the side. So to the white bears, the ⟨polar bears⟩ sea lions; & looked at the brilliant green showering trees. with sleepy birds pecking about on the grass.

6. Barbara Hutchinson and Victor Rothschild (b. 1910) announced their engagement at the end of October; he was at this time at Trinity College, Cambridge, working for a fellowship in Zoology (which he obtained and held from 1935-9); in 1937 he succeeded his uncle as 3rd Baron Rothschild.
7. The artist André Masson (b. 1896) had designed the abstract decor for *Les Présages*, a new ballet to the music of Tchaikovsky's 5th Symphony, with choreography by Massine, being performed by the Ballets Russes de Monte Carlo in their current three-week season at the Alhambra Theatre. The Woolfs had seen it on 13 July.

Vivi. E[liot]. said of the scene with Tom at the solicitors: he sat near me & I held his hand, but he never looked at me.

---

written here	He's not a poet, no; so what is he to do "... That is poetry
by mistake—	Maggie in its pre-natal stage; before it has taken wings to
damn.	itself & flown to the—" She paused at the bookcase, & took down, the Antigone, translated by Edward Pargiter . to the utmost

---

Wednesday 26 July

Miss Cashin & L. doing books—'89 here & 500 sheets' & I very sleepy after dining with Julia [Tomlin]; having tea with E. Bowen in the heat—the great heat. Another unbroken wave. When I cant write of a morning—as now—I try to tune myself on other books: couldnt settle on any save T. Hardy's life just now. Rather to my liking. He was unreasonable about critics, so that pale cold chicken Morgan says. And he felt bitter about the treatment of working men at Oxford; hence Jude. "The Marionnette" L. is reading out to Miss Cashin.[8] Quentin has mild pleurisy; Nessa gone down to Charleston; finds Raymond there; at Julia's last night Wogan [Philipps], "I think you might remainder 50 of M[arionette]. L."—Dorothy Bussy, Peter Quennell: whom I dont warm to—exiguous worm, rather: skinned: clever; cleverer than Wogan, who's nicer than Peter. Talk of Memoir Club. "But my autobiography would be too dirty" said PQ. They said—the young—that they had no group. Talk about Ann & Judith: Q. said he deprecated Amazons. I said I liked them till 20 or so. Q. I think is in trouble, so I guess, with his doll of a wife.* "Marriage—"—spoken very bitterly. Told me of a visit to Plaistow to correct proofs with Desmond.[9] Coming back in the rattling tram, D. said to him how someone (he thought Molly) had proposed to him, being a good deal more in love than he was "& they always feel the claws in their heart to this day." Odd instance of D.'s spasmodic intimacy.

* A good shot. He left her, or she him, soon afterwards

Oh if I could finish my Goldsmith & send it off. I must.

A great many visits: Miss Porter, James Stephen, half witted oaf, on business about Wilberforce, designed to push him on. Got out of meeting

8. *The Marionette* by Edwin Muir was published by the Hogarth Press in 1927 (*HP Checklist* 132).
9. *Life & Letters*, edited by Desmond MacCarthy, and to which Peter Quennell was a regular contributor, was printed by the Curwen Press at Plaistow, Essex.

Low, at Kingsley Martins, of Mrs Maloney, American editor of the
Feis's.[10] So we go off to Monks House tomorrow, & shall write: yes:
The P.'s must be dealt with in masterly manner. An exciting book to
write.

Sunday 30 July

Rodmell

Settled in again here. A question how far places influence one's mood.
Certain thoughts I always think: the downs spoilt, could we move, &c.
leading to a well known round. Quentin ill with pleurisy; may have to
have an operation—This the first illness at Charleston. We dine there
tonight. And, in order to refresh my mind for P.s I've been writing
memoirs, & cant disinfect my mind of Fitzroy Sqre. so strong is the
past—so as to read Italian. I'm telling the story of W.H. & H.Y.[11] But I
am organising life here, & so far rather well. Reading & walking &
swimming into lucid depths, powerfully—thats how I put it. And
people impend, but can be shelved for the moment—Colefax, E[lizabe]th
Read, Julia, the Wolves &c . .[12]

Mrs B.'s case is interesting. It reflects credit on humanity. Her half
cousin Lydia Hastie, a mad wandering witted old woman died in Florence
& left 17,000: half to Mrs B. This represents safety indeed luxury for life.

10. Louise Porter, see above, 3 January 1933. James Stephen (b. 1908), only son and
heir of Sir Harry Stephen, 3rd Bt., VW's cousin, with whom she shared a great-
grandmother in the person of William Wilberforce's sister Sarah. James Stephen
had written on 20 July to inform VW that the centenary of Wilberforce's birth
was about to be celebrated in Hull, where he intended to assert himself as a
descendent, and asking for her financial and moral support. (See also *V VW Letters*,
no. 2767.) David Low (1891-1963), New Zealand-born political cartoonist; Kingsley Martin had commissioned him to do a series of caricatures of prominent
people for publication in the *NS&N* and wished VW to be included. Herbert Feis
(1893-1972), Economic Adviser, U.S. Department of State, 1931-7; he was chief
technical adviser to the American delegation to the World Economic and Monetary
Conference which was held in London from 12 June to 27 July 1933, and had
previously worked for the League of Nations.
11. VW—as Virginia Stephen—lived at 29 Fitzroy Square with her brother Adrian
from 1907 until 1911. Walter Headlam (1866-1906), Greek scholar and Fellow of
King's College, Cambridge, and Hilton Young (1879-1960; see *I VW Diary*,
18 March 1918) had both to some extent engaged VW's feelings and fantasies. No
memoir concerning this chapter of her past has come to light.
12. Elizabeth Read, an admirer of VW with literary aspirations, had been a social
worker in Stepney; she lived with one Gilbert Denny and they divided their time
between a cottage in Shropshire and Sheffield where she also did social work. But
she stayed for some months in a cottage in Rodmell, and was now at Glynde.
See MHP, Sussex, letters.

Now we come down & are given all the lawyers letters. Signora Colli who looked after the dying demented Hastie—Hastie's letters to Mr Duncan in Aberdeen on politics very interesting; & her perpetual shifting of Josephus, Macaulay & so on—this Colli writes that she had expected 600 a year. And so would certainly have got it, had Miss H. signed a codicil. P[ercy]. & Mrs B. say they will offer her £50 p.a. if the other legatee will do the same. She is not grasping, Miss Colli, accounts for every penny, & Dr Potts is humane: & the B.'s full of sense & restraint—more than I, had I suddenly one thousand ⟨without working⟩. These little tributes to human nature are deserved after Hitler & Mussolini—about whom Miss Hastie often wrote. I figure her perpetually arranging her blue & gold tea set, her fathers watch, the bon bon box, & the card box made of the Fern oak in Windsor "which was mentioned in Shakespeare" in the house in Florence, where she lived with Colli aged 76.[13]

Tuesday 8 August

Since we came here I have been twice to Charleston; seen the Keyneses; been to Worthing; had Eth Read (a nice shrewd hard girl with a public mind) to tea; the Easdales & Norman Stewart (a clever, good fellow, scientist) to tea; expect Mrs Nef at 3 to discuss her scandalous memoirs: we go to London on Friday & Ethel comes on Sunday. Is this peace?[1] I'm heavy brained today—its been so hot; & I have read Mrs Nef from 10 to 12.20. Scandals about USA: but I am sworn to secrecy. I imagine a pretty youngish jumpy intellectual-fashionable American, completely disoriented; writes rather well; interesting; but all at sea.

Saturday 12 August

So naturally after Mrs Nef I was so tired—I shivered & shook. I went to bed for 2 days & slept I daresay 7 hours, visiting the silent realms again. It strikes me—what are these sudden fits of complete exhaustion? I come in here to write: cant even finish a sentence; & am pulled under;

13. For Mrs Lydia Bartholomew, wife of LW's gardener, see above, 4 June 1932. Miss Helena Lydia Hastie, who had died a month previously in Florence, had indeed bequeathed to her half of her £17,430 personal estate in Great Britain. George Duncan, Advocate in Aberdeen, was one of Miss Hastie's executors and proved her will, with its thirteen codicils allocating and re-allocating her personal possessions, some of which VW details.

1. Norman Stewart (or, according to LW, Stuart), unidentified. Elinor Castle Nef (1895-1953), wife of John Ulric Nef, a member of the faculty of the University of Chicago; he published his wife's *Letters & Notes, Volume I* after her death in 1953; it included sections related to VW.

now is this some odd effort; the sub-conscious pulling me down into her? I've been reading Faber on Newman; compared his account of a nervous breakdown; the refusal of some part of the mechanism; is that what happens to me?[2] Not quite. Because I'm not evading anything. I long to write The Pargiters. No. I think the effort to live in 2 spheres: the novel; & life is a strain; Nefs's almost break me, because they strain me so far from the other world; I only want walking & perfectly spontaneous childish life with L. & the accustomed when I'm writing at full tilt: to have to behave with circumspection & decision to strangers wrenches me into another region; hence the collapse.

Still, Saturday, I cant focus; am disoriented; sleepy; physically tired, but quite calm; the dear old repetitions soothe me again: L.; Pinka; dinner; tea; papers; music; I have a dread of 'seeing' people: increase this in anticipation: but what I dread is the wrench to another sphere.

Wednesday 16 August

And owing to Sir Alan Cobham's flying, & Angelica & Julian & fetching the boat I had another headache, & bed, & didnt see Ethel, but heard her voice & have 6 pages on the subject this morning,[3] & didnt see the Wolves, & am out here again, nibbling at The P.s & thinking Oh Lord how am I ever going to pull all that into shape! What a tremendous struggle it'll be! Never mind. I want to discuss Form, having been reading Turgenev. (but how my hand trembles after one of these headaches—cant lay hands on words or pens exactly—the habit has been broken)

Form then, is the sense that one thing follows another rightly. This is partly logic. T. wrote & re-wrote. To clear the truth of the unessential. Dostoevsky But then D. would say that everything matters. But one cant read D. again. Now Sh[akespea]re. was constrained in form by the stage (T. says one must find a new form for the old subject: but here, I suppose, uses the word differently—) The essential thing in a scene is to be preserved. How do you know what this is? How do we know if the D. form is better or worse than the T. It seems less per-

2. See *Oxford Apostles: A Character Study of the Oxford Movement* by Geoffrey Cust Faber, 1933, pp. 59f and 177f where John Henry Newman's breakdowns of 1820 and 1827 are considered.

3. Sir Alan Cobham (1894-1973), pioneer aviator, whose company National Aviation Ltd toured the British Isles in 1932 and 1933 giving air displays; the Woolfs took Julian and Angelica Bell to see it in Lewes on 12 August. On 14 August Ethel Smyth, who was staying with Maurice Baring at Rottingdean, came to Monks House but was not allowed to see VW; her long reproachful letter ('wonderful to sit in your house . . . only a board between us') of 15 August is in the Berg; for VW's reply, see *V VW Letters*, no. 2775.

manent. T.'s idea that you the writer states the essential & lets the reader do the rest. D. to supply the reader with every possible help & suggestion. T. reduces the possibilities.

The difficulty about criticism is that it is so superficial The writer has gone so much deeper. T. kept a diary for Bazarov: wrote everything from his point of view. We have only 250 short pages.[4] Our criticism is only a birds eye view of the pinnacle of an iceberg. The rest under water. One might begin it in this way. The article might be more broken, less composed than usual.

Thursday 24 August

A week ago, on Friday to be precise, having got my wind again, I dipped into The Pargiters, & determined to sweat it bare of flesh before going on, accumulating more scenes. I am rearranging too, all the first part, so as to bring it together. The death happens in the first chapter now. I think I shall reduce the size by half; it is however a little bare & jerky at present. Moreover it is rather a rush & a strain. I have just killed Mrs P. & cant shoot ahead to Oxford. For the truth is these little scenes embroil one, just as in life; & one cant switch off to a different mood all in a second. It seems to me that the realness of the beginning is complete. I have a good excuse for poetry in the second part, if I can take it. Rather an interesting experiment—if I could see the same thing from two different views.

And now I have spent the morning reading the Confessions of Arsene Houssaye left here yesterday by Clive.[5] What a vast fertility of pleasure books hold for me! I went in & found the table laden with books. I looked in & sniffed them all. I could not resist carrying this one off & broaching it. I think I could happily live here & read forever.

It is true, we have many interruptions. Yesterday, after knocking against a wild Alsatian that ran into the car—we gave him a great bang— he lay squirming—dead, I thought, then reeled up & went galloping over the field, unhurt, though he broke our lamps & bent the mud guard— after this unpleasant shock, Clive came & Julian & Frances Marshall. Clive said only one thing to hurt me—how I could not take a beating at a

---

4. 'Turgenev kept a "dossier" or set down a sort of biography for each of his characters—in this case [Fathers and Sons] a journal of the protagonist Bazarov.' Avrahm Yarmolinsky, Turgenev: The Man, his Art and his Age, a book VW had reviewed in 1927 (Kp C281). Notes VW made at this time concerning Turgenev are in the Berg (Holograph Reading Notes, Vol. I).

5. Arsène Houssaye (1815-96) went to Paris as a young man and threw himself into literary and artistic society there; in the 1850s he became director of the Comédie Française. He published four volumes of his reminiscences (Confessions) in 1885 and a further two in 1891.

game. That was a feeble effort, compared with what he can do in that line. Otherwise we were affable enough; & played bowls; & Fanny asked us to Ham Spray, where we may go, if we make our Western tour. Still, we see too many people, to my view: the Kingsley Martins, who are to me mentally & physically unattractive people; the sort of people George Trevelyan would have liked 25 years ago:[6] this struck me, for their views are 'right', & she is ugly stringy earnest plain. K. eats so sloppily. And they force themselves upon us. Into the bargain, I have heard from Tom, & from Peter [Lucas]. Tom is all artifice & quips & querks. A defence. One of these days perhaps he'll give up the trick, with marriage, or perhaps religion.[7] All the same, our quiet days, in between times, are rightly balanced, full of peace, & possibilities. How happy, when people go, to get our dinner, & sit alone, & go to bed in my airy room, where the rising sun on the apples & asparagus wakes me, if I leave the curtain open. I am reading all Turgenev, with a view to an article; for I intend to space the arduous sections of The P.s with serene criticism. This keeps me in reading while I spin fiction. A happy day today, without visitors. Hugh Jones & the Cartwrights, alas, tomorrow.[8]

Sunday 27 August

The Cartwrights werent so bad after all, though a bit of a grind—two gawky girls, & Hugh, a schoolboy, with a crest worked on his coat pocket. The girls squawked a little; too genteel over their tea, which they devoured. I had had the forethought to buy sugar cakes in Lewes, where we had to go in the morning, to take Martin's [garage] man back; for he had brought the car, refurbished from the Alsatian. And my typewriter ribbon had gone wrong. So we went in & found Lewes in festival—the corporation fidgetting about on a doorstep covered with dull red: the local tradesmen habited in blue robes with thin strips of fur, because the

6. George Macaulay Trevelyan, OM (1876-1962), the Regius Professor of Modern History at Cambridge, was R. C. (Bob) Trevelyan's younger brother; he was married to a daughter of the high-minded Mrs Humphry Ward.

7. Eliot wrote, on 16 August, to say that since his return from America he had been living quietly in the country 'observing the habits of finches and wagtails, composing nonsense verses'; and that it would give him 'great solace and satisfaction' to spend a night at Rodmell any time in September. He signed himself: 'Your obedient servant, T.S.E. (now Honorary Member of the Michael Mullins Marching & Chowder Club).'

8. Philip Hugh Jones (b. 1917) was the son of Philip Morrell and Alice Jones who had been his secretary during the war; she was now an indispensible member of the NS&N staff. Mrs Cartwright had been in charge of the Hogarth Press office from July 1925 to March 1930; she had two daughters.

troops were coming, on their economy march to Arundel.[9] We ran into them; dirty men in shirtsleeves, marching, with the flaps of their caps let down over their necks, it was so hot. The natives of Lewes stood at the bottom of Station Street waving handkerchiefs, bobbing their umbrellas up & down. Not an inspiring sight—the British army; & I disliked the credulous fat faced old women who had been dabbing their handkerchiefs in the air. But the Cartwrights had their cakes, & we played bowls. They are all 3 becoming scientists, possibly scientific chemists, science, they say being the most popular subject now, though they are doubtful about jobs. Now & again Hugh reminded me of Philip. The same green blue prominent eyes, & I thought that I detected perhaps a finer grain in him than in the others. But L. denies this. They were nice, simple, shy; why did they come, I wondered? Did Mrs C. & Mrs J. insist? We drove them over to the Sea Hotel on the front at Seaford, & I saw seaside life going on. And they seemed very young & unfitted—I mean, the average, not the exception. They bathe, running down the steps of the sea hotel into the sea. A sort of beauty too. Not that I liked the couple in evening dress who passed. She was wearing a fur coat. Why dress for dinner? To show your social standing? Home, & Tarring Neville looked very lovely.

And I forgot to say that Flush has been chosen by the American Book Society. Lord!

Wednesday 30 August

And two days ago, sitting in the garden at Charleston, Clive in his queer jerky way said he had very bad news of Francis Birrell & brought out a letter from Raymond. F. has a tumour on his brain & is to be operated on, perhaps, today. So all night I dreamt of him, my dream giving me, as my dreams often do, the essence of a relationship which in real life will never find expression. I remember sitting beside him on a sofa, & how we kissed & kissed, as friends; though in my dream I do not think that I knew he was ill. I am rather haunted by it. Think of waiting all yesterday, for an operation which may well be fatal. What should I have felt had I been him? And why was I not him? The sense of friends dying is a very terrible one.

Yesterday here was hot, baking hot; & Campbell Douglas came, 10.30: Robson 2.30. "Call me Willie" he said at 5: at 6 Vita came; Mr Neil Lyons strolled in from the road to beg bay leaves for his pickled herrings, & a sprig of hazel since he suspects himself of being a water diviner.[10]

9. The 1st Battalion, The Royal Sussex Regiment, marched from Dover to Arundel via Lewes and Brighton, where they were fêted and spent the night of 26 August.
10. Rev. the Hon. Leopold Douglas Campbell-Douglas (1881-1940), later 6th Baron Blythswood, had been a friend of LW's since university days; from 1927-31 he

Vita stayed the night; we had grouse for dinner; she spent the morning talking to me; & Mary Hutchinson has just rung up to suggest a visit. Tomorrow we go to London.

Saturday 2 September

With that usual dread of asking for news on the telephone, I rang up Raymond on Thursday & heard to my extreme relief, that F.'s case is not so bad nearly as it seemed. The growth is small, thought to [be] on the outside, & there seems no reason why he should not recover. I seemed to see him hauled up into the air again as R. spoke. The operation is next week. Curious how all ones fibres seem to expand & fill with air when anxiety is taken off; curious also to me the intensity of my own feelings: I think imagination, the picture making power, decks up feelings with all kinds of scenes; so that one goes on thinking, instead of localising the event. All very mysterious. But anyhow I expanded, & felt very fond of that dear old rattling milk lorry, & hoped he would see me out, & must bring myself to write to him. Partly selfishness, of course, this horror, that it means another extinction of one's own life: brings death nearer. But let us think no more of death. Its life that matters, to quote my quotation from Montaigne.[1]

Suddenly in the night I thought of "Here & Now" as a title for The Pargiters. I think it better. It shows what I'm after & does not compete with the Herries Saga, the Forsyte Saga & so on.[2] I have now done the first part; I mean compressed it, shall, I think, compress Eleanor's day, & then what? The rest does not admit of much compression. I think I have reduced it to 80,000 words perhaps; but it seems to me there must be another 40, to come. 80+40 = 120,00[0]. If so it will be the longest of my little brood—longer than N[ight]. & D[ay]. I imagine

As Percy says when he brings in the slop pail & I'm boiling the kettle "You've never had such a summer". No I say, "its been fine since Christmas" which is more or less the case. We have steadied the old ship & sail through blue days again. L. is having the new pond made, the old one re-grouted, & is going to pave the front garden. Flush, I think with some pleasure, has made these extravagances possible. We should net £2,000 from that six months dogged & dreary grind. What will people

---

had been vicar of Ringmer in Sussex, but now held the living of Stockcross in Berkshire. A. Neil Lyons (1880-1940), prolific author and journalist, lived at Rock Cottage, Southease.

1. 'my own version of Montaigne'; cf. *III VWD*, p. 8.
2. Hugh Walpole's series of four novels about the Herries family, later (1939) re-published as *The Herries Chronicle*; he had just sent VW an advance copy of the fourth, *Vanessa*. *The Forsyte Saga*, by John Galsworthy.

say of that little book I wonder, without great anxiety. Tom wrote yesterday, telling me, in his jaunty uneasy manner, to conceal his address, & the date of his visit. The mystery I imagine flatters him. But we shall see deeper into that dark well perhaps.[3] And I have had 2 blessed days of silence. & we walked on the marsh today, & saw a drowned sheep, & were flurried by our 3 dogs. And I have decided by the way not to accept the Leslie Stephen lectureship which has not been offered me, & feel comfortably cool & obscure & anonymous. As Lytton once said, success came to us too late to make us hop on our perches.[4]

I am reading with extreme greed a book by Vera Britain, called The Testament of Youth. Not that I much like her. A stringy metallic mind, with I suppose, the sort of taste I should dislike in real life. But her story, told in detail, without reserve, of the war, & how she lost lover & brother, & dabbled her hands in entrails, & was forever seeing the dead, & eating scraps, & sitting five on one WC, runs rapidly, vividly across my eyes. A very good book of its sort. The new sort, the hard anguished sort, that the young write; that I could never write. Nor has anyone written that kind of book before. Why now? What urgency is there on them to stand bare in public? She feels that these facts must be made known, in order to help—what? herself partly I suppose. And she has the social conscience. I have still to read how she married the infinitely dreary Catlin & found beauty & triumph in poor, gaping Holtby. But I give her credit for having lit up a long passage to me at least. I read & read & read & neglect Turgenev & Miss C. Burnett.[5] But why does my hand shake? Why cant I write clearly?

Sunday 10 September[6]

To begin with another question (just read the last pages) why am I sitting here at 10.30 on a Sunday morning, rather stiff in the back, rather

3. T. S. Eliot wrote from Cardiganshire on 31 August suggesting dates for his visit; he came to Monks House for twenty-four hours on 9 September.
4. The Leslie Stephen Lectureship at Cambridge had been founded by his friends in 1905 for the biennial delivery of a public lecture 'on some literary subject, including therein criticism, biography, and ethics'. It was not, as she says, offered to VW.
5. *Testament of Youth* by Vera Brittain (1894-1970) was published in August 1933. In 1925 she married George Catlin (1879-1979), from 1924-35 Professor of Politics at Cornell University; he had been an Exhibitioner at New College, Oxford, and VW possibly met him there when staying with her cousin the Warden, H. A. L. Fisher. Until her marriage Vera Brittain shared a flat with Winifred Holtby, whom she had met on returning to Oxford after war service as a nurse, and about whom she wrote in *Testament of Friendship* (1940). Ivy Compton Burnett's fifth novel *More Women than Men* was published in 1933; in 1929 a previous novel submitted to the Hogarth Press had been rejected.
6. VW misdated this *Sunday 13th Sept.*

sore of the lips, writing diary, not novel? Because of dear old Tom largely. 24 hours (short interval for sleep) solid conversation, preluded by 2 hours flimsy conversation with the Hutchinsons. And at 1.30 Rosamond & Wogan to lunch; & at 4.30 Charleston to tea. Hence I am sitting here. Tomorrow, in the divine peace of Monday, I shall walk on the downs & think of Tom & my parched lips with some degree of pleasure. Yes, it was worth it, though when a second day seemed on the cards my tongue fainted & my heart stood still. He is 10 years younger: hard, spry, a glorified boy scout in shorts & yellow shirt. He is enjoying himself very much. He is tight & shiny as a wood louse (I am not writing for publication). But there is well water in him, cold & pure. Yes I like talking to Tom. But his wing sweeps curved & scimitar like round to the centre himself. He's settling in with some severity to being a great man. Keats wasn't that. We talked about Keats's letters. Tom said that letter writing was a form he preferred to Times leader writing. I think this hints some change in his views. He said that he no longer ⟨thought⟩ felt quite so sure of a science of criticism. He also said that people exaggerate the intellectuality & erudition of his poetry. "For example Ross Williamson in his book on me. . . ." He says that very seriously. I couldnt quote Holtby with the same candour. Ross apparently attributed the dog, in Tom's quotation from Webster, to profound associations with the dog star. Not a bit of it says Tom: I was having a joke about Webster.[7] I connect all this with his bubbling up of life. At 46 he wants to live, to love; even seeing Rochester is an event to him. He has seen nothing, nobody, for the last 10 years. We had it out about V. at breakfast. Some asperity on Tom's part. He wont admit the excuse of insanity for her— thinks she puts it on; tries to take herself in; for this reason, mystifies Eth Bowen. I thought him a little resentful of all the past waste & exaction. I gather he will see a good deal of us: & if I had time, & if I could move the heavy stone of his self esteem an inch or two higher, I should like to talk out to Tom about writing. Only there's always the reservation—I cant talk about "my writing"; so that talk about his writing palls[?]. But I am to find him 2 rooms in Somers Town.[8] And we agreed about the infamy

7. See *The Waste Land*, line 74: '"Oh keep the Dog far hence, that's friend to men/Or with his nails he'll dig it up again!"', and *The White Devil*, V, 5 (Cornelia's dirge): 'But keep the wolf far thence, that's foe to men,/For with his nails he'll dig them up again.' Hugh Ross Williamson (1901-78), in *The Poetry of T. S. Eliot* (1932), p. 104, wrote: 'The "Dog" of course is Sirius, the Dog Star, which in Egypt was regarded as the herald of the fertilising floods of the Nile.'
8. VW did make some attempt to find rooms for Eliot (see below, 14 November 1933) and he refers to the problem in letters to her until the end of the year (copies, MHP, Sussex). However he found lodgings in South Kensington and then became a paying guest of the vicar of St Stephen's, Gloucester Road, of which church he became Vicar's Warden in 1934.

of teaching English; the idiocy of lectures; the whole hierarchy of professor, system & so on: at any rate I got him to go some way with me in denouncing Oxford & Cambridge. He learnt (1) self confidence at Oxford; (2) how to write plain English—thats all. I daresay though he will become Prof. of Poetry at Oxford one of these days.

His father was a brick merchant in St Louis; & they lived in the slums among vacant lots. & his father always gave away money; & died, alas, in 1919 before Tom had become—well, happily his mother lived to see him what she called (& I daresay Tom too) a great man.[9] What a queer naïve vanity all this is! But of course, when you are thrown like an assegai into the hide of the world—this may be a definition of genius—there you stick; & Tom sticks. To shut out, to concentrate—that is perhaps—perhaps—one of the necessary conditions. And now it is close on eleven; the bells are tolling; the leaves are very bright on pear tree & apple tree; & I think I shall dawdle over letters & books—I must read 12th night for Lydia's extortion (an article on her appearance)[10] & so drowse as quietly as possible till we have to talk incessantly till 8 o'clock—& then O Lord— quiet, dine alone, & sleep in my airy room; & no talk tomorrow or tomorrow.

(why not write a book—of Cr[itics]m in this style?)

Saturday 23 September

This summer, I may say by way of criticism, & as a warning, has been too broken up with people. Next year I intend to be more circumspect. For the past fortnight I have lived, I say, as other people live—that is outwardly. I gave up The P.s, had reached the end of the revision; & as we had the Lucas's, Angelica & [*her friend*] Eve [Younger], to stay, also to go to London, to dine with the Hutches, to have Morgan for the week end, & the memoir Club tonight, it seemed wise to attempt no concentration; but to participate with one's friends. I've had to wedge in though, that horrid tough little article on 12th night; which being tentatively roughed out this morning I write here.

And it is a thorough wet day. The ponds are filling. L.'s new pond & garden are almost done, & surprisingly good, I think. The summer is put away folded up in the drawer with other summers. By Gods grace we may get 10 or 12 days without visitors before going back, but I say this not with conviction. The truth is, I like it when people actually come; but I love it when they go. It was this subconsciously that made me assume

9. She died in 1929, aged eighty-six.
10. Lydia Lopokova was to appear as Olivia in Tyrone Guthrie's production of *Twelfth Night* at the Old Vic. The Woolfs drove to London on 20 September, dined with the Hutchinsons before the performance, and returned to Rodmell after it. VW's review was published in the *NS&N* on 30 September 1933 (Kp C339).

that Peter & Prudence were only staying the night—whereas he had suggested two nights. This was the cause of some embarrassment. We had to go to London soon after breakfast.[11] She is one of the direct shorthaired terrier kind, breaking, unexpectedly, into loud barks. Why Peter, the fastidious, should commit himself for life to her, after Topsy, I cant think. A hand raised in the High or the Low would summon 20 such instantly. For life!—good God! I could not envisage a week of that ardent, shadeless, untidy, loveless, beautyless little woman; at 22 perhaps: but think of 32, 42, 52—No. He is single eyed though; paces through life between blinkers, seeing only the high road. Perhaps Prudence serves as giglamp. She works for him in libraries. They quote Greek & Latin. And he never reads a book unless he is going to write about it, she says. And so he will pen his way through life—charming, honest, fastidious, ascetic as he is; & will leave a long trail of books behind him—which I shall never read, because he writes with frozen fingers.

Old Ethel came, grown stout. And as I say, we go to Brighton today to meet Morgan, & I shall read my memoir tonight, send off my article on Monday morning, & so consider myself quit of all duties to my friends.[12] Monday begins my holiday, my breathing space. I shall go for a long walk, I tell myself, & read Smoke [*Turgenev*] in the evening, having played a game of bowls with L. And it will be a very fine day. And I shall pull open my curtains & see the stars at night. Really a marvellous spectacle—all for nothing. I am reading Margot—"V W our greatest English authoress;" Molly Hamilton on Webbs: & Turgenev.[13]

Tuesday 26 September

Why not, one of these days, write a fantasy on the theme of Crabbe?— a biographical fantasy—an experiment in biography?[14]

11. F. L. (Peter) Lucas, having separated from his first wife Topsy (the novelist E. B. C. Jones) in 1929, in 1932 married a potter and sculptor considerably younger than himself, Prudence Dalzell Wilkinson. They came to Monks House on 19 September, and the Woolfs were committed to going to London the following day to see *Twelfth Night*.

12. The Woolfs and E. M. Forster dined with the Keyneses before the Memoir Club meeting at Tilton. VW presumably read the lost memoir centred on Fitzroy Square and 'proposals of marriage' (see above, 30 July 1933, and *Moments of Being*, p. 182). The other reader was Forster. Her article was that on *Twelfth Night* (Kp C339).

13. See *More Memories* (1933) by Margot Oxford, p. 205 fn: '. . . this year (1931) the greatest of our English authoresses—Virginia Woolf—told me that my writing had always given her pleasure.' *Sidney and Beatrice Webb* (1933) by Mary Agnes Hamilton.

14. VW's only known essay on George Crabbe (1754-1832) is that published posthumously in *The Captain's Death Bed* (Kp A30).

I had so much of the most profound interest to write here—a dialogue of the soul with the soul,—& I have let it all slip—why? Because of feeding the gold fish, of looking at the new pond, of playing bowls. Nothing remains now. I forget what It was about. Happiness. The perfect day, which was yesterday. And so on. Now I began the morning by telephoning corrections of 12th Night to the N.S., put in a comma, take out semi-colon; & so on. Then I come out here, having seen the carp, & write Turgenev.

Monday 2 October

Yes. I had to write about the memoir Club, & Molly's biting our hands. "Its torture anyhow, when one cant hear a word". Then they all came over, & we sat on the terrace; eleven people here; Julian in outline with E. Read. "Julian's going to teach me to think" she said as she went. I had to scurry back to MacCarthys. Thats all over.

Its October now; & we have to go to Hastings Conference tomorrow & Wednesday, to Vita, then back to London. I opened this in order to make one of my self-admonishments previous to publishing a book. Flush will be out on Thursday & I shall be very much depressed, I think, by the kind of praise. They'll say its 'charming' delicate, ladylike. And it will be popular. Well now I must let this slip over me without paying it any attention. I must concentrate on The Pargiters—or Here & Now. I must not let myself believe that I'm simply a ladylike prattler: for one thing its not true. But they'll all say so. And I shall very much dislike the popular success of Flush. No, I must say to myself, this is a mere wisp, a rill of water; & so create, hardly [?] fiercely, as I feel now more able to do than ever before.

Thursday 5 October

No, I will not tackle the peculiarity of Turgenev. For one thing we are starting at 11.30 sharp for Sissinghurst; & then I spent yesterday in bed; headache; infinite weariness up my back: clouds forming in my neck; half asleep; through the rift reading Steen (author of Stallion) on Hugh Walpole. My word—how Hugh can let that rotten pear lie on his name God knows. "God is Romance. God is The Character in Hugh Wal's novels" & so on.[1] And then Flush has taken his first fence, the Lit Sup, at a bound. Also to my pleasure, some obscure journalist detects no signs

1. Marguerite Steen (1894-1975), of whom, according to his biographer Rupert Hart-Davis, Walpole 'became very fond: she was his type of woman—intelligent, uninhibited, amusing and undemanding'. Her novel *Stallion* and *Hugh Walpole: A Study* were both published this year.

of whimsicality.[2] So, though I shall get some nasty raps in the weeklies, I am sunning my wings this morning: this bright soft October morning: when the pear tree has a spatter of bright leaves; Caburn is under mist; the big pond is almost full; the little pond done; & thank Heaven, L. & I are driving off, ever so happily, through Kent. This is going to be a happy day, I say;

On Tuesday we went to Hastings; a queer experience always, that conference: a door opened into a buzzing bursting humming perfectly self dependent other world. Bevan [Bevin] was vociferating when we came in. But they were all marking time owing to a compromise.[3] There are details I never get clear. When one of the tub thumpers was up, we went & sat on the balcony. The Hall is a very gay frivolous seaside hall, & the ships passed adapted for municipal concerts dances & so on. We very indifferently sat out & had coffee on a green table, & Gillies came, on the horizon & Phil Baker, & they dissected policies, again invisible to me, though Gillies threw out the remark (in deference to me, perhaps?) that he was not naturally a politician, but preferred Gardens; had been staying at Zennor: W. A. F. has a whole field of gentians &c. Phil does not truckle to the arts, for which I like him. I always think about his teeth being filed.[4] And then the Rodent—a mixture of Bob [Trevelyan] & Youngs—reminiscent of my early youth— a rather thin, water blooded kind of man, with hair parted & steel grey eyes—& a mouth like a spinsters reticule, but of course humane, vitalised by his humanity, sufferings of negroes, son who goes to Russia, vegetarian, once every 3 weeks overcome with lust for beef—ate fish—he gave us lunch at Frascati's, or some such place.[5] I had a vast plate of beef. L.

2. 'Brown Beauty', a one-column review in the *TLS*, 5 October 1933; the obscure journalist not traced.
3. The Labour Party annual Conference opened at the White Rock Pavilion, Hastings, on 2 October; the Woolfs attended on the two following days. The debate on 3 October was on the policy report, and the 'compromise' concerned the withdrawal of an amendment requiring the means 'for a rapid and complete conversion of the capitalist into a socialist system' by the next Labour government to be specified by the National Executive. Ernest Bevin (1881-1951), General Secretary of the TGWU 1921-40, and a member of the TUC General Council, was a vociferous critic of the compromise.
4. William Gillies was secretary of the International Department of the Labour Party; he had been staying with Will Arnold-Forster in Cornwall. Philip Noel-Baker (b. 1889), ex-Labour MP, was at this time assistant to the president of the Disarmament Conference at Geneva; see *II VW Diary*, 17 October 1924: 'Phil Baker is standing as a Labour candidate. Irene [his wife] will have his teeth filed and get him in—(a scrap of *real* dialogue).'
5. Charles Roden Buxton (1875-1942), whom LW described as a 'good man' and 'mentally and emotionally a nineteenth-century non-conformist Liberal . . . never completely at home in the twentieth-century Labour Party' (*IV LW*, p. 245), was

fed Pinka on the bone of his cutlet. R. in his way genial, a man of the world; a gentleman I thought as I followed him through his hotel by a secret passage out. He held himself so well. Then to the Queens Hotel where the bigwigs lodge: & then Rodent being a gentleman wished to entertain us & crooked his finger & summoned Pethick Lawrence & Mr Robertson & the lady who calls herself Mrs being in fact a Fitzroy & the friend of Mrs Walter. I talked to Pethick L.; a frost-bitten blue eyed little old man now; & he was reading Holtby on V.W. You *are* V.W.? Yes. I said; & then in my emotional way praised his speech that wet day at Brighton: which kindled him a little; & he told me about his wife, now speaking at Oxford about armament firms.[6] I was enlightened & horrified; how France & Germany combine to stir up war—were joint manufacturers of guns & so on. All this should be a government industry he said. I said What an argument against Capitalism! And then he had to go to the Con[feren]ce to hear Dalton: but we could only stand very little of Hugh; & so went out, got into the car & drove home.[7]

The night before we went to a meeting here, in the Club, & L. broached the question of a play ground. Captain Palmer talked to me—a man with one idea in his perfectly direct upright wizened tanned little being. His wife more voluptuous had been at Wye races therefore was sleepy. He had a great idea of duty to the village: called the men Back, Hubbard & so on, & thought it a disgrace that Toc H in Lewes should be asked to supply a helper to run a boys club. He was also inclined to think Mr Hancock a menace.[8] But I must get ready now for Vita.

Friday 6 October

Less jubilant, on account of Rebecca West's criticism: that F[lush] is

Chairman of the Labour Party Advisory Committees on International and Imperial Affairs of which LW was Secretary. The Youngs (see *I QB*, p. 131) were old family friends of the Stephens.

6. Frederick William Pethick-Lawrence (1871-1961) and his wife Emmeline (d. 1954) were active campaigners for Women's Suffrage and Disarmament. He had been, and was again to be, a Labour MP and a Minister; he was made a peer in 1945. VW had presumably heard him speak at the Labour Party Conference at Brighton which she attended in 1929. Mrs Walter had been VW's housekeeper for a few months in 1930 (see *III VW Diary*, p. 305); she and her husband Karl had a wide acquaintance in the Labour and Co-operative movements. Robertsons, unidentified.

7. Hugh Dalton (1887-1962), a member of the Labour Party's National Executive who, like Roden Buxton and Pethick Lawrence, had lost his seat in the 1931 election, returned to Parliament in 1935. At this time he held a post as Reader in Economics at London University.

8. Rodmell Social Club met on 2 October; Capt. Francis Palmer, MC, was a fairly recent resident of the village.

not one of my best &c: but rather braced.[9] The problem will now be how to guide oneself through popularity: a curious reversal of my old problem; but I daresay the same. An interesting problem: I like problems to change. Now for Turgenev, in my braced mood. It is better to write braced than relaxed—

[Saturday 7 October]

no doubt true; but this morning (Saturday) cheered by Bunny's praise. Says its a new venture; the best in proportion & so on.[10] And today not a word about me anywhere. So thats soothing. And if tomorrow were over, Sunday Times & Observer through, I could settle in snugly. Oh & Morgan says my memoir was 'wonderful'; which pleases me for the light it throws on Here & Now. Perhaps I can bring off that style.[11] And now, letters, packing, going from the lodge to the house; a damp dull day so far, but it will clear. However there's the cement works here; so I must balance one thing with another. A very crowded gay summer in its way. Too crowded; but what happiness, coming back that night from London with L. for example: the country at midnight. And going [?] up early; & bowls, & our solitary evenings; & cooking dinner.

Monday 9 October

52 Tavistock Square

Back again & our burden is on us. Mrs Woolf yesterday; today David Cecil; tomorrow Nessa Quentin Julian lunch; Hugh Walpole tea; Thursday Vita & Mrs St. Aubyn—& so it begins, with Sibyl & Rosamund in the background.[12] I'm through the Flush wave though. A small one,

9. *Flush: A Biography* was published by the Hogarth Press on 5 October 1933. Rebecca West, in her review 'A Dog's Life with the Brownings. Two Poets through the Eyes of a Spaniel' in the *Daily Telegraph* of 6 October, wrote: 'This is perhaps not one of the works over which Mrs Woolf's most devoted admirers will feel their greatest enthusiasm ... It sometimes produces the effect ... of a family joke that has been too hardy in leaving the four walls of its origin, and facing the rude airs of the great world.'

10. David Garnett, who in March had succeeded Ellis Roberts as Literary Editor of the *NS&N*, wrote in his 'Books in General' page on 7 October 1933: 'Most important of all, it is something quite fresh ... *Flush* is more perfectly proportioned than any of her books—as well proportioned as its subject was himself. It amused Mrs Woolf to write and it has brought out her delightful humour as nothing else has done.'

11. E. M. Forster wrote on 5 October from Abinger Hammer: 'I much enjoyed my week end, thought my own paper good and yours wonderful.' (Berg).

12. The Hon. Mrs Francis St Aubyn, *née* Gwendolen Nicolson (b. 1896) was Harold Nicolson's sister and for some years henceforward was to be Vita's most intimate

compared with others. Desmond praises: Morn P. tears me between the rough, coarse yellow feeble teeth of poor Mr Grigson.[13] So its over: & if it werent for the strain of people, dentists, clothes—but no: I'm going to master this. I'm going to let my self have room & verge enough. Talk of leaving London yesterday & moving the Press to Monks House: talk of buying a cottage in the North. We have plenty of money anyhow.

A soft day; have to take the car to Hendon, am writhing with Turgenev of a morning. Can I finish this week, & start Here & now next? Can I?

[Monday 16 October]

And then Desmond broke in; yes—but today is Monday again, the 16th; & I have lived through the scrimmage of that week, & actually at 2.30 today, delivered my Turgenev to the typist, & so have tomorrow free for Here & Now. Free—yes. After Philip W[oolf]. & Babs to supper yesterday. I pared the cold mutton & put it in the pot. Mary comes today: L. is sneezing; pray God not a cold; Miss Evans [unidentified] is pending; & I want, rather vainly, to read the Book of Job. Tomorrow & tomorrow & tomorrow. Yesterday we said Time stand still & walked up a hill outside Princes Risborough. I seem to have stopped inventing The P.s about Aug 20th then rewrote:

Friday 20 October

Did I say I was going to write Here & Now? Not a word done. L. had influenza; so Elly says. Up & about in 2 days of course. But last night I came to the decision to stop the career of the Hogarth Press; to revert to Richmond days. What is the use of drudging & sweating & curtailing Siena & entirely obliterating all Italy England Ireland & Greece for the sake of publishing Susan Lawrence & bad novels? No. Here we stop & take a fresh course—We go to Rodmell tomorrow & I shall there broach the new scheme. Look, I cant write, cant hold a pen, all for the bother & the worry. I can only hear the pump booming. Its true I wrote the Turgenev, all yesterday till my head spun. Its true we've had the devils own week. But to me the Press has lost its spring & balance, & could regain it if it now made a constriction to the old ideals. We might start the magazine.

---

friend. VW met her on 5 October when she and LW drove over to Sissinghurst for lunch.

13. See Desmond MacCarthy, 'The World of Books', *Sunday Times*, 8 October 1933, $1\frac{1}{2}$ columns on 'Two Poets and a Spaniel. Canine Biography'. Geoffrey Grigson (b. 1905), poet and critic and at this time literary editor of the *Morning Post*, wrote of *Flush* in the issue of 6 October 1933: 'Its continual mock-heroic tone, its bantering pedantry, its agile verbosity make it the most tiresome book which Mrs Woolf has yet written.'

It's possible that Flush is to be pictured. Brace yesterday talked of a substantial sum. It will fall through I suppose; but for Gods sake, why make more money? I have a thousand letters to write & Hampson to read—cant spin a sentence in the air, or even control my nib. So no more.[14]

Oh & Gerald Brenan's book is unmitigated trash—a sickly slab of plum cake iced with pink fly blown sugar, in spite of Bunny.[15]

Sunday 29 October

No my head is too tired to go on with Bobby & Elvira—theyre to meet at St Paul's—this morning. I wish I could get it full & calm & unconscious. This last is difficult, owing to Flush, owing to the perpetual little spatter of comment that keeps me awake. Yesterday the Granta said I was now defunct. Orlando Waves Flush represent the death of a potentially great writer.[16] This is only a rain drop; I mean the snub some little pimpled undergraduate likes to administer, just as he would put a frog in ones bed: but then there's all the letters, & the requests for pictures—so many that, foolishly perhaps, I wrote a sarcastic letter to the N.S.—thus procuring more rain drops.[17] This metaphor shows how tremendously important unconsciousness is when one writes. But let me remember that fashion in literature is an inevitable thing; also that one must grow & change; also that I have, at last laid hands upon my philosophy of anonymity. My letter to the N.S. is the crude public statement of a part of it. How odd last winter's revelation was! freedom; which now I find makes it quite easy for me to refuse

A man wrote to say that my letter is to be the basis of a new guild for the P. of P. See January number of something or other

14. In the Autumn Book Supplement of the *NS&N*, 14 October 1933, *Foreign English*, a novel by John Hampson, was announced for forthcoming publication by the Hogarth Press. It was never published. Perhaps once again (see 5 January 1933, n. 6) VW rejected it.

15. Gerald Brenan's novel *Jack Robinson* was published under the pseudonym George Beaton; it was eulogised by David Garnett in his 'Books in General' column in the *NS&N* of 14 October 1933: 'by far the most exciting literary event of the year, perhaps of very many years.' (In 1974 Brenan wrote of it: 'Today there is no book of mine that I dislike more.' *Personal Record*, p. 200.)

16. '. . . the deadly facility of [*Flush*] combined with its popular success mean . . . the end of Mrs Woolf as a live force. We must mourn the passing of a potentially great writer who perished for lack of an intelligent audience.' *The Granta*, 25 October 1933, in a review of *Flush*, together with the newly issued uniform Editions of *Orlando* and *The Waves*, signed F.C. (probably Frank Chapman, later a regular contributor to *Scrutiny*).

17. See *V VW Letters*, no. 2810 to the Editor of the *NS&N* on 'The Protection of Privacy', published 28 October 1933.

Sibyl's invitations, to take life much more strongly & steadily.[18] I will not be 'famous' 'great'. I will go on adventuring, changing, opening my mind & my eyes, refusing to be stamped & stereotyped. The thing is to free ones self; to let it find its dimensions, not be impeded. And though this as usual is only a pot shot, there is a great deal of substance in it. October has been a bad month; but might have been much worse without my philosophy. Its been harassed, then L. with influenza, if only for 2 days, quickens all my insight into disaster; then Nessa away; Quentin ill; with it all, however, I have forced myself to space out these horrors.

But enough. Raymond came yesterday: Francis still very much paralysed; after 10 minutes the Raymond machine clogs; an uneasy shallow sandy mind; Eth Bowen, improving; oh & the Kingsley Martins never cease to invite us to meet Low.

Shall I now read the New Testament?

The great family dinner is tonight.

I think the pump is improved, by a letter to Bentley.[19]

Sunday 12 November

I ought to have made a note on Nessa & the aeroplane—last Friday— no Friday week—at Croydon. We took them there at 7.[1] Had to be up by moonlight at 6.30. Drove across an empty delicately tinted London; lines all much marked; Croydon a great space like a green race course. We stood on the top of the roof; saw the aeroplane whirl, till the propellors were lost to sight—simply evaporated: then the aeroplane takes a slow run, circles & rises. This is death I said, feeling how the human contact was completely severed. Up they went with a sublime air & disappeared like a person dying, the soul going. And we remained. I saw the plane become a little mark on the sky. A good funeral could be arranged. And I did not at all enjoy waiting for Nessa to come back across the Alps: sat making conversation with Lady Simon. So thats over.

And our visit to Francis—the shaven Chinese Idol; old Birrell grown very soft & babyish, in slippers, with his shod stick beside him, apologis-

18. See above, 19 December 1932: 'Yes, I will be free & entire & absolute & mistress of my life by Oct. 1st 1933. Nobody shall come here on their terms; or hale me off to them on theirs.'
19. The dinner, at the Forum Club, was for Mrs Woolf's eighty-third birthday. Noise, from the buildings and the building operations in their neighbourhood, was a perpetual source of aggravation to VW which LW took what steps he could to reduce.
1. Quentin Bell had been ill since the summer; his pleurisy had now been diagnosed as tubercular, and treatment in a Swiss clinic was recommended. Vanessa flew with him from Croydon aerodrome to Geneva on 3 November; her return journey on 7 November was prolonged owing to fog over Paris.

ing in an airy way for the basin & hairbrushes—all very airy now, for he cant remember names—Vanessa or Virginia? & so on.[2] Now, this minute back from the Wogans; a lovely fox red glow from beech trees; old Oxford farm houses; theirs a large, too wide, too square & cold, old house; disguised, to me unpleasantly, by Banting's decorations—I prefer the old to the new there, unless done with more taste.[3] But how nice, easy, mobile, affectionate, & humane it all was. We talked of Lytton & Carrington last night, Wogan sent for, 30 miles, twice one day to master Ralph, who emerged from the bushes, where he was skulking, threatening suicide. And had barricaded his door against Frances. Wogan has a shrewd worldly sense for all his patter. Said Ralph play-acted; was a lonely, but boring man; brings you tea stark naked, a bull among heifers. Theyre all naked, they all comment eternally on 'parts' & breasts—a kind of rough parody of the old Ham Spray—Lytton acted in the kitchen. We walked this morning, but soft mist hid the hills; all was red brick Queen Anne, stately, arboreous—the moment of loveliness that comes to everything over it today. Harrod to lunch—a young[?] man with black eyebrows & white teeth.[4] So home to tea.

Tuesday 14 November

And I have precisely 3 minutes before tea to say that Jacqueline Stiven has taken up a great deal of time & inspired a great deal of ingenuity by sending a passage from A R of Ones O to the Statesman. L. was positive it was a hoax. But I have now been in touch with Mrs Miles Reid & Mrs Stiven the Syrian—names that will mean nothing to me in a years time.[5] We went to Islington this afternoon to look for rooms for Tom; it is a fine autumn day; Vita & Leon dined last night, & I am so dissipated I could not write a word this morning. Then Bunny came about the hoax.

2. The Woolfs went to Brighton on 3 November to see Francis Birrell, recuperating from his operation in September for a brain tumour. His father Augustine Birrell (1850-1933), the author and Liberal statesman, died on 20 November this year.
3. The Woolfs drove to Ipsden in Oxfordshire on 11 November to stay a night with Wogan and Rosamond Philipps; their house had been decorated by John Banting (1902-72), a member of the London Group, whose work showed the influence of both cubism and surrealism.
4. Roy (Forbes) Harrod (1900-78), economist, an Oxford Scholar who had studied under Keynes at Cambridge and published his biography in 1951, was at this time University Lecturer in Economics at Oxford.
5. The *NS&N* of 11 November 1933 printed a nine-line paragraph entitled 'A Dinner' over the name 'Jacqueline Stiven, *aetat* 14'; it was in fact a passage from *A Room of One's Own* sent in by a schoolgirl which the literary editor David (Bunny) Garnett, recognising the quality though not the author, decided to publish. His apology for this mistake appeared in the *NS&N* on 18 November.

So to tea, & I should add so to Westminster to hear The March of the Women, Ethel Smyth; & Rebecca speaking on married womens earnings. Instead I shall sleep over the fire, reading Tom's criticism, & Michael Field diaries, alone thank God.[6]

Thursday 23 November

Being too tired after dining with the Hutches last night to meet Michael Arlen to produce the finished article in Here & Now, perhaps I had better produce the raw. It was a real party—that is I wore my velvet dress.

But I took it in my stride. I was not much beglamoured. The drug only half worked. E[lizabe]th Bibesco came in, a ruffle of pink feathers round her shoulders, as we were ranged on the stairs coming down. Pasty, podgy, her point the eyes, which to me seemed sadder, as if she had flung away the orange. & she talked of her daughter. And I had—oh voluminously—all M.A.'s confession, as I expected.[7] He made £50,000 out of the Green hat, which money he has perpetually to atone for—as by talking of D.H.L., & how he escaped his influence, how he made his own life how he married his own wife, a dumb Greek called Atalanta,—silent, he said, but a perfect lady—& has 2 children & can keep them all, with drains games servants—all this is protest & justification. Now he is writing an intelligent novel, from real experience, lacking to highbrows. Yet oh Mrs Woolf how I envy Aldous Huxley his background—his education. I was at a 3rd rate public school, & lived in Earls Court. His father died of a broken heart when Roumania came into the war. A little scraping dingy porous clammy monkey faced man. My wife the Contessa Atalanta . . . always still justifying, but I didnt feel that need myself. Sat with Victor [Rothschild] & B[arbara]. in Mary's bedroom & V. got above himself—as he will do more & more—too butcher like in his red flesh,

6. The meeting at the Central Hall, Westminster, to which VW did not go, was in defence of the right of married women to earn; Dame Ethel Smyth there conducted her 'March of the Women', and Rebecca West was among the speakers. On 31 October T. S. Eliot had sent VW a copy of *The Use of Poetry and the Use of Criticism* (1933), the published version of the Charles Eliot Norton Lectures he had delivered at Harvard. *Works and Days: Extracts from the Journal of Michael Field*, edited by T. & D. C. Sturge Moore, was published in 1933.

7. Elizabeth Bibesco, *née* Asquith (1897-1945), was the wife of the Roumanian diplomatist Prince Antoine Bibesco; VW met her first at the Robert Cecils (see *I VW Diary*, 6 December 1919), when she also described her as 'pasty & podgy'. Michael Arlen (1895-1956), author of the best-selling novel *The Green Hat* (1924), was born Dikran Kouyoumdjian in Bulgaria, the son of an Armenian merchant, but was educated at Malvern College and became a naturalised British subject in 1922. In 1928 he married the Greek Contessa Atalanta Mercati.

too thick cut, underdone, assertive. "We do all this sort of thing in public"—fondling B.'s arm. We dont think of age, Virginia. Called me Virginia too often. "The most malicious person I've ever met". That stung a little, but not eno' to get a real rise. Talked of Dadie & Mrs Barnes.[8] Gave a sporadic account of Dadie's fathers death & so on. Was too self assured with the P[rince]ss.—the handsome irresistible young man. I shall tell him some home truths. B. called out of the room. Absent 20 minutes. Thats V. on the telephone. "How dare you call me conceited! We cant dine out together in future thats all . . . I will call you conceited—I'll write to Virginia . . . You *were* conceited . . ." & so on: always bickering. He brought her a bandbox full of the Rothschild rubies, worth £300,000 so that they cant be insured—a crown that glows & drips red light. He said there was a book in the box. No, I dont altogether like that. So home at last, leaving Eth at 44.[9]

Saturday 25 November

L.'s birthday. Off to see the Sickerts with a view to writing; see his letter.[10] Dear me. This comes however after a lull: I mean theyre sitting in Kensington Gds & I want a breath before I go on to Kitty's Party. (I at once make her say I oughtn't to have been doing this kind of thing & then I see Lord Lasswade. But stop.) [Cf. *The Years*] I was going to say old Birrell died last Monday; & is cremated—odd, to have had that last talk, in the Hotel at Brighton—odd to have seen the sharp old man at the very edge of taking off, sitting plump pink soft yet with his rather formidable acuteness, with his shod stick & his slippers. "These legs, that have taken me to so many good places wont work any more" he said, apologising for not being able to get up. "I made it a rule never to refuse what was offered". A story about C[ampbell].B[annerman]. And Frankie's brain. "They took out what was all nonsense—the Eton part—all nonsense". But at one moment the Birrell family was on the verge of extinction—⟨So I got⟩ And saying "Did you know the Souls—Oh

8. Anne Barnes's husband George was Mary Hutchinson's younger half-brother; he was at this time assistant secretary of the Cambridge University Press.
9. LW, who had dined with his mother, came to fetch VW from the Hutchinsons, and also took Princess Bibesco to 44 Bedford Square, the home of her mother Margot, Lady Oxford.
10. A retrospective of pictures by Walter Richard Sickert (1860-1942) was shown from 2-23 November at Thomas Agnew & Son, 43 Old Bond Street; after seeing it, VW, encouraged by her sister, wrote to tell him of her admiration, and he replied (copy, MHP, Sussex): 'Do me the favour to write about my pictures and say you like them'. The result was *Walter Sickert: A Conversation* (Kp A20; *HP Checklist* 355), also published, with some variations, as 'A Conversation About Art' in the *Yale Review*, September 1934 (Kp C344).

Margot—a very generous woman, believe she's coming tomorrow". The door opened, & I was beckoned off from old Birrell to Francis.[11]

Wednesday 29 November

So feebly minded after too much talk—sat to Nessa, Tom to tea, Fry's [to] dinner. I cant make way even through the shallow waters of Sickert. I am making a sketch of him at random. And so I thought I would make a footnote about the soul. I think I've got rid of vanity: of Virginia. Oh what a riddance. I've not read an article on me by a man called Peel in the Criterion.[12] I feel this a great liberation. Then I need not be that self. Then I can be entirely private. I have cut the string that ties me to that quivering bag of nerves—all its gratifications & acute despair. Time I did. It is another great discovery. One sees people lunging & striking at a thing like a straw horse & its not me at all. I sit back in comfort & look round. I wonder if Nessa has always been like this? It is calming. It is dignified. One does not seek uneasily for opinions on oneself. How have I come to this? Will it last? How will it work? I lie awake at night astonishingly happy sometimes. What a poem, for 10 minutes. The advantage is that it gives me a great deal to spend on L.; on reading; on doing what one likes. I wonder whether this is related to any of the famous human feelings. A rough note only which I meant to make some time ago.

Monday 4 December

Staying with the Fishers.[1] A queer thing, people who accept conventions. Gives them a certain force. H[erbert]. has the organisation behind him. But robs them of character, of vagaries, of depth, warmth, the unexpected. They spin along the grooves. H. to some extent anxious to impress his privileged impartial position. Many stories of "when I was in the Cabinet". Yet why not? The odd thing is that when with them one accepts their standards. And whats wrong? So nice, just, equable, humane. But how chill! And over his shoulder I see the rulers; small; but not evil;

11. Augustine Birrell had served both as President of the Board of Education and Chief Secretary for Ireland in the Liberal administrations of Campbell-Bannerman and H. H. Asquith. 'The Souls' was a group of friends in London society flourishing at the end of the last century, of which Margot Tennant (as she was before her marriage to H. H. Asquith) was a leading luminary.

12. 'Virginia Woolf' by Robert Peel, *Criterion*, October 1933, pp. 78-96.

1. VW went to Oxford on 30 November to stay a night with her cousin the historian H. A. L. Fisher (1865-1940), since 1925 Warden of New College, and his wife Lettice. In 1916 Herbert Fisher had been invited by Lloyd George to serve as President of the Board of Education in his wartime cabinet, of which Winston Churchill and Arthur Balfour were likewise members.

striving,—a complex impression. Warden[s] have lived there since 1370—
or so. How can he differ? Young men all very smooth, but talkative.
Nothing to strike on. A nice nameless boy told me he read Greek 8 hours
daily. Some like Oxford, some think it a place of restrictions. Scatters
Wilson's son said this.[2] Yes, Herbert accepts the current values, only
rather intellectualises & refines. Dismissed Tom, Clive, Maynard (partly)
in favour of the great forces of vitality—Winston, L. George. Lettice
waspish about Labour Party. L.G. their trump card—their pattern man.
No music in Tom. Ottoline dirty. Tells stories of Balfour & in the
manner of the great man—discreet, nipped, bloodless, like a butler used
to the best families. Toils at history of Europe. Is an example. Do their
duty by the college. Represent culture, politics, worldly wisdom gilt with
letters. Nothing to whizz one off one's perch at New College: all in good
taste, & very kind. But Lord to live like that!

Thursday 7 December

I was walking through Leicester Sqre—how far from China—just now
when I read Death of noted Novelist on the poster. And I thought of
Hugh Walpole. But it is Stella Benson.[3] Then why write anything,
immediately? I did not know her, but have a sense of those fine patient
eyes: the weak voice; the cough; the sense of oppression. She sat on the
terrace with me at Rodmell. And now, so quickly, it is gone, what might
have been a friendship. Trusty & patient & very sincere—I think of her;
trying to cut through, in one of those difficult evenings, to some deeper
layer—certainly we could have reached it, given the chance. I'm glad I
stopped her at the door as she got into her little car & asked her to call me
Virginia—to write to me. And she said There's nothing I should like
better. But its like the quenching of something—her death out there in
China; & I sitting here, & writing about her, & so fugitive, & yet so
true; & no more to come. How mournful the afternoon seems, with the
newspaper carts dashing up Kingsway "Death of Noted Novelist" on the
placard. A very fine steady mind: much suffering; suppressed;—there
seems to be some sort of reproach to me in her death, as in K[atherine]
M[ansfield']s. I go on; & they cease. Why? Why not my name on the
posters? And I have a feeling of the protest each might make: gone with
their work unfinished—each so suddenly. Stella was 41. "I am going to
send you my book)(" & so on. A dreary island, she lived on, talking to
Colonels.

2. Peter Cecil Wilson (b. 1913), third son of Lt.-Col. Sir Mathew ('Scatters') Wilson,
   4th Bt., was to become a director and later Chairman of Sotheby & Co.
3. Stella Benson (see above, 16 July 1932) died of pneumonia on 6 December at
   Hongay, Tonking, in Indo-China.

A curious feeling: when a writer like S.B. dies, that one's response is diminished. Here & Now wont be lit up by her: its life lessened. My effusion—what I send out—less porous & radiant—as if the thinking stuff were a web that were fertilised only by other peoples (her that is) thinking it too: now lacks life.

Sunday 17 December

I finished part 4 of, Here & Now yesterday—therefore indulge in a contemplative morning. To freshen my memory of the war, I read some old diaries. How close the tears come, again & again; as I read of L. & me at the Green: our quarrels; how he crept into my bed with a little purse, & so on: how we reckoned our income & I was given tea free for a treat.[4] The sense of all that floating away for ever down the stream, unknown for ever: queer sense of the past swallowing so much of oneself. And today we make a loop with the past by going in our grand car to see Margaret & Lilian.

Well we are very happy. Life buds & sprouts all round us: by which I mean, everybody accepts if we ask them. Joyce Wethered would 'adore' to come; & on Tuesday Stephen Spender, Miss Lynd dine, & Plomer & K. Raine come in—all young, all new.[5] And Vita lunches. And tomorrow I go to tea with the [Bruce] Richmonds. I think we live in a rich porous earth. I think we live very fully, freely, & adventurously. In short, what we made of that strange prelude is good.

The question that now fronts me as a writer is the war chapter. That I shall leave for a few days to simmer. No doubt the brew will spout out suddenly at Rodmell. We go on Thursday. This book therefore nears its end. Too thick a book.

I dined with Clive to meet Sickert the other night [15 December]. S. is sunk & old till warmed with wine. He scarcely eats. At last he expanded, & sang a French song & kissed Nessa's hand—spontaneously; mine more formally. I think a difficult old man probably. But the ingrained artist. Therese modest, suppliant.[6] Laughter—extravagance. How he was born in Germany, but not German. And lived at Munich till he was 8; & the

---

4. See I VW Diary, January-February 1915.

5. Maire Lynd (b. 1911) was the younger daughter of Robert and Sylvia Lynd, both writers; she was an Oxford Home-Student, and lived with the Fishers in the Warden's Lodgings at New College, where VW had met her on 30 November. Kathleen Raine (b. 1908) had been at Girton, and was introduced to VW by Julian Bell as a potential assistant in the Hogarth Press; see her The Land Unknown (1975), p. 56, and V VW Letters, no. 2818.

6. Thérèse Lessore (1884-1944), whom Sickert married as his third wife in 1926, was herself an artist, was the daughter of a French artist, and was formerly married to the artist Bernard Adeney.

German maid met the mad King who walked beside her, & she said—I forget. S. branches off. Then he went to Reading, a school kept by a drunken old woman, who beat a boy who had broken his arm. "And we 30 little wretches lay there cowed . ." How far he wants me to write about him, I dont know. I suspect he is changeable: that he forgets. T. prompted him with words. She knows all his stories. He gets up at 5 & goes to his garage Studio at 7 & has difficulty in lighting his stove. He reads 3 papers. He wore a pilots cap with a green brim, but no overcoat, though it was freezing cold (I bought a fur coat by the way last week). He says one paints—let me see—the canvases galloped towards me. Angry with Agnew. Not a penny from that show came his way. Never again, he said. A fine Roman head, crisp hair, thick over the ears. Small dark eyes, broad forehead. "Oh Roger's a darling—but dear me . . ." great jokes about Roger. Had wired to Lydia not to be a fool & try to act. "She's thrown away her reputation. She had a great name with the public—now she's lost it" Had lunched with the K[eynese]s. Maynard told them to listen to the WC. Sounds very audible. How she had her hour, & we must all learn to renounce, to give up: (here C. interposed one of his ring the bell sentences, about Virginia declining now from her glory & living with dogs: irritating as he meant it to be). And so we went on, a little wine-flown, but friendly & communicative, & living on our capital—I mean that we were all artists—free masonry. I cant feel very sure though of any fact or relationship; I've not seen him these 10 years, & then only to sing & joke. Yet he's chiselled, severe; has read: was reading Goldoni he said. & Flaubert's letters. And is Madame Bovary good? Is the Tentation good?[7] I'm a literary painter, romantic— You are the only person who understands me—kissing my hand. So home in the frost to find Leon sitting with L.; & he sat & sat, propounding rather fumbling questions about literature, till at 1.45 I said I was cold, moved to the fire & he—very reluctantly—went. Younger, cruder than I thought; & I'm afraid, from reading his 2nd novel in MS, not so intelligent.[8]

Thursday 21 December

I guess that my Turgenev, over which I took such tremendous pains, is not much liked. Richmond's thanks merely formal. So why go on with these essays? Why not invent a new method? I'm worried over Goldsmith. Cant be good to worry so much over transitions & packing in of ideas. But I have said this before, & say it now only because this is the relic of a morning when I should tidy, pack, write letters & so on. We lunch at $\frac{1}{4}$ to one, & then go, this yellow cold morning. No longer the great transition that it used to be.

7. Gustave Flaubert: *Madame Bovary* (1857); *La Tentation de St Antoine* (1874).
8. Derrick Leon's second novel, *Wilderness*, was published by Heinemann in 1935.

Spender & M[aire]. Lynd to dinner: a free & easy night, but both notably young & at first deferential. S. has the makings of the long winded bore. Thats odd. A handsome poetic boy to look at—& very ardent, & a great egotist. Lynd silent, secretive, hobble tongued. She will no doubt become a scribbler too, like her parents. Foolishly perhaps I denounced scribblers.

It struck me that a very plain narrative might be interesting. Yesterday I wrote Goldsmith all the morning; we lunched; Pinka's eyes are bad; we walked round the Square; then I shopped in Oxford Street; went to Warings;[9] liked the china cups: think of buying a dinner service; home at 4: L. to mother [?]: I round to Nessa's; Angelica cutting out silver paper beasts: Duncan entertaining Bradford Corporation, was given desert service; back to dinner, read a good MS by a man called Graham;[10] heard a Haydon symphony; bed. A fairly specimen day. Letter from Hugh Walpole.

The Woolfs drove to Rodmell in a fog on the afternoon of 21 December. Maynard and Lydia Keynes came to lunch, and Vita Sackville-West and her two sons to tea, on Christmas Day; and there was frequent contact with the Charlestonians.

9. Waring & Gillow Ltd, House Furnishers, 164-182 Oxford Street.
10. Probably *Good Merchant* by John L. Graham, which the Hogarth Press published in September 1934 (*HP Checklist* 340).

1934

1934

The Woolfs returned from Monks House to Tavistock Square on 14 January.
DIARY XXII continued.

Tuesday 16 January

I have let all this time—3 weeks at Monks—slip because I was there so divinely happy & pressed with ideas—another full flood of Pargiters or Here & Now (odd that Goldie's letter mentions that—The Waves is also here & now—I had forgotten).[1] So I never wrote a word of farewell to the year; not a word describing the Keynes & the Jones's; nothing about the walks I had ever so far into the downs; or the reading—Marvell of an evening, & the usual trash. And Clara died; & I sat with Mrs Woolf who said "She asked so little of life"—she crooned it, rather, lying in a daze.[2] Nothing of that has been written; & now we are back again. (And have I a touch of the flue?) What a bore, since I am floating rather rapturously in the Raid scene & dont think that 3 days in bed would be at all useful. No doubt its nothing though.

Vita dined last night, & we discussed Sparrow's book, she as always generously impartial:[3] never takes sides, or lives in a set—a good example, though without my intensity of feeling (I add immediately to recoup myself). This is rather the style of Here & Now: my random rapid letter writing style. Lyn wants me to write for her;[4] Ethel to lend my screen; that is the worst of one's friends—these little unfair demands that make one turn on the other side in the middle of the night. But it is lunch time. This

1. 'Such prose has never been written and it also belongs to here and now though it is dealing also with a theme that is perpetual and universal.' G. L. Dickinson to VW, 23 October 1931 (see above, 17 November 1931, n. 8).

2. Lady Jones (the writer Enid Bagnold) lived at Rottingdean; she came to tea at Monks House on 5 January, and the Woolfs went to tea with her at North End House on 11 January. LW's second sister Clara, Mrs George Walker (b. 1885), died on 4 January; he and VW drove to London for the day on Sunday 7 January so that he might attend her funeral; women being excluded from the synagogue, VW sustained her mother-in-law at Tavistock Square; see *V VW Letters*, nos. 2845, 2846.

3. *Sense and Poetry. Essays on the Place of Meaning in Contemporary Verse* (1934) by John Sparrow.

4. In February 1934 Lyn Lloyd Irvine produced the first of ten issues of a mimeographed fortnightly magazine, *The Monologue*, from her flat by Battersea Park; she asked VW to contribute (see *V VW Letters*, no. 2848) but in the event it was written entirely by herself.

book, alas, must continue soberly in the same cover as 1933: too wasteful to begin another & leave all this blue paper blank.

Tuesday 30 January

At this moment, 5 to 4, Ethel Smyth is about to visit Leonard on business, her infringement of the Pankhurst copyright I imagine; therefore I sit down here till 4.30 in order to escape.[6] We have Tom & Tommie [Tomlin] dining; & I am going to say I shall call you Stephen. Rather a rush of people; & a dinner to meet Noel Coward at Sybyl's on a cold foggy night. Nessa painting me again. Christmas mercifully over.[7] Nessa very hard up. Question how to make money. Talk of some caricatures. issued between us. Rather an old wives talk. Children, money, education, ways of life; I with my curious penetration playing tentatively round her mood, & afraid to impose my own.

People seen: Mary Hutch. Jack in evng dress: Ld. Castlerosse's 8/6 cigar like a jackass's penis; Nessa Angelica, Roger Duncan: Rose Macaulay, I. Davidson: Noel Coward Ld Ivor S. Churchill. Colefax's:[5]

Yesterday I went to Shapland about my watch bracelet, L.'s birthday present; came back; sat; talked; Julian came to tea; read Young's French travels: rather headachy; sleepy; strange trances in which I make up the last sentence read; to bed; sleep.[8] Today, writing Here & Now, longing

5. VW dined with the Hutchinsons on 23 January. Viscount Castlerosse (1881-1943), later 6th Earl of Kenmare, an urbane man about town and gossip writer; he was a director of Express Newspapers, and his column, 'A Londoner's Log', appeared in the *Sunday Express*. The writer Rose Macaulay (1881-1958) whom VW first met in 1921, and her friend Ivy Davison came to tea at Tavistock Square on 22 January; the latter, who had worked on the editorial staff of both the *Saturday Review* and the *Week-end Review*, was looking for work, and later came 'to write letters' for VW (see below, 14 February 1934). VW dined, again without LW, at Lady Colefax's on 24 January in company with the actor and playwright Noel Coward (1899-1973) whom she had met there in 1928, and the connoisseur and collector Lord Ivor Spencer Churchill (1898-1956).

6. Ethel Smyth in her recently published book *Female Pipings in Eden* had devoted a long chapter to the militant suffragette leader Emmeline Pankhurst (1858-1928) and her own relations with her, quoting freely from her letters; as Ethel wrote critically of Mrs Pankhurst's later life, and of her daughter Christabel, it seems probable that her use of copyright material had been called in question by the aggrieved daughter.

7. Vanessa's oil portrait of VW, signed and dated 1934, is reproduced in the American edition of *QB*; and the water-colour sketch for it in Spater & Parsons, *A Marriage of True Minds*, 1977, p. 145.

8. Shapland was a jeweller and silversmith of 207 High Holborn; VW was fifty-two on 25 January. *Travels in France during the Years 1787, 1788, and 1789* by Arthur Young records the social and economic conditions prevailing before and during the French Revolution.

to end the Raid Scene, which draws out—hence my headache; then I shall palter with something: lunch with L.: went to Danish Laundry about his collars. A nice frank spoken woman. Collars may have got among the white stuff. Women ironing. Back room with more women standing. Coppers I daresay downstairs. Looked at flats, L. home to print, I to wander to the Law Courts. Bevir Case being tried. Penetrated from end to end. Judges Chambers: a kind of vault. Kings Bench; &c. People scurrying; my sense of guilt at having no business there.[9] So to bus; home, & found my bracelet.

Wednesday 14 February

But it was rather a bad headache: 10 days recumbent, sleeping, dreaming, dipping into oh dear how many different books, how capriciously: Thackeray, Young's travels in France—but too many revolutions on hand actually: I dont want to read of them: I want turnips & peace & settlement; then a book a day from the Times, Berners, Selincourt & a stout life by Neale of Q. Elizabeth which pretending to impartiality emphasises the double chin & the wig of Mary at the critical moment: a fig for impartial & learned historians! All men are liars.[1]

And so to Rodmell for the week end, & the bees buzzing in the hyacinths: the earth emerging very chastened & sharpened from winter under a veil; which became fog as we drove up, & is fog today. In addition, the house rings with the clamour of electricians: the new bath water engine being inserted; & then the Surveyor comes & says we are weighting the floors down with books: a heavy bill threatens; so out to buy ink for my new Waterman, with which I am to take notes for a new Common Reader; & Ethel Sands to tea—my first visitor. Yesterday I had Ivy Davison for the first time to write letters. No letters therefore today. Now I have just refused the Nat. Portrait Gallery offer to draw me, thank God, & am very cautiously revising Sickert.[2]

9. *Bevir v. Burt-White*, High Court of Justice, King's Bench Division, 22-30 January 1934, before Mr Justice Horridge. Harold Bevir successfully sued Miss Dallas Burt-White for slander and was awarded £3,500 damages and costs.
1. The volumes supplied by the Times Book Club were: *First Childhood* (1934) by Lord Berners; *Dorothy Wordsworth* (1933) by Ernest de Selincourt; and *Queen Elizabeth* (1934) by J. E. Neale: 'She [Mary] was forty-four, and . . . had been a prisoner for just on twenty years. The charm of youth was gone; she was corpulent, round-shouldered, fat in the face and double-chinned; her auburn hair was false.'
2. See *V VW Letters*, no. 2857: The National Portrait Gallery 'send a wretched boy to draw one . . . then they keep the drawing in a cellar, & when I've been dead ten years they have it out & say Does anyone want to know what Mrs Woolf looked like? No, say all the others. Then its torn up. So why should I defile a whole day by sitting?' The NPG, balked on this occasion, in the 1950s acquired two represen-

Friday 16 February

Five minutes here before going to lunch with Nessa. A great Nelly row yesterday; which I hereby declare the last. It was about the workmen & her day out, & the end was that we had eggs for lunch & were forced to dine at the Cock [*Tavern, Fleet Street*], expensively & badly. No more of this, I say, & anticipate many days of ill ease, some violent scenes, & then pray God, after Easter, peace.[3]

Finished my Sickert article all the same. I put off Here & Now till next week.

Sunday 18 February

And I began Here & Now again this morning, Sunday, at the point where I left off all but 3 weeks ago for my headache. Here I note that from 2 to 3 weeks is the right space. It has not gone cold, as after 6 weeks; I still carry it in my mind, & can see how to revise. It has gone—the talk during the Raid—running all over the place, because I was tired; now I must press together; get into the mood & start again. I want to raise up the magic world all round me, & live strongly & quietly there for 6 weeks. The difficulty is the usual one—how to adjust the two worlds. It is no good getting violently excited: one must combine. And I have the Nelly question on top of me in addition to the usual grind of what Ethel calls society. Some planning is therefore necessary. I have to 'see' Ottoline, Ethel, K. Furse, Ly Cholmondeley (perhaps), E. Bowen: Lyn comes to dinner tonight to discuss her rather acid & thin blooded bantling. And I've made up my mind what I'm going to say. I will write if she lets me tell the truth.

The new electric boiler in & boiling our bath water this morning. The K. of Belgium killed mountaineering. All last week they were fighting in Vienna: this somehow comes closer than usual to our safe London life: the people shot down. why? John came to see L.: as spruce as ever; & has left his poems. We went to Angelica yesterday, & ate eggs in Mrs C.'s large Adams room. A. has to speak on Mrs Pankhurst. We watched Lacrosse. A. despises all games.[5]

---

tations of VW: a cast of the 1931 bust by Stephen Tomlin, and a charcoal sketch of 1908 by Francis Dodd.

3. See *V VW Letters*, no. 2867 of 29 March 1934 to Ethel Smyth for an extended account of 'the most disagreeable six weeks of my life', culminating in Nelly's final departure after eighteen years' service.

4. Sybil (b. 1894), wife of the 5th Marquess of Cholmondeley, was the sister of Sir Philip Sassoon whom VW had met in 1929 at Lady Colefax's. For Lyn Irvine's 'bantling', see above, 16 January 1934.

5. Albert I, King of the Belgians, fell to his death on 17 February while rock-climbing near Namur. On 12 February civil war had broken out in Austria when the Social

Tuesday 20 February

To note the interesting stages of the duel with Nelly. Today I said, do you want this quarrel to go on? I would like it to stop now; but I shall discuss it later. Whereupon she said she wished it to end, but it was all my fault. And she wished to have nothing hanging over her. So I am indifferent calm & Lord knows if I ⟨shall⟩ shant give her notice tomorrow.

[*Sunday 4 March*]

10 to eleven on Sunday March 4th—a fine day, no fog; & I'm to sit to Nessa for the last time in 10 minutes; & the house is being done, & we've taken rooms at Pippa's, &—&.[1]

As for Here & Now I'm going to start that seriously tomorrow. Kitty & Ed. in Richmond: this Chapter is to be visual & animal; spring; movement; plants; birds dogs; airs; flowers.

Yesterday at Ethel Smyth's mass. The Queen in the box: nodding from side to side; Ethel in her 3 cornered hat beside her; with her hand up. The Q. bowing, doing her duty graciously. So to Lyons—I forget the mass— where in that sordid crumby room assembled the garish Ly Diana, Ly Cunard, & the pensive Ly Lovat & ourselves; amid clerks & shop girls eating cream buns.[2] All rather strident & obvious & rubbing too much on one string as usual to be very interesting Yet it had elements— The great sun setting behind the trees in Hyde Pk. as we drove back. Oh dear me, L. is doing the books & wont let me help. Lydia's Dolls House

---

Democrats, deliberately provoked by the increasingly powerful neo-Fascist *Heimwehr*, took to arms; after four days they were defeated; their party was declared illegal, and Chancellor Dollfuss took steps to strengthen his authoritarian control of the country. John Lehmann was just back from Vienna, where he had been living; his book, published under the title *The Noise of History* in the Hogarth Living Poets, Second Series, appeared in September (*HP Checklist* 342). Mrs Curtis was the head of Angelica's Essex boarding school, Langford Grove.

1. The dust and confusion in 52 Tavistock Square during the redecoration insisted upon by their landlords caused the Woolfs to seek some refuge at 51 Gordon Square, the large house which had been Lady Strachey's, now occupied by her unmarried daughters.

2. In the early part of 1934 there was a series of events to honour Dame Ethel Smyth's seventy-five years, culminating in the performance in the Albert Hall on 3 March of her 'Mass in D' and other works, conducted by Sir Thomas Beecham in the presence of Queen Mary. Among her guests at a Lyons Tea Room afterwards were Lady Diana Cooper (b. 1892), wife of the politician A. Duff Cooper and daughter of the Duke of Rutland, and the widowed Lady Lovat, *née* the Hon. Laura Lister (1892-1965), daughter of Lord Ribblesdale.

tonight; on Wednesday Nessa's Private view;[3] Sickert here to tea—rather a rusty rat trap that man with hard little eyes. very old—no illusions about his own greatness. "They'll collect it all one of these days" he said, sublimely about his art critic[ism]s. My BBC Comtee suppressed— thank the Lord. No official positions for me.[4] Now to sit.

Wednesday 14 March

I cannot hold out any hope for the next 14 days. Theres the workmen everywhere; theres Nelly gay & garrulous as a lark. Can I do it? I must. I must. And I caught an influenza—a little shivery bout at Monks on Sunday; cant screw my brain up therefore; & yet have the feeling that some magnificent chapters wait me. If only the 14 days were over—& I in my bed again! How human beings torture each other![5]

A black day, pouring rain; dirt everywhere. Let me see: there was a lovely day at Monks. There was the suffusion of blue in white cotton wool. Mr Lavender talked at the meeting about growing mushrooms. Ethel [Smyth] came over—to deposit her horrid gnawed bone or sucked chocolate—C. St John's praise to wit—at my feet. A very ruthless shoving woman in some ways.[6] And then on the crest of the Kitty Eleanor scene

3. Lydia Lopokova played Nora in a performance of Ibsen's *A Doll's House* at the Arts Theatre Club on Sunday 4 March, given by J. T. Grein's Cosmopolitan Theatre. The private view of an Exhibition of Recent Paintings by Vanessa Bell and Elwin Hawthorne at the Lefevre Galleries was on 7 March; the catalogue had a foreword by VW (Kp B11.1).

4. Towards the end of 1933 Logan Pearsall Smith had proposed that VW should become a member of the BBC Advisory Committee on Spoken English, and she had hesitantly agreed; now, hearing that meetings were suspended pending reconstitution of the committee, she withdrew. (See *V VW Letters*, nos. 2829, 2861).

5. The Woolfs had gone to Monks House on Friday 9 March and, because VW caught a chill, did not return to London until this Wednesday, 14 March (although LW drove up and back on Monday afternoon). VW had determined to give Nelly notice before they again went to Rodmell for Easter on 28 March.

    'Western wind, when wilt thou blow,
      The small rain down can rain?
     Christ, if my love were in my arms
      And I in my bed again.' *Anon, 16th century*

6. Mr Lavender (see below 27 August 1934) gave his talk to the Rodmell Village Club. Christopher Marie St John (c. 1875-1960), drama critic of *Time & Tide* 1920-31; she lived with Edith Craig, Ellen Terry's daughter, and had edited the correspondence between the latter and Bernard Shaw (see above, 3 June 1932); they jointly produced a *Memoir* of her in 1933. Christopher St John became Ethel Smyth's biographer (1959).

comes this shiver: bed; waiting for L.; cooking dinner. Back today & a man threw a parcel containing shoes at the basement window & broke it. A thief presumably. Lady Oxford wants to meet me at Ott's. Mr Ridge the builder talking about Tenby & a little church on the rocks. The sea comes over the chapel floor. And he bought a picture in Holland Park for 7/6 that reminded him of Wales.[7] Then the bookbinder. Thats my day. Now in the rain to Nessa.

Monday 19 March

I cannot describe how the Nelly situation weighs on my spirits. I am determined not to discuss it with L. either. She pressed me this morning. You show no confidence in me; you dont treat me like a maid. Oh dear— how tempted I was then to say Then go; but I bit my tongue. And then down here, trying to make it up. I couldn't imagine it would be so hard, & the worst to come. On the top of it this hammering painting, ordering of books. And I cant get into flood therefore with H. & N., though I had I think rather a brilliant flash this morning how to compact the rather fluid Eleanor. I shall have a shot anyhow. But Nelly spoils all. And to think none of this need have happened had I stuck to my guns 3 years ago! Now I must & will.

We went to Cambridge on Saturday, lunch with Dadie, Rosamond & Wogan; I ought not to call him that. He is jealous about R.'s fame: she not. So to An. & C. & there was Shephard [J. T. Sheppard] with all the little Eton boys, like the white chaps of a Christmas pig. A dragging weak performance.[8] Lovely drive home in the twilight through the wide unmarked country. To dine with Nessa last night. Clive there. N. all a blowing & aglowing with the success of her show, & the money made. Then in came Lydia, all &c. too, owing to her success; & I felt so old so cold so dumpish, nothing flowery or fiery glowing in me owing to Nelly, but not jealous: I dont think that. Mynd [Maynard] very flown too, & Duncan too, & Clive quiet & now I think of walking round to Ott's to meet Ly Oxford & if I can change my mood—rather a violent remedy. A clear wet spring sort of day. We went to Drews & bought Cashin's present, then to L.'s hat & tailor; so home. All yesterday I did the dining room books. Today he is finishing the study & they are painting the stairs. Oh for the end of this chapter, for Rodmell & peace & freedom to use my mind again.

7. C. Ridge & Son, House Decorators, 20 Leigh Street, WC1. The little church was St Julian's chapel, Tenby.

8. *Antony and Cleopatra*, produced by George Rylands, was being performed by the Marlowe Society at the Festival Theatre, Cambridge.

Monday 26 March

"The worst is to come"—that is with Nelly.[9] Well it is now coming very near—by this time—3.30—tomorrow it will be over. And then there'll only be the one dreadful day & we shall be off. I feel executioner & the executed in one. Meanwhile it is a brilliant spring day; I'm back in my studio, white, clean, more spacious, after 3 days of Pippa's. Miss Walton is arranging books; Hugh, Stephen, William, Ott, & Vita all coming to tea & so on; I dine with Vita; then must ring up Eth Bowen about our Irish tour, & so the immitigable day passes. I face up to it without any evasion: this has to be lived I say to myself.

Tuesday 27 March

The great scene with Nelly is now over, & of course much less violently than I supposed. She stood by the drawing room door in the full light, white & pink, with her funny rather foolish mulish face puckered up. And I made my speech correctly, & even was able to say "And I expect you want to get another place too—" persuasively. She had one outburst—"I can say nothing—its all because it was my night out, & I asked you . . ." which I cut short & said we had agreed to part on good terms, gave her a cheque for £25 & a £1 note for my mending "but you dont owe me anything" she said, & so she went upstairs & I came down here. I suppose some further lamentation & argument, with L. perhaps is inevitable. But Lord what a relief now!

The Woolfs were at Rodmell for Easter, from Wednesday 28 March until 10 April; there was a Memoir Club meeting at Tilton on Sunday 8 April, for which Morgan Forster came to stay from Saturday to Monday at Monks House.

Wednesday 11 April

I am a little proud of myself; for I have just read through the last pages, & now pat myself on the back, & say that I kept to my resolution, through thick & thin, & am now back here with Nelly gone, Annie upstairs, & Mabel, declared by Ha. to be a treasure, coming to see me tomorrow.[1] So this has been definitely accomplished, after all these

9. A memory of Tennyson, *Sea Dreams*: 'The worst is yet to come'?
1. Mabel was one of two sisters who had worked for Margery Fry ('Ha') when she and her brother Roger lived in Holloway; the other, Flossie (Mrs George Riley), became the daily help at Vanessa's and Duncan Grant's Fitzroy Street studios. Annie Thomsett, the Woolfs' Rodmell daily, was temporarily helping at Tavistock Square in place of Nelly.

years. The sense of freedom & calm—no more brooding; no more possessiveness; no more sense of being part of Nelly's world; & her planted
there. Even if the cooking is less luxurious, that is all to the good. We
had a horrid day last Wednesday—a fortnight ago; she trailed about,
some how pathetic, to me, catching at me, & whimpering & revealing her
own vanity. "But they'll blame me—" However, she rattled off her spiteful
little noise at L. when the parting came, thinking only of herself as
usual; & there we left her in the kitchen, grasping a wet cloth; "No I
really couldn't Sir" she said, when L. held out his hand. How dazed &
free & quiet I felt driving down to Lewes! She has taken with her all the
cookery books, except too elementary manuals, & the chair cover—a last
spasm of possessive spite.

Tuesday 17 April

So jaded am I after last night that I cannot add a word to my Sickert or
make out a sketch of the last chapters of Here & Now. A high price to
pay for a hurried dinner at the Hutches; racing to Macbeth; talking to
Dodo MacNaghten; then to Sir Fred Pollock on the stage of Sadlers
Wells.[2]

An idea about Sh[akespea]re

That the play demands coming to the surface—hence insists upon a
reality wh. the novel need not have, but perhaps should have. Contact
with the surface. Coming to the top. This is working out my theory of
the different levels in writing, & how to combine them: for I begin to
think the combination necessary. This particular relation with the surface is imposed on the dramatist of necessity: how far did it influence
Shre? Idea that one cd work out a theory of fiction &c on these lines: how
many levels attempted. whether kept to or not.

Wednesday 18 April

A curious little fact.

Instead of smoking 6 or 7 cigarettes as I write of a morning, I now, for
3 mornings, make myself smoke one only. And rather enjoy doing without.

2. The first performance of an opera by Lawrance Collingwood (principal conductor
of Sadler's Wells Opera, 1931-46) based on Shakespeare's *Macbeth*, was given at
Sadler's Wells on 12 April 1934; the Woolfs were taken to it by the Hutchinsons on
16 April, and to a party at the theatre afterwards. Both Lady Macnaghten and
Sir Frederick Pollock were figures from VW's youth: 'Dodo'—*née* Antonia Mary
Booth (1873-1952)—was the eldest daughter of her parents' great friends Charles
and Mary Booth; and the jurist Sir Frederick Pollock, PC, KC, 3rd Bt (1845-1937)
had been one of Leslie Stephen's original 'Sunday Tramps'.

APRIL 1934

Tonight Tom & Maynard dine to discuss Tom's book; After Strange Gods.[3] Julian & E. Bowen come in afterwards. I want to try & make myself write down the discussion tomorrow, as I am keeping off fiction.

Thursday 19 April

Oh but I am much too sleepy to make even a brief note of the talk. It began at dinner. Tom & Maynard talking about his book. You have brought up again one of the primal questions, & nobody has even tried to consider it. No, said Tom, much like a great toad with jewelled eyes. Morality. And JM [Keynes] said that he would be inclined not to demolish Xty if it were proved that without it morality is impossible. "I begin to see that our generation—yours & mine V., owed a great deal to our fathers' religion. And the young, like Julian, who are brought up without it, will never get so much out of life. Theyre trivial: like dogs in their lusts. We had the best of both worlds. We destroyed Xty & yet had its benefits". Well the argument was something like that. I pressed Tom to define belief in God; but he sheered off. Then Julian came. The economic question: the religion of Communism. This the worst of all & founded on a silly mistake of old Mr Ricardo's which M. given time will put right.[4] And then there will be no more economic stress, & then—? How will you live Julian, you who have no moral strictness? We Julian said miss your morality which has landed us in psycho-analysis, but I prefer my life in many ways. Maynard accused the young of being anxious to publish too soon. Thats to make our names & make money. We want to chip in before the talk has changed said J. V. Its because you have no sense of tradition or continuity. I used to feel that the British Museum reading room was going on for ever. I felt I could take 15 years over a book; I wanted to take longer & longer. Whereas you write & publish at 18. Tom agreed. Tom agreed to most of this, but reserved his idea of God. Eth Bowen came in, rayed like a zebra, silent & stuttering. Had also been brought up to repress, by moral ancestors. Is 34. L. said Jews with great morality but no religion. Quoted his mother on immortality. M. talked about Montagu Norman the Governor of the B. of E. an elf; an artist, sitting with his cloak round him hunched up, saying "I cant remember—" thus evading all questions, & triumphing—going away disguised —going mad. Also about Douglas, the credit man, being interviewed, &

3. T. S. Eliot's three controversial Page-Barbour lectures delivered at the University of Virginia in 1933 were published in February 1934 under the title *After Strange Gods: A Primer of Modern Heresy* (Gallup A25).
4. David Ricardo (1772-1823), economist, whose 'labour theory of value' was the starting point of part of Marx's analysis of capitalism.

whenever they came to par. 7 saying "To explain this I must go back to beginning".[5]

M. on becoming a fellow of Kings.[6] The moving nature of the service; how they go to the Chapel & lock the doors & sit in their pews, & then the Provost asks Mr So & So to come up & put his hands in his hands & reads out a statement, about preserving the laws & traditions, & then they all shake hands & he is admitted to the brotherhood, a society for research, religion, &c. education. And thus he is accepted as a brother whom they will support & sustain. This is a great moment; & there is nothing very ceremonious; religious; only an admittance. I said did this society, this coming together move him, & M. said very much. Kings was full of such societies: & feelings.

The Woolfs drove to Rodmell on Sunday 22 April, and on the following Wednesday set out by car, spending one night at Salisbury and the next at Abergavenny, for Fishguard, whence they sailed overnight for the Irish Free State. After lunching at Lismore, they reached Bowen's Court, Kildorrery, the 18th century mansion inherited by Elizabeth Bowen, and stayed the night there with her and her husband Alan Cameron. On Sunday 29 April they went on to Glengariff on Bantry Bay, and spent two nights in Eccles Hotel. LW's diary (LWP, Sussex) briefly records their itinerary.

This Irish journal is written on smaller loose-leaf sheets (25 pp) inserted in DIARY XXII.

IRELAND

[*Monday 30 April*]

Glengariff

This is the 30th of April, Monday, so I think, foreign travel not leading to thought. A mixture of Greece, Italy & Cornwall; great loneliness; poverty & dreary villages like squares cut out of West Kensington. Not a single villa or house a-building; great stretches of virgin sea shore; the original land that Cornwall & much of England was in Elizabethan times. And a sense that life is receding. At Lismore the Tchekov innkeeper said Theyre all going away & leaving their houses; nothing's kept up since the war. So the old man on the island here said today—the very sad gentle old

5. Montagu Collett Norman (1871-1950), Governor of the Bank of England 1920-44; in 1931 he suffered a breakdown and was ordered abroad to recover his health. Clifford Hugh Douglas (1879-1952), consulting engineer and economist, was the propounder of the theory of Social Credit, an economic analysis urging state subsidization of purchasing power.
6. Maynard Keynes was elected a Fellow of King's College, Cambridge, in March 1909.

man who longed to talk.[7] All gone—What good did the war do anyone?
Only the Americans. And crooned & moaned leaning on the rake with
which he was heaping up some kind of weed. Yes there is great melancholy
in a deserted land, though the beauty remains untouched—miles & miles
of Killarney—the lake water lapping the stones, the butterflies flitting, &
not a Cockney there. Today, sitting on the verandah after lunch, the
German lawyer having been forced to go to the Island—a string of touts
loaf about pressing poetry & boats on one—after they had gone, the
invalid, who reminds me of Nelly Cecil began to talk as they all begin to
talk; & said she came from Limerick & when we asked if one could get a
house there, she said—she laughed a great deal yet seems hopelessly
crippled—"You can get plenty, but its not so nice when you have one."
"Servant difficulties?" I asked. "Ah, all that" she said, & one can see,
after Bowen's Court, how ramshackle & half squalid the Irish life is, how
empty & poverty stricken. There we spent one night, unfortunately with
baboon Conolly & his gollywog slug wife Jean to bring in the roar of the
Chelsea omnibus,[8] & it was all as it should be—pompous & pretentious &
imitative & ruined—a great barrack of grey stone, 4 storeys & basements,
like a town house, high empty rooms, & a scattering of Italian plaster-
work, marble mantelpieces, inlaid with brass & so on. All the furniture
clumsy solid cut out of single wood—the wake sofa, on wh. the dead
lay—carpets shrunk in the great rooms, tattered farm girls waiting, the
old man of 90 in his cabin who wdn't let us go—E[lizabe]th had to say
Yes The Ladies are very well several times.[9] And we went to the wishing
well, where there are broken cups as offerings & half a rosary & L.
wished that Pinka might not smell, which made me laugh; & then I talked
to the cook, & she showed me the wheel for blowing the fire in the windy
pompous kitchen, half underground—rather like the Bride of Lammer-
muir—Caleb showing the guests nothing[10]—no there was a fine turkey
but everywhere desolation & pretention cracked grand pianos, faked old
portraits, stained walls—& yet with character & charm, looking on to a
meadow where the trees stand in a ring called Lamb's Cradle. Talk too
much of the Chelsea bar kind, owing to C.'s—about starting a society
called Bostocks, about Ireland with Alan, a good humoured bolt eyed fat

7. The old man was one of the O'Sullivan brothers, caretakers for the Bryce family
   who owned Garnish Island and planted its locally celebrated gardens.
8. Cyril Vernon Connolly (1903-1974), later editor of the literary periodical *Horizon*,
   at this time reviewed fiction for the *NS&N*; his first wife Jean, *née* Bakewell, was
   American.
9. The garrulous 'old man of 90' was Patsy Hennessy who lived in a cabin near St
   Geoffrey's Well, the waters of which were said to be beneficial to the eyes.
10. Caleb Balderstone was the officious butler in Sir Walter Scott's novel who was
    determined to uphold the honour and conceal the impoverished circumstances of
    the Ravenswood family.

hospitable man.[11] So on here over the mountains. And pray God the C.'s
dont show their gorilla faces at dinner or invade the old Squires library in
which we sit.

Tuesday 1 May

Waterville [*Butler Arms Hotel*]

Too like its name; blowing the spray & the rain over a flat land, & a
scattering of hideous 1850 watering place houses. Mist today, wind tonight; & L. opening the first Times to come our way, said George Duckworth is dead.[1] So he is. And I feel the usual incongruous shades of feeling, one from this year, one from that—how great a part he used to play
& now scarcely any. But I remember the genuine glow, from last summer
when I went to see him—the thing that always made me laugh & yet
was marked in him. But how little he meant, after his marriage—&
yet how childhood goes with him—the batting, the laughter, the treats, the
presents, taking us for bus rides to see famous churches, giving us tea at
City Inns, & so on—that was the best which oddly enough returned of
late years a little, with the Lincoln sausages, the bottles of eau de Cologne,
the great bunch of flowers. Margaret I remember playing round him, & I
thought how happy in their way they were. But this is all happening far
off. Here I sit on my bed in the windy seaside hotel, & wait for dinner,
with this usual sense of time shifting & life becoming unreal, so soon to
vanish while the world will go on millions upon millions of years.

Wednesday 2 May

Glenbeith [*Glenbeigh Hotel*]

On again, after an extremely interesting encounter at the windy hotel
with Ireland—that is Mr & Mrs Rowlands; he is a giant, very shapely,
small head, obliterated features; she small, abrupt, vivacious. They began
directly, & so we talked,—they accepted us as their sort, & were gentry,
Irish gentry, very much so, he with a house 500 years old, & no land left.
"But I love my King & Country. Whatever they ask me to do I'd do it"—
this with great emotion. Oh yes, we believe in the British Empire; we hate
the madman de Valéra."[2] There they live, 14 miles from Cork, hunting,

11. Alan Charles Cameron (1893-1952), whom Elizabeth Bowen married in 1923, was
Secretary for Education in the City of Oxford and was soon to become Secretary
to the Central Council of School Broadcasting at the BBC.

1. Sir George Duckworth died on 27 April at Freshwater, Isle of Wight, aged sixty-
six; the announcement of his death was in *The Times* of 28 April.

2. Mr and Mrs A. Rowlands of Ballinacurra House, Midleton, co. Cork. Éamonn de
Valéra (1882-1975), the Irish Republican leader and President of the Fianna Fail
party, was from 1932-37 President of the Executive Council of the Irish Free
State, and the Minister for External Affairs.

with an old retriever dog, & go to bazaars miles & miles away. "Thats the way we live—no nonsense about us—not like the English people. Now I'll give you my name, & I'll write to my friend & she'll tell you of a house—& I hope you'll live in Ireland. We want people like ourselves. But wait, till the budget." This she said, with all the airs of the Irish gentry: something very foreign about her, like old Lady Young,[3] & yet in slave to London; of course everyone wants to be English. We think Englands talking of us—not a bit. No said the obliterated Greek torso, for such he was, when I was courting my wife—she lived in Liverpool—the young chaps used to say "now Paddy tell us one of your stories" but now they dont take any interest in us. But I'd do anything for my King & Country, though youve always treated us very badly.

So we got on to the Bowens; & established ourselves as of their sort. Yes I felt this is the animal that lives in the shell. These are the ways they live—he hunting all day, & she bustling about in her old car, & everybody knowing everybody & laughing & talking & picnicking, & great poverty & some tradition of gentle birth, & all the sons going away to make their livings & the old people sitting there hating the Irish Free State & recalling Dublin & the Viceroy.

On to Tralee & saw the gipsies coming down the road & thought of G. being buried.[4]

Thursday 3 May

Adare [*Dunraven Arms Hotel*]

Theyre looking out names on maps at this moment. "That gives us a very good idea of . . . . What I wd suggest if I might—tomorrow on the way—we're coming down from Killarney tomorrow—then another thing, wd you like to go to Glengarrif—" (they are 4 fattish unattractive but kindly women—wont take our fire, we're sitting in the hotel lounge after a long day driving & I certainly can't read Prou[s]t with such a patter going on. We have a roasting great fire.

Listen, I thought you'd made up your mind to do this part first—well then tomorrow. Listen—wd this be too much of a— I dont want to break the springs of that car. Thats another idea—we're going West.

To copy down conversation is not very interesting. People say the same thing over & over again. I wd like to describe the perfection of

3. The Youngs, of Formosa Fishery, Cookham, were old family friends of the Stephens; Lady Young (d. 1922) was born Alice Eacy, daughter of Evory Kennedy MD of Belgard Castle, Dublin.
4. The Woolfs drove from Waterville to Tralee to pick up their letters, and then to Glenbeigh. Sir George Duckworth's funeral was at his local church, St Margaret's, West Hoathly, on 2 May.

Irish conversation, which was Mrs FitzGerald's last night.[5] She is exactly the great French lady—only living in a black jersey on an Irish bog. After dinner she came in, ostensibly to lend us a paper & offer advice, in fact to indulge her genius for talk. She talked till 11, & wd. willingly be talking now: about hotel keeping, about frigidaires, about her grandmother sitting on a chair in the kitchen & saying Thats done that wants another 2 minutes & so on, never stirring herself but somehow getting it done. We have the name of being good housekeepers. Then on about bogs, she has bought several fragments because now there may be money in it. However I can give no notion of the flowing, yet formed sentences, the richness & ease of the language; the lay out, dexterity & adroitness of the arrangement. There was the story of old Julia the cook, who had gone off home in a huff jealous of the young maids; had her daughter & the London husband on her, bought them gramophone records, & now wont own that she has wasted her savings. Mrs F. is one of those bluntnosed parted haired Irishwomen with luminous brown eyes & something sardonic & secretive in her expression. Talk is to her an intoxicant, but there is as Mr Rowlands said, something heartless about the I[rish]: quite cold indifferent sarcastic, for all their melody, their fluency, their adorable ease & forthcomingness. She was very much on the spot, accurate, managing, shrewd, hard headed, analytic. Why arent these people the greatest novelists in the world?—with this facility, this balance, this fundamental (now L. has joined in & is advising the 3 ladies. Are they American?)

Its very kind of you telling us: thank you very much. Now the wireless is brawling. Everything looks nice in fine weather. I think I'll go to bed. I want you to read this. One is the director of the others, severe, but apologetic, perhaps paid for.

But why isn't Mrs F. a great novelist? Certainly the salon survives at Glenbeith, the lust for talk, & finishing one's sentence—only with complete naturalness. For instance, explaining the bogs, "saturated, now whats the opposite word?" Desiccated, L. suggested, & she adopted it with pleasure. She said one could never understand the Irish: one had to live as they did. They sit in their cottages talking about politics; they dont dance much; they have no amusements. They at once started to poach on her bog merely because she had bought it—otherwise it had been left alone for centuries. The bogs are full of trees, cant be self planted, so orderly, but now who has planted them? And they burn in a resinous way—go up—puf!—in a flash, like petrol. Suddenly she became severe & thought me a fool. "What does this good lady mean?" Her grandmother was an innkeeper; she herself went away for 25 years; Oh, as my grandmother said, one becomes able to read peoples characters before they step

5. Mrs Ida Fitzgerald was the proprietress of the Glenbeigh Hotel until ca. 1938; her reputation as a 'talker' still endures there.

over the door, & ones never wrong one way or the other. Her quickness was amazing. This morning the talk began & L. very slightly put out his hand. "Oh I know that means you wanting to be off"—& so we parted from the last representative of the French salon of the 18th Century, this strange mixture of county lady, peasant, & landlady.

Oh but the Irish loudspeaker is inferior like everything else in this down trodden land. Things cant be worse, said the one armed man—his artificial arm wore a black woollen glove—who warned us off the river walk, & then showed us the full horror of Dunraven Castle, built from 1835 to 1850 like the rest of Ireland, a French Château in grey stone costing a million, & better razed to the ground.[6]

Nessa writes that George before he died wanted Nessa & me to wire to him—which she did. What was in his mind? some old memory? some regret? I wonder.

Friday 4 May

Galway [*Great Southern Hotel*]
A phrase made this windy day: the clouds looping up their skirts & letting down a shaft of light. We picked bright blue gentians on the cliff looking towards the Aran Islands. This, though raining & cloudy, was one of our best drives—to the sea; views over folds of wild land with one or two orange & yellow white cottages: the sea blue, stone coloured or deep black: the waves tossing their hair back. People gathering sea weed & heaping carts. Extreme poverty.

So on to Galway which has 2 great bookshops, otherwise wild, poor, sordid. We saw the Claddagh; shawled women, coated men, all standing in groups together beside thatched huts, like islanders, waiting for a funeral. This the original Irish quarter; G. Thompson whom we found sitting before his Greek books in a little room looking on the sea came to the hotel after dinner & told us how they spend their lives in talk, dont mind poverty so much. He teaches 6[?] Galways Greek in Irish.[7] Directly

Galway
May 5th 6 or 7th
Sat. May 5th

he went, at 11, up started a wild pale Irishman & poured forth more talk. "I hear you're going to Dublin. Please dont miss the Guinness brewery or the 4 mummified nuns." & so on. He was agent for a Radio

6. The one-armed man was James Mullooly, caretaker at the Dunraven estate at Adare, a former member of the Royal Irish Constabulary who had lost his arm in the Troubles.

7. The bookshops were O'Gorman's and McCullagh's (now closed); the Claddagh is a district of Galway City, south-west of the River Corrib. George Derwent Thomson (b. 1903), Greek and Irish scholar, a Fellow of King's College, Cambridge, and like LW an Apostle; from 1931-34 he was Lecturer in Ancient Classics through Irish at University College, Galway.

Company & was touring Ireland; was Irish, but had lived in America; a mixture of Siegfried Sassoon & Robert Graves to look at, but internally preoccupied with breweries & nuns. Pouring wet; a gale; & off now to Dublin.[8]

Sunday 6 May

Dublin [*Russell Hotel*]

It is very windy wet & cold, & I am sitting alone after lunch in the lounge with a grey black netting woman. The scene is St Stephen's Green, an Irish attempt at Lincoln's Inn Fields, just as Merrion Square attempts Bedford Sqre & so on. We lunched at the Sherburne [*Shelburne Hotel*]; & there are the film actors; here they are too. Aran islanders, in thick tweeds, who sit over the fire downstairs singing what may be hymns. I heard Irish for the first time.[9] This is a dreary waiting moment. L. has to write letters. Then perhaps we go to the [National] Gallery. An air of inferiority sleeps or simpers or sneers or rages everywhere. A visitor from England brings back news of picture galleries, theatres. Here it is a mixture of Hampstead & Cambridge. At the Gate Theatre last night we were not sure which it was: there's an edge of difference, & the play was good: about Emmett, advanced, pseudo-Auden, I imagine.[10] Three instruments to make music. A curtain that wdnt close; much satire of the Irish love of bloodshed; satire of the attempts at culture; a sudden sense came over me of being in the midst of history—that is of being in an unsettled, feverish place, which would have its period given it in the books; anything may happen. Yet what can happen when the best restaurant in the capital is Jammets, when there's only boiled potatoes in the biggest hotel in Dublin? Everywhere they seem to be living on watered wine. At last I gather why, if I were Irish, I should wish to belong to the Empire: no luxury, no creation, no stir, only the dregs of London, rather wishwashy as if suburbanised. Yet, I thought too at the Gate, they may have a

8. The Guinness Brewery in Dublin, founded ca. 1759, covered some 600 acres and was open to visitors. The vaults beneath St Michan's Church contain an array of bodies shrivelled and mummified through the moisture-absorbent properties of the limestone structure.

9. The Aran islanders were on their way home from England, where they had spent some weeks recording and being used for publicity purposes in connection with the documentary film *Man of Aran*, made on location 1932-34 by the Canadian-born director Robert Flaherty (1884-1951). The world première had been at the New Gallery Cinema, London, on 25 April; the Woolfs went to see it there on 23 May.

10. The play was *The Old Lady Says 'No!'* by E. W. Tocher (pseudonym of Denis Johnston), first produced at the Gate Theatre in 1929; Micheál MacLiammoir played the part of Robert Emmet (1778-1803), the Irish revolutionary hero who inspired the abortive Dublin rising of 1803, was tried for treason, and hanged.

spirit in them somewhere, that could make something, if freed. But they are freed, I continue—& indeed the play said, sardonically, & only this provinciality is the result. I dont believe in the songs of the Aran islanders, or in old men who cant read—that is, theyre not of necessity Homer. Their voices penetrate the glass door. The netting lady has let the fire out. The Arans are going out in full dress. I must run & see.

And I ran, & found a hot fire downstairs; & the old woman in the red shawl has moved off. Coming in yesterday I thought here was the cream of Dublin, meeting a cauliflower faced young man of redolent charm in the hall; and a fine bluff red genial man, & the little boys—heres the ancient aristocracy of Ireland, I said, but it turned out to be the producer—who lodges at the She[l]burne—& his troop, who lodge here. A quarrel is going on between a lady & the manager. Nothing in the wide world wd. have induced me &c. This is what upsets orderly composition & makes it impossible for me to finish—

Most unsatisfactory—will you look up my postcard—inclusive board—

No, it wouldnt do living in Ireland, in spite of the rocks & the desolate bays. It would lower the pulse of the heart: & all one's mind wd. run out in talk. "Its awfully nice to see you & looking so well"—She's off with a tall Irish gentleman & silence falls.

Merrion Square is about 3 times the size of Bedford Square; at one time a passion for glory must have settled on the Irish, & then having run up street after street of Bedford Row off they went. Doctors & lawyers have crept into the 18th Century shells. Oh but theyre now discussing the character of the lady who's so angry. She's handsome, she's fine, but . . . who did she marry? & so on. Talk, talk, talk. Not as nice looking at all— in the good old days they used to come.

Grafton Street is not on the level of Sloane Street. The quays are much like the Paris quays. Bookshops. Long architectural vistas; one house after another, but some a storey too tall. Very broad streets. Our car too grand —this is what makes it impossible for me to finish Proust, I was about to say. Yet its been one of our most amusing tours. If only for the talk talk talk.

Tuesday 8 May

Worcester [*Star Hotel*]

We finished up Dublin in grand style yesterday. On the windy, indeed roaring windy Sunday we walked through Phoenix Park, where a crowd—this marks their lack of entertainment—watched a school of small girls playing hockey: had tea at Leixlip, pronounced Leeslip, an 18th century bare parlour, nice woman who had a child ill, & had been having a guest from Manitoba who said she was descended from the Kings—& then off we went down a leafy country lane—but the trees were lashing & one great bough fallen across the road—to Celbridge, where the famous interview with the blue eyes—I forget the phrase— took place. A girl said the Abbey was the big house down the road. It is a thick grey sham Gothic Abbey, but weathered now to look ancient, with sham Cathedral windows bricked up, & a great garden, all trees & bowers perhaps, leading down to the river. That was where she sat then; & she died here. But we could not see into the garden from the bank, & so drove home again.[11]

The next day which was oddly enough, yesterday, for now time & the Channel have cut off Ireland, and here in Worcester, the ancient, rich, traditional, all that shifty poverty seems blotted out—yesterday we went first to the Nat Gall. of which I say nothing—the pictures are very highly cleaned—& then to St Patrick's, where, over the door are the tremendous words; & in front of the door a diamond shaped brass, to mark the dean's tomb.[12] There beside him till a few years ago slept Stella; but the late Bishop, as the verger sarcastically remarked, pointing to his name oppro- briously on the long list, decided that she was buried at some distance, & so moved her brass plate. I suspect this was prudery; & if Swift was buried in her grave, that seems to amount to marriage. Also her epitaph which he wrote, alludes to her being celebrated by him. However the Bishop moved them—& in prudery also Lord Guiness has cased all the old pillars of Irish marble in stucco, so that they look like South Kensington, & somebody else, of equal piety, has floored the whole building with

11. Marlay Abbey, Celbridge, on the Liffey about ten miles to the west of Dublin, was the home of Esther Vanhomrigh—Dean Swift's devoted Vanessa. Leslie Stephen, in his life of Swift published in the 'English Men of Letters' series in 1882, quotes (p. 136) Pope's description of Swift's prominent eyes—'azure as the heavens'— in his account of the fatal scene with Vanessa in 1723 when he 'rode in a fury to Celbridge . . . [and] silent with rage, threw down her letter on the table and rode off.' Esther Vanhomrigh died soon afterwards.

12. The 'tremendous words', (mis)quoted by Leslie Stephen (*op cit*, p. 209), in Swift's own epitaph inscribed on a black marble tablet above the door of the Vestiaries, are: 'Ubi saeva Indignatio / Ulterius / Cor lacerare nequit.' His bust, in a roundel to the left of the door, is encircled with the translation: 'He lies where furious rage can rend his heart no more'. To the right of the door is a white marble cartouche commemorating: 'Mrs HESTER JOHNSON better / known to the World under the name of STELLA / under which she is celebrated in the Writings of / Dr JONATHAN SWIFT Dean of this Cathedral.' The two brass floor plates recording the interments of Swift (1745) and of Stella (1728)—who were probably not married, nor buried side by side—were laid after the wholesale restoration of the cathedral carried out by Sir Benjamin Guinness at his own expense in the 1860s; they were separated by Dean Lawlor in 1924, and reunited by Dean Wilson in 1935.

black & red tiles such as there are in hotels—much to the dudgeon of the old verger, who, like everybody else, regretted the old days: showed us the stalls of the Knights of St Patrick, with their helmets & arms, one the Prince of Wales's another the Duke of Connaught's "but they dont come here now"—[13] He too, like the shopkeepers & hotel keepers would gladly have done with the President of the Free State. "We dont want this hate—it does nobody any good" as the porter at Holyhead said to me this morning when he remarked how few cattle now came over. And at breakfast—the best I have ever eaten, because the coffee was good—I said to L. all the people themselves are sensible. Whats come over the politicians? And this we debated, & then took to the road in the wet & cold & drove in a downpour through Wales, through Shrewsbury (disappointing) through Much Wenlock (good) & much green & prosperous country, till we reached Worcester & took up lodging for the last time at the Star. L. told me not to stare so at the other tea drinkers, but I find it difficult not to gaze at these real English, these dwellers in the very heart of the land, who talk of horses & games all the time, & meet their men friends in the lounge, & sit drinking & laughing & bandying county gossip under pictures of famous race horses. Horses rule England, as salmon rule Ireland. In every hotel in Ireland sits a military man with poached egg eyes & sandy hair, a loud commanding voice, & spongebag coat & red slippers, after a day's fishing. There he sits & drinks; & all day he fishes—landing salmon after salmon, if its at Galway, so that they lie along the bank, to the wonder of the intellectual German lawyer, whom we met again there. He told us he saw them fishing all day, & a day costs £2, & they must give back half the fish they catch, & so much on every fish caught to the man with the gaff. He marvelled. And thats what Ireland is kept for: in every place where there's a river is built a large Inn, with town cooking & hot water & ladies & gentlemen's lavatories, though there's nothing but bog & hill for miles around, & there in the lounge the majors sit, & pay for the fishing, while the natives talk & talk & talk— about the old Kings of Ireland, presumably. Not that their folk lore is very interesting, Thompson said. An odd division of the country.

And here we are amidst the wealth of Worcester. Richer than ever it seems—this Cathedral city, set in the centre of ancient glovemaking & porcelain making, of Queen Ann[e] guildhalls, with a girdle of the usual 18th Century ecclesiastical houses, indeed in Much Wenlock there is more ancient stone & carving & architecture to be seen than in the whole of Ireland.

We are very tired of hotels & glad that this is our last night, though the comfort is extreme.

13. The Knights of St Patrick hadn't 'come here' since the disestablishment of the Irish Church in 1871.

[*Wednesday 9 May*]

[52 Tavistock Square]

This the 9th of May was our last day, & fine. So we saw Warwick-
shire—but I've been reading the Monologue & note how oddly another
style infects—at its best: thick green, thick leaves, stubby yellow stone
houses, & a fine sprinkling of Elizabethan cottages. All this led very
harmoniously to Stratford on Avon; & all crabbers be damned—it is a fine,
un self conscious town, mixed, with 18th Century & the rest all standing
cheek by jowl. All the flowers were out in Sh[akespea]re's garden. "That
was where his study windows looked out when he wrote the Tempest"
said the man. And perhaps it was true. Anyhow it was a great big house,
looking straight at the large windows & the grey stone of the school
chapel, & when the clock struck, that was the sound Shre heard. I cannot
without more labour than my roadrunning mind can compass describe
the queer impression of sunny impersonality. Yes, everything seemed to
say, this was Shakespeare's, had he sat & walked; but you wont find me
not exactly in the flesh. He is serenely absent-present; both at once;
radiating round one; yes; in the flowers, in the old hall, in the garden; but
never to be pinned down. And we went to the Church, & there was the
florid foolish bust, but what I had not reckoned for was the worn simple
slab, turned the wrong way, Kind Friend for Jesus' sake forbear—again
he seemed to be all air & sun smiling serenely; & yet down there one foot
from me lay the little bones that had spread over the world this vast
illumination.[14] Yes, & then we walked round the church, & all is simple &
a little worn; the river slipping past the stone wall, with a red breadth in it
from some flowering tree, & the edge of the turf unspoilt, soft & green &
muddy, & two casual nonchalant swans. The church & the school & the
house are all roomy spacious places, resonant, sunny today, & in & out
[*illegible*]—yes, an impressive place; still living, & then the little bones
lying there, which have created: to think of writing The Tempest looking
out on that garden; what a rage & storm of thought to have gone over
any mind; no doubt the solidity of the place was comfortable. No doubt
he saw the cellars with serenity. And a few scented American girls, & a
good deal of parrot prattle from old gramophone discs at the birthplace,
one taking up the story from the other. But isnt it odd, the caretaker at

14. Shakespeare's monument, with the coloured stone bust by Gerard Johnson the
Younger, was erected before 1623 on the chancel wall of Holy Trinity Church; the
floor stone over his grave bears the lines:
　　　　'Good friend for Iesus sake forbeare,
　　　　To digg the dvst encloased heare!
　　　　Blest be ye man yt spares thes stones,
　　　　And curst be he yt moves my bones.'

New Place agreed, that only one genuine signature of S.'s is known; & all the rest, books, furniture pictures &c has completely vanished? Now I think Shre was very happy in this, that there was no impediment of fame, but his genius flowed out of him, & is still there, in Stratford. They were acting As you like it I think in the theatre.

Duffers the biographers not to make more hum & melody out of New Place. I could, so I think. For the man told us that after the great grand daughter's death there was a sale, & why shouldn't some of his things he said, be lost, put away & come to light? Also, Queen H. Maria, Charles the 1st's Queen stayed there at New Place with the grand daughter (?) which shows how substantial it must have been.[15] That he told us, & I had never heard. And he said Gastrell, the clergyman had the original house, wh. stretched across the garden almost to the chapel, pulled down because people bothered him, asking to see Shre's house. And there (between the window & the wall) was the room he died in. A mulberry reputes to be the scion of the tree that grew outside Shre's window. Great cushions of blue yellow white flowers in the garden, which is open, so that the living go on walking & sitting there.

[End of inserted pages]

Two days after returning to Tavistock Square from her Irish journey, VW fell ill and spent a few days in bed before LW drove her to Rodmell on 17 May for the Whitsun holiday. Here she began DIARY XXIII.

Friday 18 May

I broke off, after sticking my Irish papers into the old book, & felt I suppose a little shiver. Cant be anything I said to myself after all that holiday; but it was—the flue. So I had to resign all ideas—all flood of Pargiters & the glorious & difficult end of that book: all was blotted by the damp sponge; & now it is precisely a week since I went to bed, & here we are for Whitsun at Monks; whats more amazing is that I write this with a gold Waterman, & have some thoughts of supplanting steel Woolworth. It is a sunny voluptuous day, the birds all rasping, on their nests I suppose, & cawing on the trees & early in the morning giving loud & continued bursts of song, to which I lie listening. I hear L. going about the

---

15. New Place, one of the largest houses in Stratford, originally built ca. 1483, was bought by Shakespeare for £60 in 1597, and here he died; Queen Henrietta Maria was billetted there on his daughter Mrs Hall for three days in 1643; *her* daughter Lady Bernard, having inherited Nash's House next door, sold New Place, and it was pulled down by the Rev. Francis Gastrell in 1759; but the 16th century Nash's House, which gives on to the site and gardens of the original New Place, was restored by the Trustees and Guardians of Shakespeare's Birthplace to form the New Place Museum. Shakespeare had no great-granddaughter.

garden with Percy. All is calm & profoundly comfortable, owing to the absence for ever even in the background of grumbling Nelly, & her replacement by the steady silent unselfish Mabel. Yes, we do without a Char; we are free, serene, matter of fact, oh what a relief! So if I can pull my head out of the bog, I may go back on Tuesday to the 3 months immersion. But I take a day or two more to rest myself. How infinitely modest & disillusioned & without ambition of any sort I became, all because of influenza. Couldnt believe that anyone would come & see me, let alone that I could ever again string a dozen words. Now self confidence, conceit, the blessed illusion by which we live begin to return; very gently. Smooth serenity is the first stage which I will not interrupt by writing.

Tuesday 22 May

At last today, which is Tuesday, after striking the match on the box despairingly, sterilely,—oh I was so overcome with rigidity & nothing-ness—a little flame has come. Perhaps I'm off. This refers to the devilish difficulty of starting Part 7 again after the flu. Elvira & George, or John, talking in her room. I'm still miles outside them, but I think I got into the right tone of voice this morning. I make this note by way of warning. What is important now is to go very slowly; to stop in the middle of the flood; never to press on; to lie back & let the soft subconscious world become populous; not to be urging foam from my lips. There's no hurry. I've enough money to last a year. If this book comes out next June year its time enough. The last chapters must be so rich, so resuming, so weaving together that I can only go on by letting my mind brood every morning on the whole book. Theres no longer any need to forge ahead, as the narrative part is over. What I want is to enrich & stabilise. This last chapter must equal in length & importance & volume the first book; & must in fact give the other side, the submerged side of that. I shant, I think, re-read; I shall summon it back—the teaparty, the death, Oxford & so on, from my memory. And as the whole book depends on bringing this off, I must be very leisurely & patient, & nurse my rather creaking head & dandle it with French & so on as cunningly as possible. We go back this afternoon, & the summer lap therefore now begins in earnest; Mabel &c.

Out of sheer white mist we drove to Charleston last night & my numbed torpor became slightly incandescent. Benita there. Clive Nessa Duncan Quentin all talking at once about Spencer's pictures.[16]

16. Stanley Spencer (1891-1959), elected ARA in 1932, was showing six works in the Royal Academy Summer Exhibition. His highly idiosyncratic pictures of nomi-nally biblical subjects, set in his native Cookham, were attracting widespread attention.

JUNE 1934

Monday 11 June

That hopeful page reads rather too credulous now, since I went back &
again on Friday following shivered, & ached, was stiff as a rod, talking to
Elizabeth Bowen: 101: bed: influenza: & so lay all that week, till last
Sunday to be accurate; & then went to Rodmell; & there began the
chapter again, & had a sudden fuse of ideas & then there was the opera,
the nightingale singing in the ilex tree, Christabel & Mr Olaf Hambro
telling stories about the Queen & Prince; & a very hot concert yesterday,
so I cannot, no I cannot write today.[1] Patience, as Carlyle wd. say (in
Italian). But consider—the whole system is so strained over this end, that
one tiny grit, one late night, one too tiring day—takes away all rush, all
fusing. And just as I saw it clear before me: the very intricate scenes: all
contrasting; building up: so wait till tomorrow.

Monday 18 June

Very very hot; day altered so as to go out after tea. A drought over the
world. In flood with Here & Now, praise be. Yet—very wary; only just
now I made up the scene with Renny & Maggie: a sign I am fertilising, for
I should be doing French for Janie, who comes at 5.[2] Yes, & last night we
sat in Gordon Sqre with Mary Baker—a timid housemaid little body, no
birth or breeding, but 2 dogs; lizards on her terrace, & scorpions, which
dont bite with their claws, but punch you & then bite; she had seen one,
placed in a ring of fire commit suicide; very very hot it was, the Stracheys
calling through the railings to be let in. Then James & Alix, all praising
that scramble & scream of a party which I hated so: rather shocked that
Nessa enjoyed it. So many young screaming drunks. Well, perhaps at 2 in
the morning . . . .[3] I forgot we had Aldous: a most admirable, cool, anti-
septic distempered, but humane & gentle man: with age just tempering
his brow: experience; but admirably mature, as we are not; has gone about
the world, completely sceptical, all the more humane; judging everything,
yet nothing. A little theoretical, about religion & sex; not for that reason
a novelist; infinitely elongated & bony: his blurred grey eye; his malice &

1. 1934 was the first year of the Glyndebourne Festival in Sussex; the Woolfs went to
   Figaro on Friday 8 June, and to an afternoon concert conducted by Fritz Busch on
   Sunday 10th (when Pippa, Marjorie and James Strachey lunched with them)
   before driving back to London.
2. The drought, widespread in Russia, Europe, and the United States, had lasted in
   Britain without serious interruption since November 1932. VW was now having
   twice-weekly French conversation lessons with Janie Bussy.
3. The Woolfs went to a party given by James and Alix Strachey on Friday 15 June;
   Aldous Huxley came to tea with them that afternoon.

wit; talked of Sullivan, of Ottoline; Brett; then of the French noblesse; how he visits them; and they come down, amazed to find a WC: & he had spent a weekend at Welwyn with the Sex Reformers; taken off his clothes among the cabbages & read Waste Land. Necessary to say penis & fuck; but that said, no change follows.[4] He uses every instant to the best advantage but has somehow solved the problem of remaining just, gentle,—a very sympathetic mind, & I'm glad I troubled to write to him— one of my rare fruitful actions; not to let things slip so much, to which I owe Aldous's visit, & we are to meet in the autumn.[5]

Monday 2 July

Rung up by Osbert Sitwell just now. After hopping & jumping about publishers, Holroyd Reece, lunches dinners & teas,[1] he comes out with, "And can't anything be done about this monstrous affair in Germany?" "One of the few public acts" I said "that makes one miserable". Then trying, how ineffectively, to express the sensation of sitting here & reading, like an act in a play, how Hitler flew to Munich & killed this that & the other man & woman in Germany yesterday.[2] A fine hot summers day here & we took Philip [Woolf] Babs & 3 children to the Zoo. Meanwhile these brutal bullies go about in hoods & masks, like little boys dressed up, acting this idiotic, meaningless, brutal, bloody, pandemonium. In they

4. J. W. N. Sullivan (1886-1937), Irish writer on mathematical, scientific, and musical subjects, was an old friend of Huxley's; during this year he was afflicted with the first stage of an incurable paralysis. The Hon. Dorothy Brett (1883-1977), painter, who like Huxley had lived with the Morrells at Garsington during the war, in 1924 went with D. H. Lawrence to Taos, New Mexico, where she remained until her death. For the Sex Reformers, see above, 12 July 1932, n. 13.

5. During her recent indisposition, VW had written to Ethel Smyth that she was 'now reduced to Huxley' (V VW Letters, no. 2897); she had perhaps written to him (no letter survives) in praise of his Beyond the Mexique Bay, published in April 1934, and suggested their meeting.

1. Osbert Sitwell (1892-1969) was the second of the aristocratic trio of writers, brother of Edith and Sacheverell, each of whom VW met from time to time, but did not know well. John Holroyd-Reece (1897-1969) was the founder of the Pegasus Press in Paris in 1927, the Albatross Continental Library, and in 1934 took over control of Tauchnitz editions.

2. It was on 30 June 1934 that the rivalries within the ruling Nazi party came to their climax with Hitler's decision to crush the Brown Shirts (SA) and their leader Röhm, whom he personally arrested in Munich. In all some 1200 people were done to death without trial, including—among non-Nazis whom Hitler feared or disliked and seized the opportunity of eliminating—General Kurt von Schleicher, his predecessor as Chancellor of the German Reich, who with his wife was shot 'resisting arrest' at his Berlin flat.

come while Herr so & so is at lunch: iron boots, they say, grating on the parquet, kill him; & his wife who rushes to the door to prevent them. It is like watching the baboon at the Zoo; only he sucks a paper in which ice has been wrapped, & they fire with revolvers. And here we sit, Osbert I &c, remarking this is inconceivable. A queer state of society. If there were any idea, any vision behind it: but look at the masks these men wear —the brutal faces of baboons, licking sweet paper. And for the first time I read articles with rage, to find him called a real leader. Worse far than Napoleon. Established for a thousand year says somebody. Meanwhile as I say the weather is brilliant, dry, hot; Clive gives a cocktail party, Bianca [Weiss] invites us to hear singing—& I get £300 this morning from Harcourt Brace.

Friday 6 July

Being unable to continue the P.s this morning, having indeed worked out that particular vein after 5 weeks writing I suppose, I went out & bought a pen with which I write, a Swan pen, on a broiling hot day, a real scorcher. And came in & found a letter from Stephen Spender praising The Lighthouse,[3] & was made by that to think, have I written myself out, & so read the last chapter of H. & N. disconsolately—what a silly thing to do, since, as I've just said, I'm out of that mood. We go to Rodmell this burning afternoon, & yesterday we were at Reigate, being tried for the inconsiderate act of passing the cyclist. A great red municipal building: sunburnt country gents one wreathed with a gold chain on the bench: L. stood in the box. 3 pounds I heard them whisper, & so it was. The old gents had made up their minds long before that.[4] No I dont like this pen.

Wednesday 11 July

I dont like this pattern[?] any better I think; but no matter. L. says all Swans have soft snub noses. And this feels so but less taut.[?] The heat goes on—the burning dry heat. Mabel making jam sweats: I'm forced to take a cab just now; I'm writing about belief in a city church by way of a change. I'm letting the subconscious populate. So dazed & dusty: I rather think of marking time till August & Rodmell: where we take Mabel, shall have Louie Everest I think as permanent. We saw her last week end— a merry little brown eyed mongrel who came running to meet us in the road. Yesterday tea with Nessa; & the Morris's there; today Osbert. I

3. Stephen Spender's letter, dated 4 July, is in MHP, Sussex; for VW's reply, see V VW Letters, no. 2910.
4. LW had been summonsed for careless driving.

make these marks. & hear John's voice in Miss West's room signing his name.[5] L. there.

Tuesday 17 July

I forgot to put in about the Colefax Row, curiously enough. How she wrote me a violent letter—better to break all together—can no longer have you in my life, because I put off dinner to meet Noel Coward. She pleads her most difficult life: Sir Arthur?[6]

This is one of the dryest & hottest of summers. At it again this morning. And heat brings such lassitude; & people swarm. I have let them die out, be extinct: Osbert for instance; with his very sensual Royal Guelf face; his extreme uneasiness; his childish vanity always striking the two notes: rank & genius: so easily touched by praise, so eager. Told me the story of the lady in the pink hat. He lectures in the provinces, indeed rather likes the Prince in disguise part which he plays, staying with his dentist at Gerrards X perhaps. Well, he had a letter from Verena, to say she had always posed as familiar with him: would he lend himself to the deception & recognise her? She wd wear a pink hat. So he exclaimed, out loud, Oh Verena! what a pleasure to see you! The story would have gone better had she not been Verena. So he went off to swim for an hour before dining with Princess Mary & so on. A sensitive man; voluble; august[?], uneasy; spending 6 months in China alone: & gushing words. Still I like him—why I dont know.[7]

And then the Eccles' on Sunday at Clive's & the Whistler picture, & talk of Margaret, my little owl done by command; for I went to fetch the

5. In 1929 the Woolfs had bought a cottage in Rodmell to house their domestic servant Annie Thomsett; she was now leaving to get married to Albert Penfold, and VW advertised locally for a replacement. Louie Everest (1912-1977) was engaged, started work in August, and remained as cook-housekeeper until LW's death in 1969. For her own account, see Louie Mayer in *Recollections of Virginia Woolf* (1972), edited by Joan Russell Noble, pp. 154-63. Peter Morris, a painter, and his sister Dora (later Lady Romilly), were particular friends of Duncan Grant. John Lehmann was signing the limited edition (75 copies) of his book *The Noise of History* (*HP Checklist* 342A).

6. Sibyl Colefax's husband Sir Arthur Colefax, KC (1866-1936) was a lawyer and had been a member of several Government committees and Courts of Enquiry. Her violent letter does not survive among the eleven undated and almost illegible examples now preserved in MHP, Sussex.

7. Osbert Sitwell came to tea on 11 July. His story of the 'Lady with the Pink Feather' (whom he there names Albinia) is included in his *Penny Foolish. A Book of Tirades and Panegyrics* (1935). He had returned to England in May after spending six months in the East—three of them in Peking—not alone, but in company with his friend David Horner.

picture & there was old Dick, & Margaret & I sobbed—she so soft simple
& stately—in the dining room of the hired house. A curious scene:
some sincerity welling up after all these indifferent years. L. talking
to bluff tough gruff Dick in the drawing room. M. to stay with him &
see the beech woods of Highclere. Mrs Eccles the pretty daughter of Ld
Dawson of Penn. C. called her an aristocrat. Clive very flighty & talking
French. R[oger]. looking under his eye at the Whistler. Dyou know,
I'm getting less & less sure. I'm not sure of that arm: & there's a certain
flatness . . . No, I'd rather you asked Turner's advice, which Clive explained, when R. went, because R. had been duped over a Whistler once,
when Clive was in the right.[8] Mr E. a slab faced agent de change: I put
stockbroker in French because I'm rather slick in that language now, &
have 2 weekly lessons from Janie. This is a real solid triumph, to have
made myself face that curious fear—about French—& have now, I think,
routed it.

Vita to lunch, after many weeks, yesterday, with her MS. which, L.
says, is perilous fantastic stuff, a woman flagellated in a cave. How much
will the public stand? She has a joke about the prostate gland which we
are asking her to reconsider.[9] She has grown opulent & bold & red—
tomatoe coloured, & paints her fingers & lips which need no paint—the
influence of Gwen [St Aubyn]; underneath much the same; only without
the porpoise radiance, & the pearls lost lustre.

[*Thursday 19 July*]

Is my brain dwindling, I ask myself after $1\frac{1}{2}$ hours writing at the Fact &
Fiction—that is, I am revising the first chapter of that old bugbear of
mine on fiction.[10] And I get so knotted & jaded; never mind. I shall lie
flat a little in brain, for a few days: until I feel the well full. That is, I am
priming myself for a final go at Here & Now. It is still so hot—so hot—

8. The Woolfs, Roger Fry, Duncan Grant, and Vanessa and Julian Bell all forgathered
at Clive's after dinner on Sunday 15 July; his dinner guests were David Eccles
(b. 1904), a future Conservative MP and Minister, created Viscount Eccles in
1964, and his wife Sybil, eldest daughter of the King's Physician, Lord Dawson of
Penn. Three days earlier the Woolfs had been to see the widowed Lady Margaret
Duckworth; she was the aunt of the current Earl of Carnarvon, whose family seat
was Highclere Castle, Newbury; but who Dick, or what the Whistler picture, was
has not been discovered. Percy Moore Turner (1877-1950) was an art dealer who
specialised in modern French painting.
9. V. Sackville-West's novel *The dark island* was published by the Hogarth Press
in October 1934 (*HP Checklist* 351).
10. For VW's projected but never completed book on Fiction, embarked on for the
Hogarth Press in 1925, see *III VW Diary*, 7 December 1925; above, 10 January
1931 and 3 March 1932; and below, 21 August, 10 October 1934.

my skylight painted smooth blue every morning—when we hear rain as we did last night we rush to the window. A puddle the rarest of sights. Smell of wet earth delicious. We drive to Cambridge to dine with Rothschilds tonight—home by starlight. Mary rings up to ask us to dine to meet Tom. How heavenly to drive by night she says. Cant because Jack wont. I did not go to Edith Jones cocktail or her party yesterday, & so felt assuaged; walked in Oxford St: bought a 15/- servants dress. Sun came out, though very soon: bought a melon therefore. How pleasant to have coins in one's purse. On the whole a well managed summer, if my head were more vigorous. Oh these long books, what a tremendous effort they are—to whole [hold?] the entire span on my shoulders. And as Bogy Harris said, you must go on now till you die. Which is true.[11]

No letters; no fame; rather a relief, to sit in the shade & spin. Julian trying for a Chinese professorship; will hear today.[12] He dined & brought a skatelike looking woman—[name omitted]—a mouth cut in a wide fishlike face—entirely obtuse: sucking greedy. Why does J. like such inanities?

Saturday 21 July

A new nib. But I want sometimes to describe people, & here is our visit to the Rothschilds fading in my mind.[13] We went down on Thursday, starting about 4.30, driving through that very spacious country that I always honour by planting myself down in a house in the midst of the corn. There are such houses; & the road runs by open unfenced fields. Why are fields always hedged off in England? The other way is much better. So to Merton Hall: a grey old house, half chapel, or college; half the usual rich young couples version of life: 4 kittens & a sickly pathetic marmoset; Barbara in a great hat, very pregnant, perched on a chair; long room, bowls of flowers, tea luxuriously spread at 6.30. I asked for a pale stale cup. She telephoned for the footman to bring long lemonades with gin—no without. And where is Mr R.? Asleep ma'am. Then V. came in, a slab of beefsteak, fat, thick, red lipped, in his open shirt. Sparring with B. about the rent they paid. Oughtn't I to know? Don't I pay it? & so on, partly for our edification. 'Blubsy' is one of his words. 'Barbara went blubsy.' Half asleep, he said, after a lunch party, Venetia Montagu & two

11. Henry ('Bogey') Harris (1870-1950) was a wealthy and sociable connoisseur and collector who lived in Bedford Square.

12. Through the Cambridge Appointments Board, Julian Bell had applied for the Chair of English at Wuhan University; he did not hear that he had been successful until the following year (see below, 17 July 1935).

13. Barbara Hutchinson and Victor Rothschild were married on 28 December 1933; they now lived at Merton Hall, near Cambridge.

of her lovers, one by the way Grey Walter, the son of our old cook.[14] B. sat very upright, painted, like a cornflower. Wild, vivid; & then we walked about the garden, stuck like a jam tart—little square box edged beds with single flowers in them; a pretentious uncared for garden. Go & get your note book, he jibed: no I wont. Oh but she always has a note book. One thing a little shocked me; his saying, 'I dont get much time for Barbara'. This he said perhaps boasting again, as he walked me down the narrow paths; he said he was determined not to become a specialist like the other science dons, thus spent so many hours with science, so many with books, which doesnt leave much time for Barbara. She had snapped at him; putting her heel down, when he wanted to tell me what Dadie had told her about—& the servant & the boy all in the same bed as—[names omitted]: no thats not quite it, but it was scandal on those lines. B. had been drawing (like Mary, I thought) Dadie's confidences. As it appears from this, Victor told me the story, as we walked. Then dinner on the lawn, & they refused the ice: a luxurious decorative dinner. So in to the library: a steel bookcase packed with first editions, each sealed in a red morocco case; which we had out, Gulliver's Travels, Boswell, Wordsworth, Swift, all laid on the floor; thousands of pounds worth, bought since last year, & I had set him reading with my Common Reader. Ah but this isnt the way to read, I almost said. Too easy; sitting at Sotheby's bidding. But then youth has enormous power, I said, for I liked him, rather, her a good deal; she is the more sensitive & civilised, he the more robust & triumphant. Youth can have a child in September: nothing it cant do: has 50 years ahead of it, living in this very lovely England, & he said the R. fortune is now at full flood again. Shall he remain a scientist & refuse to be a financier? Thats the sort of question youth can ask. He wont live with these pickers up of minute peas in Cambridge. He said that his professor, aged 40, comes out to dine, & tells very old very dreary smutty stories, all his energy having been sucked up by science: so that is another argument against the specialist.[15] Cant connect.

We drove home at 11, & got back at 1. A lovely cool shadowed drive through the fields again, two great steeples of light searching the sky about Ware, & an aeroplane sailing among the stars. Suddenly I saw a green star moving.

Duncan ill with very bad piles—operated on last night, or, since that

14. The Hon. Mrs Edwin Montagu, née Venetia Stanley (1887-1948), widow of a politician, was an ornament of society noted for her beauty and wit; she lived at Attleborough, Norfolk, some fifty miles from Cambridge. William Grey Walter (1910-77)—whose mother, an intellectual American who had acted as VW's cook-housekeeper for a few weeks in the summer of 1930 (see *III VW Diary*)—having taken first class honours in Physiology at King's College, Cambridge, was now a post-graduate student there.
15. This specialist has not been identified.

sounds alarming, lanced. Spoke to Janie of the snobbishness of our sympathies. Cant really sympathise with that particular disease, though the pain is terrible. Must laugh.

I have just finished, the other pen continues, though very provisionally, the first truth telling chapter: but Lord knows if I must not entirely scrap the whole thing once more.[16] At any rate I have now got a little fresh water in my well for Here & Now. I had one of my sudden rushes listening to Monti Verde last night. Last night came a letter from Henry to my dear Aunt Virginia saying that George has left me £100. I feel rather rebuked & uncomfortable, I dont altogether know why, at this final tip.[17] Shall I spend it on what? Now I have so much money. And by the way Nessa came in, rather to my shame—but again, why?—only I like noting these queer waifs in my mind—dressed in a 3/6 dress she had made herself. I know what I am going to do now: I am going to come down with both feet on this dress mania: this shyness; this tremendous susceptibility: & it is not so very difficult, once faced.

I am reading Shre plays the fag end of the morning. Have read, Pericles, Titus Andronicus, & Coriolanus.

[Sunday 22 July]

We went round, I continue, to fill in ten minutes on Sunday morning— a grey blue sky above the skylight, to Nessa with fruit; & found her sublimely in command of the situation as usual. Elly [Rendel] in a panic insisting upon a nurse: look at the haemorrhage; can you take the responsibility? Certainly I can said Nessa: anyhow I must. I'm not young, & I've seen bloodier bandages than these. This too at the nerve racking hour of dawn. So she triumphed. I doubt whether I could have. Perhaps. Walked as usual this summer in the Park; & saw the people playing bowls, & were happy to think that next week we shall have our own bowls. Also how shall we spend our legacy? Poor old George only left £7000 or so of money: what had he done with the rest? After dinner we listened to a very good concert; L. made cigarettes, & I followed my new diversion of book binding. I am covering Proust in little shiny squares of gummed paper that one buys for 6d at Kettles: a great relief to work one's fingers. Letter from Elizabeth Reed—ecstatic, highfalutin, unreal, in spite of miscarriage on the moors.[18]

16. i.e.: her book on Fiction; see MHP, Sussex, B 7a, *The Truth Tellers.*
17. Monteverdi's 'Ballet of the Ungracious Ladies' was broadcast by the BBC on Friday evening, 20 July. Henry George Austen de l'Etang Duckworth (b. 1905) was the eldest son and executor of Sir George Duckworth, who left net personality of £7,421; he made a similar bequest of £100 to Vanessa.
18. Elizabeth Read wrote on 19 July from Shropshire to say she was 'making good' although she had had a miscarriage and nearly died. See MHP, Sussex. Kettles, paper specialists, used to be in High Holborn.

Tuesday 24 July

Infinitely bored with correcting, or rather inserting a snip, into, my old Sickert for those pernickety Americans, who insist that Max shall be drag[g]ed in.[19]

Dinner last night at the Hutchinsons. Let me see. Praise of my dress— taken very philosophically. Desmond there & Tom— dinner: not very good: one element of pleasure lessened. Talk frivolous at first. Jack's jokes with Mary for being in love with Arlen. He sends her books. I do not altogether like Jack's jokes with Mary: her lovers &c. Then, Mary describes a party: a champagne cocktail. Tom gravely attentive. Talk gets upon whether we frighten or are frightened. Tom said I made him feel I saw through all his foibles; which perhaps I do. Talk of Patmore. Desmond expatiated, praised, placed him with Crashaw: described his love of great fires, his son Epiphany, all in the Sunday Times agreeable manner, not very close to the object: a love of little pictures.[20] Jack robust, rather coarse; how old Victorians always had an eye to the main chance. Tom remained on the verge; yellow, bony; but I regretted having denounced the Rock—so much melancholy in his face.[21] Yes, & then, somehow to Hitler. Desmond again describing Bottomley & Pemberton Billing.[22] I always feel he flutters & skirts, where Tom dives to the centre. And there was Leonard aquiline & lean; & so Desmond drew on to politics, & the half wit wasps whom he watched in their Hive: Fascists that is: how Hitler had dealt them a blow. So to politics & then, what with Jack's cross exam- ination, & Tom's intentness, & Desmond burbling general goodwill & human love, & Leonard's specialised convictions, the argument blazed: how the Labour party wd come in: what it would do. But how can you make any such ridiculous claim Jack boomed. What is it going to do

19. In April VW had offered her article on Sickert (see above, 25 November 1933, n. 10) to the *Yale Review*, and the editor Miss McAfee asked her to adapt it slightly for American readers (see *V VW Letters*, nos. 2881, 2908). VW inserted a paragraph of some 200 words, adverting to Max Beerbohm's caricatures, Rossetti, 'the house in Chelsea', Meredith, and Whistler's Thames, and made a number of other minor alterations.

20. Richard Crashaw (1612?-1649) and Coventry Patmore (1823-1896); both poets were converts to Roman Catholicism. Francis Epiphanius ('Piffie') was Patmore's last child born to his third wife in 1883.

21. T. S. Eliot's *The Rock. A Pageant Play* had been performed at Sadler's Wells Theatre 28 May-9 June in aid of the Forty-five Churches Fund of the Diocese of London, and was published at the same time. VW only read it, and expressed her views in a letter to Stephen Spender (*V VW Letters*, no. 2910).

22. Both Horatio Bottomley (1860-1933) and N. Pemberton Billing (1880-1948) were populist journalists and MPs whose campaigns led them to the courts: Bottomley was sentenced to seven years' penal servitude for fraudulent conversion; Pember- ton Billing was acquitted of libel, but became a persistent and dismal litigant.

about unemployment, about agriculture? All these questions were put from the view of here & now, capable business men; L. ideal by comparison. How 10 sensible men 'round a table', one of his phrases, could so manipulate the supply of locomotives & wheat that one country supplemented another. Oh if we were all men of good will, if we were all ready to be nice about it— Then Desmond as usual praised moderation, tact, the virtues of the defunct Liberal party: how civilisation runs slowly in a great wide stream, & you must slowly facilitate its course, but by no means introduce whirlpools, cut precipices & so on. The deceased Oxford [H. H. Asquith], presumably, his ideal; but this is what so depresses & baffles me in him as a critic. They heckled L. between them, & when the argument began to put its tail in its mouth, Mary asked if I would like to withdraw. We went upstairs, & she sat on the fender, & said how, being alone for the week end she had tried to write an ambitious biography. There was to be an outer story, & a second meaning; as far as I could gather. But when she had called one character George Buchanan, & another Lettice Ponsonby, they died under her hands. Could one then try to write disconnected scenes? Must they combine into a story? No need whatever I said. And she clapped her hands, as if I had given her leave; & declared that she would write scenes, & send them to me. For instance there was Syrie Maugham's party. As a person, she had not enjoyed it. I gathered that she had not had any intimacy. Then she reflected that she had danced every dance with an entirely different person: Freyberg, Arlen, & I forget who else; Lord Hambledon; had said the same thing to each; & each was entirely different.[23] As an artist then, a dispassionate observer, the party had been a great success. Not to her as Mary. One must cease to be Mary.

Then the others came; & Tom read Mr Barker's poems, chanting, intoning. Barker has some strange gift he thinks & dimly through a tangle of words ideas emerge. He thinks there is some melody some rhythm some emotion lacking in the Audens, & Spenders. Wants 5/- a week for this young man, who has wife & child.[24] So home at last. The aeroplanes were droning in the sky all the time.

On 25 July LW collected from King's Cross Station a 'sickly pathetic marmoset' (see above, 21 July 1934) called Mitz, which was henceforth to be his constant companion until it died in December 1938 (see IV LW, pp. 186-7). The following afternoon the Woolfs drove to Rodmell.

23. Syrie Maugham, *née* Barnado (1879-1955), whose uneasy marriage to the celebrated and successful writer Somerset Maugham had ended in divorce in 1929, was a fashionable interior decorator and hostess, entertaining smart society, aristocracy, art and intellect at her house in the King's Road, Chelsea.
24. George Barker (b. 1913), poet, whose *Thirty Preliminary Poems* and *Alanna Autumnal*, a prose work, were both published by Eliot's firm, Faber & Faber, in 1933.

Friday 27 July

Rodmell begins again: with this difference, we have Mabel just arrived, this instant; & Louie [Everest], who is moving in today. And the usual helter skelter, tidying, & nothing to settle to; must at once go to Worthing, then come back to a meeting. Not the kind of day I much like, & would rather have no servant in the house; but we shall see. Also, my old brain must wake & bestir itself over Here & Now.

This is written to kill time, as I cant settle in. Perhaps we have too many possessions. Too many tables & chairs.

Mrs B[artholomew]. last night: has had her hair shingled. Propped against the door talked & talked. How difficult she found it to spend money though she now has it after all those years of stinting. Had given Annie a cheque. Also pays old Grey's insurance. A queer genuine, though untamed, I mean uneducated spray—I mean so tremulous & wispish—something wild & vagrant; this becoming more quiet; in fact rather a nice sharp kind woman. Now she has a cheque book & draws cheques. Theres the money coming, she said. She wants to leave Rodmell. Percy doesn't. She advertises for rooms at Colchester. Cant get them. So there it is, when we can afford to go we cant. But she has been very kind coming up to oblige, washing up doing the rooms. She cooks a bit of meat for Mrs Grey—whose [*maiden*] name is Squelch. Oh I'm too bothered & dithered —wish to sleep—but must go to Worthing instead.

[*Saturday 28 July*]

ah hah—but now, having despatched that entirely disagreeable day, Worthing, & Mr Fears, representing Rodmell Labour party for an hour after dinner, I'm free to begin the last chapter;[25] & by a merciful Providence the well is full, ideas are rising, & if I can keep at it widely freely powerfully I shall have 2 months of complete immersion. Odd how the creative power at once brings the whole universe to order. I can see the day whole, proportioned—even after a long flutter of the brain such as I've had this morning[—]it must be a physical, moral, mental necessity, like setting the engine off. A wild windy hot day—a tearing wind in the garden; all the July apples on the grass. I'm going to indulge in a series of quick sharp contrasts: breaking my bonds[?] as much as ever I like. Trying every kind of experiment. Now of course I cant write diary or letters or read because I am making up all the time. Perhaps Bob T. was

25. The Woolfs had been to tea with old Mrs Woolf in Worthing. Mr Fears was the village postman, and a strong Labour supporter.

right in his poem when he called me fortunate above all[26]—I mean in having a mind that can express—no, I mean in having mobilised my being —learnt to give it complete, ⟨not ju⟩ outcome—I mean, that I have to some extent forced myself to break every mould & find a fresh form of being, that is of expression, for everything I feel & think. So that when it is working I get the sense of being fully energised—nothing stunted. But this needs constant effort, anxiety & risk. Here in H. & N. I am breaking the mould made by The Waves.

Wednesday 1 August

I'm black & blue from their worrying,
    They've tortured me early & late,
Some with their love,—God help me!
    The others with their hate.

Why I trouble to copy out these [*untraced*] lines which are from Heine, I dont know, except that they represent what happened to my perfect free day at Charleston yesterday. One ought not to have the illusion of perfect happiness—that it is possible; yet again I did. And then, yes my friends— this is Sybil Colefax sneering to Clive at my taking too much care of myself; & this is Clive handing it on; & then this morning, poor old Francis [Birrell] paralysed; another operation tomorrow, under which says Nessa, it is to be hoped he may die, since the cancer has come back. She sees him today. How odd, ones last day, this: here very hot & fine. & then of course he may live. How I hate going through these thoughts again, & what a jumble of meanness & sordidity & the fine, one's feelings are.

Remember, as far as S[ibyl]. C[olefax]. goes, never never to speak of health. In fact this might be useful in all connections.

Thursday 2 August

My mind, only how call it so solid a name, still running not upon dear old Frankie, who may be dying—but our convention is to be very cheerful & objective—but upon that gnat Sybil. Why didnt I remind her when

---

26. R. C. Trevelyan had sent VW a poem (see *V VW Letters*, no. 2913) which her advice to him in a previous letter (*V VW Letters*, no. 2879) had inspired him to write. It was published as 'To V.W.' in his collection *Beelzebub and other Poems* (*HP Checklist* 377) in 1935, and includes the lines:

    'Fortunate therefore must I deem all those
    Who serve that "other harmony of prose";
    And among all most fortunate must you be,
    Whose chosen art has left your spirit free
    To range through all experience, in quest
    Of such spoil as may please your fancy best.'

I wrote of the way she treated me, how she put me off twice here. What a stinging rejoinder that would have been—& I only thought of it yesterday. But perhaps I can still get it in. A curious problem: why was I not even mildly annoyed at the time, & now, in August, why am I acutely irritated. Clive's drop of poison, I suppose, managed to crystallise the whole thing; the oddly vivid & upsetting effect of knowing that one's been talked about. The reflection of myself in Courtauld's drawing room. being made the subject of her & Clive's jeers & sneers. But I dont mean to have another row, à la Eddy.

And this fly in the eye makes it impossible for me to see—no, thats not true, I can 'see' the nursing home, the bed, the surgeon; I can act ones last night, & being waked early in Welbeck St & all that—my eye is quite remorseless—but I dont feel. However, these flies gradually dismember themselves, & perish.

I'm worried too with my last chapters. Is it all too shrill & voluble? And then the immense length, & the perpetual ebbs & flows of invention. So divinely happy one day; so jaded the next.

Louie's first morning here. A leap in the dark rather. Mabel making currant jam. Vast basins of black currants which she heads & tails. Mabel had a chicken that lived with her 14 years & was called Old George.

Saturday 4 August

Waiting about to go to Annie's wedding. No signs yet. No bells ring-ing. So impossible to do anything, & here I am at 11 this hot August morning in full garden party dress. No news of Frankie. The tap tap of the boys playing cricket reminds me of our cricket sensations. What is the difference between memory, excited by sensation, & thought—the thought required by a page of Plato for instance?

Yesterday just as we had done tea, Adrian's gaunt form appeared; Karin's touseled shape, grown very thick & large. Her inferiority complex takes the form of praising Adrian. Clever old Adrian, she exclaims, if he bowls a good bowl. This is by way of saying—what? My marriage was not so bad after all? He remains perfectly unmoved, quiet, sensible; I suppose curiously immature, though able to go through all the actions correctly of a grown man, father, husband.

The night before, Enid Jones rang up & came, from 9.15 to 10.45 to discuss her book—the effect of winning the Grand National on a child, ostensibly; really another case of inferiority I think; to rub off the taste of Goodwood with Scatters Wilson.[1] Like a dog eating grass. But why shd

1. See *Enid Bagnold's Autobiography* (1969), pp. 182-4 for her own account of her disastrous outing to Goodwood with Sir Mathew Wilson (see above, 4 December 1933, n. 2), and her subsequent visit to Monks House. Her best-selling novel *National Velvet* was published in 1935.

she need to eat grass? Because, being a scallywag she married a very rich man: is neither fish flesh fowl nor good red herring; & thats an ambiguous state that requires perpetual adjustment. She shifts from self to self. We have to provide a transition. An uneasy woman. rather hard. Brandishes all her children all her responsibilities all her gaieties in our face. Uncertain whether to stay or to go.

Clive & Julian & so on to tea today. I will swear not to pick up one of the thorns so artfully administered by the Pismire—slipped in. George ring the bell & run away. I will carefully observe his method & analyse it in action.

Saxon very glad to come here next week end. We take up a conversation broken these 10 years in our natural voices. What about Pericles? & so on. A relief after Sybil's histrionics.

Certainly bright leaves do glare as Rupert said.[2] No sign of the wedding yet. I think of the craving of the human being for sympathy.

Tuesday 7 August

A rather wet Bank holiday. Tea with Keyneses.

Maynard had had teeth out, but was very fertile. For instance: "Yes, I've been 3 weeks in America. An impossible climate. In fact it has collected all the faults of all the climates. This carries out my theory about climate. Nobody could produce a great work in America. One sweats all day & the dirt sticks to ones face. The nights are as hot as the days. Nobody sleeps. Everyone is kept on the go all day long by the climate. I used to dictate articles straight off. I felt perfectly well until I left. The shipwreck was all the Captains fault. We made a bee line for the Lightship in a fog. He had the boats launched before we struck. We had the men out of the water before they were in it. Very efficient, but not a good captain. A character. A Don Juan."[3] So to German politics "They're doing something very queer with their money. I cant make out what. It may be the Jews are taking away their capital. Let me see, if 2000 Jews were each to take away £2,000—Anyhow they cant pay their Lancashire bill. Always the Germans have bought cotton from Egypt, had it spun in Lancashire:

2. Cf: 'Unconscious and unpassionate and still
                  Cloud-like we lean and stare as bright leaves stare,
              And gradually along the stranger hill
                  Our unwalled loves thin out on vacuous air.'
                                        Rupert Brooke, *Town and Country*.
       See also VW, 'Rupert Brooke' in *Books and Portraits*, 1977 (Kp A49).
3. Invited by Columbia University to receive an Honorary Degree on 5 June, Keynes sailed to New York on the liner *Olympic* (Captain John W. Binks), which on 15 May rammed and sank the Nantucket Shoals Lightship in thick fog, resulting in seven deaths.

its a small bill, only $\frac{1}{2}$ a million, but they cant pay. Yet theyre buying copper all the time. Whats it for? Armaments no doubt. Thats one of the classic examples of intn trade—Now Holden has been over & says we wont go in.[4] 20,000 people out of work. But of course there's something behind it. What is the cause of the financial crisis? Theyre doing something foolish—no Treasury control of the soldiers."

(but I am thinking all the time of what is to end Here & Now. I want a Chorus. a general statement. a song for 4 voices. how am I to get it? I am now almost within sight of the end. racing along: becoming more & more dramatic.

And how to make the transition from the colloquial to the lyrical, from the particular to the general?)

Sunday 12 August

This is Saxon's week end. He is in the house, this windy cold gray day, playing chess with L. Odd that I should think of 'honey-sweet' Queen in connection with Saxon.[5] But he has grown rather pink & chubby in face, & very mellow & in fact charming in mind. The old eccentricities have been melted in the sun—I cannot guess of what success. Is it The Treasury, or Mrs Sickert? Anyhow he is not merely a bundle of desiccated separate remarks about toothbrushes & trains: he is continuous & even suggestive. I have spent an hour or so talking with him about Shakespeare, books in general, then people: & there is some virtue in these old friends: I mean conversationally; they enrich. If I ask what about Francis? he can supplement my question with all his knowledge of the past; & that is joined to my knowledge; so that we say many things we mean. Thus, it was a good idea of mine to ask him. He stays away a good deal, it seems; has rather expanded into queer corners; the Beresfords & the Lambs.[6] And he has bought a new book on Aristotle. Barbara [Bagenal] & her children the bulls eye I imagine. But the other circles all to his liking. We had the Keynes's over. Old friends again. M. adroit & supple & full of that queer

4. Sir George Holden (1890-1937), managing director of Combined Egyptian Mills Ltd, had just returned from Berlin, where he led a delegation of Lancashire cotton spinners in discussions with German importers about the German government's refusal to allocate enough foreign exchange to pay for imports of cotton yarn. On his advice, futher deliveries were suspended pending payment.
5. Helen: You know all, Lord Pandarus.
Pandarus: Not I, honey-sweet queen.
Troilus and Cressida III i
6. Mrs Sickert, a musician, was the widow of the painter's younger brother Oswald, of an earlier generation at Trinity College, Cambridge, than LW, Saxon, and Walter Lamb—an old admirer of VW's—who from 1913-51 was Secretary of the Royal Academy. J. B. Beresford (1888-1940) was a colleague of Saxon's at the Treasury.

imaginative ardour about history, humanity; able to explain flints & the age of man from some book he has read. Silent while we gossip. Immensely amused too by little scenes, as of Mrs Hardy & the sausages [*unexplained*]. He complained that great men, Shaw & Wells, are not serious; they do their stunt. Why cant they be simple, & do no stunt? He said Shaw never said anything new, but Charlotte [Mrs Shaw] does. He has a ranging adventurous mind, which I enjoy. In short we old stagers have made a good job, on the whole—such was my feeling. They stayed late.

Duncan is still bad with the ridiculous torturing disease, & Nessa I suppose much worried.

New[s] at first, through Julian, extremely optimistic about Francis. Now nothing, but perhaps more doubtful. Oh & the drought has broken: 2 carp are dead; there is the old ugly grey welter in the sky, which I'm afraid may now become 'weather'. But all, at this moment, rather loose, random, interesting. Vita came over very late for dinner, having been kept by a row with her mother who, says M[aynard], eats pate de foie with a shoehorn. She had been accusing her footman, a cocktail party boy with fair hair called Leonard, nicknamed Lemon, of putting Lysol in her medicine.[7] Vita thinks Harold is getting soft & domestic, because he talks of grandchildren, & wants to have a butler to brush [h]is clothes & a spare room. Good Lord said Vita, as if I wanted grandchildren! for which exclamation I like her. In fact she wears, to me, in spite of G[wen]. & the Dark Island, very well. So in to roast beef & plum tart.

Friday 17 August

Yes. I think owing to the sudden rush of 2 wakeful nights, making up early mornings rather, I think I see the end of Here & Now (or Music, or Dawn or whatever I shall call it). Its to end with Elvira going out of the house & saying What did I make this knot in my handkerchief for? & all the coppers rolling about———

Its to be all in speeches—no play——— I have now made a sketch of what everyone is to say; & it ends with a supper party in the downstairs room. I think the back is broken.

It will run to something like 850 of my rough pages I imagine: which is at 200: 850

200
———

170,000

& I shall sweat it down to 130,000.

The boat came yesterday & Julian & I walloped about on the river. An

7. Growing increasingly wilful and suspicious with age, the Dowager Lady Sackville lived in a house on the cliffs near Brighton, where Vita frequently visited her; she describes her mother's last years in *Pepita* (1937), chapter VI.

expensive sail—£7.7.6 to be exact.[8] Thats what comes of saying lightly I'd like a boat. But never mind. I have George's legacy, & even if H. & N. cant be published till Oct. year, still I have £1000 or thereabouts saved.

Mabel, called now The Cow, is stiff with neuritis & very 'low' as she calls it. A very sociable summer this. I have not entered High Salvington: seeing the down made into Putney & a pneumatic drill at work; & the scented room; & Ada like a double guinea pig, pale hair en brosse; going over the windmill—such a drive & such a visit as branded itself like a new cheap villa on my brain.[9]

But I am thinking of H. & N. & it is lunch time.

Tuesday 21 August

Having taken a week off, in the middle of the last scene, which is indeed like a scene in a play, I am too jaded to write that horrid book, I mean Fiction, this morning—

Last night the ice was hard, & we decided that Mabel must go. She is a dump. She wears her shoes on one side, & has long black stockings. Also there was a hot violent gale. It was a bad day of its kind, & I dreamt ferociously all night; about Massine; & Wilmington,[10] & woke with all my back in hackles, like a cats, & the old cry Fight: upon wh L. opened the door; no letters; only burnt bread—& so I had ½ an hour in the kitchen which is crumby, with Mabel, & now I cant think: I shall moon the day away. This is what comes of driving ahead at that last chapter. It is very concentrated. I read Une Vie last night, & it seemed to me rather marking time & watery—heaven help me—in comparison.[11] Its the change of gear that so upsetting[?] Like a smash in a car; being spilt from one world to the other.

I shall go in & get a book & my watch & moon away the morning & pray for a good dinner. The week end will be intolerable. Plomer & Lyn, neither of whom do I wish to see. We are using the new room for the first time.

The lesson of Here & Now is that one can use all kinds of 'forms' in one book. Therefore the next might be poem, reality, comedy, play: narrative; psychology, all in one. Very short. This needs thinking over.

Also, a play about the Parnells.

or a biography of Mrs. P.

8. The Woolfs had bought a rubber dinghy.
9. On 14 August the Woolfs went to tea with LW's mother and Ada de Jongh, one of her Dutch relatives, at High Salvington, just to the north of Worthing, where she was staying in a private hotel.
10. Léonide Massine (1896-1979), principal dancer and choreographer in Diaghilev's and de Basil's Russian Ballet companies. Wilmington is a secluded village at the foot of the downs towards Eastbourne; VW may have seen a house for sale there.
11. *Une Vie* (1883), a novel by Guy de Maupassant.

Sunday 26 August[12]

Plomer & Lyn are talking outside the window. They are sitting in the walled garden, on the chairs we bought yesterday. We have left them there to read. We have supplied them with Ethel's books, with Blind men cross the Bridge—an immense long totally absurd (work of genius the Lit Sup calls it) novel;[13] but now they have ceased reading—indeed it is rather windy—& are talking. I catch only a word now & then. Lyn has just said that she "immensely enjoyed it". What, I wonder? I doubt that she immensely enjoys anything. She is rather faded & suppressed & literal & conscientious wearing her horn spectacles & frowning. William I think (but L. disagrees) rather aged & disillusioned. But, against my forecast, I am enjoying the week end. For one thing the cooking has been good. Mabel 'a treasure'. With Louie to help we live in greater comfort than any time these 5 years. Ethel came over to tea, yesterday and did her owl—who is a red wattled turkey cock—very vigorously. In fact she adds considerably to the entertainment of the week end. We sat & bawled, about God & Dulwich.[14] She only had time for half a remark about the Prison & her complete lack of ambition.

Thursday was a horrid day though, when we took Julian Angelica & Susan to London, on a windy day; & I had toothache & went to the dentist, & he says I must have 2 teeth out; & everything went as a nightmare—ending, after a bitter cold drive with a most depressing view of family life at Charleston, which I arranged into a climax of domesticity & was thoroughly irritated with Duncan for making Nessa into Aunt Mary—cant come here, cant go to London as long as he is ill; & with Nessa for her passive submission; & with myself for being the good fairy Aunt.[15] Lord how that role can bore me—how unreal it is—& why do I act it? These were my thoughts, soothed mercifully after dinner alone by Leonard.

12. VW has misdated this entry: *Sunday Aug* 25th.
13. See *TLS*, 23 August 1934: 'It happens . . . perhaps once in ten years or so, that we are confronted with a novel that cannot be judged by the comfortable standards applicable to the mass of fiction. . . . in recent years we have . . . such experiments as Mr E. M. Forster's "Where Angels Fear to Tread", Mrs Woolf's "The Voyage Out", or Miss Dorothy Richardson's "Pointed Roofs", and now Miss Susan Miles's "Blind Men Crossing a Bridge" . . . which unquestionably falls into the category intimated by these examples . . . a novel that . . . bears signs of genius.'
14. *The Lonely Lady of Dulwich* (1934) was a new novel by Maurice Baring which Ethel Smyth believed justified her claim 'that Baring is one of the finest novelists England has ever produced'. (See *V VW Letters*, nos. 2915, 2916, 2918.)
15. Susan Henderson was a friend of Julian's who had been staying at Charleston. Aunt Mary: Mrs Herbert Fisher (1841-1916), her mother's elder sister, was a symbol to VW of insufferable saintliness.

Monday 27 August

The week end better. I am trying to start the nameless book again; & of course find it grinding, to try to get back into those stiff boots. All the same, I enjoyed the week end. Lyn left; which was all to the good, as she has no great range poor Lyn, & W[illiam]. had, I guessed, said all he could say. Then [Neil] Lyons came, & subtly pervaded the house with a smell of stale cabbage. "At Jimmy Gunn's cocktail yesterday . . . . I said to Sickert—. dining in Mayfair." He is not merely secondrate, but almost criminal; which is amusing, once in a way. A South African Jew & sharper, Wm said. Probably the son of a small tailor. Stammers on the letter A. has a sexual delusion. He told us of a small hat black woman, who divorced her husband, 6ft 4 & in the Guards, lives at Uckfield & leaves Neil at 2. am. She drives through Lewes & blackguards the police. He would not repeat the word she used. Then Lavender the gardener is an ex-burglar: has done 14 years in gaol, & is a preventive detention man, under charge of Hancock. (This ex burglar came round the other night to borrow 15/-). He—Neil—has his prattling amiability though, & amused me with his stories of making cigarettes & gathering samphire. A nimble light fingered little monstrosity, much concerned to amuse, to impress, & much afflicted with various desires. He eats corn cobs; & may unhappily come round to bring me some, & show off his cigarettes. What a dip in the kitchen pail!

Wm. gone this morning. I doubt that I have anything to add to the portrait of Wm. save that I think he is losing charm, & perhaps adding weight. Another novel coming this autumn. No reference to the Press. Lyn gave him a scrap of her own hand to decipher, which I thought unfair.[16]

Thursday 30 August

If I cant even write here, owing to making up the last scenes, how can I possibly read Dante? Impossible. After 3 days grind, getting back, I am I think floated again.

Robson comes to tea today; & the Woolves tomorrow; & . . . another lapse making up El's speech . . "D'you know what I've been clasping in my hand all the evening? Coppers."[17]

Well anyhow I've enough in stock to last out this Chapter; I daresay another 2 or 3 weeks.

Yesterday I found a new walk, & a new farm, in the fold between Asheham & Tarring Neville. Very lovely, all alone, with the down rising

16. William Plomer had a gift for graphology. His forthcoming novel, *The Invaders*, was published by Jonathan Cape in October 1934.

17. In the 'Present Day' Chapter at the end of *The Years* Eleanor Pargiter sits clutching 'two or three coppers' throughout her sister Delia's party.

behind. Then I walked back by a rough broad overflowing grey river. The porpoise came up & gulped. It rained. All ugliness was disolved. An incredibly 18th century landscape. happily making me think less of Wilmington.

A tremendous hail storm after tea. Like white ice; broken up: lanced, lashing, like the earth being whipped. This happened several times. Black clouds while we played Brahms.

No letters at all this summer. But there will be many next year, I predict. And I dont mind; the day, yesterday to be exact, being so triumphant: writing: the walk; reading, Leeson, a detective, Saint Simon, Henry James' preface to P. of a Lady—very clever, [*word illegible*] but one or two things I recognise: then Gide's Journal, again full of startling recollection—things I cd have said myself.[18]

Sunday 2 September

I dont think I have ever been more excited over a book than I am writing the end of—shall it be Dawn? Or is that too emphatic, sentimental. I wrote like a—forget the word—yesterday; my cheeks burn; my hands tremble. I am doing the scene where Peggy listens to them talking & bursts out. It was this outburst that excited me so. Too much perhaps. I cant make the transition to E[lvir]as speech easily this morning. Another lull; but very slight, caused partly by the great tea table talk yesterday— 9 to tea; Ks. B's. Ky Martin & Kahan, the economic Jew, I forget his name.[1] We arranged lots of little cakes on two tables. And some came early, others late. And they talked (as in my book that morning) about Civilisation, owing to L.'s article on Shaw, which had, as usual upset Kingsley, even to the extent of making him consider giving up the NS. & taking a professorship. "For whats the use of the NS. if there's no future for our civilisation?" What use is there for professors in that case?[2] Clive inappropriately tried to flirt with that scrannel woman Olga. A wrung out

---

18. *Lost London. The Memoirs of an East End Detective* by Ex-Detective Sergeant B. Leeson. André Gide's *Pages de Journal, 1929-32* had recently been published in France; Roger Fry mentioned it in his last letter to VW (*II RF Letters*, no. 710 of 3 August 1934).

1. The tea-party comprised Maynard and Lydia Keynes who brought Richard Kahn, Kingsley and Olga Martin, Clive and Quentin Bell, and the Woolfs themselves.

2. In his review, entitled 'Too True to be Good' of George Bernard Shaw's collected *Prefaces*, to be published in the *NS&N* of 8 September 1934, LW wrote: 'There was no living man to whom the generations which came to maturity between 1900 and 1914 owed as much as to Mr Shaw . . . Nothing less than a world war could have prevented [him] from winning the minds of succeeding generations to truth, decency, socialism, peace, and civilization. So they made a world war, and ever since the barbarians have naturally been on top. Hitler, Mussolini, Pilsudski, Schusnigg, and Mosley!'

washerwoman's hands woman. And K[ingsley]—so histrionic, so effusive. Lydia oppressed, I thought, by the death of Cecchetti.[3] And Maynard by his week end party. The men played bowls. The girls, including M[aynard] —sat in the upstairs room. But Olga made us restrained.

I am very calm & worldly competent at the moment though. I rather like those made up words. Single words too precise. Annoyed by Duncan's scare—a temp: must be consumption & so on. Now the specialist says nothing of the kind, as I cd. have told them. Strange to be irritated by this: but I am.

Wednesday 12 September

Roger died on Sunday.[4] I was walking with Clive on the terrace when Nessa came out. We sat on the seat there for a time. On Monday we went up with Nessa. Ha came. Nessa saw Helen [Anrep]. Tomorrow we go up, following some instinct, to the funeral. I feel dazed: very wooden. Women cry, L. says: but I dont know why I cry—mostly with Nessa. And I'm too stupid to write anything. My head all stiff. I think the poverty of life now is what comes to me. a thin blackish veil over everything. Hot weather. A wind blowing. The substance gone out of everything. I dont think this is exaggerated. It'll come back I suppose. Indeed I feel a great wish, now & then, to live more all over the place, to see people, to create, only for the time one cant make the effort. And I cant write to Helen, but I must now shut this & try.

Maupassant, on writers—(true I think).

"En lui aucun sentiment simple n'existe plus. Tout ce qu'il voit, ses joies, ses plaisirs, ses souffrances, ses desespoirs, deviennent instantanément des sujets d'observation. . Il analyse malgré tout, malgré lui, sans fin, les coeurs, les visages, les gestes, les intonations."[5]

I remember turning aside at mother's bed, when she had died, & Stella took us in, to laugh, secretly, at the nurse crying. She's pretending, I said: aged 13. & was afraid I was not feeling enough. So now.

Sur l'eau 116   The writer's temperament.
"ne jamais souffrir, penser, aimer, sentir comme tout le monde, bonnement, franchement, simplement, sans s'analyser soi-meme apres chaque joie et après chaque sanglot"

---

3. The celebrated teacher of Russian ballet, *Maestro* Enrico Cecchetti, born in 1850, had died in 1928; possibly VW mistook his for some other name on Lydia's lips.

4. Roger Fry died of heart failure on Sunday 9 September at the Royal Free Hospital, following a fall two days earlier at his home in Bernard Street.

5. Guy de Maupassant's *Sur l'eau*, a journal he kept during a cruise along the Mediterranean coast in the spring of 1887, was first published the following year. Both passages quoted by VW occur in the entry dated 10 *avril*.

Saturday 15 September

I was glad we went to the service on Thursday.[6] It was a very hot summers day. And all very simple & dignified. Music. Not a word spoken. We sat there, before the open doors that lead into the garden. Flowers & strollers which Roger would have liked. He lay under an old red brocade with two bunches of very bright many coloured flowers. It is a strong instinct to be with ones friends. I thought of him too, at intervals. Dignified & honest & large—"large sweet soul"—something ripe & musical about him—& then the fun & the fact that he had lived with such variety & generosity & curiosity. I thought of this. Karin annoyed me coming in late, stumbling. That went off. They played Bach. Then the coffin moved slowly through the doors. They shut. They played again— Anon, I think: old music. Yes, I liked the wordlessness: Helen looking very young & blue eyed & quiet & happy. That is much to remember her for. I kissed her on the lips, in the courtyard. Then Desmond came up: said wdnt it be nice to walk in the garden? "Oh we stand on a little island" he said. But it has been very lovely I said. For the first time I laid my hand on his shoulder, & said dont die yet. Nor you either he said. We have had wonderful friends, he said. We walked a little, but Molly was out of it, with her deafness. So we took them to Wellington Sqre & had tea. A merry natural talk, about Roger & books & people, all as usual: Molly breaking in, about her philograph, & her books.[7] Queer isolation of deafness—breeding this rather peevish but pathetic egotism. And it was roasting hot. D'you remember the dinner we gave the Memoir Club said Desmond in the street—looking at his dinner table. Never again said Molly. Oh yes, I said; & we drove off.

Very jaded; cant write; all my books seem a complete jerked[?] failure. I must take a few days off. Ann & Judith upon us: then Dadie.

Tuesday 18 September

Dadie has been gone half an hour, & I am silent after talking incessantly, it seems, & is in fact almost true, since 1 on Saturday. A. & J. came, strode in without their box. Great brown naked legged colts. Then there was Mrs Jones & Hugh: bowls: I sat & listened to the poor womans plaints; knees that lock, cant make eno'; will I give her work; in a bungalow at

6. Roger Fry's funeral was at Golder's Green Crematorium on the afternoon of 13 September. The Woolfs drove up to London that morning; and, after the ceremony, took the MacCarthys back to their house in Wellington Square, Chelsea, before returning to Rodmell.

7. Philograph: 'An apparatus with a transparent plane on which to trace a facsimile of a view or object seen through an adjustable eyepiece' (*Webster's Dictionary*).

Seaford. Then dinner: next day Angelica's party (like the Lytton party) at Charleston. They acted;[8] I did my poor old frenzied owl; at parting Clive, who is off to Spain till November, said But you'll get over it—an arrow wh. stuck, for then I felt I had over acted. Never mind. Nessa infinitely mournful & struck, like a statue, something frozen about her. Janie. The children also saddened (not A. & J.). They acted very beautifully in Chinese clothes by the pond. Well I thought I can see this through Roger's eyes: its right to enjoy every tint. And yet how can one? This has gone out of the day—that laughter; that energy; & we were all thinned & stunted. So home. And then after A. & J. went—& I had begun to fidget because they dont wipe their mouths & eat so much—the Keynes's & Dadie came. We did not exactly repeat the funeral talk: but it loomed over us. Lydia to me rather jarring. She did not care. Nothing much loomed over her. Dear old Dadie very charming & affectionate. We talked about Cambridge; about teaching English; I held out a bare pole—I mean extended my views rashly; he was donnish, serious, very measured; believes in education; in measuring the mind, & sending youth out to Africa with 'an improved sense of leisure' & so on. But this rather broke down, & he admitted that he means to leave as soon as he can afford it. Peter [Lucas] a deathly warning. Teaching without zest a crime. Shepherd a complete buffoon; but good, because of his completeness.[9] Dadie wants to marry, to have whitehaired children & live a romantic life with a dark haired feminine wife. As it is has to comfort his most desolate mother.

I like writing this morning because it takes off the strain on the lips. A cold dull day after all this blaze. Now we have [John] Graham—& Mrs W[oolf]. but then, perhaps, peace, & an end to the book? O if that could be! But I feel 10 miles distant—far away—detached—very jaded now.

[Wednesday 19 September]

I had a notion that I could describe the tremendous feeling at R.'s funeral: but of course I cant. I mean the universal feeling: how we all fought with our brains loves & so on; & *must* be vanquished. Then the vanquisher, this outer force became so clear; the indifferent. & we so small fine delicate. A fear then came to me, of death. Of course I shall lie there too before that gate, & slide in; & it frightened me. But why? I mean, I felt the vainness of this perpetual fight, with our brains & loving each other against the other thing: if Roger could die.

8. Angelica's winter party had been overcast by the death of Lytton Strachey in 1932, as her summer party now was by that of Roger Fry. The entertainment was provided by Angelica and Janie Bussy.
9. John Tressider Sheppard (1881-1968), the classicist, was elected Provost of King's College, Cambridge, in 1933; he had entered the college in 1900.

[*Thursday 20 September*]

But then, next day, today which is Thursday, one week later, the other thing begins to work—the exalted sense of being above time & death which comes from being again in a writing mood. And this is not an illusion, so far as I can tell. Certainly I have a strong sense that Roger would be all on one's side in this excitement, & that whatever the invisible force does, we thus get outside it. A nice letter from Helen. And today we go to Worthing—dear me, that poor old very superficial content with the outsides & shows of things woman. Who never grasps anything but lives like a butterfly unable to retain or reflect; but abundant genuine of its kind unreflecting feeling. I shall have to hear all her sorrows, & 'cheer' her up: which happens quite easily. A cake, a [*word illegible*] a compliment—chatter.

[*Later*] As a matter of fact she was unexpectedly sensible & rather sympathetic about Roger. She said how terrified she had been when she came to see me first at B[runswic]k Sqre—how she had been impressed by my tapestries—had never seen such stuff.

Sunday 30 September

The last words of the nameless book were written 10 minutes ago; quite calmly too. 900 pages: L. says 200,000 words. Lord God what an amount of re-writing that means! But also, how heavenly to have brought the pen to a stop at the last line, even if most of the lines have now to be rubbed out. Anyhow the design is there. And it has taken a little less than 2 years: some months less indeed, as Flush intervened; therefore it has been written at a greater gallop than any of my books. The representational part accounts for this fluency. And I should say—but do I always say this?—with greater excitement; not, I think of the same kind quite. For I have been more general, less personal. No 'beautiful writing', much easier dialogue; but a great strain, because so many more faculties had to keep going at once, though none so pressed upon. No tears & exaltation at the end: but peace & breadth, I hope. Anyhow, if I die tomorrow, the line is there. And I am fresh; & shall re-write the end tomorrow. I dont think I'm fresh enough, tho', to go on 'making up'. That was the strain—the invention; & I suspect that the last 20 pages have slightly flagged. Too many odds & ends to sweep up. But I have no idea of the whole—

A fine, blowing day. Starlings bathing. Must now write to Helen.

Tuesday 2 October

Yes, but my head will never let me glory sweepingly: always a tumble. Yesterday morning the old rays of light set in; & then the sharp, the very sharp pain over my eyes; so that I sat & lay about till tea; had no walk, had not a single idea of triumph or relief. L. bought me a little travelling ink pot, by way of congratulation. I wish I could think of a name. Sons & Daughters? Probably used already. Theres a mass to be done to the last chapter, which I shall, I hope, dv. as they say in some circles, I suppose still, begin tomorrow: while the putty is still soft.

So the summer is ended. Until the 9th of Sept: when Nessa came across the terrace—how I hear that cry Hes dead—a very vigorous, happy summer. Oh the joy of walking! I've never felt it so strong in me. Cowper Powys, oddly enough, expresses the same thing:[1] the trance like, swimming, flying through the air; the current of sensations & ideas; & the slow, but fresh change of down, of road, of colour: all this churned up into a fine thin sheet of perfect calm happiness. Its true I often painted the brightest pictures on this sheet: & often talked aloud. Lord how many pages of Sons & Daughters—perhaps Daughters & Sons would give a rhythm more unlike Sons & Lovers, or Wives & Daughters [by Mrs Gaskell],—I made up, chattering them in my excitement on the top of the down, in the folds.

Too many buildings, alas: & gossip to the effect that Christie & the Ringmer building Co. are buying Botten's Farm to build on.[2] Sunday I was worried, walking to Lewes, by the cars & the villas. But again, I've discovered the ghostly farm walk; & the Piddinghoe walk; & such variety & loveliness—the river lead & silver: the ship—Servic of London— going down: the bridge opened.[3] Mushrooms & the garden at night; the moon, like a dying dolphin's eye; or red orange, the harvest moon; or polished like a steel knife; or lambent: sometimes rushing across the sky; sometimes hanging among the branches— Now in October the thick wet mist has come, thickening & blotting.

On Sunday we had Bunny & Julian; Bunny so thick & solid, like a beam out of an old tree; Julian rather smaller than usual. Bunny has grey wisps at his temples; talks like a heavy wardrobe; all heavy angular sentences. I noted how my own rushing pace, seemed too rushing, & after 10 minutes had adapted itself to Bunny.

How—do—you—start—an—aeroplane? This unheard cry [?], Lord what a wonder filling sheets to an inch every Friday.[4] Bunny has severe

1. In *Autobiography* by John Cowper Powys (1872-1963), published this autumn.
2. Capt. John Christie, MC, JP (1882-1962), founder of the Glyndebourne Opera Festival, was a director of the Ringmer Building Works Ltd (which built the opera house); Jasper Botten farmed Place Farm, Rodmell.
3. Until World War II there was a swing bridge over the river Ouse between Southease and Itford and cargo vessels regularly sailed up-river as far as Lewes.
4. The *NS&N*, of which David Garnett was literary editor, appeared on Fridays. He had taken up flying, and flew his own plane to Sussex this year.

small blue eyes that slowly fix themselves. All rather heavy footed. Julian silent. So we walked on the Terrace. Then Duncan & Helen came—Helen in a long coat & the funny amateur hat with the green tuft that she wore at the service. It was rather fortunate that the first meeting should be among the flowers, vegetables, improvements. Then we went upstairs & talked & laughed about Roger, easily. I felt however the worn out, the used up feeling as if she were now feeling the shallows, after the exaltation; the shingle grating, the sordid—poor Helen! All the [Fry] sisters conglomerate in B[ernard]. St. & arrange R.'s pictures—dating them wrongly. How one can hear R. laugh! see him padding about in his slippers. Margery is left literary executor. Tatlock smelling of drink comes round & says he wants to write R.'s life. Well whats to be done about our 'lives' I wonder? The EMF. Goldie thing to me quite futile.[5] But this is an aside. What we talked of was Ha & Joan & Pamela & Julian; & Helen made her usual quips & severities: but all was a little watery. Her blue & pink less bright—poor woman. She is very poor—it seems: must give up B. St. & find a flat: must perhaps give up Rodwell.[6] Then the problem of the children—how facts come trooping in, when the great rush of emotion is past. I mean, this dealing with the difficulties used to be done so much by R.: at any rate, there he was, bullying her, laughing at her: forcing her to give it all up & come out to Venice, or St Remy. Now she'll be more and more bothered, worried. But she has a great many friends.

And we went to Sissinghurst. Vita playing the Gramophone at the top of the pink tower. A blazing day. (I bought 1st edition of Mill on Floss at Websters by the way).[7] Some constraint now, of a very simple & obvious kind, because of Gwen. She came in at 2. We were sitting under a pergola, lunching. An uneasy, nerve strained woman—very tense. She told us how she had taken Miss Maddock the 70 year old secretary to the Mayfair Hotel to tea. M. had eaten crumpets & cakes. Had had no lunch. Whats to become of her? Gwen rather a doer of good. This stimulates V.'s sentimental easy going benevolence, I think. And we talked of Sibyl & Ethel; & then went; V. saying, very calmly, that the majority agreed with me in thinking the D. Island a bad book. And I dont lose any of my liking for

5. E. M. Forster, in his biography of his friend *Goldsworthy Lowes Dickinson* (1934), had had to withhold the truth about Dickinson's sexual propensities.
6. Helen Anrep bought Rodwell House, Baylham, Suffolk, in 1928 as a country retreat for Roger Fry and herself; she did not give it up. Margery ('Ha') and Joan Mary Fry (1862-1955) were the fifth and second respectively of Roger's six unmarried sisters; after his wife became incapable, each had at one time kept house for him and his children—Julian and Pamela (b. 1902, and since 1923 married to a Roumanian painter Micu Diamand).
7. The Woolfs went to Tunbridge Wells on 28 September to travel Hogarth Press books, and on to lunch at Sissinghurst. George Eliot's *The Mill on the Floss* was first published in 1860.

her gentleness, truthfulness, modesty. Ly S. has bought Long B. for £8,000.[8]

Books read or in reading:[9]
Shre.   Troilus.
          Pericles.
          Taming of Shrew.
          Cymbeline.

Maupassant.
de Vigny   } only scraps
St Simon.
Gide.

Library books: Powys
                Wells
                Lady Brooke.
                Prose. Dobrée.
                Alice James.
Many M.S.S.   none worth keeping.

Thursday 4 October

A violent rain storm on the pond. The pond is covered with little white thorns; springing up & down: the pond is bristling with leaping white thorns: like the thorns on a small porcupine; bristles; then black waves: cross it: black shudders; & the little water thorns are white: a helter skelter rain, & the elms tossing it up & down: the pond overflowing on one side. Lily leaves tugging: the red flower swimming about; one leaf flapping. Then completely smooth for a moment. Then prickled: thorns like glass; but leaping up & down incessantly. A rapid smirch of shadow. Now light from the sun: green & red: shining: the pond a sage green: the grass brilliant green: red berries on the hedges: the cows very white: purple over Asheham.

Friday 5 October

The storm is over; having sunk a few ships. And half blown us along the towing path; & tossed all the apples off the trees. We are discussing

8. Until she moved to Sissinghurst Castle in 1930, Long Barn had been Vita's home, Lady Sackville bought it, and on her death in 1936 bequeathed it to her daughter.
9. The following note appears on the page facing the diary entries for 4 and 5 October. The library books are: *Autobiography* (1934) by John Cowper Powys; *Experiment in Autobiography* (1934) by H. G. Wells; *Good Morning and Good Night* (1934) by Her Highness the Ranée of Sarawak (Sylvia Leonora, *née* Brett, wife of Charles Vyner Brook, Rajah of Sarawak); *Modern Prose Style* (1934) by Bonamy Dobrée; *Alice James: Her Brothers—Her Journal* (1934), edited with an introduction by Anna Robeson Burr.

plans for moving this lodge to the churchyard wall under the tree. Wicks' estimate is for £157—which seems extreme. considering that its only a fad: will improve the view but then perhaps an improved view is worth 157.[10] Water is also to be laid on: & I am in a mood rather to doubt my own earning capacity. That is to say the last chapter is going to give me a deal of trouble. But perhaps it is wrong to lay such stress on last chapters. They need not necessarily rise higher than the level of the book. My instinct is though that they shd. be more condensed: a summing up: a solution. If the last chapter fails does the book fail? What is the last chapter of War & Peace? I forget.

The names of the BBC committee are out: & I am interested to feel two different emotions: disappointment & relief; & a third, that it dont much matter either way.[11]

The Woolfs returned to Tavistock Square on Sunday afternoon, 7 October.

Tuesday 9 October

Back again in London. A party last night: Mary Fisher, Eddie Playfair, Rose Macaulay & Saxon. An odd mixture; but successful. We cried with laughter. This was partly Eddie's account of Carrie who went round the world with James: who died: & became 'the body'. Mountains very nice. Everything very nice. This was to prove that character is one & indivisible.[12] Rose maintained the opposite. "I'm a mere battlefield of opposite people—my ancestors" she said. "Take this as a simple illustration: I want to walk all day alone: but I also want to drive my car. We called it having "battling lizards"." That made us laugh. Saxon & Eddie represented the uniformity of the Treasury. Also we discussed commas: Rose very erudite on that subject: & her book of extracts. How she grinds! And authors' vanity; which was to be ravaged by fear of what one's Aunt thinks of a review. She professed never to care, for herself, what reviewers said, & then began uneasily a story about the hostility of the Lit. Sup. to

10. P. R. Wicks was a Lewes Builder and Decorator; he was to re-erect VW's lodge in its present position.
11. See above, 4 March 1934, n 4.
12. Mary Letitia Somerville Fisher (b. 1913) was the only child of VW's cousin H. A. L. Fisher, the Warden of New College, Oxford, and his wife Lettice; she was a scholar of Somerville College. Edward Wilder Playfair (b. 1909), was a contemporary at King's College, Cambridge, and close friend of Julian Bell; he had joined the Civil Service in 1931 and now worked in the Treasury. His father's widowed cousin, Agnes Caroline Morison, *née* Herne, and her brother James set out to visit another brother in British Columbia; throughout the long journey by boat and train, and the illness and death of James on the way, Carrie despatched a stream of letters to her family in London describing their adventures in terms of unvarying approbation—everything and everybody was 'very nice.'

her last six novels; & how they had put her Milton into small type at the
end. At which unconscious revelation we smiled.[13] She is a ravaged
sensitive old hack—as I should be, no doubt, save for L. Mary Fisher
recalls Boo; but has a mean look a sharp practical look—derived from
Lettice.[14] She puts me out of conceit with the family face. Too insipid.
The hair too mousy & untidy & the clothes dowdy. A drop of Fisher
blood dilutes & acidifies. But she is upstanding; has lived in good
company; is not a mere drudge; & adores her father, I guess. Likes
authority; loves Winchester Oxford & the very urbane intellectual
aristocracy; but I was not whizzed off my perch. The King of Jugoslavia
& Bartou murdered this evening.[15]

[? Wednesday 10 October]

Today, as I have a few minutes left, I think I have improvised another
method for P[hases]. of F[iction]. to be phases of the readers mind:
different situations. Part 2. to be in dialogue, in a hotel on the Mediterranean: each chapter to correspond with the period. Thus to rob it of
formality.

Thursday 11 October

A brief note. In todays Lit. Sup. they advertise Men without Art by
Wyndham Lewis. Chapters on Eliot, Faulkner, Hemingway, Virginia
Woolf...[16] Now I know by reason & instinct that this is an attack; that I
am publicly demolished: nothing is left of me in Oxford & Cambridge &
places where the young read Wyndham Lewis. My instinct is, not to read
it. And for this reason: well, I open Keats: & find: "Praise or blame has
167   but a momentary effect on the man whose love of beauty in the
abstract makes him a severe critic on his own works. My own
domestic criticism has given me pain beyond what Blackwood or Quarterly could possibly inflict . . . . . This is a mere matter of the moment— I

13. Rose Macaulay's 'book of extracts' was *The Minor Pleasures of Life* (1934); it
included one from *Orlando*. Her *Milton* (in Duckworth's two-shilling series
'Great Lives') had been given favourable if short notice (it was a short book—
141 pp.) in the section 'New Books and Reprints' at the back of the *TLS* of 11
January 1934.
14. Boo = Cordelia Fisher (1879-1970), VW's cousin and Mary's aunt.
15. On 9 October, King Alexander of Jugoslavia and the French Foreign Minister
Jean Louis Barthou were assassinated at Marseilles by a supporter of the Croatian
Nationalist movement.
16. Percy Wyndham Lewis (1882-1957), writer and artist, whose by now legendary
hostility to Bloomsbury dates back at least to his short-lived involvement in the
Omega Workshops in 1913; he published numerous veiled and unveiled attacks
on Bloomsbury, most famously or infamously in *The Apes of God* (1930).

think I shall be among the English poets after my death. Even as a matter of present interest the attempt to crush me in the Quarterly has only brought me more into notice."[17]

Well: do I think I shall be among the English novelists after my death? I hardly ever think about it. Why then do I shrink from reading W.L.? Why am I sensitive? I think vanity. I dislike the thought of being laughed at. of the glow of satisfaction that A B & C will get from hearing V.W. demolished: also it will strengthen further attacks. Perhaps I feel uncertain of my own gifts: but then, I know more about them than W.L.: & anyhow I intend to go on writing. What I shall do is craftily to gather the nature of the indictment from talk & reviews: &, in a year perhaps, when my book is out, I shall read it. Already I am feeling the calm that always comes to me with abuse: my back is against the wall: I am writing for the sake of writing: &c. & then there is the queer disreputable pleasure in being abused—in being a figure, in being a martyr. & so on.

Sunday 14 October

The trouble is I have used every ounce of my creative writing mind in the Pargiters. No headache (save what Elly calls typical migraine—she came to see L. about his strain yesterday). I cannot puts spurs in my flanks. Its true I've planned the romantic chapter of notes: but I cant set to.[18]

This morning I've taken the arrow of W[yndham].L[ewis]. to my heart: he makes tremendous & delightful fun of B. & B.: calls me a peeper, not a looker, a fundamental prude; but one of the 4 or 5 living (so it seems) who is an artist.[19] Thats what I gather the flagellation amounts to:

17. See *Letters of John Keats*, edited by Sidney Colvin, 1891. (VW's own copy was a reprint of 1918: see *Holleyman*, MH VII, p. 4). The extract beginning 'Praise or blame . . .' is from a letter of 9 October 1818 to J. A. Hessey (p. 167); and that beginning 'This is a mere matter . . .' from one to George and Georgina Keats of 14 or 15 October 1818 (p. 171).

18. i.e.: for VW's new approach to her interminable critical work *Phases of Fiction* which (see above, 10 October 1934) she adumbrated as a dialogue, and later entitles 'A Discourse for 4 Voices' (see MHP/B 2m, the first page of which is dated 16 October 1934). Subsequent references to 'notes for biography' (15 October), 'writing away this morning' (16 October), 'I slog away at Romance & biography of a morning' (17 October), and to 'biography and autobiography' (1 November) appear to relate to this project.

19. See *Men Without Art* (1934) by Wyndham Lewis, chapter V (*M&M*, pp. 331-8), in which no credit is given to VW as an artist. '. . . while I am ready to agree that the intrinsic literary importance of Mrs Woolf may be exaggerated by her friends, I cannot agree that as a symbolic landmark—a sort of party-lighthouse—she has not a very real significance.' He gives a teasing summary of *Mr Bennett and Mrs Brown*, and describes VW as one 'apeeping in the half-light': 'Outside it is terribly *dangerous* . . . But this *dangerousness* does, after all, make it very *thrilling*, when peeped-out at from the security of the private mind.'

(Oh I'm underrated, Edith Sitwell says). Well: this gnat has settled & stung; & I think (12.30) the pain is over. Yes. I think its now rippling away. Only I cant write. When will my brain revive? in 10 days I think. And it can read admirably: I began [Thomson's] The Seasons last night; after Eddie's ridiculous rhodomontade—or so I judge it: like Madame Tussauds: a vast book called The Sun in Capricorn: a worthless book I think; so that my intention to make a beckon in his direction is now in abeyance. No. I don't like him. Trash & tarnish; and this morbid silliness. Denzil Torrant. &c.[20]

Well: I was going to say, I'm glad that I need not & cannot write, because the danger of being attacked is that it makes one answer back—a perfectly fatal thing to do. I mean, fatal, to arrange the P.s so as to meet his criticisms. And I think my revelation 2 years ago stands me in sublime stead. to adventure & discover, & allow no rigid poses: to be supple & naked to the truth. If there is truth in W.L. well, face it: I've no doubt I am prudish & peeping, well then live more boldly. But for God's sake dont try to bend my writing one way or the other. Not that one can. And there is the odd pleasure too of being abused: & the feeling of being dismissed into obscurity is also pleasant & salutary.

Monday 15 October

Walked with L. all round Serpentine & K[ensington]. Gardens yesterday (a fine blowy day: leaves falling) & asked him these questions:
1) What is the sensible attitude to criticism?
   Not to read it.
2) What should I do now of a morning—creation flagging?
   Read.
3) Does he feel I have prevented him from going abroad?
   No. I have only prevented him from lesser activities (I think this was the answer).

We agreed to save up for foreign travel on a large scale to try to fly over America. Perhaps to go to India & China.

I now see us, far far away. A new civilisation &c.

I meant to read this morning, but got tempted into making notes for biography. Rather scrappy, but clearly the only complete escape from depression (W.L. & R[oger]'s death) is in getting the mind to work. No anodyne possible I think in the morning. But I am as slack as a piece of maccaroni: & in this state cant shake off a blackness, a blankness. Now (10 to 1) after writing & beginning to read an old life of Boswell I feel the wheels grinding.

20. *The Sun in Capricorn* (1934) by Edward Sackville-West—'writing primarily to please himself' (*TLS*, 18 October 1934)—in which Denzil Torrent is the central figure.

Ethel—oh d—n—after tea. Morgan tomorrow. Yes: creation drops the little personal body down: up we go: all that forgotten.

Oh & L. was divinely good: so direct: what an immense relief to talk to him! what a simplification. What an egress to open air & cold daylight: how dignified: yes, & I have him every day, as I so often think. So why—. &c. &c.

Tuesday 16 October

Quite cured today. So the W.L. illness lasted 2 days. Helped off by old Ethel's bluff affection & stir yesterday, by buying a blouse; by falling fast asleep after dinner, when L. went to the Robsons.

Writing away this morning.

[Wednesday 17 October]

I am so sleepy. Is this age? I cant shake it off. And so gloomy. Thats the end of the book. I looked up past diaries—a reason for keeping them—& found the same misery after Waves. After Lighthouse I was I remember nearer suicide, seriously, than since 1913.[21] It is after all natural. I've been galloping now for 3 months—so excited I made a plunge at my paper—well, cut that all off—after the first divine relief, of course some terrible blankness must spread. There's nothing left of the people, of the ideas, of the strain, of the whole life in short that has been racing round my brain: not only the brain; it has seized hold of my leisure: think how I used to sit still on the same railway lines: running on my book. Well, so theres nothing to be done the next 2 or 3 or even 4 weeks but dandle oneself: refuse to face it: refuse to think about it. This time Roger makes it harder than usual. We had tea with Nessa yesterday. Yes, his death is worse than Lytton's. Why I wonder? Such a blank wall. Such a silence. Such a poverty. How he reverberated! And I feel it through Nessa.

But selfishly, I cant throw it off as I did the first week after his death; when it became all the colours of the setting sun, in my excitement. Now theres the dulness, the cold to face & no protection. And so W.L. had the power to sting. No thats over. Only I cant get up any steam. I'm so ugly. So old. No one writes to me. I'm .... Well: dont think about it, & walk all over London; & see people. & imagine their lives. I cant read seriously. I feel so drowsy, as if my brain were dilated: cant contract: then I suddenly lapse into sleep.

Margery is going, Nessa thinks, to ask me to write about Roger. I dont

21. Following the completion and acceptance of her first novel *The Voyage Out* in 1913, VW entered a prolonged period of depression and illness during which, on 9 September 1913, she attempted suicide. For her depression after finishing *To the Lighthouse*, see *III VW Diary*, 15, 28, and 30 September 1926.

feel ready to. I dread the plunge into the past. I slog away at Romance & biography of a morning.

I would like to write down more actual conversation; but its such hard work. With Nessa & Duncan at tea:

V. Roger . . well everybody he met felt like that about him. He got very restless in the last year or two. He was always jumping up to show one something. Clive made me very angry at Charleston—He abused Roger—really for the criticism in his article.[22] He was jealous. Yes. I think it is right to have lives— What a pity that it should all be lost. Peoples impressions are good. Besides, someone will be certain to write about Roger—so it had better be by us.

Duncan. I liked Priestley's play tho I'm told all his novels are very bad. He is very dramatic. He knows how—I mean— (D. always against public opinion—lying on the sofa—has had a cold).[23]

Then Morgan, after tea, about the meeting of the Civil Liberties tomorrow.[24]

M. I hadnt thought of that. I'm dreadfully ignorant. So Leonard you would say—may I have a piece of paper? Yes, then: the point is—I will say . . .

On Saturday 20 October the Woolfs drove to Maidstone, taking Kingsley Martin with them, to attend the conference of the New Fabian Research Bureau; they stayed overnight, and returned to London on Sunday afternoon.

Wednesday 24 October

I have just written with homage in my copy of Sickert. So thats done.[25]
And Stephen Spender, did I say, has defended me against W.L.; & Rosamond & Read & Stephen are coming tonight. And I have been toiling at an article on the Queen of Roumania: by way of a rest.[26] No I cant

22. In the controversy over the attribution to Holbein of the Castle Howard portrait of Henry VIII, Fry, in his article 'The Artist as Critic' (*Burlington Magazine*, Feb. 1934), had maintained that art historians were better judges of authenticity than painters.

23. *Eden End*, a play by J. B. Priestley, author of the best-selling novels *The Good Companions* (1929) and *Angel Pavement* (1930), ran at the Duchess Theatre from September 1934 until February 1935, with Beatrix Lehmann and Ralph Richardson heading the cast.

24. The National Council for Civil Liberties, founded in February 1934 with E. M. Forster as first president, called a meeting on 18 October at the Central Hall, Westminster, to protest against the Incitement to Disaffection Bill (the Sedition Act); see P. N. Furbank, *E. M. Forster: A Life* (1978), vol. II pp. 188-9. LW was there.

25. *Walter Sickert: A Conversation* (Kp A20) was published on 25 October 1934.

26. Stephen Spender, reviewing Wyndham Lewis's *Men Without Art* in the *Spectator* of 19 October 1934, paid special attention to his 'Twelve well-filled pages of

write about Roger; & yesterday I went to see Lady Simon, in Catherine St. & looked at the conventional drawing room & tried to make out why it comes together. Two red & silver shields from Marshall & Snelgrove: a reproduction of an Italian picture; a comic parrot in watercolour; bad rugs; bears & lions; sham Adams mantelpiece; green curtains; brown fumed oak stairs & carpet—all uneasy trifles, too many details: no design: no taste: only one thing after another.

Shena on couch like Tristram.[27]

"I've been thinking—dont we lead a very narrow life at Manchester? We only see business men, university people, & social workers. Ought I to try & get artists to come?"

Rather worried & puzzled: reiterative; pale after an operation: is going to the Argentine. Tell me, how do writers see things? Are you interested in all kinds of people. So I made up a scene. Am I rather acting? inventing? Well I was tired after Pam[Diamand]'s nondescript visit: she came—why? Oh yes, I like the country. Very nice. Very nice house—& the children like it. And Micu is going to do papers for sweets. A thousand yards at a time. She is becoming the driven sweet wife; very nice; childlike: no go, or backbone: no look—of Roger: but affectionate. So I walked home from Shena across Westminster: a warm spring day: summer clothes: people strolling: streets crowded.

Friday 26 October

Yesterday at Ottoline's. Old Yeats.

What he said was, he had been writing about me. The Waves.[28] That comes after Stendhal he said. I see what you're at—But I want more humanity. Cant bear Stendhal: observant [?]: photographic; has a passion for Balzac: reads & re reads. Because his people are planted in history: there they are, sitting in the box at the opera: Tolstoy leaves them at school. I'm trying to get the Irish back to the great men of the 18th Century. Swift!

---

malice and ill-temper ... devoted to attacking Mrs Woolf.' See *M&M*, pp. 338-40. Herbert Read (1893-1968), poet, critic, and exponent of modern art, was editor of the *Burlington Magazine* 1933-39. 'Royalty', VW's article on *The Story of My Life* (1934) by Marie, Queen of Roumania, appeared in *Time & Tide*, 1 December 1934 (Kp C345).

27. i.e.: in the last act of Wagner's *Tristan und Isolde*.

28. See W. B. Yeats's introduction to his play *Fighting the Waves* (1934): 'Certain typical books—*Ulysses*, Virginia Woolf's *The Waves*, Mr Ezra Pound's *Draft of XXX Cantos*—suggest a philosophy like that of the *Samkara* school of ancient India, mental and physical objects alike material, a deluge of experience breaking over us and within us, melting limits whether of line or tint; man no hard bright mirror dawdling by the dry sticks of a hedge, but a swimmer, or rather the waves themselves.'

But did Swift like Ireland.

Read—(what? draper letter?[29]) He started the whole Irish movement—made Irish different from English. Oh the bitterness against England.

Must get their back to their own speech.

You have always been rich & powerful. You create without hatred. The need of tragedy: some cause: that is what creates literature.

Rather vague about the Ethns. Takes 300 years to absorb a war. Not yet time to create after 1914. Must get dignity into letters.

Goldsmith's English.

The Occult. That he believes in firmly. All his writing depends on it. Was walking with Robinson Ellis. The words came to him "The world is the excrement of God": 2 minutes afterwards R.E. said them. This convinced Yeats of the existence of another mind.[30] A woman accused him of being the father of her child. He went to Lady Jowett. She wrote a message in Greek—Oh sweet singer—showed it to Waley at Brit. Mus: said it was written by an Englishman[?] 200 years ago. Anyhow this proves absolutely the existence of another mind. Neither religion nor science explains the world. The occult does explain it. All in Plotinus. Has seen things. His coat hanger advanced across the room one night. Then a coat on it, illuminated: then a hand in it.[31] Is writing his memoirs. About Moore & Ly Gregory. Ave Vale all nonsense. At the age of 50 Moore found himself impotent. Hence his sex mania. 'I dont know why he minded so much'. Scene with M.'s cook & the policeman. Is there no law to defend me from omelettes like that? This went on for 1½ hours, I should say. At last Ott brought up Pudley, & the session ended.[32] I was too jaded after

29. *The Drapier's Letters*, published by Jonathan Swift in 1724, prophesying ruin to the Irish if Wood's halfpence' were admitted into circulation, 'gave him his chief title to eminence as a patriotic agitator' and 'made him the idol of his countrymen.' (Leslie Stephen).

30. Robinson Ellis (1834-1913), classical scholar and eccentric; Fellow of Trinity College and Corpus Professor of Latin in the University of Oxford; Hon. LL.D., Dublin.

31. Arthur Waley (1889-1966), orientalist and translator from the Chinese, was on the staff of the British Museum from 1913-29. Yeats's poem. 'The Apparitions' (1938), has the refrain:

> 'Fifteen apparitions have I seen;
> The worst a coat upon a coat-hanger.'

32. W. B. Yeats's diverse memoirs *Dramatis Personae 1896-1902 and other Papers* were published in 1936. George Moore's autobiography "*Hail and Farewell*" was published in three parts: *Ave* (1911), *Salve* (1912), and *Vale* (1914). For the story of Moore's cook, see Joseph Hone, *The Life of George Moore* (1936), p. 233. Lady Augusta Gregory (1852-1932) was co-founder with Yeats of the Irish National Theatre. John Sleigh Pudney (1909-77) joined the staff of the BBC in 1934; his first book of poems, *Open the Sky*, had just been published.

Rosamond Spender Read & Plomer & the incessant rather sniping talk about Grigson & Stephen's muddled theories to whip my brain: but felt Yeats' extreme directness, simplicity, & equality: liked his praise; liked him: but cant unriddle the universe at tea. He is older, less coloured & vigorous. Little burning eyes behind great glasses: ruffled hair: tweeds. Philip [Morrell] aged, whitened, fallen in: almost 70 I suppose. A new cumquhat dog: various obscure dowds: one Dilys Powell: & so on.[33] Home to sleep over the fire: & now to Rodmell.

[*Later*] Yeats said that in writing his memoirs he had to leave out himself, because no man could tell the truth about the women in his life. Also no man knew about himself. Somebody had cast his horoscope & given him a character, the very opposite of his own conception; but as he now saw, this was his real character. He believes entirely in horoscopes. Will never do business with anyone without having their horoscope. Is trying to get a play acted in London, at the Gate. But no actor can produce a play. Actors only know their own parts. They cant see that theres a piebald horse outside the window.

Yeats always has 'a narrative man' with whom he goes for walks—a man who tells a story.

Yeats said of Proust "a slow motion novel".

Monday 29 October

Reading Antigone. How powerful that spell is still—Greek. Thank heaven I learnt it young—an emotion different from any other. I will read Plotinus: Herodotus: Homer I think.

Wednesday 31 October

Too tired after dining with Helen last night & talking too much with Oliver about Roger & B[loomsbur]y—too tired to write. And must dine with Clive to meet Aldous & the Clarks. What a life I could have led if I had been born with full rich blood to my head. As it is, one late night floors me; all sand this morning. We talked too much, I think. And I sat in Roger's chair, & thought once he was there—Oliver's shoes like his. The room diminished slightly: not so rich & sonorous. Baba [Anrep] an ill favoured, rough mouthed girl. And Oliver's mistress—dear me, why mistress? Sickert I rather gather a failure: silence descends on that little flurry.

33. (Elizabeth) Dilys Powell, Hellenist and *Sunday Times* journalist and critic 1928-31 and from 1936. Her first book, *Descent from Parnassus* (on contemporary poetry) was published in 1934.

Now to read Jane Austen's Thomson's Seasons.[34]

Helen by the way asked me tentatively to write Roger's Life. Julian to collect all facts, make a skeleton; I to sum & compose. But Margery [Fry] wants to write it. Margery has the documents: is executor. I deferred. Isnt a 'Life' impossible? Yes, said Oliver. All sorts of people shd put down recollections. And unprintable. So whats to come of it? I deferred. (what exactly does that word mean?)

Thursday 1 November

Ideas that came to me last night dining with Clive; talking to Aldous & the Kenneth Clarks.[1]

About Roger's life: that it should be written by different people to illustrate different stages.

Youth.   by Margery
Cambridge. by Wedd?
Early London life . . .
Post Imp.   Clive
                   Sickert.
Bloomsbury, Desmond
                   V.W.
Later life.   Julian
                   Blunt.
                   Heard.   & so on.[2]

all to be combined say by Desmond & me together.

About novels: the different strata of being: the upper under—This is a familiar idea, partly tried in The Pargiters. But I think of working it out more closely; & now, particularly, in my critical book: showing how the mind naturally follows that order in thinking: how it is illustrated by literature.

34. In September 1933, travelling Hogarth Press books in Hastings and St Leonards, the Woolfs bought from the bookseller C. Howes four calf-bound volumes of *The Works of James Thomson*, 1773, which had belonged to Jane Austen; volume I contains 'The Seasons'. See D. J. Gilson, 'Jane Austen's Books' in *The Book Collector, Spring* 1974.

1. Kenneth Mackenzie Clark (b. 1903) and his wife Jane, who were married in 1927. Starting from a background not of culture but of wealth, he had devoted himself to the study of art to such purpose that in January 1934 he became Director of the National Gallery, and they were enjoying what he was to call (*Another Part of the Wood*, 1974), the 'Great Clark Boom'. An admirer of Roger Fry, and a good friend to artists, he had commissioned a dinner service—delivered as 48 plates each bearing the image of a famous woman—from Duncan Grant and Vanessa Bell.

2. Nathaniel Wedd (1864-1940), classical scholar and Fellow of King's College, was a contemporary and close friend of Roger Fry at Cambridge. Anthony Frederick Blunt (b. 1907), Fellow of Trinity College, Cambridge, 1932-36, art historian.

I must now do biography & autobiography.

Talk at dinner about: Yeats; Noel Coward; the plates: Clarks cant use theirs: the hostesses: Sibyl & Emerald. Ly C[unard]. says Aldous indecent: wears a false bust: their collection like playing cards; had dined & sat next Lady P. Smith; a bore;[3] the other woman a hump back; Coward at Monte Carlo, laying his hand on A.'s arm: this this is divine—a Jazz like the rest. The variety of his gifts: but all out of the 6d box at Woolworth's. Beating & beating & beating—an omelette without eggs, said A. Nothing there: but the heroic beating. Talk about the Occult: A. cant stand Auden. Nothing but a demagogue. Declaims: takes in the young. Something in Day Lewis—hasnt read Spender.[4]

Friday 2 November

Two teeth out with a new anaesthetic: hence I write here, not seriously. And this is another pen. And my brain is very slightly frozen, like my gums. Teeth become like old roots that one breaks off. He broke, & I scarcely felt. My brain frozen thinks of Aldous & the Clarks; thinks vaguely of biography; thinks am I reviewed anywhere—cant look—thinks its a fine cold day. Angelica at the Nat. Gallery. Thinks how I shall read Dante; how I did not go to Vita's lecture; how we have refused Enid Jones next week; how we should have met Wells there; I finished the Seasons last night: that is a surface reading, such as I give poetry for the first time. Ten skins to the mind. No, I cannot write at all with a frozen brain.

I went upstairs to rinse my bleeding gum—the cocaine lasts ½ an hour: then the nerves begin to feel again—& opened the Spectator & read W.L. on me again. An answer to Spender. "I am not malicious—several people call Mrs W. Felicia Hemans." This I suppose is another little scratch of the cats claws: to slip that in, by the way—"I dont say it—others do". And they are supercilious on the next page about Sickert; & so—[5] Well L. says I shd. be contemptible to mind. Yes: but I do mind for 10 minutes: I

3. Lady Pamela Smith (b. 1914) was the second daughter of the 1st Earl of Birkenhead.
4. Cecil Day Lewis (1904-1972); three books of his poems had been published by the Hogarth Press since 1929. Auden, Spender and Day Lewis were 'bound together in a holy trinity' (*V VW Letters*, no. 3085) as the new left-wing poets of the 'thirties.
5. The *Spectator* of 2 November printed a reply from Wyndham Lewis to its review (19 October) of his *Men Without Art*, rebutting Stephen Spender's charge of malice: 'Mrs Woolf is charming, scholarly, intelligent, everything that you will: but here we *have* not a Jane Austen—a Felicia Hemans rather, as it has been said: for there are some even more "malicious" than I am, I am afraid.' (See *M&M*, p. 340). The anonymous reviewer of *Walter Sickert: A Conversation* commented: 'Mr Sickert is . . . a novelist's painter . . . a painter of the school of Mrs Woolf, and that is why she can write so appreciatively about him.'

mind being in the light again, just as I was sinking into my populous obscurity. I must take a pull on myself. I dont think this attack will last more than 2 days. I think I shall be free from the infection by Monday. But what a bore it all is. And how many sudden shoots into nothingness open before me. But wait one moment. At the worst, should I be a quite negligible writer, I enjoy writing: I think I am an honest observer. Therefore the world will go on providing me with excitement whether I can use it or not. Also, how am I to balance W.L.'s criticism with Yeats—let alone Goldie & Morgan? Would they have felt anything if I had been negligible? And about 2 in the morning I am possessed of a remarkable sense of driving ey[e]less strength. And I have L.: & there are his books; & our life together. And freedom, now, from money paring. And . . . . if only for a time I could completely forget my self, my reviews, my fame, my sink in the scale—which is bound to come now, & to last about 8 or 9 years— then I should be what I mostly am: very rapid, excited, amused: intense. Odd, these extravagant ups & downs of reputation: compare the American in the Mercury . . .[6] no, for Gods sake dont compare: let all praise & blame sink to the bottom or float to the top & let me go my ways indifferent. And care for people. And let fly, in life, on all sides.

[*Monday 12 November*]

These are very sensible sayings I think. And its all forgotten & over—

What is uppermost now, is (1) The question of writing R.'s life. Helen came [*on 8 November*]. Says both she & M[argery]. wish it. So I wait. What do I feel about it? If I could be free, then here's the chance of trying biography: a splendid, difficult chance—better than trying to find a subject—that is, if I *am* free. But M. hesitates: I have heard nothing from her; & rather suspect she wants to do it herself.

We were at Monks House in a great flood of rain & storm of wind this week end; which lifted yesterday, & I took my Sunday morning walk with L. & saw the monkey that was found in the Brooks. This great yellow green ape had run all across the down from Peacehaven—a circus monkey wintering with a keeper up there. An odd sight to have met it clambering along over the downs. So I went on, to Piddinghoe, & back by the river. And my brain rose out of the mist (writing about reviewing, I mean) & I felt young & vigorous. Home with the car all acrid & yellow & red with chrysanthemums. And put them in water—a long job—& so to hear Sweeney Agonistes at the Group Theatre; an upper attic or studio: I sat by Tom: an audience, containing Ottoline & Hope & Raymond. The

6. Probably a reference to 'A Woman Pioneer', a review by Winifred Holtby of *Three Men Die* by Sarah Gertrude Millin (*London Mercury*, November 1934) in which VW is mentioned in passing.

acting made more sense than the reading but I doubt that Tom has enough
of a body & brain to bring off a whole play: certainly he conveys an emotion, an atmosphere: which is more than most: something peculiar to himself; sordid, emotional, intense—a kind of Crippen, in a mask: modernity
& poetry locked together. I liked the egg speech.[7] Talk with Hope about
her thyroid gland & her dachshund: Hope as usual eccentric impulsive
ecstatic odd. And there was a mint of notables.

Wednesday 14 November

Here I am taking a morning off to breathe in before I tackle the 9 volumes of that book.[8] And I am dissipated & rather frittered. There is no
doubt that to talk to Sibyl is very depressing. She mews & mows. Wont
speak out; complains with one breath, asks pity but cant be induced to say
what is on her mind. Perhaps there is very little there. She said 'One is no
longer so young as one was. Arthur is getting deaf. So I have to stand in a
shop all day .. But one shouldn't be—' I think she called it 'crimping'—I
forget the exact word. Oblique references were made then to our quarrel.
And I was hampered: couldnt get hold of her. Off she went, sentimentally
mournful, apologetic. And she impeded Margery who came at the same
moment—so that too remains, as they say, in abeyance. And this cringing
makes my own soul flop.

[Thursday 15 November]

And am now, 10.30 on Thursday morning, Nov. 15th, about to tackle
re-reading & re-writing The Pargiters. An awful moment.

12.45. Well that horrid plunge has been made, & I've started rewriting
the P.s. Lord Lord! 10 pages a day for 90 days: three months. The thing is
to contract: each scene to be a scene, much dramatised; contrasted; each to
be carefully dominated by one interest; some generalised. At any rate this
releases the usual flood & proves that only creating can bring about proportion: now, damnably disagreeable, as I see it will be—compacting the
vast mass—I am using my faculties again. & all the flies & fleas are forgotten.

7. Three performances of T. S. Eliot's *Sweeney Agonistes* were given by the Group
Theatre company in their rooms at 9 Great Newport Street; the Woolfs went to
that on Sunday evening, 11 November.
Sweeney: 'You see this egg
You see this egg
Well that's life on a crocodile isle.'
H. H. Crippen was hanged in 1910 for poisoning his wife. (In 1939 Eliot went as
Crippen to a fancy-dress party given by Adrian Stephen: *VI VW Letters*, no. 3483.)
8. These holograph notebooks are in the Berg; but there are only eight.

[?Saturday 17 November]

A note: despair at the badness of the book: cant think how I ever could write such stuff—& with such excitement: thats yesterday: today I think it good again. A note, by way of advising other Virginias with other books that this is the way of the thing: up down, up down—& Lord knows the truth.

Wednesday 21 November

Margery Fry to tea on Sunday. A long debate about the book on Roger: not very conclusive. She says she wants a study by me, reinforced with chapters on other aspects. I say, well but those books are unreadable. Oh of course I want you to be quite free she says. I should have to say something about his life, I say. The family— Now there of course I'm afraid I should have to ask you to be careful, she says. Agnes is stone deaf; has lived all her life in the family. I couldn't let her be hurt— And so on. The upshot of all of which is that she's to write to the NS. asking for letters: that I'm to go through them; that we're then to discuss—so it will drag on these many months, I suppose.[9] And I plan working at P.s: & getting in reading time with Roger's papers, so that by October next I could write, if thats the decision. But what?

A fog lasting several days. Both of us rather cheerful again. L. has finished the first part of Quack: & it goes along vigorously.[10] And we've seen— Lady Rhondda, Heard, Eth Williamson, Julian; Lyn; Tom; Kitchin; Hope . . . . in fact we've done our duty as party givers, & today heave a sigh of heavenly gladness because Raymond has a cold & puts our dinner with him off. I am reading, with interest & distaste, Wells;[11] I want to read a great deal; & the P.s goes at 8 or 9 pages daily. & that is why I feel content.

Tom's head is very remarkable; such a conflict; so many forces have smashed against him: the wild eye still; but all rocky, yellow, riven, &

---

9. Agnes (1869-1958) was the third—the younger twin of Isabel—of Roger Fry's six sisters. Margery Fry's letter, appealing for the loan of letters from him as material for a biography, appeared in the *NS&N* of 1 December 1934.

10. *Quack, Quack!* by LW was published in May 1935 (*HP Checklist* 380); the first part of his attack on Fascism and quackery in general was 'Quack, Quack in Politics', the second, 'Intellectual Quack, Quack.'

11. Lady Rhondda and Gerald Heard dined on Friday 16 November; Julian Bell and Elizabeth Williamson came after dinner. Lyn Lloyd Irvine lunched on 20 November. T. S. Eliot and C. H. B. Kitchin (1895-1967)—whose *Crime at Christmas* the Woolfs had published in October (*HP Checklist* 341)—dined on 19 November, and were joined after dinner by Hope Mirrlees. H. G. Wells's *Experiment in Autobiography* had been published in two volumes in September 1934.

constricted. Sits very solid—large shoulders—in his chair, & talks easily but with authority. Is a great man, in a way, now: self confident, didactic. But to me, still, a dear old ass; I mean I cant be frozen off with this divine authority any longer. Not a very good evening. Talk scattered & surface pattering. Hope & her dog distracting. Kitchin a little fat & white & cunning & not up to the mark. A rather conceited touchy man, I guess; has a good opinion of himself; & is slightly commonplace. But how little I care now, for these slight misfits. Generally there's some fun to be had—a saying, an attitude. Tom is larger minded than of old. "But thats only human" he said, when I asked him if he still liked seeing his own name in print.

Monday 26 November

At Rodmell for the week end. My Lodge is demolished; the new house in process of building in the orchard. There will be open doors in front; & a view right over to Caburn. I think I shall sleep there on summer nights. I made out a careful map of the week; & then, of course, come home & find us asked by the Kauffers to a show of Man Ray's photographs in Bedford Sq. So we go, & find Aldous, Mary & Jack, & a South American Vasta—was that what Roger called these opulent millionaires from Buenos Aires?[12] Anyhow she was very ripe & rich; with pearls at her ears, as if a large moth had laid clusters of eggs; the colour of an apricot under glass; eyes I think brightened by some cosmetic; but there we stood & talked, in French, & English, about the Estancia, the great white rooms, the cactuses, the gardenias, the wealth & opulence of South America; so to Rome & Mussolini, whom she's just seen. He was simple & kind—on purpose. She sat & forgot to call him Excellency. And he said sometimes he woke in the night & wondered Are my people happy? She said he is the Coué of Italy: repeats every day & every way &c.[13] Also spoke of women: how no great man—Bismarck, Napoleon, Caesar, needed them: how Beatrice was only Florence. And how we all make mistakes: hers had been that she made an unhappy marriage. "But now go & have a child" he told her. The time is past she said. And so to Me de

12. An exhibition of photographs by the *avant-garde* Paris-American Man Ray (1890-1976) was being shown at Messrs Lund Humphries, 12 Bedford Square; the Woolfs went to a private view on Sunday evening after returning from Rodmell. The '*Vasta*' was Victoria Ocampo (1890-1979), an Argentinian of wealth and culture, publisher in Buenos Aires of the intellectual magazine *Sur*; in the next few weeks her friendship with VW ripened rapidly. For her account of her meetings and correspondence with VW, see *Review 23*, published by the Center for Inter-American Relations, New York, 1978.

13. Dr Emile Coué (1857-1926), French psychotherapist whose formula 'every day and in every way I am becoming better and better' became proverbial.

Noailles, dying of extinguished vanity in a small flat.[14] She lay in bed, bedizened, covered with dozens & dozens of veils &c: began plucking them off; was never still a moment, lighting lamps & putting them out; demanded worship; was not old, but had outlived her fame. Nothing wrong with her but the death of her great fame. And she left letters to Barrès wh. his widow holds; & her doctor is piecing the story together. Then of a sudden we part; Man Ray says will I come & be photographed —on Tuesday 3.30.[15] Mary says she wants to come to tea. Thats the end of my planned week—almost.

[Tuesday 27 November]

Human misery is certainly very great. We wish to comfort Nessa; have her to dinner; & tell her about Julian's poems. At once she ruffles like a formidable hen. I am irritated. This is the religion & superstition of motherhood. Well—L. then speaks, emphatically but reasonably. She is also reasonable but cold. All our feelings are confused: mine discreditable. Why does it irritate me so, this maternal partiality? Anyhow, we all sit exacerbating ourselves, instead of consoling.[16] And she is like a stone wall when I hint that Julian might mend his manners—at least be more considerate—perhaps conciliate Lady R[hondda]. "Like Eddie Playfair—she said at once. No, thats not Julian's way." And "I should have thought that anyone of sense could have seen—Mrs Grant [*Duncan's mother*] thought him charming" .. &c &c. Then why does J. beg us to get him a job? No, it was not a nice evening; & she is lonely without Roger. And the S. American Okampo sent me orchids. I dislike many of my feelings. Most of all I hate the hush & mystery of motherhood. How unreal it all is!

Sunday 2 December

Isnt it odd? Some days I cant read Dante at all after revising the P.s: other days I find it very sublime & helpful. Raises one out of the chatter of words. But today (doing the scene at the Lodge) I'm too excited, I think it a good book today. I'm in the thick again. But I will stop at the end of

14. Comtesse Mathieu de Noailles, *née* Anna de Brancovan (1876-1933), poet and prominent figure in French cultural society. Maurice Barrès (1862-1923), French writer.
15. VW presumably agreed; a Man Ray portrait of her is reproduced opposite p. 176 in *IV LW*.
16. The Woolfs were critical of Julian Bell's poetry; VW had recently read and returned some MS poems he had sent her, with no suggestion that the Hogarth Press might publish him (though it did later). See *II QB*, Appendix C, for VW's feelings about Julian Bell.

the funeral scene, & calm my brain. That is I will write the play for Xmas: Freshwater a farce—for a joke.[1] And rig up my Contemporary Criticism article: & look around. David Cecil on fiction: a good book for readers, not for writers—all so elementary: but some good points made, from the outside. I've done though with that sort of criticism. And he's often wrong: gets W.H. wrong, I think: wants to have a profound theory.[2] We—B[loomsbur]y—are dead; so says Joad. I snap my fingers at him. Lytton & I the two destructors.[3]

Poor Francis lies in a hotel bedroom in Russell Sqre this rainy morning. I went in & sat with him. Quite himself with a lump on his forehead. And is aware of it all. May die under another operation, or slowly stiffen into complete paralysis. His brain may go. All this he knows; & there it was between us, as we joked. He came to the verge of it once or twice. But I cant feel any more at the moment—not after Roger. I cannot go through that again. Thats my feeling. I kissed him. "This is the first time—this chaste kiss" he said. So I kissed him again. But I must not cry, I thought, & so went. And he said, bitterly, how he had given 10 years of his life to love—to a horrid little creature. Thank God I never let you see him, he said. Gone to Russia. No I really couldnt follow him there. When I saw him first—I just came into the room—I thought I had never seen anyone so beautiful. He had talent of course. But . . . .— So we rambled & rattled. And Hubert Waley, dark & slim, poured him out whiskey, as if they now let him have what he likes.[4] He cant read. He lies there with one arm bandaged: in that bedroom, with the chrysanthemums, under a green silk quilt.

Today come Okampo & H—no I cant remember the name of the French journalist deposited on me by Peter [Lucas]. Oh damn ones friends![5]

1. VW's play *Freshwater* was conceived in 1919 (see *I VW Diary*, 30 January 1919); it was written in the summer of 1923 (see *III VW Letters*, nos. 1418, 1426, 1430), rewritten during the coming weeks and performed in Vanessa Bell's studio at 8 Fitzroy Street on 18 January 1935.
2. See chapter V: 'Emily Brontë and Wuthering Heights' in *Early Victorian Novelists* (1934) just published by David Cecil.
3. C. E. M. Joad (1891-1953), philosopher and popular expositor of ideas; in the first of two articles entitled 'The End of an Epoch' published in the *NS&N* on 1 and 8 December 1934, he posited that a post-war epoch, during which Bloomsbury had reigned supreme in the cultural sphere, began to decline in 1926.
4. The Russian defector was one Basile Kouchitachvili. Hubert Waley (1892-1968), younger brother of the sinologue Arthur, lived at one time in the same Bloomsbury house (*my father's: ed.*) as Francis Birrell; an unsuccessful artist, he became fascinated by films, and was to work for the British Film Institute.
5. Louis Gillet, writer, and editor of the *Revue des Deux Mondes*; he wrote an introduction to Charles Mauron's translation of *Flush* published in 1935 (Kp D26).

Tuesday 18 December

Talk with Francis yesterday. He is dying: but makes no bones about it: only his expression is quite different. Has no hope. The man says he asks every evening how long will this go on, & hopes for the end. He was exactly as usual; no wandering, no incoherence. A credit to atheism. The soul deserves to be immortal, as L. said. We walked back, glad to be alive: numb somehow. I cant use my imagination on that theme. What wd it be like to lie there, expecting death? & how odd & strange a death. I write hurriedly, going to Angelica's [*school*] concert this fine soft day.

On Friday 21 December the Woolfs drove to Rodmell and stayed there very quietly for just over three weeks. The Charlestonians were away at Christmas, but the Keyneses and Richard Kahn came to tea at Monks House on Boxing Day. VW's 'lodge' by the churchyard wall was now ready for her occupation.

Sunday 30 December

Since I forgot to bring my writing book, I must fill up here, on loose sheets. End the year; with those cursed dogs barking: & I am sitting in my new house; & it is, of all hours, 3.10; & it is raining; & the Cow [Mabel] has the sciatica; & we are taking her into Lewes to catch a train to London; after which we have tea at Charleston, act the play [*i.e.: rehearse Freshwater*] & dine there. It has been the wettest Christmas, I should say, drawing a bow at a venture, on record. Only yesterday did I manage my phantom farm walk; but pray God, with Christmas over, the rain will stop falling, Miss Emery's dogs barking.[6]

It was stupid to come without a book, seeing that I end every morning with a head full of ideas about The Pargiters. It is very interesting to write out. I am re-writing considerably. My idea is to ⟨space⟩ contrast the scenes; very intense, less so: then drama; then narrative. Keeping a kind of swing & rhythm through them all. Anyhow it admits of great variety—this book.

I think it shall be called Ordinary People. I finished, more or less, Maggie & Sarah, the first scene, in the bedroom: with what excitement I wrote it! And now hardly a line of the original is left. Yes but the spirit is caught I think. I write perhaps 60 pages before I catch that. And coming back I see it hopping like a yellow canary on its perch. I want to make both S. & M. bold characters, using character dialogue. Then we go on to Martin's visit to Eleanor: then the long day that ends with the King's

6. Miss Kathleen Emery (1892-1981), who lived with Miss Dicksee at Charnes Cottage next door to Monks House, bred Fox Terriers.

death. I have sweated off 80 or 90 pages, mostly due to a fault in paging though.

End of the year: & Francis transacting his death at that nursing home in Collingham Place. The expression on his face is what I see: as if he were facing a peculiar lonely sorrow. One's own death—think of lying there alone, looking at it, at 45 or so: with a great desire to live. "And so the New Statesman's going to be the best paper that ever was, is it?" He's dead though (of Brimley Johnson) spoken with a kind of bitterness.[7] None of these words are exactly right.

And here we are, chafed by the Cow's lame leg & the dogs: yet as usual very happy I think: ever so full of ideas. L. finishing his Quack Quack of a morning: the Zet [Mitz] crawling from one chair to the other—picking at L.'s head.

And Roger dead. And am I to write about him? And the stirring of the embers—I mean the wish to make up as much of a fire as possible. So to get ready for the wet drive—dogs still barking.

7. R. Brimley Johnson (1867-1932) was a publisher, editor, and writer on literary subjects.

1935

1935

The following entries for 1, 5, and 11 January, all (like that for 30 December 1934) written at Rodmell, are on loose sheets inserted at the end of DIARY XXIII.

Tuesday 1 January

We went to Charleston. Nessa explained to us that Clive had made a scene the night before about bringing six friends to the party.[1] Wouldnt come, unless he could bring 6 friends without naming them. Now why? I suppose something rankling about our not liking Raymond & so on. Final grumbles to be heard at dinner; as if he were anxious to explain. The play rather tosh; but I'm not going to bother about making a good impression as a play wright. And I had a lovely old years walk yesterday round the rat farm valley, by a new way, & met Mr Freeth, & talked about road making; & then in to Lewes to take the car to Martins [*garage*], & then home, & read St Paul & the papers. I must buy the Old Testament. I am reading the Acts of the Apostles. At last I am illuminating that dark spot in my reading. What happened in Rome? And there are seven volumes of Renan. Lytton calls him 'mellifluous'.[2] Yeats & Aldous agreed, the other day, that their great aim in writing is to avoid the 'literary'. Aldous said how extraordinary the 'literary' fetish had been among the Victorians. Yeats said that he wanted only to use the words that real people say. That his change had come through writing plays. And I said, rashly, that all the same his meaning was very difficult. And what is 'the literary'? Thats rather an interesting question. Might go into that, if I ever write my critical book. But now I want to write On being despised. My mind will go on pumping up ideas for that. And I must finish Ordinary People: & then there's Roger.[3] If I could finish O.P. in July: I would spend August in reading Roger, & writing Despised. Begin Roger in October 1935. Is that possible? Publish O.P. in Oct: & work at those two during 1936. Lord knows! But I must press a good deal of work in—remembering 53—54—55 are on me. And how excited I get over my ideas! And there's people to see—

1. i.e.: Angelica's party on 18 January at which *Freshwater* was to be performed.
2. Mr H. W. Freeth was foreman of South Farm, Rodmell. Ernest Renan (1823-1892), philologist and historian, author of 'Histoire des origines du christianisme', a series of seven historical studies including *Vie de Jésus* (1863), *Les apôtres* (1866), and *St Paul* (1869), which VW was reading.
3. 'On Being Despised' and 'Ordinary People': working titles for what became *Three Guineas* and *The Years* respectively; see above 20 January 1931, n. 8.

Sunday 6 January

Francis died on 2nd. It was a mercy, as we say, that it ended so soon. But a queer thing death. Last night I suddenly thought, how silly & indeed disgusting death, the decomposition of the body, &c. Why think of it as anything noble?

We lunched with Maynard & Lydia. The first fine cold day since we came. Talk rather sterile at first. Servant in the room. I suddenly scaled Lydia's depths; & desire to have it recognised. We were talking about Somerset Maugham. ⟨She⟩ "I said to him, do you write in the morning or the evening? And he said "This is not the time to discuss things like that" he thought me so naiv: he thought I was nothing more." "But when I write your life I will bring in the other Lydia" I said. Oh Virginia do! she exclaimed. M[aynard]. talked about the books he bought at the Gibbon sale. Geoffrey bought an Herodotus full of G.'s notes. Geoffrey's library is the best investment he ever made.[4] After lunch we got through the formal artificial. We talked about Francis: M. said he was a case of arrested development; had been a most brilliant undergraduate, & remained one. Should have his brain analysed. Then Wells—had read his Au[tobiograph]y. Thought him a little squit. Ah Maynard, you could not put that word in print. A lack of decency, said M. Shaw feels it. Shaw wd. never write of anyone he respected as he wrote of Wells. Then he read us a long magnificently spry & juicy letter from Shaw, on a sickbed, aged 77. The whole of economics twiddled round on his finger, with the usual dives & gibes & colloquialities. The most artificial of all styles, I said, like his seeming natural speaking. M.['s] own letter said that he thinks he has revolutionised economics; in the new book he is writing. "Wait ten years, & let it absorb the politics & the psychology & so on that will accrue to it; & then you'll see—the old Ricardo system will be exposed; & the whole thing set on a new footing." This he wrote in so many words: a gigantic boast; true I daresay.[5] That was why we were asked to lunch not tea—that he may write his book in the soft exciting hours. "He pots" said Lydia when we got up to go. He was potting this morning. "All the weeklies

4. Edward Gibbon's Lausanne Library was auctioned at Sotheby's on 20 December 1934; from it Maynard Keynes acquired a total of some 36 titles (now in the Library of King's College, Cambridge). His brother Geoffrey Langdon Keynes (b. 1887), surgeon, Blake scholar and bibliographer, bought Herodotus' *Historiarium Libri IX*, but later relinquished it to Victor Rothschild; it formed part of the library of 18th century books Lord Rothschild gave to Trinity College in 1952.
5. Shaw's letter (dated 11 December 1935) to Keynes is preserved in the Library of King's College, Cambridge, as are the drafts of Keynes's relevant letters (2 December 1934; 1 January 1935) to Shaw. Keynes's new book was *The General Theory of Employment, Interest and Money*, completed in December 1935 and published in 1936.

are mere homes for inferiority complexes" he said. Nobody has any dignity or nobility as a critic. Except Chesterton, struck in Lydia. What we want is impersonality, I said. And we discussed Joad's dismissal of Bloomsbury. So to our car, they hanging arm in arm. And to Lewes to get the gaiters I'm so proud of. And a teasing letter (the other night) from E[lizabe]th Bibesco.

"I am afraid that it had not occurred to me that in matters of ultimate importance even feminists cd. wish to segregate & label the sexes. It wd. seem to be a pity that sex alone should be able to bring them together"— to which I replied, What about Hitler? This is because, when she asked me to join the Cttee of the anti-Fascist Exn., I asked why the woman question was ignored. So we go on, sparring & biting. I shouldn't mind giving that woman a toss in the air [*word illegible*][6]

Friday 11 January

I have made a very clever arrangement on the new board that L. gave me for Christmas: ink, pen tray &c. I never cease to get pleasure from these clever arrangements. So death will be very dull. There are no letters in the grave, as Dr Johnson said.[7] A very long, rather formal, I mean affected letter from Tom this morning, which I must put away, as it will be so valuable. Did he think that when he was writing it?[8] L. whose modesty is enough to make me blush, heard from Brace yesterday that they anticipate a large sale for Quack Quack. Some ass wants him to call it—some asses' name. It will be out this spring. This spring will be on us all of a clap. Very windy; today: a damp misted walk two days ago to Piddinghoe. Now the trees are threshing. Nessa & Angelica & Eve yesterday.[9] We talk a great deal about the play. An amusing incident. And I shall hire a donkeys head to take my call in—by way of saying This is a donkeys work. I make

6. VW had been invited by the Princess Bibesco to support a proposed anti-Fascist exhibition initiated by the Cambridge anti-War Council; to VW's enquiry about the omission of the 'woman question' in such a project, Elizabeth Bibesco replied on 1 January: 'There will of course be a section dealing with women under the Nazi regime' and continuing in the words VW has copied. VW pasted this letter into the second volume of material collected by her relating (ultimately) to *Three Guineas* (MHP, Sussex, B 16).
7. 'As he opened a note which his servant brought to him, he said, "An odd thought strikes me: we shall receive no letters in the grave."' Boswell's *Life of Johnson* (G. B. Hill's edition, 1887, vol. IV, p. 413).
8. T. S. Eliot's letter dated 'Twelfth Night (or What You Will) 1935' with a covering letter dated 9 January, is in the Berg.
9. Eve Younger, whose doctor father died in 1928, lived in Mecklenburgh Square; she and Angelica had made friends when they were both at Miss Paul's little private school there, and she often stayed at Charleston during school holidays; she took the part of Queen Victoria in *Freshwater*.

out that I shall reduce The Caravan (so called suddenly) to 150,000: & shall finish retyping in May. I wonder. It is compressed I think. And sometimes my brain threatens to split with all the meaning I think I could press into it. The discovery of this book, it dawns upon me, is the combination of the external & the internal. I am using both, freely. And my eye has gathered in a good many externals in its time. See how much more I write about myself than Leonard does about himself. Already engagements are piling; & the lap ahead will be full of the usual jerks & strains. I am going to a Comtee I think at the Oxfords on Wednesday:[10] Tom suggests a fortnightly tea. And there's Helen . . . I never never invite anyone; but lie like an apron under an apple tree for fruit to drop.

I cant read Dante of a morning after the struggle with fiction. I wish I could find some way of composing my mind—its absurd to let it be ravaged by scenes; when I may not have read all Dante before I— but why harp on death? On the contrary, it is better to pull on my galoshes & go through the gale to lunch off scrambled egg & sausages. Louie & L. will eat liver. Lambs liver is more tender than calfs, said Louie, thus filling up a blank in my knowledge of the world.

The Woolfs returned to London on Sunday 13 January, taking Adrian Stephen with them from Charleston. VW begins a new book, DIARY XXIV.

Saturday 19 January

The play came off last night, with the result that I am dry-brained this morning, & can only use this book as a pillow.[11] It was said, inevitably, to be a great success; & I enjoyed—let me see what? Bunny's praise; Oliver's; but not much Christabel's, or the standing about pumping up vivacities with David [Cecil], Cory [Bell], Elizabeth Bowen: yet on the whole, it is good to have an unbuttoned laughing evening once in a way. Angelica ravishing of course, but of course too grown up for my taste. That is, I rather dread Bloomsbury; & rather relish the clumsy directness, the hard fact of the Stephen girls: so clumsy & large. But they will become workers—in the cause of—how the phrases one has written & listened to so many times run in the head! And Bobo [Mayor] by the way, grey-haired, silver & rose, very handsome, exacerbated me by saying I was

10. The committee of the Anti-Fascist exhibition met at 44 Bedford Square, the home of Elizabeth Bibesco's mother, Lady Oxford.
11. *Freshwater*, a comedy by VW based upon the personality of her great-aunt the photographer Julia Margaret Cameron and her Isle of Wight neighbours—Tennyson, G. F. Watts, and Ellen Terry (played by Angelica Bell)—and depending to a considerable extent upon family stories and literary allusions, was performed in Vanessa Bell's studio at 8 Fitzroy Street on 18 January; for its history, cast and text, see *Freshwater, a Comedy*, edited by Lucio P. Ruotolo, 1976.

always publishing. Am I? But I carefully extracted that thorn & put it on the mantelpiece. And Morgan said it was lovely, I mean the play. In the middle, old Gumbo [Marjorie Strachey] delivered a stout envelope, with a photograph of her mother. Old Gumbo never went to America after all. And Rosamond's play is dubious, because Gielgud has made such a success with Hamlet.[12] There is something pleasing in the misfortunes of ones friends: I wonder.

And there was Helen, & she said that Margery has all her spines erect again, about Roger: which makes me guess that she is doubtful about that biography. Roger's ghost knocked at the door—his portrait of Charlie Sanger was delivered in the thick of the rehearsal.[13] And How Francis would have enjoyed this, Leonard said. These are our ghosts now. But they would applaud the attempt. So to sleep: & now, God bless my soul, as *Tenn*: would say [*see* Freshwater], I must rinse & freshen my mind, & make it work soberly on something hard: theres my Dante; & Renan. And the horrid winter lap begins; the pale unbecoming days, like an aging woman seen at 11 o'clock. However, L. & I shall go for a walk this afternoon; & that seems to me an enormous balance at the Bank: solid happiness.

I have an idea for a 'play' Summers night. Someone on a seat. And voices speaking from the flowers.

Wednesday 23 January

Yes, I ought to have explained why I wrote the Sickert. I always think of things too late. I am reading the Faery Queen—with delight. I shall write about it. I took Angelica shopping. "Do you mind if I read the Heir of Redcliffe?" she said at tea, amusing me.[14] What a curious sense the clothes sense is! Buying her coat, mine, hearing the women talk, as of race horses, about new skirts. And I am fluttered because I must lunch with Clive tomorrow in my new coat. And I cant think out what I mean about *conception*: the idea behind F.Q. How to express a kind of natural transition from state to state. And the air of natural beauty. It is better to read the originals. Well, Clive's lunch will jump me out of this. And now that the play is over, we must begin to see people here: & go to Hamlet, & plan our spring journey. I am taking a fortnight off fiction. My mind

12. John Gielgud's Hamlet ran for 155 performances—from 14 November 1934 to 23 March 1935—at the New Theatre. Rosamond Lehmann's play *No More Music* was not performed until 1938.
13. After C. P. Sanger's death in 1930, Roger Fry gave his portrait of him to Trinity College, Cambridge; why it was now delivered to 8 Fitzroy Street is unexplained.
14. See MHP, Sussex, B 2m: notebook labelled 'Four Voices. Faery Queen'. *The Heir of Redclyffe* (1853) by C. M. Yonge.

became knotted. I think of making Theresa *sing*: & so lyricise the argument. Get as far from T (so called after my Sarah & Elvira provisionally). But oh heavens the duck squashy—this is from the pressed duck Jack [Hills] once gave us. All juice: one squab of juice. I am reading Point Counterpoint. Not a good novel. all raw, uncooked, protesting. A descendant, oddly enough, of Mrs H. Ward: interest in ideas; makes people into ideas.[15]

A man from America returns my letters & says he is glad to see me as I am.

Friday 1 February

And again this morning, Friday, I'm too tired to go on with P.s. Why? Talking too much I daresay. I thought though I wanted 'society': & saw Helen, Mary, Gillet. Ann tonight. I think the P.s however a promising work. Only nerve vigour wanted. A day off today.

Saturday 2 February

Poor old Ethel has been rooked £1600 by the Treasury on unpaid income tax. She says she wont accept a penny & will pay it out of her income, but she may have to sell Coign. This at 76—[1]

Ann to dinner last night: rather pale, rather resolute & melancholy perhaps. Talked of servants & science. She is going in for another Exn [?] at Newnham, & I had to vouch for her character to the Mistress of Girton. Rather a queer comment upon the independence of family control. Hadnt even told her parents about these formalities. Karin only seen in bed of a morning, Adrian seldom, the house full of lodgers & patients, Ann found going off alone to get a meal. An attractive girl; but uncombed; independent, proud of Stephen blood; much brought up by school mistresses; contemptuous of exams; wishes to be a doctor, & live in Geneva. Judith a great admirer of Hazlitt, & writes essays in secret.

Headachy all day. Walked to Chancery Lane in bitter rain about my spectacles, & am going to experiment with an improved version of a lorgnette. I wrote in praise of Rebecca's book to Rebecca, & have had no answer.[2] This I did because of the talk at Charleston, when they said how much pleasure such letters gave. I expect I have (somehow) given pain.

---

15. Aldous Huxley was in fact a nephew of Mrs Humphry Ward; his *Point Counter Point* was published in 1928.

1. 'Owing to the pressure put on the Treasury by her rich friends', and by their actual contributions, Ethel Smyth succeeded in reducing and eventually discharging her tax liabilities. (See *V VW Letters*, nos. 3019, 3032.)

2. Rebecca West's book, *The Harsh Voice* (1935), contained four tales, three concerned with the dominion of money.

But its no great matter. My conscience, as they say, is clear. And now I must write to Eth Williamson, about Ethel.

[?Sunday 3 February]

Notes:

Mrs W. saying she had been "happy" suddenly the night before. And once walking up Regent Street. What a divine feeling. And then it went. She did not know what caused it, or how to describe it

(2) The man in charge of the cactuses at Kew. The unreality: himself [?] become a living cactus, perhaps: or a hater of cactuses. Their involved serpentings: their grotesqueness. As a matter of fact he was a withered & bloodless old man. Gone grey, infinitely bored, by living with cactuses.[3]

Tuesday 5 February

Why should I mind so much Rebecca not answering my letter? Vanity largely, I suppose. I thought she would be glad &c. Never mind. She is a queer ill bred mind, with all the qualities I lack & fear.

Tom to tea, yesterday. An admirable way of seeing him. And how he suffers! Yes: I felt my accursed gift of sympathy rising. He seemed to have got so little joy or satisfaction out of being Tom. We—L. rather—argued, about the T & T correspondence.[4] Highly philosophical: on war: suddenly T. spoke with a genuine cry of feeling. About immortality: what it meant to him—I think it was that: anyhow he revealed his passion, as he seldom does. A religious soul: an unhappy man: a lonely very sensitive man, all wrapt up in fibres of self torture, doubt, conceit, desire for warmth & intimacy. And I'm very fond of him—like him in some of my reserves & subterfuges. Tonight Raymond & Joyce W.: and I dont look forward to it, my spirits damped by Rebecca. A vast sorrow at the back of life this winter. And then my blood rises & I create—yesterday walking by the lake in Regents Park, going to Hugo's. And I finished the difficult song chapter this morning.

After abusing booksellers yesterday for some time, I said to Tom, do you ever buy a new book? Never he said. And I said, I sometimes buy poetry, thats all. So this accounts for the problem, it strikes me, why authors dont sell: why booksellers dont stock &c &c.

3. The Woolfs had tea with Mrs Woolf on Saturday, and went to Kew Gardens on Sunday 3 February.
4. T. S. Eliot contributed the 'Notes on the Way' column to *Time and Tide* for January 1935, and his criticisms on 12 January of A. A. Milne's recently published anti-war tract, *Peace with Honour*, had provoked a correspondence.

FEBRUARY 1935

Wednesday 6 February

I open this book to record the fact, with all its psychological implications;—the fact that Rebecca's snub has now worn off. It lasted about 4 days: gave me a cold goose feather feeling every morning & every evening. It will now gradually fade out; & I shall dismiss her, & all that is implicit in that situation. But I should still be very glad if she did write to me. On the other hand, the feeling of independence is even better than the feeling of pleasure would be.

> O vanagloria dell' umane posse,
> Com' poco verde in su la cima dura,
> se non è giunta dall etati grosse!

O empty glory of human powers! How short the time its green endures upon the top, if it be not overtaken by rude ages!
Note: a reputation does not survive the generation in which it was built up, unless a gross & unenlightened age happens to follow—

> Non è il mondan romore altro che un fiato
> di vento, che or vien quinci ed or vien quindi,
> E muta nome, perchè muta lato.

> Earthly fame is but a breath of wind,
> which now cometh hence & now thence,
> And changes name because it changes direction.

a thousand years are a shorter space to eternity than the twinkling of an eye . . . Purgatorio. Canto XI. (p. 133).[5]

A story Joyce Wethered told: there is a woman who was jilted by a man for a shop girl. She now spends her life going to shops & making the shop girls cry. She is a well known figure, & always does this. The girls at Fortnums are always crying: so are the men, but not so often. They cry because the head of the department says something that hurts their feelings. They are very badly paid—girls £2 a week—men 3 or 4—& it leads to nothing. But they are always anxious to come.

Friday 8 February

Wright to lunch yesterday: Miss Delafield passes me in the square: the

5. These notes from Dante, occupying a single page, perhaps predate VW's reading notebook (MHP Sussex, B 3b) headed 'Feb. 1935/ Purgatorio'; the text and translations are copied from *La Divina Commedia*, edited by Hermann Oelsner and translated by Thomas Okey (Dent, 1933).

278

Holtby type;[6] dine with Nessa; & oh dear, how the ghost of Roger haunted us! What a dumb misery life is for her: [Kenneth] Clark had been in; hadnt seen anything of what Roger would have seen. An extraordinary sense of him: of wishing for him; of vacancy. A letter from Margery, who is bringing documents, & wants to see me next week. Excited about O[rdinary]. P[eople]. & no letter from Rebecca. My desk a failure.

Tuesday 12 February

This should be the coldest day in the year, according to averages; & it was a bitter week end [at Rodmell] & L. had a cold & I had the divine good sense to suggest staying till Monday; & Monday, when we drove up at midday was the first day of spring. We lunched at Reigate & the marmoset attracted great attention; the well of nice middle class women is bottomless; & the two men, who were talking about the mystery of razors, "I had a clean shave on Saturday . . . but this morning with the same razor . . ." & then about the County Court, poison, & the legal status of Kingswood [Surrey], being I suppose small solicitors, said Might I ask you, Sir, what that animal is? Then we came home; then Robson came to tea, & let out a number of highly sensible remarks about the rents of houses. He has—incredible though it may seem—actually, in 3 minutes, taken a perfect house in Westbourne Terrace, at an absurdly low rent, & the house, being faced with stone, not stucco, will be very cheap to repair: also the landlord is responsible for structural repairs: Willie is expecting "an addition to the family shortly". A marvellous feat: one supposes his gestation must be as long as an elephants. He retired to L.'s room. Colefax then came half an hour late: & we had it out. Lord what a drubbing you gave me in the summer, I managed to thrust in, after the usual patter about dining last night with somebody who had been dining with Ll. George. Then her defences crumpled: she flushed & quickened; so did I. She sat on the floor by the way, & pulled down some white undergarment which had become creased. She only wears one under garment & a small belt, by the way. And she twittered out how what had hurt her had been my thinking, or insinuating, that her dinner was merely a snob dinner to bring celebrities together. The truth was Noel [Coward] adores me; & I could save him from being as clever as a bag of ferrets & as trivial as a perch of canaries. And of course, I rather liked her. And she is so childishly ready to patter about her own simple love of sunsets, comparing herself to the worldly—for example Christabel & Lady Cholmondeley. That I stubbed by saying

6. Ralph Wright, who was involved in its organisation, came to discuss the anti-Fascist exhibition with the Woolfs. E. M. Delafield (1890-1943) was the author of the very successful *The Diary of a Provincial Lady* (1931); books by her on the Brontës, and on Victorian fiction, were to be published by the Hogarth Press (*HP Checklist* 366, 406).

I admired & loved those who fill their sails with the spice breezes of the great world. So she had to trim & hedge; & admit that parties are a stimulus to the imagination; & that her chief pleasure is to tell herself stories, to make up a life, a picture, as she bustles & flits. This I think was intended to be in my manner—a tribute to the imaginative, artistic life: for indeed what she cant bear is to be rated a hard society woman: as she is, partly; but then we're all curates eggs, as I was feeling: a mix: when L. came in & the political situation was again to the fore. "I was in Manchester last week . . . a cotton manufacturer told me that now Mosley has no chance in the North . . He has, I know for a fact, to shut down several branches. And he's very hard up."[7] So she went & we kissed in the hall.

This morning Mabel's brother in law, Mr Shine, said, about my studio windows, "Theres the force, the push, & the fit—to use engineering terms." This was to show us his intellectual eminence—a nice honest eyed false toothed man, who shines in the Labour world, & cant get a job. So I will keep this phrase for Mr Duffus.[8]

Wednesday 20 February

A row with Clive which spoilt my dinner at the Reads.[9] Lor! the misery of human life—our capacity for making ourselves miserable & stinging & biting like so many fleas. Not a very serious fleabite this one; only rouses my old inflammation—I mean, after all those other little pismire affairs, I always get the sense of those unhappy days. He wrote one of his absurd pompous letters to Lord Ivor, as chairman of the F. Cttee: & quoted Virginia Woolf inviting me to "strike a blow for freedom". And so Wright rang up & Mr Blunt came round, & I had to explain, & then to write a letter, which brings the blood to my head, & takes time; & sent me parched & throbbing up to that vast comfortless studio, where none of the charm of Bohemia mitigated the hard chairs, the skimpy wine, & the

7. Sir Oswald Mosley, 6th Bt. (1896-1980), founded the British Union of Fascists in 1932 following the rout of his New Party in the general election of 1931.
8. Mr Duffus is the Welsh jobbing builder in *The Years* who repairs Eleanor Pargiter's houses in Peter Street (pp. 102-7). Mabel's brother-in-law George Riley, general handyman and decorator and later Mayor of Islington, mended VW's studio windows—see below, 26 February 1935; possibly VW here mistakes the name Riley for Shine.
9. The Woolfs dined with Herbert Read and his wife Ludo (*née* Margaret Ludwig) in Hampstead on 19 February; the other guests were the sculptor Henry Moore (b. 1898) and his wife Irena, *née* Radetzky. The row with Clive concerned the anti-Fascist exhibition: VW, as a member of the committee, had written to him (and others) asking for support. Clive's belief (correct as it turned out) that the committee was communist-dominated, led him to write to the chairman Lord Ivor Spencer-Churchill, and placed VW in an awkward position. See *V VW Letters*, nos. 2983, 2988 to Clive Bell; also no. 3007 to Quentin Bell.

very nice sensible conversation. Henry Moore, sculptor & his Russian wife, something like Cordelia Fisher in the old days to look at; but more sympathetic. Respectable B[ohemi]a is a little cheerless. Better have Sybil or the real thing. But all went decorously. Steel chairs, clear pale colours; talk of pots; brainy talk, specialists talk. Read devitalised: possibly his look—a shop assistant. So this morning I cant write; only correct; & Hugh [Walpole] & Elth Bowen tonight, & tea with Nessa & Ethel Walker. Never mind.

Sara is the real difficulty: I cant get her into the main stream, yet she is essential. A very difficult problem; this transition business. And the burden of something that I wont call propaganda. I have a horror of the Aldous novel: that must be avoided. But ideas are sticky things: wont coalesce; hold up the creative, subconscious faculty: thats it I suppose. Ive written the chop house scene I dont know how many times.

Thursday 21 February

A good party last night with old Hugh. Hugh on Hollywood. What was interesting though & rather horrifying was his account of his own pain: an agony of pain in his arm, like broken bones twittering incessantly. Agony agony agony—hadnt realised there could be such pain. Once he burst into tears & sat up shouting. Was conveyed across America in an aeroplane. Saw 'the sky'. And then, just as the pain was coming on at Hampstead, at Harold's house, a parcel was delivered: a bottle of a quack medicine called Cleano. And he took a dose, & slept; & next day he was better. And has had no pain since.[10] But what was shocking was to see him an old man. All the buoyancy & taut pink skin gone. Yet difficult to say why one feels this. Something sunk & shuttered in him. Cavities in some lights. I liked him. And I liked his capacity for miraculous rebirth. Six months at Hollywood has completely changed him. When we said something about upper class, he laughed. Classes have been wiped out. He has seen through everything. Given up the Book of the Month; no longer frets about fame & reviews; & is taking to the great new art—the complex & amazing art of colour, music, words all in one. Of course there may be something in it. Mary came; Eth Bowen, & Julian, who as usual annoyed me by denouncing my "brutality". What an uncomfortable relation, Aunt & nephew. And how nice he is, & how obtuse. But it was a flourishing

10. Hugh Walpole had gone to Hollywood in June 1934 to write a scenario of *David Copperfield* for Metro Goldwyn Mayer; in November he suffered a crippling attack of arthritis, and was brought home by his chauffeur-companion Harold Cheevers. The wonder-cure was marketed as 'Ru-Mari'. See *Hugh Walpole: A Biography* (1952) by Rupert Hart-Davis. Walpole resigned from the committee of the Book Society in July 1935 but remained honorary chairman and rejoined a year later.

kind of evening: better I think than the Reads. I rather mean to write to Hugh.

Tea with Nessa & old bass voiced Ethel Walker in her serge suit & red tie. We are to go to a dinner given to her. She told some instalments of her life's history: some repetitions. Was the daughter of a hard bullying clever man. Damn you, you little brute, he said to her. And the cab horse ran away & climbed a six foot wall, while she clasped her mother, a very stout woman, & said "Screaming makes it worse".[11]

A letter of explanation & conciliation from Clive. No satire intended. So be it.

Tuesday 26 February

A very fine skyblue day, my windows completely filled with blue for a wonder. Mr Riley has just mended them. And I have been writing & writing & re-writing the scene by the Round Pond. What I want to do is to reduce it all so that each sentence though perfectly natural dialogue has a great pressure of meaning behind it. And the most careful harmony & contrast of scene—the boats colliding &c—has also to be arranged. Hence the extreme difficulty. But I hope perhaps tomorrow to have done, & then the dinner party & Kitty in the country should go quicker. At least I find the upper air scenes much simpler: & I think its right to keep them so. But Lord what a lot of work still to do! It wont be done before August. And here I am plagued by the sudden wish to write an Anti fascist Pamphlet. L. & I, after snarling over my cigarette smoking last night (I'm refraining altogether & without difficulty today) had a long discussion about all the things I might put in my pamphlet. He was extremely reasonable & adorable, & told me I should have to take account of the economic question. His specialised knowledge is of course an immense gain, if I could use it & stand away: I mean in all writing, its the person's own edge that counts. Cory [Bell] to tea.

Wednesday 27 February

And I've just written it all over again. But it must do this time, I say to myself. Yet I know that I must put the screw on & write some pages again. Its too jerky: too [blank in ms.] Its obvious that one person sees one thing & another another: & that one has to draw them together Who was it who said, through the unconscious one comes to the conscious, & then

11. Ethel Walker (1861-1951), painter of women, flowers, and decorative figure compositions, daughter of a Yorkshire Iron founder and his second wife. She had been a member of the New English Art Club since 1900. Her portrait of Vanessa, painted probably at this time, is in the Tate Gallery (no. 5038).

again to the unconscious? I rather think it was Miss West about childrens drawings last night at tea. I rather suspect she wanted to be an artist. Anyhow she knew McKnight Kauffer when he was married, & told us a very discreditable story about him. Hence I suspect his extreme fawning & flattery when we meet, & my vague discomfort.[12] A pouring wet day, after yesterdays sun; & our balmy walk across the Park to Harrods: & nobody has written to me, & I'm neglected, & I'm as safe as a sandboy; as a toad in an oak tree; & my window wont shut. Hence the draught.

I now feel a strong desire to stop reading F[aery]Q[ueen]: to read Cicero's letters, & the Chateaubriand Memoirs.[13] As far as I can see, this is the natural swing of the pendulum. To particularise, after the generalisation of Romantic poetry.

Friday 1 March

First of March: first of spring. Another blue day; & we're off to Walton on Thames, so I must cut short my Dante—dear me. Last nights party—Ann [Stephen] & Richard Ll. D.—that was to have been so dashing & easy, turned out rather a grind. Ann, poor dear, in her thick shoes—hadn't troubled to change them, or to brush her hair, mumbled, & was shy (as I used to be, I suppose, at 19). Richard, who has never been to a public school, & therefore has no inversions & perversions, ran free as a line with a salmon on it. But, then in came Janet (the image of Madge) & a great fat shiny nosed blubber lipped man, her husband: & Saxon, shrivelled & salted.[1] No: not an easy party. How parties differ! L. & I did our old owls with a vengeance. But we were all at the wrong angles: cousins, old friends, new;—no, it was not an easy evening. Janet told the story of her dismissal, because the Beit fellowship (?) decided that no woman can do research work. This led to a fruitful discussion—fruitful for my book I mean—of the jealousy of the medical male: vested interests; how its partly that they dislike competition; partly that they cling to the status quo. But I must go & lunch at 12.30 for our expedition.

12. E. McKnight Kauffer, who settled in London in 1914, had shed his legal wife, and lived with the textile designer Marion Dorn.
13. *Mémoires d'outre tombe* by François René de Chateaubriand (1768-1848) was published posthumously in 1849-50.
1. Richard Llewelyn Davies (1912-81), son of Crompton and nephew of Margaret Llewelyn Davies, and graduate of Trinity College, Cambridge, was studying architecture; he and Ann Stephen were married in 1938. Janet Maria (b. 1899), daughter of VW's cousin W. W. Vaughan and Madge, *née* Symonds, was a doctor and now assistant in Clinical Pathology at the British Postgraduate Medical School in Hammersmith Hospital; from 1930-33 she held the Beit Memorial Fellowship. In 1930 she had married David Gourlay, but continued to use the name Vaughan in her professional life.

Monday 4 March

It was a charming grey distinguished expedition too: to Walton; & we walked by the river, & said it was like a French picture. The grey trees, the weir churning, the bridge, the white cupola, & a lion in marble. L. finished Quack Quack the day before.

Yesterday I did not enjoy. What a guzzler old Ethel has become. She guzzled our very tough jobs [?*chops*], till I could not sit still. She is a greedy old woman; I dont like greed when it comes to champing & chawing & sweeping up gravy. And she gets red, drinking. Then the concert. How long how little music in it that I enjoyed! Beecham's face beaming, ecstatic, like a yellow copper idol: such grimaces, attenuations, dancings, swingings: his collar crumpled.[2] Old Hugh [Walpole] in the stalls. I went down, & saw him, tragic, sitting alone like an old man. What is there tragic now in his expression? Some loneliness, & pain. He did not know me at once: then promised of course to send Ethel a bottle that very night. Oh no, I said. "It's very slow" he said. And was for a moment touched by my concern.

So back to Ethel. In the artists room afterwards there was Zélie with the red lips, & another ex prima donna & a dissolute musician, all waiting their turn to plague Beecham. Et toi—Zélie suddenly burst into song; but it was 25 years ago that she had her success, since when . . . And they hinted & shrugged that poor old Ethel was a well known imposition upon conductors. Out she came in her spotted cats fur with her hat askew, carrying her brown cardboard despatch box, upon which they—the tight hard old prima donnas, fell on her & larded her with praise. (They had played the Wreckers overture.) Who are they I said. Havent an idea, she replied. So we had tea at the Langham, which I dont mind so much as meat & gravy.[3] And then I could stand that stab of a voice emphasising, I dont know what, no longer; & said I must go. It was a Sunday evening drizzle in the street, an 1849 night, as we padded very slowly to the Tube: & thank God, she vanished. I was out of temper. But L. miraculously enchanted me again by persuading me not to have Italian lessons from Castelli[?]. For some reason this decision has given me a divine sense of immunity which wraps me round this morning. I am a toad in an oak

2. In one of his series of Sunday concerts at the Queen's Hall, Sir Thomas Beecham, conducting the London Philharmonic Orchestra, included the Prelude to Act II of Ethel Smyth's opera *The Wreckers*, together with works by Wagner, Beethoven, Schubert and Berlioz, in the programme on 3 March. LW did not go to the concert.

3. Zélie de Lussan (1863-1949), American mezzo-soprano of French parentage, celebrated in the role of Carmen, married Angelo Franani in 1907 and retired to settle in London. The Langham Hotel in Portland Place was almost opposite the Queen's Hall.

again: neglected, at ease, completely happy. Nessa & Julian came round to us, for a wonder, after dinner. And we talked about Roger & Margery's incestuous love. Julian at his best, weighty, reasonable & mature. Thats being with Nessa, I suppose. I said how I tried to 'rattle' L. into going to the Walker dinner.

Wednesday 6 March

It was great fun at Ethel's party last night, & I enjoyed myself enormously, & I was a success (yes, I think so) with old Tonks, & obliterated Holmes, & the Charles Morgans want to dine, & all that—[4] The difficulty is to combine the two: here & there. If I did much of that I should soon lose my hold on words, I feel: yet, before dinner, I only wanted talk gaiety other people. But thats the difficulty: not to be rubbed smoothed, jerked out into their light random gale[?]. Could one manage both, then one would be a writer. Or thats my feeling. And at the age of 53 I still struggle: & still, thank Heaven, feel the rush & the glory & the agony, & never get used to any of it. But I cant write this morning.

An easy shabby party though. Nessa & Duncan made to dine alone, as we were late: I promoted to the high table,—had my little compliment, which pleased me. What I liked was the affability & character of the old saw bones Tonks, for so I called him 30 years ago when he lunched at Gordon Square & was so severe on Nessa's pictures.[5] Now he was all kindness: & distinguished; & appreciative, & regretting Bloomsbury & the distance between us & Chelsea. Talked of G.M. & Steer—who was there in a clergymans collar: almost hidebound; entirely silent, like a log removed from the fire & stood on end. Prof. Brown slept in his chairman's

4. At the instigation of Sir William Rothenstein, a dinner to honour Ethel Walker, attended by some seventy of her admirers, was given at the Belgrave Hotel on 5 March 1935. Henry Tonks (1862-1935), who abandoned a career in medicine for painting, taught for nearly forty years at the Slade School in the University of London, where he was Professor of Fine Art, 1917-30. Sir C. J. Holmes (1868-1936) had been Director of the National Gallery from 1916-28. Charles Langbridge Morgan (1894-1958), author of the prize-winning novels *Portrait in a Mirror* (1929) and *The Fountain* (1932) was from 1921 on the editorial staff of *The Times*, of which he was principal dramatic critic from 1926-39; his wife, *née* Hilda Vaughan, was also a novelist.

5. See Virginia Stephen's 1905 diary (Berg), 24 March 1905: '... Nessa was in a state of great misery, awaiting Mr Tonks. So I sat in the studio & tried to comfort her ... At one Tonks came, a great raw boned man, with a cold bony face, prominent eyes, & a look of mingled severity & boredom. ... We talked valiantly but it was not easy work. Then he reviewed the pictures, with a good deal of criticism apparently, but also some praise.' (Vanessa had studied under Tonks at the Slade for a brief period the previous autumn.)

seat:[6] Ethel sat by him, silent, muttering in her hoarse voice, with her gnarled dirty fingers, & her hair coming down; then Holmes; Nothing could have been less formidable. A great crowd, & the Morgans as I say— he a fattish man with little pig eyes sunk: the nice respectable earnest successful ashamed of being successful man I imagined. I thought he had heard how I flung The Fountain out of the window: at any rate was a little obsequious. Then his wife came up—English dog eyed woman, brown candid simple. How they would love to dine alone, on a Friday, when Charles neednt go to a theatre. So I easily flood my empty room, if I wish. And then with the surly unhappy opinionative Adrian Daintrey in full evening dress to the Café Royal, which lacks the old romance; but I was glad to snatch a sight of it, & to wonder about life there, for a second. Not many artists, all flashy people who don't belong anywhere, Daintrey said.[7] How I laughed at Nessa & Duncan made to dine alone, & let in with the dessert. It was Duncan's fault for being so late coming in. And he slept during the drone of Brown's 84 year old soliloquy: he couldnt pull up or go on. And Tonks in his airy blue eyed way—he's grown very transparent—kept interrupting. And then Mrs MacColl, in her French accent called him to order.[8] And the dinner was very bad.

Monday 11 March

How I should like, I thought, some time on the drive up this afternoon, to write a sentence again! How delightful to feel it form & curve under my fingers! Since Oct. 16th I have not written one new sentence, but only copied & typed. A typed sentence somehow differs; for one thing it is formed out of what is already there: it does not spring fresh from the mind. But this copying must go on, I see, till August. I am only now in the first war scene: with luck I shall get to Ea. in Oxford Street before we go in May: & spend June & July on the grand orchestral finale.[9] Then in August I shall write again.

6. For Tonks's recollections of VW at the Walker dinner, see *The Life of Henry Tonks* (1939) by Joseph Hone, pp. 281-2: 'By great luck on my left sat Virginia Woolf... It is many years since I properly met her ... I can only describe her as enchanting, really good looking, with a smile that was delicious.' The writer George Moore (1852-1933) and the painter Philip Wilson Steer, OM (1860-1942) were among Tonks's closest friends; Frederick Brown (1851-1941) preceded him as Slade Professor of Fine Art.
7. Adrian Daintrey (b. 1902), painter friend of Duncan's, had studied at the Slade.
8. Andrée (d. 1945) was the French wife of the painter-critic-administrator D. S. MacColl (1858-1948), both of them very old friends of Tonks.
9. The episode of Eleanor Pargiter in Oxford Street was one of the "two enormous chunks" eliminated by VW in her final revision of *The Years*; it is reprinted by Grace Radin in the *Bulletin of the New York Public Library*, Winter 1977.

It was the bitterest Sunday for 22 years: we went down [*to Rodmell*] (there was a little skirmish between us, for when I saw the snow falling I said, what about putting it off? At this L. was I thought unduly annoyed; so that we went—but Lord what a quarrel most old married couples would have made of it: & it turned to a candid joke before we were half angry). Then on Sunday we went to Sissinghurst: in the bitter wind with the country all lying in its June green & blue outside the window. Now thats an odd observation I have to make. My friendship with Vita is over. Not with a quarrel, not with a bang, but as ripe fruit falls. No I shant be coming to London before I go to Greece, she said. And then I got into the car. But her voice saying "Virginia?" outside the tower room was as enchanting as ever. Only then nothing happened. And she has grown very fat, very much the indolent county lady, run to seed, incurious now about books; has written no poetry; only kindles about dogs, flowers, & new buildings. S[issinghurs]t is to have a new wing; a new garden; a new wall. Well, its like cutting off a picture: there she hangs, in the fishmongers at Sevenoaks, all pink jersey & pearls; & thats an end of it.[10] And there is no bitterness, & no disillusion, only a certain emptiness. In fact—if my hands werent so cold—I could here analyse my state of mind these past 4 months, & account for the human emptiness by the defection of Vita; Roger's death; & no-one springing up to take their place; & a certain general slackening of letters & fame, owing to my writing nothing; so that I have more time on my hands, & actually ask people to come here now & again. (But the week fills unbidden mostly). On the other hand, I have been less harassed; & have enjoyed reading again, more, I think than for 2 or 3 years past. I have read myself to a standstill in the F.Q.: & shall not press the mood till it returns naturally: I am reading Chateaubriand; & to my joy find I can read an Italian novel for pleasure, currently, easily. Yes, this is all very peaceful & profound, & I like it. But again I am harassed by the thought that Nessa will now take to abroad again—she's off in a week or two to Italy; &—what else? No, on the whole, save for a desire to break L. of his 'habits', I am content to let things alone. I have been to a great many picture shows lately too: to the Nat Gall.; & thats a new picture which I should like to develop among my adumbrations. The truth is, ideas for other books are beginning to stir under the slab of The Pargiters.

Coming back in the snowstorm from Vita's: the snow was like long ribbons of paper; whipping, mixing, getting entangled in front of the car.

Saturday 16 March

I have had 3 severe swingeings lately: Wyndham Lewis; Mirsky; & now

10. Cf *III VW Diary*, 21 December 1925: '—she shines in the grocers shop in Sevenoaks with a candle lit radiance, stalking on legs like beech trees, pink glowing, grape clustered, pearl hung.'

Swinnerton. Bloomsbury is ridiculed; & I am dismissed with it.[11] I didnt read W.L.; & Swinnerton only affected me as [a] robin affects a rhinoceros —except in the depths of the night. How resilient I am; & how fatalistic now; & how little I mind, & how much; & how good my novel is; & how tired I am this morning; & how I like praise; & how full of ideas I am; & Tom & Stephen came to tea, & Ray [Strachey] & William [Plomer] dine; & I forgot to describe my interesting talk with Nessa about my criticising her children; & I left out—I forget what.

My head is numb today & I can scarcely read Osbert on Brighton, let alone Dante. Why did Heinemann send me S[winner]ton? to hurt me? And that does hurt 2 seconds. And Rebecca West did answer yesterday, & signs yours ever, & had been ill, & no secretary, so thats done with. And its a warm day, & I wont remind L. that we might have gone to Rodmell. Where shall we go? How happy I am. Tom's writing a play about T a Becket to be acted in Cy Cathedral. Asks us to tea—very easy & honest & kind to Stephen. Said he wrote the last verses of W[aste].L[and]. in a trance—unconsciously. Said he could not like poetry that had no meaning for the ear. Read lacking in sensuality. Poor Stephen so hurt by reviews of Vienna that he told Tom to withdraw it. Tom advises him to abstain from poetry for a time. Stephen generously praised Day Lewis. Grown heavier, less self-confident. And thats all I can twitter (Swinnerton's word for me—but then he admires Mary Webb) this morning. Brighton forward.[12]

In last weeks Time & Tide St John Ervine called Lytton "that servile minded man . . . . that Pandar" or words to that effect.[13] I'm thinking

11. For Wyndham Lewis's attack, see above, 11, 14 October 1934. Prince Mirsky's Marxist analysis of Bloomsbury occurs in his book *The Intelligentsia of Great Britain*, published in an English translation early in 1935; for the relevant excerpt see *M&M*, pp. 346-350. Frank Swinnerton (b. 1884), novelist, critic, and publisher's reader; his survey, *The Georgian Literary Scene* (1935), published by Heinemann, has a section devoted to VW (part of which is reprinted in *M&M*, pp. 356-58) in Chapter XIII: 'Bloomsbury'.

12. *Brighton* (1935), by Osbert Sitwell and Margaret Barton. T. S. Eliot's play *Murder in the Cathedral* was commissioned in 1934 for the Canterbury Festival, and was first performed in the Chapter House of the cathedral there in May 1935. Stephen Spender's long poem *Vienna*, an attempt to relate public feeling about Fascism to his own private life, had been published late in 1934 by Eliot's firm Faber & Faber. For Swinnerton on the novelist Mary Webb (1881-1927), author of *Precious Bane* &c, see *op cit*, pp. 327-9.

13. See 'The Society of Friends', a review by St John Ervine of *John Bright and the Quakers* by J. Travis Mills in *Time and Tide*, 9 March 1935: 'It was his belittlement of his intellectual and spiritual superiors which endeared that slave-minded man, Lytton Strachey, to the pigmies who loathe those who surpass them. . . . Strachey was the Pandar of his time.'

whether, if I write about Roger, I shall include a note, a sarcastic note, on the Bloomsbury baiters. No, I suppose not. Write them down—thats the only way.

Monday 18 March

The only thing worth doing in this book is to stick it out: stick to the idea, & dont lower it an inch, in deference to anyone. Whats so odd is the way the whole thing dissolves in company: & then comes back with a rush; & Swinnerton's sneers, & Mirsky's—making me feel that I'm hated & despised & ridiculed—well, this is the only answer: to stick to my ideas. And I wish I need never read about myself, or think about myself, anyhow till its done, but look firmly at my object & think only of expressing it. Oh what a grind it is embodying all these ideas, & having perpetually to expose my mind, opened & intensified as it is by the heat of creation to the blasts of the outer world. If I didn't feel so much, how easy it would be to go on—

[Wednesday 20 March]

Having just written a letter about Bloomsbury I cannot control my mind enough to go on with the P.s. I woke in the night & thought of it. But whether to send it or not, I dont know. But now I *must* think of something else. Julian & Helen [Anrep] last night. Helen much improved by her loss. Sweeter, softer, more sympathetic. We talked—I forget—easily enough, about Ha. Helen anti Ha, naturally. And Julian was twitchy but amiable. A hot spring day. Desmond rang up, asking us to dine.

L. advised me *not* to send the letter. And after 2 seconds I see he is right. It is better he says to be able to say we dont answer. But we suggest a comic guide to Bloomsbury by Morgan & he nibbles.

Thursday 21 March

Too jaded again to tackle that very difficult much too crowded raid chapter. In fact I am on the verge of the usual headache—for one thing yesterday was such a scramble—I walked so many miles, talked so much difficult political French with a man called Malraux up at Hampstead; having first gone to Q.'s private view; the usual mincing & demurring: smart young men; little Robertson whom I met at the Fishers: Clive in his blue suit; Benita in her tight black: & then the constraint with Nessa about her sons art—as usual: am I too critical? Why this difficulty in praising? Bought nothing. Couldn't think: walked in the hot sun through the Parks to W[estminste]r. Took Bus up to Hampstead; stood all the way.[14] Crowded dining room. M[alraux]. the fluent idealogical foreigner. Stephen Spender, Read—other unknowns. Exalted to a kind of eminence among this rag tag. Listened. To be a conference, of artists, in June. Paris in June—oh, too tired to note even this, so how can I tackle fiction? Rodmell tomorrow—thank goodness.

[*Friday 22 March*]

I have resolved to leave that blasted Chapter here, & do nothing at Rodmell. Yet, as I see, I cannot read; my mind is all tight like a ball of string. A most unpleasant variety of headache; but I think, soon over. Only a little change needed. Not a real bad headache. Why make this note? Because reading is beyond me, & writing is like humming a song. But what a worthless song! And it is the spring. Ethel last night—dear old woman, so wise in her way; but her voice is like a needle stabbing stuff. And so I got more tight wound than ever. But still I felt, she is generous & ample—a note to make for her portrait.

Monday 25 March

Last night at Nessa's, talk all very chippy & choppy with Clive oddly inattentive, & a sense of unreality, & a great desire for Roger. Again the sense of him coming in with his great dark eyes, & his tie pin & his brown shoes & how, speaking in that very deep voice he would have discussed Max Eastman & Epstein.[15] We only flick the surface—some means of communication—some other instrument needed to combine us all in harmony. Stories that would have amused him. How he wd have laughed at Nessa's [*lost*] story of the party at Lady Harris's when they had the lantern slides of the tigers. And all would have been deepened, & made suggestive. But never mind. This is inevitable, & we must blow on the bellows. So I tried to be nice about Quentin. And this morning, in spite of being in a rage, I wrote the whole of that d—d chapter again, in a spasm of desperation & I think got it right, by breaking up, the use of

14. The private view of an exhibition of *collages* by Quentin Bell and photographs by Curtis Moffat was at the Mayor Gallery, Cork Street, on 20 March. (VW bought a picture later: see *V VW Letters*, no. 3007.) 'Little Robertson' was probably Ian Gow Robertson, who was appointed to the staff of the Ashmolean Museum, Oxford, in 1931. VW went up to Hampstead to a meeting at Romney's House, the home of Amabel and Clough Williams-Ellis (see below, 5 June 1935), called to engage support for an International Congress of Writers 'in Defence of Culture' to be held in Paris in June, of which the French communist writer André Malraux (1901-79) was the effective organiser.

15. The topical subjects under discussion were Max Eastman's book *Artists in Uniform* (1934)—in effect a protest against the regimentation of art and letters in the Soviet Union—and Jacob Epstein's colossal carving 'Behold the Man' in the exhibition of his sculpture at the Leicester Galleries in March 1935.

thought skipping, & parentheses. Anyhow thats the hang of it. And I cut from 20 to 30 pages.

Tuesday 26 March

A very nice dinner at MacCarthy's last night. Desmond flung the door open & almost kissed me. But thats not our formula. So glad to see us—He looks firmer & pinker. And there was Hope & Dermod & Molly gay & amiable & not so deaf. And we talked of America. Very kind, quite untaught. D. never allowed to pay. He had enjoyed himself immensely. only netted £150 though.[16] And he was concerned about the attacks on Lytton & says Swinnerton has a grudge because he is selfmade. This had annoyed him more than us (a vindication of me is in the Times this morning; so we score of course by being attacked & saying nothing.[17]) Molly as I say affectionate, very happy & prosperous all the M[acCarthy]s. I think: Dermod now a doctor, a weak looking but somehow alert & alive young man, discussing germs with L.; Hope on a diet of course. He put matches on the floor to represent germs. I couldn't burrow into Desmond as Molly had to be supplied. Dear me, friendship is a very happy thing. And nothing needs to be said. And   I forget—We took Hope to her little Close, behind the Oratory, like a scene in the Meistersingers. We discussed the case of Harry Norton; the effect of discouragement—what D[esmond]. calls Almhousing—the wish he has to retire & live on tea & bread alone in obscurity. But I said something always turns up, which is true. He had been lunching with Austen Chamberlain, who says Germany can only be treated like a slave: wont contemplate giving her anything. Patriotism is the devil—yes.[18]

Wednesday 27 March

I see I am becoming a regular diariser. The reason is that I cannot make the transition from Pargiters to Dante without some bridge. And this

16. Desmond MacCarthy had recently returned from a lecture tour in America, where in six weeks' stay he had given several lectures at Eastern Universities.
17. Swinnerton (in *The Georgian Literary Scene*, p. 356) had written that Bloomsbury 'is full of what Desmond MacCarthy . . . calls "alert, original men and women" and what I call ill-mannered and pretentious dilletanti.' The anonymous *Times* reviewer of his book wrote (26 March 1935) that Swinnerton 'fails to understand her [VW]', and that 'Towards her . . . and others he is inspired by such a democratic resentment that his previously clear discernment becomes fogged.'
18. Hope Mirrlees lived with her mother at 1 Thurloe Close, opposite Brompton Oratory. Harry Norton had for many years been a source of concern to his friends, his depression and feelings of inadequacy undermining his brilliant gifts. Sir Austen Chamberlain (1863-1937), MP and influential Francophile elder statesman of the Conservatives; VW had met him in her youth when George Duckworth acted as his unpaid private secretary.

cools my mind. I am rather worried about the raid chapter: afraid if I compress & worry that I shall spoil. Never mind. Forge ahead, & see what comes next. Lydia also interrupted, carrying a copy of Mirsky in her hand, very abusive of him. She is going to write and tell him that she thinks him a dirty little cad. She cannot come to meet the Morgans, as they are off for Easter to Charleston. So thats on us.

Yesterday we went to the Tower, which is an impressive murderous bloody grey raven haunted military barrack prison dungeon place; like the prison of English splendour; the reformatory at the back of history; where we shot & tortured & imprisoned. Prisoners scratched their names, very beautifully, on the walls. And the crown jewels blazed, very tawdry, & there were the orders, like Spinks or a Regent St jewellers. And we watched the Scots Guards drill; & an officer doing a kind of tiger pace up & down—a wax faced barbers block officer trained to a certain impassive balancing. The sergeant major barked & swore. All in a hoarse bark: the men stamped & wheeled like—machines: then the officer also barked: all precise inhuman, showing off—a degrading, a stupifying sight, but in keeping with the grey wall the cobbles the executioner's block. People sitting on the river bank among old cannon. Ships &c. Very romantic: a dungeon like feeling.

So home & Elizabeth Read & Denny suddenly appeared. To have a child in August, very pretty, genuine, high principled. Talked about herself, Denny, his debts, his Dutch wife, how he is insurance agent, drives an old car about Yorkshire. They live in rooms at Sheffield, have a cottage at Caradoc. I liked her—an odd wisp, truculent, courageous, to be blown across. He a classical scholar, but a 'mut'. Cant sleep or eat. But they are going to mend matters by having a child.

Thursday 28 March

Another bridge between P.s & Dante. But I think I have actually done the Raid this morning. A nice quiet evening last night, L. at his Mit[?]; & I sitting reading over the fire. Nobody came for once. So that there is no call to make a note—unless to remind myself of the domestic atmosphere at the M[acCarthy]s: Desmond as father: the sense of other lives growing & changing. I am bothered by tomorrows dinner though. Cant get anyone to meet the Morgans, yet fight shy of a solitary evening, wrongly perhaps. Raymond going to the Grand National. William has the flu. But this is not much of a roseleaf under the pillow after all. Spring triumphant. Crocuses going over. Daffodils & hyacinths out. Some chestnut leaves in the birds claw stage in the park. The country trees & Square trees bare still. Little bushes all green. I want to make vegetable notes for my book. How soft & springy & fresh the air was yesterday—like the sea! And I think of being abroad. But we have not yet decided where to go.

Saturday 30 March[19]

Charles Morgans to dinner last night. Nessa, Duncan & [John] Graham in afterwards. Not an alarming pair, the Ms. He rather sunk eyed & official: she—oh how she interrupted! Vague, vapid, well meaning. Oh but Charles you must tell them the Hancock story—Charles you mustn't be modest &c. We were talking about the Navy: Charles wrote a book showing up the bullying of midshipmen.[20] How they were made to do "evolutions" 4 nights out of 7. Evolutions meant jumping over chairs & being beaten. Then they drank with the beaters; were then beaten again. Those who are not virgins must report that they have had such & such women of the town by Saturday. One of them wrote it in his diary, sent it to his parson father, who reported to the Admiralty. They appealed to his patriotism. He threatened to go to Carmelite House [*Daily Mail*]: there was an enquiry & his son resigned. Morgan a well meaning cultivated egoist, little sunk eyes '[*word illegible*]' like Jowitt. Lives on a plan so as to get as much out of himself as possible. Bed at 2, after the play. Breakfast at 9 in bed: writes novels from 4 to 7. So it goes on, & The Fountain is the result. Occasionally a light came in his sunk eyes; about the Dreadnought for example; but he is colourless & pale like one of the D. of Newcastle's horses.[21] She's flyaway, visualises, sees, where Charles, if theyre walking in a wood, remembers—I walked here once. Charles' father built Victoria Station & showed Charles a picture of Chatterton to dissuade him from poetry. Must have a profession & write at leisure. So at 11 he chose the Navy. Then went to Walkley, was made his understudy on the Times: will there remain, hoarding his novel money for his children. One's 8, the other 10. A very well meaning honourable but sunken man.[22] Graham roared with laughter when they left & said Mrs

19. VW has dated this *Sat. 28th March*.
20. Morgan joined the navy as a cadet in 1907; he resigned in 1913 but rejoined in 1914 for the duration of the war. His first book *The Gunroom* (1919), which took its theme from the ill-treatment he and his fellow midshipmen suffered in HMS *Good Hope*, caused a considerable stir.
21. 'The Dreadnought Hoax'—in which VW had participated—was a practical joke played on the Royal Navy in 1910; see *I QB*, pp. 157-61. An ancestor of Lady Ottoline Morrell's, William Cavendish, 1st Duke of Newcastle (1592-1676), in exile during the Commonwealth, developed a breed of cream-coloured Barbary horses and a celebrated riding school in Antwerp which, after the Restoration, he established at Welbeck.
22. Sir Charles Langbridge Morgan (1855-1940) was chief engineer of the London, Brighton and South Coast Railway, 1896-1917; the complete reconstruction of the Brighton side of Victoria Station was undertaken under his direction. Thomas Chatterton (1752-70), poet and forger, reduced to despair by poverty, poisoned himself with arsenic (Henry Wallis's celebrated picture of the subject is in the Tate Gallery). Charles Morgan became dramatic critic for *The Times* on the death of A. B. Walkley (1855-1926), who had held the post since 1900.

Morgan was the image of John Braddock's wife [*unidentified*]. Very red & young: has shaven his beard; talked to Nessa.

Saturday 30 March

Some chestnut trees in the Park just coming out. Small leaves.[23]

Sunday 31 March

Tea with Tom yesterday. A small angular room, with the district railway on one side, Cornwall Gardens on the other.[24] A great spread; rolls in frills of paper. A dark green blotting paper wall paper, & books rather meagre, stood on top of each other; bookcases with shelves missing. Not a lovely room. A coloured print from an Italian picture. Nothing nice to look at. Purple covers. Respectable china "A present" said Tom; he was perched on a hard chair. I poured out tea. There was Mrs Munro, a handsome swarthy Russian looking woman in a black astrachan cap. And it was heavy going. All about cars; the jubilee;[25] publishing; a German boy; a little literary gossip; feet conscientiously planting themselves in the thick sand; & I not liking to go too soon, & so sitting till we were all glad when Mrs M. got up, & Tom was glad, & showed us his bedroom—a section, getting the railway under it. "I forgot to ask you to drink sherry" he said, pointing to sherry & glasses on the bedroom window sill. A pallid very cold experience. He stood on the steps—it is the Kensington Rectory & he shares a bath with curates. The hot water runs very slowly. Sometimes he takes the bath prepared for the curates. A large faced pale faced man—our great poet. And no fire burning in any of us. I discover a certain asperity in him towards the woman[?]—a priestly attitude. Here he gets warmed up a little. But the decorous ugliness, the maid in cap & apron, the embroidered cloth, the ornamental kettle on the mantelpiece all somehow depressed me. And as I say it was a bitter cold day & we have seen too many literary gents. How heavenly to sleep over the fire! Tom's was a gas fire.

A long letter from Vita, by the way, about Ethel's attack on her.[26]

23. This note is on the page opposite the end of the last entry.
24. T. S. Eliot lived from 1934 until 1940 at 9 Grenville Place, Cromwell Road, the home of Father Eric Cheetham, Vicar of St Stephen's Church, Gloucester Road, of which Eliot was Vicar's Warden, 1934-59.
25. Alida Monro, *née* Klementaski (d. 1969), second wife and widow of Harold Monro of the Poetry Bookshop. 1935 was the year of the Silver Jubilee of King George V and Queen Mary, 6 May being the anniversary of his accession in 1910.
26. Vita's letter (MHP, Sussex) dated 28 March, reports that 'out of the blue' Ethel Smyth had accused her and Gwen St Aubyn of 'leading a rotten life.' See also *V VW Letters*, nos. 3002, 3003, 3004.

She asks me why? Happily I can truthfully say I told her not to write. At the same time I agree with Ethel's opinion of that menage more than I like (see whichever page it is). And I think E. though V. tries to think her absurd, has said something true, in her violent unnecessary way. But whats the use?

Monday 1 April

At this rate I shall never finish the Purgatorio. But whats the use of reading with half ones mind running on Eleanor & Kitty. Oh that scene wants compacting. Its too thin run. But I shall finish it before I go away. We think of 3 weeks in Holland & France: a week in Rome, flying there. We went to Kew yesterday, & if vegetable notes are needed, this is to signify that yesterday was the prime day for cherry blossom pear trees, & magnolia. A lovely white one with black cups to the flowers: another purple tinted, just falling. Another & another. And the yellow bushes & the daffodils in the grass. So to walk through Richmond—a long walk by the ponds. I verified certain details. And it was 5.30 when we got back —a soft lovely day; & then I read some MSS & we had out maps, & discussed the holiday & Mabel came in & said she had sat for 2 hours in the Piccadilly [Lyons] corner house, watching people & listening to the band. Many people do this, she said. They sit on & on, eating as slowly as possible. She was ashamed how long they had sat. But then they take a long time to bring things she said.

A letter of thanks & admiration from Mrs Morgan this morning. And I gather from Judith that poor old Ann has not passed.

Tuesday 2 April

But poor old Ann has not only passed, but won a minor scholarship: Judith was only indulging in chaff. We had Ann to dinner & took her to Bengal Lancers: but the virility & empire building bored her.[1] She thinks for herself, or has the youthful point of view naturally that we acquired through satire. She was not satirical, merely bored—a good sign, if she is representative.

And it was a very cold day: & I read, in this room; & was glad not to pace the streets. I have now Enid Bagnold's rather (I suspect) meretricious & much applauded book to read [National Velvet]. Whats wrong with it? My nose is sniffing already. A letter of warm gratitude— why?—from Vita: says I AM a good friend, & have never failed her.

1. Ann Stephen was awarded the Caroline Turle Scholarship at Newnham, where from 1935-38 she read Natural Sciences and Physiology. The Woolfs took her to see Gary Cooper in the 'Jubilee Year's Greatest Film', *Lives of a Bengal Lancer*, at the Carlton Cinema, Haymarket.

Some muddle I dont fathom altogether, but suspect Gwen & St. John between them have fuddled poor old V.'s not very well founded head. Rather a lesson, not to write angry letters.

And does Louie cheat? A bill for a chicken that we had at Christmas again throws doubt on her. We must have it out about the milk this week. Not a week I want altogether. Angelica's concert on Thursday: a [*Labour Party*] meeting at Rodmell. Leonard's jury again put off.

Friday 5 April

Angelica's last concert yesterday in a snowstorm. And we took the wrong turning & went in the sleet almost to Southend. Snow falling all the time across the dark yew trees. And not a very rich performance. Angelica acting. Judith reciting French with a perfect accent, mothers in the drawing room. A great tea. Mrs Curtis opulent. The usual things—& so home in the cold—Duncan asleep.[2]

L. dined at the Cranium & met James who says he means, owing to Swinnerton & other attacks, to set about a very long life of Lytton with all the letters; & he wishes to 'lay it down' that what he wants is that I should write a character of Lytton as introduction. Lytton & Roger—so my work as a biographer is cut out— I wonder. But I'm glad, I think, that there should be a full & outspoken life. Only not as a reply to criticism. And then the buggery? But it will take James a long time. The usual heartless, cold day & we go to Rodmell. And I'm tired of writing; yet must press on & do this difficult chapter; which I shall get done before we go—to Holland we think on May 1st—3 weeks & 4 days. Oh to sit in the sun & let my mind browse!

Monday 8 April

A week end of almost incessant conversation: first Mr Hancock on Wormwood Scrubs; then Maynard on the New Statesman.[3] Both were full of interest—but oh dear, how I grudge the silent evening reading gone! And it rains & rains. Came home in the rain, dined with Helen in the rain; went to Clive's: rain pouring down when we drove Nessa back. All sat in Clive's little room, as Angelica was in the big room. Talk of Dorothea & of the Statesman. Duncan snapping viciously at Kingsley.

2. The Woolfs drove Duncan and Vanessa to Langford Grove School, near Chelmsford, which Angelica was leaving after 5½ years; her friend Judith (b. 1918) was Barbara Bagenal's eldest child.

3. The Lewes Constituency parliamentary candidate F. R. Hancock was the speaker at the Rodmell Labour Party meeting on Friday 5 April; the following day the Woolfs had tea with the Keyneses at Tilton.

Duncan when he's angry snaps. Nessa is terrifically monolithic & imperious—a terrifying woman in her way. And I almost laughed myself sick over Dorothea.[4] And it was slightly empty as usual—but why? Without Roger, I suppose: & we're all so formal & going abroad for weeks— Clive so unintimate nowadays. We must ask him to dinner in June.

And it is pelting on my skylight, & the rain has come through the roof, & I am rather jangled writing this restaurant chapter, & wish we could sit in the sun, & wish I were a more solid & capable woman; & yet manage to cut along. Here's Boulestin asking us to lunch—must I go? What an effort.[5] Helen with her children rather ineffective but alive; the 2 gawks chattering easily

Tuesday 9 April

I met Morgan in the London Library yesterday & flew into a passion.

"Virginia, my dear" he said. I was pleased by that little affectionate familiar tag.

"Being a good boy & getting books on Bloomsbury?" I said.

"Yes. You listen. Is my book down?" he asked Mr Mannering.

"We were just posting it" said Mr M.

"And Virginia, you know I'm on the Co[mmi]ttee here" said Morgan. "And we've been discussing whether to allow ladies—

It came over me that they were going to put me on: & I was then to refuse: Oh but they do—I said. There was Mrs Green . . .

"Yes yes—there was Mrs Green. And Sir Leslie Stephen said, never again. She was so troublesome. And I said, havent ladies improved? But they were all quite determined. No no no, ladies are quite impossible. They wouldnt hear of it."[6]

See how my hand trembles. I was so angry (also very tired) standing. And I saw the whole slate smeared. I thought how perhaps M. had

4. The personality of Vanessa and VW's cousin Dorothea Jane Stephen (1871-1965), a 'virtuous female with Anglican propensities' (Leslie Stephen), was often a topic in family talk.
5. The Frenchman Xavier Marcel Boulestin (c. 1878-1943), writer, designer, and restaurateur, a participant since pre-war days in London's cultural life, owned the Covent Garden restaurant which still bears his name; Mabel attended cookery classes there. See *VI VW Letters*, no. 3007a, declining his invitation.
6. George Ernest Manwaring (1882-1939) was Assistant Librarian at the London Library (and a naval historian). Alice Stopford Green (1847-1929), wife and collaborator of the historian J. R. Green, author of *A Short History of the English People* (1874). Leslie Stephen succeeded Tennyson as President of the London Library in 1892; 'Widow Green' served on the library committee for many years; by 1900, when he agreed to her request to edit her husband's letters, Leslie Stephen wrote: 'I have come to think better of her.' (*Mausoleum Book*, p. 108).

mentioned my name, & they had said no no no: ladies are impossible. And so I quieted down & said nothing & this morning in my bath I made up a phrase in my book on Being Despised which is to run—a friend of mine, who was offered . . . . . one of those prizes—for her sake the great exception was to be made—who was in short to be given an honour—I forget what— . . She said, And they actually thought I would take it. They were, on my honour, surprised, even at my very modified & humble rejection. You didnt tell them what you thought of them for daring to suggest that you should rub your nose in that pail of offal? I remarked. Not for a hundred years, she observed. And I will bring in M. Pattison:[7] & I will say sympathy uses the same force required to lay 700 bricks. And I will show how you cant sit on Ctees if you also pour out tea—that by the way Sir L.S. spent his evenings with widow Green; yes, these flares up are very good for my book: for they simmer & become transparent: & I see how I can transmute them into beautiful clear reasonable ironical prose. God damn Morgan for thinking I'd have taken that . . . And dear old Morgan comes to tea today, & then sits with Bessy [Trevelyan] who's had cataract.

The veil of the temple—which, whether university or cathedral, was academic or ecclesiastical I forget—was to be raised, & as an exception she was to be allowed to enter in. But what about my civilisation? For 2,000 years we have done things without being paid for doing them. You cant bribe me now.

Pail of offal? No; I said ⟨I was a⟩ while very deeply appreciating the hon. . . . In short one must tell lies, & apply every emollient in our power to the swollen ⟨& inflamed⟩ skin of our brothers so terribly inflamed vanity. Truth is only to be spoken by those women whose fathers were pork butchers & left them a share in the pig factory.

Friday 12 April

This little piece of rant wont be very intelligible in a years time. Yet there are some useful facts & phrases in it. I rather itch to be at that book. But I have been skirmishing round a headache, & cant pull my weight in the morning. It is now almost settled that we shall drive through Holland & Germany, concealing Leonard's nose, to Rome; & so back. A giant tour on our most heroic scale. Indeed, L. has just been in to say that we have to have the car tested this afternoon; also that the first of the spring flowers is up—Mr Brace, alas. Day after day is thus blotted out.

7. Mark Pattison (1813-1884), Rector of Lincoln College, Oxford: 'For many years he was a member of the committee of the London Library, and regularly attended its meetings. But he was singularly inefficient on a board or committee. . . .' (*DNB*).

Last night I dined with Nessa, L. being at Kingsley's to hear the story of his divided mind.[8] He cant make up his mind, & must display the separated parts, like a heaving oyster, to his friends. Sometimes thinks he is going mad. Everybody turns him. He makes up his mind to refuse Aberystwyth with Maynard: in comes Gerald Barry, pours scorn on journalism, K. seizes the telephone, rings up A.; says Is there still time to put my name forward? Next day the horror of A. descends on him. Goes to a psycho-analyst. Goes to Scilly Islands with his father, meets the Arnold-Forsters—rings us up at 9 this morning; wants Cleano. Meanwhile Olga threatens divorce or claims it—I forget which—& loves another, & is rejected & lives in Fitzroy Square. But I sat over the stove with Nessa & Duncan musing & rambling & discussing old Desmond's passions for American ladies—which is the reason why Molly seeks Freiburg for six months. And they were making plates on a new system, & off today to Stoke on Trent, & so Angelica dines here—a talented youngster the Star calls her, in a paragraph that seems founded on fact.[9]

A wild wet spring. I had the courage to wear my silver corduroy. Lord, what a shivering coward I am—but not as a writer. No. I stick to that by way of compensation.

Desmond received a deputation of his children in his room the other day to ask him to give up his love, for Molly's sake. Upon which he said, that he thought he could assure them that it was the beginning of the end. The spit & image of Mr Micawber, as Nessa says. L. much upset by the inefficiency of electric lamps. I bought one at the Stores yesterday, for my travels, & it is too small to take an ordinary bulb. This is the kind of thing that genuinely annoys L. But I am merely running on, in order to waste the precious morning.

Saturday 13 April

Poor Kingsley Martin almost in tears on the telephone this morning—cant make up his mind—certainly gives me an added sense of power & happiness.

8. In February 1934 Kingsley Martin had been offered the Chair of International Relations at Aberystwyth (University of Wales); he refused the offer, but the University held it open in the hope that he would change his mind. He was still considering the matter as late as September 1936. See *Kingsley* (1973) by C. H. Rolph, pp. 205-7. Gerald Barry (1898-1968), journalist and editor, was on the Board of Directors of the *NS&N*.
9. Duncan Grant and Vanessa Bell had been invited by a commercial firm to prepare designs on blank dinner ware which were then reproduced in the Potteries; they had included a design by Angelica, which was utilised. The results were shown in an exhibition 'Modern Art for the Table' at Harrods the previous October; and further collaboration between the artists and the industry was afoot.

Sunday 14 April

Let me make a note that it would be much wiser not to attempt to sketch a draft of On Being Despised, or whatever it is to be called, until the P.s is done with. I was vagrant this morning & made a rash attempt, with the interesting discovery that one cant propagate at the same time as write fiction. And as this fiction is dangerously near propaganda, I must keep my hands clear.

Its true I'm half asleep, after the Zoo & Willy [Robson]. But he threw some coals on my fire: the horror of the legal profession: its immense wealth; its conventions: a Royal Comn. now sitting—its hidebound hoariness, & so on; worth going into one of these days; & the medical profession & the osteopaths—worth a fling of laughter. But oh dear, not now.[10] Now for Alfieri & Nash & other notables: so happy I was reading alone last night. We saw the great dumb fish at the Zoo, & the Gorillas. Storms of rain, cloud: & I read Annie S. Swan on her life with considerable respect. Almost always this comes from Au[tobiograph]y: a liking, at least some imaginative stir: for no doubt her books, which she cant count, & has no illusions about, but she cant stop telling stories, are wash, pigs, hogs—any wash you choose. But she is a shrewd capable old woman.[11]

Monday 15 April

Not a very nice last meeting at Nessa's last night, because L. suddenly turned stony in the way I know: & cut up rusty, when we got back, ostensibly because I suggested staying not 7 days but 10 in Rome. I suppose it was the old family grievance moling again; throwing up sudden hills. But this is all silly rot, I said, as I waited for him to come & he didn't come; so went in & laughed. The truth is he had spent the whole morning filling up forms for our journey—which, I say, I could have done; & then I upset his plans in favour of my family, & stayed talking. And he had 2 hours of Willy: & is tired. And come to think of it, we're both very happy. I shall be glad when we can stretch a little at Monks House, & needn't meet Bells & so start moling. By way of reward for my sweetness of temper—but what does L. think of my temper? my book went well today; I think it probably rather good.

Yesterday another defence of Bloomsbury by Ellis Roberts in the S.

10. A Royal Commission was appointed early in 1935 to consider the state of business in the King's Bench Division of the High Court, and to report whether reforms should be adopted with a view to greater dispatch.

11. VW's reading was the Italian dramatist Vittorio Alfieri (1749-1803); *John Nash, Architect to King George IV* (1935) by John Summerson; and *My Life* (1934) by the novelist Annie S. Swan (c. 1860-1943), daughter of a Scottish farmer.

Times: of me in particular (thanks I think to my 'charm' at Ottoline's;) I am the most original mind that has written novels in the past 20 years, & so on. Nessa is going to Cochran this morning about a new curtain for one of his shows, & I'm not jealous. But oh how nice to have all this done with for six weeks! Now to write a little Italian from Danaro. I will learn German next year.[12]

Wednesday 17 April

So the move, anyhow the Bell move, which heralds the flock, has begun: Angelica rushed in here at 1 yesterday with patterns for my clothes—such is her passion—and left her cap behind, & today—a fine day so far—they're off [to Rome]. Tomorrow we go to Rodmell, & when Brace, at 7, shut the door—no, I stood in the door—but slowly put on his coat, & made some very polite remark about seeing us in New York—when all this happened, I sank back & thought the holiday has begun. For I had been trying on a dress at Murray's, in the bitter cold wind. I counted 20 between one of Brace's words & the next; he has grown toad faced, but is all the same a decent long suffering man. Things looking up in America, so he said.

I forget—I had something in mind to write here, about 'the soul' perhaps. I'm jaded again, & can't go on rewriting. The book is to be sent to America in October: may be serialised—if so won't be out for a year. But I have still £990. Something about Spender's book had I in mind? To jot down a few notes on it. No. about the soul. Breaking moulds. Coming out with views. A French article calls me the Fairy of Eng. lit. Odd how this fairy works then.[13]

The Wigrams a little defensive about Jews in Germany: want to come over & see us—Susie Buchan asks us to stay.[14] Now these painful visits are

12. R. Ellis Roberts' review, 'The Georgian Authors. Gaps in Mr Swinnerton's Picture', appeared in the *Sunday Times* on 14 April 1935; VW had talked to him at Ottoline's on 20 December 1934. The showman C. B. Cochran was recruiting talent from more serious artistic sources for his next revue, *Follow the Sun*, at the Adelphi; but Vanessa's curtain design was not used. 'Danaro': unidentified.

13. Stephen Spender's book, *The Destructive Element*—'a study of modern writers and beliefs'—was published on 29 April; he sent VW an advance copy (see *V VW Letters*, no. 3018). The 'French article' untraced.

14. In preparation for their intended drive through Nazi Germany to Italy, LW thought it advisable to consult a member of the Foreign Office, Ralph Follet Wigram (1890-1936) who, with his wife Ava, née Bodley (d. 1974), had a house at Southease. (See *IV LW*, pp. 185-6.) Susan Buchan, née Grosvenor (1882-1977), whose husband John Buchan was created 1st Baron Tweedsmuir in May 1935 on being appointed Governor-General of Canada; VW had known her since before marriage, and they had recently corresponded about the publication of her book (see *HP Checklist* 360, and *V VW Letters*, nos. 2953, 2980).

in fact the real breaking up of the soul: such a labour. And L. gets more & more addicted to solitude & astute—the old wretch—at finding good reasons for it. But then his hand trembles; mine doesnt—could I overcome the clothes fear. The soul—the soul— How far could I let myself go in an anti fascist pamphlet? I think of dashing off my professions for women, can I steal a moment between Roger Lytton & proofs. All this about being so distinguished & cultivated might be knocked on the head. In E[lvira]'s soliloquy I think I have tapped a new method of argument— very short & compact: but then this is spun out with description. The sun blazes: my skylight blue; no white tufted. I'm reading, or going to read, Alfieri, Chateaubriand, Paxton, Leo Myers; Barker & Moore poetry; so Easter will fly—oh to be alone with our fine York ham.[15] No, I've forgotten the soul.

Thursday 18 April

This is written with very dirty hands after tidying up. We go [to Rodmell] after lunch. But shall we be alone? I doubt it. I foresee Julian, Wigram & Kingsley Martin, who again rang up, is now inclined to go to A[berystwyth]: but L. bets that he will stay at the N.S. And he said—I listened in—Suppose I'm walking on the Downs, might I come & see you? Oh God, I thought, divining that he has a craving for our society— that is to talk about himself. "Or do you want to be alone?" L. who is his confessor, said, as confessors must, damn them, No do come. And physically he's so repulsive. A fineish sort of day. I bought a coffee mill at Fortnum yesterday, & going to look for lamps saw [Derrick] Leon, advising customers about fabrics in their wholly disgusting room, all strewn with luxury objects in the worst most opulent heartless brainless taste: women in black with white pearls & red lips. The atmosphere of a rich princely shop is not sympathetic. A kind of halfway house: a shop not a shop; shop people pseudo gentry: an attempt to seduce & coerce. The chimney lamp was 25/6 instead of ⟨19⟩ 18/9 as at the Stores. Six shillings to pay for lipstick & scent & carpets & the casual gentlemanly manners of Mr Marshall & the strew & the carelessness. I watched a gentleman selling Easter eggs with powder puffs, to the head buyer, who might have been Christabel.

And so home. And no one came, & that was one of Gods blessings. And I'm fidgetting, getting ready. Miss West doesnt get on with Belsher; is spending Easter at Folkestone, which she dislikes. But Miss Walton is going to Amsterdam.

15. The new books on VW's reading list were: *Paxton and the Bachelor Duke* by Paxton's grand-daughter Violet R. Markham; L. H. Myers' trilogy *The Root and the Flower*; *Poems* by George Barker, and *Selected Poems* by Marianne Moore, the latter introduced by T. S. Eliot, and both published this month by Faber & Faber.

Saturday 20 *April*

The scene has now changed to Rodmell, & I am writing at the table L. made (supported on a cushion,) & it is raining. Good Friday was a complete fraud—rain & more rain. I tried walking along the bank, & saw a mole, running on the meadow—it glides rather—is like an elongated guinea pig. Pinka went & nuzzled it, & then it managed to slide into a hole. At the same time through the rain I heard the cuckoo's song. Then I came home & read & read—Stephen Spender [*The Destructive Element*]; too quick to stop to think; shall I stop to think; read it again? It has considerable swing & fluency; & some general ideas; but peters out in the usual litter of an undergraduates table. Wants to get everything in & report and answer all the chatter. But I want to investigate certain questions: why do I always fight shy of my contemporaries? What is really the woman's angle? Why does so much of this seem to me in the air? But I recognise my own limitations: not a good ratiocinator, Lytton used to say. Do I instinctively keep my mind from analysing, which would impede its creativeness? I think there's something in that. No creative writer can swallow another contemporary. The reception of living work is too coarse & partial if youre doing the same thing yourself. But I admire Stephen for trying to grapple with these problems. Only of course he has to hitch them round—to use his own predicament as a magnet, & thus the pattern is too arbitrary; if you're not in his predicament. But as I say, I read it at a gulp without screwing my wits tight to the argument. This is a method I find very profitable: then go back & screw.

In the public world, there are emphatic scares. L. brings home a bunch after every Cttee meeting. Its odd how seldom I report them. One of these days they may come true. For instance, Toller says we are on the brink of war. Wants the allies to declare war on Hitler.[16] Belgium keeps its aeroplanes at active service level, all ready to rise into the air. But as Germany could be on them before they rose this seems useless. There is a dutiful perfunctory stir about the Jubilee. We have subscribed £3 towards buns & a bus shelter in Rodmell. It is a good excuse for buying what one wants. Piccadilly is marked with Venetian masts. Seats line all the main streets. The King is said to be almost comatose. Will he get through with his bowings? C. Morgan said he cant bend any longer. And—there are incessant conversations—Mussolini, Hitler, Macdonald. All these people incessantly arriving at Croydon, arriving at Berlin, Moscow, Rome; & flying off again—while Stephen & I think how to improve the world.

16. Ernst Toller (1893-1939), writer, socialist and former pacifist, was deprived of his citizenship and exiled when Hitler came to power. In 1933-36 he lived in London.

Monday 22 April, Bank Holiday

The Wigrams to tea; she in white checks, checked shoes, yellow curls, blue eyes, disappointed, embittered, growing old, growing fat, something like an old daisy or other simple garden flower; if a flower could look very unhappy. I suppose the deformed boy, & so on. He a cripple, with iron rods down one leg, hoisting himself about on a stick. This, I suppose, faintly disgusting physically to her. I suppose she lives with physical deformity. But she is too painted & powdered, too insipidly discontented. He is very white toothed, blue eyed, lean, red cheeked—a nice rigid honest public school Englishman. Started almost at once telling us about Hitler. He had been at Berlin with Simon.[17] Got there early & stood at the Embassy window watching the crowd. They clustered, & a policeman held up his hand, & they obediently fell back. No resistance. Then the conversations began. Hitler very impressive; very frightening. A large picture of the Madonna & Child & one of Bismarck. He has a great jowl like Bismarck. Made speeches lasting 20 minutes with out a failure. Very able. Only one mistake on a complicated point. Very well coached. And all the time a tapping sound. Wigram thought An odd day to have the masons in. But it was the sentry marching up & down the passage. Everything came out. We want . . . . We have a parity in the air already. The Germans in fact have enough aeroplanes ready to start to keep us under. But if they do kill us all? Well they will have their Colonies. I want room to move about Hitler said. Must be equal, & so on. A complete reversal to pre-war days. No ideals except equality, superiority, force, possessions. And the passive heavy slaves behind him, and he a great mould coming down on the brown jelly. Talks of himself as the regenerator, the completely equipped & powerful machine. Says outright, "If I had been in control during the war, things might have gone very differently." Wigram & the rest frightened. Anything may happen at any moment. Here in England we havent even bought our gas masks. Nobody takes it seriously. But having seen this mad dog, the thin rigid Englishmen are really afraid. And if we have only nice public schoolboys like W. to guide us, there is some reason I suppose to expect that Oxford Street will be flooded with poison gas one of these days. And what then? Germany will get her colonies.

And then we walked them round the garden, & they were, or said they were, envious & impressed. But as Mrs W. said to me, I am effusive. I was brought up in France. She has been used to listen to real talk—so she says: to buy clothes twice a year on the 9th March & Autumn, & then never to

17. Sir John Simon (1873-1954), Foreign Secretary 1931-35, and his successor Anthony Eden, then Lord Privy Seal, on what was described as a visit of exploration and enquiry, had talks with Hitler in Berlin on 25 and 26 March.

think of it again.—Here in London with my sisters of the Foreign Office she is, she says, bored, discontented, thinks of cutting the London season & staying at Southease; where, I fear, we shall now be frequently asked, to help with the garden.

And then Kingsley rang up & is now imminent. So I intend to walk.

Tuesday 23 April

Kingsley coming at eleven of our first fine morning & staying till 6 has completely taken away any power I may have over the art of fiction. In order to ensure myself 2 hours of silence & air I went off to Moggery Poke. I passed 2 really happy women sitting on the slope of Itford hill. As they smiled at me, I thought I would act the scene of Eleanor & the builder—went to them & said Did you speak? No they had not spoken. But they were very happy. I then went on—but it was a grey morning—to Moggery: & home by the river. And there was K. eating cold veal & sweeping up his cauliflower on his fork. An effusive slippery mind: always on the fizz: but how undistinguished! How without hardness or fineness of texture! & now of course all dissolved by personal anxieties into a chatter of egotism: "Is there anything more we can say about my affairs?" he remarked at 3. No, I said to myself, there is nothing more. For he had been flooding us with damp proof sheets—sticky with printers ink—all the morning. Should he stay or should he go? I could only amuse myself by probing the depths of his belief in the N.S. Directly I minimised its importance, he trotted out arguments to prove its immense value to the world. The only paper that tells the truth, the stay & bread of all the serious minded in Britain. Then, directly I'm alone with him, its his arthritis. True, he's not quite in his right mind; but how tiring this shambling through the hot sand is! & how undistinguished—well meaning, good hearted, I doubt not, but self obsessed; with no ear or eye; no reflective faculty & catching at any straw to float on; talking profusely; sociable because afraid of being alone; with no core of truth or substance in him; garrulous, untidy, slovenly; 'able' as they say, quick to snatch, a snapper up of trifles, uninteresting—yes, a profoundly uninteresting man. Yet, Aberystwith is ready to pay him £1000 a year: so he must have some merchantable quality. But it is like reading a living newspaper, talking to K. He is full of short snippets. And why so dull? He runs off my mind like a torrent of lukewarm water, but leaves it stained & tired. It is like listening to a perpetual leading article, so admirable, so well meaning, so shallow.

The Woolfs returned to Tavistock Square on 24 April.

Thursday 25 April

Whether it was Kingsley or not, the usual headache wings its way about me, rather like a fowl soaring & settling & giving me a peck in my back: clouding my mind. I think I have earned a headache & a holiday. But it remains cold. And I am not going to write a word of fiction till June 1st. Weak coffee, this morning, a badly cleaned fish; which L. visits upon the Cow, who cooked us an admirable dinner last night all the same. Must she go? An inveterate instinctive dislike on L.'s part, physical not rational. So cant be overcome. I can read Pirandello almost currently; but cant write. head begins protesting. I shall space my days quietly & buy clothes: no only shoes, I think.

Saturday 27 April

All desire to practise the art of a writer has completely left me. I cannot imagine what it would be like: that is, more accurately, I cannot curve my mind to the line of a book: no, nor of an article. Its not the writing but the architecting that strains. If I write this paragraph, then there is the next & then the next. But after a months holiday I shall be as tough & springy as—say heather root; & the arches & the domes will spring into the air as firm as steel & light as cloud—but all these words miss the mark.

Stephen Spender demands a letter of criticism; cant write it.[18] Nor can I describe with any certainty Mrs Collett, with whom both L. & I fell in love yesterday. A whippet woman: steel blue eyes; silver spotted jersey; completely free, edged, outspoken, the widow of the Lord Mayor's son, who was killed before her eyes flying. After that she broke down, & the only cure she said was to go to Hong Kong & stay with Bella.[19] From that we did not expect anything much, to tell the truth; whereas she ridiculed the Jubilee, the Lord Mayor & told us all about life in the Mansion House. The L.M. spends £20,000 out of his own pocket on his year of office; 10,000 on his sheriffdom; then buys an ermine coat for £1000 in which to admit the King to Temple Bar. It rains; the King flashes past, & the coat is spoilt. I dont like my father in law, she said; he doesnt do it at all well. Her mother in law is a perfectly natural sensible

---

18. Stephen Spender wrote from Vienna on 18 April 1935 (MHP, Sussex). For VW's prevaricating reply and later letter of criticism, see V VW Letters, nos. 3018, 3037.
19. The Woolfs met Mrs Collett at tea with LW's mother; her husband, Sqn. Ldr. S. B. Collett (1896-1934), Commandant of the City of London (No. 600) Squadron, was killed on 30 June 1934 when his plane crashed during an RAF air display at Hendon. His father, Sir Charles Collett, 1st Bt. (1864-1938), was Lord Mayor of London 1933-34. Bella Woolf's second husband, now Sir Thomas Southorn, was Colonial Secretary, and at times acting-Governor, in Hong Kong from 1926-36.

woman who goes buying fish with a bag. The Queen gave her as a token of esteem 2 huge shells, engraved with the story of George & the dragon. These mercifully are left at the M[ansion] House. The L.M. wears a dress that is heavy with bullion. A terrible state of display & ugliness—but she was so nice & unexcited I actually asked her to come & see us—which, had she known it, is a compliment we never never pay even the royal family. But I cannot write even here; so shall read a story by Pirandello. James & Alix to dine to discuss Lytton's life I suppose.

Sunday 28 April

Very cold again. Trees dotted with green in the park yesterday. Chestnuts just beginning to flower. A black sky & the paper festoons looking purple & pink across the streets: large blue paper crowns & roses being delivered. Julian & Alix to dine, James having a cold. Conversation: whether one can give people a substitute for war. Must have the danger emotion: must climb mountains, fight bulls; but this emotion mixed, I say, with philosophy, doesnt last more than a few months in case of war. J. says all the young men are communists in order to gratify their desire to do things together & in order to have some danger; which will only last a few months. The Germans being very poor, think anything is better than this. But this was not the 1914 emotion. Lust & danger. Cant cut them out at once. Must divert them on to some harmless object. But what? Some fantasy must be provided. I say many people have found life exciting without war and bull fighting. Has war ever won any cause? Alix says our civil war.

I made up some of my Professions book. Obviously, Julian's quite unaware of some of his own motives, at the same time very lively & energetic. Alix like a blackshirt, all brown & tie & tailor made. No talk of Lytton: all argument; but interesting. What is the use of trying to preach when human nature is so crippled?

Tuesday 29 April

I should be tidying the room, but I'm not. Everything scattered with winters soot & cigarette ash. The great joy of having money is that one can buy small treats for the journey—new shoes. And even give way to the temptation of a 30/- dress. Murray came & I tactfully showed him the blue taffeta; our relations are an odd mix of the friendly & employed. He gave me this blouse, so I gather. But he will dress me for the part of the Dss of Malfi, even in day clothes.

A long letter of enthusiasm from Mrs Ellis Roberts; her husband is writing on me to emphasize my heart, which Swinnerton denied. Dear me. I thought W. Lewis said I was sentimental—between the 3 of them![20]

But I was about to say that everything is a little slack now I'm not writing. Odd to be off that wave. But I want to experiment with pure external living for a month—looking sharing, taking in ideas & impressions And then watch how the old trout at the bottom of the pond rise. I predict that the desire to write will become so frantic by the time were on the way back that I shall be making up all along the French roads. At the moment I start an idea but it fades; cant write it without feeling my brain stretched; cant even write to Stephen Spender about his book. A fine spring morning, very quiet, birds chirping, all London busy wrapping up parcels for the Jubilee.

The Woolfs, with their marmoset Mitz, crossed by the night boat from Harwich to Hook of Holland on Wednesday 1 May, and toured Europe by car, spending a week in Holland and three days in Germany before crossing the Brenner Pass into Italy on 13 May; they reached Rome on 16 May, and there joined Vanessa, Angelica and Quentin Bell, who were living in a rented studio. They left Italy by Ventimiglia on 24 May and drove through France, arriving at Monks House on the last day of May. LW's diary (LWP, Sussex) briefly records their itinerary.

VW's travel diary is written on thirty-two 16 × 20 cm loose-leaf pages later inserted into DIARY XXIV. It is headed by the following autograph calendar and timetable.

Journey to Holland, Germany, Italy & France.

May 1935

				Dordrecht	Zutphen	
Sunday		5	12	19	26	Alassio to Aix
Monday		6	13	20	27	Vienne
Tuesday		7	14	21	28	Moulins
Wednesday	1	8	15	22	29	Chartres
Thursday	2	9	16	23	30	
Friday	3	10	17	24	31	
Saturday	4	11	18	25		

leave London / Hague-Haarlem / Rome
Amsterdam / Utrecht

20. R. Ellis Roberts's wife Harriet was American; an unsigned review of Swinnerton's *The Georgian Literary Scene* in the April 1935 issue of *Life and Letters* (of which Roberts was at this time editor), refers to 'the depths of suffering, the profound emotion' in VW's work, to which Swinnerton is blind.

Monday 6 May

Zutphen

This is Jubilee day, it strikes me; a very hot fine day. As for Holland: in the first place the cows wear coats; then the cyclists go in flocks like starlings, gathering together, skimming in & out. Driving is dangerous. Towns are large. They are also strung out, mile on mile. We are back in 1913. Everywhere there are shops full of clothes, food, books. The people are dressed in perfect respectability. Sailors wear felt hats. From 10 to 25 the girls are elegant, dove grey, slender, skimming on their cycles in & out. From 30 to 50 they amass vast bodies. But always the bodies are tight, spruce, shoes elegant hair beautifully done (& there I've dropped cigarette ash on the perfectly clean sheets of this modest empty hotel). Every street is 16th or 17th century, with curved apricot coloured awnings. As we say, the houses are the glory of Holland—the richly carved big windowed houses; some lean a little, others are peaked; but each is a solid spruce perfectly self respecting house, in which last night I saw the Sunday diners, old men old women sitting round with children, cactuses; a cat & a dog. We have 20 people round us wherever we stop. The apzi— the kleine apzi! I forget exactly how it all goes. Towns too big of course: Amsterdam a swollen stone monster, shaved off like a ruin on the side of the marsh: our first lunch at the Hague had 20 courses. Very expensive. Meals very early. People immensely respectable. No sign of crisis or war. The man on the ferry, said like all the rest, they wished they had gone off the gold standard. No visitors. Trade with England ended. Oh but the carved doors, the curved white façades, the lilac trees: the air of swept & garnished prosperity, antiquity, air, cleanliness. Here in Zutphen—but we've only arrived 2 hours & had our Mitzi levée, & then came to this modest Inn, with a canal outside; & a broad river beyond.

Ideas that struck me.

That the more complex a vision the less it lends itself to satire: the more it understands the less it is able to sum up & make linear. For example: Shre & Dostoevsky neither of them satirise. The age of understanding: the age of destroying—& so on.

Belchamber.

A moving, in its way, completed story. But shallow. A superficial book. But also a finished one. Rounded off. Only possible if you keep one inch below; because the people, like Sainty, have to do things without diving deep; & this runs in the current: which lends itself to completeness. That is, if a writer accepts the conventions, & lets his characters be guided by them, not conflict with them, he can produce an effect of symmetry: very pleasant, suggestive; but only on the surface. That is, I cant care what happens: yet I like the design. Also disgust at the cat monkey psychology, to which he is admirably faithful. A sensitive sincere mind—Howdie, doing his embroidery, & making his acute observations. Not a snob either.[15]

Wednesday 8 May

Utrecht.

We came back to our grand inn here [*Hotel des Pays Bas*], a cold day's drive. We sat & lunched in the car & a funeral passed us. The horse draped in black like a medieval war horse. The plan of a Dutch town is: a bridge a canal: under an arch into a street: pointed, stepped houses; orange & green awnings; 1620: on brand new garages: a great red brick tower, then a vast church, shut up. The caretaker, a respectable rather invalidish man lives opposite. Some frescoes on whitewashed walls. Empty & magnificent. Very Protestant. Flights of cyclists. Immense profusion of highly civilised shops—flower shops, shoes, bicycles, books, everything the more solidly placed wealthy but not frivolous citizen can eat or wear or use: all shining spick & span. English, French German books equal to Dutch. Shops upon shops. People pullulating. Not a beggar, not a slum. Even solid wealth. Angularity. A feeling that Holland is a perfectly self respecting rather hard featured but individual middle aged woman. Conventions of 1913. No women smoking or driving cars. Only one man smokes a pipe in the streets.

Utrecht.

A very cold day. I am (this is copied from pencil notes) sitting in a teashop where 3 Dutch are having horns filled with cream. The nice girl smiles at me. L. is getting letters. (There were none, because of the Jubilee). The two children are eating cakes. Hoolarja, Dutchaboch!—it sounds like that. They dont have tea. A very spick & span shop. They laugh. I pretend to write postcards.

Thursday 9 May

Sitting in the sun outside the German Customs. A car with the swastika on the back window has just passed through the barrier into Germany. L. is in the customs. I am nibbling at Aaron's Rod [*by D. H. Lawrence, 1922*]. Ought I to go in & see what is happening? A fine dry windy morning. The Dutch Customs took 10 seconds. This has taken 10 minutes already. The windows are barred. Here they came out & the grim man laughed at Mitz. But L. said that when a peasant came in & stood with his

15. *Belchamber* (1904) by Howard ('Howdie') Overing Sturgis (1855-1920), a prosperous American expatriate, has for its principal character 'Sainty'—the Marquis and Earl of Belchamber. VW read the 'World's Classics' edition of 1935, with an introduction by Gerard Hopkins which draws a portrait of the author.

hat on, the man said This office is like a Church & made him move it. Heil Hitler said the little thin boy opening his bag, perhaps with an apple in it, at the barrier. We become obsequious—delighted that is when the officers smile at Mitzi—the first stoop in our back.

That a work of art means that one part gets strength from another part.

At Ulken: home reached late after being turned aside to make way for the Minister President.[2]

By the Rhine, sitting at the window, looking out on the river. The waiter has been talking. He has been in America: democratic; talks as if he were host. Like a little supple monkey. "Let me see now, you like good coffee. What have we nice?" & so on. Also the manager—was in the City Road—wanted to go back & keep a German hostel in Bedford Place. We were chased across the river by Hitler (or Goering) had to pass through ranks of children with red flags. They cheered Mitzi. I raised my hand. People gathering in the sunshine—rather forced like school sports. Banners stretched across the street "The Jew is our enemy" "There is no place for Jews in—". So we whizzed along until we got out of range of the docile hysterical crowd. Our obsequiousness gradually turning to anger. Nerves rather frayed. A sense of stupid mass feeling masked by good temper. So we came here, Unkel, an old country house, with curved bannister, shallow steps, a black grated stair door, & courtyard. A number of little eyes in the roof, rabbits & doves in outhouses. The innkeeper is playing cards with his wife. They all want to go away—back to Islington, back to Washington—Oh so lovely, said the waiter, who wants to go on talking.

Sunday 12 May

Innsbruck

L. says I may now tell the truth, but I have forgotten 2 days of truth, & my pen is weeping ink. Let me see. We went on from the old country house Inn, which ran their charges up high, & drove down the Rhine, & tried to see it as an engaged couple in 1840—no good. An ugly pretentious country—operatic scenery. High, but insignificant hills, bristling with black & green fir trees, with correct towers & ruins—a river that runs with coal barges like Oxford Street; traffic on the cobbled roads: & then a wall had fallen, & we were made to cross over to the right side again. And so to—to where? I begin to forget. The dullest day of them all. But we got to ⟨Augsburg; & we had a room with a bath, & then went on, to⟩ Heidelberg, which is—yes—a very distinguished University town, on the Neckar. The dons & their daughters were having a musical evening. I saw them tripping out to each others houses with pale blue Beethoven quartets

2. The Woolfs stayed at the Rheinhotel Schultz at Unkel, having unwittingly driven through a reception organised for Goering in Bonn. See *IV LW*, pp. 190-2.

under their arms. Something like the Verralls & the Darwins in old Cambridge—the same dress, & nice intelligent faces. Great rhododendrons blooming. Still hot & blue. And the river like sliding plate glass. And next day to Augsburg—a dull town, but with a bath. A room with a bath. The country steadily improves—becomes shaped & spaced. From Augsburg to Innsbruck where I sit in the empty room—the hotels quite empty, & the town quiet as the grave, & very stately. What did we see today? Great snow hills, with black rifts in them. Torrents. Lakes; one copper green. And it rained for the first time & was cold in the mountains. Fancy living with dirty snow at the door in May! Lovely, but utilitarian, pine woods. Black troops herded together. The Hitler feeling relaxed, though every village had a painted sign "Die Juden sind hier unwunscht". But this seemed to be put up by authority. Changed into Austria at last; & we are now almost out of earshot.

Monday 20 May

Rome

This is out of its place. Nor can I really flatter myself that I am going to float off the drive home from Cassenlino[Cassino] this evening—the women balancing blue green pots, the hot[?] spring, green, blue & black precipitous mountain, flowers[?], umbrella pines, the town with the perched egg shell houses. And then, globed in the luminous light, for the sunset was pouring gold all over us, St Peters, to which we drove.

Is there any 'use' in such notes? Perhaps when the editing of the mind has gone further one can see & select better. Quentin bought an Italian paper & read of Lawrence's death. Butted into a motorcycle.[3] But I will now use the half hour left before they come to dinner to copy out from the pencil book that I keep in my bag to write it when taking in petrol, waiting for something or other. Again, whats the use, but that parrot cry would stifle most things.

Brenner. *Monday 13th.* Odd to see the countries change into each other. Beds now made of layers on top. No sheets. Houses becoming Austrian, dignified. Winter lasts at Innsbruck till July. No spring. Italy fronts one on a blue bar. The Cheko Slovaks are in front going to the customs house.

Verona [*13 May*]. Written after drinking wine. I dont want to wake up. This is the lust that led many astray, but not comparable to my own private excitements. And it wears off so soon, even as I write, reason returns. I can see the world outside. The public: the grey green officer

3. T. E. Lawrence (b. 1888), 'Lawrence of Arabia', died on 19 May in Bovington Camp Hospital, without regaining consciousness after fracturing his skull in a motorcycle accident six days earlier.

reading the paper. Queer what a part wine has played in human life. Omar [Khayyam] &c. How all impressions are mixed. I am thinking of V.D. 30 years ago: Nessa: my honeymoon: Roger: looking at Verona from the train.[4] The sensation is of a tight band round the head tingling in the soles of the feet, hotness, & a spring expanding.
What would the writing of a complete drunkard be?
A Turgenev novel at lunch. The diners cosmopolitan. A woman like Alice Clifford [*unidentified*] who asked that her ashes might be buried at sea.

Florence [*15 May*]. Ash coloured houses with green doors. Smell of coffee roasting.

Perugia [*15 May*]. Came through Florence today—Saw the green & white cathedral. & the yellow Arno dribbling into shallows. A thunderstorm. Irises purple against the clouds. So to Arezzo. A most superb church with dropped hull.

Lake Trasimen. Stood in a field of red purple clover: plovers egg lake, grey olives, exquisite, subtle, sea cold, shell green. So on, regretting that we did not stay, to Perugia— [*Hotel*] Brufani where we stayed in 1908. Now all the same. The same ardent sunburnt women. But lace & so on for sale. Better to have stayed at Trasimen. I went into an Albergo yesterday to buy rolls & found a sculptured fireplace, all patriarchal—servants & masters. Cauldron on the fire. Probably not much change since 16th century: the people preserve legends. Men & women scything. A nightingale singing where we sat. Little frogs jumping into the stream.

Brufani. Three people watching the door open & shut. Commenting on visitors like fates—summing up, placing. A woman with a hard lined aquiline face—red lips—bird like, perfectly self-satisfied. French. pendulous [*word indecipherable*]—a rather poor sister. Now they sit nibbling at human nature. We are rescued by the excellence of our luggage.

Rome. tea. Tea in cafe. Ladies in bright coats & white hats. Music. Look out & see people like movies. Abyssinia. Children begging. Café haunters. Ices. Old man who haunts the Greco.[5]

---

4. VW was in Italy with Violet Dickinson and Vanessa in 1904; with Vanessa and Clive Bell in 1908 and 1909; with LW on her honeymoon journey in 1912; and with Roger Fry *en route* for Greece in 1932.
5. The Caffè Greco in the via Condotti, frequented for centuries by artists.

Sunday cafe. N[essa]. & A[ngelica]. drawing. Very cold. Rome a mitigated but perceptible Sunday. Fierce large jowld old ladies. Q. talking about Monaco. Talleyrand. Some very poor black wispy women. The effect of dowdiness produced by wispy hair. The Prime Ministers letter offering to recommend me for the Companion of honour. No.[6]

Tuesday 21 May

Oddities of the human brain Woke early & again considered dashing off my book on Professions; to which I had not given a single thought these 7 or 8 days. Why? This vacillates with my novel—how are they both to come out simultaneously. But it is a sign that I must get to pen & paper again. Yet at the moment I am going rag marketing with N. & A— who dont come.

Sunday 26 May

[Aix-en-Provence]

We went rag marketing. & suddenly out sprang, to my eyes, the old triumphant Vanessa of early married days. Why? How she would bear off in full sail with Roger Clive & me attendant. We bought pots; & a tea set, which gave her great intense potters delight more than any clothing or jewel.

And then? I'm writing at Aix on a Sunday evening, with a band playing & stopping, & children shouting, in a too luxurious hotel where the waiters bring one the menu, & I mix my French scandalously with odd scraps of my painfully acquired Italian. Still I can rattle off Gli Indifferenti lying on my bed for pleasure.[7] Oh the loveliness of the land still here & there—for instance that first morning's drive out of Rome—the sea & the lip of the inviolated land; & the umbrella pines, after Civita Vecchia: then of course all the intense boredom of Genoa & the riviera, with its geraniums & its bouganvilia, & its sense of shoving you between hill & sea & keeping you there in a bright luxury light without room to turn, so steep the vulture neck hills come down. But we slept at Lerici the first night which does the bay the brimming sea & the green sailing ships & the island & the sparkling fading red & yellow night lamps to perfection. But that kind of perfection no longer makes me feel for my pen— Its too easy. But

6. For the letter from Ramsay MacDonald's office asking VW's agreement for her name to be submitted to the King for inclusion in his Birthday Honours as a member of the Order of Companions of Honour, with VW's draft refusal on the verso, see MHP, Sussex.

7. Gli Indifferenti (1920) by Alberto Moravia. VW was in the Hotel Sextus Thermes at Aix.

driving today I was thinking of Roger—Brignolles—Corgés—my word, the olives & the rust red earth, & the flat green & the trees.[8]

But now the band has begun again, & we must go down to dine sumptuously off local trout. Off tomorrow, & home on Friday. But though I'm impatient for my brain to eat again, I can dally out these last days better than sometimes. Why? why? I go on asking myself. And feel I could soon polish off those final scenes [*in* The Years]: a possible amplification of the first paragraph occurred to me. But I dont want to grind at 'writing' too hard. To open my net wide. It occurs to me, as we drive, how I'm disliked, how I'm laughed at; & I'm rather proud of my intention to take the fences gallantly. But writing again!

Nessa you see, is always interrupted by Angelica, who has the social sense & not the contemplative. Goodbye, sweet dreams, she laughed as she waved us away on Thursday night on the Piazza di Spagna. And so she always interrupts & says, Mummy, if you're going out would you buy me some dark blue cotton. Oh yes. And then we must think about getting hair curlers. So she cant brood over pictures, which must be a divine refreshment. Never mind. I'm dipping into K.M.'s letters, Stendhal on Rome; & the Italian.[9] Cant formulate a phrase for K.M. All I think a little posed & twisted by illness & Murry; but agonised, & at moments that direct flick at the thing seen which was her gift—Then all the old Tchekov stuff about life; & the perpetual rather sordid worries & gibes, & the doll on the bed, which I detest, & something driven & forced to cram into one year the growth of five or six. So I cant judge & get [*text ends*]

Tuesday 28 May

Moulins

And here we are in yet another hotel, this time with a bath. Last night at Vienne. No bath. Water cut off by town. A great bath for common washing supplied by the squash eyed manager. Very good local dinner: crayfish: a comm. travellers hotel, also patronised by lower grade officers, who discuss military tactics & flirt with waitress. Sugar always sweetened by the hands of a woman. All this taken philosophically by a huge black lady ladling out sour milk. I can still see the last scene—how soon they rub away—like a knock I gave my shin. All day we drove from Aix in wet straight unbroken rain, mud coloured sky over us, & peasants standing to pick cherries in the rain. Trees all red spotted with cherries— only just visible in the grey downpour. A dull boring day, but got to

8. For *Corgés* probably read *Carcès*. The colours and forms of Provençal landscape were particularly dear to Roger Fry as a painter.
9. VW had the Albatross Modern Continental Library edition (1934) of *The Letters of Katherine Mansfield*, edited by John Middleton Murry and first published in two volumes in 1928.

Vienne at last; & today has been a very good day, coming across country over the wide high hills with [*text ends*]

I forgot the Casino at Monte Carlo. A bright blue & white day: carved parapets gleaming; little embayed town on the sea. I saw domes & pillars & told L. this was the Casino; so we went in, & had to produce passports, & sign a paper, & give up hat & umbrella, & then paid nothing but went into a florid but dingy hall, set with seven or eight tables, something like great billiard tables, at which sat a dingy sweaty rather sordid crew, with their faces all set & expressionless watching the gold bars sweeping this way & that in the middle. They had something peculiar. One couldnt place them. Some were dingy old governesses in spectacles, others professors with beards; there was one flashy adventuress; but most were small business men—only rather, not very vicious. It was a blazing hot Sunday morning about 12, & this, we thought is the way our culture spends its holidays. Vicious, dull, & outside lurid. So on.

Wednesday 29 May

[Chartres]

And I begin this sentence on a grey noisy evening might be mid September in Chartres, determined to let a long slide of time pass before I go motoring again. The pane of glass that is pressed firm over the mind in these travels—there I am vitreated on my seat—cant read talk or write— only look at the endless avenues—plane trees poplars—rain, rain—old man with a cart—ask the mileage—look at map light a cigarette & turn over the old problems—chiefly the same, because I cant start a new one till the cage doors are opened—all this makes the 2 last days as intolerable as the first two are rapturous.

And then it always rains; coming over the high [?] Chartres plain it was almost a fog. At Orleans it was grey as November. Only the thought of getting quiet in ones own chair again makes this racket—I write in the window looking on to a vast bare space—tolerable. But its odd how one longs to uncurl the spring in the brain—to let fly: how insipid life is without—writing is it? Yet this is the best & least distressing of all our tours. I could only have wished 2 days less coming across France.

Its the depression too of the waiters & women behind glass in the hall. But I shall enjoy my dinner. And only one day more— It'll take a day or two however to scratch off the pane of glass.

And, putting down my pen, I fetched L. & we went to the Cathedral which was almost dark & melodramatic—I mean surprising, there only the arches & shadows showing, we all alone, & the blue windows blazing in the cold grey night. In fact it was like seeing the skeleton & eyes of the cathedral glowing there. Mere bones, & the blue red eyes. The windows are all blue & red, & at one end there's the jewel burning—the great rose jewel, burning blue in coal blackness, for all the world like something worn upon a vast—what? woman['s] body wont do. The jewel of the world then—or is that sentimental? After we had sat & looked slowly grayness returned to the thick pillars but still the scooped ⟨shadowy⟩ look remained. Never had we seen it so bare, so architectural, a statement of proportions, save for the fiery & deep blue glass, for the glass varied from gloomy to transcendent. So back to a first rate dinner—a dinner thought out, & presided over by a graceful young chef, precisely like Raymond, only with greater gift & charm. For instance he concocted a sauce out of cream, French beans, mustard, salt & wine. To add the wine he held his finger which was not clean half over the mouth of the bottle. Then left the sauce to simmer over a spirit lamp: then another red brown casserole was brought, & the sauce poured over. Our dinner was rich & thoughtful: I had mushrooms in cream. And I observed the way a good waiter serves a dish with infinite care & respect, as if handling something precious. Now Chartres is quieter, & so to sleep.

Friday 31 May

[Monks House]

Home again, & how queer, as we drove up there was Pinka's basket being carried up by Percy, & she had died yesterday: her body was in the basket. Just as we were saying that we would see her in a moment. Percy was very red, very sad, screwed his eyes up, would not smile at us, & then told us. So thats whats bound to happen we said. A very silent breakfast. I had been saying how she would put out my match & all the usual jokes. And the intensity of the sense of death—even for a dog—how odd—our feeling of her character, & the grotesqueness—something pathetic, & the depression, & the I suppose fear of sentimentality & so on.

A cold misting day: Pinka's feet by the way on my blotting paper. The usual tremor & restlessness after coming back, & nothing to settle to, & some good German woman sends me a pamphlet on me, into which I couldnt resist looking, though nothing so upsets & demoralises as this looking at ones face in the glass. And a German glass produces an extreme diffuseness & complexity so that I cant get either praise or blame but must begin twisting among long words. And so I must write letters. L.'s book is reviewed in the Lit. Sup. on the day it came out & seriously without a sneer, though not with much grasp. Never a bite in that senile paper.[10]

The view as beautiful as any I've seen, by the way, even on a mud

10. The German pamphlet (written in English) was *Virginia Woolf: a Study* by Ruth Grüber, Leipzig 1935. The review of LW's *Quack, Quack*, entitled 'Reason and Quackery' was in the *TLS* of 30 May 1935.

coloured day. The frost has nipped the fruit, the box hedges have yellow tops. Lady Rhondda asks us to dinner, & so the snake renews its skin. We drove through Normandy yesterday & it was Bank holiday owing to Ascension day, so that all the people were dressed in respectable black coats & fur. A more ugly tribute to the spirit could not be. We lunched on the balcony at Caudebec, & the Bank holiday crowd was lunching too— getting blotched & red in the face: taking out mirrors & rubbing red & white too profusely into lips & noses. An old man next us who had to be hoisted into his car after eating largely I suppose to return to Paris. A long row of cars waiting. Plethoric after their lunch & wine the holiday makers walked up & down looking at each other's cars. We drove off too, got early to Dieppe, smelt the usual strong smells, gave the car up & settled down to the usual 4 or 5 hours till 10 in the hotel. Mitz provided a long discourse with the wife, daughter & mother—3 generations—in the stuffy little office. The girl was translating Caesar. She must know languages, they said, & was to come to Newhaven to learn English. A great tradition—French talk: I enjoyed the expressiveness of the old woman, describing Englishwomen during the war. She was in a shop, & they didn't know a word, but soon had the hang of it—saying Pomme, then pomme de terre. Much more style to her than to a woman of her type in Lewes. I am writing to steady the fidgets, to cover over the depression. L. has begun work, & it is only eleven, & I cant take up my book. I think that an hour of reading some good author is prescribed.

[*Saturday 1 June*]

My excuse for not beginning my book—I mean finishing it—is that I've not got the final chapter here. So what shall I do? Read the old one. But that's fussing & fidgeting. I think wait till Monday & then flash at it, & get it done by August. Holidays are very upsetting. And its cold & grey. And my hand shakes. And I want some regular hours & work. And it'll take at least a weeks agony to get back into the mood. And I shall slip back by reading about in the book, & dreaming after tea; & perhaps, if nature allows, taking a walk. L. very depressed too, about poor dear Pink. 8 years of a dog certainly mean something. I suppose—is it part of our life thats buried in the orchard? That 8 years in London—our walks—something of our play private life, thats gone? And—odd how the spring of life isn't to be tapped at will. I cant get into the swim by saying it is Saturday morning & I will write. I cant get into that stream by standing & wishing it. All sorts of habits, of being unconscious of the surface, attentive to other things, have to settle naturally. Coming back one is horribly broken up, notices surfaces. Habit is the desirable thing in writing.

[*End of inserted pages*]

The Woolfs returned to Tavistock Square on Sunday afternoon, 2 June.

Wednesday 5 June

Back here again, & the grim wooden feeling that has made me think myself dead since we came back is softening slightly. Its beginning this cursed dry hard empty chapter again in part. Every time I say it will be the devil! but I never believe it. And then the usual depressions come. And I wish for death. But I am now seeing that the last 200 pages will assert themselves, & force me to write a play more or less: all broken up: & I stop to begin making up. Also, after the queer interlude, at once life— that is the telephone beginning—starts. So that one is forcibly chafed. (I meant to make a note about the dramatic shape which forces itself upon me). Vita; Stephen Tennant; Julian; dressmaker; going to Rodmell for Whitsun. Must I go to the Paris Conference? Amabel rings up.[1]

Mrs Woolf yesterday talking admirable racy English. My head ached. The room bare, as she's going to Worthing. She asked L. to read aloud Miss Daisy Knockends? letter, a daily maid whom Cecil might have married—a decayed wastrel. "But how can one give people up?" She had been to Phil's show. "And old Queen [Mary] was led about. I enjoyed it immensely." There were lettuces & radishes for tea, but the people complained it was cold. Babs & Phil without an ounce of flesh on their faces. Such hard work—A Gymkana. And Marie won a prize.[2] And 1 often ask myself, what have I got out of life? I have brought up good men & women. . . .

Thursday 6 June

There is no doubt that the greatest happiness in the world is walking through Regents Park on a green, but wet—green but red pink & blue evening—the flower beds I mean emerging from the general misty rain— & making up phrases after a little stimulus from little Mr Murray among

1. The Hon. Stephen Tennant (b. 1906), fourth son of 1st Baron Glenconner, was a painter and aesthete, and an admirer of VW. The writer Amabel Williams-Ellis, *née* Strachey (b. 1894) was joint secretary of the English Organising Committee for the International Congress of Writers which was to open in Paris on 21 June (see above, 21 March 1935). In a letter to the *NS&N* of 11 May publicising the Congress, she had included VW's name among its supporters.
2. LW's brother Cecil (1887-1917) had been killed in the war; his youngest brother Philip Sidney Woolf (1889-1962) had married Marjorie ('Babs') Lowndes in 1922, the year he became land agent to his distant cousin James de Rothschild of Waddesdon Manor, Bucks; they had three children, Cecil, Philippa, and Marie. His 'show' was the fête and gymkhana held on 1 June by the Waddesdon and District Branch of the British Legion in aid of the North Eastern Distressed Area; it raised £486.

his clothes. He wants to become a scene maker, to design the decors for Strauss's ballet. He was trained in the law at Edinburgh, but gave it up because some friends excited him about his designs. And now he's feeling a little at a dead end, & wants more scope. Why does this serve to start phrases, so that I left my bus, wasted 2d fare, & walked across Regents Park. Not that I'm fluent with my scene this morning; very difficult on the contrary. But Rome holds no greater excitement than this. So that Mabel's terrible faux pas—she broke the gramophone—& Pinka's death, are somehow obliterated. After dinner, however, that whining & complaining disreputable egomaniac, the Polish Count, rang up & bickered, discreditably. "I am boycotted by the entire literary world. Why I ask you does the N.S. allude to me as Montalk? Miss Rebecca West is the only writer who calls me Count Potocki—" till L. became very trenchant & weighty & cut him off: but we were exacerbated. And I had a disagreeable letter from a stranger. You of course despise anyone who lives in an Avenue, you who've had a book written on your philosophy by a Frenchman. The inferiority complex is thick as a nettle bed. And I cant read Dante after a morning with my novel—too hard.

The Woolfs drove to Monks House for Whitsun on Thursday evening 6 June, returning to Tavistock Square the following Wednesday. They went twice to Glyndebourne—to a concert on Whit Sunday, and to The Magic Flute *on Tuesday 11 June.*

Monday 10 June, Whit Monday

at Monks House. Working very hard. I think I shall rush these scenes off.

[Tuesday 11 June]

Yet I cannot write this morning (Tuesday) How can I say, naturally, I have inherited the Rose & the Star!

Wednesday 12 June

I am so glad I am not lunching with Rebecca West to meet Miss E. Jenkins; at the same [time] I am so sorry that L. wants to spend 3 days at Monks House every fortnight: from Thursday night till Monday morning.

These are my troubles Mr—as the man said when the footman put on too many coals.[3] And I think I've found a bridge in that scene.

3. See Sermon No. CVIII, 'On Riches', by John Wesley (*Works*, 1872, vol. VII, p. 220): '...a gentleman of large fortune, while we were seriously conversing, ordered

Thursday 13 June

In some ways, its rather like writing The Waves—these last scenes. I bring my brain to a state of congestion, have to stop: go upstairs, run into towsled Mr Brewster; come back; find a little flow of words.[4] Its the extreme condensation: the contrasts: the keeping it all together. Does this mean that its good? I feel I have a round of great pillars to set up, & can only drag & sweat. It's something like that. Its getting barer & more intense. And then what a relief when I have the upper air scenes—like the one with Eleanor! only they have to be condensed too. Its the proper placing that strains me.

Pannickar & Morgan last night; rather difficult. P. so bubbling, always talking with a smile, swart & greased, like some animal with a thick pelt & very white teeth. Then Morgan, evanescent, piping, elusive, settling exactly *there*. Had been lunching with Rebecca; giving away prizes. My bones ached—that cold field picnic at Glynde I suppose. And Morgan divined that we would not come to Paris. Always divines the meaning & then flits off. As a matter of fact, P. had stolen 2 books of his. He did not like him.[5] M. has a razor edge to his mind. And he cant get on with "Bloomsbury" & feels, I guess, unattached, & thus takes on public work, which depresses him.

Ought I to go & see R. West? I want to for some reason—partly about fascism. Clive rang up this morning. We dine there tonight. L. says "your" cook! which annoys me. She must go, I suppose.

Then—I will now go on with the F. Queen. & finish it. The mood has come back.

Saturday 15 June

We dined with Clive, & I felt very fond of him. He has great sympathy —as when, talking of Adrian, he said, "He gets great pleasure now from his children. When I praised Ann's looks, he bridled." Yes, I'm very fond of my old Clive. And L. was charming, genial, affable, urbane. Clive said, I always say youre half cracked (to me). We were saying how many Rogers

a servant to throw some coals on the fire: a puff of smoke came out: he threw himself back in his chair, and cried out "O Mr Wesley, these are the crosses which I meet with every day." '. Both Wesley (*Standard Letters*, V, pp. 152-3) and VW (see *III VW Diary*, 15 May 1929 and below, 13 September 1935) repeat this reflection with variations in their wording.

4. Brewster: see below, 18 June 1935, n. 11.

5. Kavalam Madhava Panikkar (1895-1963), Oxford-educated Indian barrister, newspaper editor, and politician; his pamphlet, *Caste and Democracy*, was published by the Hogarth Press in 1933 (*HP Checklist* 328). E. M. Forster was to head the British Delegation to the Writers' Congress in Paris, and urged the Woolfs to attend.

& Lyttons there are. He said Segonzac thinks Nessa the best painter in England, much better than Duncan.[6] I will not be jealous, but isnt it odd—thinking of gifts in her? I mean when she has everything else. And my head is congested again, & I will not go to Paris, because I should have a weeks misery; & for all my sweating, I'm getting ahead with the P.s. No name suggests itself. Rebecca asks me to dine. The Cecils ask us to dine.

And it is drumming with rain, & we are starting off to Philip's. This amused me—L.'s complex. "He's annoyed, thats why he hasnt written." Finally, he got me to telephone last night, thinking it might be awkward if he bearded Philip who was annoyed. "Virginia? No. I never heard. But we should be delighted to see you" said Philip cordially. So we are off, in this storm.

And Nessa never writes; but why make up stories about one's relations? An odd family complex.

Sunday 16 June

So we drove to Winchendon through the rain. I was very numb in the head by the way & saw things at a great distance, which explains the bemused state, no impact, of my impressions. London spreads about 17 miles this way, suddenly stops outside Rickmansworth at Moor Park, as if some great Lord still kept an estate. Then Amersham, with the house [*market hall*] in the middle, rather like a peasant version of an Italian town; then a few bushyheaded woods; but always houses. At last we came to the gate, & there on the left in the green watery light were the children riding on copper coloured horses, going round under the trees; & Babs & Phil. And the talk began. They had found Cardinal Wolsey's arms in a rubbish heap: had them mounted into a mantelpiece. But it was badly done by the local stonemason: the fruit carving injured.[7] Tea. Proper maid. Children drinking out of Jubilee mugs. "We each have two" said Pippin who looks up under her eyes. Mary a straightnosed child Cecil sloping nosed. Talk about the great Gymkhana. P[hilip]. netted £500. All the stalls had paid. 7000 for tea. And so on. Babs has yellow front teeth; wears horn glasses. Then we walked past the wicked Lords house.[8] But I

6. André Dunoyer de Segonzac (1884-1974), *fauve* painter. Cf. letter from Clive to Vanessa Bell from Paris, 2 June 1935 (Tate Gallery Archives): '. . . last night . . . I dined and spent the evening with Segonzac . . . in his opinion you were easily the best painter in England.'

7. Philip Woolf lived from 1924-39 at 'The Wilderness', Upper Winchendon, a house standing on the site of a medieval manor which belonged to Cardinal Wolsey; a portion of a stone Tudor arch carved with Wolsey's arms and a vine-leaf decoration had been unearthed by Philip beneath a laurel bush some years before.

8. i.e.: Waddesdon Manor, the French Renaissance-style château built by Baron Ferdinand de Rothschild in the 1880s.

dont like parks. And B. talked of horses; used to break them in, teach riding; loves horses; used to teach boys, running beside them; filled all pigsties & hutches with horses. Riding now a passion: all Woolworth girls ride before breakfast, have 2/- rides. This very hard on the horses. The man next them hired 20 hunters; hunting on the hire system. One goes lame, is sent back, another supplied by Smiths. Laughed at George & Flora: child not allowed to eat ices; won't talk, spoilt;[9] family gossip: all quite running, free, what I call 'natural living'. P. walked ahead & talked politics with L. Children tipped. Asparagus given, & so home: dine at 8.30: & I slept all the evening over the fire, & dreamt of cutting my hand in a theatre, & of a professional mistress of ceremonies who had to entertain people; & somehow Mrs Clifford came in; & I woke to find L. standing over me.[10] And I have scrambled along this morning: & tonight we dine with Rhondda; but I am *not* going to Paris.

Tuesday 18 June

Yesterday, instead of reading Tom's Murder in the Cathedral, which, having run through & tested my colour sense, I expect to be good, I had to give Ralph Brewster tea. Curious teeth; gooseberry coloured staring eyes; & an air of nervous instability. Large hands, hanging: only just neat enough to have tea. A sudden amused kindling in the gooseberry eyes; & the profuse storytelling of those who have lived with savages. Would go on & on & on.[11]

[Thursday 20 June]

I am so oppressed by the thought of all the books I have to write that my head is like a bursting boiler. Half an hour ago, Margery Fry rang up to ask me to open an Ex[hibitio]n of Roger's paintings at Bristol; to speak for 15 minutes. Oh we should all love it! she said. Then it appeared that they are counting on me to write a life. She is collecting papers. This morning theres a book (in the Lit. Sup.) complaining that women have dropped their sacred task.[12] This floods me with my Professions book.

9. LW's youngest sister Flora (1886-1975) had married George Sturgeon in 1918; they had one daughter.
10. Mrs W. K. Clifford (c. 1855-1929), writer, friend of VW's parents. See *II VW Diary*, 24 January 1920.
11. Ralph H. Brewster (1905-1951), grandson of Ethel Smyth's friend H. B. Brewster and of the German sculptor Adolf Hildebrand; he had explored Mount Athos with a Greek sailor and a camera, and the resulting illustrated book, *The 6,000 Beards of Athos*, with an introduction by Ethel Smyth, was published by the Hogarth Press in October 1935 (*HP Checklist* 359).
12. See review of *The Defeat of Women* by Mary Moore, *TLS*, 20 June 1935: 'All that

Helen tells me that the Stracheys are hurt that I never offered to write about Lytton. "But I wanted to & they never asked me!" I said. Oh but they didn't like to suggest it—James says they do want it. And here I am wedged—no, buoyant—in a floating storm of scenes at the end of my book, which must be compacted & pulled out & turned & (this comes from my hair waving yesterday—from 2 to 4.45 & rather successful). And we are incessantly asked to dine lunch & 'see' people.

Tom last night: supple & sub[t]le, simple & charming. Stayed till 12.15. I never felt so much at my ease. He is a dear old fellow: one of 'us': odd: I felt I liked him as I liked Lytton & Roger—with intimacy in spite of God. First we talked of his play. He stayed with Lady Raleigh, & she gave him cocoa & Oliver biscuits but never said a word about the play. There was a canon there. And they looked out of the window & saw 3 girls in very short shorts, naked legs & large bottoms go into the Cathedral. "The dean encourages them" said Lady R. grimly. "I am in favour of St. Paul if one must be irrational" said Tom.[13] Now tell me about the marmozets view of Germany." We made a good dinner. And he said he liked Stephen —"What a charming person in many ways" no, I think he didnt even qualify his remark, so kind has he become. "Auden is a very nice rattled brained boy. Some of his plays extremely good, but its superficial: stock figures; sort of Punch figures . . ."[14] Publishers gossip. A story about a party to entertain the Reads, Ludo & her sister & German friend. Tom bought fireworks; sugar that dissolved & let out small fish; & chocolates that he thought were full of sawdust. "Theyre very greedy," he said; "And by a mistake the chocolates were full of soap. They set on me. . . . And it was not a success. So much so that I forgot the fireworks, until they were going. I then let them off on the doorstep. And poor Herbert had to pay for a cab from Bina Gardens to Hampstead."[15] This was very amusing, & not as stiff as usual. L. made cigarettes. Tom drank whisky. I mused & was at my ease. Tom wants to give me all his works, but thought I didnt read them—would always have given me all his works.

---

woman stands for—the mother-caring spirit . . . was defeated in the *debâcle* following the Great War.' &c.

13. Lady Raleigh (d. 1957) was the widow of Sir Walter Raleigh, Professor of English Literature at Oxford, 1904-22, and Fellow of Merton College, where Eliot was a post-graduate student; she now lived in the precincts of Canterbury Cathedral. The Dean of Canterbury from 1931 to 1963 was the Very Rev. Hewlett Johnson (1874-1966), known as the 'Red Dean'. See *I Corinthians* 11, 13: 'Judge in yourselves: is it comely that a woman pray unto God uncovered?'

14. Eliot's firm, Faber & Faber, had published *The Dog Beneath the Skin* by W. H. Auden and Christopher Isherwood on 30 May.

15. The party was given by John Hayward at his home (which Eliot later shared), 22 Bina Gardens, SW5.

[*Saturday 22 June, Rodmell*]

The Bees are swarming this week end, & Percy goes about in flannel trousers with a net over his head, very self important. "I'm going to get a friend to help me tonight, & we shall cut out the Queens" he's just said.

It has suddenly become full summer: droning, misting, with birds & bees. The cuckoo calling in the elm tree at 3 or 4 this morning so that I had to stop my ears. The heat came suddenly as we walked by the river on Friday. And the field in front is red with something that [*farmer*] Botten's growing in his bog. We had mushrooms—people come out at 4 or 5 to pick them. Instead of surveying all this in a torpid swoon of pleasure, illustrated by scenes from my book, Mrs W. & Harold came to tea; she stumbled on the doorstep & turned her ankle. Then there were figures passing the window—Jack & Jeremy: whereupon she lost all interest in life, poor old lady, thinking that no one would listen to her family stories. She cannot stretch to take in any stranger. But, after saying that the garden was the best they had ever seen, they went on to the [Glyndebourne] opera. Monty Shearman was strolling, all in black, outside . .[16] Harold Mrs W. & I continued our rather burbling conversation: about highbrows, & then about Maids, & the hotel. I heard all about L.'s father, & how he did not take silk till he was 45, & made his name over—I forget what case; so it comes over & over again, the story of her life, with the usual comments. "And I ask myself, what for? And I am now so lonely. I have lived alone so many years now . . ." which I mechanically turn off upon Bella: who is now Queen of Hong Kong. She is very ambitious. And so wonderfully tactful. And so popular. What dress did she wear? A beautiful white taffeta. Tom [Southorn, *her husband*] was so generous—He gave her some money to spend on clothes. She has to have so many. In the old days she did not mind how she dressed. So we droned, sitting on the terrace before this house—very successful as a sitting place on a hot day.

Why does this talk smear my mind so that I cant settle in at 6.30 to do anything but march up & down the terrace? Poor old lady. She has shrunk slightly, carries some animal with a white belly, & white gloves. Harold brings his horse down on a trailer & rides on the downs. The horse is fed by an automatic feeder invented by himself. He has given up his yatcht, as Alice [*his wife*] dislikes it. L. buying newspapers was told by the newsagent the story of Miss Wightman. She wears her fathers mackintosh & nothing underneath. It is getting old, & coming to bits. She is a poet, & has won a medal from the King which she keeps in a red morocco case, & the newsagent has seen it.[17]

16. Montague Shearman (1885-1940), barrister and picture collector, was a great friend of St John (Jack) Hutchinson, whose son Jeremy (b. 1915) was now at Oxford. Harold Sidney Woolf (1882-1967) was LW's next younger brother.

17. This eccentric poet has not been identified.

JUNE 1935

Tuesday 25 June

A curious & rather unpleasant scene with Mabel. She was in tears, because Mr Woolf never believes a word she says. And I think its true. L. is very hard on people; especially on the servant class. No sympathy with them; exacting; despotic. So I told him yesterday when he'd complained about the coffee. "If I maynt even say when the coffee is bad &c". His extreme rigidity of mind surprises me; I mean in its relation to others: his severity: not to myself but then I get up & curse him. What does it come from? Not being a gentleman partly: uneasiness in the presence of the lower classes: always suspects them, is never genial with them. Philip & Edgar [Woolf] are the same. His desire, I suppose, to dominate. Love of power. And then he writes against it. All this I shall tell him again, for it doesnt matter, to me; in our relationship; & yet I hate people noticing it: Nessa; Dadie; even Kingsley Martin—who all admire & respect him. An interesting study. It goes with great justice, in some ways; & simplicity too; & doing good things: but it is in private a very difficult characteristic. I must now get rid of Mabel, & find another. This row has precipitated it & given me a good excuse for sacking her: but I feel its unfair on her.

Thursday 27 June

A good thing for old Bloomsbury to be shaken up no doubt: a good thing to dine with R. West & Mr Andrews [*her husband*] last night in their flat in P[ortman]. Sqre. with the view, with the £750 book case, & the fish carved out of a yew branch, & the modern pictures, period furniture, letter box in the wall & which dont work (nor did Arnold Bennett's—you have to poke with a stick). But the electric light in the coat cupboard does work. And what's wrong? The plumbers nose—the miner's canary, again. I mean scenting out differences, & let us hope inferiorities. Of course its admirable in its way—impersonal, breezy, yes, go ahead, facing life, eating dinner at Savoy, meeting millionaires, woman & man of the worldly; but— no, I must add the kindness intelligence & erudition of the admirable effete spectacled swollen eyed Andrews—the cultivated don turned banker, with his devotion to R.—Cecily he calls her, for whom he buys these fish & bookcases. Whats wrong then? Where does the gas escape? I think its the emptiness, the formality, the social strata they live on—appearances, as the Apostles would say: the sense of Now we're having a dinner party & must talk till 11: tomorrow another. Hospitality to American publisher & the Woolves. Nothing said of any naturalness or spontaneity. Yet thats not quite so; that one cd. go on having dinner every night & never know each other better. No intimacy at the end of that Oxford Street. And I was a little diminished in my own esteem—

why? Because . . did they differentiate me from other people? No. Or
Leonard? But then isnt this Bloomsbury conceit—our d-d refinement? I
went on the roof with Andrews & saw all London—a magnificent metropolis so brushed up, so ornate, so continental & cosmopolitan at night in
that quarter: there's Oxford Street, theres Hyde Park, thats the new
Lyons block of flats. And the West End squares; & oblongs of white
light, & yellow light the faces, the rouged faces of offices & steeples &
cranes; all very impressive; very soigné, like Mr Ginsburg's little sharp
face: so radiant—& I so blown about, I suppose[?]. Graham came, a little
fuddled: had drunk too much I think; made heavy weather with R.[18] She
has great vitality: is a broad browed very vigorous, undistinguished
woman: but a buffeter & battler: has taken the waves, I suppose; & can
talk in any language: why then this sense of her being a lit up modern
block, floodlit by electricity?

Friday 28 June

But dinner with the [David] Cecils last night was very good: free &
spontaneous; they were all dressed for a party at the Herberts: Origo was
there, whom I like. She is young, tremulous, nervous—very—stammers a
little—but honest eyed; very blue eyed. Have I already described her?
How she came to tea.[19] Anyhow, shes clean & picks her feet up. Talk
spurted. (I hope I did not try to be brilliant?) Rachel very diaphanous,
simple, erratic, with Molly's look, some of Desmond's humour. David
growing domed & bald; his hair ruffled. We talked about: fear of people;
parties; they were all afraid; Sitwell's lunch; Osbert such a nervous host;
the gilt dolphin: rank; up in the drawing room, Origo (her name is Iris)
sat down on purpose I think by me, & oh dear was it for this I got so
free & easy?—she has read my books, & was of course full of stumbling
enthusiasm; so I made a rush, & talked about writing, spilling out ideas,
of a kind. She lives near Siena, in perfect country; they talk of the seasons;
harvest; vintage; share with peasants; have a great vintage feast off goose.
And we talked about biography & fiction; but with David pricking up

18. Mr Ginsburg was presumably the American publisher. John Graham had dined
with LW, and they both came on to Portman Square afterwards.
19. Iris Origo, née Cutting (b. 1902), daughter of the American first husband of her
thrice-married mother, Lady Sibyl Lubbock, quo Scott. She had been brought up
in Florence and, on her marriage in 1924 to the Marchese Antonio Origo, they
bought a run-down estate in the Val d'Orcia, and gradually revivified it. She came
to tea with the Woolfs at Tavistock Square on 25 June to discuss her book Allegra,
which they published in October 1935 (HP Checklist 373). The party at the
Herberts' was a dance given for Laura, youngest daughter of the late Aubrey
Herbert (Lady Margaret Duckworth's half-brother), who in 1937 married Evelyn
Waugh.

his ears across the room. So he had to be drawn in; & I think we have said the same things before—about the relevant facts; biography as an art. Then the door opened & in came Leo Myers, like a du Maurier drawing; such a perfect white waistcoat, (I had not changed—oh dear, when I have such nice clothes now) & his grizzled distinguished head. But he still looks like a sleepy viper.[20] Well then we talked about novels; & could one write down thoughts for a whole day? He had done this & torn it up. He does not keep a notebook. What shall we do about our biographies? Can one report talk? Fear. He is always afraid. And Origo was silent for half an hour, because of going to the party. But she would lose her fear after the entry was over. Leo will be unhappy the next morning. Why does one do these things? Because this is life, after all. One has to. In the street David said that LM is in love with Iris. Thats why he had come. The sleepy viper in his white waistcoat.

L.'s book selling now; & he is cheerful, & very contrite, in his way, about Mabel. Here he comes in about the question of Ethel writing an introduction to Brewster's book. And Vita writes that Gwen has to have a terrible operation. And Nessa does not write. And after thunder & heat & cold it is hot again; and in an access of generosity we have lent Monks House to Stephen Tennant, & thank God we are alone this week end.

Sunday 30 June

We went to Swakeleys Farm [Ickenham] yesterday & bought a dog— Sally. She has a fine domed head; is like a three of black diamonds very globular eyes; a bloodhounds muzzle; very affectionate, supple, 13 months old, clasps L.'s breast, climbs on to his chair, & is afraid of the basement stairs. She cost £18—dear me. Still as we say, its nice to have a good dog. And we shall breed from her. She is very distinguished looking. The only question is, has she intelligence? She has already her own rather gentle whimsical manner—fumbles, paws; is lighter, more nervous, perhaps less solid a character than Pinka. But so far she has no marked fault, unless she is perhaps fastidious about her food. Had her nose been the 18th of an inch longer, she would have been a champion like her sister, who fetched £2, or £300.

Mr Lloyd is a great expert. He lives in a trim villa residence, that is, in fact an old farm; has 1701 on the chimney. But the room where we waited was completely modernised: with all the cups & bowls, cigar cases, engraved with tributes, in what are called perhaps chiffoniers. He has made a very snug place for himself out of the passion for cockers. "A very

20. Leopold Hamilton Myers (1881-1944), a contemporary of LW's at Trinity College, Cambridge, was a man of considerable means and a serious novelist.

nice little person" he said. So did the Kennel man. They have their own language. It was broiling hot, & the garden paved with sham crazy paving: all the image of a garden.

[? *Thursday 4 July*]

Well of course its extremely interesting having to deal with so many different selves. Theres the one that enjoys external life. Will she now insist upon my enjoying external life—the mild fluent chatter of the Buchans? Yes, I did enjoy it. I liked the simplicity the swiftness, the release, the expansion. And L. says "They spend their money getting on— thats why they[re] Governor Generals" & I think thats not true. But how queer to have so many selves—how bewildering![1]

Monday 15 July

I have let the days slip I see, a good thing no doubt, as this book is too full; but I have left out a good many encounters; my visit to the Buchans, a strenuous day, which left me raddled; & we went to Monks House, where, as I have not noted, Stephen Tennant was planted; & came & talked, happily gone to Piddinghoe, though; & I slept; then there was the heat wave—still indomitably with us; & then Odette & Clive & the Brenans[2]—she [Odette] a Paris tart, with eyebrows elongated like antennae, to give her the likeness of a bird in flight, she being all for speed & vengeance & venom & vice—not a woman I like; & Clive sparred, nor did she like meeting anyone who knew her ways. Gerald to me grown commonplace & dried, like one of those hams or tongues that hang in country grocers shops: always, too, uneasily reverting to his book, which was only by way of lesson & trial; indeed he spent some time reading up facts about rogues in the Brit. Mus. But it is fatal to try to excuse one's works. His wife is a rather faded but L. says very nice, genuine & simple, American; & they go back to their lovely Malaga house, where Gerald has, as he rather ostentatiously intimated, his illegitimate children.[3] There, in an English Colony, they can live patriarchally on £200 a year; & he

1. VW went to stay the night of 2 July with Susan Buchan (now Lady Tweedsmuir) at Elsfield Manor, near Oxford. For a full account of the visit, see *V VW Letters*, no. 3040.
2. Clive Bell dined at Tavistock Square on 8 July with Odette Keun (1888-1978), a writer and journalist born in Constantinople, who lived for some years in France with H. G. Wells, from whom she separated in bitterness in 1932. The Brenans came in after dinner.
3. Gerald Brenan's book was *Jack Robinson*; see above, 20 October 1933. For his own picaresque life, see his *Personal Record, 1920-72* (1974).

can for ever turn & fumble over his books; looking, poor man, with those obstinate little eyes, for the right word. But it was a jangled evening, during which, by the way, round the corner at the Bussys, Frances Partridge gave birth to a son; or rather had him cut out: & all went well.[4]

All this time the Bristol speech was weighing on me, and making me unable to get into my swing for the last lap: so I shut down, wrote it, learnt it, said it & went to Bristol, the hottest day of the year on Friday & said it, dripping, to a large, but not I think very appropriate audience.[5] It puzzles me why such displays, using up so much nerve power, should be needed. There was Roger's face on the canvas, smiling at me, & them. But oh the heavenly relief when we drove off in the hot evening to Bradford on Avon, & slept the night in an ancient workhouse in the valley [*the Old Court Hotel*]; with a disordered garden, a stream with rotting sacks of old clothes, & the usual elderly ladies, retired business men, spaniels, bustling landladies & so on. And then, with a divine inspiration, we made across Avebury to Lechlade; went to Fairford & found the Carnival braying outside the church with the painted windows, had tea ad. lib: the milk in enamel jugs, the sugar in zinc bath tubs, under the trees; then slept at Lechlade, walked by the river, saw the moon rise, like a rose petal, & yesterday drove to Kelmscot & peeped over the wall.[6] In this country everything is made of silver grey flaky stone, & the houses cluster round, with their little gables, all crowded, ancient, with roses, with haystacks, & the river flowing in the great grass meadows, all untouched, beyond the builders ring, which begins at Abingdon, & then till London all becomes red brick Georgian; & Riverine, that is gramophontic, girls in trousers, young men in shorts, all noisy & strident & a little indecent—a bad lunch at the Quarry Hotel [Bourne End], & so home here.

Nor must I forget Mr Ellis Roberts, not that he is attractive, an inky little podgy underworld man, who came to ask me to be president of the PEN in succession to Wells. This great honour, unanimously offered with Priestly enthusiastic, would involve meeting authors, for which purpose apparently it exists—that authors should meet & discuss each others works. With E.R. in front of me—but no: how could anyone invent such a post,

---

4. Lytton Burgo (d. 1963), only child of Ralph and Frances Partridge, was born by Caesarian section on 8 July 1935.

5. In response to Margery Fry's request (see above, 20 June 1935), the Woolfs drove to Bristol on 12 July so that VW might open the Roger Fry Memorial Exhibition at the Bristol Museum and Art Gallery. Her address, printed for private circulation only (Kp A21), was reprinted in 1948 in *The Moment* (Kp A29)

6. The late perpendicular church of St Mary at Fairford has twenty-eight 16th-century stained glass windows. Kelmscott Manor, near Lechlade, was the home of William Morris from 1871 until his death in 1896; it was still lived in by his daughter May.

how could anyone accept it? He pretended, poor worm, to feel as I did; which was a lie.[7]

And now, with a brain washed cool & rid of that intolerable speech, I must dream myself back in to my own world—rather a touch & go proceeding: but its no use getting worried; the end must come. & whether its good or bad, Heaven knows.

Tuesday 16 July

A curious sense of complete failure. Margery hasn't written to me about my speech: according to Janie Pamela thought the whole thing a failure. And it was for this that I ruined my last pages! I cant write this morning. Cant get into the swing. Innumerable worries, about getting people to dine & so on, afflict me. My head is all jangled. And I have to get that d—d speech printed, or refuse to. The director has written. Never again, oh never again!

I think though that I can get the last pages right, if I can only dream myself back into them. Yes, but how dream, when I have to see Susie & Ethel, to see Miss Belsher's house, to ring up, & write notes & order this & that? Well, be still & ruminate; its only 16th: theres a fortnight before August. And I'm sure that there is a remarkable shape somewhere concealed there. Its not mere verbiage, I think. If necessary I could put it away. But I think no: merely go on & perhaps write a very rapid short sketch, in ink—thats a good plan. Go back & get the central idea, & then rocket into it. And be very controlled, & keep a hand on myself too. And perhaps read a little Shakespeare. Yes, one of the last plays: I think I will do that, so as to loosen my muscles. But oh this anxiety, & the perpetual knocking of the cup out of my hand.

Wednesday 17 July

Last night as I was sitting alone, L. dining with the [Noel-]Bakers, there were three rings, & I went down & let in Julian, who said "I have been given a professorship in China." He was very much excited, rather alarmed, naturally—it means that he must start in the middle of August & spend 3 years in China at Wu Jong, or some such place, alone on a flooded river.[8] So we talked—intimately, I mean about the past & our

7. International P[oets] E[ssayists] N[ovelists] Clubs were intended to promote friendly contacts among writers all over the world. H. G. Wells had succeeded the first president, John Galsworthy, and J. B. Priestley was to succeed him. Ellis Roberts was vice-president of the English club.

8. On 16 July Julian Bell was interviewed for and offered the post of Professor of English at the National University of Wuhan, on the Yangtze River, for which he had applied a year earlier (see above 17 July 1934). Tony = Antoinette Pirie, née Patey, one of his Cambridge friends.

lives, for the first time. I'm very sorry he's to go—the delightful, honest bubbly yet after all so sympathetic & trusty young man. Still, obviously this is his first real experience. He had to break off to answer a trunk call from Tony. He said she spoke with almost too much common sense. But he had always determined not to let his private life shackle him. Then he will travel about China in his holidays, & come back a full grown mature man, with a place in the world. He wants to write on politics & philosophy & to enter politics seriously. He says politics have got more & more on his conscience. They're on the conscience of all his generation. So he can't be merely a poet, a writer. I see his dilemma. So he goes, & I'm sorry. Three years. He will be thirty & I 56 alas.

Just now I finished my first wild retyping & find the book comes to 740 pages: that is ⟨174,800⟩ 148,000 words: but I think I can shorten: all the last part is still rudimentary & wants shaping; but I'm too tired in the head to do it seriously this moment. I think all the same I can reduce it: & then—? Dear me. I see why I fled, after The Waves, to Flush. One wants simply to sit on a bank & throw stones. I want also to read with a free mind. And to let the wrinkles smooth themselves out. Susie Buchan, Ethel, then Julian—so I talked from 4.30 till 1 am with only 2 hours for dinner & silence.

I think I see that the last chapter shd. be formed round N[orth]'s speech: it must be much more formal; & I think I see how I can bring in interludes—I mean spaces of silence, & poetry & contrast.

Friday 19 July

No. I go on getting preliminary headaches. It is no good trying to do the last spurt, which should be much like a breeze in the heavy elms, these last days here: yes, a wind blowing in the trees that are thick with green leaves. For there must be movement as well as some weight, something for the breeze to lift. And we have Edith [Sitwell] & Eddie Playfair, & Ottoline & Julian & Quentin tonight.

Yesterday we went to tea with Mr & Mrs Standgroom.[9] Coming out we said, no, L. had the technical phrase—but I cant remember it—that they have the world they want. Bedroom suites are made for them; all Tot. Court Road is theirs; the world is to their liking. And gramophones & cases of cutlery & table centres. All this they have & enjoy, genuinely, without any shyness. Standgroom is a wizened parched little man, under her thumb, a clerk in the Customs, who deals with tea. I thought them rather engaging, so pleased with having what everyone has. And Miss B. as she wishes to be called, is quite on top of the situation. Patted my

9. Peggy Belsher, the secretary of the Hogarth Press, had recently married Mr Stangroom.

shoulder. No snobbishness. No sense of class differences. And science has helped them to electric toasters: I mean their life materially is much freer & easier than ours at Hyde Park Gate. The only room she did not show us was the W.C. We saw her wedding dress—a pale pink. She does not mean to have children.

Saturday 20 July

But it turned out very well last night: headache lifted—we walked in Regents Park in the rain. Old Edith singular—very, with her great bald face—its sweep of rather repulsive brown—its shock of red hair. So beautiful in some lights; & the thin fan shaped hands & their gestures, timid, appealing, attached to this large fat clumsy body in its black rather sack like dress. She has great wit & some sharp edge of character. Quite decided. Knows her mind. She made us laugh all dinner, talking about W. Lewis, who used to paint her, letting her in, at a chink of the door. Who have you been seeing? Clive Bell? And he wore a patch over one eye; switched it on to another. as he disliked the light.[10] She has a gay rambling butterfly mind; & a good deal of sting. & humanity. In came Ottoline; rather garish, & not so quick in the mind as the rest of us. Eddie a very good listener. Then Julian, with his poems, & Quentin. It was all demonstration on Edith's part, done for our amusement very difficult to recapture. And something drenched & feeble. She has to get up at 7 to write about Queen Victoria at the bidding of Dick le Mare, who is a magician.[11] Something yielding about her, humble, & yet a lady of quality. "The horrid middle class way" said Ott. Edith echoed her. Looks like a Plantagenet tomb said Ott. So she does, with her high nose, in the air, & her thin lips & her little peering eyes—very medieval. Ottoline said you couldnt read Sh[akespea]re in India—too remote.

The Woolfs went to Rodmell for their summer break on 25 July.

Saturday 3 August

With that remark of Ott's about not reading Shre in India I broke off my London summer abruptly; though it chattered itself out in great style with a dinner to John [Lehmann]—a reconciliation dinner—& the Busseys, at which he laughed so loud & free that my restraint went; & I talked French to Simon, & went round to the Bussys & saw Clive like a

10. Wyndham Lewis's portrait of Edith Sitwell, now in the Tate Gallery (no. 5437), was begun in 1923 but was not completed until the mid-thirties as she, disliking Lewis's manner, broke off the sittings.
11. Richard de la Mare (b. 1901), son of the poet Walter de la Mare, was a director of Faber & Faber, who published Edith Sitwell's *Victoria of England* in 1936.

white robin redbreast, all got up going to a party at the Courtaulds: but I do it very seldom, he said in a huff, when Simon chaffed him. "Mon cher—vous etes arrivé."[1]

So the summer ended; & now opens again here, with Nessa back; Charleston in being, though rather intermittent, with Duncan in Rome still, Clive going to Greece, Julian to China, & Nessa proposing to paint the Queen Mary in London.[2] And the harvest is positively orange on the hill, & the country divinely coloured ripe ashcoloured & gold, as I came through Tristram's Grove up the river.

Nessa came about a cable to China; & we called in at Charleston to suggest—what its no use foraging in my rather dissipated mind to find. For, by way of a jaunt from the book—the unchristened book—I took a flight into Marryat this—& here I broke off, to go & dredge the pond I think.[3]

Friday 16 August

I cannot make a single note here, because I am so terrifically pressed re-writing—yes, typing out again at the rate, if possible, of 100 pages a week, this impossible eternal book. I work without looking up till one: what it now is, & therefore I must go in, leaving a whole heap of things unsaid: so many people, so many scenes, & beauty, & a fox & sudden ideas.[4]

Wednesday 21 August

Up in London yesterday. And I saw this about myself in a book [*untraced*] at the Times—the most patient & conscientious of artists— which I think is true, considering how I slave at every word of that book. My head is like a like a—pudding, is it—something that mildly throbs &

1. The Bussys when in London lodged at the Strachey home in Gordon Square, no. 51; Clive's rooms were next door, in no. 50.
2. Both Duncan Grant and Vanessa Bell had been commissioned by the Cunard-White Star Company to provide decorations for the SS Queen Mary, launched in September 1934. In the event Duncan's three large panels were rejected, but Vanessa's smaller decorative designs were used.
3. VW was reading *The Life and Letters of Captain Marryat* by his daughter Florence Marryat, published in 2 volumes in 1872. This was the starting point for her essay 'The Captain's Death Bed' published in *TLS* 26 September 1935 (Kp C346). See also her Holograph Reading Notes, vol. 10, in Berg.
4. People seen between the date of the last entry and this one included old Mrs Woolf and attendant family, John Graham, Keyneses, Bells, Charles Mauron, Robsons, Janie Bussy and Stephen Tennant.

cant breed a word at the end of the morning. I begin fresh enough. And I sent off the first 20 pages or so to Mabel [*typist*] yesterday.

Margery Fry comes on Friday with her hands full of papers, she says. Another book. Have I the indomitable courage to start on another? Think of the writing & re-writing. Also there will be joys & ecstasies though. Again very hot. I am going to re paint this room. Went to Carpenters [*untraced*] yesterday—chose chintzes. Is this worth writing? Perhaps.

Harvest all ready. Blackberries ripe. No mushrooms. Abyssinia. Cabinet summoned. Sitting today. Should I like to be old Baldwin? returning from Aix in this heat.[5] L. has indigestion. Mitz spent the night on the free. Janie left the door open. We have our electric stove.

Thursday 22 August

Worked in the morning. Finished Marryat. Went to Lewes, very hot day; & bought stores. also distemper. And went to the County Library; full of books. So hot after tea: walked along the river bank; a game of bowls; beaten; dined with Keynes's. Maynard not well—rather damp talk. He went. Talk of Abyssinia. Thunderstorm at 3.30. L. made me come & sleep in the upstairs room. It strikes me that I will call this book, Other People's Houses.

Thursday 29 August

I had meant to write one matter of fact note daily, but have never had time. My brain all tossing after the mornings work. Julian is leaving Newhaven at this moment I suppose for 3 years. I have been doing the scene of Eleanor's day with the usual pangs & ecstasies. On Tuesday we went to Sissinghurst; lost L.'s spectacles, & the meat on the top of the car. Saw the great new room. Vita in trousers. Rather woke my affection & regret. Harold gave me Mrs Lindbergh's book. Woke my insensate obsession—to write P & P—by telling me how a room of ones own is regarded & my American fame.[6] The big Alsatian hunting; the pink tower & the rain on the leaves, L. said, falling as he had not heard it since Ceylon. To dine at Charleston. Julian a little depressed. Duncan laughing

5. Stanley Baldwin, who had succeeded Ramsay MacDonald as Prime Minister on 7 June, cut short his holiday at Aix-les-Bains, and returned to Downing Street for a meeting of the cabinet following the breakdown of the Three-Power talks on Abyssinia in Paris.

6. Harold Nicolson had just returned from staying with the Lindberghs in America, where he revised the proofs of his biography of Dwight Morrow, father of Anne Morrow Lindbergh whose book, *North to the Orient* (1935), he gave to VW. 'P&P' appears to be another temporary title for what was to become *Three Guineas*.

about Lady Blanche—his name for G. St Aubyn. Grouse. Nessa composed. Quentin in bed with throat. I very sleepy. Kissed J. in the dark garden. We think of going to China, at any rate think so, to mitigate the parting. Yesterday very drowsy. Walked the Tristram Grove & river walk. L. came to meet me & missed me. Louie's child attacked by dog. Took it to Lewes. Mr Hancock brought in with injured leg. Very bad. Bach at night. Man playing oboe fainted in the middle. War seems inevitable. I won one game of bowls out of 3. Reading Miss Mole, Abbé Dunnet (good), an occasional bite at Hind & Panther, but brain too expanded.[7] Oh to be done with the book & my own mistress again. Piles of Roger's papers sent by Margery—a whole box. I have now 3 large boxes, but dare not look in, & am terribly obsessed by P. & P.

Friday 30 August

For a wonder, my head is clear, & my hand does not shake; but then I've been doing the Law Courts passage, which went easily: an upper air passage. Now the book seems to me very good.

Last night they sung the Belgian anthem at the Prom: out of respect for the Queen: & after that, the news-reader announced, in his most penetrated with respectful sorrow voice, the death of the Queen in a motor accident. The car ran off the road into a tree, & she was flung out; struck her head. The King kissed her, as she died "& as I could not do anything, I went on" says the most trustworthy observer, a passer by, this morning. That, in its way is a tragedy.[8] Mr Baird [*Rodmell resident*] had a fit after having tea at Southease. I distempered—the colour is too blue, but better than the green; then we walked to the river, played bowls, & now expect, alas, as I'm in the swim, a teaparty of the most ferocious description, & its a blowing rainy cold day too; the Wolves, Hugh Jones, Angelica & Eve. Not much pleasure to be had, & a tired brain tomorrow; but as I often say—what do I often say? Something to the effect that one must sweep it all up in one's stride, even as a matter of art. Could I be alone, & write & walk & read, perhaps—but no, I admit the thought at the moment has nothing but heavenly delight in it. As it is, off to Lewes, buying cakes; arrange the room; put the kettle on, & say to Mrs W. Mind the steps.

Saturday 31 August

Only the Wolves came however. Torrents & floods & rain & wind. Edgar [Woolf] like a corpse—not a pleasant one either. Yawned behind

7. *Miss Mole* (1930) by Emily Hilda Young; Abbé Dunnet, unidentified; *The Hind and the Panther* (1687) by John Dryden.
8. Queen Astrid of the Belgians died in a motor accident near Lucerne on 29 August 1935; King Leopold, who was driving, was injured.

his hand. Sylvia nervous, cat faced, making conversation. Chiefly about gold fish dogs & cars. L. valiant: I did my usual owl with Mrs W. & she said, as my reward, there was no talk she enjoyed more. Went to Lewes first, in the flood, without a rain coat; went to Helen Boyd, two nervous twittering spinsters in a panelled room, about servants: want a 3 day a week girl. Called at Mount Street. Olivers out.[9] Hugh Jones waited an hour at Southease; went home. Angelica did not come. Mercifully, as the party was damp & dismal, sitting till 6.30 in the dining room. How it rains, said Mrs W. The tap had overflowed: the window a ripple of water. Read Hind & Panther. D.H.L. by E. (good) & slept.[10]

Everybody talking about Abysinnia, wh. I cannot spell, nor can I form letters, though the morning has been fluent—E. & Parnell [*The Years, p. 120*]—too fluent. A blowing grey day, laden with water.

Wednesday 4 September

The most critical day since Aug 4th 1914. So the papers say.[1] In London yesterday. Writings chalked up all over the walls. "Dont fight for foreigners. Briton should mind her own business." Then a circle with a symbol in it. Fascist propaganda, L. said. Mosley again active. The Queen of B's funeral. Flags at half mast. Bought an umbrella for 25/-. The first good umbrella I've had for years. Man on the bus saw it was new, with a tassel.

And I think I will call the book "The Years"

L. saw Miss Swinstead Smith, a very nervous, nice, odd shabby woman, youngish; her first book; Constables almost published it but cried off on commercial grounds. We are going to do it though. She lives at Sennen in a cottage rent £12 a year.[2] I went to L[eiceste]r. Sqre & bought silk for nightgown. Mabel at the flat, very competent. Hot, windy. Home to grouse early. Now pouring. Letter from Denny, a silly gushing letter. has a son. Nature. She writes worse than she talks. Perhaps its writing to me. And Queenie Leavis also writes, a priggish letter, drawing attention to Life as we have known it, in that prigs manual, Scrutiny. All they can do is to schoolmaster.[3]

9. Helen Boyd was an agency at 14 High Street, Lewes, which presumably supplied VW with the name and address of a potential but elusive servant girl.

10. *D. H. Lawrence. A Personal Record* (1935), by E. T. (Jessie Chambers).

1. *The Times*, 4 September 1935: 'The session of the Council which begins this afternoon at Geneva is universally regarded as the most critical in the history of the League [of Nations].' It was concerned to find conciliatory means to avert the use of force by Mussolini in furthering his territorial ambitions in Abyssinia.

2. The Hogarth Press published *The Marchesa and Other Stories* by K. Swinstead-Smith in March 1936 (*HP Checklist* 398).

3. 'Denny'—i.e. Elizabeth Read—wrote to VW on 31 August (MHP, Sussex) to announce the birth of her son George. Queenie Dorothy Leavis (1906-1981),

Oh how it pours! I used my umbrella for the first time to cross the garden. Cant write today. I suppose after yesterday. Nessa in London. We saw a snake eating a toad: it had half the toad in, half out; gave a suck now & then. The toad slowly disappearing. L. poked its tail; the snake was sick of the crushed toad, & I dreamt of men committing suicide & cd. see the body shooting through the water.[4]

Thursday 5 September

I've had to give up writing The Years—thats what its to be called— this morning. Absolutely floored. Sally in bed. Cant pump up a word. Yet I can see, just, that somethings there; so I shall wait, a day or two, & let the well fill. It has to be damned deep this time—740 pages in it. I think, psychologically, this is the oddest of my adventures. Half my brain dries completely; but I've only to turn over, & there's the other half, I think, ready, quite happily to write a little article. Oh if only anyone knew anything about the brain. And, even today, when I'm desperate, almost in tears looking at the chapter, unable to add to it, I feel I've only got to fumble & find the end of the ball of string—some start off place, someone to look at Sara perhaps—no, I dont know—& my head would fill & the tiredness go. But I've been waking & worrying. Bothered about L.'s indigestion & his loss of weight, with the apple picking & the Cttee meeting autumn coming on.

A very sensational voice on the loudspeaker last night. M[ussolini]. closes the door. Deep disappointment. What next? &c. But the papers this morning are less melodramatic, & incline to think that the affair will drag on undecided for some time. I was also in a stew about war & patriotism last night. And when it comes to my thinking about my country! Thank God, John Bailey's life is out, & I shall seek consolation there. And write about Mrs Lindbergh?

Friday 6 September

I am going to wrap my brain in green dock leaves for a few days: 5, if I can hold out; till the children, L.'s nieces, have gone. If I can—for I think a scene is forming. Why not make an easier transition: Maggie looking at

---

co-editor with her husband F. R. Leavis of the critical quarterly *Scrutiny*; her article, 'Lady Novelists and the Lower Orders' in the issue for September 1935, refers to the collection *Life as We Have Known It* by Co-operative Working Women (1931), edited by Margaret Llewelyn Davies (Kp B11), and to VW's 'acute and sensitive introductory letter'. VW forwarded Mrs Leavis's letter and article to Margaret Llewelyn Davies (see *V VW Letters*, no. 3061).

4. Cf. *Between the Acts*, p. 119.

the Serpentine say; & so avoid that abrupt spring? Isn't it odd that this was the scene I had almost a fit to prevent myself writing? This will be the most exciting thing I ever wrote, I kept saying. And now its the stumbling block. I wonder why? too personal, is that it? Out of key? But I wont think. A flutter & clutter of engagements: Nessa; Stephen [Tennant], Ethel, then the children; & L., as I know, is very touchy, dear love, about his family: an inferiority complex, I call it, thinking how much more vigorous & interesting my relations are: missing Julian; yes. Still whats odd is how nice people are: children always. So there's no great harm done if I have to give up 48 hours.

Hugh, like Pipsy about the nose & eyes, Ang[e]l[ica] & Eve & Q. to tea yesterday. Bowls & archery. Into Lewes, shopping, which I dislike. Got Mrs Thompsett to come: Sandy clear skinned; was distempering kitchen, bright green; rather a good colour. I must get Rosie to make my curtains. Reading. Miss Mole: fair, but soft; & Stella Benson but I'm hard on novels, & an old dr. called Salter, & Dryden, & Alfieri.[5] How soon one gets the hang of a written language! My gift I think—the shape of the sentence. Violent wind & rain; violent sun & light; & they go on talking, threatening, advancing & retreating at Geneva. Look how clear my hand is when I don't write fiction of a morning. Head cool now at 1 instead of parboiled.

Saturday 7 September

A heavenly quiet morning reading Alfieri by the open window & not smoking. I believe one could get back to the old rapture of reading if one did not write. The difficulty is, writing makes one['s] brain so hot it cant settle to read; & then when the heat goes, I'm so tired in the head, I can only skirmish. But I've stopped 2 days now The Years: & feel the power to settle calmly & firmly on books coming back at once. John Bailey's life, come today, makes me doubt though—what? Everything. Sounds like a mouse squeaking under a mattress. But I've only just glanced & got the smell of Lit. dinner, Lit. Sup, Lit this that & the other—& the one remark to the effect that Virginia Woolf of all people, has been given Cowper by Desmond, & likes it! I, who read Cowper when I was 15—d—d nonsense.[6]

---

5. There were at least four Thomsett families living in Rodmell in the 1930s. Rose Bartholomew was Percy's sister. Stella Benson's unfinished novel *Mundos* was published posthumously in 1935. *Dr Salter: His Diary and Reminiscences from the year 1849 to the year 1932*, compiled by J. O. Thompson, 1933.

6. See *John Bailey, 1864-1931, Letters and Diaries* (1935), edited by his wife: '4 April 1927: Dined Literary Society... Our talk was chiefly of Milton and Cowper, about whom MacCarthy is very enthusiastic.. said he had given Cowper lately to Virginia

SEPTEMBER 1935

Monday 10 September

A not so heavenly morning. Children staying here.[7] Chill. L. in a stew about Stephen [Tennant]—that is he wants to come: why have S. 3 times & not Kingsley Martin. A very old, sorry, but not serious story. And yet how foolish to have even these disagreements; & yet I suppose how inevitable—magnets which draw other little straws along. Can I read, write or think though, going for a picnic, & the children—nice lively undistinguished brats—shooting. Yet how quick & hard & unexpected childrens minds are. Everything within 10 miles seen exactly; their school; the maid who's in love with the gardener; a solicitor not so good as a barrister: the rank of the girls fathers: the whole of society in one drop.

Thursday 12 September

Mornings which are neither quiet nor heavenly, but mixed of hell & ecstasy: never have I had such a hot balloon in my head as re-writing The Years; because its so long; & the pressure is so terrific. But I will use all my art to keep my head sane. I will stop writing at 11.30 & read Italian or Dryden and so dandle myself along.

To Ethel at Miss Hudson's yesterday.[8] As I sat in the complete English Gentleman's home, I wondered how anybody could tolerate that equipage; & thought how a house should be portable like a snail shell. In future perhaps people will flirt out houses like little fans; & go on. There'll be no settled life within walls. There were endless clean, well repaired rooms. A maid in a cap. Cakes on pagoda trays. A terrible array of glossy brown furniture, & books—red sham leather. Many nice old rooms, but the manor house has been embellished & made of course self consciously elaborate. A ball room: a library—empty. And Miss Hudson all brushed up with her Pekinese, a competent ex mayor of Eastbourne, with waved grey hair, & all so neat & stout, & the silver frames askew; & the air of order, respectability, commonplace. "I'm going to call on the vicars wife." Ethel immensely red & stout; churning out, poor old woman, the usual indefatigable egotism about deafness & her Mass. She must have a scene every six months. No. But of course, to be deaf, to be 76—well, back to

---

Woolf of all people, and she had caught his enthusiasm, which he thought a confirmation of his prophecy about the young.' Cf. *III VW Diary*, 28 February 1927: 'I think Cowper is a good poet. I'd like to write about him.' The Woolfs dined with the MacCarthys on 17 March 1927.

7. i.e. Pippin (Philippa) and Marie, Philip Woolf's daughters, who stayed from Sunday to Tuesday.

8. Councillor Miss Alice Hudson, JP, had been Mayor of Eastbourne in 1927; she lived in the restored and enlarged 17th century Wootton Manor, near Polegate.

Charleston with Eve & Angelica. And we called on the Wigrams & snubbed Stephen off.

Friday 13 September

What a combination for the superstitious! Driving off to visit Margaret & Lilian at Dorking; & I have got into a mild flood I think with The ⟨Ps⟩ Years. The difficulty is always at the beginning of chapters or sections where a whole new mood has to be caught plumb in the centre.

Richmond accepts my Marryat & thanks me for his poor little knighthood! L. is made all rigid by that d—d fool Brewster & his complaints about the photographs. To make matters worse, Dr Mary Gordon rings up to bother us about her life of the Ladies of Llangollen;[9] & it has turned grey & windy. Am I to ask Angelica or not? These are my troubles, as the man said . . . Yesterday L. took the car in; (but I'm making up scenes: this began in the middle of last night). Then we walked to Lewes, & found the new way, after all these years, by the Canal, under the Bridge. And home to bowls, & veal cutlets. Reading Love for Love, Life of Anthony Hope, &c. A man could live on £200 at Oxford if he lived at home.[10]

Sunday 15 September

A terrific downpour. Never was such rain, I think, as this year. Autumn showing through. Autumn birds chirping through the rain. A queer book, Hope's life—so neat, discreet, & somehow dated. An Edwardian writer making £70,000 out of books in 10 years; very much in the world, like a du Maurier; yet sensitive, depressed: much left out I guess; only a decorous shell, sitting sucking a gold knobbed cane by the Row. But genuine in its well bred way.

I am thinking I will broach the three boxes of Roger; very staidly, merely beginning to drop a few facts into my brain. Indeed I must, as people want letters & so on. But I swear I will not let it buzz me into excitement. I will keep a space for my P. P. little book. Anthony Hope lived in dread of going sterile. I dont think I ever envisage that as a possibility. I always say on the contrary, Shall I ever have time enough to write

9. Bruce Richmond, editor of the *TLS*, had been created Knight Bachelor in the King's Birthday and Jubilee honours announced on 3 June 1935. Dr Mary Louisa Gordon's book on the Ladies of Llangollen, *Chase of the Wild Goose*, was published by the Hogarth Press in May 1936 (*HP Checklist* 388).
10. *Love for Love* (1695) by William Congreve. Sir Charles Mallett's biography of Anthony Hope (author of *The Prisoner of Zenda*, &c), *Anthony Hope and His Books* (1935), is the source of the information VW notes, and which she repeated in the notes (I, 31) to *Three Guineas*.

out all thats in my head? A much happier state; though suppose what's in my head becomes sillier & feebler? But why should it? Not if I vary it sufficiently: what with pamphlets, criticism, poetry, fiction, & as I think a play perhaps. But then I'm a very slow writer. He did his book yearly. And The Years (that name is fixed; dropped like a billiard ball into a pocket) will have taken me very nearly 3 years—say I finish it by Christmas. And I never think, seriously, of dying.

Nessa & Duncan are to come to tea; Angelica & Eve to stay the night; then London, & L.'s labour party tomorrow. So the summer ends itself. A very hard working summer.

Margaret & Lilian in a pale yellow house, fitted as compactly as a ships cabin—fires let into the wall—baths turning into cupboards more or less—in a wood.[11] Very nice tree opposite the sitting room, & spotted woodpeckers. The best view of that silly pretty Surrey country: M. in a cap; L. very blind. We had so much to say, they were so starved of talk, that in fact we said things of the utmost triviality. That was queer. And had to see over the house. A pile of dull 19th Century classics that L[ilian]. wants to sell. All spick & span: very blue & yellow. M.'s melodramatic bad taste surprising. We drove through Rusper & other small dignified Surrey towns lying shut in, airless, among hedges: merely country. Now to write letter after letter. But I cant cross the garden in this rain. Percy has to hide. Even the Church bells, I think, dont ring. A black bird digging in the grass. And the rooks cawing through the down rush; through the mist of rain.

Tuesday 17 September

So they came: I mean all the Bells, & Janie, growing a little elderly & showing her grandfather the shoemaker, but very gayly dressed; a coloured comforter round her neck; a chic little knitted cap, & a black coat with silver buttons. Quentin like a large red & white sheepdog. Eve very pretty; mouse like with her pointed twitching nose. When I woke her early next morning she looked just like a white sleeping mouse. Angelica suddenly depressed. I think I did not get enough glow into the dinner, & she thought why did I want to come?

London yesterday: a violent storm of wind all night. Garden a litter of apples & branches. Percy busy staking up trees.

[Friday 20 September]

Yes it was a terrific storm; a storm to mark, I suppose. All the trees chocolate brown on the wind side; little leaves like chipped potatoes. We

---

11. Their house was Hillspur, Punchbowl Lane, Dorking, in Surrey.

went to Seaford & saw the explosions of white water over the lighthouse. The cars were stopped by a policeman. Sea coming over the road. (I passed 5 minutes making up The Years, which is now going strong: only then we have Tom for the week end of course).

People were standing under the shelter of the Buckle Inn [*facing the sea*]. I went creeping round while L. took a photograph, & saw the people standing in the upper window, looking out: very 18th century; the lower windows & cellars boarded up. Clive Angelica & Q. yesterday. I'm ashamed to say I had longed for this week to be all alone; reading; never had a quiet week all this summer, & the balm it would be—& even a tea party means apprehension, breakage. Went to Lewes; bought a cake; left the car, tried walking home; fine but a great tearing wind; so stopped at Iford & took the bus. Poor old Clive a little battered I thought. A grey tuft. He has a curious antiquity, premature age, sometimes: I suppose when the top doesn't spin. He had been spinning round Greece with Dadie, Shepherd [Sheppard], aristocrats, schoolmasters; was impressed by the beauty; enjoyed himself vastly. Must have done his owl vociferously. Was very nice, I've no doubt, & had dined God knows with what Lallas & Hoffmans & the rich & the great at Venice. All determined on war. Clive is writing a letter to the N.S. against war. War's so awful it cant be right anyhow—an argument for which I like him: his genuine humanity. Dislike of being uncomfortable himself: yes; but he dislikes other people's unhappiness too. Says Mu[ssoli]ni is mad—the Italians say so; but all the young are frothed up.[12] Very cold. Sat over the fire. Two nights ago I started reading Roger. There's all the schoolboy letters to begin on: whether its wise, I dont know. But I think I can—the boys are in the churchyard, & want to climb over & get our chestnuts, but see me— mass my day all together.

Monday 23 September

Reflections on Tom week end: that it is too long[13]. Cant write. That he is more masterly; tells a story like one who has the right; is broader & bonier & more wild eyed—long almond shaped eyes—that he means to write modern verse plays: that he is self confident although going up Charleston Lane in the dark last night (Lottie advancing in her red jacket) he told me that he has no self confidence: Joyce has; but Joyce is interminably bored with everything. What can he do when he's finished this book? Perhaps thats why he procrastinates. We dined at Charleston.

12. Clive Bell had been on a three-week Hellenic cruise, 20 August-15 September, staying at Venice en route and return. His letter on 'Sanctions' was published in the *NS&N* on 28 September 1935.

13. T. S. Eliot came to Monks House on the afternoon of Saturday 21 September and left on Monday morning.

Nessa ordered eleven grouse, having doubled the number, thinking of them halved: Clive, Janie, Angelica & Eve. Acting. A. did not remember her part.[14] We walked. Long silences. Bruce Richmond brooded over the week end. *His* week end: his rotund country gentleman ways: port hock bedroom candles; & telling little stories. Tom likes going there; is magisterially accepting new experiences. Likes, more than we do, respectability. Went to service at 8 on Sunday: a wet morning, & he hea[r]d one old woman say to another—in the churchyard, "And she was lying in bed with a still born child beside her." But he did his duty. A very nice man, Tom; I'm very fond of Tom, & at last not much knocked off my perch by him. That is, not as I was when he came here & I was writing Jacob's Room.[15] Now he cant much disturb The Years, though he makes me feel that I want to write a play.

Thursday 26 September

Why is this—that is the first scene with Sally & Maggie in the bedroom, the most difficult I have ever written?

Winifred Holtby is, I rather suspect, dying.[16] It is a very fine day. Two luggers with brown sails are moving very slowly down the river. We were in London yesterday. And London is in full swing. "The Abyssinians have mobilised!" exclaims one suburban lady to another in the bus. And the other says "That was in the paper yesterday". A great swarm in Rymans where I went to buy a case for my Roger notes. In future I shall write in loose leaf books, & so avoid these swelling pages. Mabel had a very nice lunch. I watched the men in T[avistock]ck Sqre eating on the pavement. They are having the road up with a drill. They eat with the point of the knife. They have lunch wrapped in newspaper. They warm some drink in a bucket. They have at least an hour off. But then I work my brain I say to myself. Belsher ill. Miss West travelling. Our last day up. Very glad to get back here. But the boys are making a bonfire in the field. We pray for a few days peace. Now 2 men want to come tomorrow to discuss the WEA at Rodmell.[17] This must be mastered. L. had a certain amount of row with Kingsley about the L. party & the League.

14. James Joyce worked for seventeen years on *Finnegan's Wake*, which was published in 1939. One family explanation for Vanessa's largesse is that, confused by Clive's sporting terms, she ordered a *brace* of grouse for each person, rather than the normal provision of one bird between two; see Clive Bell, *Old Friends* (1956), pp. 120-21. The entertainment was *Last Night in Old Pompeii*, a play in heroic couplets largely written by Julian Bell.
15. See *II VW Diary*, 19, 20 September 1920.
16. Winifred Holtby died, aged thirty-seven, on 29 September 1935.
17. John Bradfield, Workers' Educational Association tutor for East Sussex, 1933-40, came to see LW on 27 September.

[?Sunday 29 September]

Yesterday I saw the kingfisher again on the river. It flies across & across, very near the surface: it has a bright orange chocolate under side. And it is a tropical bird, sitting weighted on the bank. I have also seen a stoat—brown with a white tipped tail. Yesterday I went to Moggery Poke, back by the river. L. met me with Sarah [*the dog*], who wont walk with me. Her love increases. And I read the Lovers Melancholy & skimmed the top of the words; & want to go on reading things miles away—beautiful hard words. remote. Not Mrs Easdale, who is silly, egotistic, sloppy, & very conventional. I am shocked to find Rodmell patched on to those pages.[18]

Wednesday 2 October

Yesterday we went to the L[abour]. P[arty]. meeting at Brighton, & of course, though I have refused to go again this morning, I am so thrown out of my stride that I cant hitch on to The Years again. Why? The immersion in all that energy & all that striving for something that is quite oblivious of me; making me feel that I am oblivious of it. No, thats not got it. It was very dramatic: Bevin's attack on Lansbury.[1] Tears came to my eyes as L[ansbury]. spoke. And yet he was posing I felt—acting, unconsciously, the battered Christian man. Then Bevin too acted I suppose. He sank his head in his vast shoulders till he looked like a tortoise. Told L. not to go hawking his conscience round. And what is my duty as a human being? The women delegates were very thin voiced & insubstantial. On Monday one said, It is time we gave up washing up. A thin frail protest, but genuine. A little reed piping, but what chance against all this weight of roast beef & beer—which she must cook? All very vivid & interesting; but over lapping: too much rhetoric, & what a partial view: altering the structure of society: yes, but when its altered? Do I trust Bevin to produce a good world, when he has his equal rights? Had he been born a duke— My sympathies were with Salter who preached nonresistance. He's quite right. That should be our view.[2] But then if society

18. i.e.: *Middle Age: 1885-1932* (1935), in which Tea with Virginia Woolf is recorded at some length; see above, 27 September 1931. *The Lover's Melancholy*, the romantic comedy by John Ford, acted in 1628.

1. On the second day of the Labour Party Conference at Brighton, during the debate on the Party's attitude to enforcing sanctions against Italy in her dispute with Abyssinia, George Lansbury (1859-1940), Leader of the Labour Party since 1931 and a veteran idealistic socialist, resigned following a devastating attack on his pacifist stance by Ernest Bevin. See also *III LW*, p. 221 and *IV LW*, pp. 244-45.

2. Dr Alfred Salter (1873-1945), MD, MP, urged that Britain should acknowledge the evils of imperialism and deliver her tropical colonies into the hands of an international body, as an example to the Italians; new problems and dangers would only stem from the imposition of sanctions.

is in its present state? Happily, uneducated & voteless, I am not responsible for the state of society. These are some of the minnows that go round my head, & distract me from what is, after all, my work. A good thing to have a day of disturbance—2 days even—but not 3. So I didnt go; & cant really write. However I will make myself when I've done this. Odd the enormous susceptibility of my mind to surface impressions: how I suck them in & let them swirl about. And how far does anybodies single mind or work matter? Ought we all to be engaged in altering the structure of society? Louie said this morning she had quite enjoyed doing for us, was sorry we were going. Thats a piece of work too in its way. And yet I cant deny my love of fashioning sentences. And yet . . . L. has gone there, & I daresay I'll discuss it with him. He says politics ought to be separate from art. We walked out in the cold over the marsh, & discussed this. The fact is too my head easily tires. Yes, too tired to write. But a good thing to be too tired for that reason, minnows swirling, now & then. I will do some Roger.

The Woolfs returned to London on Saturday 5 October.

Tuesday 15 October

Since we came back I have been in such full flush, with Years all the morning, Roger between tea & dinner, a walk, & people, that here's a blank. And I only scamp Roger this evening because I wore a hole in my back yesterday; couldn't write this morning; & must go up & receive Miss Grueber (to discuss a book on women & fascism—a pure have yer as Lottie would say) in 10 minutes.[4] Yes, it has been 10 days of calm full complete bliss. And I thought how I shall hate it. Not a bit. London is quiet dry comfortable. I find my dinner cooked for me. No children screaming. And the sense of forging ahead, easily strongly (this petered out today) at The Years. Three days I got into wild excitement over The Next War.[5] Did I say the result of the L.P. at Brighton was the breaking of that dam between me & the new book, so that I couldn't resist dashing off a chapter: stopped myself; but have all ready to develop

Seen: Janie, Walther;[3] Joan Easdale; Nessa. Clive. Helen. Duncan. been to Richmond Park (saw snake by the Serpentine) Concert. Saw Morgan & Bob & Eth Williamson. Asked to speak at some lunch. Read all early R. letters. noted them. also library books: also Keats: also MSS.

3. Janie Bussy brought a French friend, François Walter, round to Tavistock Square after dinner on 7 October to discuss a proposed anti-Fascist organisation of intellectuals.

4. Ruth Grüber had published a feminist study of VW's work earlier in the year; see above 31 May 1935, n. 10.

5. Yet another title for the eventual *Three Guineas* (see above, 20 January 1931, n. 8).

—the form found I think—as soon as I get time? And I plan to do this sometime this next spring, while I go on accumulating Roger. This division is by the way perfect, & I wonder I never hit on it before—some book or work for a book thats quite the other side of the brain between times. Its the only way of stopping the wheels & making them turn the other way, to my great refreshment, & I hope improvement. Alas, now for Grueber.

Wednesday 16 October

What I have discovered in writing The Years is that you can only get comedy by using the surface layer—for example, the scene on the terrace. The question is can I get at quite different layers by bringing in music & painting together with certain groupings of human beings. This is what I want to try for in the raid scene: to keep going & influencing each other: the picture; the music, & the other direction—the action—I mean character telling a character—while the movement (that is the change of feeling as the raid goes on) continues.

Anyhow, in this book I have discovered that there must be contrast: one strata, or layer cant be developed intensively, as I did I expect in The Waves, without harm to the others. Thus a kind of form is, I hope, imposing itself, corresponding to the dimensions of the human being: one should be able to feel a wall made out of all the influences; & this should in the last chapter close round them at the party so that you feel that while they go on individually it has completed itself. But I havent yet got at this. I'm doing Crosby—an upper air scene this morning. The rest of going from one to another seems to me to prove that this is the right sequence for me at any rate. I'm enjoying the sequence, without that strain I had in The Waves.

Tuesday 22 October

I am again held up in The Years by my accursed love of talk. That is to say, if I talk, to Rose Macaulay from 4. to 6.30: to Elizabeth Bowen from 8 to 12 I have a dull heavy hot mop inside my brain next day & am a prey to every flea, ant gnat (as for example that I let P. Quennel misrepresent me & never answered him[6]). So I have shut the book—Sal & Martin in Hyde Park—& spent the morning typing out Roger's memoirs. This is a most admirable sedative & refresher. I wish I always had it at hand. Two days rest of that nerve is my prescription; but rest is hard to come by. I think I shall refuse all invitations to chatter parties till I'm done. Could it only be by Christmas! For instance, if I go to Edith

6. This may refer to Quennell's *A Letter to Mrs Virginia Woolf*—a response to her *Letter to a Young Poet*—which, though published three years before, may have rankled.

Sitwell's Cocktail this evening I shall only pick up some exacerbating picture: I shall froth myself into sparklets; & there'll be the whole smoothing & freshening to begin again. But *after* The Years is done *then* I shall go everywhere: & expose every cranny to the light. As it is, who doesn't come here? Every day this week I must talk. But in my own room I'm happier, I think. So I will now plod quietly through the Bridges letters, & perhaps begin to arrange all Helen's tangled mass.[7]

Sunday 27 October

Adrian's birthday, it strikes me. And we asked him to dine. No, I will *not* hurry this book. I'm going to let every scene shape fully & easily in my hands, before sending it to be typed, even if it has to wait another year. I wonder why time is always allowed to harry one. I think it rather good this morning. I'm doing Kitty's party. And in spite of the terrific curb on my impatience—never have I held myself back so drastically—I'm enjoying this writing more fully & with less strain &—whats the word? I mean its giving me more natural pleasure than the others. But I have such a pressure of other books kicking their heels in the hall its difficult to go on, very slowly.

Yesterday we walked across Ken Wood to Highgate & looked at the 2 little old Fry houses. Thats where Roger was born & saw the poppy. I think of beginning with that scene.[8] Yes, that book shapes itself. Then theres my Next War—which at any moment becomes absolutely wild, like being harnessed to a shark; & I dash off scene after scene. I think I must do it directly The Years is done. Suppose I finish The Years in Jan: then dash off The War (or whatever I call it) in six weeks: & do Roger next summer.

It is a grey dim windy day: I walked along the Euston Rd. & was beaten by its sheer gloom; came back & did Roger—P[amela]'s letters; & I'm furious with Ellis Roberts who has told the PEN I wish to be elected.[9]

Wednesday 30 October

By way of a symptom—just because, reaching for a book, I opened my first draft of What are we to do & read the first page, I cannot settle to The Years save by dint of severe prodding. My mind is once more flooded with the desire to be at that argument. It is true that this was, I suppose,

7. Robert Bridges (1844-1930), who was appointed Poet Laureate in 1913, was married to a first cousin of Roger Fry, Monica Waterhouse; he and Fry had maintained a correspondence since the latter's undergraduate days. For 'Helen's tangled mass' see MHP, Sussex, B 17f: 'Extracts from Letters to Helen Anrep, 1924 to 1934.'

8. Roger Fry was born at no. 6 The Grove, Highgate (see the first paragraph of *Roger Fry* (1940) by VW); later his father bought no. 5 next door.

9. See *V VW Letters*, no. 3074 to the General Secretary of the International PEN Club, Herman Ould.

suggested by having Miss White—nice not very highly intelligent but fresh, with a prominent nose, & eyes that oddly changed from hard to soft—to tea: (a New Zealander; her father a doctor; has been ranging about the world in Cargo steamers; now lives in a flat at Highgate)—then Miss Lynd, & Adrian & William to dinner.[10] So that no doubt my nerve tension is loosened & twangs slightly. Anyhow, here is my hour for reading Roger or a tiresome half good half bad MS—wasted in mind spinning. A very fine October day.

Went to Peace Conference, by way of a joke, yesterday, & saw several baboon faced intellectuals; also some yearning, sad, green dressed negroes & negresses, looking like chimpanzees brought out of their cocoanut groves to try to make sense of our pale white platitudes.[11] I took some notes; walked across the Green Park; bought a little Italian frame for 7/6. The woman said (when I only had 5/) "I can trust you—yes, for two days. And if you dont pay me, well then bad luck to you". So home just in time to put buns in the oven for Miss White, who said, "Oh but you see this isn't just visiting a publisher. It is seeing two famous people" & she stayed getting more at her ease, till 6.30. Then my Gray (3 volumes) had come;[12] but I had no time to cut it, for at 8 the party began, & they stayed till 12.45. And then Lynd couldn't get her mother's new car to start, & A[drian]. forgot his keys & came back to find them. A. very spruce lively & witty. We hit it off when other people are there. I have an impression that he is far more social than he was—staying away with the Lintotts. Miss L. rather too 'dressed' in red plush, with one jewel, & dark hair. Not clear cut enough about the nose & lips, a little brushed with the Lynd, I mean the professional scribbler, Priestley, Walpole brush. She said that Squire now runs about won't do anything, drinks, & has deposited Lady S. in a small ugly house in Hampstead, being no longer the old country gentleman, but merely what he was originally—that is a scallywag. Mind I suppose all rubbed away by his scribbling—if he ever had one, which L. denies.[13] Now today we have to go to tea with Mrs W[oolf]:

10. Anna D. Whyte was the author of two books published by the Hogarth Press: *Change Your Sky* (1935) and *Lights are Bright* (1936), *HP Checklist* 379 and 401.
11. A one day conference, presided over by G. P. Gooch and C. Roden Buxton, arranged by the National Peace Council was held at the Livingstone Hall, Westminster, on 29 October, to consider the relation of colonial problems to the general question of peace. There were representatives from Africa, India, and other tropical regions.
12. *Correspondence of Thomas Gray*, edited by the late Paget Toynbee and Leonard Whibley, 3 vols., 1935.
13. Henry Lintott (b. 1908), a near-contemporary of Julian Bell at King's College, Cambridge, was now a civil servant; he had married Phyllis Hamerton in 1934. J. C. Squire had been knighted in 1933; his wife, Eileen, *née* Wilkinson, now lived at 18 Rosslyn Hill, NW3.

tomorrow Clive's lunch; then M[onks].H[ouse]. & a meeting in the schoolroom; & on Monday I have to go to the BBC out of sheer curiosity, to hear a record which I have no intention of supplying. No answer from the P.E.N. I must note that not to be answered is far more crushing than to be answered. Even more than the usual shower of anti-Fascist leaflets. I go up & find that the Americans demand that I shall cable at *their* expense.

Friday 1 November

Now again I pay the penalty of mixing fact & fiction: cant concentrate on The Years. I have a sense that one cannot control this terrible fluctuation between the 2 worlds. Take the past days: Mrs Bennett touching me on the shoulder in Kensington Gardens. "This is Virginia'. A stocky little bright eyed girl in spectacles. Firing off bombs; but doesnt like the explosion. We talk about the name 'Virginia'.[1] L. emerges from the Lavatory. We go to Mrs W.; very hot; Flora there; in come the Howes [*unidentified*] Mrs H. has collected 100 seals (glass: not animal) at Caledonian market. A good day when she only spends a penny: has sometimes to spend 2/- What for? Her only stimulus—collecting glass seals. Mr H. walks. Off home. Ethel Sands asks me to see the Baroness Nostitz [*see note 6 below*]. Have to ring up & arrange to be back at 4.30. Cant get her.

Lunch with Clive. Desmond & Christabel. Confusion about Lottie & Dottie. We each sketched different characters; Lottie prehensile—Oh dear me no, said Desmond, poor girl, she's amassed thing after thing & cant order them—Oh its Lottie youre talking about. Lord Berners' Sapphist skit. No. You shall not waste your time on it. Lunch. "I've been talking about Lytton," dining with James. C. becomes emotional. Cant we put up a tablet to Francis. Saint & Wit. But where? Gerrard Street? Do we like monuments? Yes, she says. Clive chivalrously agrees. Then, just as I began to talk to Desmond, easily, about Santayana's book, C. chips in: must read us the D. of Argyll's letter, (which I had read in [*illegible*] book). This finished the lunch.[2]

(And I forgot that Ka came the night before, all in red lace, & as usual determined to assert her dignity her importance her social value, so that we spent all the time trotting out acquaintances & honours—this she

1. Dorothy Cheston lived with Arnold Bennett (whose wife refused to divorce him) and in 1925 changed her name by deed poll to Bennett; their daughter Virginia was born in April 1926.
2. Lord Berners' (privately printed) skit was called *The Girls of Radclyffe Hall*. After 1924 no. 30 Gerrard Street was the home of Birrell and Garnett's bookshop. George Santayana (1863-1952), Spanish-born, American educated philosopher, poet, and critic; his most recent book was *The Last Puritan, A Memoir in the Form of a Novel* (1935); the Duke of Argyll's letter, unexplained.

does whenever she emerges from Cornwall) Then home; Lady Howard & the Baroness for L.:[3] then up to Mary[Hutchinson]'s, because she was hurt on the telephone that we hadn't written; Rothschilds & Aldous Huxleys; more talk; sticky at the end: A. says all this signing anti-F[ascist]. rumpus is mere chitter chatter; got off on biology; Victor had a copy of Gray's Pope: in red volume. I dont like that way of book buying & so home to bed & so cant even write this. Raining & we go to Rodmell where L. speaks. Yet its fluid & amusing in a way—not a patch on the other though. I must draw in for the last lap, would my friends allow.

Tuesday 5 November

A specimen day, yesterday: a specimen of the year 1935 when we are on the eve of the Duke of Gloucester's wedding: of a general election: of the Fascist revolution in France: & in the thick of the Abyssinian war: it being mild warm November weather; at 2.30 we went to the BBC & listened to some incomparable twaddle—a soliloquy which the BBC requests me to imitate (a good idea, all the same, if one were free) with all the resources of the BBC behind one: real railway trains; real orchestras; noises; waves, lions & tigers &c; at 3. we reach Dorland Hall; a loud-speaker proclaiming the virtues of literature, the Princess Louise having just declared the show open & said that books are our best friends.[4] There we meet old stringy Rose Macaulay, beating about, like a cat a hawking odds & ends; Gerald Duckworth, covered with small prickly red squares, as if he had fallen on his face in a bramble bush; ⟨Fisher⟩ Unwin; & so out:[5] home; at 5.15: telephone; the Baroness Nostitz has arrived early; will we see her now; up she comes; a monolithic broad faced Hindenburg, bulky; cant get in or out of my chair; says Germany is the better for Hitler—so they say: but of course I'm not a politician: I want to get some young man to lecture on English poetry; has a rather hard, dominating impassive eye: slow, stately; must have been a beauty; statuesque; aristocratic.[6] Then a card: in comes the Indian; stays till 7.30. was turned out of a carriage in Bengal.

3. Lady Howard: probably the wife of the wealthy Maecenas Lord Howard de Walden.
4. The 3rd *Sunday Times* Book Exhibition was held at Dorland Hall, Lower Regent Street, from 4-18 November; it was opened by HH Princess Marie Louise (1872-1956), a grand-daughter of Queen Victoria.
5. Gerald de l'Etang Duckworth (1870-1937), VW's younger half-brother, was the founder and head of the publishers Duckworth & Co. Stanley Unwin (1884-1968) Chairman of the firm George Allen & Unwin who had published LW's book on Co-operation in 1918, was the current president of the Publishers Association.
6. Helene von Nostitz-Wallwitz (1878-1944), *née* von Beneckendorff und von Hindenburg, was a niece of the late president of Germany, Field-Marshal Paul von Hindenburg; she was a member of a German organisation of writers.

Thats an Indian! the lady cried
If you dont go, I shall kick you.

He jumped out, happily into bushes, as the train was going 15 miles an hour. Liberty, justice. A girl who shot at the Governor. Hatred of the British rule. Still, its better than the Italian. Mss [Mussolini] is paying their fare & hotel bills in order to get them to side with him. *You* are our allies. The British will be kicked out. And now Morgan rings up—what about Jules Romains? Will you meet him. May I lunch to discuss the French question. And so we go on.[7]

Another specimen day.

Sunday 10 November

Specimen days have somewhat relaxed later in the week. I seem to recall some walks—a great deal of rain: the D & Dss of Gloucester driving through the Sqre: she bright & gay: he like Cory: & then I met the royal coach empty & noted the white bottoms of the postilions, & the rather sheepish look of the footmens faces in the daylight, all dressed up.[8] Then, last night there was Day Lewis at the Book show, a man who makes queer faces; very nervous at first; with blurred eyes; a nice sensitive young man; but I think it would have been better read, his speech. All poets are misfits & therefore want communion with the common people. A good deal about the Trinity: some bite in him: to explain their desire to write not pure poetry but ——? What exactly is poetry that is part the desire to communicate with the common people? Political poetry? Certainly its not easy, one word Wordsworth poetry. Instead of the Leech Gatherer [*Wordsworth*] the tank & poison gas. Yes. Too much theory: too little gift I think & too much public speaking. But then if he wants to be in touch with the common people he must talk at Book shows. Not very anxious I think to dine with us, for which I liked him. The usual hurry & scramble of literary gents: poor red scrannel faced [Herbert] Palmer, & Rose again hawking round the area railings for scraps. So to

7. The Indian was called Chakravaty (LW's diary). Jules Romains (1885-1972), the French poet, dramatist, and novelist, author of *Les Hommes de bonne volonté*, became president of the International PEN Clubs in 1936.
8. The marriage of the Duke of Gloucester, the King's third son, and Lady Alice Montagu-Douglas-Scott took place on 6 November in the private chapel in Buckingham Palace; the couple passed up Woburn Place on their way to St Pancras Station. Mrs Stangroom (Miss Belsher) recalls: 'we always had to let her [VW] know when any royalty were going to pass by on their way to Euston Station. On these occasions a friendly policeman stayed on our stretch of pavement & would let us know when the royal car was due. Then having already been informed of the event VW would join the staff up the basement steps in time for us to wave them on. This always produced a gracious bow specially for us.'

dine at Gennaro—not very good; to N. Gallery movies—not very good; & home in the cold.[9]

A letter from Bruce R. asking me to write more leaders; from Joe, asking me to write for The Listener.[10] And L. says we are going to have a very lean year at the Press. I must consider money again for a moment—how not to make too much or too little, & so on.

Monday 18 November

Our election week end was not a wise move, personally. I was silly though. Why go to Patcham in pouring rain? Even if I didn't stay in London & hear Ethel's case, as I wished, it was foolish to have $2\frac{1}{2}$ hours trapesing in the violent wind & wet to Rodmell.[11] A wild grey white sea, & so many stops all the time, as we passed it, to take up the workmen who are building at Peacehaven. So a headache next day; & this morning a throat. I am held up & damped down. We missed Quentin & Nessa last night, from headache; and have to dine with Raymond & go to Aldous party tonight.

It struck me tho' that I have now reached a further stage in my writers advance. I see that there are 4? dimensions; all to be produced; in human life; & that leads to a far richer grouping & proportion: I mean: I: & the not I: & the outer & the inner—no I'm too tired to say: but I see it: & this will affect my book on Roger. Very exciting: to grope on like this. New combinations in psychology & body—rather like painting. This will be the next novel, after The Years.

Thursday, 21 November

Yes, but these upper air scenes get too thin. Reflection after a morning of Kitty & Edward in Richmond. At first theyre such a relief though after the other that one gets blown & flies ahead. The thing is to take it quietly; go back; & rub out detail; too many 'points' made: too jerky, & as it were talking 'at'. I want to keep the individual & the sense of things coming

9. Gennaro's restaurant, 63-65 New Compton Street, Soho. The New Gallery Cinema, Regent Street, was showing Jessie Matthews in *Just a Girl*, the news magazine programme *The March of Time*, and royal wedding scenes.
10. J. R. (Joe) Ackerley (1896-1967), writer and an intimate friend of E. M. Forster, became literary editor of *The Listener* in the Spring of 1935—a post he was to hold until 1959. VW did not write specifically for the paper until 1940.
11. The general election took place on 14 November (the Conservative leader Stanley Baldwin and his supporters winning a handsome majority); the Woolfs voted in Sussex, where LW drove voters to the polls. On that day, Ethel Smyth appeared in *Smyth* v. *British General Press* in the King's Bench Division of the High Court, before Sir Malcolm Hilbery, who found for her in an action in which she sued for the return of articles offered for publication.

over & over again & yet changing. Thats whats so difficult: to combine the two.

Last night L. was woken at one, by a man shouting abuse of Woolf & Quack in German under his window. Ought we to tell the police? I think it was a drunken undergraduate.

After our dinner at Raymond's with Aldous & the subconscious hostility I always feel there, I'm facing the fact that my next book, Professions, The Next War, will need some courage. 2 million women all longing for men, Aldous said. Raymond insisted, with his little hard squeak, that men were now unfairly treated: have to maintain a ⟨woman⟩ wife. Went on to Albany. Party for the German theyve married to the postman—for £50. I talked to crazy Bob Nichols, & had my hand pressed by the rather sordid fat [*word illegible*] greyfaced intense Naomi [Mitchison], who wants to come & see us.[12]

Friday 22 November

The four old ladies sitting round the tea table at Aubrey House last night made me think of a nest of little rats.[13] Why? One got up—Mrs Bridges—more pointed than the others. People say she's like Lady Fry. Old Eliz? pours tea; deaf; carpenters; once smoked when 9. Rachel brings out book about Aubrey House. Its a 17th Century house, like a college, with a quadrangle, & trees. Long 18th Cent looking room; all shining: with the Dutch pictures collected by Mr Alexander. "In this room there was gummed together the first petition for Women's Rights. John Stuart Mill carried it to Parliament. The Peter Taylors had this house. We've had it for 60 years."[14] Some joke about one of the sisters not being

12. From the end of 1934 the Huxleys rented a ground floor flat at Albany, Piccadilly, to which they had returned after spending the summer in France. Robert Malise Bowyer Nichols (1893-1944), was one of the soldier-poets of the 1914-18 war, since when he had lived in Tokyo and Hollywood. Naomi Mitchison, see above, 2 June 1932.

13. Aubrey House on Campden Hill, Kensington, had been bought by the banker and art collector W. C. Alexander (1840-1916) in 1873, and of his six daughters (two painted by Whistler) three still lived there. Mrs Bridges, the poet's widow—whom VW had come to meet—was the daughter of the Victorian architect Alfred Waterhouse and his wife Elizabeth, *née* Hodgkin, sister of Lady Fry, Roger's mother. The book Rachel produced was *Aubrey House, Kensington, 1698-1920*, compiled by Florence M. Gladstone, 1920.

14. Peter Alfred Taylor (1819-1891), MP for Leicester 1862-84, and an advanced radical connected with every movement for the promotion of freedom, and his wife Clementia, first secretary of the Women's Suffrage Society, lived at Aubrey House from 1860-73. On 7 June 1867, the philosopher and reformer John Stuart Mill (1806-73), MP, presented a petition in the House of Commons signed by nearly 1500 women, for the enfranchisement of women property owners.

yet 60. Three boxes of cigarettes—"My nephews". I sat over log fire with
Mrs B. who said she cdnt write. B[ridges]. refused to have a Biogy. Used
to put his feet on the mantelpiece & say "Now I'll write a letter." Did it
first in pencil & then ink. Used to say things straight out. Roger very
sensitive—used to stay with them—a 3 cornered friendship. Didnt know
his wife—she wore a check skirt—not at my ease with her—sorry about
the quarrel over the pictures. R. minded very much—Well I've really
nothing to tell you. Story of bowls at Failand. May we play bowls father?
Robert wants to. R[oger] asking Sir Edward's permission.[15]

Wednesday 27 November

Too many specimen days—so I cant write, yet, Heaven help me, have
a feeling that I've reached the no man's land that I'm after; & can pass
from outer to inner, & inhabit eternity. A queer very happy free feeling,
such as I've not had at the finish of any other book. And this too is a
prodigious long one. So what does it mean?

But oh my specimen days: Sunday Ray [Strachey] for tea; dine at the
hotel with Mrs W.: course after course, all bad; to Nessa's: she & Duncan
alone with new cat, Ruff: Monday, to the ⟨NatGall⟩ Francks [*unidentified*];
rather lost my head, too tired to think; settle my mind; Miss White
[Whyte,] Stephen S. dine: Sally Graves Helen Igor in after; Tuesday;
Stephen Tom & Edith Hales (Boston) tea.[16] Black edged card handed me.
M & Mme Gillet; all ruined. dryed: 3 hours wasted. L. annoyed. no music.
too tired to read, & cant write; & Ethel Sands to tea, & Vita lunches
tomorrow. Why cant I get quit of it all? Still happiness persists. And now
for 30 mins of Roger's letters to Helen—that vast sparkling dust heap, the
best so far; but how to dig out? how to represent? I must read & read &
wait on the moment of illumination. Cold frosty weather, dry for a
miracle, & very sunny.

15. Helen Combe, whom Roger Fry had married in 1896, became mentally deranged
    as the result of thickening of the skull, and from 1910 until her death in 1937
    lived in institutions. Fry painted three portraits of Robert Bridges: the first, of
    1923, was universally condemned and destroyed; the other two remained in the
    sitter's family. See *Roger Fry* (1980) by Frances Spalding, pp. 239-41. Failand
    House, near Bristol, was the home of Roger's father, the Quaker High Court
    Judge Sir Edward Fry (1827-1918), after his retirement from the bench.
16. Elizabeth (Sally) Graves (b. 1914), a niece of the poet Robert Graves, had recently
    come down from Somerville College, Oxford, where she was a friend of Anastasia
    Anrep. Emily Hale (1891-1969), Eliot's 'dull, impeccable Bostonian lady' (*V VW
    Letters*, no. 3084), who taught speech and drama at Smith College, Massachusetts,
    had known and corresponded with him since 1913. Her letter describing this tea
    with VW is published in *VW Miscellany*, no. 12, Spring 1979.

DECEMBER 1935

[?Thursday 28 November]

Another balk this morning: cant get the start off of the last chapter right. Whats wrong I dont know. But I needn't hurry. And the main thing is to let ideas blow, easily; & come softly pouring. And not to be too emphatic. Of course to step straight into the middle of a new character is difficult: North: & I'm a little exacerbated; meant to have a quiet week, & heres Nelly C[ecil]. & Nan Hudson both asking to come; & will I ring up: & Nan has a Turkish friend. But I will *not* be rushed. No.

Wednesday 4 December

I must take 10—no 5—minutes off before going up, & from reading Roger to Helen. I read & read & the packets hardly lessen, & I think of love, & L. & me; & the different lives. Yesterday Day Lewis wrote that his agent advises him to leave us for a larger firm, as he must make money. This revives the question of the Press—once again, once again. We both said walking at Caen Wood yesterday, we will now decide on a date & stop it. Yes: reading Roger I want to be free to travel as he was: free of MSS. Yet how keep our books? Or shall we try to hand it on to an intelligent youth? I rather doubt if such exist, or able to run it alone, & then we should still be tied. Raining. A lovely perfectly filled day yesterday: walk; alone; Romeo & Juliet in the evening. How fresh, rich, various coloured— & then think of the pale New England morality murder.[1]

Tuesday 10 December

I have only 3 minutes before the clock strikes, & not much paper left. I spend my spare hour or half hour reading Roger to Helen—that explains. And next year I shall have a loose leaf book. So many people again. Nelly Cecil yesterday. I like her. Better than Colefax who cut me for Madame d'Erlanger. Thats a joke. Clive intends to spread it & rub it in: never mind.[2]

I have promised to deliver The Years by 15th Feb. And had a bad mornings work in consequence. And Angus [Davidson] & Mary Fisher tonight. But if I want more time, I shall take it. I'm not time's fool—no.[3]

1. *Romeo and Juliet* at the New Theatre, with John Gielgud as Romeo, Laurence Olivier, Peggy Ashcroft, and Edith Evans. The Woolfs had seen T. S. Eliot's *Murder in the Cathedral* at the Mercury Theatre on 12 November.
2. Catherine d'Erlanger (d. 1959), wife of the wealthy banker Baron Emile d'Erlanger, was a vivid, generous hostess and patron of the arts, with a grand house at 139 Piccadilly. VW amplifies this example of Lady Colefax's duplicity in her memoir 'Am I a Snob' (*Moments of Being*, p. 192).
3. 'Love's not time's fool'—from Shakespeare's sonnet: 'Let me not to the marriage of true minds/Admit impediments.'

Save that I must go up to lunch. Always write as if a cynical eye, doubting were on me. Nessa I thought very sad again, dining with Clive. What thin stuff we talk compared with what we used to talk. And then people say death doesnt matter. Clive hopping on his canary perch: V. very silent: L. too. Bought stuff for a dress. pretty stuff to amuse myself.

Wednesday 11 December

It went all right last night, on the whole. Mary [Fisher] has bright, rather beautiful eyes; but her lips are thin, & her nose too pointed. But she has all the competence of the world of masters & cabinet ministers; rather a mercy. Grown more decided. But the pigeons were tough. Helen & Alix after dinner. Talk of Lear, of Huxleys; of this that & the other; till L. got silent. Letter from Sybil [Colefax]. Carefully composed lies, about a tiresome woman in Piccadilly wanting to consult her about bedroom curtains at 5.30. I wonder she thinks it worth while. And I shall reply Full up.

Saturday 14 December

Dinner last night with the [Aldous] Huxleys: not altogether a sparkler. Julian & his wife, whom I did not recognise, but later understood from his eyebrows &c who he was. A very chirpy I dont know why I think him dull, man. Full of scraps of information; & the same quickness that Aldous has—the same vivacity—but less sympathetic. And I guess that they spar—Julian & Juliette. She would have her say—about politics: he breasted her. But Maria & I talked after dinner, about Lotte Wolf—did I say I'd spent 2 hours over their Dutch writing table under the black lamp being analysed?[4] That was the evening Morgan rang up & said he had to have an operation: & I was very gloomy, in my funeral way, going to Piccadilly in the bitter cold, & walking down Regent St. by mistake. Then Morgan dined with us, & had a little private talk with L. I think he feels he may die. Naturally. Aldous has a man in Switzerland however who does the operation from behind, & its over, & the patient cured in a day. Aldous in great flow: enjoys London; is getting on well with his novel; & thus juicy, sympathetic. He has a sense of the suffering, as well as of the

4. Julian Sorell Huxley (1887-1975), biologist, Aldous's elder brother, became secretary of the Zoological Society of London in 1935; his wife, whom he married in 1919, was Juliette Baillot, a Swiss girl who had come to Garsington as a companion to the Morrell's daughter Julian. Dr Charlotte Wolff (b. 1902), a psychologist and a refugee from Nazi Germany, had been encouraged by Maria Huxley to come to London from Paris to pursue her studies of the human hand and its relation to personality and futurity; she saw VW at the Huxley's apartment in Albany on 11 December.

infamy of the world. Had been getting Bryan Guiness to subscribe towards the Prince; who sits 2 doors off us, starving under his purple robes. Cheeks sunk; pouting starving Aldous said, in a room of the flat of some people who teach Russian. And he led us down the long gallery to the cab.[5]

Monday 16 December

A question, how to do Roger. Why not begin at the end with Le Mas: a whole day; & then work backwards: give the elements in combination in action, first; & then trace them—give specimen days, all through his life.

Le Mas:[6] the mosquitoes &c. his cooking: the colour, the martins: the French novel: freedom—cast back to childhood. Quote. Then Cambridge, then America: then us. Then the end.

[Tuesday 17 December]

How terrified I'm getting of Ethel[Sands']s dressed dinner tomorrow! It makes a kind of ring round my mind. What I'm to wear: my velvet or chiffon: then my hair. When I'm there it'll be as easy as shelling peas— why this apprehension? Wolff never touched on *that* by the way.

Sally Graves to tea: stayed till 7. A resolute cornered mind, defiant rather; balanced; pleased L.: she's to write on Socialism. Told me I'm abused by the Graves' in their new magazine; said the Mag was laughable.[7] Said she was going to Paris; & I liked her; but not effusively. Too clever: too young. All in black. On the defensive. Now Bore Will [Robson] to lunch. Shopped yesterday. I sit on a rubber cushion & can so type.

Wednesday 18 December

I've had a bad morning at The Years, & feel it will spray off at the end. Thats I think because I had to see M[argery Fry]. at Holland Park &

---

5. E. M. Forster had a preliminary prostate operation on 19 December, which was completed in February 1936. Aldous Huxley's novel was *Eyeless in Gaza*, published in 1936. Bryan Guinness (b. 1905), son and heir of the 1st Lord Moyne, who had been taught by Aldous at Eton, was an aspiring poet and a generous patron of the arts; the 'Prince' towards whom his bounty was being directed was the Polish Count, Potocki de Montalk. Albany has a covered walk running its whole length from the Piccadilly entrance to Vigo Street, which gives access to the chambers within.

6. In 1931 Roger Fry had bought the Mas d'Angirany on the Route des Antiques at S. Rémy-de-Provence, which he shared with his friends the Maurons.

7. *A History of Socialism* by Sally Graves was published by the Hogarth Press in 1939. Volume I of a new magazine, *Epilogue*, edited in Majorca by Laura Riding and Robert Graves, was published in the autumn of 1935; a note to an article by Madeleine Vara, 'The Idea of God', refers to the atmosphere in VW's work of 'hermaphroditic ambiguity in which sexual distinction is blurred with pious artistry' &c.

missed my mooning airy easy afternoon—the only soother of my tired head. So started making up in bed: so tired; & have to dine with Sands tonight. & Ethel S[myth]. rings up at 8.30 inviting herself to lunch. Please God we shall set off on Friday: & dear old Morgan has his operation tomorrow. A cold fine day.

Thursday 19 December

Dinner last night: the Bruce Richmonds; the Maclagans; Leigh Ashton, & a sprinkling of elderly bachelors.[8] Not a twinge of alarm in it—only the horrid beforehand discomfort—hair doing—rose buying—& setting out in cold. And B.R. was the spryest & liveliest of the lot. L. Ashton swollen, plum pudding faced; & such silences—Elena almost stupid to extinction—unvisited by a single idea—sitting silent; rough faced; oh so commonplace & we all so elderly; & not a spark or a twinkle; a rather spare dinner; & at 11 everyone got up, & the car hadn't come. And it was for this I crossed London in evening dress—this is society.

Friday 20 December

"Its because one changes one's values" Nessa said last night, when we discussed why we cdnt paint or write after a dinner party. And thats true. Only artists know how to live. She cant paint after a party. Cant get back into those proportions—Worse for women, because they have to be more active at parties: have to throw themselves into it. She wont go anywhere now where they make her dress. The best thing about our notoriety such as it is is that we can see anyone we want here on our own terms. The bell went on ringing. Tut. Popkin. Clive & Benita—all by appointment to sign some documents in Duncan's room. And as he had stuck up a notice saying Out, Flossie had to come constantly to say Mr Popkins says he's out. Tell Popkins to go in.[9] Then Helen—And I was not glad to see her, wh. she felt—(to my disgrace) & after one cup went. And Nessa had chosen a nice rug. And had had her London Group meeting there. And this must be the last entry in this book because we are just about to go to Rodmell for Christmas.

8. Dinner with Ethel Sands at 15 The Vale, Chelsea: Sir Eric Maclagan (1879-1951), an authority on Italian sculpture, was director of the Victoria and Albert Museum from 1924-45; Leigh Ashton (b. 1897)—who succeeded him—was at this time in the Department of Ceramics at the museum, and was engaged in the organisation of the great winter exhibition of Chinese art at Burlington House.
9. 'Tut'—the nickname for a friend of Duncan's who suffered from the delusion that he was a reincarnation of the Pharaoh; Percy Popkin was a tax accountant with a considerable clientèle in Bloomsbury; Flossie Riley, Mabel's sister, was Vanessa's daily help.

DECEMBER 1935

The Woolfs drove to Monks House for Christmas on 20 December; it was a cold and wet and melancholy season. VW began another book for her diary: DIARY XXV.

Saturday 28 December

Its all very well to write that date in a nice clear hand, because it begins this new book, but I cannot disguise the fact that I'm almost extinct; like a charwomans duster; that is my brain: what with the last revision of the last pages of The Years. And is it the last revision? And why should I lead the dance of the days with this tipsy little spin? But in fact I must stretch my cramped muscles: its only half past eleven on a damp grey morning, & I want a quiet occupation for an hour. That reminds me—I must devise some let down for myself that wont be too sudden when the end is reached. An article on Gray I think. But how the whole prospect will take different proportions, once I've relaxed this effort. Shall I ever write a long book again—a long novel that has to be held in the brain, at full stretch—for close on 3 years? Nor do I even attempt to ask if its worth while. There are mornings so congested I cant even copy out Roger. Goldie depresses me unspeakably. Always alone on a mountain top asking himself how to live, theorising about life; never living. Roger always down in the succulent valleys, living. But what a thin whistle of hot air Goldie lets out through his front teeth. Always live in the whole, life in the one: always Shelley & Goethe, & then he loses his hot water bottle; & never notices a face, or a cat or a dog or a flower, except in the glow of the universal. This explains why his highminded books are unreadable. Yet he was so charming, intermittently.

Sunday 29 December

I have in fact just put the last words to The Years—rolling, rolling, though its only Sunday, & I allowed myself till Wednesday. And I am not in such a twitter as usual. But then I meant it to end calmly—a prose work. And is it good? That I cannot possibly tell. Does it hang together? does one part support another? Can I flatter myself that it composes; & is a whole? Well there still remains a great deal to do. I must still condense, & point; give pauses their effect, & repetitions, & the run on. It runs in this version to 797 pages: say 200 each (but thats liberal) it comes to roughly 157,000—shall we say 140,000. Yes, it needs sharpening, some bold cuts, & emphases. That will take me another—I dont know how long. And I must subconsciously wean my mind from it finally & prepare another creative mood, or I shall sink into acute despair. How odd—that this will all fade away & something else take its place. And by this time next year, I shall be sitting here, with a vast bundle of press cuttings—no: not in the flesh, I hope; but in my mind there will be the usual Chorus of what people have said about this mass of scribbled type writing, & I shall be saying, That was an attempt at that; & now I must do something different. And all the old, or new, problems will be in front of me. Anyhow the main feeling about this book is vitality, fruitfulness, energy. Never did I enjoy writing a book more, I think: only with the whole mind in action, not so intensely as The Waves.

Monday 30 December

And today, no its no go. I cant write a word; too much headache. Can only look back at The Years as an inaccessible Rocky Island, which I cant explore, cant even think of. At Charleston yesterday. The great yellow table with very few places. Reading Roger I become haunted by him. What an odd posthumous friendship—in some ways more intimate than any I had in life. The things I guessed are now revealed; & the actual voice gone. Clive Quentin, Nessa Duncan. A little boasting. Some laughter over Mrs Easdale. Politics—but carefully subdued.

I had an idea—I wish they'd sleep—while dressing—how to make my war book—to pretend its all the articles editors have asked me to write during the past few years—on all sorts of subjects. Shd. women smoke. Short skirts. War—&c. This wd give me the right to wander: also put me in the position of the one asked. And excuse the method: while giving continuity. And there might be a preface saying this. to give the right tone. I think thats got it.

A wild wet night—floods out: rain as I go to bed: dogs barking: wind battering. Now I shall slink indoors, I think, & read some remote book.

ABBREVIATIONS

Holleyman	Holleyman & Treacher Ltd: *Catalogue of Books from the Library of Leonard and Virginia Woolf, taken from Monks House, Rodmell, and 24 Victoria Square, London, and now in the possession of Washington State University.* Privately printed, Brighton, 1975.
Holroyd	Michael Holroyd: *Lytton Strachey. A Biography*. Revised edition, Penguin Books, 1971.
HP Checklist	*A Checklist of the Hogarth Press 1917-1938*. Compiled by J. Howard Woolmer. With a short history of the Press by Mary E. Gaither. Hogarth Press, London, 1976
Kp	B. J. Kirkpatrick: *A Bibliography of Virginia Woolf*. Third edition, Oxford University Press, 1980
LW	Leonard Woolf
	Five volumes of his *Autobiography*, Hogarth Press, 1960-69
I LW	*Sowing . . . 1880-1904* (1960)
II LW	*Growing . . . 1904-1911* (1961)
III LW	*Beginning Again . . . 1911-1918* (1964)
IV LW	*Downhill all the Way . . . 1919-1939* (1967)
V LW	*The Journey not the Arrival Matters . . . 1939-1969* (1969)
LWP, Sussex	*Leonard Woolf Papers c. 1885-1969*. University of Sussex Library Catalogue (Sx Ms 13), 1980
M&M	Robin Majumdar and Allen McLaurin, editors: *Virginia Woolf. The Critical Heritage*. Routledge & Kegan Paul, London, 1975
MHP, Sussex	*Monks House Papers*. University of Sussex Library Catalogue, July 1972
N&A	The *Nation & Athenaeum*
NS&N	The *New Statesman & Nation*
RF Letters	*Letters of Roger Fry*, edited by Denis Sutton. Chatto & Windus, London, 1972
I RF Letters	Volume I: 1879-1913
II RF Letters	Volume II: 1913-1934
QB	Quentin Bell: *Virginia Woolf. A Biography*. Hogarth Press, London, 1972
I QB	Volume I: *Virginia Stephen, 1882-1912*
II QB	Volume II: *Mrs Woolf, 1912-1941*
TLS	The *Times Literary Supplement*

VW   Virginia Woolf
                    The Letters of Virginia Woolf. Edited by Nigel Nicolson
                        and Joanne Trautmann. Hogarth Press, London,
                        1975-1980
I VW Letters   Volume I: *The Flight of the Mind, 1888-1912* (1975)
II VW Letters   Volume II: *The Question of Things Happening, 1912-
                        1922* (1976)
III VW Letters   Volume III: *A Change of Perspective, 1923-1928* (1977)
IV VW Letters   Volume IV: *A Reflection of the Other Person, 1929-1931*
                        (1978)
V VW Letters   Volume V: *The Sickle Side of the Moon, 1932-1935*
                        (1979)
VI VW Letters   Volume VI: *Leave the Letters Till We're Dead, 1936-
                        1941* (1980)
                    The Diary of Virginia Woolf. Edited by Anne Olivier
                        Bell. Hogarth Press, London.
I VW Diary   Volume I: *1915-1919* (1977)
II VW Diary   Volume II: *1920-1924* (1978)
III VW Diary   Volume III: *1925-1930* (1980)

NOTE: unless otherwise indicated the *Uniform Edition* of the Works of Virginia
Woolf, published in London by the Hogarth Press, and in New York by Harcourt Brace Jovanovich, is that used to refer to.

APPENDIX
Biographical Outlines of Persons Most Frequently Mentioned

ANREP, Helen, *née* Maitland (1885-1965), American-born of Scottish parentage, studied opera-singing in Europe, associated with Augustus John and his Bohemian circle, and in 1917 married the Russian mosaicist Boris von Anrep (1883-1969), by whom she had two children, Anastasia and Igor. She met Roger Fry early in 1925 and, some eighteen months later, after painful difficulties with her unfaithful but indignant husband, left him to live with Roger Fry and her children at 48 Bernard Street, WC1. This marriage in all but name endured until Fry's death in 1934.

BELL, Clive (Arthur Clive Heward, 1881-1964), art critic, married Vanessa Stephen in 1907, and became an important figure in VW's life. His long affair with Mary Hutchinson came to an end in 1927-28. He had an independent establishment at 50 Gordon Square, but shared Charleston with his wife and Duncan Grant as a family country home. He was a frequent contributor to the *NS&N*; and his most recent books were *Landmarks in French Painting* (1927); *Civilization: an Essay* (1928); and *Proust* (1928).

BELL, Vanessa ('Nessa'), *née* Stephen (1879-1961), painter, VW's beloved elder sister. She married Clive Bell in 1907, and their sons were Julian Heward (1908-37) and Quentin Claudian Stephen (b. 1910). After a liberating love affair in 1911 with Roger Fry, whose lifelong friendship she retained, from about 1914 she lived and worked with the artist Duncan Grant; their daughter Angelica Vanessa was born on Christmas Day, 1918. In London Duncan and Vanessa occupied adjacent studios at no. 8 Fitzroy Street.

BIRRELL, Francis ('Frankie') Frederick Locker (1889-1935), critic, elder son of the Liberal statesman Augustine Birrell, educated at Eton and King's College, Cambridge. During the war he worked in a Quaker Relief Unit with David Garnett, with whom he later opened a bookshop much patronised by Bloomsbury. He wrote dramatic criticism for the *NS&N*, and two short biographies: his life of Gladstone was published in 1933.

ELIOT, Thomas Stearns (1888-1965), American-born poet, critic, and dramatist; educated at Harvard and Oxford Universities, he worked in Lloyds Bank in the City until 1925, when he joined the publishers Faber & Faber, from whence he continued to edit *The Criterion*, the literary periodical he founded in 1922. He became a British subject in 1927, and that year was received into the Anglican

Church. His impulsive marriage in 1915 to Vivienne Haigh-Wood (1888-1947) had been unhappy and destructive, and in 1933 he left her.

FORSTER, Edward Morgan (1879-1970), novelist, educated at King's College, Cambridge, member of the Cambridge Conversazione Society (the 'Apostles'). His last novel, *A Passage to India*, was published in 1924, but he continued to write and publish criticism and stories, and, as a public figure, was active as a speaker, a broadcaster, and a supporter of civil liberties and liberal causes. He lived with his mother at Abinger Hammer, Surrey, with a *pied-à-terre* in Brunswick Square, Bloomsbury. In 1927 Forster met the young policeman Bob Buckingham who became his dearest friend and, with his wife May, a lifelong support and help.

FRY, Roger Eliot (1866-1934), art critic and painter; of Quaker stock, he was educated as a scientist at King's College, Cambridge, but took to the study and practice of art, and became an immensely stimulating and serious influence as a writer, an organiser, and a speaker; appreciation of his work as a painter was less than he hoped. His marriage in 1896 to the painter Helen Combe met tragedy when in 1910 she became incurably insane and was institutionalised. He subsequently fell in love with Vanessa Bell, and never wholly out of it; but his *ménage* during the last nine years of his life with Helen Anrep afforded him longed-for domestic stability and a profound happiness.

GARNETT, David ('Bunny', 1892-1981), writer, only child of the publisher's reader and literary talent-spotter Edward Garnett and his wife Constance, translator of the Russian classics; he studied botany at the Royal College of Science. As a pacifist he lived at Charleston during the war, working with Duncan Grant as a farm-labourer, and subsequently, in partnership with Francis Birrell, opened a bookshop in Bloomsbury from which, after the unexpected success of his first novel *Lady into Fox* (1922), he withdrew to give more time to writing. From 1932-35 he was literary editor of the *NS&N* and regularly wrote the 'Books in General' page. In 1921 he married Rachel ('Ray') Alice Marshall (d. 1940), an elder sister of Frances (who was to marry Ralph Partridge).

GRANT, Duncan James Corrowr (1885-1978), artist, only child of Major Bartle Grant of the Indian Army, youngest brother of Lady Strachey, with whose family of ten children—his cousins—Duncan was largely brought up. He was one of the inmates of the shared house, 38 Brunswick Square, in which VW and LW lived before their marriage. From about 1914 his life and work were shared with Vanessa Bell; their daughter Angelica was born in 1918. His reputation and success grew steadily, and reached its peak in the 1930s.

HUTCHINSON, Mary, *née* Barnes (1889-1977), a cousin once-removed of Lytton Strachey, married in 1910 the barrister and friend to the arts St John

('Jack') Hutchinson, KC (1884-1942). Gifted and elegant, she led a very social life, both as hostess and guest, with a particular predilection for the company of writers and artists. Her long love affair with Clive Bell, lasting some dozen years, had ended by 1928. In 1927 the Hogarth Press published her *Fugitive Pieces*.

KEYNES, John Maynard (1882-1946), economist, Fellow and Bursar of King's College, Cambridge, and University Lecturer in Economics. In 1916 he took over the lease of the Bell's house at 46 Gordon Square, and housed a floating population of friends until his marriage in 1925 to the Russian ballerina Lydia Lopokova (1892-1981), who had been a member of Diaghilev's company; shortly after this he took a 99-year lease of Tilton, a farmhouse some half-a-mile from Charleston, where in 1918 he had written his polemic *The Economic Consequences of the Peace*. He published the first of his major works on economics, *A Treatise on Money*, in 1930. He was on the board of directors of the Liberal weekly *The Nation* and, after their amalgamation in 1931, of the *NS&N*.

LEHMANN, John (b. 1907). poet, publisher, and editor, educated at Eton and Trinity College, Cambridge, where he met and became a close friend of Julian Bell (at King's) and a confiding fellow-poet. In January 1931 he became the enthusiastic trainee manager of the Hogarth Press, but the strain of working with LW and the allurements of freedom and a life in Vienna decided him to leave after eighteen months; he returned on a partnership basis in 1938.

MacCARTHY, (Charles Otto) Desmond (1877-1952), literary journalist and editor, graduate of Trinity College, Cambridge, an Apostle, and, with his wife Molly, *née* Mary Warre-Cornish (1882-1953), a long-standing friend of the Woolfs. Literary editor of the *New Statesman* 1920-27, in 1928 he succeeded Sir Edmund Gosse as senior literary critic of the *Sunday Times*, and became for five years editor of the newly-founded literary periodical *Life and Letters*.

MORRELL, Lady Ottoline, *née* Cavendish-Bentinck (1873-1938), half-sister of the 6th Duke of Portland, hostess and patroness of the arts, married in 1902 Philip Morrell (1870-1943), barrister and Liberal MP, 1906-18. During the war their country home, Garsington Manor, Oxfordshire, had provided a refuge for pacifists, writers and artists; in 1927 they returned to London to live at 10 Gower Street, WC1.

MORTIMER, (Charles) Raymond Bell (1895-1980), critic and man of letters, graduate of Balliol College, Oxford. VW had known him since 1923, when he was serving his literary apprenticeship under Desmond MacCarthy on the *New Statesman*; from 1935-1947 he was literary editor of the *NS&N*. A passionate and informed Francophile and traveller, he was a particular friend of Clive Bell, of Harold Nicolson, and of Francis Birrell.

SACKVILLE-WEST, Victoria ('Vita') Mary (1892-1962), poet and novelist, only child of the 3rd Baron Sackville whose estates and Elizabethan mansion Knole, Kent, she was by reason of her sex debarred from inheriting at his death in 1928. In 1913 she married the diplomatist Harold Nicolson (1886-1968) and, though their sexual proclivities diverged, the marriage was cemented by enduring love and children. She preferred to use her own name, and to remain in England when her husband was posted abroad. The love affair, dating from 1925, between her and VW, which bore literary fruit in the form of *Orlando* (1928), was now evolving into a more subdued friendship. In 1930 Vita and Harold bought the derelict Sissinghurst Castle in Kent, and devoted their imagination and resources to breathing new life into its fabric and gardens.

SMYTH, Dame Ethel (1858-1944), composer, author, and feminist; she studied music in Leipzig and, the daughter of an army general, was a vigorous campaigner both for the performance of her own compositions, and for the cause of women's rights and suffrage. Reading VW's *A Room of One's Own* fired her with the desire to meet the author, which she did in 1930, and thereafter, in spite of her age and her deafness, became one of VW's most devoted, demanding, irresistible, and intimate friends. She published several volumes of reminiscences—one, *As Time Went On* (1936), dedicated to VW—and continually sought her help and advice on her writing.

STRACHEY, (Giles) Lytton (1880-1932), critic and biographer; a contemporary of VW's brother Thoby Stephen, of Clive Bell, and of LW at Trinity College, Cambridge, he was one of the Woolf's oldest and dearest friends. A homosexual, he had since 1917 shared a home with his devoted admirer Dora Carrington and, after her marriage to Ralph Partridge, they all three settled in 1924 at Ham Spray House, near Hungerford, establishing a closely interdependent *modus vivendi* based on loving if not on sexual fidelity. Strachey's major books were *Eminent Victorians* (1918), *Queen Victoria* (1921), and *Elizabeth and Essex* (1931); his last was a collection of essays, *Portraits in Miniature* (1931).

STRACHEY, James Beaumont (1887-1967), psychoanalyst, the youngest of the ten children of Sir Richard and Lady Strachey, and the brother closest to Lytton, whom he followed to Trinity College, Cambridge. He married Alix Sargent-Florence (1892-1973) in 1920, when they both went to Vienna to study under Freud; and it was through James Strachey's agency that the Hogarth Press came to publish the papers of the International Psycho-Analytical Library; he became the principal English translator and general editor of Freud's *Collected Papers*, and ultimately of *The Standard Edition of the Complete Psychological Works of Sigmund Freud*, published by the Hogarth Press. James and Alix lived at 41 Gordon Square, Bloomsbury.

INDEX

Abingdon, Lady: 31 & n, 32
Abyssinia: 335 & n, 337 & n
Ackerley, J. R.: 353 & n
Action, Mosley's newspaper: edited by Nicolson, 38 & n, 39; on *The Waves*, 47 & n; 'dead', 61 & n
Aeschylus: 105
Agnew & Son, Thomas: 110 & n, 194
Aholibah, The, river launch: 66 & n
Ainslie, Douglas: *Adventures Social and Literary*, 122 & n
Albert I, King of the Belgians: 202 & n
Alexander, King of Yugoslavia: 250 & n
Alexander, W. C.: 354 & n
Alfieri, Vittorio: 300 & n, 302, 339
Allen, Clifford, 1st Baron Allen of Hurtwood: 76 & n
All Souls College, Oxford: 116
America: to visit?, 32, 34; to fly over, 252; Desmond back from, 291 & n; looking up, 301; *ref*: 11, 134, 147, 171, 276, 281, 311, 358
Anderson, James O'Gorman, husband of Stella Benson: 117 & n, 118
Andrews, Henry Maxwell, husband of Rebecca West: 167 & n, 326, 327
Anrep, Anastasia ('Baba'): 68 & n, 257, 355n
Anrep, Boris: National Gallery mosaics, 134 & n; and Ottoline's fête, 164 & n; *ref*: 68n, 163
Anrep, Helen, *née* Maitland: for Biographical Note *see* Appendix; flattering, sub-acid, 68; says good-bye, 89; signalled to, 144; dines in bedroom, 166; and Roger's death, 242, and funeral, 243; nice letter from, 245; poor woman, 247 & n; dining with, 257; and Fry's biography, 258, 260, 275; sympathetic, anti-Ha, 289; ineffective but alive, 297; her tangled mess, 348; not glad to see her, 359; *ref*: 27n, 68n, 120, 132n, 274, 276, 296, 324, 346, 355, 357
Anrep, Igor: 67, 68n, 355
Anti-Fascist Exhibition: 273 & n, 274n, 280 & n
Antigone, The: 169, 257
Apostles, The, Cambridge Conversazione Society or The Society: dinner, 162; as they would say, 326; *ref*: 120
Aran Islands: come to Dublin, 215 & n, 216; *ref*: 214

Arbuthnot, Rear-Admiral Sir Robert, distant kinsman of D. Grant: 71 & n
Argyll, Duke of: 350 & n
Argyll House, home of Lady Colefax: 40
Aristophanes: 98
Aristotle: 236
Arlen, Michael: VW meets, 189 & n; *ref*: 230, 231; *The Green Hat*, 189 & n
Arnold-Forster, Katherine ('Ka'), *née* Cox: condescending, self-approving, 78, 350-1; *ref*: 32n, 79 & n, 162, 299
Arnold-Forster, William: 32 & n, 182 & n, 299
Arundel, Sussex: 175
Asheham: grey sheds at, 85; and purple light, 248; *ref*: 39, 46, 62 & n, 240
Ashton, Leigh: 359 & n
Ashton, Mary, wife of J. W. Hills: 33 & n
Asquith (family, *see also* Oxford): 105
Asquith, Anthony ('Puffin'): 105 & n
Astrid, Queen of the Belgians: 336 & n, 337
Athenaeum, The, periodical: 72 & n
Athens: described, 90-2, 98, 99; visions of, 100; *ref*: 88, 89, 94
Atkin, Gabriel: 84 & n
Aubrey House, Campden Hill: 354 & n
Auden, W. H.: Eliot on, 231, 324; Huxley on, 259; *ref*: 105, 259n; *The Orators*, 106n; *The Dog Beneath the Skin*, 324n
Austen, Jane: her Thomson's *Seasons*, 258 & n; *ref*: 168

Bach, J. S.: 42 & n, 243, 336
Badenhausen, Ingeborg: *Die Sprache Virginia Woolfs*, 85 & n
Bagenal, Barbara, *née* Hiles: Carrington laughs at, 81 & n; no longer loves Tommy, 109; Saxon's bull's eye, 236
Bagenal, Judith: 296 & n
Bagnold, Enid (Lady Roderick Jones): at Beaverbrook party, 87 & n; a day at the races, 234-5; her meretricious book, 295; *ref*: 199, 227, 234n, 259; *National Velvet*, 234 & n, 295
Bailey, John Cann: his death, 33 & n; his life, 338, 339 & n
Baird, N. H. J., of Rodmell: 336
Baker, Mary, and mother: summons Clive, 115; underbred ... hysterical dog, 118; timid housemaid, 222; *ref*: 104 & n
Balderstone, Caleb (fict): 210 & n
Baldwin, Stanley: 163 & n, 335 & n

Balfour, Arthur: 191n, 192
Balniel, Lord and Lady: 110, 111 & n
Balzac: 255
Bank of England: 134 & n, 208, 209n
Baring, Maurice: a Regency survival, 31 & n; tea with, 87-8; Ethel Smyth's novelist, 239 & n; *ref*: 12n, 86, 87n, 128; *The Lonely Lady of Dulwich*, 239 & n
Barker, George: Eliot reads & admires, 231 & n; VW to read, 302 & n; *Alanna Autumnal*, 231n; *Poems*, 302n; *Thirty Preliminary Poems*, 231n
Barnes, Mrs Anne: 190 & n
Barnes, George: 190n
Barrès, Maurice: 264 & n
Barry, Gerald: 299 & n
Bartholomew, Mrs, of Rodmell: inherits luxury for life, 170-1 & n; spends benevolently, 232; *ref*: 108 & n
Bartholomew, Percy: prophet of doom, 85; steals anthracite, 86; beekeeper, 109, 325; and good fortune, 171; going about garden, 220; wants to stay, 232; and Pinka's death, 317; hides from rain, 342; *ref*: 24 & n, 176
Bartholomew, Rose: 339 & n
Barthou, Jean Louis, French Foreign Minister: 250 & n
Bax, Arnold: 29 & n
Baynes, Keith: 110n
Bazarov (fict): 173 & n
Bear Inn, The, Hungerford: 61, 62n, 64
Beatrice (fict): 263
Beaverbrook, Lord: 87
Becket, Thomas à: 288
Beddingham, Sussex: 28
Bedford Estate: 52 & n
Bedford Square: 49, 215, 216
Beecham, Sir Thomas: to do *Prison*, 70 & n; Shaw criticises, 107; conducts Smyth, 284 & n; *ref*: 31n, 203n
Beerbohm, Max: 'small talent . . . sedulously cultivated', 26 & n; *ref*: 155, 230
Beethoven: 10, 311; *Grosse Fuge*, 5
Bell, Angelica: Vanessa's portrait of, 32, 33n; her birthday party, 44 & n; and talk of bed, 61; her party shadowed, 64 & n, 244 & n; visited at school, 114 & n; VW dreams she's dead, 124; in fancy dress, 139; to *Don Giovanni*, 145; cutting out beasts, 195; to speak on

Mrs Pankhurst, 202 & n; her school concert, 266; and *Freshwater*, 273; ravishing but . . ., 274 & n; in school concert, 296 & n; 'talented youngster', 299 & n; drawing, rag-marketing, in Rome, 314; lacks contemplative sense, 315; to tea, 339; suddenly depressed, 342; in Charleston entertainment, 344; *ref*: 118, 143, 172, 179, 200, 239, 259, 273n, 301, 308, 336, 337, 341, 343
Bell, Clive: for Biographical Note *see* Appendix; 'Blind', 5 & n; in Cassis, 30; favourably disposed, 34; VW reads his book, 52; enquires after Lytton, 55n; bright as bullfinch, 61; tearful at Seend?, 62; dinner with, 70-2; on G. Heard, 70; on Lytton's portrait, 70, 71n; on Ralph, Carrington and Frances, 71; and Baron Corvo, 72; his shrewdness inherited, 74; dining with disliked, 104; his oblique method, 104, 105, 233, 234, 235; good tempered, and cross, 108; lyrical about lovers, 109; liberation with, 114; urges economies, goes to Claridges, 115; and Mary Baker, 115, 118; 'George, Ring the Bell & Run Away', 132 & n; in Jamaica, 147; with naked lady, 149; and Morrells, 164; feeble effort to hurt, 173-4; bears bad news, 175; dismissed by Fisher, 192; and Sickert, 193; rings & runs, 194; is quiet, 205; discusses Stanley Spencer, 221 & n; gives cocktail party, 224; very flighty, on Roger & Whistler, 226; flirts with Olga, 241; his arrow sticks, 244; 'abused Roger', 254; VW must dine with, 257, 258; and Fry's life, 258; made a scene, 271; VW must lunch with, 275; spoils dinner, 280 & n; conciliation, 282; in blue suit, 289; oddly inattentive, 290; so unintimate, 297; VW very fond of, 321-2; and Odette Keun, 329 & n; Wyndham Lewis and, 333; a white robin redbreast, 333-4; back from Greece, writes on Sanctions, 343 & n; at entertainment, 344 & n; lunch with, 350; intends to gossip, 356; hopping on perch, 357; *ref*: 15 & n, 27 & n, 37, 52n, 55, 86, 122, 225, 296, 314, 334n, 359, 361; *An Account of French Painting*, 52 & n

Bridges, Robert: & Fry biography, 348 & n; friendship with Fry, 355 & n

Bridges, Mrs Robert: 354 & n, 355

Brighton: 55, 64, 157, 180, 183, 288, 345, 346

BBC: VW & spoken English, 204 & n, 249; VW to hear record at, 350, incomparable twaddle, 351

British Museum: 'going on for ever', 208; ref: 34, 256, 329

Brittain, Vera: reports on VW, 7n; stringy metallic mind, 177; *A Testament of Youth*, 177 & n

Brontë, Emily: *Wuthering Heights*, 265 & n

Brooke, Rupert: 50n, 235 & n; 'Town and Country', 235n

Brooke, Lady, Ranée of Sarawak: *Good Morning and Good Night*, 248 & n

Brown, Frederick: 285 & n, 286

Browning, Robert: 43

Brunswick Square, No. 38: 245

Buchan, John (Lord Tweedsmuir): 301n, 329

Buchan, Susan (Lady Tweedsmuir): 301 & n, 329 & n, 331, 332

Buck, Pearl: *Good Earth*, 72 & n

Buckingham Palace: 157

Bullock, Malcolm: 49 & n

Burnett, Ivy Compton: *More Women than Men*, 177 & n

Busch Quartet: 77, 78n, 147

Bussy, Dorothy: ineffective rather, 114 & n; at Roquebrune, 155 & n; ref: 162, 169, 330, 333, 334n

Bussy, Janie: teaches VW French, 222 & n, 226; saddened by Fry's death, 244; a little elderly, 342; in Charleston entertainment, 344; ref: 155, 229, 330, 331, 333, 334n, 335, 346 & n

Bussy, Simon: 'ironic Gallic', 114 & n; at Roquebrune, 155 & n; exhibition, Leicester Galleries, 163n; in reptile house, 168; chaffs Clive, 334; ref: 162, 330, 333, 334n

Button, Jemmy: 142 & n

Butts, Anthony: 84 & n

Butts, Mary: 84 & n

Buxton, Charles Roden: 182 & n, 183

Byron: *Don Juan*, 34

Cabot, Professor Richard Clark: 113 & n

Caburn, Mount: 7 & n, 42, 57, 74, 182, 263

Carmarthen, Marquess of: 104 & n, 118

Caine, Sir (Thomas Henry) Hall: 57 & n

Camargo Ballet Society: 78 & n, 107n, 113, 163 & n

Cambridge, ethos: 101, 120

Cambridge, town: 35, 84, 111, 205, 227

Cambridge, University of: denounced, 179; Rylands on, 244; ref: viii, 5n, 52, 72, 228, 250, 258, 312, 358

Cameron, Alan, husband of Elizabeth Bowen: 209, 210-11 & n, 212

Cameron, Julia Margaret: 274n

Campbell, Jean: 38 & n

Campbell-Bannerman, Sir Henry: 190, 191n

Campbell-Douglas, Rev. the Hon. Leopold Douglas: 175 & n

Cannan, Gilbert: hurts Ottoline, 73 & n

Carlyle, Thomas: 13 & n, 222

Carrington, Dora: her death, viii; Lydia disapproves of, 56; 'will commit suicide', 61; sends news of Lytton, 64; what will happen to?, 65; can't be left alone, 66; and Ralph, 71 & n; Woolfs visit, 81-2; her suicide, 83, and its shadow, 84, 85, 102, 103, 120; lied to James, 114; ref: 56n, 73, 81n, 367

Carswell, Catherine: 126; *The Savage Pilgrimage . . .*, 127 & n

Cartwright, Mrs, and family: 174 & n, 175

Case, Euphemia (Emphie): 11 & n

Case, Janet: age & poverty, 11 & n; comes to tea, 130

Cashin, Molly, Hogarth Press clerk: 114, 169, 205

Cassis: 22, 30, 86, 109, 144

Castlerosse, Lord: 200 & n

Catlin, George Edward Gordon: 177 & n

Cecchetti, Enrico: 242 & n

Cecil (family): 104, 105

Cecil, Lord David: does not care for *Waves?*, 53 & n; gives party, 105-6; always loved pictures, 111; marries, 127 & n, 128; on fiction, 265 & n; pumping up vivacities, 274; on biography, 327-8; ref: 15 & n, 37, 78, 105n, 110, 184, 322; *Early Victorian Novelists*, 265n; *Max: A Biography*, 26n

Cecil, Lady Eleanor (Nelly): old white attenuated, 162 & n; tea with, 164; ref: 163, 210, 356

Cecil, Rachel, née MacCarthy: 127 & n, 128, 322

Cecil, Lord Robert: 164
Chakravaty, Indian visitor: 352 & n
Chamberlain, Austen: 291 & n
Chambers, Jessie (E. T.): *D. H. Lawrence. A Personal Record*, 337 & n
Chapman, Doris: Adrian's beloved, 103 & n; like a dogfish, 109; like a codfish, 115
Charles I, and Queen Henrietta Maria: 220 & n
Charleston: red cave effect of, 3; gay & uneasy at, 38; strews sand over Greece, 100; first illness at, 170; Stanley Spencer discussed at, 221 & n; its effect on illusions, 233; depressing family life at, 239; tea at, 266; 'in being', 334; dining at, 335, 336; Woolfs & Eliot dine at, 343-4; *ref*: 122, 125, 147, 149, 169, 171, 175, 178, 254, 274, 276, 292, 335, 341, 361
Charteris, Evan: clears Gosse's character, 31 & n; *The Life and Letters of Sir Edmund Gosse*, 4n
Chateaubriand: 302; *Mémoires d'outre tombe*, 283 & n, 287
Chatterton, Thomas: 293 & n
Chatto & Windus, publishers: 57
Chaucer, Geoffrey: 63, 92
Cheevers, Harold: 281 & n
Chekhov: 209, 315
Chelsea: v. Bloomsbury, 131n, 285; *ref*: 76, 146, 210
Chesterton, G. K.: 273
Chichester, Hon. Gerald (Timmy): 151 & n
Chichester, Earl of: 111 & n
Cholmondely, Lady: 202 & n, 279
Christie, Capt John, of Glyndebourne: 246 & n
Churchill, Lord Ivor Spencer: 200 & n, 280 & n
Churchill, Winston: 192
Cicero: 283
Clair, René: 147
Clark, Kenneth and Jane: 257, 258 & n, 259, 279
Clark Lectureship: offered to VW, 79 & n; *ref*: viii
Clifford, Alice, unidentified: 313
Clifford, Mrs W. K.: 323 & n
Clio, muse of history: VW as, 134 & n
Clutton-Brock, Sheelah: 17 & n
Cobham, Sir Alan: 172 & n

Cochran, C. B.: 301 & n
Cock Tavern, Fleet Street: 202
Coke of Norfolk (Thomas Earl of Leicester): 84 & n
Colefax, Sir Arthur: 39n, 40, 225 & n, 261
Colefax, Sibyl: self-inviting magpie, 39 & n; forever collecting facts, 40; dubs *Waves* a failure?, 53; works in shop, 145 & n; her dry claws, 150; & Noel Coward, 200, 225; the Colefax Row, 225 & n, 279; sneers at VW, 233; her histrionics, 235; very depressing, 261; defences crumpled, undergarment creased, 279; ... or the real thing, 281; cuts VW, 356; lies ..., 357; *ref*: 78, 85, 128, 170, 184, 247, 259
Coleridge, S. T.: 117 & n, 122, 157; *S. T. Coleridge's Unpublished Letters*, 117 & n
Collett, Mrs S. B.: 306 & n
Colli, Signora: 171
Congreve, William: *Love for Love*, 341 & n
Connolly, Cyril and Jean: 210 & n, 211
Constable, John, publisher: 337
Cooper, Lady Diana: 75, 203 & n
Cornish, Hubert Warre: 128
Cornwall: loved in childhood, 97; and Irish mixture, 209; *ref*: 126, 351
Corvo, Baron: 72 & n
Coué, Dr Emile: 263 & n
Courtauld, Samuel: 56n, 111, 234, 334
Courtauld, Mrs: 56 & n, 61, 334
Coward, Noel: VW meets, 200 & n; adores VW, 279; *ref*: 225, 259
Cowper, William: 339 & n
Crabbe, George: fantasy on?, 180 & n
Craik, Mary, Lady: 40 & n
Cranium, The, dining club: 296
Crashaw, Richard: 230 & n
Creevey, Thomas: 157 & n, 159; *The Creevey Papers*, 157n
Crippen, Dr H. H.: 261 & n
Criterion, The, periodical: 191 & n
Cromwell, Oliver: 43 & n
Crosby (fict): 347
cummings, e. e.: *The Enormous Room*, 4 & n
Cunard, Emerald, Lady: 15 & n, 203, 259
Curtis, Mrs, Angelica's headmistress: 202 & n, 296

Daintrey, Adrian: 286 & n
Dalton, Hugh: 183 & n

Eiffel Tower, restaurant: 48 & n
Eleanor, see Pargiter, Eleanor
Elgin, Lord: 99 & n
El Greco: 111
Eliot, George: *The Mill on the Floss*, 247 & n
Eliot, T. S.: for Biographical Note *see* Appendix; 'poor man', 123; the Norton lectures, 123n; and Shelley quote, 124 & n; VW writes to, 143 & n; deserts wife, 167 & n; wife to pray for?, 168; scene at solicitors, 169; all artifice & quips, 174 & n; uneasy mystery, 177 & n; to stay, on *Waste Land* & Webster, 178 & n; a great man, 179; VW seeks accommodation for, 188; reading his criticism, 189 & n; dismissed by Fisher, 192; dines & discourses, 208 & n; VW sees through?, 230; on Barker, Spender & Auden, 231 & n; Wyndham Lewis on, 250; *Sweeney* performed, 260, 261 & n; his remarkable head, 262-3; calculating correspondent?, 273 & n; suggests fortnightly tea, 274; how he suffers, 277; writing *Murder*, 288 & n; easy & honest, on writing *Waste Land*, 288; in the rectory, 294 & n; his '*Murder...*' expected to be good, 323; one of 'us', in spite of God, 324; weekend visitor, 343 & n; 'very fond of', 344; & Emily Hale, 355 & n; 'New England morality', 356 & n; *ref*: ix, 5 & n, 11, 15 & n, 21, 73, 118, 122, 178n, 191, 200, 227, 262n, 277n, 302n, 324n; *After Strange Gods*, 208 & n; *Murder in the Cathedral*, 288 & n, 323, 356 & n; *The Rock*, 230 & n; *Sweeney Agonistes*, 260, 261 & n; *Thoughts After Lambeth*, 21 & n; *The Use of Poetry and the Use of Criticism*, 189 & n; *The Waste Land*, 178n, 223, 288
Eliot, Vivienne, *née* Haigh-Wood: wild as Ophelia, 123; deserted by Eliot—LW her executor, 167 & n; fund for?, 168; scene at solicitors, 169; Eliot 'thinks she puts it on', 178; *ref*: 73, 122
Elizabeth I: 77
Ellis, Robinson: 256 & n
Elvira, see also Sara (fict): & VW's identity, 148; in bed, 149; the difficulty, 152; scene finished, 163; her soliloquy, new method, 302; *ref*: 132

& n, 134, 139, 147, 168, 186, 221, 237, 241, 276
Emery, Kathleen, Rodmell dogbreeder: 266 & n
Emmett, Robert: 215 & n
Epstein, Jacob: 290 & n
Ervine, St John: attacks Strachey, 288 & n
Eton College: 63, 111, 190, 205
Eugénie, Empress: 14 & n
Euripides: 98
Everest, Louie, cook-housekeeper: moving in, 232; leap in dark, 234; brings comfort, 239; furnishes knowledge, 274; cheats?, 296; enjoys job, 346; *ref*: 224, 225n, 336

Faber, Geoffrey: *Oxford Apostles: A Character Study of the Oxford Movement*, 172 & n
Faber & Faber, publishers: 57, 167 & n
Failand House, home of Sir Edward Fry: 355 & n
Farrell, Sophia: like a born lady, 131 & n; fine old type, 165; *ref*: 48n, 61
Faulkner, William: 250
Fears, Mr, Rodmell postman: 232 & n
Feis, Herbert: 170 & n
Field, Michael: journals of, 189 & n
Firle, Sussex village: 27
Fisher, Cordelia ('Boo'): 250 & n, 281
Fisher, H. A. L.: visit to described, 191-2; *ref*: 191n, 193n, 289
Fisher, Lettice, *née* Ilbert: 191 & n, 192, 193n, 250, 289
Fisher, Mary ('Aunt Mary'): 239 & n
Fisher, Mary Letitia Somerville: 249 & n, 250 & n, 356, 357
Fitzgerald, Mrs Ida, Irish hotel proprietress: conversationalist, 213-14; *ref*: 213n
Fitzroy Square, No. 29: 170 & n
Fitzroy Street, No. 8: 30, 139, 144, 274n
Flaubert, Gustave: *Madame Bovary*, 194 & n; *La Tentation de St Antoine*, 194 & n
Florence: 156, 170, 171 & n, 263, 313
Follett, Mary: 113, 118
Ford, John: *The Lover's Melancholy*, 345 & n
Forster, E. M.: for Biographical Note *see* Appendix; *The Waves*—'a classic', 52 & n, 53; he alone matters, 54; comes to lunch, 112; preferred guest, 115 & n;

377

advises Goldie, 120; comes in, 147; on Goldie, 162; pale cold chicken, 169; for weekend, 179, 180 & n, 206; praises VW's memoir, 184 & n; 'futile' on Goldie, 247 & n; & Civil Liberties, 254 & n; in critical balance, 260; 'Freshwater' lovely, 275; nibbles at Bloomsbury guide, 289, 297-8, 321; London Library incident, 297-8; evanescent, piping, elusive, & writers' congress, 321 & n; to have operation, 357, 358n, 359; *ref*: 253, 346, 352; *Goldsworthy Lowes Dickinson*, 54n, 247n

Fra Angelico: 144

France: and armaments, 183; holiday in?, 295; visited, 314-17; Fascist revolution in, 351; *ref*: ix, 17, 20, 27n, 30, 71, 85, 88, 153, 159, 160, 304, 308

Fraser, J. G.: *The Golden Bough*, 159 & n

Freeth, H. W., Rodmell farm foreman: 271 & n

Fry, Agnes: 262 & n

Fry, Sir Edward: 355 & n

Fry, Helen, *née* Combe: 355 & n, 356

Fry, Joan: 247 & n

Fry, Julian, cattle rancher: 93 & n, 247

Fry, Margery ('Ha'): to visit Greece, 86, with Woolfs, 88; 'the Yak', 89-90; well-instructed, 91; her inferiority complex, 91, 97; remembers Canada, 93 & n; paints & sketches, 93, 94; with goat girl, 95; her humanity, & prison reform, 96; lacks charm, 97; commiserates, 98; & London Squares campaign, 164 & n; recommends Mabel, 206; Roger's literary executor, 247; and his biography, 253; wants to write it, 258, wants VW to write it, 260; in abeyance, 261; debates biography, 262, doubtful about?, 275; bringing documents, 279, 335, 336; her incestuous love, 285; Helen anti, 289; and Fry Memorial Exhibition, 323, 331; *ref*: 247n, 262n, 358

Fry, Lady: 354 & n

Fry, Pamela *see* Diamand, Pamela

Fry, Roger: for Biographical Note *see* Appendix; Vanessa accommodates, 38; violent impressions from, 39; sedulously avoided, 53; Oliver Strachey on, 66 & n; Woolfs visit, 67, 68; designs curtains, 68 & n; dines *chez* Clive, 70-2;

on G. Heard, 70; his portrait of Lytton, 70-1, 71n; loves facts, 71; worries about painters, 72; lecturing on French art, 76 & n; excited about Jesus, 77; to dine, 80; to visit Greece, 86, with Woolfs, 88; embarks, 89; on Venice and Ruskin, 90; plays chess, 90, 97; on Athens, & Byzantine church, 91; 'awfully swell' at Aegina, 92; talking about Eastman, 93; painting & sketching, 93, 94; slung with paintboxes, 96; paints at Parthenon, 97; Francophile, 98; to have operation, 115; visits Goldie, 120; less volatile?, lecturer's egotism, 144; in Tangier, 147; dinner *chez*, exhibits at Agnews, 166 & n; Sickert jokes about, 194; duped over Whistler, 266; his death—the poverty of life now, 242 & n; his funeral, 243 & n; haunts party—& the universal feeling, 244, 245; can hear him laugh, 247; his death felt, 252, 265, 287, worse than Lytton's, 253; admired by Vanessa, abused by Clive, 254; cant write about, 254-5; his daughter, 255; and Bloomsbury, 257; his biography, 258, 260, 267, 275, 296; his Sanger portrait, 275 & n; Nessa & his ghost, 279; his incestuous love, 285; & Bloomsbury baiters, 289; absent harmoniser, 290, 297; remembered in Italy, 313, 314, & in Provence, 315 & n; how many Rogers?, 321; Memorial Exhibition, 323, 330 & n; intimate liking for, 324; piles of papers, 336; three boxes of, 341; started reading, 343; will do some, 346; his birthplace, 348 & n; & Bridges, 355 & n; & Helen, 355 & n, 356; always in the succulent valleys, 360; odd posthumous friendship, 361; *ref*: viii, 27 & n, 122, 132, 191, 200, 226n, 263, 302, 344, 353; *Characteristics of French Art*, 144n

Furse, Charles: 112n, 113

Furse, Katharine: 112 & n, 118, 143, 202

Gage, Henry Rainald, 6th Viscount: 39 & n, 131

Galsworthy, John: lies stark dead, 146-7 & n; not competing with, 176; *The Forsyte Saga*, 176 & n

Galsworthy, Mrs: 147

Gandhi: 8 & n

Gregory, Lady: 256 & n
Grenfell, Florence: 31 & n
Grey, Mrs, *née* Squelch, of Rodmell: 123, 124-5 & n, 232
Group Theatre: 260, 261n
Grigson, Geoffrey: 185 & n, 257
Grüber, Fraülein Ruth: 34n, 317n, 346 & n, 347
Guinness, Sir Benjamin: 217 & n
Guinness, Bryan Walter: 358 & n
Gulde, Fraülein: 34 & n
Gumbo *see* Strachey, Marjorie
Gunn, James: 240

Ha *see* Fry, Margery
Hale, Emily: 355 & n
Halifax, Lord: 151 & n
Hambledon, Lord: 231
Hambro, Ronald Olaf: 151 & n, 222
Hamilton, Molly: *Sidney and Beatrice Webb*, 180 & n
Hamlet (fict): 70, 123
Hamnet, Nina: 51, 52n
Hampson, John: 142 & n, 186 & n; *Foreign English*, 186n
Hampstead: 147, 149, 281, 289, 349
Hampton Court: 152
Ham Spray House: Woolfs visit, 64 & n, and again, to see Carrington, 81 & n, 82; rough parody of, 188; *ref*: 55n, 56 & n, 89
Hancock, F. R., Lewes Labour candidate: 17n, 44, 46, 183, 240, 296, 336
Harcourt Brace, publishers: 224, 273
Hardy, Florence: wishes VW had written Hardy's life, 118-19, 119n; *ref*: 237
Hardy, Thomas: VW's article on, 118-19 & n; Forster on, 169; *Jude the Obscure*, 169
Harris, Frank: *Bernard Shaw*, 106 & n
Harris, Henry ('Bogey'): 227 & n
Harris, Mrs Leverton: 78, 79n
Harris, Lilian: visit to described, 342 & n; *ref*: 165 & n, 193, 341
Harrod, Roy: 188 & n
Hartington, Lady: 128
Harvey, Gabriel: 53n, 54
Hastie, Lydia: 170, 171 & n
Hawkesford, Mrs: 85-6, 86n
Haydn: 195
Hayward, John: 48 & n, 324n
Hazlitt, William: 276
Headlam, Walter: 170 & n

Heard, Gerald: essentially a nobody, 67-8; his character examined, 70; advises Goldie, 120; & Fry's biography, 258; *ref*: 54 & n, 68n, 262 & n
Heine: quoted, 233
Heinemann, William, publishers: 87, 287n, 288
Hemans, Felicia: 259 & n
Hemingway, Ernest: 250
Henderson, Joan Cedar ('Toby'): 14 & n
Henderson, Susan: 239 & n
Hennessy, Patsy: 210n
Herbert (family): 327 & n
Herbert, A. P.: *Tantivy Towers*, 14 & n, 15
Herodotus: 257, 272 & n
Highclere Castle, Newbury: 226 & n
High Salvington, Sussex: 238
Hills, John Waller ('Jack'): & marriage allowance, 33 & n; *ref*: 276
Hills, Stella, *née* Duckworth: 33n
Hitler, Adolf: Bruno Walter on, 153; crushes brownshirts, 223-4; and Fascists, 230; & incessant conversations, 303; described by Wigram, 304; 'Heil . . .', 311; 'The Hitler feeling,' 312; *ref*: 81, 171, 223n, 273, 303n, 304n, 351
Hodgson, Ralph: 74 & n
Hogarth Press: durability & Desmond, 28; contributes to bonus, 33; in the event of death, 55; 'dear old', 63; should net £2,000, 89, but at a cost, 101; re-arrangements at, 104, 146 & n; melting again, 141; directed from Italy, 158; & Logan's version, 162; move to Monks?, regain old ideals, 185; lean year forecast, 353; question of revived, 356; *ref*: ix, 5n, 6, 17n, 21n, 25, 56n, 121, 240; *see also under* Lehmann, John *and* Woolf, Leonard (2)
Holden, Sir George: 236 & n
Holland: Woolfs to visit, 295, 296, 298; visited, 308-10; *ref*: ix
Holmes, Sir C. J.: 285 & n, 286
Holroyd-Reece, John: 223 & n
Holtby, Winifred: writing on VW, 13 & n; on *The Waves*, 45; fails to cause tremor, 125; to tea, 146; and Vera Brittain, 177 & n; couldn't quote her, 178; is dying?, 344 & n; *ref*: 143, 147, 183, 260n, 279
Homer: 92, 216, 257

Letters of D. H. Lawrence, 126 & n; *The Man Who Died,* 28 & n; *Sons and Lovers,* 20, 28, 246; *Women in Love,* 73n

Lawrence, Susan: 148 & n, 165 & n, 185

Lawrence, T. E.: 312 & n

Lea, Miss, *see* Wright, Lizzie

Leaf, Walter: 116 & n

League of Nations: 344

Leavis, Q. D.: 337 & n

Leeson, Ex-Detective Sergeant: *Lost London. The Memoirs of an East End Detective,* 241 & n

Lehmann, Beatrix ('Peggy'): 110 & n, 254n

Lehmann, John: for Biographical Note *see* Appendix; & Hogarth Press, ix; to be seen, 5 & n; 'may do', 6; praises *Waves* —inspires Letter, 44 & n; doubtful candidate, 52; wants to be manager, 63; fractious & irritable, 78; will not stay?, 89; his 'feelings' discussed, 101 & n; emotional & grasping, 102; 'no John', 104; stays . . . as adviser, 109; craves authority, 110 & n; is ill, 114; throws up sponge, 123 & n; in tears— consults lawyer, 131; Rosamond sisterly, 140; & Logan's version, 162; back from Vienna, leaves poems, 202 & n, signs copies, 225 & n; reconciliation dinner with, 333; *ref:* 43, 61, 74, 113; *The Noise of History,* 225n; *Thrown to the Woolfs,* 101n, 110n

Lehmann, Rosamond (Mrs Wogan Philipps): liked by VW, 37 & n; dinner guest, 115n; talks about brother, 140 & n; her husband jealous, 205; her play dubious, 275; *ref:* 178, 184, 188 & n, 254, 257; *A Note in Music,* 37n; *Dusty Answer,* 37n; *No More Music,* 275 & n

Lenare, photographer: 124 & n

Leon, Derrick: 130 & n, 188, 194 & n, 302; *Livingstones,* 122 & n, 130n; *Wilderness,* 194 & n

Leonardslee, Sussex: 162 & n

Leopardi: 165

Leopold, King of the Belgians: 336 & n

Leslie Stephen Lectures: 177 & n

Lewes: in festival, 174-5; Races, 120; gaiters from, 273; style of woman in, 318; servant hunting in, 337 & n, and shopping, 339; new way to, 341; *ref:*

56, 62, 122, 143, 183, 207, 240, 246, 266, 271, 335, 336, 343

Lewis, Lady: 9 & n, 10

Lewis, Percy Wyndham: hostile jibings, viii; pain from anticipated, 250, and registered, 251-2; pleasant & salutary, 252; 'the W. L. illness', 253; Spender counterblasts, 254 & n, is rebutted, 259 & n, 260; calls VW 'sentimental', 308; & Edith Sitwell, & Clive Bell, 333 & n; *ref:* 287, 288; *The Apes of God,* 250n; *Men Without Art,* 250, 251n, 254n, 259n

Lindbergh, Anne Morrow: 335 & n, 338; *North to the Orient,* 335n

Lintott, Henry and Phyllis: 349 & n

Listener, The, periodical: 353 & n

Lloyd, Marie: 140 & n

Lloyd, Mr, dog-breeder, of Ickenham: 328

Lloyd George, David: 192, 279

London: the season in, 86; not enough, 97; curious day in, 121; talk of leaving, 185; delicately tinted, 187; safe life in, 202; and Irish gentry, 212; back again in, 249; walk all over, 253; prepares for Jubilee, 308; magnificent metropolis, 327; broken summer in, 333; fascist graffiti in, 337; in full swing, 344; quiet dry comfortable, 346; enjoyed by Huxley, 357; crossed in evening dress, 359; *ref:* 10, 16, 26, 30, 38, 41, 61, 96, 106, 139, 143, 151, 153, 176, 179, 180, 181, 184, 213, 239, 246, 254, 257, 258, 266, 274, 287, 305, 318, 330, 334, 338, 342, 353

London, University of: 165, 166n

London Group: 359

London Library: & 'impossible' ladies, 297-8, 297n, 298n; *ref:* 166 & n

London Mercury, periodical: 74n, 260 & n

Long Barn, former home of Nicolsons: 63, 248 & n

Lopokova, Lydia, *see* Keynes, Lydia

Lovat, Lady: 203 & n

Low, David: 170 & n, 187

Lowndes, Mrs Belloc: 87 & n

Lucas, F. L. ('Peter'): not a writer, 50 & n; marries giglamp?, 180 & n; 'a deathly warning', 244; *ref:* 17 & n, 174, 179, 265

Lucas, Prudence, *née* Wilkinson: 179, 180 & n

Ludby, Cotter, *née* Helen Cotter Morison: 145 & n
Lussan, Zélie de: 284 & n
Lynd, Maire: 193 & n, 195, 349
Lynd, Robert: 349
Lyons, Neil: 175 & n, 240

Mabel, domestic: silent unselfish, 221; chicken & jam, 234; 'The Cow'—must go, 238; 'a treasure', 239; has sciatica, 266, 267; sits in Corner House, 295; LW dislikes, 306; breaks gramophone, 320; & LW's class consciousness, 326, 328; makes nice lunch, 344; *ref*: 206 & n, 232, 280
McAfee, Helen, of *Yale Review*: rejects VW's article, 77 & n
Macaulay, Lord: 171
Macaulay, Rose: erudite on commas, & author's vanity, 249-50; & VW's love of talk, 347; old stringy, 351; hawking for scraps, 352; *ref*: 147, 200 & n, 250n; *The Minor Pleasures of Life*, 250n; *Milton*, 250 & n
MacCarthy, (Charles Otto) Desmond: for Biographical Note *see* Appendix; can't handle book—much obliterated, 26; publishes with Putnam, 28; steals articles, 35; his sneer at *Mrs Dalloway*, 42 & n; & pays price, 42-3; on *Waves* —his damnable tepidity, 56 & n; lacks screw, 57; his maniacal lies, 61; Shaw's biographer?, 106 & n; can't dint butter, 110; on *Jacob's Room*, 110n; his book so bad, 111; his tepid praise, 119; gives daughter away, 127 & n, 128; claws in the heart, 169; and *Life & Letters*, 169 & n; praises *Flush*, 185 & n; burbling, depressing, baffling, 230, 231; on Patmore, 230; attends Fry's funeral, 243 & n; & Fry's biography, 258; dinner with—America & Swinnerton discussed, 291 & n; as father, 292, 299; & American passion, 299; & VW & Cowper, 339 & n; at Clive's lunch, 350; *ref*: 15, 26n, 78, 110, 147, 168, 181, 289, 327; *Criticism*, 110 & n; *Portraits*, 26 & n
MacCarthy, Dermod: 128, 291
MacCarthy, Michael: thrown to the leopards, 43 & n
MacCarthy, Mary ('Molly'): a pouter pigeon—at daughter's wedding, 127,

128; claws in the heart, 169; bites our hands, 181; after Fry's funeral, deafness & egotism, 243; not so deaf, 291; children campaign for, 299; Rachel's resemblance to, 327; *ref*: 73, 243n, 292
MacCarthy, Mrs Charles, Desmond's mother: 128
MacCarthy, Rachel *see* Cecil, Rachel
MacColl, D. S. and Andrée: 286 & n
MacDonald, Ramsay: 303, 314n, 335n
MacLagan, Sir Eric: 359 & n
McLaren, Christabel: dubs *Waves* a failure?, 53; suggests caricature, 57; telling stories, 222; 'worldly', 279; *ref*: 15 & n, 30, 31, 32, 55, 105, 151, 274, 302, 350
Macnaghten, Antonia ('Dodo'), *née* Booth: 207 & n
Magdalena—'Maggie' (fict): 132 & n, 134, 168, 169, 222, 266, 338, 344
Maloney, Mrs, American editor: 170
Malraux, André: 289, 290 & n
Manchester, University of: offers honour to VW, 147, 148 & n; *ref*: viii, 149
Manchester Guardian: 51 & n, 75 & n
Mansfield, Katherine: met beyond death, 29; her letters, 38 & n; on Ottoline, & Bertrand Russell, 73 & n; reproach of her death, 192; VW cant judge, 315 & n; *The Letters of Katherine Mansfield*, 315 & n
Mansfield, Mrs, London charwoman: 12
Manwaring, George Ernest, of London Library: 297 & n
Marie-Louise, Princess: 351 & n
Markham, Violet R.: *Paxton and the Bachelor Duke*, 302 & n
Marryat, Frederick (Captain): 334 & n, 335, 341
Marshall, Archibald: *Out and About, Random Reminiscences*, 166 & n
Marshall, Frances, *see* Partridge, Frances
Martin (fict): 266, 347
Martin, (Basil) Kingsley: unattractive, 174; unceasing invitations from, 187; histrionic about civilization, 241, 242; viciously snapped at, 296; and Aberystwyth, 299 & n, 302; LW his confessor, 302, 305; notices LW's class consciousness, 326; & the old story, 340; LW rows with, 344; *ref*: 45 & n, 89, 170 & n, 254, 306

No . . . No . . . No, 164 & n; Fisher
thinks her 'dirty', 192; violent remedy,
205; to tea, 206; hostess to Yeats &
VW, 255, 256; sees Eliot's *Sweeney*,
260; her opinions, 333; *ref*: 33, 34, 70,
78, 131, 149, 202, 205, 223 & n, 301,
332

Morrell, Philip: discusses Dryden, 73;
'works' next door, 74; reads aloud,
140; & Ottoline's honour, 164 & n;
aged . . . fallen in, 257; and offspring,
339; *ref*: 162, 175, 223n

Morris, Peter, and sister Dora: 224, 225n

Mortimer, Raymond: for Biographical
Note *see* Appendix; uneasy dialogue
with, asked to stay, 38; violent
impressions from, 39; admired by
Heard, 70; in tiger sweater, 76; with
Mrs Keppel, 80 & n; needs arboreous
bush, 108; in drawing rooms, 109;
with Ethel Sands, 140; and Francis
Birrell's health, 175, 176, 187; shallow
sandy mind, 187; not liked, 271;
attends Grand National, 292; hostility
chez?, 354; *ref*: 15, 26, 169, 260, 262,
277, 353

Mosley, Lady Cynthia: 160 & n

Mosley, Sir Oswald: recruits Nicolson, 38
& n, 39, 61; no chance in North, 280
& n; active in London, 337; *ref*: 160n

Mozart: *Don Giovanni*, 145; *Figaro*, 222n;
The Magic Flute, 107, 320

Muir, Edwin: *The Marionette*, 169 & n

Murray, Ronald, dressmaker: by appointment, 150, 301; VW's relations with,
307; his ambitions, 320; *ref*: 161

Murry, John Middleton: and K. Mansfield,
315 & n; *ref*: 96, 106; *Son of Woman.
The Story of D. H. Lawrence*, 96n

Mussolini: 171, 263, 303, 337n, 338, 343,
352

Myers, Leo: 328 & n; *The Root and the
Flower*, 302 & n

Napoleon: 224, 263

Nash, John, architect: 300 & n

Nation, The, New York: 42 & n

National Council for Civil Liberties: 254
& n

National Gallery, London: 259, 287, 355

National Libraries, Friends of the: 163 & n

National Portrait Gallery: offers to draw
VW, 201 & n

National Society for Women's Service:
6 & n, 7 & n, 145, 146n

Neale, J. E.: *Queen Elizabeth*, 201 & n

Nef, Elinor Castle: 171 & n, 172

Nelly *see* Boxall, Nelly

Nevinson, Henry Woodd, and spouse:
148 & n

Newcastle, Duke of: 293 & n

New College, Oxford: 191n, 192

Newhaven, Sussex: 17, 18 & n, 62, 318,
335

Newman, Cardinal: 172 & n

Newnham College, Cambridge: 276

New Place, Stratford-on-Avon: 220 & n

New Statesman & Nation, periodical: LW
as Wayfarer?, 34 & n; and Harold
Nicolson?, 89 & n; VW letter on
Privacy to, 186 & n; a hoax of one's
own?, 188 & n; & Kingsley Martin's
despair, 241 & n; & Kingsley's future,
299 & n, 302, 305; Clive Bell's
'Sanctions', 343 & n; *ref*: 4n, 13n, 129
& n, 179n, 181, 262, 267, 296, 320

Nichols, Robert: 354 & n

Nicolson, Harold: at docks with VW, 15
& n; edits Mosley's *Action*, 38 & n, 39;
thinks *The Waves* a masterpiece, 47
& n; *Action* folds, 61n; on Vita's
shoulders, 63 & n; nobler and poorer,
party with Enid, 87; *NS&N* candidate,
89 & n; drivelling snapping, 114 & n;
sailing to America, 134n; soft &
domestic, 237; & Mrs Lindbergh's
book, 335 & n; *ref*: 109, 122

Nicolson, Nigel: 168

Noailles, Comtesse Mathieu de: 263-4 & n

Noel-Baker, Philip and Irene: 182 & n, 331

Norman, Montagu Collett, Governor of
the Bank of England: 208, 209n

North (fict): 332, 356

Northease, Sussex farm: 3, 36, 37

Norton, Charles Eliot, lectures: 123n,
189n

Norton, Henry Tertius James: and Lytton,
71 & n; and discouragement, 291 & n

Nostitz, Baroness von: 350, 351 & n

Observer, The: 184

Ocampo, Victoria: 263 & n, 264, 265

Olivier, Lord: *The Myth of Governor Eyre*,
149 & n

Ophelia (fict): 123

Origo, Marchesa Iris: 327 & n, 328

200 & n; by appointment, in 3-cornered hat, 203 & n; ruthless shoving woman, 204; bawls about Baring, 239 & n; her bluff affection, 253; £1,600 tax demand, 276 & n; what a guzzler, at concert, 284 & n; dear old woman, 290; rows with Vita, 294 & n, 295; usual indefatigable egotism, 340; *v. British General Press*, 3˙3 & n; *ref*: 5 & n, 9n, 10n, 21, 31, 48n, 63, 70n, 88n, 89, 109, 118, 119n, 125, 143, 145, 146, 171, 180, 189, 202, 247, 277, 323 & n, 328, 331, 332, 339, 359; *Der Wald*, 69 & n; *March of the Women*, 189 & n; *Mass in D*, 203 & n, 340; *The Prison*, 9n, 12 & n, 13n, 27n, 29, 70 & n, 119n, 239; *The Wreckers*, 46 & n, 48 & n, 49, 69n, 119n, 284 & n; *A Three-Legged Tour in Greece*, 95n; *Female Pipings in Eden*, 88n, 200n

Snowden, Ethel: 70 & n

Society for Sexual Information and Progress: 119 & n, 223

Sophocles: 98

Souls, The: 190, 191n

Southease, Sussex: 28, 305, 336, 337

Southorn, Bella, *née* Woolf: Queen of Hong Kong, 325; *ref*: 67 & n, 167, 306 & n

Southorn, Sir Thomas: 306n, 325

Sparrow, John: 105 & n; *Sense and Poetry*, 199 & n

Spectator, The, periodical: Wyndham Lewis attack in, 259 & n

Spencer, Stanley: 221 & n

Spender, Stephen: in *New Signatures*, 128n; his stature, 129; bore potential, 195; praises *Lighthouse*, 224 & n; Eliot on, 231; defends VW against Lewis, 254 & n; his muddled theories, 257; hurt by reviews, 288; admired, 303; demands criticism, 306 & n; liked by Eliot, 324; snubbed off, 341; *ref*: 128, 193, 206, 259, 290, 308, 355; *The Destructive Element*, 301 & n, 303; *Vienna*, 288 & n

Spenser, Edmund: *Faery Queen*, 275 & n, 283, 287, 321

Sprott, Sebastian: Lytton's amanuensis, 73 & n

Squire, Lady: 349 & n

Squire, Sir John Collings: Montaigne opposed to, 42 & n; flimsy on Lytton,

74 & n; measured by Lawrence, 127; his style, 164; scallywag, 349 & n

Stangroom, *see* Belsher, Peggy

Star, The, newspaper: 299

Steen, Marguerite: *Hugh Walpole*, 181 & n; *Stallion*, 181 & n

Steer, Philip Wilson: 285 & n

Stendhal: 33 & n, 255, 315; *De l'amour*, 33

Stephen, Adrian: loses allowance, 33 & n; his party, 103, 104; to separate, 109; garrulous & cheerful, 114; fretted to death, 115; his suicidal face, 118; on father, 162; curiously immature, 234; daughter seldom sees, 276; dines on birthday, 348, 349; *ref*: 4n, 50n, 119, 122, 123, 274

Stephen, Ann: likes action, 150; Amazon, 169; naked legged colt, 243; at Charleston, 244; clumsy & large, 274; her character vouched for, 276; poor dear, 283 & n; wins scholarship, 295 & n; *ref*: 14 & n, 150n

Stephen, Dorothea: & *NS&N*, 296; sickeningly funny, 297 & n

Stephen, Sir Harry: 147

Stephen, James: 169, 170n

Stephen, Judith: candid as boy, 150; Amazon, 169; naked legged colt, 243; at Charleston, 244; clumsy & large, 274; admires Hazlitt, 276; indulges in chaff, 295; *ref*: 122, 151n

Stephen, Julia: 12

Stephen, Karin: odd character, 65 & n; deaf, twisted . . . baffled, 103; to separate, 109; with tattoo, 162; her inferiority complex, 234; late for funeral, 243; only seen in bed, 276; *ref*: 4n, 122

Stephen, Leslie: and Stella's marriage settlement, 33n; takes Scott seriously, 41 & n; at St Ives, 43 & n; VW's, article on, 123 & n, 129, 130; utterly bad?, 162; eponymous lectures, 177 & n; and London Library, 297 & n; & widow Green, 297 & n, 298; *ref*: 12, 156n

Stephen, Thoby: and *The Waves*, 10

Sterne, Laurence: & VW's sensibility, 75 & n

Stewart, Jean: 29 & n

Stewart, Norman: 171 & n

Stiven, Jacqueline: a hoax of one's own, 188 & n

Stocks, Mary (Baroness Stocks): 148 & n

Strachey (family): their stout constitution, 55; attending Lytton, 61-2; begot by Ruby, 65 & n; think Carrington: 'morbid', 82; 'hurt' by VW, 324; ref: 70

Strachey, Alix: & Carrington's death, 83; red Indian, 112, 114; editor-translator, 112n; praising party, 222 & n; like a blackshirt, 307; ref: 89, 103, 146, 357

Strachey, (Giles) Lytton: for Biographical Note see Appendix; his literary virtues, 26; dislikes *Waves?*, 53 & n; seriously ill, 54-5, 55n; 'my old serpent,' & the Keyneses, 56; 'if anything better,' 57; attended by Stracheys and others, 61-2; now better, now not so well, 63; Woolfs visit, 64; his death —intolerable impoverishment, 64-5; Oliver on, 65, 66; leaves books to Senhouse, 65; autopsy, 66; Easter at Corfe, 66 & n; portraits of—by Bell, Fry, Grant & Lamb, 70-1, 71n; letters unpublishable, 71, 72; cremated, 72 & n; unverified feelings about, 72-3; Ottoline on, 73; Squire on, 74 & n; Mary's intimacy with, 75, 81; and Senhouse, 75, 82; Maynard on his funeral, 78; Carrington on, 81-2; and Shakespeare, 82; & Carrington's death, 83; odd he didn't write more, 86; 'the result' of his death, 88; his literary remains—and intentions, 89; a longing to speak to, 102; & brother James, 103, 114, 146; measured by Lawrence, 127; thought of, 134; on Bunny's style, 142; on late success, 177; post-Lytton parody, 188; measured against Fry, 253; 'destructor', 265; on Renan, 271; attacked by Ervine, 288 & n; Desmond concerned about, 291; his biography, 296, 324; no talk of, 307; how many Lyttons?, 322; ref: viii, 26n, 53n, 70, 120, 244, 302, 350; *Elizabeth and Essex*, 53 & n; *Eminent Victorians*, 70-1, 71n; *Portraits in Miniature*, 26 & n

Strachey, James: for Biographical Note see Appendix; witnesses Lytton's cremation, 72n; & Lytton's letters, 73; is cautious, 82; on Lytton's things, 83, 146; and literary remains, 89; holding on, 103; offers books, 114; praising

party, 222 & n; plans Lytton biography, 296, 324; has cold, 307; ref: 50n, 51, 55, 162, 350

Strachey, (Joan) Pernel: & Lytton's last illness, 61; integrity's the word, 150; ref: 17 & n

Strachey, Julia (Mrs Stephen Tomlin): 81 & n, 118, 119, 130, 169, 170; *Cheerful Weather for the Wedding*, 81n

Strachey, Marjorie ('Gumbo'): has genius for obscenity, 140 & n; ref: 144, 275

Strachey, Oliver: & Lytton's last illness, 61; his discourse, 65-66; & Roger & Bloomsbury, 257, 258; ref: 62n, 65n, 274

Strachey, Philippa: & National Society for Women's Service, 6 & n; & Lytton's last illness, 61; sobbing, 64; autopsy kept from, 66; cautious, 82; VW joins her society, 130; 'looks unhappy', 149; puts Woolfs up, 203, 206; ref: 83

Strachey, Ray: wants *babies*, 65 & n; at Corfe, 66 & n; to dine, 288; ref: 355

Strachey, Richard: taken for ghost, 104 & n; ref: 65n, 103 & n; *A Strachey Child*, 65n

Stratford-on-Avon: 25, 219-20 & n

Stulik, Rudolf: 48 & n

Sturgeon, George and Flora: 323 & n, 350

Sturgis, Howard Overing: *Belchamber*, 309, 310n

Suddaby, Elsie: 9 & n

Sullivan, J. W. N.: 223 & n

Sunday Times: on *Flush*, 185 & n; Book Exhibition, 351 & n; ref: 184, 230, 300-1, 352

Swan, Annie S.: *My Life*, 300 & n

Swift, Dean: & Vanessa & Stella, 217 & n; Yeats on, 255, 256; ref: 228; *Gulliver's Travels*, 228; *The Drapier's Letters*, 256 & n

Swinnerton, Frank: hostile jibings, viii; ridicules Bloomsbury, dismisses VW, 288 & n, 301n, 307, 308n; effect of his sneers, 289; MacCarthy on, 291 & n; *The Georgian Literary Scene*, 288n, 308n

Swinstead-Smith, K.: *The Marchesa and Other Stories*, 337 & n

Sydney-Turner, Saxon: helps during Lytton's illness, 62 & n; witnesses cremation, 72n; Chinese mandarin, 141; after 10 years, 235; honey-sweet

new author, 337; forecasts lean year, 353

(3) *Political activities*. Fabian Society meeting, 32n; on Sino-Japanese conflict, 71 & n; attends Labour conferences, 125 & n, 182 & n, 183 & n, 345 & n, 346; voices specialised convictions, 230-1; Rodmell Labour Party, 232, 296 & n; & New Fabian Research Bureau, 254; politics to the fore, 280; brings home scares, 303; talks politics, 323; London meeting, 342; rows with Kingsley, about Labour & League, 344; speaks at Rodmell, 351

After the Deluge, 30 & n, 51 & n, 54, 61; *A Village in the Jungle*, 30 & n; *Quack, Quack!*, 262 & n, 267, 273, 284, 317 & n

Woolf, Marie, *née* de Jongh (Mrs Sidney Woolf): odd spurt of sex in, 37 & n; birthday dinner, 52 & n; described at tea, 67 & n; dying & recovering, 146-7; at Leonardslee, 162; on daughter's death, 199 & n; unexpectedly sensible, 245; and 'happy', 277; admirable racy talk of, 319; & mind smearing talk, 325; enjoys VW's owl, 337; tea with, 349, 350; *ref*: 184, 232n, 336, 355

Woolf, Marie, daughter of Philip: 319 & n, 322, 340

Woolf, Philip: organizes fête, 319 & n, 322; Woolfs visit, 322-3; & LW's family complex, 322; & class consciousness, 326; *ref*: 185, 223, 322n, 340n

Woolf, Philippa ('Pippin'), daughter of Philip: 319n, 322, 340

Woolf, Sylvia, wife of Edgar: 162 & n, 337

Woolf, Virginia. Entries are divided thus: (1) Early life and relationships; (2) Personality and health; (3) Relationship with LW; (4) Diversions, parties and travel; (5) Domestic matters; (6) Literary activities; (7) Her own published books and pamphlets.

(1) *Early life and relationships*: thoughts of Thoby, 10; and Janet Case, 11 & n; Jack Hills's allowance, 33 & n; father at St Ives, 43 & n; and Sophie Farrell, 48n, 61, 131; 'uneducated child', 79; love for Cornwall, 97; the Italy one used to visit, 156; *aetat* 13, 242; Tonks remembered, 285 & n; mixed impressions, 313 & n; Hyde Park Gate, 333

(2) *Personality and health*: private sorrows, public rewards, viii; attitude to Press, ix; several resolutions—& Charleston depression, 3; excited, 6; headaches, 7; delight of skirmishing, 8; stethoscope rites, 9; despair over hair, 11, & general misery, 11-12; can't deny the young, 14; flushed by wine, hair down, 15; on Bennett's death, 15-16, 23, & funeral, 24; repulsive correcting, 16, 29, 30, 34, 35, 230; 'Hancock's Horror', 17 & n, 46; White Hart bettered, 22; tourist racket hated, 24; a happy life, 25-6; black holes, 25, 27; headache—flashes of light, 27; 'hammer, hammer, hammer', 29; celebrated sensibility insulted, 29; dreams of K. Mansfield & others, 29; why so happy?, 30; given picture of Angelica, 32; allowance stopped, 33 & n; tight spun brain, 34; reading *Don Juan*, 34; in jubilation, 36; sculpted by Tomlin, painted by Nessa, 36-37; headache—bitterness, 38; 'vibrational', 39; on Colefax, 40-1; bed & headache, 41; attacks Desmond, 42-3; inspired by praise, 44; Donne v. Gold Standard, 45; less naked than usual, 46; trembling with pleasure, 47; 'godmother', 50 & n; damped & disheartened, 51; substantial pleasure, 52; dreams of Vita, 54; perpetual headache, & younger generation, 55; & Lytton's illness, 55 (*see under* Strachey, G. L.); dispassionate, 57; youngest person on bus, 63; the money-trap, 64; sobbing, 64; on LW's mother, 67; on fame, 72, 73; *sic transit*..., 78; on Ka's patronage, 78-9; on Mrs Keppel, 80-1; & Carrington, 81-3; faults preferred, 85; & Greek temples, 85; Our Transition Age, 86; desire to be with friends, 88; little girl's writing, 89; a writer's view, 89; 'Now I'm 50', 91; becoming a peasant, 94; happy, easy, friendly, 96; on charm, & a hot new season, 97; heroism on Orient express, 99, 100; process of detachment, 100; sordid

300; breaking moulds—odd fairy, 301; at Fortnum's, 302; 'not a good ratiocinator', 303; usual headache, 306; Julian & war, 307; pure external living, 308; the Hitler feeling, 310-11, 312; CH declined, 314 & n; on K. Mansfield, 315; on Pinka's death, 317; grim wooden feeling, 319; an odd dream, 323; on Eliot, 324, 344; and Bloomsbury, 326-7; a new dog, 328-9; different selves, 329; on Brenan, 329-30; & Fry Memorial Exhibition, 330, 331; complete failure, 331; Julian & China: reactions, 331-2; on Edith Sitwell, 333; most patient artist, 334; war inevitable, 336; most critical day, 337; absolutely floored, 338; rapture of reading, Desmond's d——d nonsense, 339; hell & ecstasy, 340; enough time?, 341-2; longing to be alone, 343; hand & brain, 344; tears over Lansbury, 345; complete bliss, 346; accursed talk, 347; specimen days, 351, 352, 355; on Mortimer, 354; at Aubrey House, 354-5; on artists' values, 359; almost extinct, 360; too much headache, 361

(3) *Relationship with LW*: happy alliance, ix; pathos for, a squirrel for?, 6; day ruined for us both, 8-9; Woolfs compared with Huxleys, 11-12; 19 years with, 18; France v. England, 23; divine goodness of, 27; not jealous of, 34; family argument, 38; perfectly happy, 40; VW's sensibility: insanity, 43; Mandrill walk revisited, 46; 'We makers of masterpieces', 50; mother & little boy, 51; 'too good', 53; talk about death, 55; sobbing together, 56, 62; another 20 years?, 63; divided over aristocracy, 69; LW on Clark lectures, 79-80; discussing suicide, 83; in mood for ventures, 83-4; his immense responsibility, 102; beneficial conversation, 103; vigorous & young, 113; benefactors, 115; too aloof & absorbed?, 119; how happy, 125-6; so happy, 130; reciprocal judgment, 132; LW's disappointment, 134; 'stay this moment', 135; no to Riviera, 155; happy day, 182; what happiness, 184; a great deal to spend on, 191; remembered at Richmond, 193; birthday

present for, 200; the Nelly situation, 205; in VW's dream, 238; thoughts soothed by, 239; congratulatory gift, 246; question & answers, 252; LW—divinely good, 253; our life together, 260; rather cheerful, 262; solid happiness, 275; snarling over cigarettes, 282; trying to rattle LW, 285; little skirmish, 286; what a quarrel, LW's habits, 287; won't remind him, 288; his advice, 289; LW cuts up rusty, 300; and Mabel, 321; LW: not a gentleman —his attitude to servant classes deplored, 326; thoughts of China, 336; LW very touchy, 339; very old story, 340; & love, 356

(4) *Diversions, parties and travel*: foreign travel, ix; resolved against parties, 3; attends *Prison* rehearsal, 9-10, and performance, 12; no adventure, no travel, 11; to *Tantivy Towers*, 15; fortnight in France, 17, 18-24; at Fontevrault, 19; *chez* Montaigne, 21; at French movies, 22; and Chinon, 22-3; Mrs Hunter's sale, 25; to Gala opera, 30, 31-2; dining at Eiffel Tower, 48; have read Faust, Coningsby &c, 55; *chez* Fry, 67-8; *chez* Clive, 70-2, 104, 108-9; at Fry's lecture, 76; to Busch Quartet, 77, 78n; to Camargo Ballet, 78 & n; to East Anglia, 83-4; to Sissinghurst, 87; Greek adventure, with Frys, 88, 89-100; Lord David's party, 105-6; Hyde Park observed, 108; Hutchinson dinner, 110-11; dining with K. Furse, 112-13; to Labour party conference, 125 & n; at Cecil wedding, 127-8; entertaining peerage, financing Music Room, 131; to Angelica's party, 139-41; and *Pomona*, 144; to *Don Giovanni*, 145; outings & entertainments, 147; to Hayling Island, 148; to Bedford, 149-150; to Italy, 153-60; to Leonardslee, 162; Covent Garden gala, 163; lunch with Shaws, 163-4; dinner at Roger's, 166; at the Hutchinsons', 168; a great many visits, 169-70, and more, 171; Lewes festival, 174-5; cakes & bowls, 175; bowls, 180; to Sissinghurst, 181; and Labour conference, 181, 182-3; to see Sickert pictures, 190 & n; to Ethel Smyth's *Mass*, 203; to Cambridge, &

Nessa's, 205; to Ireland, 209-18; at Bowen's Court, 210-11; in Galway, 214-15; in Dublin, 215-16, 217-18; at Stratford, 219-20; party hated, 222; dining with Rothschilds, 227-8, with Hutchinsons, 230-1; Annie's wedding, 234; Keyneses to tea, 235-6; an expensive sail, 237-8; Angelica's party, 244; to Sissinghurst, 247-8; a party, 249-50; to *Sweeney Agonistes*, 260-1 & n; lunch with Keyneses, 272-3; party with Hugh Walpole, 281; an uneasy party, 283; expedition to Walton, & Smyth & the prima donnas, 284; Ethel Walker dinner, 285-6; Quentin's private view, 289; MacCarthy dinner, 291; to the Tower, 292; tea with Tom, 294; *Bengal Lancers*, 295; holiday plans, 295, 298; journey to Holland, Germany, Italy & France, 308-18; rag-marketing in Rome, 314; at Monte Carlo, 316; at Chartres, 316; dining with Clive, 321-2; to Winchendon, 322-3; dining with R. West, 326-7, and the Cecils, 327-8; Bach on radio, 336; to Peace Conference, 349; to movies, 353; to *Romeo and Juliet* and *Murder in the Cathedral*, 356 & n; dinner with Huxleys, 357-8

(5) *Domestic matters*: resolution regarding, 3; not fuming over, 4; solid middle-class household, 6; regrets for Monks, 17; 2 frigidaires & everything handsome, 25; intolerable lamps, 27-8; material blessings, 36; apple baskets in drawing room, 46; a new lease?, 52; O these dogs, 61, 63; another view lost, 62; servant meanness, 77; fleas, beetles & mice, 115; 35 Gordon Square?, 146; great Nelly row, 202 (*see under* Boxall, Nelly); redecoration, 203 & n; back in studio, 206; what a relief, 221; we shall see, 232; thoughts of Wilmington, 238, 241; new Lodge, 249, 263; Cow & dogs, 267 (*see also under* Mabel); does Louie cheat?, 296; rain through roof, 297

(6) *Literary activities and opinions*: ideas for articles, 4; 'All About Books', 4n; 'Edmund Gosse', 4 & n, 7, 16n; another *Orlando?*, 5, 32; 'Poetry, Fiction and the Future', 5 & n;

'Phases of Fiction', 5n, 79-80, 80n; conflicting styles, 6; addresses Pippa's society, 6, 7; an author's note, 8; images & symbols, 10-11; on Aldous Huxley, 12; six articles for *Good Housekeeping*, 12 & n, 15 & n, 16n; 'Great Men's Houses', 13 & n; on Arnold Bennett, 15-16; 'This is the House of Commons', 16; 'Lockhart's Criticism', 16n; 'Aurora Leigh', 16n; D. H. Lawrence read, 20, 25, Strachey comparison, 26, decline traced, 28; my bibliography, 21; *incommunicado*, 22; on Lytton's talent, writing v. nonwriting, 26; factual biography, poetic fiction, 40; Scott v. Walpole, 41; Elizabethan prose, 42; 'Donne After Three Centuries', 44 & n, 45, 70, 77; 'The Tree' envisaged, 48; 'a cook's talk,' 48 & n; 'The Strange Elizabethans', 50 & n; another book, 53; embodying exact shapes, 53; *Q.Eth.* disliked, 53; some simpler means of writing, 53-4; 'Diary or Calendar', 54; Desmond & the screw, 56-7; the, appalling novel', 57; a closer screw?', 61, a quicker cut, 115; another 4 novels—20 year programme, 63; writing—harder & harder, 66; article on Skinner, 77 & n; *Arcadia* finished, 78; and Clark lectures, 79-80; 'Dorothy Osborne', 80 & n; two books on VW, 85 & n; 'De Quincey's Autobiography,' 86, 89, 111; 'Dr Burney's Evening Party', 87 & n; on Lawrence's method, 95, and Letters, 126; the male virtues, 95; how to take criticism?, 100-1; 'David Copperfield', 101n, 102; more articles, 104; 'The Novels of Thomas Hardy', 'I am Christina Rossetti'—how tired one gets of one's own writing, 113; Mrs Hardy's wish, 118-19; 'Leslie Stephen, the Philosopher at home . . .', 123n, 129, 130; 'Old Mrs Grey', 123, 124, 125n; novel of fact, 129, 133, 142; 'Middlebrow', 129 & n; Bunny's falsetto, 142, 'Oliver Goldsmith', 149, 150 & n, 151, 160, 161, 166, 169; a nip from Gissing, 150 & n; 'The Novels of Turgenev', 151; on Henry James, 157; amused by diary, 167; on Hardy, 169; on form, Turgenev and Dostoievsky, 172-3; on

Vera Brittain, 177; on T. S. Eliot, 178-9; criticism scheme?, 179; on *Twelfth Night*, 179 & n, 181; Crabbe fantasy?, 180 & n; to read memoir, 180 & n; 'The Novels of Turgenev', 181, 184, 185, 194; on Hugh Walpole, 181; Forster's praise, 184; might start magazine?, 185; on Brenan's book, 186; 'The Protection of Privacy', 186 & n; on Michael Arlen, 189; why go on with essays?, 194; 'Oliver Goldsmith', 194, 195; caricature collaboration?, 200; on Shakespeare, 207; £300 from America, 224; 'Fact and Fiction', that old bugbear, 226 & n, must scrap?, 229, horrid book, 238; inserting Max, 230; Rupert Brooke, 235 & n; play about Parnells or . . .?, 238; quotes Maupassant, 242; 'Phases of Fiction', another method, 250, *ref:* 251 & n, 252, 254, 259; 'Royalty', 254 & n; about novels, 258; on *Sweeney Agonistes*, 261; 'Contemporary Criticism', 265; idea for a 'play', 275; anti-fascist pamphlet, 282, 302; 'Professions for Women', 302, 307, 314; satire, 309; on *Belchamber*, 309-10; on Eliot's *Murder*, 323, 356; and PEN, 330, 350; 'The Captain's Death Bed', 334n, 335, 341; 'Life As We Have Known It', introduction, 337 & n; new combinations—the next novel, 353; 'Am I A Snob?', 356n; article on Gray, 360; my War book, 361 (see under *Three Guineas* below)

(7) VW's published books and pamphlets:

Between the Acts: 338n

Common Reader, The: (1st Series): 21n, 228; (2nd Series): second thoughts about?, 74; proves credentials, 77 & n; can't correct any more, 86; finishing, 110, 111; not quite done, 113; ready, 115; proofs corrected, 121; sent off, 123; not a tremor, 125; published, 128; strain of, 142; *ref:* ix, 42, 50, 53 & n, 57, 70

Flush: cannot write, serves purpose, 40; freak of writing, 123; cooling effect of, 132; what a waste, 133, 134, 153; abominable dog, 139; glad to be quit of, 141; another week of, 142; 'finished', 142; stiffens neck, 143;

researched in Wimpole Street, 144 & n; cannot despatch, 144; despatched, 145; proofs, 151; that silly book, 153; Book Society takes, 160 & n; a blank wall, 161; taken in America, 175; reaping rewards of, 176; pre-publication self-admonishments, 181; takes first fence, 181-2 & n; R. West on, 183-4 & n; praised by Bunny, 184 & n; and Desmond, 185 & n; torn by Grigson, 185 & n; to be pictured?, represents VW's 'death', 186 & n; *ref:* vii, 37 & n, 38, 57, 175, 245, 332

Freshwater: a farce, a joke, 265 & n; rehearsal, 266; rather tosh, 271 & n; donkey's work, 273; great success, 274 & n; *ref:* 275

Jacob's Room: vii, 110n, 133, 344

Letter to a Young Poet, A: inspired to write, 44 & n; just finished?, 66; out tomorrow, 114 & n; passes unnoticed, 119; *ref:* 47, 57, 78, 347n

The London Scene: 12n

Mr Bennett and Mrs Brown: 251 & n

Orlando: 5, 32, 132, 133, 186

Roger Fry: A Biography: question of, 258, 260; long debate on, 262; to write?, 267; begin in October?, 271; M. Fry's doubts, 275; documents for, 279, 335, 336; will do some, 346; accumulating, 347, 348; reading, 349; how to do?, 358; can't even copy, 360; *ref:* vii, 302, 353

Room of One's Own, A: sequel to, 6 & n; & *NS&N* hoax, 188 & n; *ref:* 25, 28

Three Guineas (for alternative working titles see p. 6 n.8): sequel to *A Room . . .*, 6; sucking at my brain, 7; wish to write, 28; Squire's provocation, 42; what's its name?, 75; to have 4 pictures, 77; freedom to write, 79, 80; thinking of again, 95; and Clive Bell, 132n; ideas for, 271, 361; feminism & fascism, 273 & n; and London Library, 297-8; unwise to sketch, 300; & women's 'sacred task', 323 & n; 'P & P', 335 & n; obsessed by, 336; Anthony Hope's Oxford, 341 & n; wild excitement over, 346; desire to be at that argument, 348; courage, 354; *ref:* vii, 57, 63, 102

Wordsworth, Dorothy: 82 & n
Wordsworth, William: one word poetry, 352; *ref*: 82n, 157, 228; *Resolution and Independence* ('The Leech Gatherer'), 352
Workers' Education Association: 344 & n
Worthing, Sussex: 37, 171, 232, 245, 319
Wright, Joseph and Lizzie: respected by VW & described, 115-16 & n
Wright, Ralph: 278, 279n, 280

Yale Review, periodical: 16n, 190n
Yeats, W. B.: at Ottoline's, 255-7: on *The Waves*, 255 & n, 260, Balzac, Tolstoy, 255, Swift, 255, 256 & n, the Occult, 256 & n, George Moore, 256 & n, horoscopes, and his 'narrative man', 257, & Proust, 257; eschews the 'literary', 271; *ref*: ix, 259; 'The Apparitions', 256n; *Dramatis Personae*, 256n; *Fighting the Waves*, 255n
Yonge, C. M.: *The Heir of Redclyffe*, 275 & n
Young (family): 182 & n, 212 & n
Young, Arthur: *Travels in France* . . ., 200 & n, 201
Young, Emily Hilda: *Miss Mole*, 336 & n, 339
Young, Hilton: 170 & n
Young, Lady: 212 & n
Younger, Eve: plays Queen Victoria, 273 & n; very pretty, 342; in Charleston entertainment, 344; *ref*: 179, 336, 339, 341

Zennor, Cornwall: 182
Zuckerman, Solly: 103 & n, 104; *The Social Life of Monkeys & Apes*, 103n